ST PATRICK'S
PURGATORY

EARLY ENGLISH TEXT SOCIETY
No. 298
1991

*For my father and
in memory of my mother*

ST PATRICK'S PURGATORY

Two versions of OWAYNE MILES
and
THE VISION OF WILLIAM OF STRANTON
together with the long text of the
TRACTATUS
DE PURGATORIO SANCTI PATRICII

EDITED BY

ROBERT EASTING

Published for
THE EARLY ENGLISH TEXT SOCIETY
by the
OXFORD UNIVERSITY PRESS
1991

Oxford University Press, Walton Street, Oxford OX2 6DP

Oxford   New York   Toronto
Delhi   Bombay   Calcutta   Madras   Karachi
Petaling Jaya   Singapore   Hong Kong   Tokyo
Nairobi   Dar es Salaam   Cape Town
Melbourne   Auckland

Associated companied in Beirut   Berlin   Ibadan   Nicosia

Oxford is a trade mark of Oxford University Press

British Library Cataloguing in Publication Data

Easting, Robert
St Patrick's Purgatory.—(Early English Text Society.
Original Series; 298).
I. English literature, history, 1066–1400.
I. Title   II. Series
820.9354
ISBN 0–19–722300–1

Set on a Lasercomp at
Oxford University Computing Service
Printed in Great Britain by
Ipswich Book Co. Ltd.

PREFACE

This edition is a revision of the corresponding parts of my unpublished Oxford D.Phil. thesis (Bodleian Library, MS D.Phil. d. 6202) presented in 1976. Since that date much has been published on medieval vision literature; I have endeavoured to take this into account and bring my own work up to date.

I wish to record here my gratitude to those who have assisted me in the preparation of the edition in either of its forms. I am indebted to Professor Douglas Gray, a kind and generous supervisor and mentor; my examiners, Miss Celia Sisam and Professor John Burrow, for their careful attention and encouragement that I should publish the edition; Professor Michael Benskin for information from the Middle English Dialect Project; the late Professor Norman Davis for the loan of his microfilm of the Book of Brome; Dr Pamela Gradon, with whom I first discussed the revision for publication, and Dr Malcolm Godden, her successor as Editorial Secretary of EETS, for his supervision of the volume's preparation for the press; Professor Dr Peter Dinzelbacher for giving me access to the notes of the late Professor Ludwig Bieler concerning the *Tractatus* manuscripts; and Monsignor Thomas Flood for his permission to visit Station Island, the site of St Patrick's Purgatory, in 1979. My work has also profited from contacts with Dr Nigel Palmer, Dr Yolande de Pontfarcy, and Dr Carol Zaleski. At Victoria University of Wellington I thank Adrienne Carley for typing the Glossary; the staff of the Reference Section of the University Library for busily procuring materials unavailable in New Zealand; the Internal Research Committee for grants towards the cost of purchasing microfilms and photocopies; and the Leave Committee for granting me sabbatical leave in 1987 to complete the book. I am also grateful to the Computing Services Centres at Victoria and Oxford universities for their help.

For permission to print from manuscripts in their possession, I thank The British Library Board; The Trustees of the National Library of Scotland; Yale University Library; and His Grace the Archbishop of Canterbury and the Trustees of Lambeth Palace Library. I thank Barbara A. Shailor of the Beinecke Rare Book and Manuscript Library at Yale for her particular kindness. The plates are reproduced by permission of the British Library and Yale University Library.

Lastly, I gratefully acknowledge the invaluable personal support and encouragement of family, friends, and colleagues, in particular Susi Easting, Dr Christine Franzen, Dr Ian Jamieson, Mr Harry Orsman, and Dr Kathryn Walls.

The dedication is small recompense for my long and distant absence.

R.E.
Wellington
New Zealand

CONTENTS

LIST OF PLATES

SIGLA

Middle English
A   National Library of Scotland, MS Advocates' 19.2.1
      —The Auchinleck manuscript (*OM*1)
C   BL MS Cotton Caligula A ii (*OM*2)
Ld   Oxford, Bodleian Library, MS Laud Misc. 108 (*pa*)
SA   BL MS Additional 34,193 (*VWS*)
SR   BL MS Royal 17 B xliii (*VWS*)
Y   Yale University Library, MS 365
      —The Book of Brome, formerly MS Hamilton (*OM*2)

Anglo-Norman
F   CUL MS Ee. 6. 11 (AN)

Latin
α MSS of *T*
Ar   BL MS Arundel 292
B   Bamberg, Staatliche Bibliothek, MS E. VII. 59
H   BL MS Harley 3846
U   Utrecht, University Library, MS 173

β MSS of *T*
L   Lambeth Palace Library, MS 51—base text in this edition
R   BL MS Royal 13 B viii
S   Cambridge, Sidney Sussex College, MS 50

ABBREVIATIONS AND SHORT TITLES

Excluded from this list are abbreviations commonly in use for reference works such as *English Dialect Dictionary, Middle English Dictionary*, and *Oxford English Dictionary*, and grammatical abbreviations used in the Glossary.

α	short version of the *Tractatus*, represented by ArBHU
β	long version of the *Tractatus*, represented by LRS
a.	*ante*
AASS	*Acta Sanctorum Bollandiana*, ed. Jean Bollandus (Antwerp, 1643 *et seq.*)
AB	*Analecta Bollandiana*
AN	Anglo-Norman translation of *T*, contained in F
ANT	*The Apocryphal New Testament*, trans. M. R. James (Oxford, 1924, corrected ed. 1953)
Auchinleck MS	*The Auchinleck Manuscript: National Library of Scotland, Advocates' MS. 19.2.1*, with an introduction by Derek Pearsall and I.C. Cunningham (London, 1977)
BEH	*Bede's Ecclesiastical History of the English People*, ed. Bertram Colgrave and R.A.B. Mynors (Oxford, 1969) [Citations also give pagination (contained in *BEH*) of C. Plummer ed., *Venerabilis Baedae Opera historica*, 2 vols. (Oxford, 1896)]
BL	British Library
BN	Bibliothèque Nationale
Briquet	C.M. Briquet, *Les Filigranes*, 4 vols. (Geneva, 1907, republished with supplementary material ed. Allan Stevenson, Amsterdam, 1968)
c.	*circa*
Common-place Book	Lucy Toulmin Smith ed., *A Common-place Book of the Fifteenth Century* (London and Norwich, 1886)
CUL	Cambridge University Library
Dialogues	*Grégoire le Grand: Dialogues*, ed. Adalbert

	de Vogüé, 3 vols., Sources chrétiennes, 251 (1978), 260 (1979), 265 (1980)
Dobson	E.J. Dobson, *English Pronunciation 1500–1700*, 2 vols., 2nd ed. (Oxford, 1968)
EETS, ES, SS	Early English Text Society, Extra Series, Supplementary Series
ES	*English Studies*
EStn	*Englische Studien*
Haren & Pontfarcy	*The Medieval Pilgrimage to St Patrick's Purgatory: Lough Derg and the European Tradition*, ed. Michael Haren & Yolande de Pontfarcy, Clogher Historical Society (Enniskillen, 1988)
HRHEW	*The Heads of Religious Houses England and Wales 940–1216*, ed. Dom David Knowles, C.N.L. Brooke, and Vera C.M. London (Cambridge, 1972)
IER	*Irish Ecclesiastical Record*
Index	Carleton Brown and Rossell Hope Robbins, *The Index of Middle English Verse* (New York, 1943)
JEGP	*Journal of English and Germanic Philology*
K	Eugen Kölbing's edition of C, in *EStn*, i (1877), 113–21
K1	Kölbing's corrections to K, in 'Berichtigungen zu Band 1', *EStn*, i (1877), 540
K2	Kölbing's reply to Wu1, in 'Zu Anglia 1. p. 373ff', *EStn*, i (1877), 541–2
K3	Kölbing's review of Wu, in *EStn*, iv (1881), 499–500[1]
K4	Kölbing's further corrections to K, in 'Nachträge und Besserungen zu den Englischen Studien', *EStn*, v (1882), 493–4
KA	Kölbing's edition of A, in 'Zwei mittelenglische Bearbeitungen der Sage von St. Patrik's Purgatorium', *EStn*, i (1877), 98–112
KB	Kölbing's notes to KA, *ibid.*, pp. 112–13
KC	Kölbing's corrections to KA, in 'Vier romanzen-Handschriften', *EStn*, vii (1884), 181–2[2]

---

1. K2 and K3 are not listed in *Manual*, 2, V [321] c.
2. Not listed in *Manual*, 2, V [321] b.

Kr   G.P. Krapp's print of SR in *The Legend of Saint Patrick's Purgatory: Its Later Literary History* (Baltimore, 1900), pp. 58–77

L   the edited β text of the *Tractatus* (*T*) in this edition, based on Lambeth Palace Library, MS 51, with variants recorded from R, S, and W β

LALME   Angus McIntosh, M.L. Samuels, and Michael Benskin, *A Linguistic Atlas of Late Mediaeval English*, 4 vols. (Aberdeen, 1986)

Luick   Karl Luick, *Historische Grammatik der englischen Sprache*, ed. F. Wild and H. Koziol, 2 vols. 1914–1940, repr. (Stuttgart, 1964)

MA   *Medium Aevum*

Manual   *A Manual of the Writings in Middle English 1050–1500*, ed. J. Burke Severs, Albert E. Hartung *et al.* (New Haven, 1967–)

ME   Middle English

MGH   Monumenta Germaniae Historica

ES   Epistolae selectae

PLAC   Poetae latinae aevi carolini

SRM   Scriptores rerum merovingicarum

MLN   *Modern Language Notes*

MLR   *Modern Language Review*

MRHEW   *Medieval Religious Houses England and Wales*, ed. David Knowles and R. Neville Hadcock, 2nd ed. (London, 1971)

MRHI   *Medieval Religious Houses Ireland*, ed. A. Gwynn and R. Neville Hadcock (London, 1970)

NM   *Neuphilologische Mitteilungen*

NQ   *Notes and Queries*

N.F.   Neue Folge

NS   New Series

OM1   *Owayne Miles*, six-line tail-rhyme stanza version (*aabccb*) represented by A

OM2   *Owayne Miles*, couplet version represented by C and Y

Owst, *LPME* G.R. Owst, *Literature and Pulpit in Medieval England*, revised ed. (Oxford, 1961)

Owst, *PME*   *Preaching in Medieval England: An Introduction to Sermon Manuscripts of the Period c.1350–1450* (Cambridge, 1926)

pa   SEL 'St Patrick', translated from an α text

	of *T*. (This abbreviation is used by Manfred Görlach, *The Textual Tradition of the South English Legendary* (Leeds Texts and Monographs, NS, 6, Leeds, 1974))
PL	*Patrologia Latina*
Picard & Pontfarcy	*Saint Patrick's Purgatory: a twelfth century tale of a journey to the other world*, translated by Jean-Michel Picard with an introduction by Yolande de Pontfarcy (Dublin, 1985)
PRIA	*Proceedings of the Royal Irish Academy*
RC	*Revue celtique*
RES	*Review of English Studies*
RF	*Romanische Forschungen*
RP	*Romance Philology*
RR	*Romanic Review*
RS	Rolls Series, Rerum Britannicarum medii aevi Scriptores (London, 1858–96)
SEL	South English Legendary
Sm	readings common to Sm1 and Sm2
Sm1	Lucy Toulmin Smith's first edition of Y, in 'St. Patrick's Purgatory, and the Knight, Sir Owen', *EStn*, ix (1886), 1–12 [text pp. 3–12]
Sm2	Lucy Toulmin Smith's revised edition of Y, in *Common-place Book*, pp. 82–106
Supplement	Rossell Hope Robbins and John L. Cutler, *Supplement to the Index of Middle English Verse* (Lexington, 1965)
s.v.	*sub verbo*
T	*Tractatus de Purgatorio Sancti Patricii*
Top. Hib.	Giraldus Cambrensis, *Topographia Hibernica et Expugnatio Hibernica*, ed. James F. Dimock, RS, 21.v (London, 1867)
Trip. Life	*The Tripartite Life of Patrick with other Documents relating to that Saint*, ed. and trans. W. Stokes, 2 vols., RS, 89 (London, 1887)
VCH	The Victoria History of the Counties of England
VEL	E.M. Thompson, 'The Vision of Edmund Leversedge', *Notes and Queries for Somerset and Dorset*, ix (1904), 19–35 [text pp. 22–35]
VWS	*The Vision of William of Stranton*,

	represented by SA and SR
VSP	ME *Vision of St. Paul*, ed. C. Horstmann, 'Die Sprüche des h. Bernhard und die Vision des h. Paulus nach Ms. Laud 108', *Archiv für das Studium der neueren Sprachen und Literaturen*, lii (1874), 35–38
VSP I/IV	*Visio Sancti Pauli* redactions I and IV, ed. H. Brandes, *Visio S. Pauli: Ein Beitrag zur Visionslitteratur mit einem deutschen und zwei lateinischen Texten* (Halle, 1885), pp. 65–71 and 75–80
W	Warnke's editions of the *Tractatus* (α and β texts), in Karl Warnke, *Das Buch vom Espurgatoire S. Patrice der Marie de France und seine Quelle* (Bibliotheca Normannica 9, Halle/Saale, 1938)
Whiting	B.J. Whiting and H.W. Whiting, *Proverbs, Sentences and Proverbial Phrases from English Writings mainly before 1500* (Harvard, 1968)
Wu	R.P. Wülcker's edition of C255–460,[1] in *Altenglisches Lesebuch*, 2 vols. (Halle, 1874–79), II. 22–26
Wu1	Wülcker's review of K, 'Englische Studien ... Heilbronn, 1877', *Anglia*, i (1878), 376–7[2]
Wu2	Wülcker's notes to Wu, in *Altenglisches Lesebuch*, II. 235–7
Z	J. Zupitza's corrections to KA in a review, 'Englische studien ... 1 band', *ZfdA*, xxii N.F. 10 (1878), 248–9
Z1	Zupitza's review of K, in *ZfdA*, xxii N.F. 10 (1878), 250–1
ZfcP	*Zeitschrift für celtische Philologie*
ZfdA	*Zeitschrift für deutsches Altertum*

---

1. Not ll. 250–460 as reported in *Manual*, 2, V [321] c.
2. Not listed *loc. cit.*

INTRODUCTION

1. ST PATRICK'S PURGATORY

Since the late twelfth century St Patrick's Purgatory has been the most renowned and continually frequented pilgrimage site in Ireland. Today, during the 'season' from 1 June to 15 August, tens of thousands of pilgrims annually perform the three-day vigil on Station Island in Lough Derg, Co. Donegal. At this place God is said to have revealed to St Patrick an entrance to the other world in order that the saint might more readily convert the pagan Irish. From the thirteenth century onwards the belief was widespread that whoever spent twenty-four hours in the 'cave' or 'pit' of the Purgatory would be exempt from purgatory after death.

The earliest surviving account of the founding of the Purgatory and of the penitential rites undergone there is in the Latin prose *Tractatus de Purgatorio Sancti Patricii* (*T*) composed *c.*1180–1184 by a Cistercian monk, H[enry] of Sawtry (Saltrey), Huntingdonshire.[1] This work recounts the visit to the Purgatory (*c.* 1146/7) of an Irish knight named Owein, and his spiritual passage (spoken of as a physical journey) through purgatory and the Earthly Paradise, to which the 'cave' entrance was believed to give access. Henry's informant was another Cistercian, one Gilbert, formerly of Louth Park, Lincolnshire and ex-abbot of Basingwerk, Flintshire. Gilbert had spent two and a half years in Ireland helping to found a monastery, probably Baltinglas. During this time (*c.*1148–51) Owein served as his interpreter and frequently told Gilbert of his experiences at St Patrick's Purgatory.[2] *T* was copied frequently in the following three centuries and was widely translated.[3] It has been called 'one of the best-sellers of the Middle Ages'.[4] The popularity of Owein's story is not hard to

1. For convenience I use the name Henry, traditionally assigned to the author, who gives only his initial; see Commentary L3–4. For references to discussions of the date, see below, p. lxxxiv n. 1.
2. For a fuller discussion of these historical matters, see Easting, 'Owein at St Patrick's Purgatory', *MA*, lv (1986), 159–75.
3. For references to the translations, see Easting, 'The South English Legendary "St Patrick" as Translation', *Leeds Studies in English*, xxi (1990), 119–40, esp. nn. 16–25. For a modern English translation see Picard & Pontfarcy.
4. Shane Leslie, *Saint Patrick's Purgatory: A Record from History and Literature* (London, 1932), p. xvii.

explain for it combines the fascination of an other-world journey and matter from a long tradition of vision literature with the actual, yet geographically remote, location of the purgatorial 'cave'.[1] The story was influential in shaping people's ideas about the other world[2] and prompted a large number of overseas visitors to make the pilgrimage and leave their own accounts.[3]

1. For these aspects of the story see, for example, Thomas Wright, *St. Patrick's Purgatory: An Essay on the Legends of Purgatory, Hell and Paradise, current during the Middle Ages* (London, 1844); C. Fritzsche, 'Die lateinischen Visionen des Mittelalters bis zur Mitte des 12. Jahrhunderts. Ein Beitrag zur Kulturgeschichte', *RF*, ii (1886), 247–79 and iii (1887), 337–69 (esp. pp. 358–61); E.J. Becker, *A Contribution to the Comparative Study of Medieval Visions of Heaven and Hell, with Special Reference to the Middle-English Versions* (Baltimore, 1899), pp. 87–93; Philippe de Félice, *L'Autre Monde: mythes et légendes. Le Purgatoire de saint Patrice* (Paris, 1906); St. John D. Seymour, *Irish Visions of the Other World: A Contribution to the Study of Mediaeval Visions* (London, 1930), pp. 168–87; August Rüegg, *Die Jenseitsvorstellungen vor Dante und die übrigen Voraussetzungen der 'Divina Commedia'*, 2 vols. (Einsiedeln and Cologne, 1945), I, 395–405; F. Bar, *Les Routes de l'autre monde: Descentes aux enfers et voyages dans l'au-delà* (Paris, 1946), pp. 93–101; H.R. Patch, *The Other World according to Descriptions in Medieval Literature* (Cambridge, Mass., 1950, repr. New York, 1970), pp. 114–16; D.D.R. Owen, *The Vision of Hell: Infernal Journeys in Medieval French Literature* (Edinburgh and London, 1970), pp. 37–47, 64–75; and Easting, 'An Edition' (1976), pp. cxxxviii–ccxxxvii. See further Peter Dinzelbacher, *Vision und Visionsliteratur im Mittelalter* (Stuttgart, 1981); Carol Zaleski, *Otherworld Journeys: Accounts of Near-Death Experience in Medieval and Modern Times* (New York and Oxford, 1987); and for recent work on the background tradition of late classical and early Christian other-world material see Alan F. Segal, 'Heavenly Ascent in Hellenistic Judaism, Early Christianity and their Environment' in *Aufstieg und Niedergang der römischen Welt*, II.23.2 (1980), 1333–94; John S. Hanson, 'Dreams and Visions in the Graeco-Roman World and Early Christianity', in the same volume, pp. 1395–1427; and Jacqueline Amat, *Songes et visions: l'au-delà dans la littérature latine tardive* (Paris, 1985). For fuller bibliography on St Patrick's Purgatory and other ME visions of the other world, see Easting, 'Legends of the After-Life', in *Saints' Legends*, Middle English Volume 8 of *An Annotated Bibliography of Old and Middle English*, general editor Tom Burton (in preparation).
2. See, for example, A.B. van Os, *Religious Visions: The Development of the Eschatological Elements in Mediaeval English Religious Literature* (Amsterdam, 1932), pp. 58–67, and Jacques Le Goff, *La Naissance du purgatoire* (Paris, 1981), esp. pp. 259–73, trans. Arthur Goldhammer, *The Birth of Purgatory* (Chicago and London, 1984), pp. 193–201. For a response to Le Goff's treatment of *T*, see Easting, 'Purgatory and the Earthly Paradise in the *Tractatus de Purgatorio Sancti Patricii*', *Cîteaux: Commentarii Cistercienses*, xxxvii (1986), 23–48, and add Graham Robert Edwards, 'Purgatory: "Birth" or Evolution?', *Journal of Ecclesiastical History*, xxxvi (1985), 634–46.
3. For references to these accounts, see H. Delehaye, 'Le Pèlerinage de Laurent de Pasztho au Purgatoire de S. Patrice', *AB*, xxvii (1908), 35–60 (pp. 36–40), and 'A Fifteenth Century Pilgrimage to St Patrick's Purgatory', *New Ireland Review*, xxxi (1909), 1–9, and R. Verdeyen and J. Endepols, *Tondalus' Visioen en St Patricius' Vagevuur*, I (Ghent and 's Gravenhage, 1914), pp. 167–87.

The later literary and social history of St Patrick's Purgatory through to the present day still remains to be adequately written.[1] There are three Middle English translations of 'St Patrick's Purgatory' derived from T.[2] The earliest (*pa—Manual*, 2, V [321] a) is found under 'St Patrick' in the South English Legendary, late thirteenth century.[3] The present volume contains the two later translations, both (somewhat confusingly) known as *Owayne Miles*:[4] the earlier (*OM1—Manual*, 2, V [321] b), early fourteenth century, is found in the Auchinleck manuscript (A); the later (*OM2—Manual*, 2, V [321] c and d), late fourteenth or early fifteenth century, in BL MS Cotton Caligula A ii (C) and Yale University Library MS 365 (Y).

This edition also contains *The Vision of William of Stranton* (*VWS—Manual*, 2, V [321] h), a fifteenth-century prose text, which tells of another vision seen at St Patrick's Purgatory by one William from Stranton, Co. Durham, in 1406 or 1409. It shows a knowledge of the T, but is an independent work. *VWS* is here presented in parallel texts from the two extant manuscripts, BL MSS Royal 17 B xliii (SR) and Additional 34,193 (SA).

Apart from *pa*, this edition therefore contains all the major ME accounts of visions at St Patrick's Purgatory.[5] The volume also contains the first edited text of the complete long β version of T,

---

1. There are numerous partial studies: see, for example, G.P. Krapp, *The Legend of Saint Patrick's Purgatory: Its Later Literary History* (Baltimore, 1900); G. Dottin, 'Louis Eunius ou Le Purgatoire de Saint Patrice', *Annales de Bretagne*, xxvi (1910–11), 781–810; Shane Leslie, *Saint Patrick's Purgatory* (1932) and *Saint Patrick's Purgatory* (Dublin, 1961); St. John D. Seymour, *St. Patrick's Purgatory: A Mediæval Pilgrimage in Ireland* (Dundalk, 1918); Alice Curtayne, *Lough Derg: St. Patrick's Purgatory* (London, 1944), and see the review by Aubrey Gwynn in *Studies*, xxxiii (1944), 550–4; Victor Turner and Edith Turner, *Image and Pilgrimage in Christian Culture: Anthropological Perspectives* (New York, 1978), pp. 104–39; Carol Zaleski, 'St. Patrick's Purgatory: Pilgrimage Motifs in a Medieval Otherworld Vision', *Journal of the History of Ideas*, xlvi (1985), 467–85. The most recent and most comprehensive treatment of St Patrick's Purgatory in the medieval period is to be found in Haren & Pontfarcy.
2. See Francis A. Foster, 'Legends of the After-Life', in *Manual*, 2, pp. 453–4, and 646–8, and Easting, 'Middle English Translations of the *Tractatus de Purgatorio Sancti Patricii*', in *The Medieval Translator, Volume II*, ed. Roger Ellis, Westfield Medieval Publications, 1991.
3. See also above, p. xvii n. 3.
4. On the name, see below, p. xliii.
5. *Manual*, 2, V [321] e, f, and g, are, respectively, the 'Harley fragment' of a revised quatrain version of *pa*; the 'Hearne fragment'; and a translation from the account in the *Legenda Aurea*. *Manual* is in error here for the 'Hearne fragment' is not a separate version; it is in fact a print of part of the 'Harley fragment': see Easting, 'The Middle English "Hearne fragment" of St Patrick's Purgatory', *NQ*, NS, xxxv (1988), 436–7. For other mentions of St Patrick's Purgatory in Middle English, see Easting, 'The English Tradition', in Haren & Pontfarcy, pp. 58–82.

from which $OM1$ and $OM2$ both ultimately derive; this edited text is hereafter referred to as L.

2. MANUSCRIPTS AND LANGUAGE

i. Owayne Miles (OM1) Auchinleck

A

National Library of Scotland, MS Advocates' 19.2.1, the Auchinleck manuscript, contains the only extant copy of the six-line tail-rhyme stanza (*aabccb*) version *OM1* (*Index* 11*, *Supplement* 303.6*, *Manual*, 2, V [321] b) on ff. 25ra–31vb. A full description here of this famous manuscript of about 1330–40 is rendered unnecessary by the publication of *Auchinleck MS*, the facsimile with introduction by Derek Pearsall and I.C. Cunningham.[1]

In the present state of the manuscript *OM1* is the sixth item; the original number, xi, is still visible in the top margin of ff. 26r, 28r, 29r, 30r, though it has been wholly or partially cropped away elsewhere. The original first five items have been lost. *OM1* occupies folios 3–8 of the present fifth gathering and folio 1 of the sixth gathering of eight leaves. The catchwords *& honourep nouȝt her* are written at the foot of f. 30vb at the end of the fifth gathering. The present first sixteen items, which occupy the first two booklets and the beginning of the third,[2] are mainly religious legends and didactic pieces, including the two romances *Þe King of Tars*[3] and *Amis and Amiloun*. *OM1* is preceded, in their original order, by *The Legend of Pope Gregory, Þe King of Tars, The Life of Adam and Eve, Seynt Mergrete*, and *Seynt Katerine*, and followed immediately by *Þe desputisoun bitven þe bodi & þe soule* and *The Harrowing of Hell*.

OM1 is incomplete, the beginning having been lost when folio 2 of the fifth gathering was excised, leaving a narrow strip of parchment. This folio was probably removed for the sake of the miniature at the head of *OM1*; the opening sections of seventeen

---

1. See also A.J. Bliss, 'Notes on the Auchinleck Manuscript', *Speculum*, xxvi (1951), 652–8; G. Guddat-Figge, *Catalogue of Manuscripts containing Middle English Romances* (Munich, 1976), pp. 121–6; O.D. Macrae-Gibson ed., *Of Arthour and of Merlin*, II, EETS, 279 (1979), pp. 35–40; and Maldwyn Mills ed., *Horn Childe and Maiden Rimnild* (Middle English Texts 20, Heidelberg, 1988), pp. 11–16.

2. (1) ff. 1–38 (2) ff. 39–69 (3) ff. 70–107. See P.R. Robinson, 'A Study of Some Aspects of the Transmission of English Verse Texts in Late Medieval Manuscripts', unpublished B.Litt. thesis, University of Oxford, 1972, pp. 135–6, where she distinguishes 12 booklets in all, and see her full description, pp. 120–38.

3. *The King of Tars*, ed. Judith Perryman (Middle English Texts 12, Heidelberg, 1980), postdates the listings in the facsimile.

other items have suffered similarly.[1] Now only five miniatures remain, on ff. 7r, 72r, 167r, 256v (defaced), and 326r. These miniatures and the other decorations have been identified by J.J.G. Alexander as 'a later product of the Queen Mary Psalter *atélier*, which operated in the first half of the fourteenth century', possibly in the east of England.[2] The excision of the miniature at the head of *Þe desputisoun bitven þe bodi & þe soule* has caused the loss of most of 13 lines of *OM*1, 177:2–179:2[3] (f. 31ra). It is fairly certain that at the beginning of *OM*1 32 lines have been lost.[4] This can be demonstrated as follows. The preceding article, *Seynt Katerine*, is also extant in a revised and complete version in Gonville and Caius College, Cambridge, MS 175 (*Index* 1158), which adheres closely line by line to the earlier Auchinleck text. The incomplete Auchinleck *Seynt Katerine* contains 660 lines, the Caius copy 796 lines,[5] though Auchinleck omits 4 lines found at Caius 625ff. After the point where Auchinleck breaks off, Caius has another 132 lines,[6] 665–796. We may therefore take it that 132 more lines on the missing folio would have completed the Auchinleck text. As this part of the Auchinleck manuscript is regularly ruled for two columns of 44 lines this means that *Seynt Katerine* has lost exactly three full columns. *OM*1 would, therefore, originally have started at the top of column two on the verso of the folio preceding the present f. 25, and the 44 lines of that column would most likely have contained: i) a two-line heading, ii) a ten-line miniature,[7] iii) five complete six-line stanzas plus two lines of the stanza of which the remaining four lines form the present opening of the poem, i.e. 2 + 10 + (5 × 6) + 2 = 44. This is what one would expect considering the stage in the story at which *OM*1 now opens. It would give space to call attention, to protest the truth of the tale to be told, to introduce St Patrick and proclaim his fame, and to state how he came to find the pagan Irish in need of conversion.[8] The full text of *OM*1 therefore probably contained 203 stanzas (1218 lines); A currently contains 1186 lines, including the lacuna on f. 31va.

---

1. See *Auchinleck MS*, p. xv col. 2.
2. See Robinson, 'A Study', pp. 135–6.
3. References to A (*OM*1) are in the form stanza:line.
4. Pearsall suggested 'about 40 lines are lost', *Auchinleck MS*, p. xx.
5. See C. Horstmann ed., *Altenglische Legenden: Neue Folge* (Heilbronn, 1881), pp. 242–59.
6. Not, as Pearsall reports, 130, *Auchinleck MS*, p. xix.
7. The rough excision of the miniature at the head of *Seynt Katerine* caused the loss of 11 lines (122–32) on f. 21vb.
8. See Commentary A1.

*OM*1 was copied by Kölbing's[1] scribe *a*, Bliss's[2] scribe 1, who wrote down some 72% of what survives, in a straightforward, legible book hand with sparse use of abbreviation. The end of most lines is marked by a full point. Some corrections have been made by the scribe, interlining missing letters, striking through repetitions, and rewriting over wrong letters. These do not usually present any difficulties in *OM*1. Each six-line stanza is marked off by a paraph, drawn alternately in red and blue ink. At one point this has been misplaced, at line 71:6 instead of 72:1. An additional paraph occurs at line 23:4. The initial letter of each line has been ruled off one letter space from the rest of the line and touched in with red ink. Two-line initials with flourishes occur at the beginning of stanzas 29, 76, 83, 90, 105, and 145, marking new episodes in the narrative's action. A four-line initial with flourish occurs at stanza 96. These have been recognized by in-setting the text at these places.

Language of A

L.H. Loomis' contention that the manuscript is the product of a London bookshop has been substantiated by later studies and is now widely accepted, though with qualifications.[3] The London origins of the language of scribes 1 and 3 have been demonstrated by E. Zettl[4] and K. Brunner[5] respectively. The language of scribe 1 has been described as an early form of London Standard by M.L. Samuels,[6] and in *LALME* it is placed on the London/Middlesex border and entered in Middlesex.[7]

---

1. E. Kölbing, 'Vier romanzen-Handschriften', *EStn*, vii (1884), 183. In his description of the MS, pp. 178–91, he identified five scribes.
2. Bliss, 'Notes on the Auchinleck Manuscript', detected six scribes. Robinson, 'A Study', reckoned there were only four, but six has been maintained by A. McIntosh, 'Towards an Inventory of Middle English Scribes', *NM*, lxxv (1974), 621 n. 2, and by Cunningham in *Auchinleck MS*, p. xv.
3. See 'The Auchinleck Manuscript and a Possible London Bookshop of 1330–1340', *PMLA*, lvii (1942), 595–627, and for references, see *Manual*, 2, [52], and the discussions in *Auchinleck MS*, pp. viii–xi, and Perryman, *The King of Tars*, pp. 35–41. See also Timothy A. Shonk, 'A Study of the Auchinleck Manuscript: Bookmen and Bookmaking in the Early Fourteenth Century', *Speculum*, lx (1985), 71–91, and Mills, *Horn Childe*, pp. 79–81.
4. *The Anonymous Short English Metrical Chronicle*, EETS, 196 (1935), pp. cxviii–cxxiii.
5. *The Seven Sages of Rome*, EETS, 191 (1933), p. xxvi.
6. 'Some Applications of Middle English Dialectology', *ES*, xliv (1963), 81–94 (esp. p. 87), and *Linguistic Evolution* (Cambridge, 1972), pp. 166–8.
7. *LALME*, I. 88, LP 6510, III. 305–6, Grid 532 190, IV. 339.

The evidence of rhymes suggests that the language of the original of *OM*1 was not significantly different from that of the A copyist, and may also be ascribed to a London provenance. It is probable that the poem was translated in the Auchinleck bookshop;[1] there is no reason to press its date of composition much earlier.[2] The following are the rhyme forms which do not usually occur within the line; they are all, however, attested in other London works and elsewhere in scribe 1's output.

1) *a* in *gan*, inf. 'go', rhymes with (r.w.) *Satan* (75:1–2). Cf. *Metrical Chronicle* 1156. Doubtless this is a concession to rhyme.
2) *a* in *yknawe/þrawe* (58:4–5). This is not decisive for the sound quality, being a self-rhyme, but cf. *Of Arthour and of Merlin* (*AM*) 901.
3) *a* in *þare* (for *þere*) r.w. *bere* pa. t. pl. (45:3–6), and r.w. *totere* pa. t. pl. (73:1–2), and *bare* pa. t. sg. (89:4–5). Cf. *AM* 1286.
4) *a* in *man* pl., r.w. *þan* (91:1–2). Cf. *Kyng Alisaunder*[3] 5551, 5870.
5) *e* in *wes* ('was') r.w. *pes* (76:5–6) and *les* (OE *lēas*) (30:1–2). Cf. *AM* 98.

It is now understood that the following features in scribe 1's work are also acceptable London forms.

1) Pr. p. in *-and*, e.g. *boiland* (78:3), *glow(e)and* (70:2, 79:2), *stinkand* (93:1).[4]
2) *wald* (34:5, 75:4) beside *wold*, and *warld* (12:2, 52:4) beside *world*.[5]
3) One example of pr. 3 sg. in *-es; regnes* (86:3).[6]

Kölbing[7] attempted to show that *OM*1 was composed by the author of the *Sayings of St Bernard* (*Index* 3310) and the version of the *Vision of St Paul* (*Index* 3089) found in Bodleian MS Laud Misc. 108, ff. 198rb–199rb and 199rb–200vb respectively. Brandes[8] accepted his attribution of these three poems to the same author; Varnhagen[9] remained unconvinced. Kölbing's evidence, based on the rhymes and the proportion of romance to

1. See below, p. xlvi.
2. *MED* dates *OM*1 *c.*1330 (?*c.*1300).
3. Ed. G.V. Smithers, EETS, 237 (1957).
4. See O.D. Macrae-Gibson, 'The Auchinleck MS.: Participles in *-and(e)*', *ES*, lii (1971), 13–20.
5. See Macrae-Gibson, EETS, 279 (1979), p. 63 n. 1.
6. Cf. Smithers, EETS, 237 (1957), p. 50.
7. In *EStn*, i (1877), 92–98.
8. H. Brandes, *Visio Sancti Pauli: Ein Beitrag zur Visionsliteratur auf einem deutschen and zwei lateinischen Texten* (Halle, 1885), pp. 58–59.
9. H. Varnhagen, 'Zu mittelenglischen Gedichten', *Anglia*, iii (1880), 60.

native words, is insufficient convincingly to prove the same dialect in the originals, let alone the same author.[1] In fact, he admitted that his observations 'nicht ganz erschöpfend sind'.[2] The author of *OM*1 certainly has made use of the same version of the *Vision of St Paul* as that in the Laud MS,[3] but I do not believe that it can be proved that he was the author of both or all three of these poems.

*OM*1 contains a number of words or forms which are unrecorded in or antedate *MED* and/or *OED*;[4] others are either first citations[5] or evidently early uses;[6] they are noted in the Commentary.[7]

ii. Owayne Miles (OM2) Cotton

C

BL MS Cotton Caligula A ii[8] contains the earlier of the two extant copies of the octosyllabic couplet version *OM*2 (*Index* 982, *Manual*, 2, V [321] c) on ff. 91va–95rb. The volume consists of two originally separate paper manuscripts bound together before 1654. The first, ff. 3–139 (formerly MS Cotton Vespasian D viii), containing 39 items, is followed by two paper leaves, ff. 140–141, and a parchment bifolium, ff. 142–143, which may originally have been the cover of the second manuscript, ff. 144–210 (formerly MS Cotton Vespasian D xxi), containing Statutes of the

1. The dialect of MS Laud Misc. 108, ff. 1–200 is N.W. Oxon; see *LALME*, LP 6920.
2. *EStn*, i (1877), 96.
3. See below pp. li–liii.
4. *acordaunce* 156:2, *breke* her notes 145:4, *caroly* 143:1, 5, 144:6, *chaundelers* 136:4, *honestly* 170:1, *last* pa. t. 3 sg. 111:2, *last* n. 189:4, *misours* 102:5, *pinacles* 132:6, *plou3* 86:5, *queyntaunce* 79:4, *redempcioun* 123:5, *regnes* pr. 3 sg. 86:3, *sarmoun to make* (without article) 2:1, *semblaunce* 156:1, *tabernacles* 132:1, *tonicles* 154:5.
5. *causteloines* 131:5, *celestien* 165:4, *charbukelston* 132:4, *creaunce* 15:1, *cristal* 131:1, *eglentere* 147:4, *feþerfoy* 147:4, *jaspers* 131:1, *knottes* 132:5, *ouerfle* 167:3, *ribes* 131:4, *safer-stones* 131:3, *salidoines* 131:4.
6. *arches* 132:4, *burdoun* 145:5, *carol* 142:1, *colombin* 147:5, *coral* 131:2, *diamaunce* 131:6, *dominical* 123:1, *flaumbe* 183:2, *flaumme* 105:2, *fulfild of* 2:4, *hautein* 145:5, *licorice* 148:6, *margarites* 131:2, *mene* 145:5, *mint* 147:4, *onicles* 131:5, *ouerþrewe* 72:5, *paintour* 133:2, *quic brunston* 78:2, 99:6, *primrol* 147:3, *sautry* 142:5, *spourged* 162:2.
7. See also Easting, 'Some Antedatings and Early Usages from the Auchinleck *Owayne Miles*', in *Sentences for Alan Ward*, ed. D.M. Reeks (Southampton, 1988), pp. 167–74.
8. For other descriptions, see Ward, *Catalogue of Romances*, II. 482–4; E. Rickert ed., *Emaré*, EETS, ES 99 (1906), pp. ix–x; F.E. Richardson ed., *Sir Eglamour of Artois*, EETS, 256 (1965), pp. xi–xii; M. Mills ed., *Lybeaus Desconus*, EETS, 261 (1969), pp. 1–2; Robinson, 'A Study', pp. 160–3; Guddat-Figge, *Catalogue of Manuscripts*, pp. 169–71; Frances McSparran ed., *Octovian Imperator* (Middle English Texts 11, Heidelberg, 1979), pp. 10–13; and Rodney Mearns ed., *The Vision of Tundale* (Middle English Texts 18, Heidelberg, 1985), pp. 45–47.

Carthusian Order, 1411–1504. Ff. 1, 2, 140, 141 are thinner paper than the rest, and may have been added when the two manuscripts were originally bound together.[1] The shelfmark 'Vespasian D. 21' has been crossed out at the head of f. 140r. The present binding with new outer flyleaves dates from August 1957, when the leaves were mounted on paper strips about 35mm wide. It is impossible to determine the original collation; there are no catchwords or signatures. There are two systems of foliation for the 210 leaves: the earlier began with the first item *Sussan* (now f. 3r) and disregarded ff. 141–3, 149–55, 207–8; the present foliation begins with the seventeenth-century *Elenchus*[2] and includes all the leaves. Robinson (p. 160) distinguishes two booklets in the first manuscript, ff. 3–13, 14–139. One scribe seems to have copied all these folios except for medical recipes on f. 13v (in a sixteenth-century hand) and a continuation of the Latin *Cronica* to the reign of Richard III, f. 110v.

Rickert dated ff. 3–139 between 1446 and 1460, the earlier date determined by the inclusion of *The Nightingale* (ff. 59r–64r, *Index* 931),[3] the latter by the *Cronica* extending to the reign of Henry VI (ff. 109r–110v). Mills ascertained the *raisin* of the watermarks of ff. 3–13 as 1451–6. McSparran (p. 13) has suggested a possible *terminus a quo* of 1454, based on Carleton Brown's belief (shared by MacCracken) that the Cotton text of *O mors quam amara est memoria tua* (ff. 57v–58r, *Index* 2411) is a later, revised version of the poem found in BL MS Harley 116, and that it has been purposefully changed to efface all the personal references found in Harley to the death in 1454 of Ralph, Lord Cromwell and his wife. However, Rosemary Woolf's argument, that Harley inserts these references rather than that Cotton omits them, seems the more convincing.[4]

In the present state of this manuscript, which contains eight romances,[5] *OM2* follows a section containing two hortatory religious pieces and a religious tale: *Carta Jhesu Christi* (ff. 77ra–79rb), *Ypotys* (ff. 79va–83ra), *Þe stacyonys of Rome* (ff.

---

1. See Rickert, p. ix n. 5.
2. This includes 'A poem intitled swaine [*sic*] miles'. The first letter of the title is uncertain but appears to be a long *s*.
3. See O. Glauning ed., *Lydgate's Minor Poems*, EETS, ES 80 (1900), pp. xxxvi–xxxviii. The Lydgate attribution was disputed by H.N. MacCracken ed., *The Minor Poems of John Lydgate*, I, EETS, ES 107 (1911), pp. xxxiii–xxxiv.
4. See Carleton Brown ed., *Religious Lyrics of the XVth Century* (Oxford, 1939), pp. 243–5 and notes pp. 339–40, and Rosemary Woolf, *The English Religious Lyric in the Middle Ages* (Oxford, 1968), p. 340, with reference to MacCracken in *MLN*, xxvi (1911), 243–4.
5. See Mills ed., *Lybeaus Desconus*, p. 1.

83rb–86va), *Trentale Sancti Gregorij* (ff. 86vb–88ra), and *Quindecim Signa* (ff. 89ra–91rb). *OM2* is immediately preceded by *Vpon a lady my love ys lente* (f. 91rb, *Index* 3836) and followed by *Tundale*, its most fitting companion. Mearns has argued that this part of the manuscript containing the *Fifteen Signs*, *OM2*, and *Tundale* (ff. 95va–107vb) 'may constitute a quire, possibly even a booklet', which for convenience he terms 'the Eschatological Booklet'.[1]

OM2 is written in two columns of between 40 and 43 lines each. The leaves, which have been trimmed throughout the manuscript, here measure on average 220 × 140mm and the written space 177 × 120mm. The hand is a regular-sized mixed cursive; Guddat-Figge speaks of a 'very small, crowded Secretary', with the running titles (and titles and colophons) in Anglicana Formata (*Owayne myles* on ff. 91v, 92v, 94v, and *Owayne Miles* on f. 93v).[2] The ink is dark brown and in this section of the manuscript initials, flourishes and the first letter of each line are touched in with yellow ink. There is no punctuation. The overall impression is plain and workmanlike; there are no miniatures or large coloured initials, though spaces have been left for capitals on ff. 17r, 39r, and 111r. The large proportion of narrative romance and the smaller assembly of devotional and didactic material also suggest that the manuscript may have been copied in a bookshop,[3] 'with a specific readership, if not a reader or readers, in mind'.[4] In connection with *Sir Thopas* and the Auchinleck manuscript, L.H. Loomis has said of Cotton Caligula A ii that Chaucer may have 'had access to some fourteenth-century prototype of this fifteenth-century manuscript'.[5]

Language of C

The language of the C copyist has been called a late indistinctive standard, with southern provenance suggested by the preservation as late as *c*.1450 of *hem* and *her* as the usual forms for 'them' and 'their'.[6] In *OM2* there are two examples of *þem*, one *þer,* and one *þur* (perhaps only because of a slip in the use of the abbreviation). M.L. Samuels speaks of 'a south-eastern stratum of dialect mixed

---

1. Mearns ed., *Vision of Tundale*, p. 45.
2. See Plate facing p. 35.
3. See Richardson ed., *Sir Eglamour*, p. xi.
4. Mearns, p. 47.
5. See W.F. Bryan and G. Dempster eds., *Sources and Analogues of Chaucer's Canterbury Tales* (London, 1958), p. 489, and see the discussion by Mills ed., *Lybeaus Desconus*, pp. 39–40.
6. Görlach, *Textual Tradition*, p. 119, and see p. 259 n. 216.

with one or more other strata'.[1] He lists 26 texts in which occurs the replacement of /ð/ by /d/ found in C, e.g. in *OM2 dyþur* 141, 176 and *de* 'thee' 167, and points out that apart from this feature and a few others 'the forms are preponderantly those of the copyist's originals and not his own'.[2] As he says, an exhaustive study of the scribe's work is still required to localize the latest stratum of the language. A detailed discussion of the scribe's language by McSparran points to a SE or SE Midland origin,[3] and Mills's evidence would support the SE Midland claim by showing the closeness of the C copyist's dialect in *Lybeaus Desconus* to the original of that poem.[4]

On the basis of the 268 items on its analysis sheet which I submitted to the Middle English Dialect Project, Professor Michael Benskin suggested (in private correspondence) that many of the forms in *OM2* which imply spoken language equivalents are in general reconcilable with an area in SE Worcestershire and the border of Warwickshire, around Evesham. It is possible that the C copyist's exemplar derived from this area. The language of C is, however, mixed, and certain orthographic variants which are probably scribal, e.g. *ll/l* in 'will' and 'shall', *sch/sh* in 'shall', do not match this region.

The following orthographic features are of some interest.

1) The *þ/d* interchange[5] mentioned above is also found in *þore* 'door' 201, and non-initially in *cloded* 'clothed' 533, *forde* 'forth' 353, *swide* 220, 485, *wordy* 'worthy' 588.

2) There is considerable variation in the vowel used in unstressed final syllables. Occurrences are as follows, with the figures for abbreviations in parentheses.

-es 82 (2)   *-us* 14 (18)   *-ys* 2
-er 29 (6)   *-ur* 2 (89)   *-yr* 1
-en and *-e* always
-ell 4   *-ull* 7   *-yll* 10   *-all* 1

1. 'Kent and the Low Countries: Some Linguistic Evidence', in *Edinburgh Studies in English and Scots*, ed. A.J. Aitken, Angus McIntosh and Hermann Pálsson (London, 1971), p. 13.
2. *Ibid.*, p. 19 n. 73.
3. *Octovian Imperator*, pp. 20–25.
4. *Lybeaus Desconus*, pp. 28–40.
5. On this feature in the C scribe's work see also A.J. Bliss, 'The Spelling of *Sir Launfal*', *Anglia*, lxxv (1957), 281–4 and ed., *Sir Launfal* (London and Edinburgh, 1960), p. 11, and McSparran ed., *Octovian Imperator*, p. 23.

iii. Owayne Miles (OM2) Yale

Y

Yale University Library MS 365, formerly MS Hamilton,[1] the Book of Brome,[2] contains the later of the two extant copies of OM2 (Index 1767, Manual, 2, V [321] d)[3] on ff. 28r–38r. The history of this late fifteenth-century manuscript, its rediscovery and subsequent twentieth-century changes of ownership, together with the collation and a list of contents, have been reported by Norman Davis.[4]

Part of the manuscript was written by Robert Melton of Stuston, Suffolk, who worked for the Cornwallis family in the late fifteenth and early sixteenth centuries. The manuscript was rediscovered about 1880 at Brome Hall, Suffolk by Sir Edward Kerrison. In the 1930s it was in the possession of the Hon. Mrs. R. Douglas Hamilton of Oakley House, Diss, and in 1959 became the property of Mr. Denis Hill-Wood of Sherborne St John.[5] After a sojourn in the Ipswich and East Suffolk Record Office in Ipswich, it was purchased from Mr. Laurence Witten, 23 December 1966, and given to Yale by Edwin J. and Frederick W. Beinecke in 1967.[6]

The manuscript at present contains 81 paper leaves (originally 94) measuring approximately 205 × 140mm and dated from watermarks about 1465–75.[7] It is bound in original limp heavy

1. So designated in the *Index* and *Manual*.
2. The complete manuscript was edited by Miss Lucy Toulmin Smith, *A Common-place Book of the Fifteenth Century* (London and Norwich, 1886). (The spine and half-title read *The Boke of Brome*).
3. *Manual* lists C and Y as 'Early couplet' and 'Late couplet', as if they were separate versions, but they are independent and substantially variant copies of the same version, and hence printed in parallel in this edition.
4. See *Non-Cycle Plays and Fragments*, EETS, ss 1 (1970), pp. lviii–lxii.
5. Hence Y is called 'Hillwood' in *Supplement* 1767.
6. I am indebted to Christina M. Hanson and Barbara A. Shailor of The Beinecke Rare Book and Manuscript Library, Yale University, for information on the manuscript. Ms. Shailor kindly showed me a draft of the description of Y in the second volume of her catalogue of the Yale manuscripts (see following note). See also R.L. Greene, 'The Book of Brome: Appearance and Disappearance', *Yale University Library Gazette*, xlii (1968), 107–9, and Stanley J. Kahrl, 'The Brome Hall Commonplace Book', *Theater Notebook*, xxii (1968), 157–61.
7. For descriptions of the manuscript see Barbara A. Shailor, *Catalogue of Medieval and Renaissance Manuscripts in the Beinecke Rare Book and Manuscript Library Yale University, Volume II: MSS 251–500* (Medieval & Renaissance Texts & Studies 48, Binghamton, New York, 1987), pp. 210–14, and W. Cahn and J. Marrow, 'Medieval and Renaissance Manuscripts at Yale: A Selection', *Yale University Gazette*, lii (1978), 241–2. On the watermarks see also Thomas E. Marston, 'The Book of Brome', *Yale University Library Gazette*, xli (1967), 141–5, and *Non-Cycle Plays and The Winchester Dialogues: Facsimiles of Plays and Fragments ... Introductions and a Transcript of the Dialogues by Norman Davis*

vellum, with a flap covering the open end; the back is heavy cowhide. The manuscript is written by two main hands.[1] The first, a professional looking cursive, is responsible for the verses on ff. 1–26v, 28r–44r, 79v, and 80v–81r, which include a cipher and sayings, anti-feminist puzzles, a poem on fortune-telling by dice, and five longer works: the *Dialogue of Adrian and Epotys* (ff. 5r–14v, *Index* 220);[2] the play *Abraham and Isaac* (ff. 15r–22r, *Index* 786); the *Fifteen Signs before Doomsday* (ff. 23r–26v, *Index* 1823) incomplete; *OM2*; and a life of *St Margaret* (ff. 39r–44r, *Index* 2673) incomplete. The first hand also wrote certain legal forms of charters and bonds in Latin with an English translation (ff. 68r–77r). From a form of indenture written apparently in the same hand on the inside of the front parchment cover, it appears that this first scribe was alive in May 1492.[3] The second hand, that of Robert Melton,[4] wrote a motley collection of items, including rent records, a list of prayers, and accounts dated from 1499 to 1508; these are scattered through the remainder of the manuscript. A copy of one document is dated 1454. It seems most likely that the poems were copied by the first scribe in the third quarter of the century and that space was left for further such works, but that the original moral purpose of the collection was abandoned, and that later Robert Melton used the blank pages for documents of more practical importance, just as the first scribe had begun to do.

OM2 is written in one column of 32 lines per page. The written space is on average 155×65mm. There are pen work decorations on the initial capitals on ff. 28r, 29v, and 36v, and elongated ascenders on the top line of each page. The first line of the poem is written in red in bold formal letters; the first letter of each line is also touched with red. The couplets of f. 28r are bracketed, with double brackets for the last couplet on the page.

(Leeds Texts and Monographs, Medieval Drama Facsimiles V, Leeds, 1979), pp. 49–50 (facsimile pp. 51–65).
1. A third and later hand contributes a record of payments, ff. 60v–61r. Other odd names betoken further contributors: see Davis, *Non-Cycle Plays and Fragments*, pp. lx–lxi.
2. See frontispiece facsimiles of ff. iv and 14v accompanying Lucy Toulmin Smith, 'Notes on A Common-place Book of the Fifteenth Century, with a Religious Play of Abraham & Isaac', *Norfolk Antiquarian Miscellany*, iii (1887), 115–67.
3. See the reply to Kahrl by N. Davis, 'The Brome Hall Commonplace Book', *Theater Notebook*, xxiv (1970), 84–86.
4. See *LALME*, I. 219, LP 8640, III. 364, Grid 617 305, IV. 339.

Language of Y

The language of the Y copyist of *OM2* is consistent with the original home of the manuscript near Diss on the Norfolk–Suffolk border.[1] Norman Davis[2] has given an account of the spellings and language of the scribe as evidenced in the play *Abraham*, and as the same forms tend to be found in *OM2* I shall only note different instances and other features of interest.

ar for earlier *er* in *ȝarn* 380, *sward* 463, *wardly* 'worldly' 517. Conversely *er* for *ar* in *herche-boschoppe* 56.

e for earlier *i* in *hethyr* 159, 235, *medys* 464, *reche* 48, 52, *swech(e)* 206, 307, *wentyr* 207. *reyth* 327 appears beside usual *ryth(e)*, and *ryght* 381.

g is usual in *ageyn*, with one instance of *ȝ, aȝen* 102. *ȝ* is prefixed to an initial front vowel in *ȝend* 375.

ȝ is usual for the initial consonant in 'give', with one example of *g, geffe* 148.

sch- is used for the initial sound in 'chains', *schenys* 364, and in 'canon(s)' (from Central French *chanoine*), *schanown(ys)* 82, 184 beside *chanownys* 652. *sch-* is also used for *schall* 57, *schallte* 279, *schude* 28, though *x-* is usually used for the forms of 'shall', e.g. *xall* 73, *xulde* 303. *-sch* is used for the final *-s* in the rhyme *wysche* (< OE *wissian*) /*heuyn-blysche* 3–4; see Dobson, II. § 373.

The initial sound of words earlier beginning with *hw-* is usually written *w-*, e.g. *wereof* 512, *wy* 448 (beside *why* 402), though *wh-* is frequent in *what, whan, wher*. There is one instance with *q-, qwhan* 135. Cf. the inverted spelling of *who* 'woe' 284, 313 alongside *wo(o)* 173, 239.

Words containing earlier *-ht* are usually spelt with *-th*, e.g. *knyth* always, *myth* 1, *ryth(e)* 2, 4, *bowth* 13, 247, *browth* 188, *dyth* 319, *nyth(e)* 68, 299, *noth* 512, *nowth* 322, *thowth* 525, but there is also considerable variation, e.g. *browte* 507, *nowt(e)* 137, 260 *thowt(e)* 120, 362, *nyte* 166, *nygth* 79, *ryght* 467. There are no instances with *ȝ*, and the preponderance of forms lacking the fricative seems to indicate that this was no longer part of the Y scribe's pronunciation. Note also that *-th* for *-t* appears in *felth* 488, *fryuth* 572, *seynth* 40, 99, 235, *wenth* 673 and *whath* 105.

h- is inserted before an initial vowel in *harte* 159, *hentre* 92, *heuery* 53, *howyn* 'own' 151, and *Howyn* is the usual spelling for the name Owein. These may be direct spellings indicating aspiration of initial vowels, or they may be inverted spellings showing the loss of [h], though there are no spellings lacking *h* where it is required.

[g] seems to be unvoiced to [k] in *purcatore* 99, *purcatory* 580, *porcatory* 33.

v is used for *w* in *vax* 679, and *vetyn* 353, and *w* for *v* in *schrywe* 123, 657 (beside *schryve* 587) and *dewyll* 495. Intervocalic [v] is lost in *delys* 335.

Excrescent letters appear in *downg* 190 and *stafte* 59, 672; *klepynd* 111 and *cryend* 313 show metathesis.

'Bishop' is nowhere spelt with an *i*, but there are numerous spellings with *o(y)*, e.g. *bochoppe* 77, *bosschoppe* 50, *boyschoppe* 96. Such spellings probably indicate the sound [u], a rounding of [ɪ] perhaps via [y], after *b* and reinforced by following [ʃ]. Compare the sound in 'will' to judge by the spelling *woll* 58, 113. See Dobson, II. § 85 and notes 2 and 5.

Enclitic object pronoun 'it' is suffixed to verbs in *baryth* 55, *clepete* 59, *ʒyldyth* 277, *hant* 106, *loket* 91, *selydyth* 151, *syngth* 649. This feature is also found in the Y scribe's copy of *Abraham*: *hydygth* 165, *fyndygth* 300, 304.

The spelling *wyll(e)* is used to cover six words: 'will' *n.* 157; 'weal' 575; 'well' *adv.* 64, 86 (beside *woll* 6, 105); 'well' *v.* 425; 'wheel' *n.* 373, 376, 383; 'while' *adv.* 197 and *n.* 174, 508.

Verbal inflexions.

Pr. 2 sg. ends variously, e.g. *cum* 270, *comys* 582, *comyst* 274; *may* 413, 466, *mayis* 625; *hast(e)* usually, beside *hate* 580.

Pr. 3 sg. ends in -*yth*, syncopated in *syth* 'sits' 406 and *leste* 681.

Pr. pl. is without ending, except for *fyttyn* 608. 'Have' appears as *han* usually, with *haue*, and *hath* once 253. The usual form of 'to be' is *be* or *byn*, with two occurrences of *arn* 52, 574.

Pa. t. 3 sg. -*th* in MS *semyth* 380 seems to stand for -*d*, and has been thus emended. This is the reverse of -*d* for -*th* noted by Davis in pr. 3 sg. endings.[1] The same may be intended in *bernyth* 379 for *bernyd*, but here I have retained the MS reading, it being equally acceptable as present tense.

Pr. p. ends in -*yng*, but once in -*ynd*, *wepynd* 665.

Personal pronoun 3 pl. is usually *þey/they*, with *þi* 325, *þie* 353; oblique usually *them*, with *hem* five times, 5, 171, 237, 349, 587; possessive usually *ther*, with *hyr* 355, 533, *hyre* 346.

---

1. *Ibid.*, p. lxix.

iv. The Vision of William of Stranton (VWS) Royal
SR

BL MS Royal 17 B xliii,[1] a fifteenth-century quarto, contains 187 parchment leaves (iii + 181 + iii) numbered consecutively throughout, plus modern endpapers. It comprises three originally separate manuscripts, bound, or rather re-bound, together in the eighteenth century; the leather cover is stamped 1757. Seymour, followed by Guddat-Figge, thought there were four separate manuscripts, one for each of the four items, but I follow Ward[2] in believing that the second and third items originally belonged to the same manuscript; they may be distinguished as separate booklets. The contents of the three manuscripts are as follows.

1   ff. 4–115, i–xiv[8], Mandeville's *Travels* (incomplete).
2 i   ff. 116–31, i–ii[8], *Sir Gowther* (*Index* 973).
  ii ff. 133–48, i–ii[8], *VWS* (*Manual*, 2, V [321] h)
3   ff. 150–84, i[8–1], ii[8], iii–iv[10] *Vision of Tundale*[3] (*Index* 1724) (incomplete).

On f. 184r after *Explicit Tondale* is written:

scriptum [in later hand] /Anno domini millesimo quadringentesimo quinquagesimo primo /Anno regni regis henrici sexti post conquestum anglie vicesimo nono[4]

This colophon is followed by a scribbled extract from the lyric *Mankend I cale* (*Index* 2086), beginning *Com home agayne*, continuing to f. 184v. Folios 132 and 149 are not part of the regular gatherings, but are separate leaves inserted to carry coloured drawings (on the versos) introducing the two otherworld visions; these drawings are probably by the same executant.[5] Folio 132v shows a figure probably meant to represent St John of Bridlington, one of William of Stranton's guides,

1. For other descriptions, see K. Breul ed., *Sir Gowther: Eine englische Romanze aus dem XV. Jahrhundert* (Oppeln, 1886), pp. 1–3; Ward, *Catalogue of Romances*, II. 484–6; G.F. Warner and J.P. Gilson, *Catalogue of Western Manuscripts in the Old Royal and King's Collections*, II (London, 1921), 233–4; M.C. Seymour, 'The English Manuscripts of *Mandeville's Travels*', *Edinburgh Bibliographical Society Transactions*, iv (1966), 185–6; Guddat-Figge, *Catalogue of Manuscripts*, pp. 211–13; and Mearns ed., *Vision of Tundale*, pp. 54–60.
2. Ward, *Catalogue of Romances*, II. 433.
3. Ed. from this manuscript by A. Wagner, *Tundale: Das mittelenglische Gedicht über die Vision des Tundalus* (Halle, 1893).
4. See Andrew G. Watson, *Catalogue of Dated and Datable Manuscripts*, I (London, 1979), 156, no. 902, and vol. II plate 520 for the hand of *Tundale*.
5. Seymour is misleading when he suggests that ff. 132 (not 131) and 149 were extraneous leaves which 'may have been inserted' in the eighteenth century. The drawings certainly do not appear to be from the eighteenth century and are clearly designed to match the texts they precede. See further, Mearns, pp. 54–55.

or conceivably the bishop met by William in the Earthly Paradise (see SR614–17). He stands on a small patch of green, wearing his robes and mitre with halo, holding a staff with a cross on top in his left hand and raising his right hand in blessing.[1] On his right, two devils are tormenting three or more souls; the devil above has a face on its stomach. On his left, a cauldron above flames bears three souls, with a devil above right and another below applying the bellows.[2] F. 149v shows a bearded figure (probably Tundale's guardian angel) in a brown hat and green gown (both made of feathers?) over a red and orange striped garment; he is aiming a bow and arrow tipped with a star at a globe, the left half of which is green, the right half brown. The figure stands on a small patch incompletely coloured green (cf. the bishop in the other drawing); he has three devils on his right and one on his left.

It is probable that ff. 116–31 and 133–48 were prepared by the same hands and possibly copied by the same scribe.[3] The parchment is very similar for both items, and is generally rather rougher and thicker than that for manuscripts 1 and 3. 2 i and 2 ii were originally separate booklets, both of two quires of eight. The outer leaves of both booklets, indeed of each of the four quires, show signs of wear, suggesting separate use before binding. The dimensions are the same, 205 × 145mm, but the leaves may have been trimmed when all three manuscripts were bound together. This is suggested by the close cropping of some of the annotations in the outer margins. The single-line four-sided frame ruling is identical in dimensions (150 × 98mm) and appears to be drawn by the same or a similar stylus. There are no line rulings; the top line of text on each page is written above the frame. The treatment of the ascenders in the top margin and of the descenders in the bottom margin is the same in both texts: they are touched in with red, and crudely elaborated in the form of fishes in the bottom margin. Guddat-Figge speaks of the hands in these two items as very similar Secretary hands, that in 2 ii being 'rather calligraphic'; she compares Parkes' plate 12 (ii).[4]

---

1. St John is shown mitred, with cope, stole, and crozier, in a window, 1450–60, in the parish church of St Lawrence, Ludlow: see J.S. Purvis, *St. John of Bridlington* (The Journal of the Bridlington Augustinian Society, No. 2, August, 1924), fig. 3 opp. p. 6. On 15 October 1409 Pope Alexander V granted that in honour of St John 'Prior Thomas and his successors should wear the mitre, ring, and other pontifical *insignia*' (*A History of Yorkshire* (VCH), iii (1913, repr. 1974), p. 202 col. 2).
2. This drawing is reproduced in black and white by Leslie, *Saint Patrick's Purgatory* (1932), opp. p. 28.
3. Mearns (p. 55) says they are 'in different hands'.
4. See M.B. Parkes, *English Cursive Book Hands 1250–1500* (Oxford, 1969).

Seymour's description of the letter forms suggesting different hands is misleading: with one exception, every form of every letter he selects is in fact found in both texts; the sole exception is that only the open backward-curving *g* occurs in 2 ii, whereas in 2 i both the backward- and forward-curving forms occur. If the overall 'look' of 2 ii is slightly more regular than 2 i this is probably because of the constraints of space in the prose text: 2 i averages 22 lines per page; 2 ii in the same space averages 25 lines (the limits are 23 and 27).

In 2 ii punctuation is by oblique red strokes; capitals are also touched in with red. There are frequent flourishes but few marks of abbreviation and contraction. On f. 133r the initial capital *H* is principally coloured blue, and the capital *Y* is red with green in the middle. On f. 144 there is an unfilled space left for a capital *A*. Contrary to Seymour and Guddat-Figge I detect no signatures in 2 i and 2 ii, but 2 ii does have the catchword *hondes* on f. 140v at the end of the first of its two quires.

Guddat-Figge is non-committal about another error made by Seymour. In the right-hand margin of f. 134r, next to the place in the text where St John of Bridlington first reveals his name to William, a later hand (16th century?) has repeated *Jo: Bridlington*. Seymour mistakenly took this as the name of an owner of the manuscript, and accordingly included Jo. Bridlington in his list of sixteenth-century owners of the Mandeville manuscripts.[1]

Language of SR

The provenance of the dialect of the copyist of the Mandeville MS has been localised by M.L. Samuels as the extreme south of Herefordshire, between Broad Oak and Marstow. Angus McIntosh places the *Tundale* MS in N. Derbyshire, between Bakewell and Tideswell. Seymour suggested NE Midlands for *Sir Gowther*. I submitted an analysis sheet on *VWS* to the Middle English Dialect Project and Professor Michael Benskin has established that it fits very convincingly in west central Warwickshire, within the area roughly between Warwick, Kenilworth, Solihull, and Henley-in-Arden, bounded by the *LALME* LP's 4680, 85, 7901, and 7890.[2]

Rather than give any analysis here, therefore, I shall only mention two uncommon spelling features.

1. Seymour, 'English Manuscripts of *Mandeville's Travels*', pp. 186, 207.
2. Again, I am indebted to Professor Benskin for his kind assistance and information on these identifications.

Pr. p. most frequently ends in *-ing, -yng,* but there are at least fourteen occurrences of *-eng,* e.g. *brynneng* SR163, *singeng* 599, *suffreng* 641, plus one occurrence of *-and, apperand* 65.[1]

Noun plurals usually end in *-(e)s, -is,* but occasionally in *-ous, monkous* SR406, *perlous* 188.

An interesting indication of the scribe's spelling variations is found where he apparently recopies a section. Lines SR70–72 *be sent heder ... be perisshid* are repeated anyway at 76–77, but the section *And þan ... be sent heder* 72–76 is also repeated at 77–81. Within this short section the spelling of approximately one third of the words is given in different forms: *thei/þei, thiself/þiself, this/þis, therefore/þerfore, thow/þow/þou; them/hem; ageyn/aȝen; no/not;* v. *passen/passe, spillyn/spil;* pr. pl. *louen/loue, ben/be;* pa. t. pl. *saiden/said;* pp. *sent/send, pershid/perisshid.* The only substantive change is that for *bi þem* (73) the repeat reads *bi the help of owre lord Jhesu Crist* (78). In addition *þat* (75) is omitted in the repeat (80), *which* (75) becomes *þe which* (81), and there are two different forms of *right* and *which,* with and without a flourish.[2]

The following words in SR are of interest for their spelling, form, or date; the Commentary includes notes on them: *abstinded* SR407, *arders* 353, *behouefull* 435, *bitellis* 353, *costluer* 676, *disworship* 192, *gyngeles* 169, *noselyng* 350, *plunchyng* 492, *pressis* 443, *revershid* 615, *siluers* 677, *smolder* 291, *stompyng* 356, *stowpeng* 251, *tredyng* 356, *wullepak* 235.

v. The Vision of William of Stranton (VWS) Additional
SA

BL MS Additional 34,193 is a fifteenth-century folio volume of 228 parchment and intermixed paper leaves, comprising 32 quires and five singletons, re-bound with separately mounted quires in 1982. It contains a miscellaneous collection of religious and moral treatises and poems. Nothing is known of the manuscript's early history.[3]

---

1. For pr. p. in *-eng(-)* see *LALME,* I. 391 map 347.
2. Cf. G.L. Brook, 'A Piece of Evidence for the Study of Middle English Spelling', *NM,* lxxiii (1972), 25–28, and T.M. Smallwood, 'Another Example of the Double-Copying of a Passage in Middle English', *NM,* lxxxvii (1986), 550–4.
3. See *Catalogue of Additions to the Manuscripts in the British Museum in the years 1888–1893* (London, 1894), pp. 225–6; Curt F. Bühler ed., *The Dicts and Sayings of the Philosophers,* EETS, 211 (1941 (for 1939)), pp. xxvi–xxvii; and for a fuller collation and descriptive list of contents, W.F. Nijenhuis ed., *The Vision of Edmund Leversedge* (Capelle aan den IJssel, 1990), pp. 1–8. A few paper leaves at the end of the manuscript bear watermarks resembling Briquet's no. 15100, dated 1480.

VWS, incomplete at the end, and with various lacunae, is in three sections, all on parchment, each beginning 'on a blank space left in a page of another article':[1] ff. 99rb–100vb, 106ra–106vb, and 119v–125v. This text was doubtless incorporated because of the prominent place given to other-world visions in the first half of the manuscript. *The Pilgrimage of the Soul*, an English prose version of the poem by Guillaume de Deguileville, occupies ff. 5r–98v.[2] The rubric to *VWS* starts halfway along a line after *Quibus* at the beginning of a sentence of an abandoned copy of a Latin account of St James the Apostle, from the *Legenda Aurea*. This text started at the top of the same leaf. Here the ruling is the same as for the *Pilgrimage of the Soul* preceding: single pricking, double for the next to bottom line, writing below the top line, in double columns of 33 lines. Ff. 101r–106r contain the Latin *Narratio de Spiritu Guidonis*, unruled. *VWS* resumes where this text ends and completes the remainder of f. 106 in two roughly ruled columns of unequal width. Ff. 107r–119v contain Latin and English versions of the *hymnal de tempore*, 'O first fownder and hevenly creature' (*Index* 2433). *VWS* resumes after this text, first with a line right across the page, then reverting to the double column format of ff. 99r–100v, crudely ruled, without apparent prickings, to approximate to the ruling of the *Pilgrimage*. The text continues through to f. 125v where it breaks off shortly before the end with the loss of the succeeding folio. There follows in the present state of the manuscript another vision, seen by Edmund Leversedge at Frome, Somerset in May 1465, ff. 126ra–130vb (i.e. *VEL*).[3]

The present foliation, in pencil, 1–228, runs from first to last folios, excluding the two flyleaves at the beginning and end. An earlier system of pagination, in ink, ran 1–5 (f. 2r–4r) and then, from the beginning of the *Pilgrimage*, 1–446 (ff. 5r–228v). The pages measure 280 × 185mm, and the written space for *VWS*, 195 × 145mm. In the lower margin at the foot of f. 100vb the scribe has written *The vj^te leffe*, which directs the reader to turn six leaves, where the text duly resumes at f. 106r. Similarly, at the foot of 106vb is written *The xiii^te leffe*, and turning thirteen leaves one finds the text continuing on f. 119v. At the foot of f. 125vb is written *The leffe befor þe kalendar*, but there is now no calendar nor the leaf which stood before it, and so the end of *VWS* is missing.

1. See Ward, *Catalogue of Romances*, II. 487–9.
2. *Ibid.*, pp. 584–5. A note on f. iv mistakenly reads: 'The Pilgrimage of the Soul Compiled and wrote by William de Stanton in the year of our Lord 1416'.
3. See also the edition by Nijenhuis (above p. xxxvi n. 3).

The hand, which appears nowhere else in the manuscript, is a rather crude, upright, and careless book hand, with abbreviations often represented by a dot. Most capitals have been touched in with red ink. Red is also used for the opening rubric (SA1–4), the Latin prayer (13) and for the following capitals: *T* in *Then* or *Than* at 156 (two-line), 242, 259, 292, 306, 318, 336, 368 (in error for *A*), 420, 584; *A* in *And* at 216, 400 (two-line), 506, 615, 663. Punctuation is by an occasional point.

Language of SA
The dialects of all the English hands of this manuscript have been located by Angus McIntosh in the N. Midlands, in a fairly small area, probably in E. Leicestershire or a little farther north in E. Nottinghamshire. The hand responsible for *VWS* is located in Nottinghamshire.[1]

The following words and forms are associated with the North or NE Midlands.

abown(e) SA452, 576, *apon* 261 usual (beside *vpon* once 385), *batte* 403, *clede* pp. (<ON *klaeddr*) 23, *gare* 406, *gartt* 485, *kyrke* 130, *na* 624, *pyke* 319, *ryffe* 307, *stange* (inf.) 406, *stangyd* 386, 403 (<ON *stanga*, see *OED* stang v.1; *MED* stangen v.), *thowffe* 137, *wardely* 270, *ware* 404, *warlde* 69, *warse* 383, *wrachys/-es* 237, 250, *wsyd* 'used' 395, *yll* 111. Spellings with vowel + *i/y* may indicate long vowels, a northern practice, e.g. *greytte 334,* *hoytte* 243, *leyde* 'plumbum' 217, *prevays* 244, *sowroys* 358, *theis* 197 (beside *thes* 296 and *thyes* 206), *thoys* 191 (beside *thows(e)*, *þos(e)*, *thos, thowys*), *wayke* (<ON *veikr*) 560, *wreyke* 410. Another northerly feature is that spellings suggest OE *ō* + *h* is not diphthongized, e.g. *boght(e)* 203, 104, *broght* 576, *thoght(e)* 23, 83; cf. OE *ō* + *g*, in *loghe* 'laughed' 27, and OE *ā* + *ht*, in *taghtt* 84.

The following spelling features are also of interest.

Initial sound of 'showed' is represented by *ch-*, in *chewyd* SA368; cf. *fleche* 181 (beside *fleschely* 75).

Final *-y* is occasionally replaced by *-e*, e.g. *bode* SA200, *lade* 119, *mane* 89. Final *-e* is occasionally duplicated, e.g. *esee* 641 (beside *eese* 651), *hyee* 464, and *platees* 432.

Final *-t* is frequently duplicated, e.g. *amendementt* SA143–4, *att* 205, *bott* 97, *complentt* 126, *hertt* 200, *hytt* 51, *ryghtt* 110, *sprett* 111.

t for *th* in *fort* SA259, *mowtes* 245 (beside *mowthes* 193); *th* for *t* in *hoth* 260.

---

1. Communicated to me in private correspondence by Professor Benskin, and see *LALME*, I. 101.

OE *ā/á* (> *ǫ*) is rendered *ow* in *bowth* SA293, *cowlde* 369 (beside *cold(e)* 522, 523), *howt* 319, *thows* 392. Note also the use of *w* in *howge* 'huge' 447, *howgyste* 534 (beside *hoghe* 550).

u/v/w are used interchangeably in e.g. *saules* SA321, *savles* 261, *sawles* 131, and *saue* 179, *save* 306, *saw(e)* 3, 169 (beside *saghe* 457) for pa. t. 'saw'.

The spelling of 'saint' always seems to indicate shortening and loss of diphthong, e.g. *Sant(e)* SA19, 56, *Santt* 100, *santtys* 614.

In unstressed final syllables before -*n* the vowel is frequently *o* (beside more usual *y* or *e*), e.g. *bondon* SA260, *get(t)on* 130, 280, *molton* 217, *oxon* 272, *smeton* 228, *wrytton* 422.

As SA has not previously been printed and, apart from the brief extracts included in footnotes to Kr, has not been used by the compilers of the *MED*, I include here a list of words that are of interest because of their spelling, form, or date; the Commentary includes notes on them: *bowlynge* SA219, 225, 228, *dreynynge* 185, *dyspetyusly* 357, *fowynge* 244, *gave* pp. 486, *gyngyles* 174, *jaggys* 172, *pycturede* 70, *pylyde* 455, *streynynge* 184, *tobownede* 400, *tomangylde* 310, *vemunsume* 378.

3. PREVIOUS PRINTED EDITIONS[1]

1. Owayne Miles
a. Stanzaic Version (*OM1*)—Auchinleck
Henry Weber made an unpublished transcription preserved in a manuscript volume entitled 'Metrical Romances', pp. 45–66, held in the Abbotsford Library, Press N, shelf III.[2]
OM1 has been printed twice.
  i. *Owain Miles and other Inedited Fragments of Ancient English Poetry*, Edinburgh, 1837. The Bodleian copy (shelfmark 37.1186) has a hand-written note on the flyleaf: 'Only 32 Copies printed.[3] [Edited at Edinburgh by David Laing, W.B.D.D. Turnbull and others].' This pioneering print has a brief introduction (pp. 3–12), and prints the text of A (pp. 13–54) without comment, emendation, or punctuation. Misreadings are common and there is no strict adherence to the spelling of the manuscript. It is to be noted that the title of the volume has been adopted from C, where it appears in the top margin of each verso;[4] there is no running-title in A and the head title has been lost. Laing printed two extracts from C (ll. 1–44, 545–603) to cover those parts of the tale lost in A (pp. 55–58).
  ii. E. Kölbing, 'Zwei mittelenglische Bearbeitungen der Sage von St. Patrik's Purgatorium', *EStn*, i (1877), 98–112 (KA). Here A is followed by the first complete printing of C, and preceded by an introduction (pp. 57–98) wherein Kölbing compared some Latin, French, and English versions,[5] and attempted to define the

---

1. Some selections and modernisations are listed in *Manual*, 2, V [321] b, c, d, h.
2. I am indebted to Dr. W.E.K. Anderson, Eton College, for arranging that a photocopy be sent to me.
3. See also p. iii, 'the impression of this little volume has been limited to THIRTY-TWO copies, intended for private distribution by the Editors.' (This rare book is now available from University Microfilms International, M1A-OP25384.)
4. See above, p. xxvii, and below, p. xliii. Sir Walter Scott had called the poem *Legend of Sir Owain* when he quoted eleven stanzas on the 'Brig o' Dred' (116–126) in his introduction to 'A Lyke-Wake Dirge' in *Minstrelsy of the Scottish Border*, 2 vols., I (Kelso, 1802), 228–30.
5. Latin: 1) J. Colgan's text in *Triadis thaumaturgae ... acta*, II (Louvain, 1647), 273–81; 2) BL MS Royal 8 C xiv; 3) BL MS Harley 3776; 4) BL MS Cotton Nero A vii; 5) BL MS Arundel 292; 6) Matthew Paris in *Chronica Majora*, s.a. 1153; French: 1) Marie de France; 2) BL MS Cotton Domitian A iv; 3) BL MS Harley 273; 4) BL MS Lansdowne 383 (a fragment); English: 1) *pa* in C. Horstmann, *Altenglische Legenden* (Paderborn, 1875); 2) A; 3) C. Kölbing showed, somewhat

original dialect of *OM*1. Both A and C are unsatisfactorily printed, with little close regard for the spelling of the manuscripts and many misreadings. KA is followed by twenty-two brief notes on pp. 112–13 (KB). J. Zupitza made several corrections in his review in *ZfdA*, xxii, N.F. 10 (1878), 248–9 (Z). Kölbing printed a list of revised readings in *EStn*, vii (1884), 181–2 (KC).

b. Couplet Version (*OM*2)—Cotton and Yale
C
Extracts from C were printed by Laing (see above a.i.), and ll. 255–460 were printed by R.P. Wülcker, *Altenglisches Lesebuch*, II (Halle, 1879), 22–26 (Wu), with notes, pp. 235–7 (Wu2). The only complete text is Kölbing's in *EStn*, i (1877), 113–21 (K—see above, a.ii.), which is without notes or linguistic comment. He printed some corrections on p. 540 (K1); Wülcker's review in *Anglia*, i (1878), 376–7 (Wu1) provided a few more. Kölbing replied in *EStn*, i. 541–2 (K2). Zupitza reviewed K in *ZfdA*, xxii, N.F. 10 (1878), 250–1 (Z1). Kölbing reviewed Wu in *EStn*, iv (1881), 499–500 (K3), and provided further corrections to K in *EStn*, v (1882), 493–4 (K4).

Y
Y has been printed twice by Miss Lucy Toulmin Smith:
i. 'St. Patrick's Purgatory, and the Knight, Sir Owen', *EStn*, ix (1886), 3–12 (Sm1) with an introduction (pp. 1–3);
ii. a slightly altered text was reprinted in her edition of the complete manuscript, *A Common-place Book of the Fifteenth Century* (London and Norwich, 1886), pp. 82–106 (Sm2), with an introduction (pp. 80–82).
I use Sm to denote readings common to both these texts. Miss Toulmin Smith supplied missing lines by inserting the corresponding lines of C from K, and she followed Kölbing's line numeration by using letters to indicate lines peculiar to Y. Misreadings are few, but some obvious manuscript errors have been retained; there is no commentary.

2. *The Vision of William of Stranton*
SR was printed by G.P. Krapp, *The Legend of Saint Patrick's Purgatory: Its Later Literary History* (Baltimore, 1900), pp. 58–77, with an introduction (pp. 53–58) and summary (pp. 35–40). On p. vi he called his print 'an inedited text', and on p. 58

confusingly, that in his opinion none of these French or English versions derives directly from any of the other texts examined; cf. below, p. xliv.

pointed out that 'no attempt has been made to normalize the text, except partially in capitalization and punctuation'. His transcription has only a few small errors. He included a few brief extracts from SA, principally the different beginning and ending, in footnotes to the text; the spelling of these is frequently inaccurate. Apart from these few extracts, SA has not previously been printed, nor cited in *MED*.

3. Tractatus de Purgatorio Sancti Patricii
See below, Chapter 6.

4. OWAYNE MILES

The two versions of this story edited here, the Auchinleck stanzaic version (*OM*1) and the Cotton/Yale couplet version (*OM*2), recount the founding of St Patrick's Purgatory and the visit to the site by an Irish knight named Owein. We are told how Owein entered the Purgatory after preliminary rites, how he was advised by a number of men in white about what torments and rewards he might expect, how he witnessed and suffered the pains of purgatory and afterwards visited the Earthly Paradise before retracing his path to the entrance to the Purgatory. Subsequently he made a pilgrimage to the Holy Land and returned to Ireland a holy man.

The title *Owayne Miles* derives from the running-title in C;[1] there is no title in A and Y. As this name has been used in the *Index* and *Supplement* to apply to both the versions (which I distinguish as *OM*1 and *OM*2), I have similarly retained it.[2] Foster counts C and Y as separate versions, 'early' and 'late couplet',[3] but I deal with them as variants of the same couplet version *OM*2. In A the name of the hero is usually spelt *Owain* (23 times), alongside *Owayn* (once), *Owein* (twice), and *Oweyn* (once, cf. 30:1); in C *Owayne* predominates (11 occurrences) alongside *Owayn* (once), *Oweyn* (thrice), *Oweyne* (once), and *Owen* (once); Y uses only *Howyn* (16 occurrences). Foster speaks of *Owayn*; I use *Owein* to match the spelling in L207.

*OM*2 is not derived from the earlier *OM*1. Both versions are independent of the other main ME account (*pa*), found under 'St Patrick' in the South English Legendary, which is earlier than *OM*1. *OM*1 and *OM*2 are also unrelated to the Harley fragment (which is based on *pa*), and the 1438 translation of the *Legenda Aurea*.[4]

The ultimate source of these and all other vernacular accounts of Owein is the widely copied Latin prose *Tractatus de Purgatorio Sancti Patricii* (*T*), composed by 'Henry' of Sawtry, Huntingdonshire, in the early 1180s. A full critical edition of *T* has yet to be

---

1. See above, p. xxvii.
2. *The Cambridge Bibliography of English Literature* uses the title *Owain Miles* for *OM*1, following the print by Laing and Turnbull (see above, p. xl).
3. In *Manual*, 2, 453–4 and 647, V [321] c and d.
4. See above, p. xix.

prepared;[1] this will ideally sort out the interrelationships of the many different forms of the text preserved by the numerous surviving manuscripts (some 150 at least). At present, therefore, I rely on the basic division of the *T* manuscripts into two groups that was made by Ward.[2] Warnke followed this division (into *a* and *β* groups) when he printed editions of both versions parallel to his text of Marie de France's translation *Espurgatoire S. Patrice*,[3] and it is his text of *a* that I quote as *a* W. *pa* follows *T* more faithfully than *OM*1 and *OM*2, and is a translation of an *a* text.[4] *OM*1 and *OM*2 derive from *β* texts of *T*, as I show below.[5] All quotations from *β* are from my edition below, referred to as L.

OM1—Auchinleck Stanzaic Version
i. The relationship of *OM*1 to the *Tractatus* via an Anglo-Norman translation

Although, as will be shown, *OM*1 derives ultimately from a *β T* text, it is not translated directly from the Latin, but is a translation and reworking of an Anglo-Norman verse translation of *T*.[6]

This source has not been recognised by previous writers on the poem. Thomas Wright stated that in his opinion *OM*1 'is probably a translation of one of the French poems, and like them is very long'.[7] Wright, however, knew only three French texts: that of Marie de France; BL MS Cotton Domitian A iv; and BL MS Harley 273, and he does not show any sign of having checked to see if *OM*1 is related to any of these. In fact, it is not. Kölbing used the same three French texts and also the fragment in BL MS Lansdowne 383, but found no convincing or useful relationships.[8] Paul Meyer, in his review of Kölbing's study, pointed out that Kölbing did not seem to know a further French text, CUL MS Ee. 6. 11 [F], and Meyer printed the beginning and ending of this text.[9] In 1891 Meyer listed seven French texts, and referring to

1. See below, p. lxxxvi n. 2.
2. *Catalogue of Romances*, II. 435–54.
3. Karl Warnke, *Das Buch vom Espurgatoire S. Patrice der Marie de France und seine Quelle* (Bibliotheca Normannica 9, Halle/Saale, 1938), 2–169.
4. See Easting, 'The South English Legendary "St Patrick" as Translation', *Leeds Studies in English*, xxi (1990), 119–40.
5. See also Easting, 'Middle English Translations'.
6. For further brief discussions of *OM*1 see Easting, 'The English Tradition', pp. 62–66, 'Some Antedatings', and 'Middle English Translations'.
7. *Saint Patrick's Purgatory* (London, 1844), p. 61. *DNB*, under 'Henry of Saltrey', also says of the Auchinleck version, that it 'is probably a translation of one of the French versions'.
8. See above, p. xl n. 5.
9. See *Romania*, vi (1877), 154–5.

the three ME translations (*pa, OM*1, and *OM*2) said, 'Aucune de
ces versions ne parait faite après l'un des poèmes français qui nous
sont parvenus'.[1] M. Mörner in 1917 said of the French texts,
'Elles tirent leur origine du *Tractatus* indépendamment l'une de
l'autre et ne se rattachent non plus à aucune des versions anglaises
de la légende'.[2] In a footnote (p. xx note 4), she recognized that
Kölbing knew only the Lansdowne fragment of her fourth version
(which I call AN), and she rightly listed this fragment as being of
the same version as F. In 1927 Zanden[3] printed F together with
readings from Lansdowne, but he did not deal with the Middle
English texts at all. The most recent writer on these manuscripts,
D.D.R. Owen, is likewise concerned with them as an example of
the French transmission of the tale and makes no study of the
Middle English versions. He thinks it is likely that AN is based on
an 'α-type manuscript of the *Tractatus*',[4] but as I shall show, it is
in fact clearly based on a β text. Only McAlindon, as far as I
know, has noted that there is a link between *OM*1 and AN,
though he confines himself to mentioning two small items
common to both.[5]

None of these writers has noticed that there is a substantial link
between *OM*1 and AN, the Anglo-Norman translation of *T*
represented by F (the sole extant complete copy) and the
Lansdowne fragment. *OM*1 is not a complete translation of AN,
but F must be very close to the text used for translation by the
author of *OM*1. There are a number of distinctive and important
features in *OM*1 translated directly from AN that do not occur in
T, nor in *pa*, nor in *OM*2, nor in any other Anglo-Norman, Old
French, or other vernacular version. *OM*1 is a fairly free and
condensed translation of AN. A probably originally contained 203
six-line stanzas,[6] that is 1218 lines, as against F's 1794. There are
between 170 and 190 lines of AN which may be said to have been
directly influential on the precise wording of A in about 160 +

---

1. See *Notices et Extraits des Manuscrits de la Bibliothèque Nationale*, XXIV, i
(1891), 238 n. 3, and also *Histoire littéraire de la France*, xxxiii (1906), 371–2.
2. *Le Purgatoire de Saint Patrice par Berol* (Lund, 1917), p. xx.
3. C.M. van der Zanden, *Etude sur le Purgatoire de Saint Patrice, accompagnée
du texte latin d'Utrecht et du texte anglo-normand de Cambridge* (Amsterdam,
1927).
4. *The Vision of Hell: Infernal Journeys in Medieval French Literature* (Edinburgh and London, 1970), p. 71.
5. T.E. McAlindon, 'The Treatment of the Supernatural in Middle English
Legend and Romance, 1200–1400' (unpublished Ph.D. thesis, University of
Cambridge, 1960), pp. 123, 132 n. 1.
6. See above, p. xxii, where I suggest that 32 lines have been lost at the
beginning of the poem, apart from the 12 lines 177:3–179:2.

different lines, or 13–14% of the surviving 1174 lines of A. There are nearly thirty occasions where *OM*1 has kept the same or the equivalent word form in rhyme, on ten occasions single rhyme words being retained,[1] on eight occasions a pair of rhyming words,[2] and in one instance a sequence of three rhyming words.[3] I believe that the author of *OM*1 did not use a text of *T*: where he departs from AN he also departs from *T*. There is no substantial evidence that *OM*1 includes any details from *T* that are not also found adequately in AN.[4] The author did incorporate borrowings from a Middle English version of the *Vision of St Paul*[5] in the account of purgatory, and probably made use of some other account(s) of the Earthly Paradise, for this section of the poem expands considerably on the details found in AN, but if so I have not been able to identify them. That A is translated and adapted from Anglo-Norman fits the pattern for many of the texts in the Auchinleck manuscript; indeed, 'nearly all the romances are based on known or putative French or Anglo-Norman sources ...'.[6] '[I]t seems that translation and versifying were as much the activities [of the bookshop which apparently produced the manuscript] as scribing, illuminating, binding and selling'.[7]

All the close verbal correspondences between A and F are given in the Commentary, where I quote F from Zanden's edition, which I have checked with the manuscript and find accurate. CUL MS Ee. 6. 11 is a small parchment volume of 84 leaves. It contains three items: 1) an Anglo-Norman *Life of St Margaret*; 2) AN ff. 13r–37v in double columns of approximately 30 lines, with the colophon *Explicit liber de Gaudio Paradisi terrestris*; 3) Marie de France's *Fables*. The manuscript has been variously dated, from 'the early part of the xivth century',[8] or the first half of the thirteenth century.[9] Meyer distinguished the

1. A2:4 = F57, A3:1 = F66, A7:6 = F96, A16:6 = F148, A25:5 = F201, A35:4 = F273, A38:4 = F331, A121:2 = F1116, A127:5 = F1184, A165:4 = F1609.
2. A5:4–5 = F89–90, A15:1–2 = F139–140, A38:1–2 = F325–6, A47:4–5 = F401–2, A79:4–5 = F(787–)8, A147:1–2 = F1289–90, A156:1–2 = F1325–6, A180:3, 6 = F1619–20.
3. A176:4–6 = F1475–7.
4. See Commentary A72:2 for a single minor detail where A seems dependent on *T* independently of F.
5. See below, pp. li–liii.
6. *Auchinleck MS*, p. viii col. 1, and see also L.H. Loomis in *PMLA*, lvii (1942), 607.
7. *Auchinleck MS*, p. ix col. 2.
8. C. Hardwick and H.R. Luard, *A Catalogue of the Manuscripts preserved in the Library of the University of Cambridge*, II (Cambridge, 1857), 260–1.
9. J. Vising, *Anglo-Norman Language and Literature* (Oxford and London,

handwriting[1] of items 1) and 2) as being from the second half, and 3) from the first half of the thirteenth century.[2]

The following examples show, under 1: that A follows AN in details not found in *T*; under 2: that A follows AN in details found in β *T* but not in α; and under 3: that F follows β *T* in details which A omits.

1:1   A5:1–3   When Sein Patrike herd þis,
Michel he card forsoþe, ywis,
And sore he gan desmay.

Cf. F85–86   Quant sein Patriz iceo oÿ,
Mult en fu dolent e marri ...

1:2   A7:5–6   Sone he fel on slepeing
Toforn his auter.

Cf. F96   Il s'endormist devant l'auter ...

1:3   A18   When Seyn Patrike o slepe he woke,
Gode token he fond and vp hem toke
Of his sweuening:
Bok and staf þer he fond,
And tok hem vp in his hond,
And þonked Heuen-king.

Cf. F153–9   E quant sein Patriz s'eveilla,
Enseignes bones i truva
Ke i n'out mot de mensunge
De kanke il out veü en sunge:
Ceo fut le livre oud le bastun
Dunt Deu li aveit fait le dun.
Il en ad mut Deu mercïé ...

2:1   A35:4   Þei þou me wost comandy ...
Cf. F273   Si vus le volez comander ...
following β *te precipiente* (L217); not in α.

2:2   A41:1–3   Namore liȝtnesse nis þer yfounde
Þan þe sonne goþ to grounde
In winter sikerly.

Cf. F350–2   Kar clarté y ad autretant
Cum en iver avum ici
Quant le soleil est recunsi ...

This follows β:

1.   See the photograph of f. 19r printed by Zanden, *Etude*, opp. p. 89.
2.   P. Meyer in *Romania*, xv (1886), 268.

Lux autem ibi non apparuit nisi qualis hic in hyeme
solet apparere post solis occasum (L261–2).

Cf. α W48:15–17:

Lux ibi non habebatur nisi qualis hic uespertinis
horis in hieme habetur.

Whereas in *T* this section occurs in the narrative of Owein's
descent, in both F and A it has been brought forward and inserted
in the prior's warning speech at the entrance to the Purgatory.

2:3   A176   Hereof spekeþ Dauid in þe sauter,
Of a þing þat toucheþ here,
Of God in Trinite,
Opon men, þat ben in gret honour,
And honoureþ nouȝt her creatour
Of so heiȝe dignite.

Cf. F1473–7 Pur ceo mustra David e dist,
Ke le sauter traita e fist,
Ke home, kant il fust en honur
U le aveit mis sun creatur,
Ne tendi pas sa digneté ...

This follows the reference to Psalm 48:13 (Vulgate) found only in
β:

Et quia, cum in honore esset, non intellexit, comparatus est iumentis insipientibus et similis factus
est illis (L845–7).

3:1   F832   Un cercle enter de fu ardant ...
Cf. β   circulus igneus integer ... (L461)
not found in α (see α W82:27), nor in A.

3:2   F1095–6 Nus vus ferum commuvant
Esturbiluns e vent si grant

This follows β 'nos autem, uentos et turbines commouentes ...'
(L543–4), not α 'nos autem auram commouebimus et uentus ille
...' (α W96:16–18). This detail is not retained as such by A; see
A118.

3:3   The pagan Irish say they will not believe St Patrick's words:
F67   Pur miracle ne pur sermun ... after β:
nec pro miraculis que per eum uidebant fieri nec per
eius predicationem ... (L112–14).

α omits the reference to preaching; see W20:72ff. A reduces this
to 'bi his techeing' (3:3).

3:4   The souls nailed down in the first field of torment cry for
mercy:

F619–20 Mes la n'i aveit nul pur veir
          Ke vousist de eus merci aveir ...
after β:

          Sed non erat in loco qui misereri nosset aut parcere.
          (L379).
Cf. α W68:55–57: 'Sed qui eorum ibi misereretur non habebant.'
In A this simply becomes:
    A66:4   Merci nas þer non, forsoþe.

3:5   F1146–8 Ke tant de laür i truva
           Ke deus chares i purent aler
           E sur le punt sei encuntrer.
This follows β:

          tantum creuit pontis latitudo ut etiam duo carra
          exciperet sibi obuiantia (L562–3).
Cf. α W98:59–62: 'latitudo pontis exciperet carrum onustum, et
post modicum uia erat ita larga ut sibi obuiarent in ea duo carra.'

3:6   F1150   Al pié del punt en pes esturent ...
follows β:

          ad pedem pontis steterunt ... (L566).
Cf. α W100:64–65: 'in ripa fluminis restiterunt ...'

Other significant details are as follows.
4:1   The perilous bridge is described in F as:
    F1116   trenchant cum un rasur ...
a detail not found in T, but translated in A:
    A121:2   as scharpe as a rasour ...
A ignores the slipperiness of the bridge found in F and T, making
the three perils of the bridge (in order) height, sharpness,
narrowness (A121:1–3), as opposed to slipperiness, narrowness,
and height in T (L548–54), and height, sharpness, slipperiness
in F1113–22. There is no need to suppose that the narrowness in
A was directly derived from T, for it is the commonest feature of
perilous other-world bridges, and could be inferred anyway from
the sharpness in AN.
    F1140   Il ne senti nule escrillure ...
follows β:

          Nichil igitur lubrici sub pedibus sentiens ... (L559–
          60).
This is not found in α. In A this slipperiness becomes sharpness:
    A125:5   No feld he no scharp egge.

4:2   F elucidates a passage in A where St Patrick builds his
church; the manuscript reads:

A20:4-5   In þe name of Godes glorie,
              Seyn Patrike and our leuedy . . .
Though a church may be dedicated to its founder, it reads a little
oddly to find St Patrick establishing an abbey in his own name.
But F reads:
F168-71   Une eglise en le honorance
              De Damnedeu e de sa mere
              E del bon apostle seint Pere
              Ad sein Patriz illoc fait fere . . .
On the basis of this reading I have emended A20:5 to *Seyn Peter*
. . .[1] The MS reading may be a copying error, the scribe's eye
having been caught by the opening of
A21:1   Seyn Patrike maked þe abbay.
There is no mention of Peter in *T*.

4:3   The English author points indirectly to his Anglo-Norman
couplet source:
A29:6   As it seyt in þis rime.[2]
This is more specific than the usual phrase, *so seyt þe boke* (A46:4,
cf. 110:2).

ii. *OM*1 and the treatment of sources
Following AN, *OM*1 omits certain sections of *T*. These sections
may have been omitted from the β copy of *T* used by the
translator who composed AN. They are the opening section
(L3-76), the tale of the bestial Irishman (L82-107), the tale of the
one-toothed prior (L154-71), the two homilies (L577-750 and
918-1044), and everything after Owein's return from the Holy
Land, i.e. from L1070 onwards. These episodes are also omitted
from *OM*2[3] and *pa*. In other words, all three Middle English
versions concentrate on St Patrick's founding of the Purgatory
and the narrative of Owein's visit to the other world. In the first
part of *OM*1, stanzas A1-127, a few other incidents contained in
F have also been omitted: the letter from the bishop to the prior
of the Purgatory, F297-320 (A37); the devils' talk of the 'false' pit
of hell, F1049ff (A115); and the devils throwing hooks at Owein
as he crosses the perilous bridge, F1165ff (A126). One section has
been misplaced: the episode of the purgatorial mountain and the
stinkand river (A90-95) should follow the bath-house (A96 104)
as it does in T and F, with the bath-house at L465-87 and
F841-910, and the mountain and the river at L489-506 and

1. See Commentary A20:5.
2. See below, p. lv.
3. See Table, below, pp. lxxxviii-lxxxix.

F911–64. There is no apparent reason why these sections have been transposed in A, and nothing is either gained or lost by it. It is very likely the result of a copying error, the scribe having initially copied *Þai ladde him forÞer wiÞ gret pain* (90:1) instead of *ForÞ Þai ladde him swiÞe wiÞalle* (96:1). Apart from these instances, the A text faithfully follows the order of events in AN, which itself more closely follows *T*.

Of all the Middle English versions *OM*1 includes the most material not ultimately derived from *T*. Apart from the details inherited from AN, *OM*1 also expands the account of purgatory by using details from one of the Middle English versions of the *Vision of St Paul* (*VSP*).[1] The account of the Earthly Paradise has also been expanded, though, as mentioned, I have not identified any other specific source(s) for this section. It will be convenient to deal with these two parts of the poem in order.

Purgatory

The treatment of purgatory is considerably altered in *OM*1 by the inclusion of moralizing passages naming the sins for which the souls are punished, and listing Owein's sins in the process. These additions are adapted from *VSP*, which has the same six-line tail-rhyme stanza form as *OM*1. The author of A hereby rectifies what was evidently felt to be a deficiency in AN. *T* is unusual in this regard for unlike the majority of other-world visions it does not specify the sins being punished. In A, however, Owein is accused by the fiends of pride and lechery (58:3), lechery and gluttony (74:2–3), covetousness (87:2), and *okering* (usury, 103:4). The narrator tells us moreover that sloth is punished in the first field of torment (67:2), where souls are nailed down, the implication being that they are thereby suitably immobilized from all action; gluttons are eaten (71:4), rather than eating, in the second field; hot lechers are cooled by the cold wind (73:4), in the third field; thieves hang by the feet (80:5) and backbiters by the tongue (81:4), along with swearers *on Þe halidom* and false witnesses (82:4–5), in the fourth field. The ever-revolving wheel punishes the covetous who cannot ever have enough (86:2), and *ond* (hatefulness) *was Þe windes blast* (95:4) which blows souls into the stinking cold river from the top of the fiery mountain. Usurers (102:1) are punished by eating fiery pence from the money bags which hang about their necks.[2] The pit is, of course, the place of pride (112:5). This predominantly successful matching of pains to

1. *Index* 3089, Bodleian MS Laud Misc. 108, ff. 199r–200v, printed by C. Horstmann in *Archiv*, lii (1874), 35–38.
2. See Commentary A101:4–102:1.

sins reveals an insistence on the moral impact of the tale which is absent from the stark accounts in *T* and F. The narrator of *OM*1 is also keen to impress upon his audience directly the necessity to leave sin (81:5–6, 102:2–3). Whereas some of the manuscripts of *T* include the two homilies, *sanctorum patrum exhortationes* (L1256), to bring home to the original Cistercian audience the moral significance of the tale, F omits them, and *OM*1, aimed at a secular audience, incorporates its own commentary in the body of the narrative.

Kölbing[1] pointed out some of the parallels between A and *VSP*, and unconvincingly tried to demonstrate by a brief study of their language that they were by the same author.[2] All significant verbal parallels will be found in the Commentary to A. *VSP* contains a list of sins and sinners found in hell, for St Paul did not visit a purgatory. The sins specified are lechery (stanzas 7 and 10), 'jangling' in church (11), seeking one's neighbours' harm (12), usury (15), backbiting (17), and pride (32). This provided the model for the author of *OM*1, but the details are his alone, based upon a long tradition in other-world visions of apportioning punishments to fit the crime.[3]

Apart from this naming of the sins and the transfer of several lines describing the tortures, *OM*1 has also adopted the furnace with seven seals from *VSP* and applied it to the pit. In *T* and F the pit is the 'false' hell, the true hell lying beneath the waters under the perilous bridge. In *OM*1 the pit has been altered by superimposing the account of the true pit of hell from *VSP*.

VSP 19:1–3   He let him seon a put bi cas.
                     þat with seouen seles a seled was.
                     þat gan foule stinke.

VSP 23–25:2   Powel saiȝh a fuyr glowe grimme.
                     Of seue colours was þat leiȝe þar inne.
                     At seuen holes hit out wende.
                     Sunfole soules weren þar inne.
                     For huy deiden in dedlich sunne.
                     Heore sunnes forte amende.

                     þat o leyȝe was puy[r] snouȝh ȝwyȝht.
                     þat oþur ase hayl þat lyȝt in dyȝt.
                     þat þridde ase fuyr him brennez.
                     þat feorþe was hewene ich wene.

1. *EStn*, i (1877), 91ff.
2. See above, p. xxiv.
3. See, for example, Martha Himmelfarb, *Tours of Hell: An Apocalyptic Form in Jewish and Christian Literature* (Philadelphia, 1985), chapter 3.

þat fiȝfte ase naddres on to seone.
þare was luyte wunne.

þe sixte leyȝe ful cold was.
þe seouenþe stonke foule alas.

In *OM*1 the pit is described as follows.

A106   Of seuen maner colours þe fer out went,
         Þe soules þerin it forbrent;
         Sum was ȝalu and grene,
         Sum was blac and sum was blo;
         Þo þat were þerin hem was ful wo,
         And sum as nadder on to sene.[1]

Where St Paul testified to the pit with seven seals being the true
hell, the author of *OM*1 has transferred this testimony to the true
hell of *T* and F beneath the bridge.

VSP 20   Also þo dominical it tellez.
         Hit is þe meste pine of helle.
         Powel bereth witnesse.
         þe soules þat comez in þat prisoun.
         Of heom nis no mencion.
         Noþer more ne lesse.

A123   So þe dominical[2] ous telle,
         Þer is þe pure entre of helle:
         Sein Poule berþ witnesse.
         Whoso falleþ of þe brigge adoun,
         Of him nis no redempcioun,
         Noiþer more no lesse.

The *OM*1 poet has retained the rhyme sounds while adapting
VSP 20:4–5 to fit the transference from the *prisoun* of the pit to
falling from the *brigge adoun*, and has particularized the loss of
souls in hell by saying there is no redemption, which replaces the
mencion of *VSP*.[3] *OM*1 hereby forcefully distinguishes between
purgatory, whence redeemed souls pass safely across the bridge to
the Earthly Paradise, and hell beneath the bridge, whence *nulla est
redemptio*.

    The presentation of purgatory in *OM*1 is also altered from the
source AN by the introduction of several dramatic and descriptive
details seemingly of the author's own invention, albeit within a

1. See Commentary A106.
2. See Commentary A123:1.
3. See Commentary A123:5.

clear tradition of fiends and torments. As in *OM*2, the speeches of
the devils display a livelier sense of irony than is found in *T* or *F*.
They refer to their *daunce* (56:5, cf. C282) and *play* (56:6, 119:4),
and with nice incongruity promise to bring Owein home *wiþ fine
amour*.[1] They also make fun of Owein as *Sir kniȝt*, their leader
falling on his knees to welcome him (55:2), and introducing him
to their *courtelage* and *castel tour* which is the pit (107–8). Some of
the fiends are briefly visualized as having sixty eyes or hands
(114), and faces on their *touten* (54:2). The complete absence of
description of the demons in *T* and F is notable. (It is a deficiency
which by the fifteenth century was rectified in *VWS*, SR89–93,
SA90–95.) Other details with which the author of *OM*1 has
elaborated on his prime source include the fiery red aspect of the
purgatorial mountain (90:3, 93:2); the angel who bears Owein
from the tormenting wheel (89:4); and the fact that Owein's *clopes
wer al torent* after his adventure in the pit (113:3). This last idea is
implicit later when Owein enters the Earthly Paradise and a cloth
of gold is brought mysteriously to him, which when donned heals
all his wounds (see 89:1–2, 113, 128 and Commentary).

The Earthly Paradise

This brings us with Owein to the Earthly Paradise and the second
part of the poem, stanzas 128 to the end. It is here that the *OM*1
poet has added most to his prime source AN. In richness of
description *OM*1 here far surpasses all the other versions of the
tale, both Latin and vernacular, by the addition of catalogues of
precious stones (131), of the inhabitants (137–9), of flowers (147),
of the rivers of paradise (151–2), and of dress (154). Emphasis is
also laid on the music and heavenly carolling (141–3) (which
contrasts with the devils' dance), the elaborate bird-song (145–6)
and architectural finery (132–3). It is note-worthy that these latter
passages preserve some of the earliest occurrences of several
words as recorded in the *MED* and *OED*.[2] There is a particularity
in the naming of individual flowers that shows an infiltration of
the spirit found in such descriptions in romance literature.[3] This
amplification in the presentation of paradise expands on that
begun in AN[4] and distinguishes *OM*1 clearly from *T, þa*, and

1. See Commentary A57:4.
2. See above, p. xxv.
3. See E. Willson, *The Middle English Legends of Visits to the Other World and
their Relation to the Metrical Romances* (Chicago, 1917), pp. 34ff.
4. Owen, *Vision of Hell*, p. 73 says of AN: 'the section dealing with Paradise is
developed more fully than that describing Hell—an unusual occurrence, and a
point in the poet's favour'.

*OM*2; it is a refreshing and satisfying counterbalance to their heavier emphasis on the pains of purgatory. McAlindon pointed out the conscious attempt in A to emphasise the contrast between the earthly and the other-worldly,[1] a characteristic feature of romance literature. In fact the whole poem is shot through with comparisons to bring out the superlative quality of St Patrick's mission, the Purgatory, the pains therein, and the delights of paradise,[2] and this strain is supported by the prolific use of hyperbole and similes, often proverbial.[3] Everything is *richer ywrou3t* in the Earthly Paradise than anything found in the middle-earth of our ordinary existence. The idea of Christ as *queinter þan goldsmitþe oþer paintour* (133:2) marks out the gates of the Earthly Paradise as the masterpiece of God's handiwork.

A130:4–6   Tre no stel nas þeron non,
              Bot rede gold and precious ston
              And al God made of nou3t.

The unseen hand of God operates in the way *Þe gates bi hemselue vndede* (134:1) and in the arrival of the *cloþ of gold* (128:1) which heals Owein's wounds.

Morality and romance

By such emphasis on the wonderful *OM*1 is well suited for its inclusion in the Auchinleck collection of romances and religious tales. The opening of the poem is lost, but the narrator intrudes, in a fashion suitable for recitation and familiar from romances, to exhort the audience to attention when Owein is introduced (28:4–6, here following AN), and to appeal to his source as *þe storie* (24:6, 42:3 (spoken by the prior), 192:1). At 67:3 such an appeal follows one of our author's own additions, and similarly at 29:6, where he refers significantly to *þis rime*,[4] the appeal follows the new information that Owein was a knight from Northumberland. In *T* it is clear that Owein was Irish, and the unwarranted claim for his English origins was probably suggested by the *OM*1 poet recalling the well-known Northumbrian hero in Bede's account of the Vision of Drihthelm, or by the thought that that distant part was a fittingly remote birthplace for so remarkable a knight as Owein. Freed from any necessity to adhere to the likely historical authenticity of *T* regarding Owein's visit to St Patrick's

---

1. 'Treatment of the Supernatural', pp. 130ff.
2. E.g. 9:2–3, 12:2–3, 21:3, 40:5, 44:2, 96:3, 122, 136:5, 142:2, 148, 151:5, 165:6, 169:4–6, 170:5.
3. E.g. 41:1–3, 48:2, 52:3–6, 84:1, 90:3, 93:3–4, 106:6, 114:4–6, 116:4, 121:2, 133, 149:2, 181:1–3, 189:4–5, 191:3.
4. See above, p. l.

Purgatory, the *OM1* poet's fallacy of making Owein an English-
man is not apparent, and the appeal to an English audience is
enhanced.[1]

The romance element inherent in the structure of the tale of
Owein is most fully developed in the *OM1* version. To return to
the first part of the poem for a moment, we find that Owein is
presented in the popular mould of a valiant knight, *a douhti man
and swiþe wi3t* (29:5); *wel michel he couþe of batayle* (30:4), but he
was *swiþe sinful* nevertheless. The bravery requisite for facing the
trials of purgatory in the flesh had been well appreciated by
Henry of Sawtry in his preface:

> Notum est autem multos multociens quesisse qualiter anime a
> corporibus exeant, quo pergant, quid inueniant, quid percipiant
> quidue sustineant. Que, quia a nobis sunt abscondita, magis nobis
> sunt timenda quam querenda. Quis enim umquam cum securitate
> in incerto perrexit itinere? (L34–39)

But the repeated emphasis in *T* on the spiritual valour of Owein
as Christ's knight, armed with the armour of God, *ferro durior,
fide, spe, et iusticia* (L249–50),[2] is omitted from *OM1* and *OM2*.
Instead, the fear and dread suffered by Owein the *douhti man*
show the true horror of the situation (51:4–6, 52:3, 120:3);
compare such expressions as *animo impauido* (L307–8) and *diuina
uirtute* (L312) which tend to characterize Owein's progress in *T*.
Indeed, where *T* stresses the power of repentance and true faith,
OM1 stresses the trials and sufferings of a mortal knight fighting
the forces of evil. In *T* Owein is nearly always released by his
prayer before suffering the threatened pains, except for his brief
torments in the first fire in the hall, on the wheel, and in the river.
Only in the depths of the pit (*grauiorem penam pertulit*, L523–4)
does Owein almost forget his prayer, but he is saved *Deo tamen
inspirante* (L525). In *T* the devils' attempts to torture Owein are
repeatedly frustrated by his talismanic prayer. In *OM1*, on the
other hand, Owein actually suffers the pains:

> A68:1–3 Þis was þe first pain apli3t
> Þat þai dede Owain þe kni3t:
> Þai greued him swiþe sore.[3]

T's formula is followed at A75:4–6 and 104.

In the Earthly Paradise there are several features which parallel
the common stock of marvels that permeate the romance world
and which derive at least in part from Celtic other-world

1. See Commentary A29:4.
2. See also, e.g. L295–6, 312, and F455ff.
3. See also 60:1–2, 63:3, 89:1–2, 113:3–6.

literature. Such is the sweet smell which gives Owein strength
(134), like the *swete smal of al gode* which is the *soule fode* of the
inhabitants of paradise, the daily meal of the *holi gost in fourme of
fer*, which is but a mere foretaste of *Godes fest* as enjoyed in
paradis celestien (182–4). The *foules of heuen*, whose song also
sustains Owein (146:1–3), are reminiscent of many a company of
singing birds in Celtic other worlds, such as those in the
Navigatio Sancti Brendani. There is no reason to suppose that any
particular work was the 'source' for such a feature.

The moral bias of the first part of the tale is continued in the
account of the Earthly Paradise, where the poet combines his
description of the scenic and other delights with a certain
doctrinal interest which is again considerably more developed
than in AN or *OM2*. He reveals the exclusiveness of the *carol* in
paradise, only those *clene of sinne* and folly being admitted.[1] The
narrator's intrusion in the first person is used to emphasize the
analogy of *þe ioies of paradis* being like *þe sterres clere* in that they
are *nouȝt al yliche* (156–7). Much space is given to the explanatory
speech of the 'bishops' (158:4–167). The part of the speech
devoted to the story of Adam's fall follows AN in being longer
than in *T*, but is not given at second hand by the bishops: in *OM1*
it has been transferred to the narrator (171–179). It is clearly
stated that Owein has been through purgatory,[2] and the distinction between *paradis terestri* and *paradis celestien* is clearly defined
(164–166, 170–171).[3] In stanza 167 the author has added information on the relative speed of purgation of a new-born infant
and an old man *þat long in sinne haþ be*. This is not found in *T* or
F. It is also interesting to note that the valiant knight of the
purgatorial section of the poem is thrice called *seyn(t)* or blessed
after he reaches the Earthly Paradise (149:4, 188:1, 198:4). On this
last occasion Owein seems well nigh to have been canonized![4]
Certainly, *OM1* most clearly suggests the parallel between
descent into St Patrick's Purgatory and Christ's Harrowing of
Hell, when finally Owein, *Godes kniȝt*, emerges from the cave
amidst a bright *lem of liȝt*, which he proves *þat he was holy man*
(193–194).

1. See 141:5, 143:4, 152:1–3.
2. See 160:6, 165:1, 166:2, 194:5.
3. See further, Easting, 'Purgatory and the Earthly Paradise', pp. 42–46.
4. See also Commentary A94:1–3.

OM2—Cotton/Yale Couplet Version

i. The relationship of *OM2* to the *Tractatus*.

As a translation of *T, OM2* is less complete than *OM1* and *pa*, and much less faithful to *T* than the latter.[1] Together with the likelihood of memorial transmission in Y, these factors make it less immediately obvious which group of *T* texts the couplet versifier used. (There is no evidence to link CY with any of the extant Anglo-Norman or Old French versions.) Overall there is, however, sufficient evidence to say that *OM2* derives from a β *T* text; there is the limited possibility that an α text may have been used in one section, but as I show below it is not necessary to assume this use.

CY and β T

1. One of the most important pieces of evidence to link CY and β *T* is in the lines telling of St Patrick founding the abbey of Reglis.

C87–88 And chanonus gode he dede þerinne,
Vnþur þe abbyt of Seynt Austynne.

This follows β

beati patris Avgustini canonicos uitam apostolicam
sectantes in ea constituit (L138–9).

No mention is made of Augustine in α.

2. CY follow β in the image of the half-light found after the immediate darkness of the cavern.

C213–14 Such was hys ly3th whan hyt was beste,
As in þe wynter when þe sonne goth to reste.

For the β and α passages, see above, p. xlviii section 2:2.

3. When Owein is crossing the perilous bridge, the demons let out a tremendous roar:

C451–2 That crye, hym þow3t, greuede hym more
Then all þe payne he hadde before.

This follows β

intolerabilior ei uideretur huius horror clamoris
quam preteritarum aliqua penarum quam sustinuerat ab ipsis (L568–70).

Cf. α

magis esset uocum illorum terrore percussus quam
illatione tormentorum antea fuerat excruciatus
(W100:68–71).

4. C454 In God was all hys entente.
This follows β

---

1. For further brief discussion of *OM2*, see Easting, 'Middle English Translations'.

piique ductoris sui reminiscens (L571).
There is no equivalent in α.

5.   Y502–3   So brod was the brygge thoo,
                 Tweyn cartys myth þeron goo.
This follows β; for the passages in T see above, p. xlix, section 3:5.

6.   In the Earthly Paradise two of the inhabitants, who seem like
bishops, take Owein with them,

C514–16   Forto bere hym company,
          And schewede hym, þat he my3th se,
          The fayrnesse of þat cowntre.

This follows β

          militem in suo comitatu susceperunt secumque
          duxerunt quasi patriam et eius amenitatis gloriam ei
          ostensuri (L781–2).
Cf. α   patriam ei ostensuri in suo eum ductu et comitatu
          susceperunt (W112:65–67).

7.   These bishops (*quasi archiepiscopi* L780–1) subsequently tell
Owein:

C553–4   We haue gone þe way þer þou was,
          And we haue passed þat ylke plas.

This more likely derives from β *per illa loca transiuimus* (L861)
than from α *in illis locis ... fuimus* (W124:51–52).

8.   CY give fifteen as the number of God's messengers who meet
Owein in the underground cloister-like hall (C226, Y221). This
follows the usual β reading (see L269–70 and Commentary).

9.   The fifteen messengers warn Owein to make haste on his
return, for the prior of the Purgatory will be expecting him at
dawn.

C645–9   Aftur masse, wythoute delaye,
          The pryour of þe abbey,
          Bothe wyth preste and chanoun,
          They wyll come wyth processyoun
          To þe entre the agayne ...

This is based on β

          prior ecclesie, post missarum solempnia cum pro-
          cessione sua ueniens ad portam ... (L1058–9).
Cf. α   prior post missam portam aperiens ... (W138:29–
          30).

C Y and α?

All the lines of CY which appear to derive from an α text occur at
one point in the story, just before Owein enters the Purgatory
(C153–202).

In α, the story is as follows.

α i   In *T* MSS UB Owein is sent by the bishop to the prior of the Purgatory without any letter being mentioned, merely *secundum morem predictum* (Zanden, *Etude,* p. 10) which refers to the preceding general account of the procedure for entering the Purgatory. In MSS HAr we find the bishop gives a letter to Owein to take to the prior (W40–42).

α ii   The prior tries to dissuade Owein from undergoing penance in the Purgatory, but Owein stays fifteen days in the church, and is then led out to the Purgatory *cum processione et letanie cantu* (W42:67–69).

α iii   In direct speech, the prior warns Owein to change his mind, for many have perished in the Purgatory (W42: 72–44:84).

α iv   Owein replies, in direct speech (W44:85–87).

α v   The prior's second direct speech, telling Owein what he will find in the Purgatory (W44:88–103).

In β the pattern of events is somewhat different.

β i   Owein is sent by the bishop to the prior with a letter (L225–6).

β ii   The prior, recognizing why Owein has come, *cognita ipsius causa* (L228–9), tries to dissuade Owein, but Owein stays fifteen days in the church, and is then led out *sicut supradictum est* (L235), referring to the preceding account of the ritual procedures for entry to the Purgatory (L188–92).

β iii   The prior warns Owein in indirect speech: *iterum enumeratis tormentorum intolerabilium generibus* (L236–7). Cf. α iii.

β iv   Owein makes no direct reply: *Milite uero constanter in proposito permanente . . .* (L238). Cf. α iv.

β v   The prior, in direct speech, tells Owein what he will find in the Purgatory.

In CY the order is changed as follows.

CY i   C153–8 follow β i. The bishop gives Owein a letter to the prior. The seal is not mentioned in *T*.

CY ii   C159–63 follow the opening of β ii. The prior receives Owein and reads the letter. C162 *Sone he wyste þe knyȝthes wylle . . .* follows *cognita ipsius causa* (L228–9).

CY iii C164–74 give a new direct speech[1] by the prior, which appears to owe something to α iii.

---

1. See below, p. lxxiii.

C167–9   But I de rede þat þou do not so,
         Noþur for wele ner for wo.
         Aftur my rede þou do anoþur ...
Cf. a   Sed si nostris acquieueris consiliis, ab hoc pro-
         posito omnino reuerteris et uitam tuam ... alio
         modo corriges (W42:73–77).
C170 repeats the idea of the bishop's speech at C146.

CY iv   C175–8 Owein's reply in direct speech follows a iv.
         C177–8   Thyþur y wyll, for my synnus alle,
                  To haue forȝeuenesse, what so befalle.
         After a Pro peccatis meis intrabo absque retractione
                  (W42:85–87).

CY v   C179–82 The prior replies in words reminiscent of the
         end of a iii.
         C182   ... þe perelles we shall þe telle ...
         Cf. a   dicam tibi quid tamen primo inuenies (W44:82–
                  84).

CY vi   C183–96 Owein is put in church, and then led to the
         Purgatory after fifteen days; cf. a ii.
         C192–4   Wente wyth hym yn processyoun,
                  And as lowde as þey myȝth crye,
                  For hym þey songe þe letanye ...
         Cf. a   cum processione et letanie cantu ... (W42:67–69
                  and also 34:51–52).
         Even where β ii refers the reader back—sicut supradictum
         est (L235)—to the earlier account of the procession, the
         English author would have found no reference to 'sing-
         ing' the litany: cum processione et letania (L191). Note that
         Y187 reads seyd ... þe letaney.

CY vii   C197–200 There are no speeches at the door of the
         Purgatory, for CY have transferred them all to the time
         before Owein was admitted to the church for fifteen days.

It may be that the English author of OM2 had access to a β text
which incorporated the a speeches in this section. I know of no
such β manuscript, however, and until such a copy is discovered it
may be more plausible to assume that the English versifier was
working from both a β and an a text, probably using a to make
good a missing or defaced page in his β text.

However, the case may be argued differently. The details
seemingly drawn here from a are not decisive.

a)   The 'singing' of the litany in CY vi could easily have been
      supplied by the English author or a copyist; as noted Y reads
      seyd for C's songe.

b)   The perelles of CY v might more easily derive from

tormentorum in β iii (L236), or *plurimorum perditionem periculumque* in β ii (L229).

c)   The new direct speech in CY iii and Owein's reply in CY iv fit the widespread tendency of *OM2* to introduce direct speech and also extend some of the speeches, as I note below, p. lxxiii. The correspondence with α in CY iii is not particularly close except for C169, and the following injunction *Take þe abyte* ... (C170) repeated from C146 suggests that the *rede* of C169 may echo C145.

d)   C175–8 are corrupt: note the rhyme *well/wyll* and the repeated and inverted lines 176–7. Y168–71 seem more authentic and less close to α.

e)   The only significantly close translation in the whole section, that in CY ii, is from β.

In other words, it is possible that no α text was used in the preparation of *OM2*. This is the only such complicated passage; as shown above (*CY and β* T), the rest of *OM2* witnessed by CY shows clear evidence of derivation from a β text of *T*.

ii. Textual comparison of Cotton and Yale

C and Y are independent copies of the same version *OM2*: C contains 682 lines, Y 685 lines; approximately 480 lines are recognizably common to both C and Y, and of these about 140 lines are the same or nearly so.

C omits the following lines contained in Y: 84–85, 216–17, 316–45, 350–419, 462–3, 643–4, 684–5, a total of 110 lines.

Y omits the following lines of C: 5–8, 41, 108, 147–9, 173–4, 257–8, 297–8, 303–8, 329–30, 335–64, 378–80, 409–12, 415–16, 465, 467–70, 501–4, 507–8, 531–2, 541–4, 551, 561–74, 589–94, 597–8, 601–2, 609–10, 621–2, 642, 661–2, 669–70, a total of 113 lines. These lists are necessarily approximate, for, in Y particularly, much has been rewritten.

Cotton

C presents a fairly continuous text, except for the omission of Y316–45, 350–419, a large section dealing with the fields of torment in purgatory. It is hard to understand why C should omit such a popular and central feature of the whole tale. It may be that the copyist left off his work at C368, at the culmination of an episode, and wrongly resumed at C369 = Y420, his eye having been caught by the rhyme *before/more* (Y416–17) reminding him of C367–8 *more/byfore* where he had left off, but there is no evidence in the hand or ink that C368 represents the end of a stint. It is more likely that the copyist of C or of C's exemplar

genuinely wished to omit the scenes of torment, in C's case
perhaps knowing that he intended to copy similar scenes in the
Vision of Tundale, which follows *OM2* in the present state of the
manuscript, or to suit the taste of a particular reader.[1]

The other omissions in C as against Y are merely five sets of
couplets. The loss after C88 of Y84–85, containing the important
information on the name of the abbey *Regelys* (cf. Y412), may be
due to homoeoteleuton, the rhyme *abeye/today* (Y84–85) being
the same as that in Y80–81 and C85–86 *today/abbey*. Y643–4 seem
not so much to have been omitted by C as invented by Y,
expanding the adequate couplet C637–8 into two couplets with
the same rhyme sound, Y641–4. Similarly, the final lines Y684–5
are only a conventional expansion of the valedictory formula
which is quite sufficient as it stands in C681–2. Thus in effect
there are only two other couplets, Y216–17, 462–3, which C
appears simply to omit. We may say, therefore, that C preserves a
reasonably good copy of *OM2*, except for the 100-line omission of
Y316–45, 350–419; the general superiority of the readings and
metre of C support this.

Yale

The quality of the text preserved in Y is poor in comparison: its
metre is frequently faulty; there are many false readings; and the
nature of the numerous and scattered omissions, transpositions,
and other errors seems to indicate that Y, or one of its antecedent
copies, was written from memory. Nevertheless, it is valuable for
what it preserves in Y316–45, 350–419, the section missing from
C, and for various other preferable readings. The didactic,
apocalyptic, and dramatic poems in the Brome commonplace
book make an interesting setting for this tale of knightly prowess
in the face of other-world trials and demonic adversaries, which
obviously appealed sufficiently to the late fifteenth-century col-
lector at Brome to warrant preserving a copy, even if a faulty one.

Y's omissions

On five occasions in Y single lines have been lost: C41, 108, 465,
551, 642. In three of these instances the remainder of the couplet
is left hanging: Y37, 104, 647. Such a practice points to writing
down from memory at some stage in the transmission. The cause
of the loss of C108 is clear.

---

1. The C copyist also omits from *Tundale* the long description of Lucifer (ll.
1305–72); see Mearns, *Vision of Tundale*, p. 46.

C107–8   Of peynus, þat þey syȝ þoo,
              And of mykyll joye also.
Y104   Of peynys that þey seyn ther.

By substituting *ther* for *þoo* Y has lost the rhyme word *also*, and therefore omitted C108 altogether. Y has lost C41 by substituting the infinitive form *gon* (Y37) for *go* (C42) which rhymes with *so* (C41). The infinitive with final -*n* is common within the line in Y, but it has here been used detrimentally in the rhyme. Y has lost the second half of C642 *For ryȝth now spronge þe day* and used *For ... now* to lead straight into a corrupt version of C643:

        To pryme þey wyll þe belle rynge,

which becomes Y648:

        For now the pryme bell ryngyth.

Y is then constrained to try and rhyme *ryngyth* with 'sing it' spelt *syngth* (Y649). At Y580–2 an attempt has been made to patch up the loss of C551 by making a triplet. Y has also (poorly) patched up the loss of C465:

C464–6   Hym þowȝte hyt lasted ynto þe ayr;
           Hyt was whyte and bryȝth as glasse
           He cowþe not wyte what hyt was.
Y511–13 That ran, hym thow, vp to þe eyre.
           He cowd noth wyte wereof yt was,
           Into the eyere yt was.

The second line of the couplet (C466) has been preserved as the first line of Y's couplet 512–13 and a poor, metrically deficient, new line has been introduced (Y513) by repeating the idea of the last part of Y511, or indeed more closely the end of C464 *ynto þe ayr*, and *yt was* from Y512 or even the beginning of the lost line C465. As a result, no doubt, of this confusion, Y has lost the following two couplets, C467–70.

On two occasions Y has lost a group of three lines. Y has lost C147–9, and contrived to make a triplet, Y143–5, by inserting a couplet which occurs properly later as C171–2, Y166–7. Y has lost C378–80:

C377–80 Some wer þerinne vp to þe chynne,
           And ȝet hadde þey noȝt bete her synne;
           And some wer vp to the pappus,
           And some wer yn to [þe] shappus ...
Y428–9   Summe stod theryn vp to the chyn,
           Summe to þe pappys and summe to þe schyn.

It must have been the more complex idea in C378 which caused the line to be forgotten. Y has therefore invented a new rhyme word *schyn* (Y429) and filled the line by use of *pappys* remembered from the rhyme of the missing couplet C379–80.

A similar patching process can be seen at Y605–6:

> And here we dwellyd at Goddys wyll,
> In joy and blysse to abyd styll ...

This couplet follows the loss of C589–94 and precedes the loss of C597–8, the intervening couplet C595–6 having been retained in Y607–8. Y605–6 is made up of fragments remembered from these lost passages, and as such have not been counted among the list given above of C's omissions of lines contained in Y. Y605 recalls C598: *Her we abyde Goddes wylle* ..., and perhaps also C591 *And at hys ordynaunce we be.* Y606 has taken *In joy and blysse* from C592; *to abyd* from C598; and *styll* is new to make up the rhyme, in place of *ylle* in C597.

C661–2 may have been omitted from Y because of the difficulty of remembering the assonantal rhyme *blyþe/alyue*, and the slightly unusual rhyme *self/helf* may have caused the loss of C257–8, which itself compromises with the more usual *self/half.* Again, the unusual form *mow3th* in rhyme with *sow3th* may have caused Y to lose C297–8.

There seems to be no other explanation apart from a faulty memory to account for the loss of the couplets and couplet groups C173–4, 409–12, 415–16, 501–4, 531–2, 609–10, 621–2, 669–70.

Of the remaining omissions, the fourteen-line section C561–74 in the 'sermon' in the Earthly Paradise, together with the omission of other lines spoken by the bishops (C597–8, 601–2) may indicate that the Y copyist or one of his predecessors had less relish for the moralizing and didactic strain of the poem than for the description of the pains of purgatory, which is more fully preserved in Y than in C. This may also apply to the loss of C5–8 in the long introductory passage about God's envoys on earth, which has no origin in *T.* The loss in Y of the lines comparable to C303–8, 329–30, 335–68 will be discussed below.

Common omissions

Taking C and Y together we find there are common omissions of material in *T,*[1] that presuppose an omission in their common ancestor, or perhaps in the archetype of *OM2.* Both copies omit such major items as the third field of torment, possibly because it repeats ideas from the first and second fields; the purgatorial hill and the cold river; the 'false' pit of hell; the heavenly mountain and the gates of the celestial paradise. It is noteworthy that at C397ff (Y448ff) we have the speech of the demons who in

---

1.   That is, apart from those omissions noted above, p. l.

L528–35 meet Owein after he has emerged from the pit of the 'false' hell, and they duly say:

C399–400   'They tolde þe þat þys was helle,
            But oþurwyse we shull þe telle.'

They take Owein off to *þe deuelus mowth* (C402) under the water beneath the perilous bridge. But CY omit the passage referred to by these demons (L508–28), and their speech is thus a *non sequitur*. Whether an earlier copy and the archetype retained the episode of the 'false' hell, or whether the English versifier was merely unskilful in choosing what to translate cannot be ascertained.[1]

Transpositions and errors in C and Y

Apart from their omissions, C and Y are also differentiated by the transposition of lines and sections, the greatest such corruption being in the description of the first and second fields of torment in purgatory. In the first field in *T* (L370–88) Owein sees souls nailed to the ground, *uentre ad terram uerso* (L374–5). In the second field in *T* (L390–411), souls are again nailed to the ground, but the difference is that whereas in field one their stomachs are turned to the earth, here in field two they lie on their backs (L393–5).

In C we find field one (C319–63), clearly identified by

C330–1   Þey ete þe erþe, so wo hem was,
          Her face was nayled to þe grownde,

following *pre dolore uidebantur terram comedere* (L376–7) and L374–5 quoted above, together with the souls' cry *Spare ... a lytyll stownde!* (C332) after *Parce! Parce! uel Miserere! Miserere!* (L378–9). At the end of field one C loses the second field; the third field, also omitted from Y[2] (L413–27); the fourth field, of diverse torments (L429–47); the fifth field, containing the wheel (L449–63); and jumps straight to the bath-house (L465–87). These omissions are where C has lost the 100-line section preserved in Y316–45, 350–419.

In Y the text is more complicated. Fields one and two have been confused, part of field one being lost (C329–30, 335–64), and another part of field one (Y346–9) being incorporated in field two. The sequence as the text stands is as follows. At Y316 we switch from field one to field two: *Vpward ther belyys wer cast* is the equivalent of *dorsa terre herebant* (L394–5). Field two extends to Y335, though between Y317 and 318 should occur Y350–5. In

1. See Table, below, pp. lxxxviii–lxxxix.
2. Cf. incidentally, Commentary A72–73.

Y336–345 we have the introduction to field two, displaced because of the switch at Y316. This introduction can be identified by Y341 *Many an edder and many a tode*, after *Dracones igniti ... serpentes igniti ... Buffones ...* (L395, 397–8, 400), for beasts do not appear in field one. At Y346–9 we switch back to a fragment of field one paralleling C331–4, identified by:

> Y346–7   Hyre facys wern turny[d] to the grownd,
>   They seydyn, 'Spare vs somme stond!'

With Y350–5, which should follow Y317, we return to field two for an elaboration of *T, The todys sotyn on euery herre* (Y352) being derived from *Buffones ... super quorundam pectora sedere* (L400–1). At Y356ff Owein moves on to the fourth field, the third having been omitted altogether, as noted above.

The confusion in this whole section, Y316–56, has itself been caused by the repetitious nature of fields one and two. For instance, Y326–33 in the second field are very close to C353–60[1] in the first field, though the couplet Y328–9

> Whyll þat þey streynyd forth hys fete,
> He clepyd to hym þat ys so swete

is so superior to Y's usual attempts to pad or rewrite that it is convincing evidence that these parallel passages do belong to the two different fields (cf. C355–6). The similarity of these sections is explained by the fact that at the end of field two in *T* the reader is referred back to field one (*sicut et superius* (L409–10)) for the description of the demons' attempts to nail Owein down, *clauis eum figere* (L410, cf. L386–7). The English adaptor would have turned back to field one, *prostrauerunt eum in terram* (L386), and translated: *Anon þe fyndys leydyn hym downe* (Y324). Assuming that the archetype of *OM*2 was at least faithful to *T* in the order of events in fields one and two, this section can be reconstructed by reading in the following order: C367, Y339–45, Y316–17, Y350–5, Y318–36, Y357ff. This reading accounts for all the lines between Y316 and Y356 except for 337–8, 346–9, 356.

> Y337–8   Sweche another he neuer behylde:
>   It was lenger mych more ....

is one of the repeated formulae linking the different fields, and is superfluous in a reconstructed ordering as the true introduction to field two I take to be

> C365–6   Full ferre into anoþer felde,
>   In such on bare he neuur shelde.

Y has lost the distinctive line C366, and merely substitutes at Y337 a variant of the formula found also at Y357. Y346–9 belong

---

1. They have been so numbered by Miss Toulmin Smith.

to the first field (paralleling C331–4) and have been misplaced.
Y356 is a duplicate of the formula at Y336. In the printed texts
below, the manuscript order is followed, but I have left gaps
between Y315 and 316, between Y317 and 318, and indented
Y356 (the beginning of the fourth field), to show where the
disjointed passages collide. After Y315, Y has lost C329–30. The
gap between Y317 and 318 is six-lines long, the equivalent of
Y350–5 which should fit there. The spacing on page 55 allows the
reader to see in parallel the similar passages in the first field
(Cotton) and the second field (Yale).[1]

Of the remainder of C's large omission Y316–45, 350–419,
lines Y357–419 comprise the following: Y356–71 present the
fourth field of torment; Y372–91 the fifth field, the wheel; and
Y392–419 the introduction to the bath-house, outside which
Owein stops before being moved on and in by the demons. At this
point the C text resumes, C369.

There are other instances where lines have been transposed in
Y.

> C343–4 For bettyr hyt ys þy sowle be yn woo,
> Then þy sowle and þy body also . . .

from the first-field passage missing in Y have been recalled and
inserted earlier in a similar speech at Y284–5, though they fit the
context there slightly awkwardly.

> Y444–5 'Jhesu,' he seyd, 'I thanke the;
> Euer at nede þou helppyst me.'

These lines also seem to be recalled from the end of the first field
(C361–2), and have been placed by Y in a similar position at the
end of the bath-house scene.

In the description of the Earthly Paradise lines Y546–75 are
confused. C follows more closely the pattern of *T*.[2]

There are a number of other errors in Y, many of which might
be as well attributed to misreading or mishearing as to faulty
memory.[3] There are also numerous instances where the rhyming
word or sound has alone been retained and the rest of the line
rewritten or the sense altered, invariably for the worse.[4] That
there are so many instances of this type of change is the clearest
indicator that Y or one of its immediate ancestors, or indeed both,

---

1. A tentative reconstruction of the whole poem (786 lines) is included in my
thesis, pp. 201–25.
2. See Commentary C509ff, Y546ff.
3. E.g. 25, 69, 70, 79, 103, 107, 122, 245, 262, 505, 561.
4. E.g. 63, 74, 110, 124, 134, 163, 186–7, 193, 204, 208, 222, 240, 253, 256–7,
263, 265, 278, 295, 296–7, 304, 311, 442, 449, 477, 483, 498–9, 509, 513, 525, 534,
545, 555, 558, 578–9, 581, 590, 600, 601, 606, 617, 623, 628, 642–4, 665.

was written from memory.[1] No such thorough rewriting and deterioration can be explained merely by careless copying.

Other evidence which suggests memorial composition of Y is the repetition of familiar lines when C retains a more distinctive reading. Take, for example, the passage at Y294–7, C301–10. When the first fire from which Owein escapes is extinguished by his prayer, C reads:

> C301–2   All þat fyre was qweynte anone,
>   Þe fendes flowen away euurychone . . .

where 301 follows *extinctus est tocius rogus incendii* (L349–50). Cf.

> Y294–5   The fendys fledyn eueryschon,
>   And lettyn Syre Howyn all alon.

Y has lost the distinctive first line of C's couplet, retained a variant of C302, had to find another line to complete the couplet, and therefore resorted to one used elsewhere at a similar point in the story:

> Y332–3   The fyndys fledyn euery on,
>   And let Syre Howyn all alon.

That this couplet formula stuck in the scribe's mind is shown at Y348 where he wrote *The fendys fledyn*, struck out *fledyn* and corrected with *woldyn*. It would seem that the loss of C301 caused the Y copyist to forget the next six lines (C303–8), and to resume idly by repeating the idea of Y295 in 296: *And as he stod þer all alone* . . . He then had to complete this couplet with Y297: *Oþer deuelys abowte hym gan gone*. He has thus caught up the original rhyme word *go* (C310) in *gone*, but the *deueles oþur* of C309 has been inverted by reference to another known couplet, Y334–5, which follows on from Y332–3 which have already been used.

> Y334–5   And as he stod and lokyd abowte,
>   Other delys ther comme on a rowte.

abowte in Y297 is doubtless taken from this rhyme. This couplet formula was also well known to the copyist, having been applied earlier to the messengers of God, Y220–1 (C225–6):

> As he stod and lokyd abowte,
>   Ther com .XV. men on a rowte . . .

It also occurs later at Y446–7 (C395–6):

> As he stod and lokyd abowte,
>   Off othyr fyndys þer camme a rowte.

The same procedure in Y, of forgetting distinctive lines preserved in C and patching by reference to repeated formulae, can be seen when Owein is dragged off to the river of hell.

---

1. I am mindful of the indicators noted by G. Kane, *Piers Plowman: The A Version* (London, 1960), p. 144.

C403–4 They drewe hym be þe hatere,
        Tyll þey come to a gret water.

No doubt the uncommon word *hatere* in rhyme caused the loss of
C403 in Y, which reads:

Y454–5 As they haddyn hym forth more
        A woll mych watyr he say before.

a gret water has been remembered as the important feature,
becoming *A woll mych watyr* in Y, but for the whole couplet Y has
relied on another repeated formula found at Y392–3:

        Fast þey hadyn hym ferder more,
        A woll mych howsse he sawe before . . .

where even *A woll mych* is ready to hand. Once again a scribal
error confirms that the Y copyist had this couplet structure well
in mind because he deletes *inne* after *ferder* in Y392, recalling a
variant form found at the previous shift from field to field:

Y372–3 As they haddyn hym ferder inne,
        A woll myche wylle he sawe þerinne.

Cf. also Y418–19

        As they hadyn hym ferder inne,
        Ther he sawe woll mykyll onwyn.

For another example, see

C263–4 For all þe worlde, so hyt ferde,
        And þerto a lowde crye he herde.

Y256–7 In that wedyr so yt faryd,
        Yt made Syre Howyn sore aferde.

C's good couplet has been woefully corrupted in Y. *For all þe
worlde*, an admittedly loose adaptation of *si totus commoueretur
orbis* (L309, see Commentary C263), has been weakened to the
less plausible *In that wedyr*, where *wedyr* perhaps represents a
misread or half-remembered *world*. C264 follows *cepit audiri
tumultus* (L309). Y, having lost this sense, patches by using a line
which occurs variously as

Y267   Syre Howyn wos aferd, I trowe . . .

and Y462   Therof he wos full sore aferd.

There are further instances of scribal error which suggest
the Y copyist was writing from memory. In Y440 *klepyd* is
deleted before the true rhyme word *calde* is restored. One may
compare other occasions where in Owein's appeal to Christ Y
used *klepyd* where C used *called* (Y487 = C440, Y490 = C443,
and Y329). In Y380 *faste* is deleted before restoration of the
rhyme word ʒarn, for ʒerne. Elsewhere Y shows a more cavalier
attitude to rhyme.

MS Y494–5 Whan he comme yn to the myde bryge
          Euery dewyll to other chyd.

This couplet matches C447–8 well, except that the scribe has mentally and physically added the *bryge*. Compare MS Y121–2

> To þe boschope of that cuntre
> He went and fond hym yn þat sete ...

where C126 reads ... *yn hys se*. Such errors reveal the Y copyist's mind running ahead and his pen following after. This might be the result of the scribe's saying the lines to himself as he copied another manuscript, but taken with all the other evidence it strongly suggests that the Y copy was written down from memory. The frequent severe metrical lapses point to the same conclusion, e.g. short lines like Y359–61, or hypermetric lines like Y350, 357, 367.

However, in a few cases Y retains a better reading than C.[1] Instances will be pointed out in the Commentary, along with all occasions where the Latin of *T* can assist in determining which reading is preferable. For example, Y503 is to be preferred to C456 in the description of the perilous bridge.

> Y503   Tweyn cartys myth þeron goo.
> C456   That waynes my3th þeron haue goo.

It seems likely that C's *That waynes* was influenced by *Tweyn*, a case of misreading or faulty memory at some stage in the ancestry of C. Y's reading is more correct, following *duo carra* (L563), though it lacks the metrically requisite auxillary *haue* of C. (Compare also the *pa* reading *tuei cartes* (Ld439[2]).) Unfortunately, because of the large amount of rewriting in CY and the apparent freedom of adaptation in the original translation, *T* is not always as immediately helpful as this.

iii. Cotton/Yale and the treatment of the *Tractatus*

OM2 is by no means a straight translation of *T*: there is some evidence of inventiveness in the adaptation; some passages and details have been added or significantly altered. Like *OM1* and *pa*, *OM2* omits all the parts of *T* extraneous to the founding of St Patrick's Purgatory and the tale of Owein.[3] Nevertheless, the opening 28 lines are new and give an overall context for the story by rehearsing God's continuing revelation of *the ryght way to heuen-blysse* (C4) by wise men sent to instruct mankind. God has sent prophets, Christ himself, the apostles and bishops, a succession which leads up to St Patrick preaching in Ireland about

---

1. E.g. Y147, C152; Y168–9, C175–6; Y184, C191; Y308–9, C321–2; Y496–7, C449–50; Y549, C536; Y593–4, C577–8; Y637, C633.
2. Cited from Carl Horstmann ed., *The Early South-English Legendary*, EETS, 87 (1887), 213.
3. See above, p. l.

heaven, hell and purgatory.[1] This section is balanced towards the
end of the poem by the extended treatment of the instruction
about purgatory and repentance, given to Owein by the 'bishops'
in the Earthly Paradise. Details have been added about the Tree
of Life (C525), the *frwyte of wysdom* (C527), and Adam after the
Fall (C581ff). (Possibly the copyist of Y or of one of his
antecedent sources thought this discussion too long, for there are
several passages missing from it in Y.[2]) The main intention of
OM2, however, seems less doctrinal than to present an exciting as
well as instructive story. God tells St Patrick that whoever
successfully completes the pilgrimage to the Purgatory, be he
sqwyer or knaue (C79), will not only be exempt from purgatory
after death, but *Mony a meruayle he may of telle* (C76). Accordingly, the marvelous aspects of the story figure largely, though
not as obviously as in *OM1*. As noted above,[3] moralizing passages
in *T*, like that on the spiritual armour recommended by the fifteen
men in white, well suited for the original monastic audience, are
omitted. Instead, Owein's fear and suffering are stressed, e.g.
C273-4, 352, or 384, where he is actually cast into the bath of
molten brass. Owein discovers that the fields of torment in
purgatory are indeed different from the battlefields in which he
has previously borne his shield (C365-6). Owein is in a *grete
aventur* (C236, cf. C622), and added physical details—his groping
in the dark (C208), his near swooning with the odour of paradise
(C472)—serve to remind the reader of his human frailty and
devotion, perseverance and knightly prowess. *Syr Owayne*, as he
is repeatedly called (C196, 202, 203, 212, 273 etc.), was a *dow3ty
mon and bolde* (C119). There is a lively appeal to a secular
audience's imagination, as in the stress on emperors, dukes, earls,
and barons, alongside friars and hermits, in the paradisal congreg-
ation. Other new details include, for example, the bishop's seal
(C156), the barrenness of the other world before the hall
(C218)—the hall itself is the more surprising here as the prior's
preparatory speech has been omitted—the gruesomely incon-
gruous hint of luxurious living (Y350-1), and the descriptions of
the cold and the demonic clatter (C259ff, C315-16). As in *OM1*,
the devils are clearly a favourite part of the story. In Y406-7 they
promise to show Owein *owre maystyr and owre kyng* in the
bath-house, and something of the relish of their irony is apparent
in new details added in their speeches, e.g. C278, 282, 284, 286,
290, where in each case the second line of the couplet contains a

1.   See further, Easting, 'Middle English Translations'.
2.   Y omits here lines C551, 561-74, 589-94, 597-8, 601-2.
3.   See p. lvi.

new thrust. Indeed, it is in the speeches that *OM2* most differs
from *T*, for throughout the poem *oratio obliqua* has been replaced
by *oratio recta*, new speeches have been introduced and translated
ones expanded.[1]

Though less elaborate than *OM1*, *OM2* makes the most of a
story that combines the best of many worlds: a physical entrance
to the other world in a geographical place remote enough to be
both credible and marvelous; a secular knight triumphant over the
devils and torments of purgatory by his own fortitude and by the
grace of God; his reward, a welcome to the Earthly Paradise and a
taste of the *ryche brede* (C614), sweet and hot (C609), which daily
feeds the saved; and a sinner who becomes *a mon of goode
deuocyoun* (C676) and passes *þe ryȝte way* to everlasting bliss
(C681–2, cf. C4, quoted above, p. lxxi). The concluding prayer
would incorporate the reader in that saving passage from fear to
love.

1. See C72–80, 141–8, 149–52, 164–74, 175–8, 291–2 (cf. *nichil penitus
respondens* L337), 299–300, 348–50, 357–8, 361–2, Y322–3, Y330–1, Y402–13,
Y414–17, C389–90, 427–36, 438, 616, 617–18.

5. THE VISION OF
WILLIAM OF STRANTON

i. The Texts

The two extant copies of this fifteenth-century prose text are presented in parallel below, pages 78–117. They are imperfect and independent copies, the Royal manuscript (SR for 'Stranton—Royal') tending to expansiveness and verbosity, the Additional manuscript (SA) tending to conciseness in the narrative, but with a freer treatment of the speeches. In these respects it is difficult to say how far either approximates to the original text.

SA, though less carefully copied, preserves several better readings than SR.[1] For instance, SA accurately preserves the name of *prior Matheus, keper of the same Purgatory* (SA9–10). Matthew is attested as prior at Saints' Island, Lough Derg in 1411 in the Vision of Laurence Rathold in BL MS Royal 10 B ix, ff. 43r–v: *Matheus prior Purgatorii Sancti Patricii Clothof Raynes (Clogherensis) dioceseos.*[2] SR corrupts this to *prior of Seint Mathew* (SR9). SA has preserved several superior readings where SR has become confused and verbose, e.g. in the description of the two ways (SR33–37, SA32–36), and the repeated assertions of the 'friendly' devils (SR69–81, SA74–82).

SR, on the other hand, preserves the correct name of the diocese of *Cleghire* (Clogher) (SR7), where the Purgatory is situated; SA reads *Jalcet* (SA8).

The date of William's entry into the Purgatory is different in the two manuscripts. SA gives Easter Day (14 April) 1406 (SA4, 8); SR gives Friday, 20 September 1409, *the Friday next after the*

1. For discussion of *VWS* with an account of SA, see also Easting, 'The English Tradition', pp. 67–80. For earlier discussions of SR, see Thomas Wright, *Saint Patrick's Purgatory* (1844), pp. 140–51; the résumé by G.P. Krapp, *The Legend of Saint Patrick's Purgatory* (1900), pp. 35–40; R. Verdeyen and J. Endepols, *Tondalus' Visioen en St. Patricius' Vagevuur*, I (1914), 267–9; and St. John D. Seymour, *St. Patrick's Purgatory* (1918), pp. 45–52.
2. See H. Delehaye, 'Le Pèlerinage de Laurent de Pasztho au Purgatoire de S. Patrice', *AB*, xxvii (1908), 58 l. 4, and see p. 57 l. 31. Prior Matthew is 'most probably a Mac Craith and related to, but hardly identical with' the Matthew whose death is recorded under the year 1440 in the *Annals of the Kingdom of Ireland by the Four Masters*, III. 918–19, 'Magrath, Matthew, son of Marcus, Coarb of Termon-Daveog, died', and the *Annals of Ulster*, III. 146–7: see P.O. Gallachair, 'The Parish of Carn', *Clogher Record*, viii (1975), 301–80 (p. 346, and see also p. 306).

Fest of þe Exaltacion of þe Crosse (SR2–4), *the Friday next after holyrode day in harvest* (SR8–9). The twofold statement here may indicate that SR confidently preserves the true date. SA's *Ester day* follows the incorrect *Jalcet*, and may have been substituted as being a suitable day on which to descend *ad inferos*.[1] As for the year, there is no way of determining which is correct as *vi* may have been misread for *ix* or vice versa. In any case William's pilgrimage falls between those of Ramon de Perellós in 1397[2] and Antonio Mannini and Laurence Rathold of Pászthó, November 1411.[3] Both manuscripts agree that William entered the Purgatory early in the day, *the viij^te owre before none* (SA8–9, cf. SR7–8).

SR preserves the full form of the prayer used to ward off the devils: *Jhesu Christe, fili dei viui, miserere michi peccatori* (SR13). This is the same as that given to George Grissaphan who visited St Patrick's Purgatory in 1353,[4] and to Laurence Rathold in 1411.[5] SA characteristically shortens the prayer to *Jhesu, fili dei, miserere mei* (SA13).

1.   E.g. in the *Vision of the Monk of Eynsham* Edmund fell into an ecstasy the night before Good Friday 1196 and woke up before compline on Saturday, Easter Eve; see ed. Salter, pp. 289, 291. It is interesting to note that he had previously prayed frequently for a vision of the future world, pp. 295–6, cap. IX, ll. 8–16.
2.   On which see M. de Riquer, *História de la Literatura Catalana*, revised ed., 3 vols., II (Barcelona, 1980), 309–33, 389–404, and Dorothy M. Carpenter, 'The Pilgrim from Catalonia/Aragon: Ramon de Perellós, 1397', in Haren & Pontfarcy, pp. 99–119.
3.   On Mannini see Jean-Michel Picard, 'The Italian Pilgrims', in Haren & Pontfarcy, esp. pp. 180–9, and on Rathold see Michael Haren, 'Two Hungarian Pilgrims', in Haren & Pontfarcy, pp. 159–68.
4.   See *Visiones Georgii*, ed. L.L. Hammerich (Copenhagen, 1930), p. 97, and for discussion, see Haren in Haren & Pontfarcy, pp. 121–59.
5.   See Delehaye, 'Le Pèlerinage', p. 50 ll. 10–11. Cf. also the accounts of the visits of Ramon de Perellós and Montalban's 'Ludovico Enio' (see Krapp (1900), pp. 26, 16, 39), and also Jacobus de Varagine's account of the descent of Nicolaus, *Legenda Aurea*, cap. L (49) ed. Th. Graesse, 2nd ed. (Leipzig, 1850), p. 214. I would interpret the figure in an attitude of prayer beneath St Patrick's outstretched arm in the Todi fresco as this same Nicolaus; he may be thought of as uttering this talismanic prayer. Mac Tréinfhir says that the subscript to this figure is almost indecipherable, though 'Those with whom I have spoken in Todi favour the reading, Dominus Nicolaus.' He then says, 'It is difficult to accept this reading. The figure is probably that of the patrician who paid for the work.' But if the reading is correct this identification would not be surprising. Mac Tréinfhir mentions the *Legenda Aurea* (p. 148), but does not make the connection with the name Nicolaus, substituted for Owein in *LA*. See Noel Mac Tréinfhir, 'The Todi Fresco and St Patrick's Purgatory, Lough Derg', *Clogher Record*, xii (1986), 141–58, esp. p. 150, and now also Picard, in Haren & Pontfarcy, pp. 171–2, who interprets the fresco as I do. (The fresco is reproduced at the end of Haren & Pontfarcy.)

Further brief examples of superior readings in SR are: *backes* (SR352) against *wombys* (SA356); *pipis or tonnes* (SR393) against *towrys* (SA401); and *toes* (SR394) against *tayllys* (SA401). SA285–91 preserves a better reading in the passage on false executors, against SR274–80.

There are also a few repeated verbal variants which are characteristic of each text. For example, when in danger, William always repeats the prayer he was taught and writes the first word, *Jhesu*, on his forehead:[1] in SA this is always expressed, *I blyssyd my forhede/me wyth my prayer*; in SR *y markid my forhede/me with my praier*. The personal note seems stronger in SA, for when explaining the torments, St John usually begins by saying, *Loo, Wyllyam . . .*; this is not found in SR. In fact, the name William is used 23 times in SA as against 13 times in SR. In SA William repeatedly asserts the veracity of his vision by use of the emphatic 'truly' (14 instances); in SR this word does not occur at all. It is probable that in these last two matters SA more closely represents the original, but this cannot be proved. In SA, when St John points out the souls, he usually says *thes were thay þat*; in SR *þoo yender ben thoo*. Other repeated verbal variants include: *stynke* (SA) and *stench* (SR); *st(e)yle* of a ladder (SA) and *rong* (SR); the more northerly verb 'rive' (SA273, 307, 481) and 'tear' (SR); and SR uses forms of *þilk/thilk* 26 times, SA never.

Krapp (p. 56) writes: 'The differences of phraseology, orthography, etc., are such as would naturally arise in two independent transcriptions of a single MS.' However, there is no evidence to suggest that SR and SA were transcribed from a single manuscript. Though following the same sequence of events, both copies omit different sections and make different mistakes which would be hard to explain as arising naturally from the same exemplar. It seems likely that the copyists of SA and SR, or of their antecedents, each made their own variations in phraseology as they went along, and probably rewrote whole sentences and made additions as they thought fit.

The following is a list of different categories of omissions and variations in the two texts. The lists are not exhaustive, but representative. Because of the high degree of variation between the texts it is not always possible to say strictly that one text has omitted material preserved in the other. Some of the categories necessarily overlap, e.g. nos. 5, 6 and 7.

1. Passages preserved in SR, which have been omitted from SA, thereby leaving *non sequiturs* or other inadequacies in SA:

---

1. See Commentary SR12.

i.   omission due to repetition of a word or phrase: SR99–100, 136, 190, 269–71, 319–20, 324–5, 646–7;

ii.   error at the change of column: SR444–67;

iii.   other omissions: SR157, 272–3, 609–32;

iv.   loss of final folio: approximately SR700–9.

There are no significant instances where SA preserves passages that can be shown to have been accidentally omitted from SR to the detriment of the sense.

2. Passages preserved in SR, which are lacking in SA apparently because of scribal error, but where the lacunae do not materially affect the continuity of the sense: SR16 *if þei ... evel*, 207–8 *summe ... metall*, 342–5 *Thenne ... God*, and possibly also 335–6, 354–6, 535–7, 578–9, 681.

3. Other passages preserved in SR, which also seem to have been lost in SA: SR290–2, 298, 311–14, 475–6, 522 *and the .xv. psalmes*, 594 *And þere ... faire contree.*

4. Passages preserved in SA which may have been omitted by SR: SA91 *iiij heddys*, 213–15, 424 *heddys ... and into ther ...*

5. Passages where SA may have expanded and there is no real equivalent in SR: SA37–39, 184–5 *streynynge ... fende*, 204–6, 209–11, 330–5, 431–2, 491–7.

6. Otiose repetition in SR: 77–81.

7. Parallel passages that appear to have been largely re-written along independent lines: SR1–4, SA1–4; SR192–6, SA198–204; SR237–48, SA250–8; SR389–91, SA395–9; SR408–9, SA416–17; SR426–38, SA435–50; SR664–78, SA635–49; SR696–9, SA666–72.

Because neither copy, either in substantial readings or stylistically, can be shown to represent a version notably closer to the original, I present both copies for the first time in full. Where individual words or phrases have been accidentally omitted and can be supplied from the other copy, this I have done to facilitate reading. Otherwise the parallel setting enables the reader to see at a glance where the larger changes have been made, and to appreciate the different tone of each copy, something which can scarcely be done with a mass of alternative readings at the foot of the page.

ii. The Vision

Nothing is known of William of Stranton apart from what little can be inferred from the vision. I have adopted the form of his name given here from SA as most likely preserving the original reading. SR calls him William Stavnton. William specifies that he comes from the bishopric of Durham, and Stranton is a coastal area south of West Hartlepool, so there is little doubt that the form in SA with the name of the town is the correct one.[1] The name of the area is also known as Straunton,[2] and the Warwickshire copyist (or an antecedent) of SR has substituted the more usual family name of Staunton. The existence of a family of Stauntons in Co. Meath, and of a William Staunton there testified in the 1380s[3] I take to be coincidental; Staunton was one of the earliest English names in Ireland, and Stauntons are found in Mayo and Connaught.[4] There is nothing in *VWS* to suggest that William lived in Ireland, apart from his pilgrimage to St Patrick's Purgatory, and indeed his familiarity with the local saints John of Bridlington and Hild of Whitby suggests that he may have spent most of his life in or near his native home of Stranton, Co. Durham.

In SR St Hild of Whitby is replaced by St Ive of Quitike or Quethiock in Cornwall. Ward argued that the association of St John of Bridlington and St Ive 'could hardly have occurred, as a correction, to a mere copyist' and that SA's St Hild was 'a name not unlikely to be due to a guess'.[5] This argument is itself not unlikely, but Ward here underestimates the adaptive powers of a 'mere copyist'. It must be remembered that before founding the monastery at Whitby (Streoneshalh) in 658, St Hild was from 649 abbess at Hartlepool; she would therefore have an especially close significance for William of nearby Stranton. It is more likely that the scribe of an antecedent copy of SR, 'for the sake of local color, or in order to honor a home saint, has substituted St Ive for St Hilda.'[6] It is interesting to note that when asked by William who he is, St John replies in SA, *In yor contre they call me ...* (SA54–55), which may well be the original reading, William's

1. 'William of Stranton' is the form of the name used by Seymour, *St. Patrick's Purgatory*, pp. 45–52, and also in the *Index of Manuscripts in the British Library*, IX (Cambridge, 1985), 383. Without giving evidence, Jonathan Hughes speaks of 'William Stranton, an armigerous knight from the parish of Stranton in Durham', in *Pastors and Visionaries: Religion and Secular Life in Late Medieval Yorkshire* (Woodbridge, 1988), p. 342, and see p. 57: 'William Stauton [sic], who was from an armigerous Durham family'.

2. See C.E. Jackson, *The Place-Names of Durham* (London, 1916), p. 100; A. Mawer, *The Place-Names of Northumberland and Durham* (Cambridge, 1920), p. 191, and *A History of Durham* (VCH), III (London, 1928), 365–76.

3. See R.J. Hayes ed., *Manuscript Sources for the History of Irish Civilisation*, IV (Boston, Mass., 1965), 523 col. 2, and also IX. 82 col. 2 and IX. 83 col. 3.

4. See E. Maclysaght, *The Surnames of Ireland* (Shannon, 1969), pp. 202, 85.

5. *Catalogue of Romances*, II. 487–8.

6. Krapp, p. 55. Krapp wrongly says that SR 'is in the southern dialect', and he also mistakenly equates St Ive with St Ives (p. 58); see below, Commentary SR52–54, SA54–57.

contre being Northumberland like John's.[1] In SR John replies, *I am cleped in northcontree ...* (SR52–53), which may suggest an adaptation by a more southerly copyist.

John de Thweng/St John of Bridlington (prior 1366, died 10 October 1379, canonized 24 September 1401)[2] was renowned for his visions,[3] miracles (e.g. walking on water, raising the dead),[4] and prophecies; his shrine attracted 'a numerous resort of pilgrims, and many miracles were reported to be wrought at his tomb'.[5] He says to William, '*Thow hast often cum to me, wher my body lyes, and to my syster, Sant Hylde*' (SA61–62). His relics had been translated 'to a splendid shrine east of the high altar' at Bridlington priory on 11 March 1404.[6]

William of Stranton presents himself then as a pious sinner, who was in the habit of making pilgrimages to two of the most important local shrines, as well as his pilgrimage to St Patrick's Purgatory. He mentions that his uncle, who died sixteen years before they met in purgatory, had been a priest. William is rebuked by St John for having opposed the marriage of his sister, who, with her lover, meets them in purgatory to make her complaint. No names are given, however, nor any further information about the other acquaintances William meets among the torments. He certainly seems confident lambasting the consistory courts, the venality of bishops and the regular clergy, and the abuses of a prioress, and also knowledgeable in his exhaustive list of means by which both clerics and secular men may aid souls in purgatory (SR518ff, SA512ff). But William does not directly make these attacks or give this advice in his own person; they are spoken by St John, by the bishop in the Earthly Paradise, and by the fiends. William presents himself as one receiving instruction, a stance which is a familiar feature of vision literature, to be found, for instance, in the *Visio Tnugdali*, the *Divina Commedia*, the *Visiones Georgii*, and a host of accounts by other-world visitors who, like St Patrick and William, *abode the*

1. One of St John's miracles was saving three Hartlepool sailors from shipwreck: see *AASS*, Oct. V, p. 142 col. 1B. One of his bones was venerated at Durham: see J.S. Purvis, *St. John of Bridlington* (1924), p. 18.
2. See *A History of Yorkshire* (VCH), III (London, 1913, repr. 1974), 202 col. 2.
3. See John Bale, *Index Britanniae scriptorum*, p. 184.
4. See *DNB*, X. 888.
5. M. Prickett, *An Historical and Architectural Description of the Priory Church of Bridlington* (Cambridge, 1831), p. 25. See also Krapp, p. 57, and add P. Grosjean, 'De S. Iohanne Bridlingtoniensi collectanea', *AB*, liii (1935), 101–29, and Hughes, *Pastors and Visionaries* (1988), esp. pp. 98–101, 302–5, 337–9.
6. See Purvis, p. 18.

reuelacion of Goddes angellis (SR20–21). By this means the reader
is enabled to identify with the intrepid but ignorant other-world
explorer, and the 'guide' can convey the author's doctrine both to
the visionary and to the audience, that is, *al cristen men þat heryn
or redyn this* (SR707).

William gives no details of the exact location or nature of St
Patrick's Purgatory, apart from the hour at which he entered and
the name of the prior. William was obviously acquainted with the
Tractatus, for some features of the structure of his vision bear the
traces of its influence, though William's vision is an independent
work and not merely a variant version of *T.*[1] Like Owein in *T*,
William does not actually suffer the torments he views, but then
he does not claim, as Owein did, to have passed bodily through
purgatory! Rather he *sumwhat slumbered and slepte* (SR22), so we
can take it that all that William saw of purgatory and paradise was
vouchsafed in a dream. Unlike Owein, William is also attended by
a guide, St John. St John and St Hild, dressed in white, advise
William in the same way the fifteen men in white advised Owein
of the imminent dangers, and the *restynge-place of Sante Patrike*
(SA19) where William meets them recalls the cloistral hall of *T*.
Krapp (p. 39) points out that:

> the disquisition at the beginning of the vision of the Earthly
> Paradise on the efficacy of prayer and alms-giving in relieving the
> sufferers in Purgatory is an evident remembrance of the first
> sermon in the Latin account.

This is true, though William's account recalls only a small part of
the first homily: cf. SR517ff, SA511ff and L693ff. The episode of
the bridge over the river of hell separating purgatory from the
Earthly Paradise is altered by William, the bridge being one built
by a vainglorious priest. William tells later how, when St John left
him, *euer I lokyde after a bryge ouer that water, weche I had harde
speyke of, þat is to say, of þe bryge ful of pykys* ... (SA531–3).
William had probably *herd say in þe world* (SR540) of the bridge
in the *Vision of Tundale*,[2] for Owein's bridge had no *pykys* upon
it. William eventually crosses the river (without mention of hell)
by means of a ladder and cord sent down from a tower on the
opposite bank.

Once in the Earthly Paradise, William is greeted, as was
Owein, by *a fayre cumpany of monkys and chanouns and prestys,
and all clede in whytt aray* (SA595–7), and he experiences the

---

1. Nor is it a 'deversification' of *OM2*, as Mearns implies in *Vision of Tundale*,
p. 55 and n. 63.
2. See Commentary SA531–3.

usual savour, sweeter *then all þe spysse schoppys of all þe warlde* (SA587–8), of the Tree of Life, and hears the bird song. There is *no gresse growynge* in the Earthly Paradise, but all is *whytt and clere as cristall* (SA585–6). Whereas two men *quasi archiepiscopi* (L780–1) instruct Owein, a single bishop explains to William the sins of the world. The description of the Earthly Paradise is much shorter than that in *T*. Following a pattern established by the *Visio Sancti Pauli* (*ANT*, p. 534), William is allowed to witness the judgement of a newly arrived soul, that of a prioress. It is a new idea perhaps that a soul should undergo the Particular Judgement on top of a high hill in the Earthly Paradise, and that fiends should be able to gather there to accuse the soul of past sins. The topography, however, obviously did not concern William of Stranton as much as the opportunity to attack the extravagant secular vices of this 'religious' lady. The bishop pronounces sentence on her and she is sent to purgatory *to payne enduryng evermore til þe day of dome* (SR689–90). Again there is no mention of the possibility of hell.

It seems that the main purpose of *VWS*, in the section on the Earthly Paradise as well as in the part devoted to purgatory, is to castigate the sins of the world, especially those of priests, vicars, and bishops, and to terrify the reader into repentance with an abhorrent conglomeration of tortures. William visits nine numbered fires of purgatory, and afterwards a high rock and stone wall, two towers, two more fires, a great walled house and the river. In each place of torment the devils are found torturing the souls in innumerable different diabolic ways. The influence of the *Visio Sancti Pauli* may be found in the detailing of the sins for which the souls are punished, and in this William's vision is quite distinct from *T*. The sins and sinners punished are briefly as follows: pride and gaudy array (1st fire); swearing by God's members (2nd fire); breaking of Holy days (3rd fire); dishonouring parents (4th fire); thieves and false executors (5th fire); false witnesses (6th fire); murderers (7th fire); lechery (8th fire); failure to chastise one's children (9th fire); backbiters (on the rock, walled in); evil bishops and prelates (two towers); monks and other religious that *lyffyde natt after þer ordyr* (fire, SA416); parsons and vicars who neglect divine service (fire); more false *men of holy chirch* (SR454–5) for multifarious forms of neglect and vanity (walled house); vainglory and lechery (river). At least seven of the Ten Commandments are thus reinforced by showing the fate of their transgressors.[1]

1. For further discussion of the ways souls are grouped in other-world vision literature, see P. Dinzelbacher, 'Klassen und Hierarchien im Jenseits', *Miscellanea*

There is also a constant attack on gaudy and ostentatious clothing, extravagant spending, neglect of the poor and of the fabric of church buildings, and many of the other abuses so continually harangued in sermon material of the period. The stress on the evils of extravagant dress is exemplified in the image of moths emerging from the large presses of clothes *þat þei might haue holpen with þe nedy people* (SR462). This theme is taken up in another vision which follows *VWS* in SA. The *Vision of Edmund Leversedge* (*VEL*), who in 1465 apparently died of the pestilence but also revived, is largely concerned with this gallant excess, and the doublets worn by the religious in *VWS* become the actual clothing worn by the fiends in the later vision:

> shorte gownes and dowblettes, closse hosyn, longe heere, vpon here browes, pykes on ther shon of a foot in lengh and more, hygh bonettes I my selfe sume tyme vsid . . .[1]

This vision draws many details from both *T* and *VWS*.[2]

In William's vision the emphasis on the claims of the poor recurs, as in the passage condemning the prelates for their gluttony, who shut themselves *wythin þer hyee howses when thay schulde ete, for thay wold nat here þe pore pepyl crye* (SA466-8). Earlier, William had himself heard the souls of the poor crying out against the canons, monks, and friars who squandered what might have helped the poor. All sections of the ecclesiastical hierarchy come under attack, from bishops to friars, monks, and priests, and it is principally against ecclesiastics that the complaints are raised. There seem to be very few of the laity in William of Stranton's purgatory. Bishops' servants who had been allowed to live in sin and lechery join with the devils in torturing their masters.

Purgatory is presented exclusively as a place of pain with no mention of purification; it is full of amazingly gruesome torments all fittingly selected to correspond with the sins committed. For instance, those who wore long *pokes* on their sleeves have the skin of their shoulders slit off *like to pokes* (SR182); those who had stuffed themselves at the tavern so that they *cast vp aȝen* (SR245) are stuffed with filth as one would *stoppe a wullepak* (SR234-5);

Mediaevalia, xii (1979), 20-40, and 'Reflexionen irdischer Sozialstrukturen in mittelalterlichen Jenseitsschilderungen', *Archiv für Kulturgeschichte*, lxi (1979), 16-34. *T* briefly lists the different groups of souls in the Earthly Paradise, L772-7, 808-14.
1. *VEL* p. 25.
2. See *VEL* p. 22. For a fuller discussion of the sources and analogues and an improved transcription of this text, see now the edition by W.F. Nijenhuis.

and backbiters are eaten on the back and limbs by cats and beetles along with the more usual adders and toads. The devils, as ever, are unflaggingly energetic, *stompyng and tredyng on here backis forto encrese here paynes* (SR356–7). A recurrent phrase of St John's is that in each torment sinners will remain *duryng þe wyll of God*, thus clearly distinguishing the place as purgatory, and, as mentioned above, he tells William at length all the means by which clerics and the laity may assist souls in purgatory. There is no mention of hell in the vision; purgatory has become the immediate and overwhelming threat, aimed as deterrent at those whom no *prechyng, ne techyng, ne counseill in shrift* (SR197–8) could deter from their sins. The tone as a whole is hortatory, even to the parenthetic warning against idolatory (SR610–13). The bishop in the Earthly Paradise sounds the prevailing note of distress at man's sinful and wilful opposition to God: *Alas! þat worldly men will not take hede in here hertes* . . . (SR694–5). William is finally instructed to tell what he has seen *to them þat þis bilongith to. And lyve rightfully and þow shalt come to everlestyng ioy* (SR702–3). Like Owein, William has successfully completed the testing pilgrimage of St Patrick's Purgatory.

6. TRACTATUS DE PURGATORIO SANCTI PATRICII

Previous editions of the Tractatus

Messingham, Thomas, *Florilegium insulae sanctorum seu vitae et actae sanctorum Hiberniae* (Paris, 1624), pp. 86–109.

Colgan, John, *Triadis thaumaturgae seu diuorum Patricii Columbae et Brigidae, trium veteris et maioris Scotiae, seu Hiberniae sanctorum insulae . . . acta . . .*, II (Louvain, 1647), pp. 273–81.

Migne, J.-P., *PL*, clxxx, 971–1004.

Mall, E., 'Zur Geschichte der Legende vom Purgatorium des heil. Patricius', *RF*, vi (1889), 139–97.

Jenkins, T.A., 'The Espurgatoire Saint Patriz of Marie de France, with a Text of the Latin Original', *The Decennial Publications of the University of Chicago*, 1st series, vii (1903), 235–327.

Zanden, C.M. van der, *Etude sur le Purgatoire de Saint Patrice, accompagnée du texte latin d'Utrecht et du texte anglo-normand de Cambridge* (Amsterdam, 1927).

Warnke, Karl, *Das Buch vom Espurgatoire S. Patrice der Marie de France und seine Quelle* (Bibliotheca Normannica 9, Halle/Saale, 1938).

Caerwyn Williams, J.E., 'Welsh Versions of *Purgatorium S. Patricii*', *Studia Celtica*, viii–ix (1973–74), 121–94.

The *Tractatus*, written by 'H[enry]' of Sawtry *c.*1180–1184,[1] is the earliest account of St Patrick's Purgatory and the ultimate source for all the accounts of Owein's visit.[2] It was widely copied

---

1. F.W. Locke, 'A New Date for the Composition of the *Tractatus de Purgatorio Sancti Patricii*', *Speculum*, xl (1965), 641–6, proposed a date between 1208 and April 1215. That this date is too late I demonstrated in 'The Date and Dedication of the *Tractatus de Purgatorio Sancti Patricii*', *Speculum*, liii (1978), 778–83, where I argued that *T* was composed 'after 1173 and before 1185/6 . . . most likely . . . c. 1179–81'. Yolande de Pontfarcy has preferred within this period the year 1184: see 'Le *Tractatus de Purgatorio Sancti Patricii* de H. de Saltrey: sa date et ses sources', *Peritia*, iii (1984), 460–80, pp. 461–5.

2. For further recent discussion of *T*, see Pontfarcy, in Haren & Pontfarcy (1988), pp. 7–14, 48–57, in Picard & Pontfarcy (1985), pp. 9–33, and 'Le *Tractatus*' (1984); Zaleski, *Otherworld Journeys* (1987), pp. 35–39, and 'St. Patrick's Purgatory: Pilgrimage Motifs in a Medieval Otherworld Vision' (1985), pp. 470–80; Röckelein, *Otloh, Gottschalk, Tnugdal* (1987), pp. 121–71 and *passim*; Easting, 'Purgatory and the Earthly Paradise in the *Tractatus de Purgatorio Sancti Patricii*' (1986), 'Owein at St Patrick's Purgatory' (1986), and 'An Edition of

and translated[1] in the ensuing three centuries, and has previously
been printed in several forms. Early editors were Messingham
and Colgan. Messingham's text, which includes comments by
David Rothe of Ossory and extracts from Matthew Paris's
version[2] in *Chronica Majora* under 1153, was reprinted by
Migne. Colgan's text was reprinted by Mall, collated with BL MS
Arundel 292 (Ar—Mall used siglum K). Mall (pp. 143–97)
printed this in parallel with Bamberg, Staatliche Bibliothek, MS
E. VII. 59 (B—Mall's siglum A). Mall wrongly claimed that B is a
representative of the earliest form of *T*; B is, however, heavily
rewritten. Jenkins published BL MS Harley 3846 (H) parallel
with his text of Marie de France's translation, *Espurgatoire S.
Patrice* (pp. 241–303), and also provided a diplomatic reprint of a
transcription made by J. A. Herbert of BL MS Royal 13 B viii (R)
(pp. 310–27). Zanden (pp. 4–24) printed Utrecht, University
Library, MS 173 (U), which he claimed closely represented the
earliest form of the text, and also printed Ar (pp. 159–78).
BUHAr are the α MSS from which Warnke (W) produced his α
text. For his β text, Warnke collated R with Munich, Bayerische
Staatsbibliothek, MS C.L. 15745 and Paris, BN f. lat. 13434,
which was one of Colgan's three manuscripts. Warnke also took
occasional readings from six other β MSS.[3] Caerwyn Williams

---

Owayne Miles' (1976), pp. lxix–xc; Jacques Le Goff, *L'Imaginaire médiéval* (1985),
pp. 127–35 and see also pp. 103–119, and *La Naissance du purgatoire* (1981), pp.
259–73.

1. For incomplete lists of manuscripts, see M. Esposito, 'Notes on Latin
Learning and Literature in Medieval Ireland—V' *Hermathena*, 1 (1937), 162–7;
Manuscript Sources for the History of Irish Civilization, ed. R.J. Hayes, II (Boston,
Mass., 1965), 455 col. 2–456 col. 3, and *First Supplement 1965–1975*, I (1979),
673–6. Hayes's lists do not always distinguish manuscripts of *T* from chronicle
reductions and vernacular translations. My own lists, corroborated by the papers
of the late Professor Ludwig Bieler, comprise at least 150 manuscripts of *T*. For
translations, see above, p. xvii n. 3.

2. Copied from Roger of Wendover's adaptation of an α text.

3. Heidelberg, University Library, MS Salem 931; Wolfenbüttel, Landes-
bibliothek, MS 2331(5); Vienna, Nationalbibliothek, Bibl. Pal. Vind. MS 592;
Basle, University Library, MS A.VI; Munich, Bayerische Staatsbibliothek, C.L.
7547 and C.L. 18286.

Care must be taken when consulting earlier discussions of *T* MSS for Warnke's
use of α and β (which I follow) unfortunately inverts that found in L. Foulet,
'Marie de France et la légende du Purgatoire de Saint Patrice', *RF*, xxii (1908),
599–627 (p. 599 n. 3); *Le Purgatoire de Saint Patrice par Berol*, ed. M. Mörner
(Lund, 1917), pp. xxii–xxxiv, and Mörner ed., *Le Purgatoire de Saint Patrice du
manuscrit de la Bibliothèque Nationale fonds français 25545* (Lund, 1920), p. VII n.
1; and Antonio G. Solalinde, 'La primera versión espanola de "El Purgatorio de
San Patricio" y la difusión de esta leyenda en España', in *Homenaje ofrecido a
Menéndez Pidal*, II (Madrid, 1925), 219–57 (pp. 233–48).

printed R parallel to his edition of the Welsh prose translation (pp. 152–81).

The text below is the first to be edited of the complete β version. The β text was used by the translator of OM2 and by the Anglo-Norman translator of AN, the prime source for OM1.[1] My text is based on Lambeth Palace Library, MS 51 (L), collated with R, and Cambridge, Sidney Sussex College, MS 50 (S). LS have not previously been collated. β W, based on R, omits most of the first homily and all of the second homily, for Warnke was providing T texts only in so far as they indicated the sources for Marie de France's translation. Caerwyn Williams' text of R omits both homilies and everything after the second homily, for these parts are not found in the Welsh translations. Jenkins' diplomatic print of R is thus the only complete β text to have been published until now. None of the editions to date has any commentary, apart from a few notes provided by Colgan and introductory remarks by Warnke. My edition of T does not pretend to be the definitive critical edition, but is rather for the convenience of the reader of the Middle English texts in this edition; none of the printed β texts is readily available. A full critical edition of T still remains to be undertaken.[2]

I know of five complete β MSS, of which LRS are the earliest, being catalogued as late twelfth century or c.1200. Of these L is the only dated manuscript, started in the year 1200. A fourth complete copy is found in Oxford, Oriel College, MS 17, from the fourteenth century. R was the exemplar for the copyist of the fifth manuscript, CUL MS Ff. 1. 27, which also contains copies from R of Giraldus Cambrensis' *Topographia Hibernica, Expugnatio Hibernica* and *Itinerarium Kambriae*.[3] I know of four other β MSS which include both homilies, but all lack other sections: Oxford, Bodleian Library, MS Digby 34 omits the Prologue; MS Digby 172, and BL MSS Harley 261 and Cotton Nero A vii omit the

---

1. See above, p. xlvii.

2. I am informed (1987) that an edition is to be prepared by Jean-Michel Picard and Yolande de Pontfarcy for the New History of Ireland. As all previous accounts of the large corpus of T manuscripts and their relationships should be superseded by Picard and Pontfarcy's edition, I have not engaged in that discussion here. In my thesis, pp. lxix–xc, I argued that β may represent a closer approximation to the original shape of T, as Henry of Sawtry either composed it or revised it, and that the shorter α versions represent a reduction of β rather than that β is an expansion of α, as Warnke argued. See further, Pontfarcy, 'Le *Tractatus*', pp. 470–2.

3. See J.F. Dimock ed., *Giraldus Cambrensis Opera*, V, RS, 21.v (London, 1867), pp. xx–xxiv.

Epilogue. Of the nine β MSS used by Warnke, only R is complete.[1]

L is described by James.[2] *T* is the first item in Book One of Peter of Cornwall's huge collection of visions of the other world, which occupies the entire manuscript, entitled *Liber Reuelationum*.[3] *T* is followed by the unique account of another vision seen at St Patrick's Purgatory,[4] and then by Peter's account of visions and miracles experienced by members of his own family.[5] The epilogue to *T* is slightly reworded and there is a lacuna of some fifteen lines in the second homily, here made good from RS. L and S provide different rubrics for some sections of the narrative.

R is described in Ward, *Catalogue of Romances*, II. 435–52, and G.F. Warner and J.P. Gilson, *Catalogue of Western Manuscripts in the Old Royal and King's Collections*, II (London, 1921), 94–95.

S[6] contains *T* on ff. 5rb–13va; the remainder of ff. 13v and 14 are blank. It is written in double columns of 44 lines, ruled, with writing above the top line. The leaves measure 218 × 144mm, the written space 166 × 109mm. The ink is black, the hand small and regular. Paragraphs are marked by two-line capitals in red; rubrics are in red, though capital I's are in brown. The catchword *videntes* at the bottom of f. 8v is in a different hand and ink.

S corroborates different readings in L and R, and is the only manuscript I know to give (correctly) the name of the dedicatee of the *T*: *hugoni* is written in the rubricator's hand in the right-hand margin of f. 5r (see L3 apparatus).

1. The following eighteen β MSS that I have checked omit all or part of the homilies and some other sections: Oxford, Lincoln College, MS Lat. 28; Corpus Christi College, MS 293a; MS Bodley 509; Cambridge, Corpus Christi College, MS 462; BL MSS Harley 103, 2851, and 3776; MS Cotton Vespasian A vi; MSS Royal 8 C xiv and 9 A xiv; Lambeth Palace Library, MS 238; Paris, BN, MSS f. lat. 3338, 3855, 5137, 11759, 12618, 14553, and f. lat. n. a. 217.
2. See M.R. James and C. Jenkins, *A Descriptive Catalogue of the Manuscripts in the Library of Lambeth Palace*, pt. 1 (Cambridge, 1930), pp. 71–85.
3. On f. 9vb is the list of *capituli* for Book One with the rubric: *Incipiunt breues commemorationes Rubricarum et capitulorum primi libri reuelationum a Petro priore collectarum*. *T* is there listed as *Pvrgatorium Patricii. .i.*; it is followed by the rubrics for the appendix of 'hermit' tales: *Heremite bonus et malus. .ij.*; *Demones rapiunt escam auari. iij.*; *Sacerdos et filia eius spiritualis. iiij.*.
4. See Easting, 'Peter of Cornwall's Account of St. Patrick's Purgatory', *AB*, xcvii (1979), 397–416.
5. See Easting and Sharpe, 'Peter of Cornwall: The Visions of Ailsi and his Sons', *Mediaevistik*, i (1988), 207–62. For further bibliography on Peter of Cornwall and the *Liber Reuelationum*, see Michael Lapidge and Richard Sharpe, *A Bibliography of Celtic-Latin Literature 400–1200* (Dublin, 1985), pp. 28–30.
6. See M.R. James, *A Descriptive Catalogue of the Manuscripts in the Library of Sidney Sussex College, Cambridge* (Cambridge, 1895), pp. 33–36.

T	L	OM₁	C = OM₂	Y
Dedication & Prologue	3–76	—	—	—
Tale of the bestial Irishman	82–107	—	—	—
Revelation of the Purgatory	78–82	1–28	1–82	1–77
	+110–152			
Tale of the one-toothed prior	154–171			
Ritual for admission to the Purgatory	172–204			
Introduction of Owein	206–255	29–43:3	83–112	78–104
Owein enters the Purgatory	256–269	43:4–45:3	113–202	105–195
Messengers of God greet Owein	269–305	45:4–51	203–224	196–219
Devils torment Owein	307–353	52–61	225–256	220–251
Devils drag Owein away—wind	355–368	62–64	257–308	252–295
1st field of torment—nails, souls face-down	370–388	65–68:4	309–318	296–305
2nd field of torment—nails, dragons, snakes, etc., souls face-up	390–411	68:5–71	319–363	306–315 +346–349
3rd field of torment—nails, winds	413–427	72–75		316–345 +350–355
4th field of torment—suspension, roasting, etc.	429–447	76–82		356–371
Fiery wheel	449–463	83–89		372–391
Bathhouse	465–487	96–104	364–394	392–445
Mountain, wind, river	489–506	90–95	—	—
Flaming pit	508–528	105–115		
Devils say pit is not hell	529–535		395–402	446–453
River, perilous bridge	537–575	116–127	403–460	454–507

1st homily	577–750	—	—	508–577
Earthly Paradise	752–829	128–158:3	461–546	578–613
Address by 'archbishops'	830–884	158:4–167	547–605	614–630
Owein receives heavenly food	884–909	168–187	606–626	631–636
Owein leaves Earthly Paradise	909–916	188–190:3	627–632	—
2nd homily	918–1044	—	—	—
Owein returns via the hall	1045–1062	190:4–191	633–656	637–661
Owein returns to earth & visits Jerusalem	1062–1070	192–198	657–682	662–685
Gilbert meets Owein	1070–1096	—	—	—
Testimony of Gilbert	1097–1128	—	—	—
Testimony of 2 Irish abbots	1130–1135	—	—	—
Testimony of Florentianus	1135–1159	—	—	—
Testimony of Florentianus's chaplain	1159–1248	—	—	—
including: Tale of the bad hermit	1162–1170	—	—	—
Tale of the rich peasant	1174–1187	—	—	—
Tale of the priest & girl	1191–1248	—	—	—
Epilogue	1249–1264			

The preceding table briefly outlines the contents of T and gives the references to the corresponding passages in $OM1$ and $OM2$.

7. THE PRESENTATION OF THE TEXTS

Square brackets indicate editorial alteration or insertion; where applicable these new readings have been taken or adapted from the parallel text or from earlier editions, otherwise they are my own. Editorial deletions are indicated in the apparatus. Missing portions of the text, and words or letters supplied from earlier editions where the manuscript is now no longer legible, have been indicated by angle brackets; scribal and later interlineations are marked with ` ´. Emendation is conservative; rhyme spellings are emended only where the emended form occurs elsewhere in the same copy of the text: e.g. the MS rhyme *were/lore* (C27–8, Y22–3) is emended to *wore/lore* only in C, which uses *wore* also at 111 and 512; *wore* does not occur in Y. In all the above cases the manuscript reading or necessary explanation is supplied in the apparatus. All abbreviations and contractions have been silently expanded in accordance with the scribes' practice where the same or similar words have been written out in full. Thus, for example, a superscript minim normally expanded *ri* has been printed *ry* in *pryour* (C158) and *pryowr* (Y663) on the model of the same spellings in C93, Y651. All ampersands have been printed as *and*. Where interpretation of any abbreviation is open to question it is discussed in the Commentary. Word division has been regularized, and punctuation and capitals introduced according to modern usage. Scribal *y* with the function of *þ* has been printed *þ*, and manuscript *u/v* distinction retained. Manuscript *ihu* has been printed *Jhesu* in C, Y, SA, SR, but as *Ihesu* in A, this being the more likely form at the earlier date; otherwise capital *I/J* are distinguished according to function. *i/j* distinction has been retained to the extent that *i* is printed for *j* when the manuscript clearly does not have the long-tailed form, but regularized insofar as *j* is not printed for *i*.

Where not otherwise specified the first reading after the lemma in the apparatus is the manuscript reading. Earlier editors' substantively different readings are noted; their slips and variations in spelling are ignored. *em.* = emendation.

1. Auchinleck (A)
Abbreviations and contractions are sparsely used, as can be seen from the manuscript facsimile. The usual figure 9 abbreviation

representing *con-* or *com-* is used, e.g. in *conseily* 42:4, *compeynie* 140:2. A small horizontal stroke usually indicates missing *m, n,* or *e*. In the printed text the first words of stanzas 29, 76, 83, 90, 96, 105, and 145 have been inset to acknowledge large initial capitals in the manuscript. The six-line stanzas, each marked by a paraph in the manuscript, have been numbered consecutively to facilitate reference to KA.

2. *Cotton* (*C*)

Abbreviations for *ur, er/re,* and *us* have been expanded; the following generally ignored: stroke through *ll, ght, 3th, th*; tail on final *-r* and *-n*; and redundant strokes over *n*, e.g. in *syñne* 235, *wenteñ* 255. Horizontal stroke over *o* followed by two minims is printed *-oun*; horizontal stroke over *o* followed by four minims is ignored and also printed *-oun*.

3. *Yale* (*Y*)

The scribe's practice is erratic and it is not always possible to be fully consistent in treating abbreviations. The tail on final *-n* and stroke through *th* and *ll* have generally been ignored. Long-tailed and curving flourishes on final *-r* are usually expanded to give *-re*.

The text has been inset at lines 460 and 500 to correspond to manuscript paragraph marks. At lines 109 and 562 the text is inset to match manuscript initial flourishes.

Cotton and Yale are printed in parallel so that their omissions with respect to each other can be immediately recognized, and so that a clearer idea can be gained of the scope and form of the original text of the *OM*2 version. Special notice should be taken of the layout on pp. 53–55, for which, see above, p. lxviii.

4. *Royal* (*SR*)

As the scribe is inconsistent in the use of final flourishes and final *-e*, the printed text is not rigorously consistent; the flourish is usually ignored except where it is deemed significant, e.g. where the final *-e* has elsewhere been regularly written out by the scribe in the same word. Stroke through *ll* and a curved line over words ending in *-th, -ch* have also been ignored. Final *-on* with a long tail is printed *-ion*, e.g. in *reuelacion*; where the tail occurs on *-io* followed by two minims it is ignored. The tail for plural endings is printed *-es*. Initial *ff-* has been retained on words in mid-sentence.

Paragraphs are editorial though most follow some mark by the rubricator. They are provided liberally to facilitate comparison of the parallel texts.

5. Additional (SA)

The tail for plural endings is printed -*ys*. The form *Wyllyam* has been adopted regularly following the spelling where the scribe has written the name in full, at SA134, 250, 581. It is, however, variously abbreviated as *Wyllya* with stroke over *a* SA1; and *Wyllam* (with horizontal stroke variously over *a, m*, or between *a* and *m*) SA5, 29, 49, 71, 116, 197, 206, 266, 278, 296, 359, 413; *Wyllm* (horizontal stroke with or without final hook) SA387, 616, 624; *Wylla* with sideways final *m* SA237, 427, 482, 511. The last three forms may stand for *Wyllam(m)*.

The manuscript uses several capitals that I have ignored, usually on nouns that the scribe must have deemed important, e.g. *Juges* SA2, *Prior* 9, 11, 14, 18, *Couente* 11, *Enmy* 205, *Eme* 428, *Commendacyon* 517, *Chapman* 582, *Monkys* 596, *Chanouns* 596, *Prestys* 596, *Jugement* 630, *Relygion* 642, *Emperyce* 650.

SA and SR are printed in parallel by page and paragraph.

6. Tractatus—Lambeth (L)

The rubrics are those from the base text, L. Where R and S have different rubrics, they are included in the apparatus. Paragraphing follows L.

OWAYNE MILES
AUCHINLECK VERSION (*OM*1)

AUCHINLECK

1   <. . . . .>
         <. . . . .>

f. 25ra   And liued in dedeli sinne.
Seyn Patrike hadde rewþe
Of hir misbileue and vntrew[þ]e,
Þat þai weren inne.

2   Oft he proued sarmoun to make,
Þat þai schuld to God take
And do after his rede.
Þai were fulfild of felonie;
Þai no held it bot ribaudie
Of noþing þat he sede.

3   And al þai seyd commounliche,
Þat non of hem wold sikerliche
Do bi his techeing,
Bot ȝif he dede þat [sum] man
Into helle went þan,
To bring hem tiding

4   Of þe pain and of þe wo
Þe soulen suffri euermo,
Þai þat ben þerinne;
And elles `þai´ seyd, þat nolden hye
Of her misdede nouȝt repenti,
No her folies blinne.

5   When Sein Patrike herd þis,
Michel he card forsoþe, ywis,
And sore he gan desmay.
Oft he was in aflicc[i]oun,
In fasting and in orisoun,
Ihesu Crist to pray,

1:5   vntrewþe] vntrewe, untrewþe *suggested* KB.
3:4   sum man] roman KA, *the* o *appears to be written over a minim; the first
letter may originally have been* n *not* r; *em. suggested* Z.
4:4   seyd þat] d *and* þ *partially obscured.*   4:6   folies] e *partially obscured.*
5:1   Patrike] at *partially obscured.*   5:4   afliccioun] afliccoun.

6   Þat he him schuld grace sende,
      Hou he miȝt raþest wende
      Out of þe fendes bond,
      And do hem com to amendement
      And leue on God omnipotent,
      Þe folk of Yrl[on]d.

7   And als he was in holy chirche,
      Godes werkes forto wirche,
      And made his praier,
      And bad for þat ich þing,
      Sone he fel on slepeing
      Toforn his auter.

8   In his chapel he slepe wel swete,
      Of fele þinges him gan mete
      Þat was in heuen-blis.
      As he slepe, forsoþe him þouȝt
f. 25rb   Þat Ihesu, þat ous dere bouȝt,
      To him com ywis,

9   And ȝaf him a bok þat nas nouȝt lite:
      Þer nis no clerk þat swiche can write,
      No neuer no schal be;
      It spekeþ of al maner godspelle,
      Of heuen and erþe and of helle,
      Of Godes priuete.

10   More him þouȝt, þat God him ȝaf
      In his hond a wel feir staf,
      In slepe þer he lay;
      And Godes Staf, ich vnderstond,
      Men clepeþ þat staf in Yrlond
      Ȝete to þis ich day.

11   When God him þis ȝif hadde,
      Him þouȝt þat he him ladde
      Þennes þe way ful riȝt
      Into an gret desert;
      Þer was an hole michel apert,
      Þat griseliche was of siȝt.

12   Rounde it was about and blak;
      In alle þe warld no was hi`s´ mack,
      So griselich entring.

6:6   Yrlond] yrluod.   10:1   him] i *?corrected from* e.

When þat Patrike yseye þat siȝt,
Swiþe sore he was afliȝt
In his slepeing.

13 Þo God almiȝten him schewed and seyd,
Who þat hadde don sinful dede
Oȝaines Godes lawe,
And wold him þerof repenti,
And take penaunce hastily,
And his foliis wiþdrawe,

14 So schuld in þis ich hole
A parti of penaunce þole
For his misdede;
A niȝt and a day be herinne,
And al him schuld [be] forȝiue his sinne,
And þe better spede.

15 And ȝif he ben of gode creaunce,
Gode and poure wiþouten dotaunce,
And stedfast [of] bileue,
He no schuld nouȝt be þerin ful long,
Þat he ne schal se þe paines strong—
Ac non no schal him greue—

f. 25va 16 In wiche þe soules ben ydo,
Þat haue deserued to com þerto,
In þis world ywis;
And also þan sen he may
Þat ich ioie þat lasteþ ay,
Þat is in paradis.

17 When Ihesu had yseyd al out,
And yschewed al about
Wiþ wel milde chere,
God, þat bouȝt ous dere in heuen,
Fram him he went wiþ milde steuen,
And Patrike bileft þere.

18 When Seyn Patrike o slepe he woke,
Gode token he fond and vp hem toke
Of his sweuening:
Bok and staf þer he fond,
And tok hem vp in his hond,
And þonked Heuen-king.

14:5 be] *added* Z.   15:3 of] *added* Z.

19   He kneld and held vp his hond,
     And þonked Ihesu Cristes sond
     Þat he him hadde ysent,
     Wharþurth he miȝt vnderstond
     To turn þat folk of Yrlond
     To com to amendement.

20   In þat stede wiþouten lett
     A fair abbay he lete sett
     Wiþouten ani dueling,
     In þe name of Godes glorie,
     Seyn [Peter] and our leuedy,
     Forto rede and sing.

21   Seyn Patrike maked þe abbay:
     Þat wite wele men of þe cuntray,
     Þat non is þat yliche.
     Regles is þat abbay name,
     Þer is solas, gle and game
     Wiþ pouer and eke wiþ riche.

22   White chanounes he sett þerate
     To serue God, arliche and late,
     And holy men to be.
     Þat ich boke and þat staf,
     Þat God Seyn Patrike ȝaf,
     Ȝete þer man may se.

23   In þe est ende of þe abbay
     Þer is þat hole, forsoþe to say,
     Þat griseliche is of siȝt,
     Wiþ gode ston wal al abouten,
     Wiþ locke and keye þe gate to louken,
     Patrike lete it diȝte.

24   Þat ich stede, siker ȝe be,
     Is ycleped þe riȝt entre
     Of Patrikes Purgatorie:
     For in þat time þat þis bifelle,
     Mani a man went in to helle,
     As it seyt in þe storie,

25   And suffred pein for her trespas,
     And com oȝain þurth Godes gras,
     And seyd alle and some,

f. 25vb

20:5   Peter] patrike.   24:2   ycleped] *letter erased after* c.

Þat þai hadde sen sikerliche
Þe paines of helle apertliche,
When þai were out ycome.

26   And also þai seyd wiþ heye,
Apertliche þe ioies þai sei3e
Of angels singing
To God almi3ti and to his:
Þat is þe ioie of paradys;
Ihesu ous þider bring!

27   When alle þe folk of Yrlond
Þe ioies gan vnderstond,
Þat Seyn Patrike hem sede,
To him þai com euerichon,
And were ycristned in fonston,
And leten her misdede.

28   And þus þai bicom, lasse and more,
Cristen men þurth Godes lore,
Þurth Patrikes preier.
Now herknes to mi talking:
Ichil 3ou tel of oþer þing,
3if 3e it wil yhere.

29   Bi Steuenes day, þe king ful ri3t,
Þat Inglond stabled and di3t
Wel wiselich in his time,
In Norþhumberland was a kni3t,
A douhti man and swiþe wi3t,
A[s] it seyt in þis rime.

30   [O]weyn he hi3t, wiþouten les,
In cuntre þer he born wes,
As 3e may yhere.
Wel michel he couþe of batayle,
And swiþe sinful he was saunfayle
O3ain his creatour.

31   On a day he him biþou3t
Of þe sinne he hadde ywrou3t,
And sore him gan adrede,
And þou3t he wold þurth Godes grace
Ben yschriue of his trispas,
And leten his misdede.

f. 26ra

29:6 As] at, *em.* KA.   30:1 Oweyn] Vweyn.

32   And when he hadde þus gode creaunce,
He com, as it bifel a chaunce,
To þe bischop of Yrlond,
Þer he lay in þat abbay,
Þer was þat hole, forsoþe to say,
Penaunce to take an hond.

33   To þe bischop he biknewe his sinne,
And prayd him, for Godes winne,
Þat he him schuld schriue,
And legge on him penaunce sore:
He wold sinne, he seyd, no more,
Neuer eft in his liue.

34   Þe bischop þerof was ful bliþe,
And for his sinne blamed him swiþe,
Þat he him hadde ytold,
And seyd he most penaunce take,
ȝif he wald his sinne forsake,
Hard and manifold.

35   Þan answerd þe kniȝt Owayn,
'Don ichil,' he seyd, 'ful feyn,
What God me wil sende.
Þei þou me wost comandy
Into Patrikes Purgatori,
Þider ichil wende.'

36   Þe bischop seyd, 'Nay, Owain, frende!
Þat ich way schaltow nouȝt wende;'
And told him of þe pine,
And bede him lete be þat mischaunce,
And 'Take,' he seyd, 'sum oþer penaunce,
To amende þe of sinnes þine.'

37   For nouȝt þe bischop couþe say,
Þe kniȝt nold nouȝt leten his way,
His soule to amende.
Þan ladde he him into holy chirche,
Godes werkes forto wirche,
And þe riȝt lawe him kende.

f. 26rb 38   Fiften days in afliccioun,
In fasting and in orisoun
He was, wiþouten lesing.

33:5   sinne] i *?corrected from* e.

Þan þe priour wiþ processioun,
Wiþ croice and wiþ gonfanoun,
To þe hole he gan him bring.

39   Þe priour seyd, 'Kniȝt Oweyn,
Her is þi gate to go ful gain,
Wende riȝt euen forþ;
And when þou a while ygon hast,
Liȝt of day þou al forlast,
Ac hold þe euen norþ.

40   Þus þou schalt vnder erþe gon;
Þan þou schalt finde sone anon
A wel gret feld apliȝt,
And þerin an halle of ston,
Swiche in world no wot y non;
Sumdele þer is of liȝt.

41   Namore liȝtnesse nis þer yfounde
Þan þe sonne goþ to grounde
In winter sikerly.
Into þe halle þou schalt go,
And duelle þer tille þer com mo,
Þat schul þe solaci.

42   Þritten men þer schul come,
Godes seriaunce alle and some,
As it seyt in þe stori;
And hye þe schul conseily
Hou þou schalt þe conteyni
Þe way þurth purgatori.'

43   Þan þe priour and his couent
Bitauȝt him God, and forþ hy went;
Þe gate þai schet anon.
Þe kniȝt his way haþ sone ynome,
Þat into þe feld he was ycome
Þer was þe halle of ston.

44   Þe halle was ful selly diȝt,
Swiche can make no erþeliche wiȝt,
Þe pilers stode wide.
Þe kniȝt wonderd þat he fond
Swiche an halle in þat lond,
And open in ich side.

45   And when he hadde long stond þerout,
And deuised al about,

f. 26va   In he went þare.
Þritten men þer come,
Wisemen þai war of dome,
And white abite þai bere,

46   And al her crounes wer newe schorn;
Her most maister ȝede biforn
And salud þe kniȝt.
Adoun he sat, so seyt þe boke,
And kniȝt Owain to him he toke,
And told him resoun riȝt.

47   'Ichil þe conseyl, leue broþer,
As ichaue don mani anoþer
Þat han ywent þis way,
Þat þou ben of gode creaunce,
Certeyn and poure wiþouten dotaunce
To God þi trewe fay;

48   For þou schalt se, when we ben ago,
A þousend fendes and wele mo,
To bring þe into pine.
Ac loke wele, bise þe so,
And þou aniþing bi hem do,
Þi soule þou schalt tine.

49   Haue God in þine hert,
And þenk opon his woundes smert,
Þat he suffred þe fore.
And bot þou do [as] y þe telle,
Bodi and soule þou gos to helle,
And euermore forlore.

50   Nempne Godes heiȝe name,
And þai may do þe no schame,
For nouȝt þat may bifalle.'
And when þai hadde conseyld þe kniȝt,
No lenge bileue he no miȝt,
Bot went out of þe halle;

51   He and alle his fellawered
Bitauȝt him God, and forþ þai ȝede
Wiþ ful mild chere.

49:4   as] *added KA.*   49:5   þou] þ *corrected from another letter.*
50:1   Nempne] *second n partially obscured.*
50:2   do þe *canc. after* þe.

Owein bileft þer in drede,
To God he gan to clepi and grede,
And maked his preier.

52   And sone þerafter sikerly
He gan to here a reweful cri;
He was aferd ful sore:
Þei alle þe warld falle schold,
Fram þe firmament to þe mold,
No miȝt haue ben no more.

f. 26vb

53   And when of þe cri was passed þe drede,
Þer com in a grete ferrede
Of fendes fifti score
About þe kniȝt into þe halle;
Loþly þinges þai weren alle,
Bihinde and eke bifore.

54   And þe kniȝt þai ȝeden abouten,
And grenned on him her foule touten,
And drof him to heþeing,
And seyd he was comen wiþ flesche and fel
To fechen him þe ioie of helle
Wiþouten ani ending.

55   Þe most maister-fende of alle
Adoun on knes he gan to falle,
And seyd, 'Welcome, Owein!
Þou art ycomen to suffri pine
To amende þe of sinnes tine,
Ac alle gett þe no gain,

56   For þou schalt haue pine anouȝ,
Hard, strong, and ful touȝ,
For þi dedli sinne.
No haddestow neuer more meschaunce
Þan þou schal haue in our daunce,
When we schul play biginne.'

57   'Ac no for þan,' þe fendes sede,
'ȝif þou wilt do bi our rede,
For þou art ous leue and dere,
We schul þe bring wiþ fine amour
Þer þou com in fram þe priour,
Wiþ our felawes yfere;

56:2 touȝ] o *appears to be corrected from* u.

58   And elles we schul þe teche here,
        Þat þou has serued ous mani ȝer
        In pride and lecherie;
        For we þe haue so long yknawe,
        To þe we schul our hokes þrawe,
        Alle our compeynie.'

59   He seyd he nold wiþouten feyle:
        'Ac y forsake ȝour conseyle;
        Mi penaunce ichil take.'
        And when þe fendes yherd þis,
        Amidward þe halle ywis
        A grete fer þai gun make.

f. 27ra 60   Fet and hond þai bounde him hard,
        And casten him amidward.
        He cleped to our driȝt;
        Anon þe fer oway was weued,
        Cole no spark þer nas bileued,
        Þurth grace of God almiȝt.

61   And when þe kniȝt yseiȝe þis,
        Michel þe balder he was ywis
        And wele gan vnderstond,
        And þouȝt wele in his memorie,
        It was þe fendes trecherie,
        His hert forto fond.

62   Þe fendes went out of þe halle,
        Þe kniȝt þai ladde wiþ hem alle
        Intil an vncouþe lond;
        Þer no was no maner wele,
        Bot hunger, þrust and chele;
        No tre no seiȝe he stond,

63   Bot a cold winde þat blewe þere,
        Þat vnneþe ani man miȝt yhere,
        And perced þurth his side.
        Þe fendes han þe kniȝt ynome
        So long þat þai ben ycome
        Into a valay wide.

64   Þo wende þe kniȝt he hadde yfounde
        Þe deppest pit in helle-grounde.
        When he com neiȝe þe stede

60:2   him] *final two minims badly formed.*

He loked vp sone anon;
Strong it was forþer to gon,
He herd schriche and grede.

65   He seiʒe þer ligge ful a feld
Of men and wimen þat wern aqueld,
Naked wiþ mani a wounde.
Toward þe erþe þai lay deueling,
'Allas! Allas!' was her brocking,
Wiþ iren bendes ybounde;

66   And gun to scriche and to wayly,
And crid, 'Allas! merci, merci!
Merci, God almiʒt!'
Merci nas þer non, forsoþe,
Bot sorwe of hert and grinding of toþe:
Þat was a griseli siʒt.

67   Þat ich sorwe and þat reuþe
Is for þe foule sinne of slewþe,

f. 27rb   As it seyt in þe stori.
Who þat is slowe in Godes seruise
Of þat pain hem may agrise,
To legge in purgatori.

68   Þis was þe first pain apliʒt
Þat þai dede Owain þe kniʒt:
Þai greued him swiþe sore.
Alle þat pain he haþ ouerschaken;
Vntil anoþer þai han him taken,
Þer he seiʒe sorwe more

69   Of men and wimen þat þer lay,
Þat crid, 'Allas!' and 'Waileway!'
For her wicked lore.
Þilche soules lay vpward,
As þe oþer hadde ly donward,
Þat y told of bifore,

70   And were þurth fet and hond and heued
Wiþ iren nailes gloweand red
To þe erþe ynayled þat tide.
Owain seiʒe sitt on hem þere
Loþli dragouns alle o fer,
In herd is nouʒt to hide.

70:2 gloweand] l corrected from r.   70:5 dragouns] dragrouns.

71 On sum sete todes blake,
Euetes, neddren and þe snake,
Þat frete hem bac and side.
Þis is þe pain of glotoni.
For Godes loue, be war þerbi!
It rinneþ al to wide.

72 Ȝete him þouȝt a pain st`r´ong
Of a cold winde blewe hem among,
Þat com out of þe sky;
So bitter and so cold it blewe,
Þat alle þe soules it ouerþrewe
Þat lay in purgatori.

73 Þe fendes lopen on hem þare,
And wiþ her hokes hem al totere,
And loude þai gun to crie.
Who þat is licchoure in þis liif,
Be it man oþer be it wiif,
Þat schal ben his bayli.

74 Þe fendes seyd to þe kniȝt,
'Þou hast ben strong lichoure apliȝt,
And strong glotoun also:
Into þis pain þou schalt be diȝt,
Bot þou take þe way ful riȝt
Oȝain þer þou com fro.'

f. 27va

75 Owain seyd, 'Nay, Satan!
Ȝete forþermar ichil gan,
Þurth grace of God almiȝt.'
Þe fendes wald him haue hent:
He cleped to God omnipotent,
And þai lorn al her miȝt.

76 Þai ladde him forþer into a stede
Þer men neuer gode no dede,
Bot schame and vilanie.
Herkneþ now, and ben in pes!
In `þe´ ferþ feld it wes,
Al ful of turmentrie.

71:6 *Paraph here instead of at* 72:1 *where the scribe's sign to the rubricator is clearly marked.*
73:1 þare] þere KA (*Kölbing claimed first* e *corrected from* a, *but though* ar *poorly formed I see no clear evidence of a change to* er).
73:6 his] *first stroke of* h *corrected from* i?
74:2 lichoure] ho *partially obscured.*

77 Sum bi þe fet wer honging,
   Wiþ iren hokes al brening,
   And sum bi þe swere,
   And sum bi wombe and sum bi rigge,
   Al oþerwise þan y can sigge,
   In diuers manere.

78 And sum in forneise wern ydon,
   Wiþ molten ledde and quic brunston
   Boiland aboue þe fer,
   And sum bi þe tong hing,
   'Allas!' was euer her brocking,
   And no noþer preiere.

79 And sum on grediris layen þere,
   Al glowand oȝains þe fer,
   Þat Owain wele yknewe,
   Þat whilom were of his queyntaunce,
   Þat suffred þer her penaunce:
   Þo chaunged al his hewe!

80 A wilde fer hem þurthout went,
   Alle þat it oftok it brent,
   Ten þousend soules and mo.
   Þo þat henge bi fet and swere,
   Þat were þeues and þeues fere,
   And wrouȝt man wel wo.

81 And þo þat henge bi þe tong,
   Þat 'Allas!' euer song,
   And so loude crid,
   Þat wer bacbiters in her liue:
   Be war þerbi, man and wiue,
   Þat lef beþ forto chide.

f. 27vb 82 Alle þe stedes þe kniȝt com bi
   Were þe paines of purgatori
   For her werkes wrong.
   Whoso is lef on þe halidom swere,
   Or ani fals witnes bere,
   Þer ben her peynes strong.

83 Owain anon him biwent
   And seiȝe where a whele trent,
   Þat griseliche were of siȝt;

82:1 *No paraph.*

Michel it was, about it wond,
And brend riȝt as it were a brond;
Wiþ hokes it was ydiȝt.

84 An hundred þousand soules `and´ mo
Opon þe whele were honging þo,
Þe fendes þertil ourn.
Þe stori seyt of Owain þe kniȝt,
Þat no soule knowe he no miȝt,
So fast þai gun it tourn.

85 Out of þe erþe com a liȝting
Of a blo fer al brening,
Þat stank foule wiþalle,
And about þe whele it went,
And þe soules it forbrent
To poudre swiþe smal.

86 Þat whele, þat renneþ in þis wise,
Is for þe sinne of couaitise,
Þat regnes now oueral.
Þe coueytous man haþ neuer anouȝ
Of gold, of siluer, no of plouȝ,
Til deþ him do doun falle.

87 Þe fendes seyd to þe kniȝt,
'Þou hast ben couaitise apliȝt,
To win lond and lede;
Opon þis whele [þou] schal[t] be diȝt,
Bot ȝif þou take þe way ful riȝt
Intil þin owhen þede.'

88 Her conseyl he haþ forsaken.
Þe fendes han þe kniȝt for`þ´ taken,
And bounde him swiþe hard
Opon þe whele þat arn about,
And so loþly gan to rout,
And cast him amidward.

89 Þo þe hokes him torent,
And þe wild fer him tobrent,
f. 28ra   On Ihesu Crist he þouȝt.
Fram þat whele an angel him bare,
And al þe fendes þat were þare
No miȝt him do riȝt nouȝt.

84:1 and] *ampersand.*   87:4 þou schalt] he schal, *em.* KA.

90   Þai ladde him forþer wiþ gret pain,
          Til þai com to a mounteyn
          Þat was as rede as blod,
          And men and wimen þeron stode;
          Him þou3t, it nas for non gode,
          For þai cride as þai were wode.

91   Þe fendes seyd to þe kni3t þan,
          'Þou hast wonder of þilche man
          Þat make so dreri mode:
          For þai deserued Godes wreche,
          Hem schal sone com a beuereche,
          Þat schal nou3t þenche hem gode.'

92   No hadde he no raþer þat word yseyd,
          As it is in þe stori leyd,
          Þer com a windes blast,
          Þat fende and soule and kni3t vp went
          Almest into þe firmament,
          And seþþen adon him cast

93   Into a stinkand riuer,
          Þat vnder þe mounteyn ran o fer,
          As quarel of alblast,
          And cold it was as ani ise:
          Þe pain may no man deuise,
          Þat him was wrou3t in hast.

94   Seyn Owain in þe water was dreynt,
          And wex þerin so mad and feynt,
          Þat nei3e he was forlore;
          Sone so he on God mi3t þenchen ou3t,
          Out of þe water he was ybrou3t,
          And to þe lond ybore.

95   Þat ich pain, ich vnderstond,
          Is for boþe niþe and ond,
          Þat was so wick liif;
          Ond was þe windes blast
          Þat into þe stinking water him cast:
          Ich man be war þerbi!

96   Forþ þai ladde him swiþe wiþalle,
          Til þai com to an halle,
          He no sei3e neuer er non swiche.

96:3, 4   *Initial letters* h *and* o *partially obscured by decoration on capital* F *at*
96:1.

f. 28rb
Out of þe halle com an hete,
Þat þe kniȝt bigan to swete,
He seiȝe so foule a smiche.

97   Þo stint he forþer forto gon.
Þe fendes it aperceiued anon,
And were þerof ful fawe.
'Turn oȝain,' þai gun to crie,
'Or þou schalt wel sone dye,
Bot þou þe wiþdrawe.'

98   And when he com to þe halle dore,
He no hadde neuer sen bifore
Haluendel þe care.
Þe halle was ful of turmentri:
Þo þat were in þat bayly
Of blis þai were ful bare,

99   For al was þe halle grounde
Ful of pittes þat were rounde,
And were ful yfilt
To þe brerdes, gret and smal,
Of bras and coper and oþer metal,
And quic bronston ymelt;

100   And men and wimen þeron stode,
And schrist and crid, as þai wer wode,
For her dedeli sinne;
Sum to þe nauel wode,
And sum to þe brestes ȝode,
And sum to þe chin.

101   Ich man after his misgilt
In þat pein was ypilt,
To haue þat strong hete;
And sum bere bagges about her swere
Of pens gloweand al of fer,
And swiche mete þer þai ete:

102   Þat were gauelers in her liif.
Be war þerbi, boþe man and wiif,
Swiche sinne þat ȝe lete.
And mani soules þer ȝede vpriȝtes,
Wiþ fals misours and fals wiȝtes,
Þat fendes opon sete.

97:1   stint] s *written over* c?

103 Þe fendes to þe kniȝt sede,
'Þou most baþi in þis lede
Ar þan þou hennes go;
For þine okering and for þi sinne
A parti þou most be wasche herinne,
O cours or to.'

f. 28va 104 Owain drad þat turment,
And cleped to God omnipotent,
And his moder Marie.
Yborn he was out of þe halle,
Fram þe paines and þe fendes alle,
Þo he so loude gan crie.

105　Anon þe kniȝt was war þer,
Whare sprang out a flaumme o fer,
Þat was stark and store.
Out þe erþe þe fer aros,
Þo þe kniȝt wel sore agros;
As cole and piche it fore.

106 Of seuen maner colours þe fer out went,
Þe soules þerin it forbrent;
Sum was ȝalu and grene,
Sum was blac and sum was blo;
Þo þat were þerin hem was ful wo,
And sum as nadder on to sene.

107 Þe fende haþ þe kniȝt ynome,
And to þe pit þai weren ycome,
And seyd þus in her spelle,
'Now, Owain, þou miȝt solas make,
For þou schalt wiþ our felawes s'ch´ake
Into 'þe´ pit of helle.

108 Þis ben our foule's´ in our caghe,
And þis is our courtelage
And our castel-tour;
Þo þat ben herin ybrouȝt,
Sir kniȝt, hou trowestow ouȝt,
Þat hem is aniþing sour?

109 Now turn oȝain or to late,
Ar we þe put in at helle-gate;
Out no schaltow neuer winne,

103:4　þine] þ *corrected from two minims.*　　107:5　þ (?) *erased after* wiþ.

For no noise no for no crie,
No for no clepeing to Marie,
No for no maner ginne.'

110   Her conseil þe kniȝt forsoke.
Þe fendes him nom, so seiþ þe boke,
And bounde him swiþe fast;
Into þat ich wicke prisoun,
Stinckand and derk fer adoun
Amidward þai him cast.

111   Euer þe neþer þat þai him cast
Þe hatter þe fer on him last;
f. 28vb   Þo him gan sore smert.
He cleped to God omnipotent,
To help him out of þat turment,
Wiþ gode wille and stedefast hert.

112   Out of þe pit he was yborn,
And elles he hadde ben forlorn
To his ending-day.
Þat is þe pine, þat ich of rede,
Is for þe foule sinne of prede,
Þat schal lasten ay.

113   Biside þe pit he seiȝe and herd
Hou God almiȝten him had ywerd,
His cloþes wer al torent.
Forþer couþe he no way,
Þer him þouȝt a diuers cuntray;
His bodi was al forbrent.

114   Þo chaunged Owain rode and hewe;
Fendes he seiȝe, ac non he no knewe,
In þat diuers lond;
Sum sexti eiȝen bere,
Þat loþeliche and griseliche we[re],
And sum hadde sexti hond.

115   Þai seyd, 'Þou schalt nouȝt ben alon,
Þou schalt hauen ous to mon,
To teche þe newe lawes,

As þou hast ylernd ere,
In þe stede þer þou were
Amonges our felawes.'

116 Þe fendes han þe kniȝt ynome,
To a stinkand water þai ben ycome;
He no seiȝe neuer er non swiche.
It stank fouler þan ani hounde,
And mani mile it was to þe grounde,
And was as swart as piche.

117 And Owain seiȝe þerouer ligge
A swiþe strong, naru brigge.
Þe fendes seyd þo,
'Lo, sir kniȝt, sestow þis?
Þis is þe brigge of paradis,
Here ouer þou most go;

118 And we þe schul wiþ stones þrowe,
And þe winde þe schal ouer blowe,
And wirche þe ful wo.
Þou no schalt, for al þis midnerd,
Bot ȝif þou falle amidwerd
To our fe[la]wes mo.

119 And when þou art adoun yfalle,
Þan schal com our felawes alle,
And wiþ her hokes þe hede.
We schul þe teche a newe play—
Þou hast serued ous mani a day—
And into helle þe lede.'

120 Owain biheld þe brigge smert,
Þe water þervnder, blac and swert,
And sore him gan to d`r´ede,
For of o þing he tok ȝeme:
Neuer mot in sonne-beme
Þicker þan þe fendes ȝede.

121 Þe brigge was as heiȝe as a tour,
And as scharpe as a rasour,
And naru it was also;

115:4 ylernd] KA *claimed* n *corrected, but though first minim is squeezed*
against r *and slightly blurred I see no sign of correction.*
118:1 wiþ] þ *corrected from long* s.   118:6 felawes] fewes, *em.* KA.
120:3 drede] KC *claimed superscript* r *in different hand, but this is not certain.*

And þe water þat þer ran vnder
Brend o liȝting and of þonder,
Þat þouȝt him michel wo.

122   Þer nis no clerk may write wiþ ynke,
No no man no may biþinke,
No no maister deuine,
Þat is ymade, forsoþe ywis,
Vnder þe brigge of paradis,
Haluendel þe pine.

123   So þe dominical ous telle,
Þer is þe pure entre of helle:
Sein Poule berþ witnesse.
Whoso falleþ of þe brigge adoun,
Of him nis no redempcioun,
Noiþer more no lesse.

124   Þe fendes seyd to þe kniȝt þo,
'Ouer þis brigge miȝt þou nouȝt go,
For noneskines nede.
Fle periil, sorwe and wo,
And to þat stede, þer þou com fro,
Wel fair we schul þe lede.'

125   Owain anon him gan biþenche
Fram hou mani of þe fendes wrenche
God him saued hadde.
He sett his fot opon þe brigge,
No feld he no scharp egge,
No noþing him no drad.

f. 29rb   126   When þe fendes yseiȝe þo,
Þat he was more þan half ygo,
Loude þai gun to crie,
'Allas, allas, þat he was born!
Þis ich kniȝt we haue forlorn
Out of our baylie.'

127   When he was of þe brigge ywent,
He þonked God omnipotent,
And his moder Marie,

122:6   þe] *descender of* þ *corrected.*
123:1   dominical] dm̄cal.   124:5   þou] þ *corrected from* c.
125:2   fendes] *first* e *obliterated.*   126:6   baylie] b *corrected from* v?

Þat him hadde swiche grace ysent,
He was deliuerd fro her turment,
Intil a better baylie.

128 A cloþ of gold him was ybrouȝt,
In what maner he nist nouȝt,
Þo God him hadde ysent.
Þat cloþ he dede on him þere,
And alle woundes hole were,
Þat er þen was forbrent.

129 He þonked God in Trinite,
And loked forþer and gan yse
As it were a ston wal.
He biheld about, fer and neiȝe,
Non ende þeron he no seiȝe,
O red gold it schon al.

130 Forþermore he gan yse
A gate, non fairer miȝt be
In þis world ywrouȝt;
Tre no stel nas þeron non,
Bot rede gold and precious ston,
And al God made of nouȝt:

131 Jaspers, topes and cristal,
Margarites and coral,
And riche safer-stones,
Ribes and salidoines,
Onicles and causteloines,
And diamaunce for þe nones.

132 In tabernacles þai wer ywrouȝt,
Richer miȝt it be nouȝt,
Wiþ pilers gent and smal,
Arches ybent wiþ charbukelston,
Knottes of rede gold þeropon,
And pinacles of cristal.

133 Bi as miche as our Saueour
Is queinter þan goldsmitþe oþer paintour,
Þat woneþ in ani lond,
So fare þe gates of paradis
Er richer ywrouȝt, forsoþe ywis,
As ȝe may vnderstond.

f. 29va

134 Þe gates bi hemselue vndede:
Swiche a smal com out of þat stede,

As it al baume were;
And of þat ich swetenisse
Þe kniȝt tok so gret strengþe `y´wis,
As ȝe may forþeward here,

135 Þat him þouȝt he miȝt wel,
More bi a þousand del,
Suffri pain and wo,
And turn oȝain siker apliȝt,
And ogain alle fendes fiȝt,
Þer he er com fro.

136 Þe kniȝt ȝode þe gate ner,
And seiȝe þer com wiþ milde chere
Wel mani [in] processioun,
Wiþ tapers and chaundelers of gold,
Non fairer no miȝt ben on mold,
And croices and goinfainoun.

137 Popes wiþ gret dignite,
And cardinals gret plente,
Kinges and quenes þer were,
Kniȝtes, abbotes and priours,
Monkes, chanouns and frere Prechours,
And bischopes þat croices bere;

138 Frere Menours and Jacobins,
Frere Carmes and frere Austines,
And nonnes white and blake;
Al maner religioun
Þer ȝede in þat processioun,
Þat order had ytake.

139 Þe order of wedlake com also,
Men and wimen mani mo,
And þonked Godes grace
Þat haþ þe kniȝt swiche grace ysent,
He was deliuerd from þe fendes turment,
Quic man into þat plas.

140 And when þai hadde made þis melody,
Tvay com out of her compeynie,
Palmes of gold þai bere;

136:3 in] om.   137:1 dignite] n subpuncted before g.
139:2 r canc. after mani; KA read it as an ampersand.

. 29vb

To þe kniȝt þai ben ycome
Bitvix hem tvay þai han him nome,
And erchebischopes it were.

141 Vp and doun þai ladde þe kniȝt,
And schewed him ioies of more miȝt,
And miche melodye;
Mirie were her carols þere,
Non foles among hem nere,
Bot ioie and menstracie.

142 Þai ȝede on carol al bi line,
Her ioie may no man deuine,
Of God þai speke and song;
And angels ȝeden hem to gy,
Wiþ harpe and fiþel and sautry,
And belles miri rong.

143 No may þer no man caroly inne,
Bot þat he be clene of sinne,
And leten alle foly.
Now God, for þine woundes alle,
Graunt ous caroly in þat halle,
And his moder Marie!

144 Þis ich ioie, as ȝe may se,
Is for loue and charite
Oȝain God and mankinne.
Who þat lat erþely loue be,
And loueþ God in Trinite,
He may caroly þerinne.

145   Oþer ioies he seiȝe anouȝ:
Heiȝe tres wiþ mani a bouȝ,
Þeron sat foules of heuen,
And breke her notes wiþ miri gle,
Burdoun and mene gret plente,
And hautain wiþ heiȝe steuen.

146 Him þouȝt wele wiþ þat foules song
He miȝt wele liue þeramong
Til þe worldes ende.
Þer he seiȝe þat tre of liif
Wharþurth þat Adam and his wiif
To helle gun wende.

141:4 þere] þ *corrected from* n.   143:1 may] y *corrected from* n.

147   Fair were her erbers wiþ floures,
      Rose and lili, diuers colours,
      Primrol and paruink,
      Mint, feþerfoy and eglentere,

      Colombin and mo þer were
      Þan ani man mai biþenke.

148   It beþ erbes of oþer maner
      Þan ani in erþe groweþ here,
      Þo þat is lest of priis.
      Euermore þai grene springeþ,
      For winter no somer it no clingeþ,
      And swetter þan licorice.

149   Þer beþ þe welles in þat stede,
      Þe water is swetter þan ani mede,
      Ac on þer ʼisʼ of priis,
      Swiche þat seynt Owain seiȝe þo,
      Þat foure stremes vrn fro,
      Out of paradis.

150   [P]ison men clepeþ þat o strem,
      Þat is of swiþe briȝt lem,
      Gold is þerin yfounde.
      [G]i[h]on men clepeþ þat oþer ywis,
      Þat is of miche more priis
      Of stones in þe grounde.

151   Þe þridde strem is Eufrates,
      Forsoþe to telle, wiþouten les,
      Þat rinneþ swiþe riȝt.
      Þe ferþ strem is Tigris;
      In þe world is make nis,
      Of stones swiþe briȝt.

152   Who loueþ to liue in clenesse,
      He schal haue þat ich blisse,
      And se þat semly siȝt.
      And more he þer yseiȝe
      Vnder Godes glorie an heiȝe:
      Yblisced [be] his miȝt!

148:2 *Second half of line legible, though partially obscured by paper strip attached to mend cut caused by excision of miniature on f. 31v.*
150:1 Pison] dison.   150:4 Gihon] fison.   152:6 be] *om., added* KA.

153　Sum soule he sey3e woni bi selue,
　　　And sum bi ten and bi tvelue,
　　　And euerich com til oþer;
　　　And when þai com togiders ywis,
　　　Alle þai made miche blis
　　　As soster doþ wiþ þe broþer.

154　Sum he sei3e gon in rede scarlet,
　　　And sum in pourper wele ysett,
　　　And sum in sikelatoun;
　　　As þe prest ate masse wereþ,
　　　Tonicles and aubes on hem þai bereþ,
　　　And sum gold bete al doun.

30rb

155　Þe kni3t wele in alle þing
　　　Knewe bi her cloþeing
　　　In what state þat þai were,
　　　And what dedes þai hadde ydo,
　　　Þo þat were ycloþed so,
　　　Whi[l]e þai were mannes fere.

156　Ichil 3ou tel a fair semblaunce,
　　　Þat is a gode acordaunce
　　　Bi þe sterres clere:
　　　Sum ster is bri3ter on to se
　　　Þan is bisides oþer þre,
　　　And of more pouwere.

157　In þis maner ydelt it is,
　　　Bi þe ioies of para[d]is:
　　　Þai no haue nou3t al yliche;
　　　Þe soule þat haþ ioie lest,
　　　Him þenkeþ he haþ aldermest,
　　　And holt him also riche.

158　Þe bischopes o3ain to him come,
　　　Bitven hem tvay þai him nome,
　　　And ladde him vp and doun,
　　　And seyd, 'Broþer, God, herd he be!
　　　Fulfild is þi volente,
　　　Now herken our resoun.

159　Þou hast yse wiþ ei3en þine
　　　Boþe þe ioies and þe pine:
　　　Yherd be Godes grace!

155:3 were] weren. 155:6 While] whise, *em.* KA. 157:2 paradis] parabis.

We wil þe tel bi our comun dome,
What way it was þat þou bicome,
Er þou hennes pas.

160 Þat lond þat is so ful of sorwe,
Boþe a[n e]uen and amorwe,
Þat þou þus com bi—
Þou suffredes pain and wo,
And oþer soules mani mo—
Men clepeþ it purgatori.

161 And þis lond þat is so wide,
And so michel and so side,
And is ful of blis,
Þat þou hast now in yhe,
And mani ioies here yse,
Paradis is cleped ywis.

f. 30va 162 Þer mai no man comen here
Til þat he be spourged þere,
And ymade al clene.
Þan comeþ þai hider,' þe bischop s`e´de,
'Into þe ioie we schul hem lede,
Sumwhile bi tvelue and tene.

163 And sum ben so hard ybounde,
Þai nite neuer hou long stounde
Þai schul suffri þat hete;
Bot ȝif her frendes do godenisse,
Ȝif mete, or do sing messe,
Þat þai han in erþe ylete,

164 Oþer ani oþer almos-dede,
Alle þe better hem may spede
Out of her missays,
And com into þis paradis,
Þer ioie and blis euer is,
And libbe here al in pays.

165 As hye comeþ out of purgatori,
So passe we vp to Godes glori,
Þat is þe heiȝe riche,
Þat is paradis celestien;
Þerin com bot cristen men:
No ioie nis þat yliche.

160:2 an euen] auen.
165:4 celestien] celestian *with a* subpuncted *and* e *written above.*

166 When we comen out of þe fer
Of purgatori, ar we com her,
We no may nouȝt anon riȝt,
Til we han her long ybe,
We may nouȝt Godes face yse,
No in þat stede aliȝt.

167 Þe child þat was yborn toniȝt,
Er þe soule be hider ydiȝt,
Þe pain schal ouerfle.
Strong and heui is it þan,
Here to com þe old man,
Þat long in sinne haþ be.'

168 Forþ þai went til þai seiȝe
A mounteyn þat was swiþe heiȝe,
Þer was al gamen and gle.
So long þai hadde þe way ynome,
Þat to þe cop þai weren ycome,
Þe ioies forto se.

169 Þer was al maner foulen song,
Michel ioie was hem among,
And euermore schal be;
Þer is more ioie in a foules mouþe,
Þan here in harp, fiþel or crouþe,
Bi lond oþer bi se.

30vb

170 Þat lond, þat is so honestly,
Is ycleped paradis terestri,
Þat is in erþe here;
Þat oþer is paradis, Godes riche:
Þilke ioie haþ non yliche,
And is aboue þe aire.

171 In þat, þat is in erþe here,
Was Owain, þat y spac of here,
Swiche þat les Adam;
For, hadde Adam yhold him stille,
And wrouȝt after Godes wille—
As he oȝain him nam—

167:4 þan] *followed by an otiose stroke.*
169:4 *Paraph, no scribal indication visible.*
170:2 Is] *a second i subpuncted before* s.   170:4 oþer] þ *corrected from* u?

172   He no his ofspring neuermo
       Out of þat ioie no schuld haue go;
       Bot for he brac it so sone,
       Wiþ pike and spade in diche to delue,
       To help his wiif and himselue,
       God made him miche to done.

173   God was wiþ him so wroþ,
       Þat he no left him no cloþ,
       Bot a lef of a tre,
       And al naked ȝede and stode.
       Loke man, ȝif hye ner wode,
       At swiche a conseil to be.

174   Þo com an angel wiþ a swerd o fer,
       And wiþ a stern loke and chere,
       And made hem sore aferd;
       In erþe to ben in sorwe and wo,
       Þerwhile þai liued euermo,
       He drof hem to midnerd.

175   And when he dyed to helle he nam,
       And al þat euer of him cam,
       Til Godes sone was born,
       And suffred pain and passioun,
       And brouȝt him out of þat prisoun,
       And elles were al forlorn.

176   Hereof spekeþ Dauid in þe sauter,
       Of a þing þat toucheþ here,
       Of God in Trinite,
       Opon men, þat ben in gret honour,
f. 31ra   And honoureþ nouȝt her creatour
       Of so heiȝe dignite.

177   Alle þat ben of Adames kinne,
       Þ < at here in erþe haue don sinne >,
       S < . . . . . . >
       O < . . . . >
       < H. . . . . >
       < A. . . . . . >

176:4   *Below column, catchwords* and honoureþ nouȝt her.
177:2   *After Laing and* KA; *now only initial* þ *and upper parts of* haue don s *are legible.*
177:3–179:2   *Lost on the back of excised miniature. MS neatly patched. Initials* H, A, Th *after Laing, not in* KA.

178 <. . . . .>
<. . . . .>
<. . . . . . .>
<. . . . .>
<. . . . .>
<. . . . . . .>

179 <Th. . . . .>
B<. . . . .>
In þe paine of purgatori;
And bot he haue þe better chaunce,
At domesday he is in balaunce
Oȝaines God in glorie.

180 Þe bischopes þe kniȝt hete
To tellen h[e]m, þat he no lete,
Wheþer heuen were white or biis,
Blewe or rede, ȝalu or grene.
Þe kniȝt seyd, 'Wiþouten wene,
Y schal say min aviis.

181 Me þenkeþ it is a þousandfold
Briȝter þan euer was ani gold,
Bi siȝt opon to se.'
'Ȝa,' seyd þe bischop to þe kniȝt,
'Þat ich stede, þat is so briȝt,
Nis bot þe entre.

182 And ich day ate gate o siþe
Ous comeþ a mele to make ous bliþe,
Þat is to our biheue:
A swete smal of al gode,
It is our soule fode.
Abide, þou schalt ous leue.'

183 Anon þe kniȝt was war þere,
Whare sprong out a flaumbe o fer,
Fram heuen-gate it fel.
Þe kniȝt þouȝt, al fer and neiȝe,
Þer ouer al paradis it fleiȝe,
And ȝaf so swete a smal.

179:2 *Initial b legible and in KC.*
179:3 of purgatori] *upper parts obscured.*   180:2 hem] him.
180:3 white] *first stroke of h corrected from* i?
180:4 *Erasure (?two letters KC) after* ȝalu; grene] g *unusual form.*
181:2 *Erasure above* þan.   182:3 beheue] *final e corrected from* i.

184 Þe holy gost in fourme o fer
Opon þe kniȝt liȝt þer,
In þat ich place;
Þurth vertu of þat ich liȝt
He les þer al his erþelich miȝt,
And þonked Godes grace.

185 Þus þe bischop to him sede,
'God fet ous ich day wiþ his brede,
Ac we no haue noure neiȝe
So grete likeing of his grace,
No swiche a siȝt opon his face,
As þo þat ben on heiȝe.

186 Þe soules þat beþ at Godes fest,
Þilche ioie schal euer lest
Wiþouten ani ende.
Now þou most bi our comoun dome,
Þat ich way þat þou bicome,
Oȝain þou most wende.

187 Now kepe þe wele fram dedli sinne,
Þat þou neuer com þerinne,
For nonskines nede.
When þou art ded, þou schalt wende
Into þe ioie þat haþ non ende;
Angels schul þe lede.'

188 Þo wepe seynt Owain swiþe sore,
And prayd hem for Godes ore,
Þat he most þer duelle;
Þat he no seiȝe neuermore,
As he hadde do bifore,
Þe strong paines of helle.

189 Of þat praier gat he no gain.
He nam his leue and went oȝain,
Þei him were swiþe wo.
Fendes he seiȝe ten þousand last,
Þay flowe fram him as quarel of alblast,
Þat he er com fro.

190 No nere þan a quarel miȝt fle,
No fende no miȝt him here no se,
For al þis warld to winne;
And when þat he com to þe halle,

Þe þritten men he fond alle,
O3aines him þerinne.

191   Alle þai held vp her hond,
And þonked Ihesu Cristes sond
3Iva A þousand times and mo,
And bad him hei3e, þat he no wond,
Þat he wer vp in Yrlond,
As swiþe as he mi3t go.

192   And as ich finde in þis stori,
Þe priour of þe Purgatori
Com tokening þat ni3t,
Þat Owain hadde ouercomen his sorwe,
And schuld com vp on þe morwe,
Þurth grace of God almi3t.

193   Þan þe priour wiþ processioun,
Wiþ croice and wiþ goinfainoun,
To þe hole he went ful ri3t,
Þer þat kni3t Owain in wende.
As a bri3t fere þat brende,
Þai sei3e a lem of li3t,

194   And ri3t amiddes þat ich li3t
Com vp Owain, Godes kni3t.
Þo wist þai wele bi þan,
Þat Owain hadde ben in paradis,
And in purgatori ywis,
And þat he was holy man.

195   Þai ladde him into holi chirche,
Godes werkes forto wirche.
His praiers he gan make,
And at þe ende on þe fiften day,
Þe kni3t anon, forsoþe to say,
Scrippe and burdoun gan take.

196   Þat ich holy stede he sou3t,
Þer Ihesus Crist ous dere bou3t
Opon þe rode-tre,
And þer he ros fram ded to liue
Þurth vertu of his woundes fiue:
Yblisced mot he be!

197   And Bedlem, þer þat God was born
Of Mari his moder, as flour of þorn,
And þer he sti3e to heuen;

And seþþen into Yrlond he come,
And monkes abite vndernome,
And liued þere ȝeres seuen.

198 And when he deyd, he went ywis
Into þe heiȝe ioie of paradis,
Þurth help of Godes grace.
Now God, for seynt Owain's loue,
Graunt ous heuen-blis aboue
Bifor his swete face! Amen.

f. 31vb

Explicit

197:6   þere] þ *corrected from* ȝ.

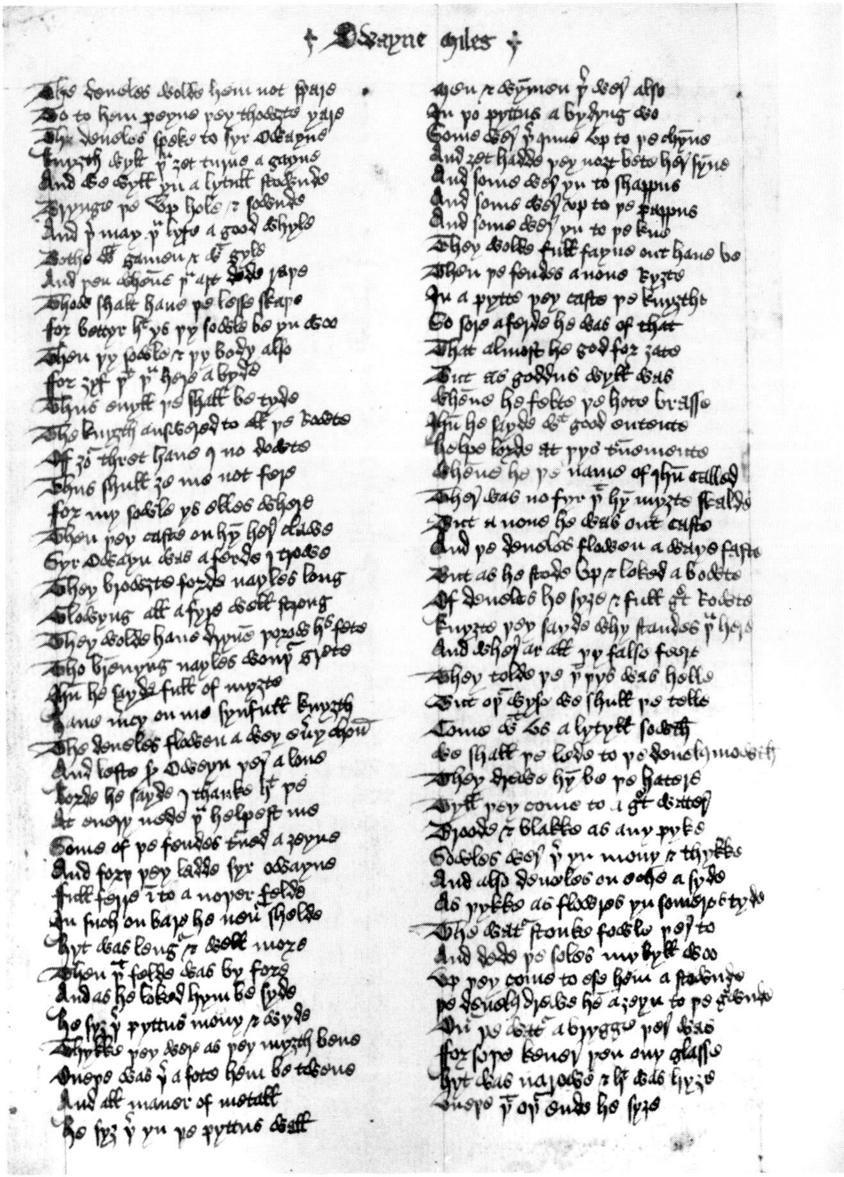

London, BL MS Cotton Caligula A ii, f. 93v

They sottyrd forth þe way tyll strong

stormys yn wond and reyn full long

whyll þ rey stroppyd forth þey soto

he cleryd to hym þ was yt so swoto

Sir he seyd full oft myth

have mercy on me þ gentyll knyth

the hyndys fledyd owt on

And þey þer gowyrd all a ton

And as he stod and lokyd a bowto

Other þolyg þer come on a rowto

And lodyrd hym yn to a nothyr fylde

Swocthe a nothyr he now þe gylde

þe way longer myth more

than þ tothyr he sawe he fore

he sawe yn that fylde brode

Many an odder and many a tode

Men and women he sawe þoo

They yn þ fylde bodyrd noo

ffor they her fobyll and woll lond

And fayrd theyts dw ony hyrd

þer fayr wond tmuny to þ grolond

They soydynd spard wey fuuhd stond

The hyndys fledynd woldyrd hym nay spard

to don hem poythyg they wer full zar

Ther hodyg þ wer worth for to be kempte full oft

And on fysloleyg layne full softe

The todyg sotyrd ow ony hyrro

Ther myth men wdyrd heath þ wore

Coderyg todyg and other woomps

yn hyr bodyors wer ther gawsyy

they raddyn hym yn to a nothyr fylde

The wyche woly brodoþ þ he dw þe gylde

But ther wach neythyr game nor songe

Word to þem a mongs

OWAYNE MILES
COTTON AND YALE VERSION (*OM*2)

COTTON

f. 91va God þat ys so full of myght,
That mendede wronge and made ryght,
He sente men vs to wysse
The ryght way to heuen-blysse.
Fyrste hys prophetys þat wer bold,   5
Off þat was comyng þey vs told;
But þe folke þat wer yn londe
Ne myght hem not vnþurstonde.
To teche vs more redylye,
He come hymself full pryuely,   10
And almoste þre and þrytty ȝer
Sothefaste mon he dwelled here.
Both yn wordes and tokenes fele
He tawȝte men her sowles to hele,
And at þe laste, for monnus goode   15
He dyed hymself vpon þe rode,
And bowȝte vs wyth hys blody syde
[Fro hym that was] lorn þorow pryde;

And hys apostelus forsoþe he sende,
That þey shulde þe folke amende,   20
And to tell hem of heuen-ryche,
Ȝong and olde, pore all ylyche.
He hadde bysshoppus gode also
And oþur prechorus mony mo,
That shewed her mony a tokenyng   25
That he ys God and sothefast kynge;
Holy byschoppus somtyme þer w[o]re;
That tawȝte men of Goddes lore.
In Irlonde preched Seynt Patryke,
In þat londe was non hym lyke.   30
He prechede Goddes worde full wyde,
And tolde men what shullde betyde.
Fyrste he preched of heuen-blysse,
Whoeuur go þydur may ryght nowȝt mysse;
Sethen he preched of helle-pyne,   35
Howe wo þem ys þat comeþ þerinne;

18 Fro ... was] All hem þat were.   27 wore] were.

YALE

f. 28r Jhesu þat ys moste of myth,
        And of wronge makyth ryth,
        Sendyth wyssemen vs to wysche
        The ryth weye to heuyn-blysche.

        To teche hem more redely,   5
        Cryste com hymcelfe woll preuely,
        And allmoste iij and xxxti ȝere
        A stedfaste man that dwellyd here,
        Bothe in word and tokenys felle,
        He tawte men ther sowll-helle.   10
        Aftyrwarde for manys good
        He dede hymselfe vpon þe rode,
        And bowth vs wyth hys blody syde
        Fro hym that was lorn for pryde;
        And or than he to heuyn wente,   15
        Hys apostollys forth he sente

        To telle men of heuyn-reche,
        ȝonge and olde, all aleche.
        ȝet we [had] boschepys alsoo,
        And holy precherys many moo,   20
        That schewyd vs many tokenyng
        That he ys God and stedfast kyng;
        Holy bochoppys sumtyme þer were,
        That tawte men of Godys lore.
        In þe lond prechyd Seynt Pertryke,   25
        In all þat lond wos hym non lyke.
        He prechyd Goddys wordys full wyde,
        And tolde men wat schude betyde.
        Fyrste he spake of heuyn-blysse,
        Howso go theder he go not amysse,   30
        And sythyn he spake of helle-peyn,
        Who ys he þat comyth theryn;

---

1   Eight-line decorative capital J and flourish, distinct from J of Jhesu. First line
written in formal bookhand.
1–5   Slightly inset.   19   had] and.

And þen he preched of purgatory,
As he fonde in hys story.
But ȝet þe folke of þys contre
Beleued not þat hyt myȝth be, 40
And seyde, but ȝyf hyt were so,
That eny mon myth hymself go
And se all þat and come ageyn,
Then wolde þey beleue fayn.
Seynt Patryke hymself beþowȝth, 45
And Jhesu faste he besowȝth,
That he wolde som tokyne shewe,
So þe pepull myȝth þe bettur knowe,
And þat he myȝth þorow hys leue
Turne hem ynto þe ryȝth beleue. 50
Our lord come to hym vpon a day,
As he yn hys bedys lay;
Two ryche þynkes he hym ȝaf,
A booke of gospellus and a staf.
Wyth full glad chere þe byschop hem toke, 55
Boþe þe ryche staffe and þe booke,
And ȝet be þo ryche relyquus þere,
And at euery feste-day yn þe ȝere
They ben bore yn processioun
Wyth full gret deuocioun. 60
The archebysshop of þat lond
Shall bere þat staffe yn hys honde.
Whoso wyll wyte what hyt hatte,
'Jhesu staffe' men calle hyt ȝette.
    God spakke to Saynt Patryke þo 65
By name, and badde hym wyth hym go.
He ladde hym ynto a wyldernesse,
Wher was no reste, more ne lesse,
And shewed, þat he myȝth se
Into þe erþe a pryue entre; 70
Hyt was yn a depe dyches ende.
'What mon,' he sayde, 'þat wyll heryn wende,
And dwelle þeryn a day and a nyȝth,
And holde hys byleue [a]ryȝth,

39 þys] þs *slightly spaced instead of usual* þˢ, þe K4.
65 *Para. sign in left-hand margin.*
66 *Oblique stroke separates* hym *from* go.
74 aryȝth] *ampersand before* ryȝth, and ryȝth K.

f. 91vb (line 41)

f. 28v And ȝyt he spake of porcatory,
        As yt ys wretyn in þe story.
        The folke þat wer in þe contre   35
        Wolde not beleue yt myte `so´ be,

        But ı m[an] myth hymselfe gon,
        And syn all þat and cum ageyn,
        Than many wolde hym beleuyn fayn.
        Seynth Pertryke hym bethowthe;   40
        Jhesu he than besowth,
        That he wolde hym sum tokenys schowe,
        That in þe lond yt myth be knowe,
        That he myth throwr hys beheue,
        Bryng þat folke yn a beter beleue.   45
        Cryste peryd to hym vpon a day,
        As he yn hys bed lay;
        Tweyn reche thyngys he hym ȝaffe,
        A boke of gospell and a staffe.
        Wyth good chyre þe bosschoppe yt toke,   50
        Bothe þe staffe and þe boke;
        ȝyt arn thes reche relekys [þore],
        And heuery heyr feste b[o]re;
        Wyth full good devocyun,
        The boschoppys baryth [yn] prosessun.   55
        The hercheboschoppe of þat lond
        Schall bere þe staffe yn hys hand.
        He þat woll wete wat þe staffe hyte,
        'Jhesu' þe stafte men clepete rythe.
        Cryste spake to Seynt Partryke tho   60
        Be name, he bade hym [wyth hym] goo.
        He led hym ynto a wyldyrnesse,
        Ther neyther man nor beste was,
        And schowyd hym, þat he wyll myth se
f. 29r Into the erthe a preuy entre;   65
        Yt was in a depe dekys ende.
        'What man,' he seyd, 'þat wold hereyn w[e]nde,
        And dwellyn hyryn a day and a nythe,
        And [holde hys byleue] arythe,

36   so] *inserted above line with caret below.*
37   ı] one Sm; man] myth; gon] o *blotted.*
44   beheue] be heue, *the first* e *in* heue *reverse* e *slightly blotted.*
52   þore] ȝowre.   53   bore] bere.   54   f *canc. in same ink after* good.
55   yn] *om.*   58   þe] *superscript* e *blotted.*
61   wyth hym] *om.*, wyt hym *added* Sm.   67   wende] wynde.
69   holde hys beleue] howo he ys be louyd.

And come aȝeyn þat he ne dwelle,   75
Mony a meruayle he may of telle;
And all þo þat doth þys pylgrymage,
I shall hem graunt for her wage,
Wheþur he be sqwyer or knaue,
Oþur purgatorye shall he non haue.'   80
Als sone as he hadde sayde hym so,
Jhesu wente þe bysshoppe fro.

f. 92ra Seynt Patryke þen anon ryght,
He ne stynte ner day ne nyght,
But gatte hym help fro day to day,   85
And made þer a fayr abbey,
And chanonus gode he dede þerinne,
Vnþur þe abbyt of Seynt Austynne.

Seynt Patryke lette make ryght well
A dore bow[n]den wyth iren and stele;   90
Lokke and key he made þerto,
That no mon shulde þe dore vndo.
The key he betoke þe pryour
And badde hym lokke hyt as tresour,
And euur close þe entre so,   95
That no man myȝth þeryn go,
But ȝyf hyt were þorow þe assente
Of þe pryour and þe couente;
Of þe bysschop he moste haue a lettur,
Elles hym were neuur þe better.   100
Ȝet ys þat stede called yn memorye
Seynt Patrykus Purgatorye.
In hys tyme some were þeryn,
To haue forȝeuenesse of her synne,
That come aȝeyn on þe morow;   105
I wote, þey tolde of mykell sorow,
Of peynus, þat þey syȝ þoo,
And of mykyll joye also.
What þey sen þer as þey wente yn,
Forsoþe, hy[t] was yn book wryten.   110
Some wente yn þat bolde wore,
But out come þey neuurmore.

And commyn ageyn [þat he ne dwell],   70
Meruellys talys he may tell.
What man þat goth thys pylgrymmage,
I xall hym grante for hys wage,
Be yt man, woman, ore knaue,
Oþer porcatory xall he neuer haue.'   75
As sone as he to hym had seyd soo,
Jhesu went þat bochoppe froo.
Seynt Partryke went anon rygth,
He not stode, day nor nygth,
But get hym helpe fro day to day,   80
And ded make þer a reche abey.
Schanonys good he dede þeryn,
Vnder þe cunsel of Seynt Austyn;
Thus men clepyd þe reche abeye
Regelys, þat hath þe same [to]day.   85
Seynt Partryke ded make full wyll
A dore bowndyn wyth yryn and stell;
Loke and keye he made þertoo,
That no man schuld that dore ondoo.
The key he toke to þe preyor   90
And bad hym loket as hys tresor.
Ther he loked þat hentre thoo,
That no man myth þeryn goo,
But yf he wer at the seynt
Of þe preyor and hys couent;   95
Ȝyt fro þe boyschoppe he muste haue a letter,
f. 29v Or ellys he wer neuer the better.
Ȝyt ys thys stede yn rememure
Klepyd Seynth Partrykys Purcatore.
In hys tyme sum were theryn,   100
To gette forȝeuenes of ther syn,
And cum aȝen all on the morow;
God wyth þem, toldyn of mykyll sorow,
Of peynys that þey seyn ther.

Whath þey seyn, woll þey wete,   105
For þey hant yn bokys wryte.
Sum wentyn yn that bodyn care,
And comyn ageyn neuermore.

---

70 þat he ne dwell] he note wyll, he note [d]wyll Sm1.
84 reche] *first* e *blotted.*   85 today] day.   89 ondoo] *second* o *blotted.*
96 fro] with *long-tailed* r, *corrected from* for *with* 2-shaped r; he] e *blotted.*
105 wete] t *has a curved tail above* -e.   106 hant] haith Sm.

In Steuenes tyme, y vnþurstonde,
That was kyng of Inglonde,
Ther was a knyȝt men called Oweyn;   115
He was þeryn and come agayn.
What he þer syȝ, y wyll ȝou telle,
Bothe of heuene and of helle.
Thys knyȝt was dowȝty mon and bolde,
And among [men] mykyll of tolde;   120
But þys knyȝte fell ynto synne,
And long tyme he lay þerinne.

f. 92rb At þe laste hym rependede soore,
And þowȝte he wolde do no more,
But to þe bysshoppe of þat countre   125
He wente and fonde hym yn hys se.
To hym he gon hym forto shryue
Of all þe synnus yn hys lyue.
The bysshoppe blamede hym yn þat hete
For hys synnus mony and grete.   130
Sethen he sayde to hym at þe laste,
That all hys lyf he moste faste,
Forto amende her hys mysdede,
Of þat he hadde mysdone and sayde.
'Syr,' he sayde, 'y þe beseche,   135
As þou art my sowles leche,
Graunte me þat y mote gone
To Saynt Patrykes Purgatorye anone;
And when y am comen agayn,
All ȝour wyll y wyll do fayn.'   140
The bysshoppe sayde, 'Dyþur shalt þou nowȝth,
For mony a fole hath þydur sowȝth;
To moche vpon hemself þey tryste,
Whyþur þey wente, no mon wyste.
I rede þe for þy deuocyoun,   145
That þou take þe abyte of relygyoun,
And ȝyf þou wylt þy synne lete,
In þys wyse may þou heuen gete.'
'Syr,' he sayde, 'y þe pray,
Thow ȝeue me leue to go þat way.   150
I hope y woll bothe come and wende,
Thorow þe grace of God [so hende].'

In Steuys tyme, I vndyrstond
Þat þer wos a knyth yn Ingelond,   110
A knyth þer wos men klepynd Syr Howyn;
He was þeryn and come ageyn.
What he sawe þer, I woll yow telle,
Bothe of heuyn and of helle.
The knyth was a dowty man and a bold,   115
Amo[n]ge me[n] mekyll he was of told,
Tyll throw folly he fell yn synne,
And long letyd hym therynne,
And aftyrward bethowte hym s[o]re,
And thowte of synne he wolde no more.   120
To þe boschope of that cuntre
He went and fond hym yn þat se.
To hym anon he gan hym schrywe
At hys myth of all hys lywe.
The boschoppe blamyd hym yn þat hete   125
For hys synnys many and grete,
And sythyn seyd, at þe laste,
That all hys lyve he muste faste,
f. 3or Forto amend hys myssedede,
That he hath done and seyd.   130
'Syre,' he seyd, 'I ȝow beseche,
As ȝe be my sowle leche,
A bone þat ȝe grante me also,
To Seynth Partrykys wey to go;
And sythyn qwhan I cum ageyn,   135
I xall fulfyll ȝowre word full fayn.'
'Seyrteyn,' seyd þe boschoppe, 'þat xall I nowte,
For many [f]ollys thedyr han sowte;
So mykyll on hemselfe they troste,
Wher þey becum, no man woste.   140
I rede the for they devociun,
Thow take abyth of relygiun,
So myth thow, both nythe and day,
Serue God wyll to pay.'

'Ȝefe me lefe to gon my wey.   145
I hope ryth wyll to cum and wynde,
Throw Goddys grace þat ys so hynde.'

109   In] *three-line decorative capital* I *touched with red.*
111   Howyn] H *touched with red.*
116   Amonge] a moge;   men] mem.   119   sore] sere.
122   se] sete.   138   follys] sollys, *initial long s lacks cross-bar of* f.

The bysshop ȝaf hym leue þo,
On Goddes name he badde hym go.
Anon he made hym a letter wele,   155
And seled hyt wyth hys owne sele.
He toke hys leue and wente hys way
To þe pryour of þat abbey.
When he to þe pryour come,
Of þe knyȝte þe lettur he nome.   160
He hyt redde and stode full stylle;
Sone he wyste þe knyȝth[es] wylle,
And wellcomed hym yn fayr manere.
'Syr,' he sayde, 'þou art wellcome here.

f. 92va By þys lettur yn myn honde   165
I haue þy wyll vnþurstonde;
But I de rede þat þou do not so,
Noþur for wele ner for wo.
Aftur my rede þou do anoþur;
Take þe abyte and become our brodur;   170
So þou may, boþe nyȝth and day,
Serue God full well to pay.
Then may þy sowle to heuen wende,
And haue þer blysse wythowten ende.'
'Syre,' he sayde, 'þou redest me well,   175
But for my synnus, dyþur y wyll.
Thyþur y wyll, for my synnus alle,
To haue forȝeuenesse, what so befalle.'
Then sayde þe pryour, 'Ȝyf þou wylt so,
God kepe þe fro kare and wo.   180
But a lytyll whyle þou moste dwelle,
And þe perelles we shall þe telle.'
Fyftene dayes he dwelled þore
In almesse-dedes and holy lore.
At þe fyftene dayes ende,   185
The knyȝth began forth to wende.
Fyrst amorow he herde masse,
And afturwarde he asoyled was
Wyth holy water and holy book,
And ryche relykes forth þey toke.   190

---

155   letter] *long-tailed* r *blotted.*
157–8   *MS order inverted.*   162   knyȝthes] knyȝth.
163   manere] marere, *with the first* re *subpuncted and* ne *written above.*
173   *Oblique stroke separates* heuen *from* wende.
186   began] g *incompletely written over erasure,* gan *separated from* be.

The boschoppe geffe hym leue thowe,
A Goddys name forto goo.
Anon he worthe hym a letter wyll, 150
And selydyth wyth hys howyn sell.
The knyth yt toke and wente hys wey
To þe preyore of that abbey.
As sone as he to þe pryowre cam,
Of hym þe letter þe pryowre nam. 155
He yt rede and stod full styll;
Anon he knewe þe knythtys wyll,
And spake to hym yn fayer maner,
'Syr, þou harte wolcum hethyr.
Be thys letter yn my hand 160
I haue rythe wyll þi wylle vnderstond;
But I rede not the so forto doo,
For grette perellys yt ys theder to goo.
I rede the dwell her and be owre brother,
And take abyte and do no nother; 165
So myth thow, bothe nyte and daye,
Serue God wyll to paye.'

'Syre,' he seyd, 'I felle my wy[kk]e,
For my synnys many and thyke.
Thedyre I wyll, what so befalle, 170
To gette forȝeuenes of hem alle.'
Than seyd þe pryowre, 'Syn þou wylte soo,
Jhesu the saue fro sorow and woo,
But ȝet a wyll wyth vs þou xalte dwell,
And of thow perellys I xall þe tell.' 175
Fyftene dayes he dwellyd ther
In fastyng and in holy lore,
And at the .xv. dayes ende
The knyth muste forth hys wey to w[e]nde.
Fyrste on mowrow he hard messe, 180
And sythyn howsyld he wos;
Holy watyr and holy boke,
Ryche relykys forth he toke.

f. 30v (margin at line 161)

---

167 *Following* C, Sm *added* full *after* God.
168 wykke] wytte.   179 wende] wynde.   183 toke] o *blotted*.

Euury prest and euery [chanoun]
Wente wyth hym yn processyoun,
And as lowde as þey myȝth crye,
For hym þey songe þe letanye,
And browte hym fayre ynto þe entre,   195
Ther as Syr Owen wolde be.
Ther þe knyȝth kneled adown,
And þer [toke] al þur benesoun.
The pryour onlokked þe dore þo,
In Goddus name he badde hym go,   200
And lokked þe þore and turned agayn,
And lafte þer Syr Owayne.
Forth wente Syr Owayne, þat bolde knyȝth,
A whyle he hadde a lytull lyȝth,

_f. 92vb_ But he wanted hys lyȝth full sone,   205
For þer shone neyþur sonne ner mone.
Hee hadde no mon hym to lede,
He groped hys way, as he moste nede.
When he come furþur wythinne,
A lytull lyȝth þer gan begynne,   210
Sone þeraftur a lytull more:
Glad was Syr Oweyn þerfore.
Such was hys lyȝth whan hyt was beste,
As in þe wynter when þe sonne goth to reste.
Then wente he faste, when he myȝth se,   215
Tyll he come to a grete countre.
Hyt semed well þe more wyldernesse,
For þer grewe noþur tre ner grasse.
As he behelde an hys ryȝth honde,
A swyde fayr halle he syȝe þer stonde;   220
Hyt was both longe and wyde,
And hyt was open on euery syde,

As a cloyster yn all wyse;
Hyt was made yn selkowth wyse.
As he þer stoode and loked abowte,   225
Ther come fyftene vpon a rowte.

191   chanoun] man.
198   toke] _om._, receiued K;   al] K _apparatus wrongly claimed this could be_
read as w.   219   behelde] be hellde, _with second_ l _subpuncted._
220   _Letter erased after_ syȝe.

Iche pryste and schanown
Wente wyth hym yn proseyssun. 185
All for hym þey gan to prey,
And seyd for hym þe letaney,
And browth hym to þat entre,
Ther þat Syre Howyn wolde be.
There þe knyth knelyd downg, 190
And toke þe pryowrys benycyoun.
The pryowre onded the dore tho,
f. 31r And lete Syre Howyn yn goo,
And lo[k]kyd þe dore and turnyd ageyn,
And they preyed for Syr Howyn. 195
Forth than wente þat bolde knyth,
And wyll he had lytyll lyth,
But he faylyd lyte full sone,
For þer schon neyther son nor mone.
He had nothyng hym forto lede, 200
He gropyd þe wye as he had nede.
Forth he wente ferder ynne,
A lytyll lyth he saw begynne,
A lytyll lyght þer hym before;
Glad wos Syre Howyn þerfore. 205
Sweche was hys lyght whan yt was beste,
As yt ys in wentyr at the sunne-reste.
Whan he had lythe, forth wente he
Tyll he cam yn a grete cuntere.
It semyd wyll forto be wyldyrnes, 210
For ther was neyther tre nor gres;
But as he behylde hym on hys ryth hond,
A woll fayur halle he sawe þer stond.
It was hey, both long and wyde,
But yt wos opyn on euery syde; 215
Sengyll pyllerys theron were
That metely þe walys bare.
Yt was made of sylkeweth gyse,
Lyke an cloyster on all wyse.
As he stod and lokyd abowte, 220
Ther com .xv. men on a rowte.

185   hym] m changed from n with upward tail (cf. 324).
192   onded] e blotted.   194   lokkyd] lolkyd.
199   son] o changed from ?u.
204   lytl changed to lyty then canc. by stroke in red ink after A.
208   he canc. in same ink after forth.

The eldest of hem, þat he þer sye,
Furste he sayde, 'Benedycyte!'
To Owayne þey 3af har benesoun,
And aftur by hym þey sette hem down.　　230
All hadde newe crownes shafe,
As prestes oweth forto haue.
The eldest mon, as hyt wolde falle,
He spake anon for hem alle.
'Kny3th,' he sayde, 'for þy synne　　235
A grete aventur þou art inne;
But God, þat dyed on þe rode,
Fulfylle þy wyll yn all gode.
We may no lengur wyth þe dwelle,
But be sente þe to telle　　240
Of þe fowndyng þe shall befalle;
God graunte þe to ouurcome all!
Full sone when we be wente þe fro,
The shall come oþur to do þe wo;
But loke þy þow3th on God be styffe,　　245
And be stedfast yn þy belefe.
Yf þey woll þe bete or bynde,
Loke þou haue þys worde yn mynde:
'Jhesu, as þou arte full of my3th,
Haue mercy on me, synfull kny3th!　　250
And euurmore haue yn þy þowght
Jhesu, þat þe so dere hath bowght.
We ne may no lenger þe preche,
But God of heuen we þe byteche.'
These holy men wenten þens þo,　　255
But þen bygon þe kny3tes wo.
　　As he sat þer alone by hymself,
He herde grete dyn on eche half;
As all þe layte and all þe þondur
That euur was herde heuen vndur,　　260
And as alle þe trees and all þe stones
Shulde smyte `to´gedyr ry3th at oonus,
For all þe worlde, so hyt ferde,
And þerto a lowde crye he herde.
Ne hadde he be well ytaw3te byfore,　　265
He hadde ben loste for euurmore,

f. 93ra

249　full] full full.　　　　257　*Para. sign in left-hand margin.*

The eldes man gan forto sey,
Fyrst he seyd, 'Benedicite!'
Syr Howyn toke ther benysun,
And all be hym þey setyn down.   225

f. 31v Alle ther crownys wer new schauyn,
As prystys befalle wyll forto hauyn.
The eldes man of them all,
Fyrste he spake as befall.
'Knyth,' he seyd, 'for þi synne   230
Gret perellys þou puttyste þe ynne;
But God, þat deyed vpon þe rode,
Fullfyll thy wyll yn all goode.
We may no lenger wyth þe here dwell,
We wer sey[n]th hethyr þe to tell   235
Off thow perellys þat [shall] þe befall;
God ȝeyffe þe grace to schape hem all!
As sone as we be gon þe fro
Ther xall cum other to do þe wo;
But loke þat þou throw thy behaue   240
Be stedfast yn þi beleue,
And yf þey wyll þe bete or bynd,
Euermore haue thys word yn mynd:
"Jhesu, God sun, full of myth,
Haue mercy of me, þi gentyll knyth!"   245
And ha[ue] euermore yn thy thowth
Jhesu, þat hath the euer bowth.
We may no lenger wyth þe preche,
But Jhesu Cryste we þe beteche.'
Thyes holy men wente hym fro,   250
And than began the knythtys wo.

As all þe le[m]e and all þe thundyre
That men hath seyn of myche wondre,
And all þe tryn and all þe stonys
Had row togedyr all at-tonys,   255
In that wedyr so yt faryd,
Yt made Syre Howyn sore aferde;
And he had nowth be tawte before,
He had be rewyd fore euermore.

233 goode] *second* o *inserted partially over the* d.
235 seynth] seyth.   236 shall] Jhu.   246 haue] hath.
252 leme] lenne, *first* e *blotted.*
259 euermore] *possible erasure, three letters' space, between* euer *and* more.

For fle my3te he naw3te, but moste abyde.
Then come þer deueles on euury syde,
Wykked gostes, I wote, fro helle,
So mony þat no tonge my3te telle;   270
They fylled þe hows yn two rowes,
Some grenned on hym and some made mowes.
Syr Owayne was aferde, y trowe,
For 3yf he hadde my3th, he wolde haue flowe.
Some deueles stode hym full ny3e,   275
That sayden to hym all on hy3e,
'Thow haste don wele to come betyme,
For þou shalte beleue on owre lyme.
Oþur come not tyll þey be dede,
But þou haste don a well bettur rede.   280
Thow comeste hydur to do penaunce,
Wyth vs þou shall lede þe daunce.
Thow haste serued vs mony a day,
We shall þe qwyte, 3yf we may.
As þou hast don, so shalte þou haue,   285
All þy kynne shall þe not saue.
Neuurþelesse, syth þou art hende,
3yf þou wolte a3eyn wende,
And lyue and do as þou haste don,
We shall þe spare tyll efteson.'   290

f. 93rb Þen sayde þe kny3th, 'I dowte you now3th.
I betake me to hym þat me hatht wroght.'
Þen þe fendes made a fyre anone
Of blakke pyche and of brenstone.
Þey caste þe kny3th þeryn forto brenne,   295
And all þey begonne on hym to grenne.
Þe kny3th þat payne full sore he þow3th,
To Jhesu he called whyle he mow3th.
'Jhesu,' he sayde, 'full of pyte,
Help and haue mercy on me.'   300
All þat fyre was qweynte anone,
Þe fendes flowen away euurychone,
And þen þe kny3th anone vp stode,
As hym hadde ayled now3t but gode,

291 you] yo^u.   300 he *subpuncted and canc. after* Help.

f. 32r Flyen myth he nowt, he muste abyd.   260
         They com yn on euer[y] syyd,
         Wykyd gostys owte of helle;
         Ther may corage hym full telle.
         [They fylled] þe howsys, rowys be rowys,
         And many stodyn wythowte þe wowys.   265
         Summe fyndys gernyd and summe made a mowe,
         Syre Howyn wos aferd, I trowe;
         And summe fyndys þat stode hym by
         Seydyn to hym, all on hey,
         'Thow haste wyll done þat þou cum here,   270
         Thus betyme to be owre fere.
         Oþer cum not tyll they be dede,
         But thow haste a woll better rede;
         Thow comyst hethyr `to´ do penawns,
         And wyth vs þou xalte lede the dawns.   275
         Thow seruyd vs many a day;
         We xall the ȝyldyth, yf we may.
         Thow hast be to vs a woll good knawe;
         As þou hast seruyd, thow schallte haue.
         But neuerþelesse, wyll þou harte hynd,   280
         Yf þou wylte ageyn wynd,
         And gone and leuyn as þou haste down,
         We xall þe sp[are] tyll eftsunne.
         Bettyr yt ys thy sowle haue who,
         Than body and sowle allso.'   285
         'Nay,' seyd þe knyth, 'þat wyll I nowte;
         I take me to hym þat hath me bowte.'
         The fyndys madyn a fyere anone,
         Off blake pyke and brymeston,
         And kyste þe knyth þeryn to b[re]nne,   290
         And all on hym they gan grenne.

f. 32v 'Jhesu,' he seyd, 'full of myth,
         Haue mercy on me, þi gentyll knyth.'
         The fyndys fledyn eueryschon,
         And lettyn Syre Howyn all alon.   295

261 euery] euer; syyd] *second* y *corrected from* n.
264 They fylled] Full.   274 to *inserted above line with caret below.*
283 spare] sprer.   289 brymeston] brymteston.
290 brenne] berne *with flourish on* n, *em.* Sm.

All alone belefte yn þat place,   305
And he þonked God of all hys grace.
Then was he bolder forto stonde,
Ȝyf þat þey wolde hym more fonde.
Ther come deueles oþur mony mo,
And badde þe knyȝth wyth hem to go,   310
And ladde hym into a fowle contreye
Wher euur was nyȝth and neuur day,
For hyt was derke and wonþur colde;
Ȝette was þer neuur man so bolde,
Hadde he neuur so mony cloþus on,   315
But he wolde be colde ȧs ony stone.
Wynde herde he none blowe,
But faste hyt frese, boþe hye and lowe.
They browȝte hym to a felde full brode,
Ouer suche anoþur neuur he yode,   320
For of þe lenghte non ende he knewe,
Therouer algate he moste nowe.
As he wente he herde a crye,
He wondered what hyt was and why.
He syȝ þer men and wymmen also   325
That lowde cryed, for hem was woo.
They leyen þykke on euury londe,
Faste nayled boþe fote and honde
Wyth nayles glowyng all of brasse;
Þey ete þe erþe, so wo hem was,   330
Her face was nayled to þe grownde,
'Spare,' þe`y´ cryde, 'a lytyll stounde!'
The deueles wolde hem not spare,
To [d]o hem peyne þey thowȝte yare.
Th[e] deueles speke to Syr Owayne,   335
'Knyȝth, wylt þou ȝet turne agayne,
And we wyll yn a lytull stownde
Brynge þe vp hole and sownde;
And þer may þou lyfe a good whyle,
Bothe wyth gamen and wyth gyle.   340
And þen whenne þou art dede raþe
Thow shalt haue þe lesse skaþe,

f. 93va

317   blowe] blowle.   326   cryed] y *corrected from* e.
328   wᵗ *subpuncted after* nayled.   334   do] to.
335   The] e *partially obliterated.*

And as he stod þer all alone,
Oþer deuelys abowte hym gan gone,
And ledyn hym ynto a fowle cuntre
Th[er] euer ys nyth and neuer daye.
Ther yt was both therke and colde;   300
Ther was neuer man so boold,
That thow hys clothys wer purfuld,
Sone hys [he]rt[e] xulde be colde.
Than felte he þer wynd blowe,
And ȝyt yt blewe boþe hey and lowe.   305
They ledyn hym ynto a fyuld brode,
Ouyr sweche on he neuer rode.
The lenkyth þerof cowd he not tell,
Therouer he muste, so yt befell.
And as he ȝyd he hard a cry,   310
And he lokyd what wos hym by.
He sawe þer men and women tho
That lowd cryend fore who;
They loyn thyke on euery lond,
Fast naylyd, fute and hond.   315

Vpward ther belyys wer cast,
And ynto þe erth naylyd fast.

The fyndys spokyn to þe knyth,
'Syste þou how theys folke be dyth?
But yf þou wylte to owþer cunsell turne,   320
Hyre xall þou ly[en] and make þi mone.'

299   Ther] That.   303   herte] thyrth.   321   lyen] lynth.

For bettyr hyt ys þy sowle be yn woo,
Then þy sowle and þy body also,
For ȝyf þat þou here abyde,   345
Thus euyll þe shall betyde.'
The knyȝth answered to all þe rowte,
'Off ȝour thret haue I no dowte.
Thus shull ȝe me not fere,
For my sowle ys elleswhere.'   350
Then þey caste on hym her clawe,
Syr Owayn was aferde, I trowe.
They browȝte forde nayles long,
Glowyng all afyre well strong.
They wolde haue dryuen þorow hys fete   355
Tho brennyng nayles wonþur grete.
'Jhesu,' he sayde, 'full of myȝte,
Haue mercy on me, synfull knyȝth.'
The deueles flowen awey euerychon,
And lefte Syr Oweyn þer alone.   360
'Lorde,' he sayde, 'I thanke hyt þe,
At euery nede þou helpest me.'
Some of þe fendes turned aȝeyne,
And forþ þey ladde Syr Owayne
Full ferre into anoþer felde,   365
In such on bare he neuur shelde.
Hyt was lengur and well more
Then þat felde was byfore.

'Nay,' seyd þe knyth, 'þat wyll I nowth.
Myne hope ys yn hym þat hath me bowth.'
Anon þe fyndys leydyn hym downe,
To don hym peyne þi wer all bone.   325

f. 33^r They fettyn forthe naylys strong,
Bernyng yt wern and reyth full long.
Whyll þat þey streynyd forth hys fete,
He clepyd to hym þat ys so swete,
'Jhesu,' he seyd, 'full of myth,   330
Haue mercy on me, þi gentyll knyth.'
The fyndys fledyn euery on,
And let Syre Howyn all alon.

And as he stod and lokyd abowte,
Othyr delys ther comme on a rowte,   335
And ledyn hym ynto anothyr fylde,
Sweche another he neuer behylde:
It was lenger mych more
Than þe tother he sawe before.
He sawe yn that fylde brode   340
Many an edder and many a tode.
Men and women he sawe thoo,
That yn þat fylde bodyn woo,
For they wer febyll and woll lene,
And loyne thyke on euery kyne.   345
Hyre facys wern turny[d] to þe grownd,
They seydyn, 'Spare vs summe stond!'
The fyndys woldyn h[e]m not spare,
To don hem peynys they were full ʒare.
Ther hedys þat wer wont forto be kempte full ofte,   350
And on pyllowys layne full softe,
The todys sotyn on euery herre,
Ther myth men vetyn wat þie were.
Edderys, todys and othyr wormys,
In hyr bodyes wer ther howsys.   355

324 hym] m *changed from* n *with upward tail* (*cf.* 185).
329 wos *canc. in same ink after* þat.   338 *Change of ink and nib.*
346 turnyd] turny, *em.* Sm.
348 fledyn *canc. in red ink after* fyndys;   hem] hym, *em.* Sm2.
353 þie] ie *superscript.*

They leddyn hym ynto another fylde,
The wyche was brodest þat he euer behylde,
But ther was neyther game nor songe
Neuer wyth them amonge.

f. 33v Iche man, of·hys turment,   360
The knyth sawe as he went.
He thowte ryth wyll to beholde
Men and women, ȝynge and olde,
Wyth schenys bernyng as the fyer,
Many þer hynge be the sqwyer;   365
Summe be the tongys and summe be þe chynnys,
Summe be the membrys and summe be þe novelys,
Summe hynge hey and summe hynge lowe,
Many he knewe that he þer sawe.
Summe hynge on hokys be þe chynne,   370
Mykyll sowrow þey hadyn for ther synne.
As they haddyn hym ferder inne,
A woll myche wylle he sawe þerinne;
It was brod and yt wos heye,
[Vneþe] to þe ouerest ȝend he seye.   375
The halfe wylle yn þe erthe ranne,
And theron hyngyn many a man.
Benethyn wos fyer and brynston
That bernyth them euer anon.
Yt semy[d] a trendyll, yt ran so ȝarn,   380
Ryght as a ston of a qwerne.
They tokyn hym be þe handys th[e]n
And kestyn hym on þe wylle to brene.
Anon wos the knyth wyll,
And ther he stoke styll.   385
Anon he klepyd onto Jhesu Cryste,
So þat no more herme he wyste.
The fyndys seyn þey myth note spede,
They grenyd on hym as woluys [wede];
All abowte hym they gan goo,   390
They wolde fayn a don hym woo.
Fast þey hadyn hym ferder more,
A woll mych howsse he sawe before,

f. 34r The lenkyt þerof he cowd note ame;
Owte of the dore comme a grete flame.   395

375 Vneþe] And nedys.
380 semyd] semyth; yt] þat Sm; faste *canc. in same ink after* so, *but later
correction?*   382 then] than.   389 wede] in wode.
391 don] d *written over another letter.*
392 inne *canc. in same ink after* ferder.

And as he loked hym besyde,
He syȝ þer pyttus mony and wyde;   370
Thykke þey were as þey myȝth bene,
Oneþe was þer a fote hem betwene,
And all maner of metall
He syȝ þer yn þe pyttus wall.
f. 93vb Men and wymmen þer wer also   375
In þo pyttus abydyng wo;
Some wer þerinne vp to þe chynne,
And ȝet hadde þey noȝt bete her synne;
And some wer vp to þe pappus,
And some wer yn to [þe] shappus,   380
And some wer yn to þe kne;
They wolde full fayne out haue be.
Then þe fendes anone ryȝte,
In a pytte þey caste þe knyȝthe.
So sore aferde he was of that,   385
That almost he God forȝate;

Ther was so mych s[t]yn[k]e and smeke,
Yt wold a made an heyll man seke.
The knyth styntyd and þer wythstod,
For þat stynke he was nere wod.
The fyndys turnyd ageyn,   400
And gresely spake to Syre Howyn,
'Why goste þou so faste? And þou halte,
Wyll þou [n]yll [þou], forth thow xalte.
Syst thow now ȝyn grete gatys?
Ther byn owyr bate fatys.   405
Ther syth owre maystyr and owre kyng;
He ys full glad of thy comyng.
Thow seruyst hym full wyll at home;
He ys woll glad þat thou arte cumme.
Syste thow thy home, wyll þou soo,   410
Or thow wylte ageyn goo,
Ageyn to þi gatys of Re[g]e[l]ys,
Than may þou seyn þou ha[ste] byn at þe develys.'
'Nay,' seyd the knyth, 'that wyll I nowte;
That xall neuer cume yn my thowte.   415
God hath holpe me hethyr before,
And ȝyt, I hope, he wyll do more.'
As they hadyn hym ferder inne,
Ther he sawe woll mykyll onwyn.
As he lokyd hym besyde,   420
He sey ther pyttys many and wyde;
Thykker myth they not byn,
All but a fote them betwyn.
Eche maner of metell
He sey yn þo pyttys wyll.   425
Men and women he sawe tho
That yn tho pyttys bodyn full mych wo;
f. 34v Summe stod theryn vp to the chyn,
Summe to þe pappys and summe to þe schyn;

Summe stod þeryn vp to the kne,   430
All owte they wold fayn a be.
The fyndys hentyd anon ryth,
And to þe pyttys þey keste þe knyth.
So sore aferd he was of that,
Tyll allmost Jhesu he had forȝette;   435

396   stynke] skynte, em. Sm.
398   stynd changed to stynt then canc. by stroke in red ink after knyth.
403   nyll þou] wyll.   412   þi] þi, þe Sm;   Regelys] relegys, em. Sm.
413   haste] hath;   develys] first e written over another letter.
418   inne] long i written over a minim.   425   þo] o superscript, þe Sm.
426   he] e partially blotted, looks more like a.

But as Goddus wyll was,
Whenne he felte þe hote brasse,
'Jhesu,' he sayde, wyth good entente,
'Helpe, lorde, at þys turnemente.'   390
Whenne he þe name of Jhesu called,
Ther was no fyr þat hym myȝte skalde,
But anone he was out caste,
And þe deueles flowen awaye faste.

But as he stode vp and loked abowte,   395
Of deueles he syȝe [a] full gret rowte.
'Knyȝte,' þey sayde, 'why standes þou here?
And wher ar all þy false feere?
They tolde þe þat þys was helle,
But oþurwyse we shull þe telle.   400
Come wyth vs a lytyll sowth,
We shall þe lede to þe deuelus mowth.'
They drewe hym be þe hatere,
Tyll þey come to a gret water,
Broode and blakke as any pyke;   405
Sowles wer þeryn, mony and thykke,
And also deueles on eche a syde,
As þykke as flowres yn someres tyde.
The watur stonke fowle þerto,
And dede þe soles mykyll woo.   410
Vp þey come to ese hem a stownde,
Þe deuelus drewe hem aȝeyn to þe grownde.
Ouur þe watur a brygge þer was,
Forsoþe kener þen ony glasse.
Hyt was narowe and hyt was hyȝe,   415
Vneþe þat oþur ende he syȝe.
f. 94ra The myddyll was hyȝe, þe ende was lowe,
Hyt ferde as hyt hadde ben a bent bowe.
The deuell sayde, 'Knyȝte, her may þou se
Into helle þe ryȝte entre.   420
Ouur þys brygge þou moste wende;
Wynde and rayne we shull þe sende.

396   a] *ampersand, em.* K.
404   water] *lobes of two-compartment* a *partially obliterated.*
421   moste] o *partly blotted.*

But sythyn wan Goddys grace was,
Whan he felte þe hoote bras,
'Jhesu,' he seyd, wyth good yntent,
'Helpe me, lord, yn thys turment.'
As sone as he to Jhesu calde, 440
Ther was no metell myth hym schalde,
But all besyd was caste;
The fyndys fleddyn awey full faste.
'Jhesu,' he seyd, 'I thanke the;
Euer at nede þou helppyst me.' 445
As he stod and lokyd abowte,
Off othyr fyndys þer camme a rowte.
'Knyth,' they seyd, 'wy sta[n]dyst þou here?
And all we byn felowys yn fere.
All þey seydyn that her was hell, 450
But owtherweyes we xall þe tell.
Cume her forth ynto þe sowth,
We xall the bryng to hell-mowth.'
As they haddyn hym forth more,
A woll mych watyr he say before 455
That was brod and blake as pyke.
Men and women ther wern thyke;
Fyndys stodyn on euery syde,
As thyke as motys yn somer-tyde.

Ouer the water a bryg was; 460
Yt wos glyddyr as ony glasse.
f. 35r Therof he wos full sore aferd,
Yt was as scharp as ony sw[e]rd.
The medys wer hey, þe endys wer lowe,
Yt faryd ryth as a bent bowe. 465
'Knyth,' seyd a fynd, 'here may þou see;
Loke toward hell the ryght entre.
Ouer thys bryg þou muste wynd;
Wynd and wether we xall the send.

437   þe] superscript e blotted.
438   yntent] y possibly changed from two minims.
440   klepyd canc. in same ink after Jhesu.
448   standyst] stadyst, em. Sm.
460   Brown and red paragraph sign in left-hand margin.
463   swerd] sward.

We shull þe sende wynde full goode
That shall þe caste ynto þe floode.'
Syr Owayne kneled þer adowne,   425
To God he made hys orysowne:
'Lord God,' he sayde, 'full of my3te,
Haue mercy on me, synfull kny3te.
Wynde and rayne ys at þy wyll,
And all wederes lowde and styll.   430
Thow kanste make wynde to blowe,
And when þou lyst, to lye full lowe.
Sende me, lorde, þy swete grace,
That y may þys brygge passe.
Help, lorde, þat y þerin not falle,   435
Forto lese my labour all.'
To þe brygge anon he 3ede,
'Jhesu,' he sayde, 'help at þys nede.'
Hys on foote he sette fyrste þeron,
And called to Jhesu ry3th anoon.   440
He felte hys foote stonde stedfastly,
And þat oþur foote he sette þerby.
He called to helpe yn þat place
Jhesu, þat euur shall be and euur was.
The brygge wax a lytyll bradder   445
Then waxe Syr Owayne gladder;
But when he come ynto þe mydde,
Euury deuell wyth oþur chydde,
And for he sholde falle by,
All þey toke vp a grete cry.   450
That crye, hym þow3t, greuede hym more
Then all þe payne he hadde before.
Neuurþelatter, forth he wente,
In God was all hys entente.
So brode þe brygge wax þoo,   455
That waynes my3th þeron haue goo.
Ouur þat he come full sone,
Then was þe deuell power done.
He þonked God yn all hys þow3th,
That hadde hym harmelese ouur brow3th.   460

457   þat] þᵗ *with* t *blurred*, þer Wu.

We xall the send wyndys wood;   470
Thowe xall caste þe ynto owre flood.'
Ther the knyth knelyd adown;
To Jhesu he made hys orysun.
'Jhesu', he seyd, 'full of myth,
That made bothe day and nyth;   475
Wynd and weder at thy wyll,
Forto blow and foreto be styll.
Thow makyst the `wynd´ foreto blowe,
And whan thow wylte, to be lowe.
Send me here thy grete grace,   480
That I may thys bryg pace.
Helpe me, lord, þat I nowte fall,
That I lece nowth my travell.'
To the brygg anon he ȝydde,
'Jhesu,' he seyd, 'helpe me at nede.'   485
Hys ɪ fote he sette thervpon,
And klepyd to Jhesu euer anon.
He felth [hys fote] stand stedfastly,
He sette another fote þerby,
And klepyd to hym euer a pasce,   490
That ȝet ys and euer was.
The brygg waxyd a lytyll broder,
So mych was Syr Howyn þe glader.
Whan he comme ynto the myde,
_f. 35v_ Euery dewyll to other chyd,   495
And all they setyn owte a cry,
Forto a don hym fall fro[m] hey.
The cry mad hym aferd more
Than all þe tother he saw before.
     Neuerthelesse, forth he wente,   500
On Jhesu Cryste full wos hys yntente.
So brod was the brygge thoo,
Tweyn cartys myth þeron goo.
He com to þe end woll sone,
Than was the develys pray done.   505
He thankyd Jhesu wyth harte and thowth,
That he had hym ouer browte.

486 ɪ] one Sm.
488 hys fote] _added_ Sm. _following_ C;   stand] d _written over another letter?_
494 myde] myde bryge.   497   from] fron.
499 Than] a _changed from_ e.
500 _Paragraph sign in left-hand margin;_   Neuer] N _three-line flourish on_
first stroke.   506   thankyd] d _blotted._

f. 94rb   Forth he wente a lytull whyle,
The mowntenance of halfe a myle.
He sawe a wall wondyr fayr,
Hym þowȝte hyt lasted ynto þe ayr;
Hyt was whyte and bryȝth as glasse,   465
He cowþe not wyte what hyt was.
When he was nyȝ þerat,
Agayne hym openede a fayr ȝate,
Full craftyly for þe nones,
Of metall and of presyous stones.   470
Out at þe ȝate come a smell,
Well nyȝ for joyc downe he fell.
As þer hadde ben all maner of flourres,
Such w[er] þ[e] swete sauourres;
Non erdely sauour, be a þowsandfolde,   475
Myȝth not to þat sauour be tolde.
Then hym thowȝte he was so lyȝte,
Off þat sauour and of þat syȝte,
That all þe sorow þat he hadde sene,
And all þe payne þat he hadde yn bene,   480
All was forȝeten yn hy[s] þowȝth,
And of hyt he sette ryȝth nowȝth.
As he stode and was so fayne,
Hym þowȝth þer come hym agayne
A swyde fayr processyoun   485
Of all maner men of relygyoun.
Fayre vestymentes þey hadde on,
So ryche syȝ he neuer non.
Myche joye hym þowȝte to se
Bysshopes yn her dygnyte.   490
Ilkone wente oþur be and be,
Euery man yn hys degre.
He syȝ þer monkes and chanones,
And freres wyth newe shauen crownes;
Ermytes he sawe þeramonge,   495
And nonnes wyth full mery songe;
Persones, prestes and vycaryes,
They made full mery melodyes.
He syȝ þer kynges and emperoures,
And dukes þat hadde casteles and tourres;   500

472   downe] d *changed from* ȝ.
473   flourres] *MS uses* ur *abbreviation,* floures K.
474   wer þe] was þat;   sauourres] *MS uses* ur *abbreviation,* sauoures K.
481   hys] hᵗ.
500   tourres] *MS uses* ur *abbreviation,* toures K.

Forth he wente a lytyll wyll,
He thowt yt myth a byn a myll;
He sey a w[a]ll wondyrly fayere,   510
That ran, hym thow, vp to þe eyre.
He cowd noth wyte wereof yt was,
Into the eyere yt was.

Owte of þe gate cam a smell.
Allmost for yoy dow[n] he fell.   515
Thow all þe flowyr[ys] and all þe erbery,
And all the wardly spycery
[Wer ther, swech] smell, be a hundre-fold,
To þat swetnes myth [not] be tolde.
Than was he so mery and so lyt,   520
Off that savor and that syth,
That all þe peynys he had yn ben,
And all þe sorow he had syn,
All was forȝete yn hys thowth,
Hym thowth yt grevyd hym noth.   525
As he stod, he was woll fayn,
Owth of the gate cam hym ageyn
f. 36r A woll fayer proseyssyun
Off euery man of relygyoun.
Fayer vestemens they haddyn vpon,   530
Swech sawe he neuer non.
Woll mych joy yt was to see
Boschoppys yn hyr dygnyte,
And other maysterys þer sey he,
Eche man yn hys degre.   535
He sey ther mvnkys and schanonys,
And fryerys wyth ther brode crownys,
And ermytys them amonge,
And nonnys wyth ther mery song[e];
Personys, prystys and vekerys,   540
They madyn hym many meladys.
He sey kynggys and emprorys,
Devkys, castelys and towerys,

510 wall] wyll; fayere] r *poorly formed.*   511 thow] thowt Sm.
514 smell] *long s may be corrected from* f.   515 down] dow.
516 flowyrys] flowyre.   518 Wer ther, swech] Yt myth not.
519 not] *om.* 520 was] *large s written over another letter.* 528 A] And a.
538 amonge] *cross through letter* ?k *between* a *and* monge.
539 songe] songys.   543 Devkys] Devlys Sm.

Erles and barones fele
That sometyme hadde þe worldes wele.
Oþur folke he sy3 also,
Neuur so mony as he dede þoo.
Wymmen he sy3 þer that tyde,   505
Myche was þe joye þer on euery syde,

f. 94va For all was joye þat wyth hem ferde,
And myche solempnyte þer he herde.
Fayre þey wellcomed Syr Oweyne,
All þat þer was of hym were fayne.   510
Then come to hym þore
Two bysshoppus, as hyt wore.
They welcomede hym and 3ode hym by,
Forto bere hym company,
And schewede hym, þat he my3th se,   515
The fayrnesse of þat cowntre.
Hyt was grene and full of flowres
Of mony dyuers colowres;
Hyt was grene on euery syde,
As medewus are yn someres tyde.   520
Ther were trees growyng full grene,
Full of fruyte euurmore, y wene;
For þer was frwyte of mony a kynde,
Suche yn þys londe may no mon fynde.
Ther þey haue þe Tree of Lyfe,   525
Theryn ys myrthe and neuur stryfe.
Frwyte of wysdom also þer ys,
Of þe whyche Adam and Eue dede amysse.
Oþur maner frwytes þer were fele,
And all manere joye and wele.   530
Moche folke he sy3 þer dwelle,
Ther was no tonge þat my3th hem telle.
All wer þey cloded yn ryche wede,
What cloþ hyt was he kowþe not rede,

520   someres] *second* e *blotted.*

And women he sey on euery syde,
That merthys madyn yn þat tyde. 545
All þey wer clothyd yn reche wed,
What clothyn yt was cowd he noth red,
But schap they had on euery maner
As men wer wonte to were here.
Be ther clothyn men myth them know, 550
As they stod eche on a row,
Ʒownge and held, more and lesse,
Off wat degre that þey wasse.
Fayer they spokyn to Syre Howyn;
All the folke of hym were fayn. 555
Anon he gan metyn ther
Tweyn boysschoppys hym thow þat þey were,
And both they went forth hym by,
And bore Syre Howyn cumpany.
They schowyd hym, þat he myth se, 560
The forest of that cuntre.

f. 36v   It was grene on euery syd,
As medowys byn yn summer-tyd,
And all so full of fayer flowerys,
Off many dyuers colorys. 565
Tryn he sawe wyth leuys grene,
Full of frute euermore, I wene;
Frut of so many kynd
In thys ward can no man fynd.
Ther he sey the Tre of Lyffe, 570
That they haue wythowtyn stryffe.
Fryuth of wesdam allso ther ys,
Therof ete Adam and ded amys;
And other frutys þer arn full felle,
And all maner of joy and wylle. 575

545–6   *See Commentary C509ff, Y546ff on misplaced lines.*
553   *Three letters, probably* ded, *canc. in red ink after* Off.
557   thow þat] thow þᵗ, thowyt Sm.
562   It] *four-line decorated* I *touched with red.*
562–5   *Slightly inset.*   572   *Scribe's new stint, new nib.*

But shapte þey hadde yn all maner   535
As folke þat wonede somtyme her.
By þe cloþus men myȝthe hem knowe,
As þey stode vpon a rowe,
Ȝonge and olde, more and lasse,
As hyt her owene wyll was.   ·   540
Ther was no wronge, but euur ryȝth,
Euur day and neuer nyȝth;
They shone as bryȝth and more clere
Then ony sonne yn þe day doth her.
The two bysshopes turnede aȝeyne,   545
And speke fayr to Syr Owayne.
'Blessed be þou,' þey sayden þoo,
'That haddeste wyll þys way to goo.
Purgatorye þou haste ben inne
To haue forȝeuenesse of þy synne;   550
Loke þat þou do synne no more,
For þou shalt neuur efte come þore.
We haue gone þe way þer þou was,
And we haue passed þat ylke plas.

f. 94vb   So shall yche man aftur hys day,   555
Pore and ryche, go that way,
For þer ys mony a mon alyue,
That hath no power hym to shryue,
Tyll at þe laste he shryueth hym for drede;
Somme penaunce þey mote suffre nede: 560
If þey woll nowȝth do here,
They shall do hyt elleswhere.
Suche maner men, erly or late,
To purgatorye þey mote algate.
Ther mote þey dwelle stylle,   565
And abyde Goddes wylle,
But somme frende for her mysdede,
For hem do oþur synge or rede;
For þus may man þorow suche dyuyne,
The soner come out of hys pyne.   570
And þou art mon ȝet alyue,
And haste gon þorow swythe;

Thow tweyn boschoppys turnyd ageyn,
And fayere spake to Syre Howyn,
'Blyssyd byn they euerychon
That mad þe thys wey to gon.
Purcatory thow hate be inne   580
To do penans for thy syne,

For purcatory comys þou neuer more yn.
We wote wyll where thow was,
For we han passyd all tho pas.
So xall iche man aftyr hys day,   585
Pore and reche, gon that wey.
Many han hem forto schryve,
Ner don penans of all ther lyve,
But at the laste he comyth for drede;
Summe to don they muste nede.   590

576   ageyn] yn *may have been corrected.*
577   d *canc. after* fayere.
581   *Long-tailed letter* (s?) *erased after* thy.
581–2   *Between these lines* Sm *inserted missing line* C551, *and in* Sm552 (Y582)
moved yn *to follow* þou.   584   tho] thow
590   Sm *added* [penaunce] *after* Summe.

Thorow grace of God and good entent
Thow art passed þat turnement,
And þou arte comen to joye and blysse;   575
I shall þe telle what hyt ys:
Thys ys Erþly Paradyse.
Her wer Adam and Eue þat wer not wyse;
For an appull þat þey ete,
All her joye þey forlete,   580
And nyne hondredde ȝer and fyftene
He lyued aftur yn erþe wyth sorow and tene,
And fowr þowsande and vi hondred and iiij. ȝere
He was yn helle wyth Lucyfere,
Tyll þat Goddes wyll was   585
To fecche hym out of þat place,
And all hys kynde þat were hym by,
That wordy were to haue mercy;
And ledde hem forth wyth hem, ywysse,
Ryȝth ynto hys owene blysse.   590
And at hys ordynaunce we be,
In joye and blysse wyth solempnyte.
But when we come hym byfore,
Then shall our joye be mykyll more.
And euery day we wexen moo,   595
But angeles called some vs froo.
All ȝyf we be out of penance ylle,
Her we abyde Goddes wylle,
For ȝet haue we not þat dygnyte
To come before hys mageste;   600
f. 95ra But oon and on, as he wyll calle,
At þe laste we shall come all.
Euery day comeþ our fode
Of hym þat for vs shedde hys blode,
And þat þou shalte fele or þou go.'   605
As he stode and sayde hym so,
Ther come a gleme anon full bryȝth,
And spradde ouur þat lond ryȝth.

574 Thow] *corrected from* That?

Thow þat arte cum to joy and blysse,
We woll the tell wat yt ys:
Ertely Paradyse thys ys.
Hereyn dwellyd Adam and dede amyse,
For on appyll that he ete,   595
f. 37r Alle hys joy he forȝete.
ix hundyrd ȝere and .xv.
He levyd yn desert wyth sowrow and tene.
iiij thowsond, vj hundred and iiij ȝere
He lay yn peynys wyth Lussyfere.   600
Aftyrward th[r]owe Goddys grace,
He toke hym fro that fowlle place,
And all hys kynne [þat] was hym by,
That wordy wos to haue mercy,
And here we dwellyd at Goddys wyll,   605
In joy and blysse to abyd styll,

And eche day we wax moo,
And angellys fyttyn vs summe froo;

Ȝyte haue we nowte þat dygnyte
To cum befor hyys magyste.   610

Euery day cum[yth] owre fode
Fro hym þat for vs bled hys blode;
That xall þou syn or that þou goo.'
As he stode [and] seyd hym soo,
Ther cam a gleme was wondyrly bryth,   615
T[h]at spredde ouer all þe lond full ryth.

600   lay] layll, em. Sm.
601   throwe] thowe, em. Sm.
603   kynne] for nn scribe has written three minims and added one above the line;
Sm reads kymre;   þat] om.
611   cumyth] cumme.   614   and] he.
615   glene canc. in same ink after a.
616   That] Tat, em. Sm; spdde canc. in red ink before spredde.

Hyt was swete and hyt was hote;
Into euery monnus mowþe hyt smote.   610
The knyȝte felde þat yn glyde;
He ne wyste wher he was þat tyde,
Ne wheþur þat he was qwykke or dede,
Such hym þowȝte þat ryche brede.
Then sayde þe bysshoppe þat be hym stode,   615
'How þowstedest þou, knyȝte, was þys gode?'
'Oo, lorde,' he sayde, 'þyn oore!
Let me dwelle her euurmore.'
'Nay, sone,' he sayde, 'þou may not so.
Agayn þou moste algate go,   620
And telle oþur men what þou haste sene,
And yn what aventure þou haste bene,
For yn þe worlde þou most dye onus,
And leue þer þy flesh and þy bonus,
And come yn sowle hydur agayne,   625
Then wyll we of þe be fayne.'
The knyȝte sye þat he moste go,
And wepynge þen he ȝode hem fro.
Anone ryȝte þer he fell adowne,
And toke all þer benesowne,   630
A redy way anon he fonde
Ryȝth ynto hys owene londe.
To þe hole hys way lay,
That he come fro þat oþur day.
The fyftene men he fonde þore   635
That he hadde speken wyth before.
They wellcomede hym anon ryȝth,
And þonked God full of myȝte.

They prayde faste he sholde gon,
And so he wente forth anon   640
Home ynto hys owne contreye,
For ryȝth now spronge þe day.
f. 95rb 'To pryme þey wyll þe belle rynge,
And afturwarde þe masse synge.

---

609 swete] *loop of first* e *blotted,* swote K.
636 speken] *loop of first* e *blotted,* spoken K.

That he sey on euery syd,
He nere woste what he ded þat tydde,
Nor wyther he was qwekke or dede,
So blyssyd hym that reche brede.   620
Than seyd he to þe knyth þat be hym stod,
'How seyste þou, knyth, wos thys good?'
'A, lord, mercy,' he seyd them there,
'Lete me dwell ere euermore.'
'Nay, nay, son, thow mayis notte soo.   625
Ageyn allgatys þou muste goo,

And yn þat ward deyen onys,
And ther yn erth to bery þi bonys.
Sythyn þi sowll xall cum ageyn,
Therof we xall be full fayn.'   630
The knyth sey he muste nedys goo,
f. 37v Wyth wepyng and wyth wolle myche wo;
Anon he knelyd ther adown,
And fayer toke ther benycyun.
Ther anon a wey he fond   635
Hom ynto hys owyn lond.
To þe halle the wey laye,
That he com by the tother day.
The fyftene men he fond there,
That he had spake wyth before.   640
They thankyd God full of myth,
That sent grace to that knyth,
To ouercum þe fyndys myth,
Wyth þe grace of God full ryth.
They blyssyd hym euerychon,   645
And sythyn bad hym go hom
Into hys howyn cuntre.

'For now the prime bell ryngyth,
And sythyn messe xall they syngth;

639   fond] *first minim of* n *corrected from* r.
647   *Smudged erasure after* hys.

Aftur masse, wythoute delaye,   645
The pryour of þe abbey,
Bothe wyth preste and chanoun,
They wyll come wyth processyoun
To þe entre the agayne,
And of þy comynge be full fayne.   650
And now be good forth all þy lyue,
And loke þat þou de ofte shryue,
And when þou art dede, þen shalt þou wende
To þe blysse wythouten ende.'
Thenne swyþe to go well hym lyst,   655
And he come hom er he wyste.
To þe dore come Syr Owayne,
And þer þe pryour come hym agayne,
And chanonus wyth mery songe,
Wyth mony a wepynge tere amonge.   660
All þey wer both gladde and blyþe
That God hadde saued þe knyȝte alyue.
Fyftene dayes he dwelled þore
Wyth þe chanonus, and somdele more,
And tolde what he hadde sene,   665
And in what payne þat he hadde bene;
And ofte he tolde hem, to make þem wyse,
Of þe joyes of paradyse.
Thenne þey wryten aftur hys mowth,
That yn londe now hyt ys kowþe.   670
Then he toke þe crosse and þe staf yn honde,
And wente forth ynto þe Holy Londe.
Agayn he come, hole and sownde,
And aftur þat lyuede a grete stownde
In bedes and yn holy orysowne,   675
As a mon of goode deuocyoun.
And aftur, when he wexede olde,
And hys body wex vnboolde,
He dyede, and wente þe ryȝte way
To þe blysse þat lastes aye.   680
To þat blysse he vs brynge,
That of all ys lorde and kynge.
                    Explycit Owayne

645   wythoute] o *badly formed.*
649   entre] *long* r *written over earlier* e?
667   make] k *blotted and corrected from another letter.*

And aftyr messe, wythowte delay,   650
The pryowr of that abey,
Both wyth prystys and chanown,
That cum hym wyth yn prosessyoun
To þe entre ther ageyn,
And of the they xall be full fayn.   655
Be a g`o´od man all thy lyue,
And loke þou do þe oftyn schrywe,
And whan þou arte ded, þan xall þou wende
To þat joy that hath non ende.'
The knyth to gon full wyll he lyste,   660
He was at hom long ar he wyste.
To þe gate cam Syre Howyn,
Ther was þe pryowr redy hym ageyn,
Wyth schanownys and wyth mery songe,
And summe wepynd allwey amonge.   665

xv dayes and summewat more
Wyth the chanownys he dwellyd there,
And told them wat he had syn,
And wat peynys he had yn byn,
f. 38r And oftyn he tolde [t]h[e]m ta make [t]h[e]m wysse,   670
Off the joy of paradysse.

Ther toke he stafte and crosse yn hond,
And wenth ynto the Holy Lond,
And cam ageyn bothe heyll and sownd,
And sythyn leuyd a woll good stownd   675
In bedys and yn oryson,
As men of good relygyon.
Whan he was full wyll of held,
That hys body gane vax onwylld,
He deyed, and went the ryth wey   680
To the blysse that leste euer and ay.
To blysse brynge vs he
That euer wos and euer xall be;
That ys lord of mythtys moste,
Fadyr and þe sunne and þe holy goste. *Finis*   685

652   chanown] chanownys.
657   of *canc. in same ink after* þe.   660   gon] o *corrected from two minims.*
670   them] him.   677   relygyon] o *corrected from two minims.*
685   Finis] *in simple scroll decoration in red.*

cryst and sen þi pier and ther shal bowd & be knddre
to the such as ther be and afterward þu shalt see and
here more gostly syghtes and swete sowites of the Whych
þu shalt be sore adradde but haue in mynd as y sayd þe
of owre lord passion & yau shal do the mone harm
¶ Thanne y William sayd if it myghit be pleasynt to god
and to þe forto haue knowlacte of þe þ so mocke kind
nesse haue shewid to me And y requyre þe for þe loue of
owre lord ihu cryste if it be this Wil ¶ Thanne he sayd y
Wil gladly þ yow mete . I am clepyd in northcountree John
of Bridlyngton & so y am and yne woman is saynt
¶ ye my syster pat woned in Antike And y sayd A:
worshipful lord and holy fader worshyp mote þe be
in heuen and in erthe þ dayneth to not to come to so
synful a man þt so mykell nede hath and it pyne And
than he sayd þu hast often tymes comen to me Whare
my body lyeth and to my swete syster here sent þre
more disesynyg ye pan owre comynys Withe be And þt
þu he blyssid me Wt his hond And went his way And
y William ras me up and went infolowyng þe same
way þ yei passyd And sone after y come to þe wranes
þt he spak to me of And sond in the way on þe bryght
hond as saynt John had sayd smit men bi sutthit appa
rayd to me ye Which Weden as by shyp in the world
and as be wold of þem And yu sayd to me Wheder
Wilt yow tho And y sayd the Way pit ye stonde in

Jo: Bridlm
ton.

London, BL MS Royal 17 B xliii, f. 134r

stone. And thay in wyde oppyn fast
bonden & all stynkyng smoke of all ye
forsayde fyres penaunce restyde on ye most
thes. And on ye nepses & on ye eynes on ye.
Wombys saw I dragowes snakys & toodys
& many other grysly bestes gnawynge
& cryinge woodyr dyspetynsly. & all to
creyse ye paynes & sorwoys. The sant
Jon sayde to me wyllm thys ar bakly
tes & thay were besy wt ye shrode talys
to go fro howse to howse speykynge evyl
of ye cryn crysten havynge reiosynge
of ye neghebor harme. & sorynes of ther
welfare. puttynge the ewt of ye gud name
too ye yll. & thys horrabyll syne wold thay
neu leve for no pchynge nor techynge
And ye for shall thay suffer ye horrabyll
paynes vnto ye day of dome wt owte
inge for thay had no insy on ye cryn crp
ten. And then sant Jon led me furdyr
and chewyd me too towres ye orfull of bry
nynge fyre. And ye other ful of cowlde yse. In
ye towre ful of fyre I saw many sawles so
sore burnynge yt hytt semyd yt thay shuld
neu mellte for ye passynge hete. And sothe
ly then toke fendys the ewte wt grett cro
kys & kest the in to ye other towre. And ye
fendys wt showsryllys kest apon them
yse & snawe. & ye payne was soo kowld yt
trewly hyt passyd many other paynes
And the saw I many other
sawles cumynge wt [....] fyrebrondys

my handys. & ye bodyes hangyng full
of snakys & towdys eddyrs. & many
dyuse venmuse wormys. And rose
sawlys knokkyd at ye zate of that
towre wt thys sorow aray abowt
them. And as sowne as thay were
lettyn in thay kest ye brondys of fyre
at ye other sawlys yt were before in
payne. And then thay toke ye brond
agaynys bett wt the ye sawlys and
ye grevyd the warse & more then
all ye other paynes. And wt ye all
ye orrabyll wormys yt hange a
pon the lepe owte vpon ye sawlys
yt were before soo bett. And boette
the stagyd the thorow ye badyes
the sant Jon sayde loo wyllm
thys were furyme bysschoppys &
plates of & anetf of holy kyrke &
shulde hane pchyrd ye law of god
to ye pepull. and gyffyn them in
sanpyll of gud lyffyng. And sothe
ly thay dyd nak & therfore thay
hcwe thys grett penaure of howe
and colde. And thowse sawlys in
fyrebrowdof wt futyme yt snadys
and lyffynge ou moche i pryde. And
many dysserynes of ye arraye thye
spentf toodes & eddyrse & snakys
were ye jaggys yt thay wt spd furyote
igrett ptr. And all ar turnyd the
te solow & care whyll ye god wyll.
And ye ar besthoppys & other plates
pynyde of ye snadys for thay wold

London, BL MS Additional 34,193, f. 122r

THE VISION OF
WILLIAM OF STRANTON

ROYAL

f. 133ʳ Here begynneth þe reuelacion the which William Stavnton saw
in Patrik is Purgatorie, the Friday next after the Fest of þe
Exaltacion of þe Crosse, in þe yere of owre lord M^l. CCCC.^mo
ix.

Y, William Stavnton, born in þe bisshopryche of Dereham of   5
Englond, bi Goddes grace entred into þe Purgatorie of Seint
Patrik in the bisshopriche of Cleghire in Irlande, þe .viij. owre
bifore þe none on the Friday next after Holyrode day in
harvest. I was put in by þe prior of Seint Mathew of þe same
Purgatorie with precession and devougte prayers of þe same   10
priour; and þe covent toke me an orison to blesse me with, and
to write þe first worde in forehede, þe which prayer is this:
Jhesu Christe, fili Dei viui, misereri michi peccatori. And þe
priour taught me to say this prayer when ony sprit good or evel
appered vnto me, or when y herd ony noyse þat y shuld be   15
afered of, if þei were good sprites or evel. If þei were good
spritis, þei wold abyde stil with me; if þei were evil, þei shuld
voyde and þe ferful noyse cese.

And after þat, by the techyng of þe priour I cam to a restyng-
f. 133ᵛ place of Seint Patrik, in þe which / he abode the reuelacion of   20
Goddes angellis when he passed þat way in his tyme, and there
y abode and sumwhat slumbered and slepte. And after y was
ware of a litel light afer as it had be the dayng of þe day. And
me thought y sawe a man and a woman boþe cladde in white;
the man in a chanons is abite, and þe woman in the same abite   25
with a vayle on hir hede as a nonne. And when y saw hem first
y, dredyng sumwhat, said my prayer and marked my forhede as
the priour taught me; þan thei laughed and said, 'God spede,'
and þan y was sumwhat reioysed, and y said, 'Þe spede of God
be welcome vnto me.' And þat man said vnto me, 'William,   30
thow art welcome and þow hast take on hond a grete þyng, but

---

1   Here] *large decorated* h, *ascender in upper margin, body over three lines high*;
two-line capital E (*1*).   5   Y] *two-line boxed decorated capital.*
18   cese] *second* e *partially obliterated.*

ADDITIONAL

f. 99rb Here begynnes the boke of Wyllyam of Stranton, the weche
berys wyttenes of sothefastenes and of all ferdfull juges, the
wh[e]che he herde and saw when he was in Patrike Purgatory,
in the 3e`re´ of owre lorde M⁰ cccc⁰ and vj.

    In the name of Gode, Amen. I, Wyllyam of Stranton, borne   5
in the bysschoppryke of Dorham in Ynglonde, thorht Goddys
grace enterde into Purgatory of Saynt Patrike in the
f. 99va bysshoppryke / off Jalcet in Irelande on Ester day the viijte
owre before none. And I was putt in by þe prior Matheus,
keper of the same Purgatory, wyth procession and deuote   10
prayers of the same prior and couente, the wheche techyd me
on orisoun to blysse me wythe, and to wrytte the fyrst worde in
my forhede, weche is thys: *Jhesu, fili Dei, miserere mei.* And the
prior taugh[t]e me to say thys oryson when any sprette gud or
evyll apperyde to me, or yf I herde any noyse þat I schulde be   15
aferde of; ffor yf thay were gud sprettys thay schulde abyde
wyth me, and yf thay were evyll, thay schulde voyde fro me.

    And after, thorow þe techynge of the prior, I cam to a
restynge-place of Sante Patrike, in þe weche he abode the
reuelacyon of Goddys angellys when he wolde passe þat way in   20
hys one tyme, and þer I abode and sumwhat I slomered and
slepyde. After þat I was ware of more lyghte cummyng to me,
and me thoghte þat I saw a man and a woman bothe clede in
f. 99vb whytte; the man in abbett of chanon, / and the woman in the
same abett wyth a velle as a nonne. And when I saw them fyrst   25
I was sumwhat dredde, and sayde my prayer and blyssyd my
forhede. Then they loghe on me and bade, 'God spede.' Then I
was sumwhat reioysyd and sayd, 'Þe spede of Gode be
welcum.' Than þe chanon sayde to me, 'Wyllyam, þow hase
takyn [on hand] a grett thyng, bott thorow þe mercy of God   30

1–4 *In red.*   3 wheche] whche.   5 In] *eight-line decorated capital* I.
6 *Later hand in right-hand margin reads* Durham in England.
14 taughte] taughe; thys] s *superscript.*
20 *Later hand in left-hand margin reads* revelation.
21 þer] er *superscript.*   22 was *canc. before* ware.
28 sayd] *added in left-hand margin,* d *superscript.*   30 on hand] *om.*

bi the mercy of God þow shalt wel do and wel fare. And here
fast by þow shalt fynde .ij. waies: one on thi righ[t h]ond,
another on þi lefte honde. The way on thi right hond is faire
and brode, and the way in thi lifte hond is more and sumdel   35
fowle in the bigynneng, and it is faire and clene to sight; but
leve þe way on þe left hond and take þe wai on þe right hond.
But thow shalt fynd men in þi right hond þe which shul lete þe
'to´ passe by here power, þe which men shullen be lich in shap
and colour to men of thi owne contree þat ben levyng, but þei   40
ben evel spirites of which þow shalt be evel aferd. And þerfore
f. 134r haue þow in thi mynde þe passion of owre lord Jhesu / Crist,
and sai þi praier and thei shul voide and be knowe to the such
as thei be. And afterward þou shalt see and here more grisly
sightes and evel spirites of the which þou shalt be sore adradde;   45
but haue in mynd, as y said þe, of owre lordes possion and þai
shal do the none harm.'

Thanne y William said, 'If it myght be plesyng to God and
to þe forto haue knowlage of þe þat so moche kindenesse haue
shewid to me, and y require þe for þe love of owre lord Jhesu   50
Criste, if it be thi wil.'

Thanne he saide, 'Y wil gladly þat þow wete. I am cleped in
northcontree John of Bridlyngton, and so y am; and þis woman
is Seint Ive, my suster, þat woned in Quitike.'

And I said, 'A! worshipful lord and holy fader, worship mote
þou be in heven and in erthe þat dayneth not to come to so
synful a man þat so mykell nede hath and is ynne.'
And than he said, 'Þou hast often-tymes comen to me whare
my body ligh and to my suster here Seint Eve, more disesyng
þe þan owre comyng dothe vs.' And with þat he blissid me with   60
his hond and went his way. And I William roos me vp and
went in folowyng þe same way þat þei passed.
And sone after y come to þe waies þat he spak to me of, and
fond in the way on þe right hond, as Seint John had said,
diuers men bi sight apperand to me, þe which leveden as by   65
shap in the world and as bi colour of them. And þai said to me,

---

33   right hond] righond.   35   and (*1*)] *preceded by ampersand.*
53   *Later hand (16th century?) in right-hand margin reads* Jo: Bridlington.
56   to *canc. after* dayneth.   59   suss *canc. before* suster.

þow shall well doo and wel fare. And here fast by þow schall
fynde two wais: on on the ryght hande, and on `on´ the left
hand. The way on the ryght hande is narrow and sumdele
fowle in the begynnyng, and þe way on þe lefte hand is ffayre
and clene in syght; bott leve þat way, and take þe way on þe 35
ryght hand. Bott þou shall mette men in þat way þe weche shall
lett þe to passe, bot þou schall say to them on thys wyse:
"Sertenly, þis way wyll I passe, throgh þe help of God". And
then they shall haue no powre to lett þe. Þos men schal be lyke
in schappe and in colowre to men off thy contre weche ar ӡett / 40
f. 100ra levyng. Neuerþelesse, thay ar no men bott evylle sprettys;
þerfore haue in þi mynde þe passyon of owre lorde Jhesu
Criste, and say þi prayer, a[nd] thay schal vode fro the, and be
knowen to þi syght what they are. And afterwarde þou schall
see more greisely syghtys and more vgely þer of euyll spretys, 45
þe weche þou schal be mekyll adrede of. Bott loke þou haue os
I sayde before: haue owre lordes passion in þi thoght, and thay
schall doo þe no harme.'

Then I Wyllyam sayde, 'And hyt myght be plesyng to God
and ӡow forto haue knolege off yow, þat thus mekyll kyndnes 50
hathe schewyde vnto me, I desyre hytt grettely; and that I
beseke yow for the luffe of owre lorde Jhesu Crist, yf hyt be hys
wyll, þat ӡe tell me hytt.'

Then he sayde, 'I wyll gladly þat þou wytt what I am. In yor
contre they call me John of Bredlyngton, and so I am; and thys 55
woman is my sister, Sant Hylde of Whytby, that wonnyde
þerin sumtyme.'

And þen I sayde, 'Worschypfull lorde, lovyde myght he be in
f. 100rb / heuen and in erthe þat sende to me, so sympyll a wreche as
me, now in thys grett nede þat I am in.' 60

And then he sayd, 'Thow hast often cum to me, wher my
body lyes, and to my syster, Sant Hylde. That more desesyd þe
then owre cumynge doose huse.' And wyth þat he blyssyd me
wyth hys hande and wentte hys way. Then I rosse and folowde
þe same way that þai passyde. 65

And sone after I cam to the wayes that Sant John tolde me
off. And in the way on the ryght hande I fande, os Sant John
sayde, many dyuers men by syght þat apperyde to me, the
weche I know ӡett levynge in thys warlde, as by schappe

---

34 and *canc. before MS* And þe.   38 þis] is *superscript.*
39 *Three or four letters erased after* þe. 40 on *canc. after* ӡett.
43 and] A.   45 spretys] *written over an erasure.*
50 kyndnes] s *superscript.* 58 þen] en *superscript*; be god *canc. after* lovyde.
62 more] *added in left-hand margin.*   65 þai] ai *superscript.*
67 tolde me *canc. after* John.   69 warlde] a *?corrected from* u.

'Wheder wilt þow go?' And I said, 'The way þat ye stonde in /
f. 134v I shal go, bi the help of owre lord Jhesu Crist.'

Than þei said, 'This way thow shalt not go; for knowe vs
well, we be thi frendes, and none evel spirites, the which be   70
sent heder bi God to teche þe [the] right way, so þat þow shalt
not be perisshid.' And þan I said to them, certeyn þat y wold
go bi þem, and þei said to me ageyn, 'Þow shalt not passe this
way, for þow wilt spil thiself. We wil no suffre the, for þou
knowest wel þat we be thi frendes which loue þe, and þerfore   75
we be sent heder bi God to teche þe the right way, so þat þow
shalt not be pershid.' And þan I said to hem, certayn þat y
wold go, bi the help of owre lord Jhesu Crist; and thei saiden to
me aȝen, 'Þou shalt not passen þis way, for þow wilt spillyn
þiself. We wil not suffre the, for thow knowest wel we be thi   80
frendes þe which louen þe, and therfore we ben send heder.'
     Than y had mynde on þe passion of owre lord Jhesu Crist,
and marked me in the forhede with my praier þat was tawght
me byfore. And sodenly þilk folk sodenly vaneshid fro me. And
þan appered to me evel spirites; but tho y was more sekerer þan   85
y was before, for þo wist y wel þat my praier was of vertu.

     And than y went forthe þat way, and sone ther appered to me
many fereful and horrible spirites, of the which y was moch
afered and dred. And summe of þo spirites had .iiij. visages,
summe with .vij. hornes and summe with .v.; summe had a   90
f. 135r visage in euery elbowe, / summe on every kne. And þei maden
to me an hudious noyse with creyes and with bleryng owt of
here brennyng tanges and other many noyses mo þan I can tell,
for y was so aferd þat y hadde no mynde on God, ne on my
praier, ne on none other thinge þat shuld me help, but only on   95
þat noyse, and so y was negh in point of perishyng.
     Then cam þat blisful virgyn Seint Ive, and [said] to me, 'Þou
madman, haue mynde in thi hert of þe passion of owre lord
Jhesu Crist, Goddes sone of heuene, and mark þe with þi
praier.'   100
     And þan I said, 'Jhesu Crist, Goddis sone of hevene, for thi
passion þat bowghtest me and all sinfull on erthe with þi
precious blode, haue mercy on my sinful bodi, and graunte me

71 the] *om.*   89 .iiij.] *inserted above canc.* twoo.
92 and *canc. after* noyse.   97 said] *om.*, [seyd] Kr.

pycturede, and by all maner of colowre. And þose men sayde to   70
me, 'Wyllyam, whether wyllte þou goo?' And I answerde, 'Þe
way þat ӡe stande in schall I goo, wyth þe helppe of owre lorde
Jhesu Crist.'

Then þai sayde, 'Thys way þat we stande in schall þou natt
goo, for þou knowes well þat we ar þi fleschely frendys and no   75
evyll sprettys, and we ar sende hether thorow grace to teche þe
f. 100va the ryght way, þat þou schall nott be peryshyd.' / 'Sothely,'
sayd I, 'thys waye schal I go thorow Goddys grace.' 'Sekerly,'
sayde `þei´, 'þow schall nat passe thys way, ffor þou wolde kyll
þiselffe yf we wolde suffer þe. Þou knowes well we ar thy   80
fleschely frendes, and therfore ar we sentt hedyr to saue þe, þat
þou spyll natt thyselffe.'

Then I thoght on þe passion of Crist, and blissede me on my
forhede wyth þe prayer þat was taghtt me before. And then
sodenly þe men they flewe fro me away in liknes of evyll   85
sprettys as they were. Then was I more sekyr and more bolder
þen I was before, ffor then I knew þat my prayer was of mekyll
vertu.

Then I went þat way forthe, and sone apperyde to me mane
grysely sprettys weche I drede ful mekyll, ffor sum of the   90
sprettys hade iiij heddys, and sum iiij visages in þer heddys;
sum wyth vj hornes, sum wyth v. Sum of them hade a visage
on ylke elbowe, and sum on ylke knee. And they made `to´ me
mekyll noyse wyth cryinge, wyth bleryng owt ther tongys, and
many other noyses they made, [more] then I can tell, þat I was   95
f. 100vb soo ferde þat I hade no thoght on Gode nor / [on] my prayer,
nor on nothyng þat schulde helppe me, bott only on the noyse
and crye þat they made.

Then cam þat blyssyd uergyn Sant Hyllde, weche I saw
before wyth Santt John, and she sayd vnto me, 'Made man,   100
haue in thy thoght þe passyon of owere lord Jhesu Criste,
Goddys son of hevyn, and [mark þe with þi praier.'

And þan I said, 'Jhesu Crist, Goddis sone of hevene,] for thy
herde passyon þat þou boghte me wyth and all synfull men,
and for thy preciose blode, haue mercy on me, synful wreche,   105

85   Þa *erased after* flewe.   87   was (2)] s *superscript.*
95   made] e *partially obliterated;* more] *om.*
96   on] no.   97   nothyng] no *canc. but retained here for the sense.*
102-3   mark ... hevene] *from SR.*

grace so to do þat is most plesyng to the and sauacion to my
ˋbodi andˊ sowle.' And tho y markid me with my praier and al   105
þe evel spirites vaneshid fro my sight.

Þan I was right glad and thongkid God and hild forþe my
way. And so y passid forthe without sight of ony spiretes goode
or evell to þe space of a myle. And þan y mette with Seint John
and Seint Ive, and a suster of myne þat was dede long tofore in   110
a pestilence tyme, and anothir man which I knewe well þat my
suster loved wel, whiles thei leved in this world. And þan I
honowred Seint John and Seint Ive.

f. 135v   And Seint John said to me þan, 'Þow were evel agast / of
other spirites.'   115

And I said, 'So y was; blessid be God and owre ladi þat y am
comen to yow ageyn.'

Þan he saide, 'Þou haddest evell mynde on þe passion of
owre lord Jhesu Crist, and on thi praier, for þow art not
stedefast on þi beleve, and also to simpell to [t]ake such a viage   120
on honde, savyng only þe merci of God.'

And whan he had þus said to me, my suster spake and said,
'Holy [fader], ye be here in Goddis stede, and y make my
complaint to yow on my brother þat here stondeth, þat he hath
synned in holy chirch aȝen God; for þis man þat stondeth here   125
loued me and y loved him, and ether of vs wold haue had other
in þe law of God, as holy chirch techeth, and shuld haue geten
on me .iij. sowles to God; and my brother lettid vs to go
togeder, ffor he said, and we didden, we shuld nothir haue ioye
of other, and for þat cause we lefte hit.'   130

Tho Seint John said, 'Whi diddest þou þis trespas aȝen God
and thi owne sowle? For y tel the, þer nys no man þat letteth
man or woman to go togeder in the bond of God, þow the man
be a sheperd and all his auncestres, and the woman be comyn
of kingis or of emperours; or if þe man be comyn of never so   135
high kynne, and þe woman of never so lowe kynne, if þei loue
other otheir, he synneth in holy chirche aȝenst God and his
cristendome indede, in þat he letteth hem, whoever he be, and
þerfore shall haue moch payn and tribulacion, but he come to

110 Ive] *followed by wavy line-filler*.   119 beleve *canc. after* thi.
120 take] make.   121 savyng] a *partially obliterated*.
123 fader] *om; nota in left-hand margin*.   138 þat] þat at.

and gyff me grace so to doo þat hytt be plesyng to þe and
saluasyon for my body and my saule.' And then I blyssede me
wyth my prayer, and as sone as I hade blyssed me, thos evyl
sprettys vanyschyde owt of my syghte.

Then was I ryghtt glade and lovyde God, and wentt forthe   110
and or I mett any sprett gud or yll, to þe space of a myle; and
ther I mett agayn Sant John and Sant Hylde, and a syster of
myne owne þat was dede, and another man weche I knewe well
luffyde my syster in hyr lyffe. Then I com and I dyde
worschyppe to Sant Jon a[n]d Santt Hylde.   115

f. 106ra   Then Sant John sayde to me, 'Wyllyam, / þou was grettely
aferde of evyll sprettys.'

And I answeryd and sayde, 'Forsothe, so I was; blyssyde be
God and owre lade þat I am comyn to yow agayn.'

Þen he sayd, 'Thow hade lytyll mynde of þe passion of owre   120
lord Jhesu Crist, and of þi prayer, ffor þou art natt stedfaste in
þi beleffe, and ouersympul to take suche a vyage on hande, save
þe mercy of Gode.'

And then when he hade þus sayde to me, then my syster
spake and sayde, 'Heyll, fader, ȝe are here in Goddys steyde, 125
and I make my complentt to yow of my broder þat here
standys: that is to say, þat he hase synnyde grettly agene Gode,
for thys man þat here standys luffyde me, and I luffyde hym,
and eder of hus wolde haue hadde other after þe law of Gode,
as holy kyrke teches, and he scholde haue geton and I born /   130
f. 106rb thre sawles to Gode; and my broder lett hus to go togedyr, for
he sayde, yff we soo dyde, ther scholde noder of hus haue joye
of oder, and for þat cause we lefte [hyt].'

Then sayde Sant John, 'Why, Wyllyam, dyde þou þat
tryspasse agayn God and thyne awne sowle? Forsowthe, I tell   135
þe þat þer is no man nor woman þat lettys man and woman to
go togedyr in þe law of God, thowffe þe man be a schepparde
and all hys auncetorys, and þe woman be commen [of] kyngys
or emperowres; or yf þe man be commyn off neuer so hyghe a
f. 106va kynne / [and þe woman of never so lowe kynne], and they luffe 140
ether odere, he þat lettys hytt synnys dedly agayn God and
cursyde he is of þe dede, whatsoeuer he be; and therfor schall

---

107   And] d <i>superscript.</i>   115   and] ad.
116   <i>In the bottom margin at the foot of f. 100vb MS direction</i> The vj^{te} leffe.
120   Þen he sayd] <i>reaches into right-hand margin.</i>
126   y <i>canc. after</i> complentt.
131   and] <i>repeated at the end of a line and the beginning of the next.</i>
132   e <i>canc. after</i> hus.   133   hyt] <i>om.</i>
138   of] <i>om.</i>   140   and ... kynne] <i>from SR.</i>

f. 136r amendement, for / þat synne greveth God gretelich. And þou   140
was never shreven therof, ne diddest never penaunce þerfore;
but [had] it comyn into þi mynde, þou haddest shreven þe
þerof and ytake þe penaunce þerfore, and therfore hath
graunted the owre lord Jhesu Crist [grace] bi þe praier of Seint
Patrik; so þat when þow comest to the worlde agayn, shryve the   145
to þe priour of þ`i´s Purgatorie, and what penaunce þat he
gefeth the, s[e] þat it be done mekely. And loke, for if þow
haddest shryve þe þerfore, and forȝete þi penaunce vndo
þerfore þat þe prest had yeve the, þow shuldest haue had
penaunce þerfore here er þou haddest hens passed.' And `y´   150
lokyd after my suster and she and þat man þat come with hir
were vaneshid away owt of my sight.

And þan Seint John said to me, 'William, seist þou þe yender
fier fer fro þe?'

And y said, 'Y se yender a smoke þat is like a fire to be þere.'   155

And Seint John said, 'Þo yender is a grete fire and styngkyng, and certeyn, were it possible þat all `þe´ people in þe
world, men, women, and children, felden þe smych of yender
fire, þei shuld not endure so long with hire lifes as a man shuld
turne his honde vp and downe; þerfore go we bitwene þe fire   160
and þe wynde, and loke wel what þou seist þeryn.'

And þan I went so nygh þat y myght know what maner of
paynes were þeryn; and þere y saw þilk fire brynneng diuerse
men and women, and summe þat y knew when þei levid in þe
f. 136v world, / as it appered there to my sight. I saw summe there   165
with colors of gold abowte here neckis and sum of siluer; and
summe men y saw with gay girdels of siluer and gold and
harneist hornes abowte here neckes; summe with mo iagges on
here clothis þan hole cloth; sum hire clothis ful of gyngeles and
belles of siluer al oversette, and summe with long pokes on hire   170
sleves; and women with gownes trayleng bihinde hem a moche
space; and summe other with gay c[h]apeletes on hir hedes of
gold and perles and other precious stones. And þan I loked on
him þat y saw first in payn, and saw the colers and the gay
girdels and bawderikes brennyng and the fendes drayng hem bi   175
.ij. fyngermele and more withynne here flessh, al brynneng as

142 had] *om.*   144 grace] *om., added* Kr.   145 wol *canc. before* worlde.
147 se] so, se Kr *(without comment).*   148 þe *canc. after* and.
150 y] *in red.*   167 iagged clothes *in left-hand margin.*
172 chapeletes] clapeletes, chapeletes Kr *(without comment).*
175 b *canc. after* girdels;   point before bi.
176 wᵗ *canc. after* fyngermele; withynne] wᵗ thynne.

he haue mekyll payn and tribulacion, bott he cum to amendementt, ffor þat syne grevose God grettely. And þou was neuer
schryvyn þerof, nor neuer dyde pennanse þerfor; neuertheles,   145
and hytt hade cummyn to þi mynde, þou hade bene schrevyn
þerof and done penance þerfor, and þerfor owre lorde Jhesu
Criste hathe grantyd þe grace thowroo þe prayer off Sant
Patrike; soo þat when þou cummyste to þe warlde, schryfe þe to
þe prior of þe Purgatory, and what penance he injones þe   150
þerfor, lowke þat hytt be done. For yf þou hade bene schrevyn
þerof and forgetyn þi penance þat þe pryst gaffe þe therfor,
therfor vndone, þou schulde þerfore haue hade thy penance here
or þou hade hense passyde.' And then I lokyde after my syster
and sche was vanyschyde away. /   155

f. 106vb   Then Sent John sayde to me, 'Seeys þou 3ondyr 3eon fyre a
lytyll froo the?'
         And I sayde, '3e, fyr. I see 3eondyr a smoke and lyke þer ys
to be a fyre.'
         Then he answerde, 'Yondyr is a grett fyre and a stynkynge,   160
and sekyrly, were [it possible þat] all þe pepyll in þe warlde,
men and wemen and chylder, felde þe stynke of þat wonderful
fyre, they schulde natt indewre as longe wyth þe lyfe as a man
schulde turne hys hande abowte; and therfor goo we betwene
þe fyre and the wynde, and loke what þou seys þerin.'   165
         And then I went so nere þ[at] I myght well knaw what maner
of paynes were þerin. And þer I saw dyuerse men and wemen
brynnyng and sum þat I knew well wene they levyde in þe
worlde, as apperyde þer to my syght. I sawe þer sum wyth
colers gyltyde abowte þer nekkys, and sum of syluer and sum   170
of golde, and sum wyth gaye gyrdyls of syluer and of golde, and
hernessede hornes abowte þer nekkys; sum wyth many jaggys
and cuttyngys in þer clothys thay ware all clede; and sum wyth
gyrdyllys full of gyngyles and bellys of syluer ther
clothys ouersett; and sum wyth longe pokys on þer slevys, and   175
f. 119va wemen wyth gownys traylyng byhynde a mekyll space; / and
other wyth gaye chappelettys on þer heddys of golde and perlle
and other precyvse stones. And then I lokyde to them þat I
saue fyrst in paynes and I sawe þe gyrdyllys and þe bawdrykes
brynnynge, and þe fendys drawynge them a hand-brede   180

156   Then] two-line capital T.   161   sekyrly] l blotted; it ... þat] from SR.
166   þat] þⁱ.   170   nekkys] s superscript.
171   and (3)] added in left-hand margin.   175   pokys] pokykys.
176   and other canc. after space; in the bottom margin at the foot of f. 106vb MS
direction The xiiiᵗᵉ leffe.
176–7   and ... and] written across the page; from perlle in two columns.
178   lokyde] l changed from k?   179   gyrdyllys] s superscript.

fire; and y saw þe iagges þat men were clothed ynne turne al to
addres, to dragons, and to todes, and many other orrible bestes,
sowkyng hem and bityng hem and styngyng hem with al here
myght; and thorowout euery gyngel I saw fendes smyte   180
brennyng nayles of fire into here flessh. I saw also fendes
drawyng down þe skynne of here shulders like to pokes and
kittyng hem of and drawyng hem to þe hedes of whom þai cut
þem fro, al brynnyng as fire. And þo I saw þe women þat had
side trayles byhinde hem, and þo side trayles cut of with fendes   185
and ybrent on here hedes; and summe toke of / þe cuttyng all
brennyng and stopped þerwith here mowþis, hire noses, and
hire eres. I saw also hire gay chapeletes of gold, of perlous and
other precious stones yturned into nailes of yren brennyng, and
fendes with brennyng hamers smytyng hem into hire hedes.   190

f. 137r

And þan Seint John said vnto me, 'Tho yender men, thei
disworship God with hire pride of hert and of aray, takyng
more hede to þe bodi for þe vanite of þe world and of þe nyse
vsage þat is hadden þerynne þan þei had nede of; ffor euerych
man owght to plese his God with mekenesse of hert and of   195
body acordaunt þerwith. And thilk men and women deden not
so, ffor þey nold not leve hire nyse pride, for no prechyng, ne
techyng, ne counseill in shrift, forto atte last, þan þey had
shrift and no space of penaunce sufferyng, and þerfor þei
shullen suffre euermore without mercy þese paynes til þe dai of   200
dome.'

And than Seint John ledde me forth to another fier, and þere
y saw bras and lede and other diuers metals molten togedre,
wherynne y saw many sowles of men and women, and fendes
among hem with swerdes, knyves, and brochis brennyng,   205
smyteng owt hire yen and fillyng þe holes of þe yen with þat

180   gyngel] gyngels.   200   nota *in left-hand margin.*
205   Swerers *in right-hand margin.*

f. 119vb and more wythin þe fleche, all brynnynge as fyre. / And I saw
þe jaggys þat men were clede in turnyde all to eddyrs,
dragonse, towdys, and odyre orrabyll bestes, sowkynge and
byttynge and nowynge them wyth all þer myghte, streynynge
and dreynynge owte of ylke gyngyll a fowle fende. Also trevly I   185
f. 120ra saw fendys smyttynge rede / fyre naylles thorow þe belles and
þe gyngyllys into þer flesche. Also I sawe fendys dravyng þe
skyne ouer þer scholdyrs þat weyryde þe powkys on ther slevys,
and threw hytt all brynnynge on þer hedeys. And I saw þe
wemen wyth þe longe traynes byhynde them, fendys cuttynge   190
of thoys traynes and brynnynge them on þer heddys; and
sum of þe fendys toke parcels of þe traylys, and all on fyre
stoppyd þer mowthes, þer nose, and þer erys þerwyth. And
I saue gay chappelettys of perle and odyr preciuus stones
turnyd into nayllys of brasse all brynnynge, and wyth brynnyng   195
[hamers] fendys smyttynge [them] into ther heddys.

And than Sant John sayde to me, 'Wyllyam, theis þat þou
seeys in þe grett payne ar bothe men and wemen þat displesyde
Gode thorowe þer grett pride þat thay vsyde in þer lyffe, bothe
in hertt and in clothynge; more forto pleyse þe bode and þe   200
false warlde for a false plesynge of vayneglory of pride and aray
þat now is vsyde, then to plese God and kepe hys cummande-
menttys þat made them and boght them wyth hys byttyr /
f. 120rb passyon. Alas, why wolde they be so wode as to luffe more the
fende ther enmy, then Gode þat is euer redy tyll hus att owre   205
nede, as owre sofferande frende. And certenly, Wyllyam, thyes
þat ar pynyde for ther fowle pride and wolde nat leve þer nyse
aray, for no prechyng nor no techynge, ne conselle of any man,
to hytt were for pouerte, vnluste of age, or sekenes made them
to leve hytt, and þat was natt for þe luffe of Gode; and ȝett were   210
they vnnethe schrevyn wyth repentance, bott space of penance-
doynge theme lakkyde, and þerfor schall they haue penance
wythowte mercy to þe day of dome. And better hade thay ben
to haue levyde þer syne and ther fowle pride [of] aray be consell
of þer gostely faders or of oder gud lyffers.'   215

And then Sent John lede me forthe to I cum to another grett
fyre, and in þat fyre saw I dyueres metellys molton, as leyde,
brasse, coper, and tyne. And in þat metell I saw many sawles
bowlynge, bothe of men and of wemen. And amonge them I
sawe many fendys wyth swerdys, knyvys, and brochys bryn-   220

181 fleche] c *blotted, but apparently no* s.   184 o *canc. after* and.
191 heddys] s *superscript.*   196 hamers, them] *after* SR.
212 doynge] *in right-hand margin in different ink, with caret after* penance.
214 of] *om.*
216 *Space and swung dash before* And *with large capital* A *and capital* N.

f. 137v brynnyng metall; summe makyng woundes with here / swerdes
and fillyng the woundes with þe same brennyng metall; summe
drayng of þe nayles of here fingers with brynnyng tonges of
yren and settyng hem on aȝen with þat metall molten; summe   210
smytyng of here armes, puttyng hem on þe fire brochis and
fillyng thilk places where armes were with molten metall al on
fire, and þei drow þe armes on þat other membris into the
molton metall, and when þei weren al on fire, þei toke hem vp
aȝen and set hem on hire places aȝen, and þus þei dide   215
continulich.

And y herd þe armes, as me thowght, verely crie and sai,
'Jhesu Crist, Goddis sone of heven, rightwous iugge, we haue
not servid þis payne, but only the hert and þe tonge.' And þan
þe fendes token owt þe hert and þe tounges and clevid hem on   220
tweyne and filt hem ful of þat hote brynneng metall, and put
ham into þe bodi aȝen.

And than Seint John said, 'Þese ben þei þat sweren bi
Goddes menbres, as bi his yen, bi his armes, bi his woundes, bi
his nayles and other his membris; and thei þus dismembrid   225
God in horrible swerynge bi his lymmes, þerfore þei be þus
turmentid in hire membris and shul be duryng the willyng of
God.'

And þan Seint John ledde me forthe into þe .iij. fire, and þat
fire was of grete stenche and hete, for theryn was cast fen and   230
dirt as had ben of gonges and of oþer maner of fylthe. And þere
f. 138r I sawe sowles of men / and women with fendis stoppeng hem ful
of þat filthe; summe other takyng brondes of fire, stoppeng and
shovyng þe felthe downe into here bodies, as þe[i] wold stoppe
a wullepak; and other fendes comyng with pottes ful of leme of   235
þat fire, yetyng it into them.

And þan Seint John said, 'Þo yender ben tho þat broken here
haly-daies; ffor on þe hali-day a cristen man shuld go to chirche
and bid hertely his prayers and shryve him, if he hadde nede,
to him þat hath power of his sowle, and foryeven all tho þat   240
haue gilt him as he woll be foryeve of God. But þese folk did
not so, for þei dispendid here haly-dai in gloteny and dronknesse in taverns and other places, takyng and fillyng hemself
owte of mesure more þan hem nedid, so mykel þat summe of
hem cast vp aȝen; and other diuers filthes and synnes thei vsid   245
in þe holi-dais, and þerfore þei shullen suffer þe yonder fillyng

213   drow] *em.* threw Kr.   214   of *canc. after* al.   220   *Point after* on.
224   nota *in left-hand margin in feint later hand.*
232   brekers of halidays *in right-hand margin.*   234   þei] þe.
237   nota *in right-hand margin in feint later hand.*

nynge, wyth the weche they smotte owt þe yne of the sowles,
and fyllyd þe holles wher þe eyne were wyth þe brynnyng
*. *120va* mettell. And thay drewe of þe nalys / of þer fyngers and of þer
towse wyth brynnynge tongys, and sett them on agayne wyth
þe same metell al hott bowlynge. Sum schare of there armes   225
and fyllyde agayn þer thay stode wyth þe brynnynge metell,
and thay threw þe armys and þe other membyrs þat thay hade
smeton of into þe bowlynge metell, and then thay toke them vp
agayne and sett them in þer places, and þus thay dyde
contynually þat grett ruthe was to se.   230

And trewly I herde, as me [thoght], þat [þe] armes cryde and
sayde, 'Jhesu, Goddis son of hevyn, we haue natt deservyde
thys horrabyll penance þat we suffyr, bott owre herttys and
owre tongys, thay dyde þe tryspasse.' And then þe fendys toke
owt þe hertt and þe tongys, and clevyd them in too and fyllyde   235
them ful of metell, and putt them into ther bodyes agayn.

Then Sent John [sayde], 'Loo, Wyllyam, thyes wrachys
suffers thyes paynes for thay dysmembyrde Gode wyth swerynge of hys body, hys armys, hys eyne, hys sydes, hys wondys,
hys naylles, hys sowle, and other of hys membyrs, and þerfore   240
Goddys wyll here endurys þat behovysse them to suffer thys.'

Than Sant John lede me to þe thyrde fyre, and trewly, þer
was an opyn stynke and hoytte also. And `in´ þat fyre was cast /
*. *120vb* fowynge and dyrtt, as hytt hade bene of prevays and many odyr
dyuerse fylthys. And þer dyuerse fendys stoppyd þe mowtes of   245
them, bothe of men and wemen, full of fylthe, and thryst hyt
wyth fyre-brondys down into þer throttys and into þer bodyes.
And other fendys com wyth pottys full of coles and cast in
after.

And then Sent John sayde, 'Lo, Wyllyam, thes wraches ar   250
thay þat brake þer haly-des, goynge to tauernys, to playes, to
vanytes of þe worlde, byinge and sellyng, and other bargynnes
makyng, when thay schulde haue gon to þe kyrke and sayd þer
prayers; and yf thay were, thay sayd and prayde jangyllynge
wyth other neghburse, and lettyd them that thay myght nat   255
praye, nother for themselfe nor for odyr; and þerfore now thay
have sorowe inoght and schal haue euer whyll Goddys wyll
lastys.'

231 thoght] *after* SR;   þe] *from* SR.   237 sayde] *after* SR.
241 Goddys] s *superscript.*   245 ff *canc. after* mowtes.
252 vanytes] s *superscript.*   257 inoght] I noght.

and stoppyng ful of filthe and stench with fendes, during þe
will of God.'

Thanne Seint John led me forth to þe .iiij. fire, and þere y
saw many sowles bounden with bondes of fire, and the fendes   250
stondyng and stowpeng here erses toward þe sowles, and
shityng owt of here erses stench and fen, with brondes of fire
þat failed not, but smote hem thorowe þe hedes and thorow al
here lymmes of here bodi whereever þat hit cam.

f. 138v   Tho Seint John said, 'Þese ben þoo þat dishonour here fader   255
| and here moder, and therefore þei shullen suffre here þis
dishonour of fendes ersis duryng þe wil of God.'

Tho Seint John led me to þe .v. fire, there y saw sowles with
all maner of goodes brennyng on hire backes; summe with
swerdes and knyves smytyng and stikeng hemself; summe   260
horses and oxen and oþer diuers bestes bityng hem and teryng
hem asonder.

Than Seint John said to me, 'Þoo yonder ben thefes and
robbers of trewe menis godes.' And hem y saw take owt of þat
payne þat þai were yn and cast to other, and other sowles take   265
owt of þilk payne þat þei were yn and sett by.

And þan `he´ said, 'Þoo sowles þat þow seist take owt of
yonder paynes and set by ben þe sowles of þoo men þat þe
yender thefes robbeden and stalen þere goodes from hem; and
as moche fawte as þoo true men suffreden in lak of her goodes,   270
so moche payn þei shullen suffre for hem, for thei made never
satesfaction in will nothir in dede; and therfore þei shullyn
suffre þere yender payn duryng þe will of God.'

And in þilk paynes y saw executours punysshid as long tyme
as þei delayn and not fulfillyn þe dethis will; and þilk   275
executours þat tokyn þe dedis goodes to here owne vse, for þe
sowles of þe owners were passid owt of purgatorie; þe help of
goodes þat were done afterward turned to þe help and reles of
other þat had nede, and þo þat withilden them were punysshid
f. 139r   therfor / with fendis in hudious paynes, duryng the wil of God.   280

Then Seint John lad me forthe to þe .vj. fire, and in þat fire y
saw many sowles ypayned; and summe fendes meltyng gold
and siluer and yet it into them. And y sawe oþer where wodes,
rochis, hilles, and londes [were] brennyng and fallyng vppon
them.   285

249   in canc. after forth;   f canc. after þe.   250   bondes] brondes;
honour fader and moder in right-hand margin.   258   f canc. after þe.
264   nota Thefes in left-hand margin.   265   to canc. before other (2).
267   he in different ink.   274   nota Executours in left-hand margin.
275   ded canc. after þe.   284   were] om.

Then Sant John lede me to þe fort fyre, and ther I saw many
sawlys bondon wyth grett bandys of yrene hoth gloynge, and   260
apon þe savles stode fendys and put þer vggely ersys to þer
121ra vysage, me thoght, / and kest on them wyth þer erses horrybyl
stynke of donge and dyrtte, wyth sparkys of fyre amonge, þat
smotte thorow the wrechyd saulys whereuer hytt felle on
thame.   265

Then Sant John sayde, 'Lowe, Wyllyam, thyes ar thay þat
dyshonord God, and þerfor thay schall suffyr þe same of fendys
ercys dewrynge þe wyll of God.'

Then Sant Jon lede me to þe v^te fyre, and trevly I saw sawles
þer wyth all maner of wardely gowdys in þer nekkys al   270
brynnynge; sum wyth knyvys, sum wyth swerdys stykkynge on
them; sum wyth oxon, sum wyth horses and odyr dyuerse
bestys byttynge them and ryvynge them in sundyr.

Then Sant Jon sayd to me, 'Thyes were thevys and robbars
of men.' And þen I saw þat thyes sawles were takyn owt of þer   275
paynys, and othyr sawlys takyn owte of þer paynys and sett by
them.

And þen Sant Jon sayde, 'Loo, Wyllyam, thes savles þat ar
fechyde fro þer owne paynys and sett by thyes thevys ar thyes
þat thay robbyd fro þer trew getton guddys, [and as moche   280
fawte as þoo true men suffreden in lak of her goodes, so moche
payn þei shullen suffre for hem]; and for thay made no
satisfaccyon in worde nor in dede, [therfore þei shullyn suffre
þere yender payn duryng þe will of God].'

In þat payn I saw exhecutores paynyd ful sore as longe as   285
thay delayde þe wyll of them to whom thay were executores;
and thyes executoures also þat toke þe dede gudys vnto þer one
vse schuld abyde þer to thay þat made þe testament and aghte
. 121rb þe guddys were / delyueryd owt of purgatory; ffor the helpe þat
was done wyth thowys gudys helpyd nat þe executours owt of   290
ther payn, bott turnyde into help of them þat hade nede.

Then Sant Jon lede me to þe vjte fyre, and þer were grett
paynes, ffor I sawe bowth gold and syluer molton `and´ cast
into þer bodyes that were in þat fyre. Also I saw grett hyllys
and roches, woddys and landys al brynnynge fall apon them.   295

259   sayd *canc. after* John; fyre *canc. after* þe.
271   swerdys] *final* s *superscript.*
275   þen] en *superscript.*
279   re *canc. after* thevys.
283–4   therfore ... God] *from* SR.
287   gudys] u *corrected from* o?

276   sawlys] *final* s *superscript.*
280–2   and ... hem] *from* SR.
286   d *canc. after* whom.
293   bowth] h *badly formed.*

Than Seint John said, 'Þoo yender be thoo þat bare false witnesse in diuers enquestes and assisis, sum for gold and summe for siluer, and now þat gold and þat siluer molten paynes them as þou seist, and so of londes and wodes, and payneth hem in .iij. maners: one is it shall bren hem; another it 290 shal brose hem; þe .iij. it shal smolder hem and hold hem ever vnder.' Tho y saw diuers sowles stondyng abowte þat fire but felyng no payn of it.

And Seint John said, 'Þo yender sowles ben of þo men þat haue suffred wrong bi thilk turmentid in þe fire, and there þei 295 shal se none other payn but se them turmentid and punysshid for her gilt, as long tyme as þei shuld haue sufferd hemself; and þilk paynes þei shul suffre duryng þe will of God.'

Thanne Seint John lad me to þe vij. fire. Theryn y saw many
f. 139v sowles ypayned with fendis teryng hem / with brennyng crokes 300 of brennyng yren, euerych lymme of þe bodi fro other, and other fendes with speris, swerdis, and knyves, smytyng the hedes of the sowles, and the other parties of þe body hewyng on sonder, fallyng into þilk fiere, the fendis takyng hem vp brennyng ful of fiere and settyng on the hedes aȝen; and þus þei 305 did continuelich.

Than sayde Seint John, 'Þilk ben þe sleers and murdres of true men.' And þere I herd a gresly crye sayng, 'Jhesu Crist, Goddes sone of heven, þow rightful iugge, we axen veniaunce on hem þe which kylden vs and distroyed vs, and þei no cause 310 had.' Thanne Seint John said, 'Þo yender ben tho sowles þat were kilde and distroied; now þei axen veniaunce on thoo yonder mysdoers, and in þe same maner þei þat killyn giltles men, þei shal be turment in þis fire duryng the will of God.'

Thanne Seint John browght me to þe .viij. fiere, and þat fire 315 was hote owt of mesure and blak as ony pych, and smale lemes as blew as ony brymston comyng owt þerof; and in þat fire y saw many sowles boþe of men and of women hongyng bi þe prevy membris with cheynes of brennyng yren, summe bi the hert and summe bi þe yen, and fendes betyng vppon hem with 320 hamours of brennyng yren.

Than Seint John said, 'Þo yendur ben þei þat leved here lif in lecherye: thei þat synned in dede ben hangid bi þe menbris; and thei þat synned in desire ben hanged bi the hert, for the
f. 140r hert was in / wil forto do þe dede; and thei þat wold not hold 325 here yen stable, but biholden faire women, and also women of men, and bi hire sight fillyn into more synne in dede, þerfor þei

286   nota Questmongers *in right-hand margin.*
287   sum for gold *canc. after* gold.
289   and (3)] *em.* it Kr.   294   said *canc. after* And;   yender *canc. after* þo.
295   þer *canc. after* there.   297   shuld] d *badly formed, possibly added later.*
301   for *canc. after* bodi.
307   sayde *added in right-hand margin in later hand.*
317   luxuria *in left-hand margin.*

Then Sant Jon sayde, 'Loo, Wyllyam, thes were thay þat
bare fals wyttenes agane ther evyn-cristen in syses and other in
enquestys; sum for gold and syluer, and that poneschies them
now a[s] þou seys; sum for landys and feese þat fallys on þem
all brynnynge.' And trewly I sawe many saullys stande abowt   300
the fyre and had þerof no payne.

Then Sant Jon sayd to me, 'Thyes ar the sowlys of them þat
by thyes false jvrours lost þer londys and þer guddys, and thay
haue no dyssese bott sees them poneschyde for þer synnys, for
trewthe wold hytt had bene gevyn agayn.'   305

Then Sent Jon lede me to þe vij^te fyre, and þer I save a
dulful syght, for þer I saw fendys ryffe sawlys wyth crokys of
yren al brynnynge eche lyme from other. Sum of þe fendys
smotte of þe heddys of þe saulys wyth kene swerdys, and all þer
_121va_ / other lymmys thay all tomangylde and kest them into þe fyre,   310
and´ all brynnynge toke them owt agayn and sett them on þer
bodyes, and þus were thay seruyde continually.

Then Sant Jon sayd, 'Þes saulys were sleyers and murderars
of trew men.' And trewly I herde þer a doleful cry þat sayd on
þis wyse, 'Jhesu Crist, Goddys son of hevyn, of thy ryght-   315
wasnes we aske vengance of them þat slene hus and dystrevd
hvs, and we gaffe them no cause.'

Then Sant Jon lede me to þe viij^te fyre, and þer sothely þat
fyre was howt owt of mesore and blak as any pyke, and small
sparkelyng lyghttys of blew lyke vnto bronston com owt þerof.   320
In þat fyre were many saules, bothe of men and wemen, sum
hyngyng by þer prevey membyrs wyth chenys of yryne brynnyng, and sum by [the hert, and summe bi] þer eene, and
fendys bettyng on them wyth brynnyng hamerys.
Then Sant Jon sayd, 'Thyes a[r] thay þat lede þer lyfe in   325
lechery; and for thay synnyd in dede, thay ar hangyd by þe
membyrse; and thay þat synnyd in wyllyng and in desyre ar
hangyde by þe [hert, for the hert was in wil forto do þe dede;]
and thay þat kepyd nat þer eene fro vanites, bot wyth them
lokyd on wemen and on þer gay areye and vanytes of þe warlde,   330

---

299 as] all;   þem] em _superscript._   309 þe (_1_)] þer _abbreviated._
311 and _in different ink._   313 Þes] es _superscript._   315 þis] is _superscript._
323 the ... bi] _from_ SR.   325 sayd] d _superscript;_ ar] as.
328 þe (_1_)] _followed by_ eene; hert ... dede] _from_ SR. 330 l _canc. after_ þer.

ben payned in here yen, and shullyn suffre þat payne duryng
the wil of God.'

Tho Seint John led me forth to the .ix. fier, and þere y saw   33c
many sowles of men and women and children in thilk hote fire,
and c[h]yldren betyng here owne fader and moder with
brondes of fire; þe fader sayng, 'My faire sone, y gat the;' tho
saing the moder, 'My faire child, y bare and norshid the with
my pappis;' and rehersid many kyndnesse done by the fader   33s
and moder to here children. Tho y herd þe children sayng to
here fader, 'Wrecche, þow gast me;' and to here moder,
'Wrecche, þow barest me, and we know well all the tendernesse
þat ye haue done to vs; but for ye chastynde vs not, and in
defaute of yowre chastement, we muste suffre these bitter   34c
paynes; and for ye betid not vs for owre mysdedes, we shul bete
yow with these fire-brondes, as Goddis wil is.' Thenne Seint
John said, 'Thilk yender ben þoo þat chasten nowght here
children, and þe yonder payn þei shal haue þerfore duryng the
will of God.'   34s
     Thoo Seint John bad me loke above my hede, and þere y saw
a roch hovyng over þe leme of al þe fires and payns þat y before
had seen. And þan he lad me vp above that roche, and there y
f. 140v saw many sowles closid / with a wal of stone, and þyulk sowles
lay noselyng on the growmd and grouelyng, and all the stench   35c
and þe smych of al the fires toforesaid rysyng vp in here
mouthes, noses, yen, and al here bodies. And on here backes y
saw dragons, arders, and snakes, todes, cattes, bitellis, and
other fowle bestis, gnawyng on here backes and on al the
lymmes on here bodies; and y saw many grisly devellis   35s
stompyng and tredyng on here backis forto encrese here
paynes.
     And þan Seint John said, 'Þe yender ben bacbiters þat
wolden never sece of saing evel of here neghbours, puttyng
hem owt of here good name into evel; never levyng it in youghe   36c
ne in age, for prechyng ne for councelyng in shrifte of hire

---

331 hod *canc. before* hote.   332   chyldren] clyldren.
333 Chaste þi child *in right-hand margin.*   358   nota *in left-hand margin.*
360 Bakbiters *in left-hand margin.*

121vb and / wemen þat behold þe stowte aray of oder wemen, þat
turnyde þer herttys to so grett vanyte, þat thay covytt passynge
þer astatte, al yf þer husbondys and þer chylder þ[er]fore weyre
in greytte dette, and by þat covytys fel into more synne, therfor
thay ar pyned in þer eyne.'   335

Then Sant Jon lede me to þe ix^te fyre, and þer I save many
saules of men and wemen pyned in þat gryssely fyre. And þer I
saw chylder bette þer owne faders and þer moders wyth grysely
brandys of fyre; and I herd how þe faders and moders sayd to
þer chylder: the fader sayd, 'Fayre chyld, I gatt yow;' and the   340
moder sayde, 'Fayre chyld, I bare yow wyth grett care and
sorowe, and noreschyde yow on my brest.' Then þe chy[l]der
sayd agayn to þer faders, 'Wryche, þou gatt hus;' and to þe
moder, 'Wreche, þou bare hus, and well we know al þe tendyr
dedes þat yow dyde for hus. Bott for yow chastyd natt hus,   345
þerfor behovys huse to suffer thyes bytter paynes; and for yow
bett nat huse for owre tryspasse, wee schall bette yow wyth
thyes fyre-brandes, for þat is Goddys wyll.'

Then Sant John bade me loke aboue my hede, and I dyde
soo, and I saw a grett roche hangyng and resayuynge þe smoke   350
and þe low of al þe fyres befor-sayde. And then Sant Jon lede
me aboue þe roche, and þer I saw many saulys closyd wythin a
122ra wall of / stone, and thay la[y] wyde oppyn fast bonden, and all
stynkyng smoke of all þe forsayde fyres [of] penanse restyde on
þer mowthes, and on þer neyses, and on þer eyne; and on þer   355
wombys saw I dragow[n]es, snakys and toodys, and many other
gryesly bestes, gnawynge and etynge wondyr dyspetyusly, and
all to increyse þer paynes and sowroys.

Then Santt Jon sayde to me, 'Wyllyam, thyes ar bak[b]yters
and that were besy wyth þer schrode talys to go fro howse to   360
howse, speykyne evyl of þer evyn-crysten, havynge reiosynge
of þer neghebor harme, and sorynes of ther welfare, puttyng

333   husbondys] *final* s *superscript*;   þerfore] þ^t fore.
342   noreschyde] o *badly formed; first stroke of* f *or long* s *canc. after* my;
chylder] chyrder.   352   *Otiose stroke before* me.
353   lay] la.   354   of] *om.*   356   dragownes] dragowes; snakys] k *blotted.*
359   bakbyters] baklyters.   360   that] *MS corrected from* thay.

goostly fader, forto it laste hem at what tyme was no space of
penaunce; and therfore þei shullyn evermore endure in those
paynes into þe day of dome, without mercy.'

Thanne Seint John lad me forth a grett space fro þat other   36~
turmentes, and there he shewed me twey towers, þat on ful of
brynnyng fire, and þe other ful of yse and snowe; and in þat full
of fire y saw many sowles ypayned and made hote in poynte
forto mylt, and sodenly with fendes þei were cast owt of þat
passyng hete into þat other tower ful of yse and snowe, and   37~
fendes with shovelis castyng yse and snow vppon hem; and þat
payned hem full sore. And thanne y saw many sowles with fire-
f. 141r brondys `bre[n]nyng´ in here hondes, / hauyng here bodies ful
of serpentes, snakes, todes, and diuers other orrible wormes,
knockyng at þe yate of þe towre; and when þei were letyn yn,   37~
thei cast the brondes of fire to thilk oþer sowles þat were cast
yn paynes, and beten h[e]m with þe same brondis, and payned
them wonderly sore; and al tho serpentes, todes, and other
orrible wor[m]is lopen from here bodies to þilk oþer þat were
payned in þat cold, and stongyn and beten hem wonderly sore.   38~

Thanne Seint John said vnto me, 'These were bisshoppes
and other diuers prelates of holy chirch þat shuld haue prechid
and geve good ensampell of levyng to þe comyn people; for thei
did not þus, now thei be punysshid and payned with this fire
and þis cold sodaynly, duryng þe will of [God]. And these   38~
sowles with þese fire-brondes þat payneth them were here
seruauntes lyveng in pride and oþer disgisyng of þe world. And
þilk serpentes, snakes, todes, and other wormes ben here iaggis
and daggis þat þei vsidden; and now thei styngen and byten
þese prelates for thei wold not correcte here meyne of here nyse   39~
aray.'

369   sod (d *incomplete*) *canc. after* and.   372   and þan *canc. after* thanne.
373   brennyng] *only three minims for* nn; hondes] *written like a catchword at
the right of bottom margin.*
377   hem] him.   379   wormis] wordis, *em.* Kr.
380   cl(?) *canc. before* cold.   381   sai *canc. after* Thanne.
384   done nat *canc. before* did.   385   God] *om., added* Kr.

them owt of þer gud name into þer yll; and thys horrabyll syne
wold thay neuer leve, for no prechynge nor techynge, and
þerfor schall thay suffer þis horrabyll paynes vnto þe day of   365
dome wythowte mercy, for thay had no mersy on þer evyn-
crysten.'

[A]nd then Sant Jon lede me fardyr and chewyd me too
towres, þe on full of brynnynge fyre, and þe other ful of cowlde
yse. In þe towre ful of fyre I saw many sawles so sore burnynge   370
þat hytt semyd þat thay schuld meltte for þat passynge hete.
And sothely then toke fendys them owte wyth grett crokys and
kest them into þat other towre, and þer fendys wyth schowffyllys kest apon them yse and snaw, and þat payne was soo kowld
þat trewly hytt passyd many other paynes. And then saw I   375
many other sawlys cummynge wyth fyre-brondys / in þer

*. 122rb many other sawlys cummynge wyth fyre-brondys / in þer
handys, and þer bodyes hangyng full of snakys and towdys,
eddyrs and many dyuerse vemunsume wormys. And þose
sawlys knokkyd at þe ȝatte of that towre wyth thys sorow[ful]
aray abowt them. And as sowne as thay were lettyn in thay kest   380
þe brondys of fyre at þe other sawlys þat were before in payne.
And then thay toke þe brondys agayn and bett wyth them þe
saulys, and þat grevyd them warse and more then all þer other
paynes. And wyth þat all þe orrabyll wormes þat hange apon
them lepe owte vpon þe saulys þat were before soo bett, and   385
bootte them and stangyd them thorow þe bodyes.

Then Sant Jon sayde, 'Loo, Wyllyam, thyes were sumtyme
bysschoppys and prelates and curetys of holy kyrke, and
schulde haue prechyde þe law of God to þe pepull, and gyffyn
them insampyll of gud lyffyng. And sothely, thay dyd natt, and   390
therfore thay have thys grett penance of hotte and colde. And
thows saulys wyth fyre-brongdys we`r´ sumtyme þer seruan-
dys, and lyffynge ouermoche in pryde and many dysgysyngys
of þer araye. Thyes serpenttys, toodes, and eddyrse, and snakys
were þer jaggys þat thay wsyd sumtyme in grett pryde, and all   395
ar turnyd them to sorow and care whyll þat God wyll. And þus
ar beschoppys and other prelates pynyde of þer seruandys, for

365 þis] is *superscript*; horrabyll] *otiose stroke over* a.
368 And] Tnd.
371 neuer after schuld *here omitted as destroying the sense.*
375 paynes] s *superscript*.   376 fyre-brondys] s *superscript*.
377 bodyes] s *superscript*.   379 sorowful] sorow.
387 *Three- or four-letter word erased after* Jon.
388 of *canc. after* prelates.   394 Thyes] s *superscript*.

And þan y saw another fire, and sowles brynnyng theryn þat
were a[s] gret as it were pipis or tonnes al toswollyn. And owt

f. 141v of here / fingers and owt of here toes come diuers wormes, as
adders, snakes, and todes, turnyng aȝen into þe same bodies,   395
sowkyng hem vnto þe tyme þat here bodies were smalle aȝen,
and þen eftesone styngyng aȝen forto þat þei were swollen aȝen,
as þus þei did continulych, and fendes blowyng the fire forto
make þe serpentes to styng hem more besely.

And þan y herd mony diuers noyses cryeng and sayng,   400
'Jhesu Crist, Goddes sone of hevene, rightfull doumsman,
awreke vs on þis people; for þei hadden þe goodes of holy
chirch more þan them nedid, and suffred vs to peressh for
defaute.'

And þan Seint John said, 'These were religious men, as   405
monkous, chanons, and other, þat shuld haue lyved in con-
tinence and abstinded of here bodi; and for thei did not þus,
now thei be payned with þis fire and þise wormen sowkyng and
payneng hem in diuers maners. And þese sowles þat axe
veniaunce on hem beth þe people þat myght haue be relevid bi   410
the goodes þat þei spendid in wast.'

Thenne Seint John shewid to me diuers sowles payned in
another fire, and summe were closid with plates of yren
brennyng al abowte, and on þe platis weren letters and wordes
wel wreten, and þorow þe wordes nayles of yren hote bryn-   415
neng, smeten into here bodies. And þan y saw fendes take owt
þe tonnges and þe hertes of somme of þo sowles, shredyng hem
smalle, and castyng in here faces as it were brynnyng fire. And
among thilk sowles y saw on so punysshid, of þe which Seint

f. 142r John said, 'Þilk is / thi eme, William, þat was person of suche a   420
place.' And I wist well þat he was dede xvj. wynter tofore þat
time.

Thanne Seint John said, 'Þese ben þe sowles of persones and
vicaries and prestis. And þe letters þat þow seist was Goddes
seruice þat þei shuld haue said with deuocion; but for þei had   425
more lust in pleyng and other flesshly and wor`l´dly lustes and

---

392   xi *in left-hand margin.*   393   as] at, *em.* Kr; town *canc. after* or.
394   religious *in left-hand margin.*   397   styngly *canc. after* eftesone.
402   f *canc. before* hadden.
407   abstinded] *curved flourish above,* abstinence Kr (*without comment*).
408   þise] s *corrected from another letter?*   411   Feint xj *in left-hand margin.*
412   persones vicares *in left-hand margin.*   417   tonnges] *could be* tounges.

*. *122va* thay wold / suffer them to lyve in pryde and foly, and
reprevy[d] them nott, bott suffyrd them þerin.'

Ande then I saw in another fyre saulys all tobownede grett as   400
towrys, and owt of þer fyngers and tayllys cum eddyrs, snakys,
towdys, wormys, and other fowle bestys. And then waxide thay
small agayn, and thyes bestys batte them and stangyd them,
and sone þai waxyde grett agayn as thay ware before. And in
þis grett payn thay were contynually, and fendys bloynge the   405
fyre to gare þe wormys bytt[e] on them and stange them þe
more bytterly.

And then I herde many voces and dyuerse cryenge on þis
wyse, 'Jhesu Cryst, Goddys sone of hevyn, rygh[t]ewose
domysman, wreyke hus on thy`e´s `pepul´, for thay have þe   410
guddys of holy kyrke more þen thay nedyde, and suffyrde hus
to paryche for defawte of gude.'

Then Sant Jon sayde, 'Loo, Wyllyam, thyes were men of
relegyon, as chanons, monkys, freres, and other, þat schulde
haue levyde in contemplacyon and abstynence of þer body; and   415
for thay lyffyde natt after þer ordyr, therfore thay suffyrde and
schall suffyre here thyes wofull paynes. And thowes þat askys
vengance on them ar þe savles of powre men þat myght have
*. *122vb* bene relevyde thorow þe guddys / þat thay dyspendyd in wast.'

Then Sant Jon schewyde me other dyuerse sawlys, and sum   420
were closyde abowt wyth plates of yrene al brynnynge, and on
the plates were letters and wordys wele wrytton, and thorow þe
wordys were nalys of yrene al brynnynge smyttyn into þer
heddys and so into ther herttys and into ther bodyes. And
amonge thyes sowlys I saw on þat hys tong and hys hertt were   425
takyn owt and schorne small, and fendys keste them on hys
face agayn. Then sayd Sant Jon to me, 'Loo, Wyllyam, thys
was thy eme þat was person of syche a towne.' And I wyst welle
þat he wase dede xj ȝere before þat tyme.

And Sant John sayde to me, 'Thyes ar þe savles of vicars,   430
and persons, and other prestys also, and þe letters þat ar
wryttyn on þe platees weche are smeton on þer heddys
betokyns deuine serues, þat thay schulde haue sayd and done

---

399   reprevyd] reprevyng (*last three letters in right-hand margin over an
erasure*).   400   Ande] *two-line* A *and capital* N.
401   tayllys] s *superscript.*   404   þai] ai *superscript.*
405   þis] is *superscript*; ta *canc. after* payn.   406   bytte] bytto.
408   þis] is *superscript.*   409   ryghtewose] ryghewose.
411   þen] en *superscript.*
418   powre] *long-tailed* r *poorly formed and added as a correction.*
422   and (2)] d *superscript.*   428   sch *canc. after* of.

myrthes than yn here seruice, therefore now þus thei be payned
with þese brynnyng nailes in there flessh. And for thei were
never well, as them thowght, but if þei myght be occupied in
hakyng or huntyng or oþer diuers synnes and vaniteis, levyng   430
Goddes service, holy prayers, and other goostly deuocions þat
is longyng to Goddis pristes, and yoven evel ensample to þe
comen people bi hire lewid levyng, and with hire tongis not
occupied in devowght praiers and Goddis seruice and
behouefull to þe people, but hire hertes and hire tungis   435
occupied in thowghtis and wordes of synne and vaniteis,
therfore fendes payneth hem nowe, shredyng and cuttyng here
tunges and hertes in hudious payn and wo to hem.'

And þan Seint John shewid to me a grete hous stronglich
ywallid abowte, and þat hous was al [o]p[en] aboue, and in þat   440
hous was þe most stench þat ever y feld; and þere y saw sowles
al nakid, and þere among hem was passyng cold. And there y
f. 142v   saw dyvers pressis ipiled wyth clothis, and owt of / þat clothe
come mothis and other diuers wormes. And þe fendes toke þoo
wormes, stoppeng and puttyng them into þe moughthes and   445
throtes of þo sowles. And there y saw many dowblettes ythrow
of fendes vppon þo sowles, þe which dowbelettes were not
hote, but yet with them þei were gretely payned and punysshid. And þan I saw the fendes turnyng here arses toward þe
sowles, shytyng vppon hem, the which dirt stonk so fowle þat it   450
was a passyng payn. And into þat hous come grete passyng
haulstones owt of þe eyr, smytyng summe of þo sowles, summe
on þe hedes, and summe on þe bodies, and al tobrosid hem.
Then Seint John said, 'Þese ben þe sowles of men of holy
chirch, as persones, vicaries, and other prestes, þat shuld haue   455
tawght good doctrine, and good exemple haue yevyn to þe
comen people; ffor þei did noght so, now thei be punysshid
diuerslich in þe paynes þat thow seist; and þei suffren now this
passyng cold to teche hem what þe pore and þe nakid people
suffreden when thei myght haue refresshid hem. These wormes   460
þat comyn owt of þese clothes were þo mothis þat engendred in
here clothis þat þei might haue holpen with þe nedy people,

427   þus] u *superscript.*   440   open] vp.
442   among hem *canc. after* there.   443   of clothe *canc. after* pressis.
453   hedes *canc. after* þe (2).   454   h *canc. after* men.

euery day wyth grett deuocyon. Bott thay have more false
devocyon and lust in hawkynge and hunttynge and other levde   435
playes and ydyll occupacyonys and wardely myrthys, then in
þe seruece of Gode, and therfor are thay þus pynede wyth
horrabyll payens. And yf thay had servyd God as thay schuld
haue done, by reson of þer charge þat thay toke, greettys blysse
. 123ra in hevyn myght thay have hade. Alas! þat syche / prestys   440
schuld be callyd Goddys knyghtys, þat feghtys euery day
agayne þer lege lorde. And þerfore thay schal be callyde be
ryght of ther false gouernance, the dewlys knyghtys and
Goddes traytores, and for syche ar they now pynyde, and schal
be whylys Goddys wyll is. And for þer herttys and þer tongys   445
were occupyde in ydyll thoght and ydyll speche, þerfore thay
suffyr now so howge payn; for when thay wolde nat purches
them blys, as thay myght haue done, and þat full mykylle, God
wyll þat thay haue now þer purchese, and þat is mekyl care and
sorow, more then any tonge can tell.'   450

And Sant Jon schewyd me a grett howse strongely wallyd
abowt, and that howse was all open abown, and trewly þer was
þe most stynk þat euer I felde. And þer I saw many sawles al
nakyd, and amonge them was a passynge colde. And þer I saw
dyueres pressys off clothes, and euery presse pylyde wyth   455
dyueres clothes and þat many. And owt of thyes clothes cam
many moghtys and other wormys; and þan I saghe to / < . . .

---

449   that *canc. after* now.   454   þer] *abbreviation mark blotted.*
457   *Following section lost presumably through scribal oversight when changing*
columns.

and now þei shul not be fed with none other mete but with þe
same wormes. And the dowblettes þat þow seist draw on /

thilk sowles weren dowblettes that nyse prestes vsid in this 465
world, as þei had ben secular men; for þer cam no frute of þe
curates and pristes of teching and of good ensample yevyng to
the comyn people, but stynkyng synne and vnklene levyng,
therfore þei shullyn now suffre þe stench and þe dirt of þese
fendes duryng þe will of God. And þilk sowles þat þow seist 470
smyten and brusid with the grete hailstonis ben þe sowles of
thik persones and vicaries þat rayn, haill, and snow defowled
here auters and here chauncelles bi hire myskepeng where
Goddis body shuld be sacred and diuine seruice said, spendyng
þe goodes þat God sent hem to kepe with þat charge and many 475
other, in synne and wrecchidnesse. And now all these sowles
`ben´ closid in þese high walles for as moch as thei closid
hemself, whiles thei leveden in þis world, in hire owne houses,
for þei wold not here þe crie of þe pore and the nedy people.'

   And þan Seint John led me forthe toward a water, the which 480
was blak and fowle to sight, and yn thilk water were mony
fendes, yellyng and makyng gresly noyse. And over þat water y

saw a gret brygge and brode, as me semed, and on þat brigge / I
saw a bisshop goyng and with him mony clerkes and diuers
officers and many other mayne. And when he had go a good 485
while on þat brigge, y saw fendes with grete strenghe pullyng
and teryng adown the pilers of þe brigge, and the bisshop
sodaynly fallyng into þe water and his meyne with him. And in
the fallyng my thowght y saw a bright angell takyng away the
myter and the cros fro þe bisshop and vaneshid away. And than 490
y saw many diuers sowles and fendes among hem takyng þilk
bisshop, teryng, drawyng, and plunchyng him in þat blak
water, and he suffred þerynne many diuers turmentes and
moche woo.

   And þan Seint John said, 'This was a bisshop which leved 495
not wel to the plesyng of God as his degre and his astate asked;
and therfore he is now payned with this diuers paynes. Þat
brigge þat þow seist was a brigge þat he lete make in the world
whiles he was on lyve, for esement of þe comen people; but for

465   sowles] canc., but retained here for the sense; dowblettes] first t looks like a
c.   487   him(?) erased after teryng.
491   and fen canc. after fendes.
492   kyng canc. at the beginning of a new line after plunchyng; it appears that
the scribe first wrote plunch-/kyng, and then wrote yng in the right-hand margin
after plunch.   495   bisshop canc. after This.

f. 123rb   > 'have holpen þ[er]wyth þe commyn pepyll, bot stynkyng
syne of lechery and other synfull lyffynge; þerfor thay schall
nedes suffyr now þis horribull stynke of fendys arses durynge   460
þe wyll of Gode. And thyes other saules all smytten wyth the
holestones and all tobryssed, ar þe savles of thos persons and
vicars, hayl, and snaw, and rayne fall into þer chansell or apon
þer hyee auters þer God schuld be worschyped and deuine
seruece sayde. And now all thyes saules ar closyd wythin thyes   465
hye wallys, for as myche as thay closyd them wythin þer hyee
howses when thay schulde ete, for thay wold nat here þe pore
pepyl crye.'
     Then Sant John lede me forthe towarde a water, and þat
water was blak as pyke. In þat water was many fendys, ȝellyng   470
and makynge a grysely noyse. And ouer þat water I saw a grett
bryge and a brode, and on þat bryge I saw a bysschope go and
wyth hym many clarkys and dyuerse offecers and many other
in feloschyppe. And when [he] hade gon a grett way on þe
f. 123va bryge, I saw fendys wyth a grett maleyce myne / and pulle   475
away pyllers and sodenly þe bysschoppe and all þe meny þat
were wyth hym fell into þe horrabyll water. And in þat fallynge
hytt semyde to me þat I saw an angell take þe crosse and þe
myter fro þe bysschoppe and vanyschyd away. And then I saw
many dyuerse saules as well as fendys takynge þe besschopp   480
and ryvynge hym, and plukkyng hym in þat ylke fowle water.

     Then Sant Jon sayd, 'Loo, Wyllyam, þat was a bysschopp
þat lyffyd nat after þe law of Gode, as hys degre was and hys
estate askyd, and þerfor is he now poneschyde wyth dyuerse
paynes and tormentys. And þis bryge þat he gartt make whyle   485
he levyd in erthe, for esement of the commyn pepull gave,

---

458   holpen] o *badly formed, perhaps a correction*; þerwyth] *MS lacks*
abbreviation mark for þer; *possibly whole word intended to be canc. as* þ *is badly*
formed, possibly struck through, and wᵗ *has small dot beneath; however, this*
scribe's deletions are usually more obvious.
460   þis] *is superscript*; aes *canc. after* fendys.   470   p *canc. after* as.
474   he] I.   476   pyllers] pyllers kyrke.   485   þis] *is superscript*.

as moche as he did it to be made principally for vaynglorie, and   500
also þe goodes þat it was made with weren falslich goten, taken
yerlych bi his office, gold and siluer, maynteyneng þe synne of
moche people in lecherie, therfore God hath suffred þese
fendes to draw down this brigge; for if it had be made with
godes trulych goten, it shuld haue `y´stondyn him now in grette   505
f. 144r stede. And these sowles þat þow seist paynenge him / in these
paynes ben þe sowles of thoo þat he suffred in þe world to liue
in synne for loue and covetise of worldly lucor, which he myght
haue amendid if he had don is dever; and therfore it is þe wil of
God þat he and his officers þat suffred hem in synne, be   510
punysshid with hem in these paynes duryng the wil of God.'
             Fin[i]s reuelacionum penalium.

And when Seint John had shewid me al þese paynes and
many mo þan y can or may tell or bithink, y said to him, 'May
ther be ony remedi or mytigacion to þese sowles þat be þus   515
ypayned in these diuers paynes?'

And he said thus, 'William, God forbede it els; for þow shalt
vnderstond þat þese sowles may be holpen owt of þese paynes
principallich bi the mercy of God, and bi þe good dedis þat her
frendes and þe people levyng in þe world may do for hem; as to   520
lernyd men, as bi masses singyng, saing of sawters, Placebo and
Dirige; commendacions, .vij. salmes and the .xv. psalmes with
þe letenye; bi almes-dede, and bi pilgrimage; and also bi lewid
men with þe Pater noster, þe Aue Maria, and þe Crede; almes-
dede, fastyng, and pilgrimage; and bi many other good dedis.   525
f. 144v For right as thow seist if a man is / hond or his fote were put
into a vessell ful of hote scaldyng water, yf a man put þerto a
quantite of cold water, sumwhat the hete of the scaldyng water
wold abate; and so ofte he myght put þerto more cold water
and more þat þe hete shuld not greve him; in the same wise, so   530
many prayers and good dedes may be do for þo sowles þat ben
in payn of purgatorie, þat [bi] þe goodnesse and bi the mercy of

504 him *canc. after* draw.
505 ystondyn] *two minims subpuncted before* d.
512 Finis] *second* i *erased.*
513 And] *scribe's small* a *in unfilled space for two-line capital; capital* N.
528 w *canc. after* water (1).   532 bi] *om.*

trevly the cause of hys makyng was vaneglory, to haue thank
and praysyng of þe pepull; and also þe gudys þat hytt was made
wyth were falssely goten for þe most parte, ffor he toke thorow
hys offecers, knowyng hymselffe þat hytt was wyth wrong   490
geton, both gold and syluer, and sufferd þerfor men and
wemen to contenue in þer syne, vnponyschyde in lechery, and
f. 123vb other contractys of matrimonie lettyde—an / evyll dede, mede
for them—and suffyrde þe partys to travell and spende þer
gudys fro [chapetor to] chapetor and consistorie to consistore,   495
to thay hade no more to dyspende, and then behovys them
nedys to leve þer trew maters, and all in faute of trewe offecers.
And þerfor hase God suffyrde fendys to draw down þat bryge,
for yf hytt had ben made wyth guddys treuly gotyn, hytt
schuld haue stande in grett stede. And the savles þat poneschys   500
them in þat water [ar] þe saulys of them þat thay suffyrd to
lye in syne for mede, for thay hade full powre to correcte
them, and dyde nat, and þerfor þe wylle of God ys þat he and
hys false offecerse be ponyschyd of them for þe grett syne,
whyll hys blyssyde wyll is.   505

And when Sant Jon hade schewyd me thyes horrabyl paynes
þat ar befor sayde, and many moo then I can tell or thynke, I
sayd to Sant Jon, 'Holy fader, may þer be no remedy nor
mittigacyon to thyes saulys þat þus ar poneschyde in dyuerse
tormentys?   510

f. 124ra And he answarde and / sayde, '3ys, Wyllyam, God forbede
ellys; for þou schal vndyrstande þat thyes savles may be
refresshyde and holpyn owt of thyes payns princypally by þe
mercy of God, and by þe gude dedys þat þer frendys and other
pepull lyffynge in þe warlde may doo for them; as prestys   515
masses syngyng, Placebo and Dirige, and psauters sayd by
them, or by clarkys commendacyon and þe vij psalmes wyth þe
latyne; by almys-dede and by pylgramage; also by lewde men
wyth Pater noster, Aue, and Crede; almus-dede, fastyng, and
by many other dedys. For yf a mannys hand or hys legge wer   520
putt into a vessell full of scaldynge hott water, yf a man put
þerto a lytyll colde water, sumwhat þe hette of þe scaldynge
wolde abate; and so ofte þerto he myghtt put cold water, þat þe
hette wold all abate and nothyng greve hym. Ryght on þe same
wyse, so many prayers and gud dedys may be done for thes   525
saulys þat or in payne, þat thorow þe mercy of God and gud

487   cause *added in right-hand margin.*
495   chapyeo *canc. after* fro; chapetor to] *om*;   consistorie] consistorise.
499   madi *canc. after* ben.   501   ar] *om.; erasure after* water.
502   correcte] t *blotted.*   517   psalmes] *final* s *superscript.*
520   legge] *final* e *superscript.* 523   he *canc. after* ofte; myghtt] *first* t *blotted.*

God and þe good dedis done for hem, þat þei myght be
delyuerid owt of payn.'

Then Seint John went with me a litill space and sone he   535
vanysshid owt of my sight, and thanne y was mochel adred
when he was gone fro me, and forth y ȝede bi the water side,
the which water was greislych and depe, and moche greisly
noise y herd þerynne, and vnderstode þat þere shuld have ben a
brigge over þat water as y had herd say in þe world. And y saw   540
none, and was the more agast and adrede. Thanne y herd a
more grislich noyse of fendys comyng bihind me þan ever y
herd bifore; and bi þat noyse my sprite and my wittes failidden
me, so þat y had no mynd on the passion of God, ne of none
other prayer.   545

And þan þat blissid virgen Seint Yve cam bihinde me and
f. 145r   saide, 'Thow madman, haue mynde / in þi hert of the glorious
passion of owre lord Jhesu Crist, Goddis sone of hevene, and
mark the with thi praier.'

And þan y said, 'Jhesu Crist, Goddis sone of heuene, for þi   550
passion þat þow suffredist for me and al synful on erthe, haue
mercy on my sinful bodi, and if me grace so forto do þat is
most plesaunt to the, saluacion for my bodi and my sowle.'
And than y markid me with my praier. And þan al þat noise þat
y herd vaneshid away fro me, and y went forth bi the water side   555
on my right honde. And on þat other side of the water y saw
nothyng but an high roche; and so long y went on þat water
side þat y saw an high towour on the ferther side of þat water,
and there y saw mo light þan y did on al þe way bifore. On þe
top of þe towre y saw a fayre woman stondyng and lokid to me;   560
and þan y was right gladde, and knelid down on my kneis, and,
with as good hert and deuocion as y had, said .v. Pater in þe
worship of owre lordis .v. woundes, and .v. Aues in þe worship
of owre ladi is .v. ioyes, and markid me with my praier. Or y
rose, I lokid to þe towour and saw a ladder fro þe top of þe   565
f. 145v   towour reching vnto the grownd where y knelid; and / for
gladnesse I rose vp and went to the ladder. And hit was so litill,
as me thowght, þat it wold onnethe bere onything; and þe first
rong of the ladder was so [hye] þat onnethe might my fynger
reche therto; and þat rong was sharper þan ony rasor, as me   570
thowt, and anone y drow my hond therfro. And þan I herd a
grisly noyse comyng fast toward me and y markid me with my

dedys done for them, thay may be delyueryd owte off þer
payn.'

Then Sant Jon went away, and I went by þe water þat was so
deppe and so grysely on to see, and mekyll gryssely noyse I   530
hard þerin. And euer I lokyde after a bryge ouer that water,
weche I had harde speyke of, þat is to say, of þe bryge ful of
pykys. And when I saw non I was þe more adrede. And wyth
þat þer cam behynd me þe gretyste and the most howgyste
noyse of fendys þat euer I harde befor; and thorow þat noyse   535
f. 124rb my wyttys and my sprete faylyde me, so þat I forgat þe /
passyon of owre [lorde] Jhesu Cryst and also my prayer.

And then þe blyssyd uergyn Sant Hylde cam behynde me
and sayd, 'Thow man, haue mynde of þe glorius passion of
owre lorde Jhesu Criste, Goddys sone of hevyn, and blyse þe   540
wyth thy prayer.'

And þen I sayde, 'Jhesu Criste, Goddys sone of hevyn, for þi
passion þou suffyrde for me and all synfull in erthe, haue mercy
on me, synfull wreche, and forgyff me all my synnys, and gyfe
me grace to do þat is most plesyng to þe and saluacyon of my   545
body and my saule.' And then I blyssyd me wyth my prayer,
and belyve, all þe orrabyll noyse wentt away þat was so grysely.
And then I went forthe on my ryght hand by þe water syde,
and on þat other syde on þe water I saw no other thyng bott a
hoghe roche. And so longe I went by þe water syde þat I saw   550
on þe other syde a hyghe towre. And þer I saw a grett[er] lyght
then I dyde in all þe way before. And on þe toppe I saw a fayre
woman standyng and lokynge to me. And then I was glade, and
sett me down on my knesse wyth gud deuocyon, to I hade
sayde v Pater noster and v Ave Maria in þe worschypp of owre   555
lorde v wondys and of owre lade v joyes; ant then I blyssyd me
f. 124va wyth my / prayer; and or I rose vp, I lokyd to þe towre, and þer
I saw a ledder fro þe toppe of þe towre rechyng to þe grownde
þer I knelyde. And for gladnes I rosse vp and went to þe
leddyr; and forsowthe me thoght hytt was so ryght wayke, þat   560
me thoght hytt wold bere nothynge þat hade any weght. And
þe fyrst style was so hye þat vnnethe I myght reche my fynger
þerto, and þat was scharper then any rasowre, and for drede I
toke my hande away. And wyth þat I harde a thowsandefolde

---

537 lorde] om.   542 þen] n superscript.
543 s or f and maybe another letter canc. after synfull; large minim canc.
after haue.
546 sal canc. before saule.   551 gretter] grett.   563 as canc. after was.

praier and al þat noyse vanyshid away. And þan y lokid to þat
ladder and þere y saw a corde comyng fro þe top of the towre to
þe fote of þe ladder, and þat woman bad me knitte þat corde   575
abowte my myddell, and so y did, an yede to þat ladder aȝen,
and reght my hond to þat rong, and þo y feld þe rong of no
sharpnesse; and bi þe help of þat woman and of myne owne
grypyng, y steied vppon þat ladder. And þo y herd a
thowsand[fold] more noyse grisly and hidowus, in þe water   580
vnder me, ꞌandꞌ in þat lond þat y com fro, þan y herd ony tyme
bifore. Þan bi þe help of owre lord Jhesu Crist and his merci
and þat woman þat was aboue þat towour, y was sone brough[t]
to þe top of þat towour, where y was passid al maner of drede.

And þo y fel on kneis and elbowis tofore þat faire woman,   585
and said, 'Jhesu Crist, Goddes sone of heven, mot quite yow
and worship yow for yowre grete and gracious help, and for
yowr corde.'

And þan þat faire woman said, 'The yender cord is thilk
f. 146r   corde þat þou / yavest to the chapman þat was robbid wi[th]   590
iwes, when he cam where þow ꞌwereꞌ, asking almes, for the loue
of God.'

And þan þe woman went evyn fro þe towre, and y folowid.
And þere we cam into a faire contree, and al the erthe of þat
contree was clere as cristal ston, and no gras growyng in þat   595
contree, but there growid many treis, and þe fairest þat ever y
saw with myne yen, and swetter of sauour þan al þe spicers
shoppes þat ever [were]; and many wonderfull breddes on the
treis, singeng on hire singyng mony dilectable songus, and
suete notes makyng and singyng.   600

In þat contre me thowght wonder meri, and fayn y wold
haue biden þeryn, and wonder fast y ȝede in þat contree forth.
Þe ferther þat y ȝede and sowght, the better me likid. And þere
cam aȝenst me a faire company of monkis, channons, and
pristes, clothid al in white, and welcomed me wel tenderlich, as   605
þowgh y had be here owne born brother, of oon fader and of
oon moder. And ofte þei lowtid and thonkid God hertly þat y
was passid al thilk peroles and gresly sightes þat y had bifore
sein, herd, and be yn. And þat ever y did ony good dede in this
world, þei thonkid me therfore, yn so moche þat for a candell   610
þat y set sumtyme in a chirch bifore an ymage, not for þe
ymage, but in worship of þat seint þat þe ymage bitokened, y
was thonkid þerfore.

580   thowsandfold] fold *om;*   þan *canc. after* water.
583   brought] brough *with flourish,* broughte Kr.   590   with] wiht.
598   were] *om.;* Kr *omits* þat ever *and adds* of all þe warlde, *after* SA.

more gryselly noyse cum to me-warde then euer I herde before;   565
and as fast as I blyssyd me wyth my prayer, belyve hytt
uaneschyde away. And then I lokyde to þe leddyr, and I saw a
corde cummynge fro þe toppe of þe towre to þe fote of þe
ledder, and þe woman bade me knytt þe roppe to my myddyll,
and so I dyde, and went then to þe leddyr agayn, and put my   570
hand to þe steyle, and then I felyde þe steyle of no scharppenes.
Bot then I harde a thowsande more folde more grysely noyse
then I harde afore, vndyr me in þe water, and on the lande,
then euer I harde at any tyme in all my way. Then thorow þe
help of þe mercy of owre lorde Jhesu Criste and þe woman þat   575
f. 124vb was abowne ther / on þe towre, I was sone broght to the towre
toppe, and then was I past al drede.

      Then I fell on knesse and inclyned before þat fayre woman,
and sayd, 'Jhesu Crist, Goddys sone in hevyn, qwytte yow for
yor gud dede and helpe and yor corde.'   580

      Then þe fayre woman sayde, 'Wyllyam, thys ys þe corde þat
þow gaffe þe chapman for rewthe when he was robbyde of
thevys, when he askyd þe sum of thy gud, for þe luffe of Gode.'

      Then the woman went fro þe towre and I folowde after. And
all þe erthe of the cuntre was whytt and clere as cristall, and   585
there was no gresse growynge, bot the fayryst tree þat euer I
saw growyde þer and swett[er] of sauere then all þe spysse
schoppys of all þe warlde; and many fayre byrdys of dyuerse
colowres were in þat tree, ful merely syngynge wyth many
swete noyse and dilectabyll, passynge all þe songys þat euer I   590
harde.

      And in þat cuntre wold I fayne a bydden for hytt was so
passynge mery in þat cuntre. I went ryght fast forthe; farthermore I went þe better, and þe ferthermore more mery and
gladder I was. And trewly, þer cam agayne me a fayre cumpany   595
of monkys and chanouns and prestys, and all clede in whytt
aray; and they welcumyd me and walkyd wyth me ful gudly /
f. 125ra and ful gentylly, as I hade bene þer borne brother by fader and
moder. And oft thay lovyde God and thankyd hym wyth gud
hertt þat I was passyde al þat peryll and gresely syghtys þat I ·   600
hade sene.

---

566   blyssyd] d *superscript*.   571   steyle (2)] *first* e *superscript*.
578   inclyned] d *badly formed, possibly corrected from* t; *followed by minim with*
stroke, which may be I *canc.*   584   me *canc. after* fro.
585   towre was whytte *canc. after* the.
587   swetter] swettyst;   spysse] spyssers Kr (*p. 74 n. 1*).
593   cuntre] t *badly formed.*   595   to me *canc. after* cam.

And [as] y stode, talkyng with hem, ther come a bisshop
f. 146v revershid with a cros / in his hond, and on that cros an ymage   615
of owre lord Jhesu Crist as he suffred paine on the rode. And
þe bisshop was barefote, and so were al tho þat were there; and
whan þe bisshop cam neigh, thei fellen al on kneis, and askid
his blessyng, and he yaf it þem with good wille. And y, in a side
bi myself set on my kneis, askid þe bisshop his blessyng as þat   620
oþer compeny did, and he with his hond blissid me.

Thanne said þe bisshop, 'Loved an heried be God, William,
þat þow art welcome heder þat hast passid a perilous place.
Worship be owre lorde Jhesu Crist, Goddes sone of heven.'
And the bisshop said to me many wordes. And among other, he   625
said, 'Alas! alas! William. Alas! for mekill people in the world
synneth in trust of Goddis mercy, and þat bigileth many, man
and woman;' and these ruful wordes rehersid abowte a .xij.
times. 'Alas!' he said, 'whi nel not þe people in þe world take
hede to þe grete goodnesse þat owre lord Jhesu Crist hath do   630
for hem, þat þei wold for his love and his kindenesse þat he
hath shewid to them, lefe here synnes and hire wikkidnesse or
here synnes lefe hem, with ynward sorow of hert shryveng hem
clene of here synnes to them þat power haue; and shew how
f. 147r ofte and þe tyme, and the place, / and the degre of the person   635
þat þei have synned with, and hire onkindenesse and turnyng
aȝen to synne; and wilfulli and mekely take penaunce and fulfil
it, and thanne continue in good levyng; and than þei shul nat be
punysshid in þo orible paynes þat þow sawest, but thei shul
haue grete thonke of owre lord Jhesu Crist, ffor þei for his loue   640
forsakyn and withstoden here synnes, suffreng þe burdon of
many temptacions; and seintes in heuen shull be ioifull and
worship hem therfore.'

And whan þis bisshop had talkid with me a good while, he
said, 'William, þow passe aȝen into þy contree, and be þow a   645
good man in thi leuyng, and þan þow shalt come heder to vs;
and if þow turnest to thi synne aȝen, thow shalt come to thilk
paynes which þow now hast ascaped.'

And þan y said, 'Holy fader, if it be plesing to owre lord
Jhesu Crist, I beseche yow for his loue þat y myght a while rest   650
me in þis contree, for here to be me thinkith ful mery.'

614 as] *om.*   627 nota *in left-hand margin.*   634 nota *in left-hand margin.*
645 þy] y *changed from another letter.*   651 place *canc. after* þis.

Then thay sayd, 'God [gyf] euer[y] cristen man and woman
gra[ce] to leve ther syn or hytt leve them, and wyth inwarde
sorow of hertt schryve them clene of þer synnys to them þat
hase powre, and tell how often, where, and what tyme, and þe   605
person, bott nat þe name, þat thay haue synnyde in and wyth;
and þer grett vnkynden[e]sse agaynste owre lord Jhesu Criste;
and wyth gud wyll take þer penance and mekely fulfyll hytt,
and afterward contenew in þer gud levynge, and thay shal nat
be poneschyde in thowys horrabyll paynes þat þou hase sene.   610
For trewly, mekyll thanke schall thay haue of owre lorde Jhesu
Criste, þat wyll after varey repentance and clene schryfte wyth
gud wyl do þer penance and wythstand temptacion. And
moreouer, all þe santtys in hevyn schal be reiosyde.'

And when þe bysschyppe hade talkyd þus to me a grett   615
whylle, then he sayde, 'Wyllyam, the behovys to turne agayn
f. 125rb into thyn one cuntre; and loke þou be a gud / man in levynge,
and þou schall cum [heder to vs; and if þow turnest to thi synne
aȝen, thow shalt come] agayne to þe paynes þat þou art in now
efte, par auenture, and be ponyschyde sore þerin.'   620
And then I sayde, 'Holy fader, yf hytt be plesynge to owre
lorde Jhesu Criste, I beseche yow þat I myght abyde here in
thys blyssyd contre, for trewly here is mery abydynge.'

602   gyf] om.; euery] euer.   603   grace] gra (at end of line).
607   vnkyndenesse] vnkyndensse.   609   haue canc. after shal.
613   Two letters canc. after penance.   617   a(?)ne canc. after thyn.
618–9 heder … come] from SR.   622   lorde] e blotted.

And þan þe bisship said to me, 'Let be, William. Þow maist
not abide here as now; but be a good man, and þow shalt come
heder. And y counsaill the þat þow aske nothing þat is
displesyng to Goddes will, for y say the, it is synne to covete it.   655
But thow shalt wend aȝen in the blissyng of God and myne.
f. 147v But yet er thow goo / thow shalt se examinacion of a prioresse
of a nunnery, for hir sowle is comen hether now to here
iugement.'

And tho the bisshop and þe company went forth, and y   660
folowid after forto þat y come to þat place on an high hill where
þat sowle abode; and there were wonder many fendes abowte
þat sowle. And anon, on of the monkis þat come with the
bisshop opend a boke of þe nonnes rule and law, after which
she shuld haue levid, and of euery poynt bi himself askid how   665
she hadde rulid hir, and as wel of hire sustern, the which she
shuld haue gouerend also as hirself. And certayn she had litil
defens for hirself; for there þe fendis accusid hir, a[n]d said þat
she come to religion for pompe and pride, and forto haue
habundaunce of the worldes riches, and for ese of hire bodi,   670
and not for deuocion, mekenesse, and lownesse, as religious
men and women owght to do.

And þo the fendes said, 'It is wel knowen to God and to al
his angels of heven, and to men dwellyng in that contree where
she dwellid ynne, and all the fendes of hell, þat she was more   675
costluer in puler weryng, as of girdelles of siluer and overgilt,
and ringes on hir fingers, and siluers bokeles and overgilt on hir
shone; esy lieng in nyghtes, as it were [a quene] or an emprise
in the world, not daynyng hir forto arise to Goddis servis; and
with all dilicate metes and drinkes she was fedde.'   680

f. 148r And þan yn certayn, that nonne in gret / wepyng said, 'It is
wel knowen to owre lord Jhesu Criste, Goddis sone of heuen,
þat y [had] / scrift and ful repentaunce of al my misdedis done
bifore þat tyme; and in ful purpos was to leve my synne and
nice vaniteis an`d´ pride, and forto haue take me only to   685
Goddis seruice; ffor y know me gilti in gouernaunce, and
therfore y forsake his rightful iugement, and take me holy to
his grete mercy.'

668   and] ad,   677   siluers] em. siluer Kr,
678   a quene] *from* SA.   679   *Two or three letters erased after* not.
681   at *canc. after* nonne.   683   had] *from* SA.
684   *Minim canc. after* tyme.   687   gouu *canc. after* rightful.

And then þe besschopp sayd, 'Na, Wyllyam, thow may nat
abyde here now, bott loke þou be a gud man, and þou schall   625
cum hether; and loke þou aske nothynge of God þat may
dysplesse hym, for þat is a grett syne to þe to covytt to abyde
here ʒett, ffor þe behovys nedys to go agayne. And þou schall
see an examynacion of a prioresse, for hyr saule is cummyn
hether now to haue hyr jugement.'   630

And wyth þat þe besschoppe and all þe cumpany wentt
forthe vnto a hyghe hyll wher the savle was abydynge, and I
felowde after. And trevly þer were many fendes abowt þat
saule. And then on of þe monkys that cam wyth þe byschoppe
opynde a boke of all evyll dedes þat sche hade done, and sche   635
f. 125va was examynde how sche hade gouernyde / hyrselfe and hyr
coventt. And trevly, þer was a straytt examynacion, bott
sertenly, agayn hyr owne person he hade bott lytyll gylte. And
then þe fendys accusyde hyr and sayde þat sche cam to þe
religeon all for pomppe and pride, and forto have abundance of   640
wardely esee and riches, and nott for devocyon nor mekenes
and lawnes of hertt, as relygion askys to doo, bothe of men and
of wemen.

And ʒett sayde þe fendys that hytt is well knowne to God and
all þe angellys of hevyn, and to men dwellynge in þat cuntre   645
where sche wonnyde, and to all þe fendys of helle, þat sche
agayne hyr ordyr was of mysgouernance, in werynge of
pelleure, and gyrdyllys of syluer, and golde rynges on hyr
fyngyrs, and sylluer bokyllys on hyr schone; and lyggynge on
nyghttys lyke a quene or an emperyce, nothynge dessyrynge   650
bott eese and reste, and not rysyng on nyghttys to God seruice;
and wyth all delycate mettys and drynkys sche was fede.
f. 125vb 'Agayne, hytt / is well knoue to owre lorde Jhesu Crist
Goddys son of hevyn,' sche sayde, 'þat I hade schryfte and full
repentance of my mysdedys and my wykkydnes done before   655
thys tyme, and in ful purpasse was to leve my syne and all þe
vanytes of pride, and to haue takyn me hollely to Goddys
seruice. And for I know my gylte and mysgouernance, þerfor I
forsake hys ryghtwys jugement, and take me to hys mercy.'

628   behovys] s superscript.   633   fendes] n partially obliterated.
636   hyrselfe] erasure after hyr.   637   trevly] otiose stroke over y.
639   of canc. after hyr.

And þan þe bisshop enioyned hir to payne enduryng
evermore til þe day of dome, for þat she wol not forsake ne leve   690
hir pride and evel gouernaunce forto it forsoke hir, and þan sho
had no space of penaunce-doyng.

And þan þe bisshop lokid to me, and so dud al his company,
and þei saiden ful tenderly wepyng, 'Alas! þat worldly men will
not take hede in here hertes how moch kindenesse and mercy   695
God sheweth to hem, and do kindenesse aȝen kindenesse; but
thei do not so, for þei be evir rebell aȝenst þe wil of God, doyng
pride and al other synne; and therfore þe[i] shul haue ful
mychell woo, payn, and tribulacion, but þei amend hem.'

Than þe bisshop said to me, 'William, passe thow home in   700
`þe´ blissyng of God and myne, and say as þow hast herd and
seen to them þat þis bilongith to. And lyve rightfully and [þ]ow
shalt come to everlestyng ioy; and drede þe noght of thi way as
f. 148v   thow passist homewarde, for thow shalt / see none evil sprites
that shul disese the; thow shalt not faile of thi way.' And with   705
that y toke my leve. Anone y was at the dore where y went first
ynne. Wherfore al cristen men þat heryn or redyn this, I
beseche yow for the loue of God, þat ye haue me in yowre
praier, and ye shul be yn myne.
                          Explicit.   710

689   a *canc. after* bisshop.   698   þei] þe.
702   þow] yow, þow Kr (*without comment*).
706   a *canc. after* Anone *at beginning of a new line.*

And þer þe byschoppe domyd hyr to payne to þe day of   660
dome, and principally for sche wolde nat forsake synne, to syne
forsoke hyr, for then sche had no space of penance.

And then þe bisschoppe lokyd to me, and hys cumpany, and
all thay sayd wyth grett wepynge, 'Alas! alas! þat wardely men
wyl nat take hede wyth all ther myght, how mekyll kyndenes   665
and mercy owre lorde Jhesu Criste hase schewyde vnto all
vnkynde wrechys in erthe, that euery day feghttys agayn hym,
and agayn hys cummandementys, ande synnys in þe vij dedely
synnys in ther v inwyttys; weche vnkynde saulys be callyde
vnwytty, for ther wyttys turnys them to foly; ffor God ordende   670
them to gett them hevyn wyth them, and thay purches them
helle. For þer / <...

660   *Two (?)* letters erased before *payne.*
672   *In the bottom margin at the foot of f. 125vb* MS direction The leffe afor þe
kalender.

TRACTATUS
DE PURGATORIO SANCTI PATRICII

TRACTATUS DE PURGATORIO SANCTI PATRICII

f. 11ra *Incipit primus Liber Reuelationum*
De Purgatorio Patricii

Patri svo in Christo preoptato, domino .H. abbati de Sartis,
frater .H., monachorum de Saltereia minimus, cum continua
salute, patri [filius], obedientie munus.   5
   Iussistis, pater uenerande, ut scriptum uobis mitterem, quod
de Purgatorio in uestra me retuli audisse presentia. Quod
quidem eo libentius aggredior, quo ad id explendum paterni-
tatis uestre iussione instantius compellor. Licet enim utilitatem
multorum per me prouenire desiderem, non nisi iussus tamen   10
talia presumerem. Uestram uero minime lateat paternitatem
me numquam legisse quicquam uel audisse, unde in timore et
amore Dei tantum proficerem. Et quoniam beatum papam
Gregorium legimus multa dixisse de hiis, que erga animas fiunt
terrenis exutas, et corporali narratione plurima proposuisse, ut   15
et tristibus negligentium animos terreret et letis iustorum
affectum ad deuotionem inflammaret, fiducialius quod iubetis
ad profectum simplicium perficiam. In multis enim exemplis
que proponit ad exitum animarum angelorum bonorum siue
malorum presentiam adesse dicit, qui animas pro meritis uel ad   20
tormenta pertrahant uel ad requiem perducant. Sed et ipsas
animas, adhuc in corpore positas, ante exitum multa aliquando
de hiis, que uentura sunt super eas, siue ex responsione
conscientie interiori siue per reuelationes exterius factas prescisse fatetur. Raptas etiam et iterum ad corpora reductas   25
uisiones quasdam et reuelationes sibi factas narrare dicit siue
f. 11rb de tormentis impiorum seu de gaudiis iustorum / et in hiis

---

1   R *rubric* Incipit prefatio de purgatorio sancti Patricii; S *rubric* De loco
purgatorii in hibernia et de Milite quodam qui ibi diuersas penas pertulit.
3   .H.] S *reads* hugoni *in right-hand margin with insertion marks in red ink
and hand of rubricator.*
4   Saltereia] Salteria S.   5   filius] R, *om.* LS.
8   aggredior] faciam S (*over an erasure*);   quo] RS, quod L.
24–5   prescisse] *in* S *first* s *added above the line, in different ink (?),* precisse R.

tamen nichil nisi corporale uel corporibus simile recitasse:
flumina, flammas, pontes, naues, domos et nemora, prata,
flores, homines nigros uel candidos, et cetera qualia in hoc   30
mundo solent uel ad gaudium amari uel ad tormentum timeri;
se quoque, solutas corporibus, manibus trahi, pedibus duci,
collo suspendi, flagellari, precipitari et multa huiusmodi, que
nostre minime repugnant narrationi. Notum est autem multos
multociens quesisse qualiter anime a corporibus exeant, quo   35
pergant, quid inueniant, quid percipiant quidue sustineant.
Que, quia a nobis sunt abscondita, magis nobis sunt timenda
quam querenda. Quis enim umquam cum securitate in incerto
perrexit itinere? Hoc uero omnibus certum habetur quod uitam
bonam mors mala non sequitur. Et licet usque ad mortem   40
maneat meritum et post mortem reddatur premium, pena
tamen post mortem esse dicitur, que purgatoria nominatur, in
qua hii, qui in hac uita in quibusdam culpis, iusti tamen et ad
uitam eternam predestinati, uixerunt, ad tempus cruciabuntur,
ut purgentur. Vnde, quemadmodum a Deo corporales pene   45
dicuntur preparate, ita ipsis penis loca corporalia, in quibus
sunt, dicuntur esse distincta. Creduntur tamen tormenta maxima, ad que culpa deorsum premit, `in´ imo esse, et maxima
[uero] gaudia, ad que sursum per iusticiam ascenditur, in
summo; in medio autem bona esse et mala [media]; quod et   50
hu`i´c uidetur congruere narrationi. Et quidem infernus subtus
terram uel infra terre concauitatem quasi carcer et ergastulum
f. 11va   tenebrarum a quibusdam esse creditur, narra/-tione ista ni-
chilominus asseritur. Et quod paradysus in oriente et in terra
sit, narratio ista ostendit, ubi fidelium anime, a penis pur-   55
gatoriis liberate, dicuntur aliquandiu morari iocunde. Dicit
uero beatus Augustinus animas defunctorum post mortem
usque ad ultimam resurrectionem abditis receptaculis con-
tineri, sicut unaqueque digna est, uel in requiem uel in
erumpnam. Quod et beatus Augustinus et beatus Gregorius   60
incorporeos spiritus dicunt pena corporalis ignis posse cruciari,
ista uidentur etiam affirmari narratione. In pena uero purgatoria, qua post exitum purgantur electi, certum est alios aliis
plus minusue pro meritis cruciari; que quidem ab hominibus
non possunt diffiniri, quia ab eis minime possunt sciri. Ab eis   65

29   et] om. R.   34   repugnant] pugnant S.   37   a] om. RS.
38   cum] in S.   45   corporales] om. S.   47   sunt] sint W.
48   in] in different ink, om. R;   et] om. RS.   49   uero] RS, om. L.
50   oooo] om. R¡ media] W, om. LRS.
51   congruere uidetur R, congrue uidetur S;   quidem] quod W.
54   oriente / terra] inverted S.
62   uidentur] uidetur W.   64   que] Quod R.

tamen, quorum anime a corporibus exeunt et iterum iubente
Deo ad corpora redeunt, signa quedam corporalibus similia ad
demonstrationem spiritualium nuntiantur, quia, nisi in talibus
et per talia ab animabus corporibus exutis uiderentur, nullo
modo ab eisdem, ad corpora reuersis, in corpore uiuentibus et   70
corporalia tantum scientibus, intimarentur. Vnde et in hac
narratione a corporali et mortali homine spiritalia dicuntur
uideri quasi in specie et forma corporali. Quis uero eam mihi
retulerit et quomodo eam agnouerit, in fine narrationis in-
dicabo. Quam quidem narrationem, si bene memini, ita   75
exorsus est.

De Purgatorio Patricii

Dicitur `Magnus´ sanctus Patricius, qui a primo est secundus.
Qui dum in Hybernia uerbum Dei predicaret atque miraculis
f. 11vb gloriosis chorus/-caret, studuit bestiales hominum illius patrie   80
animos terrore tormentorum infernalium a malo reuocare et
paradysi gaudiorum promissione in bonum confirmare. 'Eos
uero', inquit relator horum, 'bestiales esse, ueraciter et ipse
comperi. Cum enim essem in patria illa, accessit ad me uir
quidam ante Pascha cano quidem capite et etate decrepita,   85
dicens se corporis et sanguinis Christi numquam percepisse
sacramentum et in illo die proximo Pasche se tanti sacramenti
uelle fieri participem. Et, quoniam uidebat me et monachum
esse et sacerdotem, mihi per confessionem uitam suam mani-
festare curauit, quatinus ad tantum sacramentum securius pos-   90
set accedere. Et quoniam illius patrie linguam ignoraui, interpretem mihi adhibens, eius confessionem recepi. Qui cum
finem confessionis sue faceret, ipsum per interpretem inter-
rogaui, si `hominem´ umquam interfecisset. Qui respondit se
pro certo nescire si plures quam quinque tantum homines   95
interfecisset. Ita dixit paruipendens et quasi satis innocens
esset in eo quod tam paucos occidisset. Multos uero a se
uulneratos asseruit, de quibus ignorauit si inde obierint an non.
Putabat enim homicidium esse non peccatum dampnabile. Cui
cum dicerem grauissimum hoc esse peccatum et in hoc creato-   100
rem suum dampnabiliter offendisse, quicquid illi pro peccatorum suorum absolutione preciperem, gratanter suscipere et
absque ulla retractacione uelle se perficere respondit. Habent
enim hoc quasi naturaliter homines illius patrie ut, sicut sunt

---

77   R *rubric* Incipit de purgatorio sancti Patricii; S *rubric* De sancto Patricio.
89   esse *follows* sacerdotem RS.   94   unquam hominem RS.
96   innocens satis RS.   99   dampnabile] dapnabile R.
103 retractacione] retractione RL.

alterius gentis hominibus per ignorantiam proniores ad malum,   105
ita, dum se errasse cognouerint, promptiores et stabiliores sunt
ad penitendum.' Hec ideo proposui ut eorum ostenderem
bestialitatem.

De Purgatorio Patricii

Igitur, cum beatus Patricius, ut predixi, gentem prefatam et   110
terrore tormentorum et amore gaudiorum ab errore conuertere
uoluisset, dicebant se ad Christum numquam conuersuros nec
f. 12ra pro miraculis que / per eum uidebant fieri nec per eius
predicationem, nisi aliquis eorum et tormenta illa malorum et
gaudia bonorum posset intueri, quatinus rebus uisis certiores   115
fierent quam promissis. Beatus uero Patricius, Deo deuotus,
etiam tunc pro salute populi deuotior in uigiliis, ieiuniis et
orationibus atque operibus bonis effectus est. Et quidem, dum
talibus pro salute populi intenderet bonis, pius dominus Ihesus
Christus ei uisibiliter apparuit, dans ei textum ewangeliorum et   120
baculum unum, que hucusque pro magnis de pretiosis reliquiis
in Hybernia, ut dignum est, uenerantur. Idem autem baculum
pro eo, quod illum dominus Ihesus dilecto suo Patricio con-
tulit, baculus Ihesu cognominatus est. Quicumque uero in
patria illa summus fuerit archiepiscopus, hec habebit, id est   125
textum et baculum, quasi pro signo summi presulatus illius
patrie. Sanctum uero Patricium Dominus in locum desertum
eduxit, et unam fossam rotundam et intrinsecus obscuram
ibidem ei ostendit, dicens, quia quisquis ueraciter penitens
uera fide armatus fossam eandem ingressus unius diei ac noctis   130
spacio moram in ea faceret, ab omnibus purgaretur tocius uite
sue peccatis, sed et per illam transiens non solum uisurus esset
tormenta malorum uerum etiam, si in fide constanter egisset,
gaudia beatorum. Sicque ab oculis eius Domino disparente
iocunditate spirituali repletus est beatus Patricius tam pro   135
Domini sui apparitione quam pro fosse illius ostensione, per
quam sperabat populum ab errore conuersurum. Statimque in
eodem loco ecclesiam construxit et beati patris Avgustini
canonicos uitam apostolicam `sectantes´ in ea constituit. Fos-
sam autem predictam, que in cimiterio est extra frontem   140
ecclesie orientalem, muro circumdedit et ianuas serasque apposuit, ne quis eam ausu temerario et sine licentia ingredi
presumeret. Clauem uero custodiendam commendauit priori
eiusdem ecclesie.

---

121   de] et W.   123   Patricio suo S.   124   Ihesu] Ihesus RS.
128   et (1)] om. RS.   129   ostendit ei S.   135   spirituali] spiritali RS.

. 12rb / Ipsius autem beati patris tempore multi penitentia ducti 145
fossam ingressi sunt, qui regredientes et tormenta se maxima
perpessos et gaudia se uidisse testati sunt. Quorum relationes
iussit beatus Patricius in eadem ecclesia notari. Eorum ergo
attestacione ceperunt alii beati Patricii predicationem suscipere. Et quoniam ibidem homo a peccatis purgatur, locus ille 150
Purgatorium sancti Patricii nominatur. Locus autem ecclesie
Reglis dicitur.

Item de Purgatorio Patricii
Post obitum sancti Patricii erat prior quidam in eadem ecclesia,
uir quidem sancte conuersationis, ita decrepitus ut pre sen- 155
ectute non haberet in capite nisi tantummodo dentem unum.
Et, sicut beatus Gregorius dicit, 'Licet senex sit sanus, ipsa
tamen senectute sua semper est infirmus,' uir iste, ne senectutis
sue infirmitate uideretur aliis inferre molestiam, iuxta
canonicorum dormitorium parari sibi fecit cellulam. Porro 160
iuniores fratres senem uisitantes sepe ex amore iocando dicere
consueuerant, 'Quamdiu, pater, in hac uita uis morari? Quando
uis hinc abire?' Et ille, 'Mallem,' inquit, 'fili, hinc abire potius
quam ita uiuere. Fiat uoluntas Dei! Hic enim non sentio nisi
miseriam. Alibi uero magnam habebo gloriam.' Porro illi 165
canonici in cella senis angelos audiebant a dormitorio suo
sepius circa eum cantantes. Cantus autem eorum hunc habebat
modum: 'Beatus es tu, et beatus est dens qui est in ore tuo,
quem nunquam tetigit cibus delectabilis!' Eius enim cibus erat
sal et panis siccus, potus autem eius aqua frigida. Qui tandem, 170
ut optauit, feliciter ad Dominum migrauit.

f. 12va Hoc autem sciendum / quod et tempore sancti Patricii et aliis
postea temporibus multi homines Purgatorium intrauerunt,
quorum alii reuersi sunt, alii in ipso perierunt. Redeuntium
uero narrationes a canonicis eiusdem loci scripto mandantur. 175
Est autem consuetudo, tam a sancto Patricio quam ab eius
successoribus constituta, ut Purgatorium illud nullus introeat
nisi qui ab episcopo, in cuius est episcopio, licentiam habeat et
qui propria uoluntate illud intrare pro peccatis suis eligat. Qui
dum ad episcopum uenerit et ei propositum suum manifes- 180
tauerit, prius eum hortatur episcopus a tali proposito desistere,
dicens quia multi illud introierunt qui nunquam redierunt. Si
uero perseuerauerit, perceptis episcopi litteris ad locum fest-
inat. Quas cum prior loci illius legerit, mox eidem homini

154 obitum] obitum autem RS.　　　157 Et] Et quia W.
158 est semper S.　　163 inquit] *om.* RS.　　164 ita] ita diu W.
168 dens] deus R.　　175 uero] autem RS.

Purgatorium intrare dissuadeat et ut aliam penitentiam eligat   185
diligenter ammoneat, ostendens ei in eo multorum periculum.
Quodsi perseuerauerit, introducit [eum] in ecclesiam, ut in ea
.xv. diebus ieiuniis uacet et orationibus. Quibus peractis
conuocat [prior] uicinum clerum, maneque missa celebrata
munitur penitens sacra communione et aqua ad idem officium   190
benedicta aspergitur sicque cum processione et letania ad
ostium Purgatorii deducitur. Prior autem iterum infestacionem
demonum et multorum in eadem fossa perditionem, ostium ei
coram omnibus aperiens, denuntiat. Si uero constans in proposito fuerit, percepta ab omnibus sacerdotibus benedictione et   195
omnium se commendans orationibus propriaque manu fronti
sue signum crucis inprimens, ingreditur, moxque a priore
ostium obseratur, sicque processio ad ecclesiam reuertitur, que
f. 12vb   die altera iterum mane de ecclesia ad os/-tium fosse ingreditur,
ostiumque a priore aperitur. Et si homo reuersus fuerit, cum   200
gaudio in ecclesiam deducitur, in qua aliis quindecim diebus
uigiliis et orationibus intentus moratur. Quod si die altera
eadem hora reuersus non apparuerit, certissimi de eius perditione, ostio a priore obserato, uniuersi recedunt.

Item de Purgatorio Patricii   205
Contigit autem hiis temporibus nostris, diebus scilicet regis
Stephani, militem quemdam nomine Owein, de quo presens est
narratio, ad episcopum, in cuius episcopatu prefatum est
Purgatorium, confessionis gratia uenire. Quem cum pro peccatis increparet episcopus Deumque offendisse grauiter diceret,   210
intima contritione cordis ingemuit seque condignam penitentiam acturum ad episcopi libitum deuouit. Cumque ei episcopus
penitentiam secundum peccati modum iniungere uoluisset,
respondit, 'Dum, ut asseris, factorem meum in tantum offen-
sum habeam, penitentiam omnibus penitentiis grauiorem as-   215
sumam. Vt enim remissionem peccatorum accipere merear,
Purgatorium sancti Patricii te precipiente ingrediar.' Episcopus
autem hoc ei presumere dissuasit, sed uirilis animi miles
episcopi dissuasioni non consensit. Episcopus uero quam pluri-
mam in Purgatorio perdicionem, ut eum ab hac auerteret   220

185   dissuadeat] dissuadet W.   186   ammoneat] ammonet R.
187   eum] R, *om.* LS.
189   prior] RS, *om.* L.   190   et] *om.* S.   191   aspergitur] aspergatur RS.
199   ingreditur] regreditur R.   205   S *rubric* De Milite.
210   Deumque] illumque RS, grauiter offendisse R; illumque grauiter Deum
offendisse W.
219   Episcopus] Epc (*final letter written over the first of two partially erased
minims*);   uero] *om.* S.   220   Purgatorio] eo RS.

intentione, narrauit; sed uere penitentis et uere militis animum
nullo terrore flectere potuit. Admonuit episcopus ut monachorum uel canonicorum susciperet habitum. Miles uero respondit hoc se nulla ratione facturum, donec prefatum intrasset
Purgatorium. Episcopus igitur, illius uidens penitudinis con-   225
stantiam, misit per ipsum epistolam illius loci priori, quatinus
eundem penitentem secundam penitentium morem in Purgatorium intromitteret. Quo cum peruenisset, cognita ipsius
13ra causa, ei plurimorum perditionem periculumque pro/-posuit,
ut eius animum ab hac intentione reuocaret. Miles uero, se   230
grauiter offendisse Deum reminiscens et uere penitens, feruore
penitudinis uicit suasionem prioris. Prior igitur eum in
ecclesiam intromisit, in qua secundum morem quindecim
diebus ieiuniis et orationibus uacauit. Quibus expletis a fratribus et a uicino clero, sicut supradictum est, ad Purgatorium   235
ducitur, ubi iterum enumeratis tormentorum intolerabilium
generibus dissuasum est ei a priore huiusmodi subire penam.
Milite uero constanter in proposito permanente hoc a priore
dictum accepit, 'Ecce nunc in nomine Domini intrabis, tamdiu
per concauitatem subterraneam iturus, donec exeas in campum   240
unum, in qu[ó] aulam unam inuenies mira arte fabricatam.
Quam cum intraueris, statim ex parte Dei nuntios habebis, qui
tibi quid facturus es uel passurus diligenter exponent. Illis
autem exeuntibus et te solo in ea remanente statim temptatores
accedent. Sic enim habetur euenisse hiis qui ante te intro-   245
ierunt. Tu uero in Christi fide constans esto.' Miles autem
uirilem in pectore gerens animum, quod alios audiuit absorbu-
isse, periculum non formidat. Et qui quondam ferro munitus
pugnis interfuit hominum, modo, ferro durior, fide, spe, et
iusticia, de Dei misericordia presumens, ornatus, confidenter   250
ad pugnam prorumpit demonum. Primo namque se commen-
dans omnium orationibus et dextera eleuata fronti sue inprimens sancte crucis signaculum, confidenter hilariterque per
portam intrauit. Quam prior statim de foris obserauit et cum
processione ad ecclesiam rediit.   255
    Miles itaque nouam et inusitatam cupiens exercere militiam,
pergit audacter, licet solus, ac diutius, confidens in Domino,
per foueam. Ingrauescentibus magis magisque tenebris, lucem
amisit in breui tocius claritatis. Tandem ex aduerso lux paruula

---

221   uere (2)] *followed by* confessi *inserted above the line in different ink* S.
226   ipsum] illum S.   232   suasionem] dissuasionem W.
232–3   eum *follows* ecclesiam S.   235   supradictum] supra scriptum RS.
241   unum] *om.* W;   quo] W, qua LRS.   245   accedent] RS, accedunt L.
246   fide Christi R.   256   exercere cupiens R; miliciam exercere cupiens S.

f. 13rb cepit eunti per foueam tenuiter lucere. / Nec mora ad campum   260
predictum peruenit et aulam. Lux autem ibi non apparuit nisi
qualis hic in hyeme solet apparere post solis occasum. Aula
uero non habebat parietem integrum, sed columpnis et archiolis erat undique constructa in modum claustri monachorum.
Cumque circa aulam diutius ambulasset eius mirabilem mir-   265
ando structuram, ingressus est in eam, infra cuius septa uidit
eam multo mirabiliorem. Sedit itaque in aula aliquandiu,
oculos huc illucque iactans, eius apparatum et pulcritudinem
satis ammirans. Cumque solus aliquandiu sedisset, ecce quindecim uiri quasi religiosi et nuper rasi, albis uestibus amicti,   270
domum intrauerunt et, salutantes illum in nomine ‘Domini’,
consederunt. Et, tacentibus aliis, unus cum eo loquebatur, qui
quasi prior et eorum dux esse uidebatur, dicens, 'Benedictus sit
omnipotens Deus, qui in corde tuo bonum confirmauit propositum et ipse in te perficiat bonum quod incepit. Et quoniam   275
ad Purgatorium uenisti, ut a peccatis tuis purgeris, aut uiriliter
agere ex necessitate compelleris aut pro inertia, quod absit, et
anima et corpore peribis. Mox enim, ut egressi fuerimus,
replebitur inmundorum spirituum domus ista, qui tibi grauia
inferent tormenta et inferre minabuntur grauiora. Ad portam,   280
qua intrasti, te illesum ducturos, si eis ut reuertaris assenseris,
promittent, conantes si uel hoc modo te decipere possint. Et si
quolibet modo, uel tormentorum afflictione uictus uel minis
territus seu promissis deceptus, illis assensum prebueris, et
corpore et anima pariter, ut dixi, peribis. Si uero firmiter in   285
f. 13va fide spem totam in Domino / posueris, ita ut nec tormentis nec
minis nec promissis eorum cesseris, sed constanter quasi
nichilum contempseris, non solum a peccatis omnibus pur-
gaberis, uerum etiam tormenta, que preparantur peccatoribus,
et requiem, in qua iusti letantur, uidebis. Deum semper habeas   290
in memoria, et cum te cruciauerint, inuoca Dominum Ihesum
Christum. Per inuocationem etenim huius nominis statim a
tormento liberaberis. Tecum autem non possumus hic morari
diutius, sed omnipotenti Deo te commendamus.' Sicque, data
benedictione uiro, recesserunt ab eo. Miles itaque, ad noui   295
generis militiam instructus, qui quondam uiriliter oppugnabat
homines, iam presto est uiriliter certare contra demones. Armis

261   apparuit] apparuerit S (i *in different ink*).
263   parietem non habebat RS.
269   Cumque] Cum RS;   sedisset aliquamdiu S.   270   amicti] induti S.
271   Domini] *added by later* (?) *hand in margin.*   276   purgeris tuis S.
279   spirituum immundorum R.   293   autem] enim RS.

igitur Christi munitus exspectat quis eum demonum ad certamen primo prouocet. Justicie lorica induitur; spe uictorie salutisque eterne mens, ut capud galea, redimitur; scuto fidei protegitur. Habet etiam gladium spiritus, quod est uerbum Dei, deuote uidelicet inuocans Dominum Ihesum Christum, ut eum regio munimine tueatur, ne ab aduersariis infestantibus superetur. Nec enim eum Domini pietas fefellit, que confidentes in se fallere nescit.

De Purgatorio Patricii
Miles igitur, ut dictum est, cum in domo solus sederet, animo inpauido demonum pugnam exspectans subito circa domum cepit audiri tumultus, ac si totus commoueretur orbis. Etenim si omnes homines et omnia animantia terre, maris et aeris toto conanime pariter tumultuarent, ut ei uidebatur, maiorem tumultum non facerent. Vnde, nisi diuina uirtute protegeretur et a uiris predictis commodius instrueretur, ipso tumultu amentaretur.

De Purgatorio Patricii
| Et ecce post horrorem talis auditus sequitur [horribilior] demonum uisibilis aspectus. Visibiliter etenim undique cepit innumera multitudo demonum formarum deformium in domum irruere, cachinnando ac deridendo illum salutare et quasi per obprobrium dicere, 'Alii homines qui nobis seruiunt non nisi post mortem ad nos ueniunt. Unde tibi maiorem mercedem recompensare debemus, quod societatem nostram, cui studiose deseruisti, in tantum honorare uoluisti, ut, sicut alii, diem mortis nolueris exspectare, sed uiuendo corpus tuum et animam simul nobis tradere. Vt maiorem a nobis remunerationem acciperes, hoc fecisti. Recipies ergo a nobis habundanter qu[e] meruisti. Huc enim uenisti, ut pro peccatis tuis tormenta sustineres: habebis igitur nobiscum quod queris, pressuras uidelicet et dolores. Verumptamen pro eo quod hactenus nobis seruieris, si nostris adquiescendo consiliis reuerti uolueris, hoc tibi pro munere faciemus quod ad portam, qua intrasti, illesum te ducemus, quatinus uiuens adhuc in mundo gaudeas, ne totum quod suaue est corpori tuo funditus amittas.' Hec ei promiserunt, quia aut terrore aut blanditiis eum decipere uoluerunt. Sed uerus miles Christi nec terrore concutitur nec

300

305

310

315

. 13vb

320

325

330

335

298 quis] qui S. 304 enim] *om.* R; eum] *om.* S; pietas Domini S.
309 si ac R; commoueretur] commeueretur R, *with first* e *erased.*
316 horribilior] RS, *om.* L. 327 que] RW, quod LS.
328 igitur] ergo S. 334 quia] qui S.

blandimento seducitur. Eodem enim animo et terrentes con-
tempnebat et blandientes, nichil penitus respondens.

De Purgatorio Patricii

Demones igitur, a milite se contempni cernentes, horribiliter
fremebant in eum struxeruntque in eadem domo maximi   34c
incendii rogum, ligatisque manibus ac pedibus militem in
ignem proiecerunt uncisque ferreis huc illucque per incendium
clamantes traxerunt. Primo igitur missus in ignem graue sensit
tormentum. Sed uir Dei, tam regis sui munimine septus quam
a prefatis uiris nuper instructus, arm[a] militie spiritalis nequa-   34£
f. 14ra quam oblitus est. / Cum enim aduersarii eum in incendio
torrerent, pii Ihesu nomen inuocauit statimque de illo incendio
utpote de primo eorum assultu liberatus est. Inuocato enim
piissimi saluatoris nomine dicto citius ita extinctus est tocius
rogus incendii, ut nec scintilla inueniretur ipsius. Quod dum   35c
miles cerneret, audatior effectus est, constanter animo pro-
ponens eos deinceps non formidare, quos ad inuocationem
sancti nominis tam facile conspicit se posse euincere.

De Purgatorio Patricii

Relinquentes igitur demones domum, cum eiulatu et horrido   35£
tumultu secum traxerunt militem. Egredientes uero alii ab aliis
discesserunt. Quidam autem eorum militem per uastam regionem diutius traxerunt. Nigra erat terra et regio tenebrosa, nec
quicquam preter demones qui eum traxerunt uidit in ea.
Ventus quidem urens ibi flauit qui uix audiri potuit, sed tamen   36c
sui rigiditate corpus suum uidebatur perforare. Traxerunt
autem illum uersus fines illos ubi sol oritur in media estate.
Cumque illuc euntes uenissent quasi in fine mundi, ceperunt
de[xtr]orsum conuerti et per uallem latissimam contra austrum
tendere, scilicet uersus locum quo sol oritur media hyeme.   365
Illucque diuertendo cepit quasi uulgi tocius terre miserrimos
clamores et eiulatus et fletus audire, et quo magis appropiauit,
eo clarius clamores eorum et fletus audiuit.

De Purgatorio Patricii

Tandem itaque tractu demonum in latissimum et longissimum   37c
peruenit miles campum miseriis ac dolore plenum. Finis autem

338   S *rubric* De demonibus.
343   Primo igitur] Primitus ergo R, Primus ergo S.
344   uir] ubi R.   345   arma] W, armis LRS.   346   in] *om* S
348   eorum] illorum S.   350   incendii rogus RS.
353   euincere posse RS.   364   dextrorsum] R, deorsum LS.
370–1   in *follows* miles RS;   et longissimum] longissimumque RS.

illius campi pre nimia longitudine non potuit a milite uideri.
Ille itaque campus hominibus utriusque sexus [diuerseque]
etatis in terra iacentibus nudis plenus erat, qui, uentre ad
f. 14rb terram uerso, clauis ferreis candentibus / per manus pedesque   375
defixis in terra extendebantur. Hii uero aliquando pre dolore
uidebantur terram comedere, aliquando autem cum fletu et
eiulatu miserabiliter clamare, 'Parce! Parce!' uel 'Miserere!
Miserere!' Sed non erat in loco qui misereri nosset aut parcere.
Demones enim inter eos et super eos uidebantur discurrere,   380
qui non cessabant flagris eos dirissimis cedere. Dicunt ei
demones, 'Hec tormenta que uides sentiendo experieris, si
nostris non adquieueris consiliis: hoc est, ut a proposito cesses
et reuertaris. Quod si uolueris, ad portam per quam uenisti te
pacifice ducentes illesum te abire permittemus.' Hoc autem eo   385
renuente, prostrauerunt eum in terram et clauis eum trans-
figere conati sunt. Sed, inuocato Ihesu nomine, nichil in eo
conanime profecerunt.

De Purgatorio Patricii

Igitur ab illo campo recedentes traxerunt militem ad alium   390
campum, maiori miseria plenum. Iste itidem campus hominibus utriusque sexus [diuerseque] etatis clauis in terra fixis
erat plenus. Istos inter autem et alterius campi miseros hec erat
diuersitas, quod illorum quidem uentres, istorum dorsa terre
herebant. Dracones igniti super alios sedebant et quasi   395
c[om]edentes illos modo miserabili dentibus ignitis lacerabant.
Aliorum autem colla uel brachia uel totum corpus serpentes
igniti circumcingebant et, capita sua pectoribus miserorum
inprimentes, ignitum aculeum oris sui in cordibus eorum
infigebant. Buffones etiam mire magnitudinis et quasi ignei   400
uidebantur super quorundam pectora sedere et, rostra sua
deformia infigentes, quasi eorum corda conarentur extrahere.
Qui ita fixi et afflicti a fletu et eiulatu nunquam cessabant. /
f. 14va Demones etiam inter eos et super eos transcurrentes flagris eos
uehementer cedendo cruciabant. Finis huius campi pre sui   405
longitudine uideri non potuit nisi in latitudine, qua intrauit et

---

373   diuerseque] W, et LRS.   374   uentre] RS, uentrem L.
377   comedere] commedere.
378–9   clamare *follows one* miserere R, *and follows second* miserere S.
381   dirissimis] durissimis W.   386   et] et sicut R, et sicut alios W.
391   campum] *om.* RS.   392   diuerseque] W, et LRS.
393   Istos inter autem] Inter istos tamen RS.
396   comedentes] W, cedentes LRS; ignitis lacerabant] *written over an*
erasure and extends into the right-hand margin.

exiuit; in transuersum enim campos pertransiuit. 'Hec,' inquiunt demones, 'que uides tormenta patieris, nisi ut reuertaris
assenseris.' Cumque eos contempsisset, conati sunt, sicut et
superius, clauis eum figere, sed non potuerunt, audito Ihesu   410
nomine.

De Purgatorio Patricii
Transeuntes igitur inde duxerunt demones militem in tercium
campum miseriis plenum. Iste etenim campus hominibus
utriusque sexus [diuerseque] etatis plenus erat, qui ita in   415
terram clauis ferreis candentibusque fixi iacebant ut pre multi-
tudine clauorum a summitate capitum usque ad digitos pedum
locus uacuus non inueniretur quantus digiti unius summitate
tegeretur. Isti uero uix uocem ad clamandum formare
potuerunt, sed, sicut homines qui morti proximi sunt, ita   420
utcunque uocem emiserunt. Nudi et isti, sicut ceteri, uidebantur et uento frigido et urente flagrisque demonum cruciabantur. 'Hec,' inquiunt demones, 'tormenta patieris, si nobis ut
reuertaris, non assenseris.' Et cum eum, contempnentem
eorum comminationes, figere uoluissent, inuocauit nomen   425
Ihesu Christi nec quicquam amplius ei ibidem facere
potuerunt.

De Purgatorio Patricii
Hinc ergo militem trahentes, peruenerunt in quartum campum
multis ignibus plenum, in quo omnia genera inuenta sunt   430
tormentorum. Alii suspendebantur cathenis igneis per pedes,
alii per manus, alii per capillos, alii per brachia, alii per tibias,
capitibus ad ima uersis et sulphureis flammis inmersis. Alii in
f. 14vb ignibus pende/-bant, uncis ferreis in oculis fixis, uel auribus,
uel naribus, uel faucibus, uel mamillis, aut genitalibus. Alii   435
fornacibus sulphureis cremabantur; alii quasi super sartagines
urebantur. Alii uerubus igneis transfixi ad ignem assabantur,
quos demonum alii uertunt, alii diuersis metallis liquescentibus
deguttauerunt, quos tamen omnes discurrentes demones flagris
ciciderunt. Omnia genera tormentorum que excogitari possunt   440
ibidem uisa sunt. Ibi etiam uidit quosdam de suis quondam
sociis et eos bene cognouit. Eiulatus et clamores miserorum et

---

408 nisi] nisi nobis W.   410 eum] *om.* RS.
415 diuerseque] W, et LRS.
421 utcunque] ?uirum S; emiserunt uocem S.
424 eum, contempnentem] eo contempnente S.
425 comminationes] commonitiones W; figere] trans *interlined before in
different ink.*   426 ibidem ei RS.
430–1 tormentorum sunt inuenta S.   436 sartagines] cartagines S.

fletus quos audiuit nulla sufficit hominum exprimere lingua.
Hii autem campi non solum crutiatis hominibus, sed etiam
pleni erant excrutiantibus demonibus. Cumque illum ibidem   445
torquere uoluissent, inuocato Ihesu Christi nomine mansit
illesus.

De Purgatorio Patricii

Cumque transissent inde, apparuit ante eos rota ignea mire
magnitudinis, cuius radii et c'h´anti uncis igneis erant undique   450
circumsepti, in quibus singuli homines infixi pendebant. Huius
dum rote medietas sursum in aere stabat, alia medietas in terra
deorsum mergebatur. Flamma uero tetri sulphureique incendii
de terra circa rotam surgebat et in ea pendentes miserrime
torrebat. 'Hoc,' inquiunt demones, 'qu[od] isti patiuntur   455
patieris, nisi reuerti uolueris. Que tamen tolerant, prius uidebis.' Demones igitur ex utraque parte alii contra alios uectes
ferreos inter rote radios inp[in]gentes, eam tanta agilitate
rotarunt ut in ea pendentium omnino nullum ab alio uisu
posset discernere, quia pre nimia celeritate cursus sui uide-   460
batur circulus igneus integer esse. Cumque iactassent militem
super rotam et in aerem rotando leuassent, inuocato Christi
nomine descendit illesus.

De Purgatorio Patricii

Procedentes igitur inde cum milite demones traxerunt eum   465
f. 15ra uersus domum unam / grandem horribiliter fumigantem, cuius
latitudo nimia fuit, longitudo uero tanta ut illius non poss[i]t
ultima uidere. Cum autem adhuc ab ea aliquantum longius
essent, pre nimio calore, qui inde exibat, substitit, procedere
formidans. Dixerunt ergo ei demones, 'Quid tardas? Bal-   470
nearium est quod uides. Velis nolis illuc usque progredieris; in
eo cum ceteris balneabis.' Ceperunt autem de domo illa
miserrimi fletus et planctus audiri. Introductus autem domum
uidit diram uisionem et horrendam. Etenim domus illius
pauimentum fossis rotundis erat plenum, que sibi inuicem ita   475
coherebant ut uix inter eas aut nullatenus iri potuisset. Erant
autem fosse singule metallis diuersis ac liquoribus feruentibus
plene, in quibus utriusque sexus et 'diuerse´ etatis mergebatur
hominum multitudo non minima. Quorum alii omnino erant

---

450 chanti] canti RS.   451   singuli] singulis W.   455   quod] W, que LRS.
458 inpingentes   ]   impingentes   W,   inpuggentes   L,   impungentes   R,
inpungentes S;   tanta] tante S.
461 militem] eum RS.   466   uersus] uersum R.
467 possit] RW, posset LS.   472   balneabis] balneaberis W.
473 domum] in domum W.   478   diuerse] in different hand, om. RS.

inmersi, [alii usque ad supercilia], alii ad oculos, alii ad labia,   480
alii ad colla, alii ad pectus, alii ad umbilicum, alii ad femora,
alii ad genua, alii ad tibias; alii uno pede tantum tenebantur,
alii utraque manu uel una tantummodo. Omnes pariter pre
dolore plangentes clamabant et flebant. 'Ecce,' inquiunt demones, 'cum istis balneabis.' Subleuantesque militem conati   485
sunt eum in unam fossarum proicere. Sed audito Christi
nomine defecerunt in suo conanime.

De Purgatorio Patricii
Recedentes autem a loco illo perrexerunt contra montem
unum, in quo utriusque sexus et diuerse etatis super digitos   490
pedum curuatam tantam uidit sedere multitudinem nudorum
hominum quod pauci uiderentur ei omnes quos ante uiderat.
Hii omnes, quasi mortem cum tremore prestolantes, uersus
aquilonem intendebant. Cumque miles miraretur quid hec
misera multitudo prestolaretur, ait unus demonum ad eum,   495
f. 15rb   'Forte miraris quid / cum tanto timore populus hic exspectat.
[Nisi nobis consentiens reuerti uolueris, scies quid tam treme-
bundus expectat.]' Vix demon uerba finierat, et ecce ab aqui-
lone uentus turbinis ueniebat, qui et ipsos demones et quem
duxerunt militem totumque populum illum arripuit et in   500
quoddam flumen fetidum ac frigidissimum flentem ac miserabiliter eiulantem longe in aliam montis partem proiecit, in
quo inestimabili frigore uexabantur. Et cum niterentur de
aquis emergere, currentes demones super aquas eos incessanter
inmerser[u]nt. At miles, adiutoris sui non immemor, nomen   505
ipsius reclamans, in alia ripa se sine mora repperit.

De Purgatorio Patricii
Necdum militis Christi demones iniuria saciati, accedentes
traxerunt eum contra austrum. Et ecce uidit ante se flammam
teterrimam et sulphureo fetore putentem quasi de puteo   510
quodam ascendere et quasi homines nudos et igneos utriusque
sexus et etatis diuerse sicut scintillas ignis sursum in aere
iactari, qui et, flammarum ui deficiente, reciderunt iterum in
puteo et igne. Quo approximantes dixerunt militi demones,

480   alii ... supercilia] R, *om.* LS;   oculos] occulos L.
482   tantum pede R.
485   balneabis] balneaberis W;   Subleuantesque] Subleuantes S.
486   Iesu *interlined in different ink before* Christi.   494   miraretur miles RS.
495   eum] illum R.   497 8   Nisi ... expectat] RS, *om.* L; exspectat S.
500   illum] *om.* S.   501   ac (2)] et RS.
505   inmerserunt] immerserunt R, inmerserant L, ?ibi merserunt S *with* ibi
mers *over an erasure.*   514   approximantes] approximante R.

'Iste flammiuomus puteus inferni est introitus. Hic est habi-   515
tacio nostra. Et quoniam nobis hucusque seruisti, hic sine fine
nobiscum manebis. Omnes enim qui nobis seruiunt hic sine
fine nobiscum manebunt. Quo si semel intraueris, in eternum
et anima et corpore peribis. Si tamen nobis consenseris, illesus
ad propria remeare poteris.' Illo uero de Dei auxilio pre-   520
sumente illorumque promissa spernente, precipitauerunt se
demones in puteum, trahentes secum militem. Et quo profun-
dius descendit, eo latiorem puteum inuenit, sed et grauiorem
. 15va penam pertulit. Adeo namque fuit intolerabi/-lis ut pene sui
saluatoris sit oblitus nominis. Deo tamen inspirante rediens ad   525
se, ut potuit, nomen Domini Ihesu Christi clamauit. Statimque
uis flamme cum reliquis sursum eum in aerem proiecit. De-
scendensque iuxta puteum solus aliquandiu stetit. Cumque se
ab ore putei subtrahens stetisset, ignorans quo se uerteret,
egressi sunt alii demones de puteo, `ab´ eo, ut ita dixerim,   530
ignoti. Qui dixerunt ei, 'Quid ibi stas? Quod hic esset infernus,
tibi dixerunt socii nostri. Mentiti sunt. Consuetudinis nostre
semper est mentiri, ut quos non possumus per uerum fallamus
per mendacium. Non est h[i]c infernus, sed nunc ad infernum
te ducemus.'   535

De Purgatorio Patricii
Inde igitur trahentes militem cum magno tumultu et horribili
peruenerunt ad flumen quoddam latissimum et fetidum, totum
quasi sulphurei incendii flamma coopertum demonumque mul-
titudine plenum. Dixerunt ergo ei, 'Sub isto flammante flum-   540
ine noueris infernum esse.' Vltra flumen illud quod uidebatur
pons unus protendebatur. Dixeruntque demones [ad militem],
'Oportet te per hunc pontem transire; nos autem, uentos et turbines commouentes, de ponte proiciemus te in flumen. Socii
uero nostri qui in eo sunt te captum in infernum demergent.   545
Volumus tamen te prius probare quam tutum tibi sit per illum
transire.' Tenentes igitur manum eius ducebant super pontem.
Erant autem in eodem ponte tria transeuntibus ualde formid-
anda. Primo uidelicet, quod ita lubricus erat ut, etiamsi
latissimus esset, aut uix aut nullatenus quis in eo pedem figere   550
posset; secundum, quod ita strictus et gracilis erat ut uix aut
nullo modo in eo aliquis stare uel ambulare posse uidebatur;

524   intollerabilis fuit S.   526   Domini] *om.* R.   530   ut *subpuncted before* eo.
534   hic] RS, hoc L.   535   ducemus te R.   542–3   ad militem] RS, *om.* L.
545   nostri uero S.   547   ducebant] fricabant R.
549   Primo] Primum RS;   quod] quia S.
552   uidebatur] uideretur W (*comparing* uideretur *l. 554*).

f. 15vb tercium / quod adeo alte protendebatur in aere ut etiam
horribile uideretur ad ipsius altitudinem oculos erigere.
'Si tamen,' inquiunt, 'adhuc nobis assenseris ut reuertaris, etiam   555
ab hoc discrimine securus ad patriam remeare poteris.'
Cogitans autem intra se fidelis Christi miles de quantis eum
periculis liberauerit aduocatus eius piissimus, ipsius inuocato
nomine cepit super pontem pedetemptim incedere. Nichil
igitur lubrici sub pedibus sentiens, firmius incedebat, in   560
Domino confidens. Et quo alcius ascendit, eo spaciosiorem
pontem inuenit. Et ecce post paululum tantum creuit pontis
latitudo ut etiam duo carra exciperet sibi obuiantia.

De Purgatorio Patricii

Porro demones, qui militem illuc [usque] perduxerant, ulterius   565
progredi non ualentes, ad pedem pontis steterunt, quasi lap-
sum militis prestolantes. Videntes autem eum libere transire,
ita clamoribus aerem concusserunt, ut intolerabilior ei uideretur huius horror clamoris quam preteritarum aliqua penarum
quam sustinuerat ab ipsis. Cernens tamen eos subsistere nec   570
ultra progredi ualere piique ductoris sui reminiscens, securius
incedebat. Demones autem supra flumen discurrentes uncos
suos ad eum iaciebant, sed illesus ab eis preteriit. Securus
tandem procedens, uidit latitudinem pontis in tantum ex-
crescere ut uix ex utraque parte posset aquam aspicere.   575

De Purgatorio Patricii

Comparentur igitur, karissimi, passiones huius uite predic-
torum locorum tormentis et miserie. Qu[e] si igitur inuicem
opponantur in mentis statera, quasi inconparabilis harene
multitudo maris leuissime comparata pluuie, grauior apparebit   580
eorundem locorum inestimabilis miseria. [Carn]eis ut credo,
motibus sane mentis nemo delectabitur, quamdiu puro mentis
intuitu talia contemplabitur. Et quibus grauis et aspera uidetur
f. 16ra   in monasterio sui ipsius pro Christo / temporalis abnegatio,
reminiscantur, oro, quam amara sit illorum tormentorum   585
diuturna excrutiatio. Incomparabiliter enim leuior est uita
claustralis et districtissime regule rigor discipline cenobialis,
ubi tam corporum quam animarum necessaria sine sollicitudine

---

553   protendebatur] protentabatur S.   565   usque] RS, *om*. L.
567   autem] *om*. S.   568   intolerabilior] intolebilior R.
575   aspicere] inspicere R.   577   Comparentur] Comparantur S;
igitur] ergo RS.   578   Que] W, Quod LRS.
581   Carneis] RS, cum eis L.   585   reminiscantur] reminiscatur R.
586   Incomparabiliter] Incompabiliter R.   588   ubi] ut R.

queruntur, quam supradicta penarum loca in quibus miseri pro
peccatis in hac uita non emendatis, non tantum maximis sed   590
etiam minimis negligenter multiplicatis, diuturna miseria
cruciari creduntur. Sunt autem peccata que minima uel parua
siue leuia dicuntur, non quia parua uel leuia sint, sed quoniam
in hac uita uere penitentibus leuiter a Deo dimittuntur. Quod
si quis ea emendanda in futurum distulit contempnendo, non   595
leuia sed grauia immo grauissima in penis ea sentiet ex-
periendo. Nemo se de peccatorum leuium leuitate, quia ita
apellantur, blandiendo seducat. Quanto etenim fuerint leuiora,
tanto fit culpe grauioris eorum in interni iudicis examine
corrigendi negligentia. Nullum igitur omnino peccatum   600
paruum estimare debemus. Anselmus. Vtinam districtus iudex
parui existimaret aliquod peccatum! Nonne omne peccatum
per preuaricationem Deum exhonorat? Quod ergo peccatum
audet quis dicere paruum? [Deum enim exhonorare quis sane
mentis dicturus est paruum?] Quid respondebimus cum   605
exigetur a nobis usque ad ictum oculi tocius uite presentis
cursus? Tunc quippe condempnabitur quicquid in nobis
inuentum fuerit operis ociosi uel sermonis, uel eciam silentii
inemendatum usque ad minimam cogitacionem. Quis uel
mente captus audeat affirmare peccata fore leuia quibus amara   610
debetur gehenna? Ve, quot peccata proruent ibi ex inprouiso
quasi ex insidiis, que modo paruipendimus. Certe plura et
forsitan terribiliora hiis que grauia iudicamus. Quot que non
esse mala putamus, quot etiam que nunc sub specie religionis
uelata bona ualde existimamus, ibi nudata facie apparebunt   615
f. 16rb teterrima. / Ibi procul dubio recipiemus prout in corpore
gessimus, siue bonum, siue malum, tunc cum iam non erit
tempus misericordie; tunc cum penitentia non recipietur, cum
emendatio non promittetur. Hec autem, karissimi, non mea sed
sanctorum patrum sunt uerba. Hic, hic cogitemus que ges-   620
simus, et que in futuro pro hiis accepturi sumus. Si multa
bona, pauca mala: multum gaudeamus. Si multa mala, pauca
bona: multum lugeamus. O peccator inutilis, nonne hec tibi
sufficiunt ad inmanem rugitum; ad eliciendum sanguinem et
medullas in lacrimas? Ve mirabilis duritia, ad quam confrin-   625
gendam leues sunt tam graues mallei! Augeamus ergo, miseri,
augeamus superioribus erumpnis pondus, addamus terrorem
super terrorem, ululatum super ululatum. Nam ipse nos iudicabit, ad cuius contumeliam spectat quicquid ordinis et uoti
preuaricator inobediens Deo et Dei personam inter [n]os   630

595   ea] *om.* RS;   distulit] distulerit RS.
604–5   Deum . . . paruum?] RS, *om.* L.   630   nos] R, uos LS.

gerentibus peccauerit. Meminerimus, dilectissimi uoti, quod
sponte Deo uouimus et ipsius uicariis. Exigetur enim a nobis
usque ad nouissimum quadrantem, aut hic cum benignitate et
misericordia, aut in futuro, quod absit, cum seueritate et
iusticia. Ille quidem iudicabit qui cum esset Deo Patri coequ-   635
alis pro nobis factus obediens usque ad mortem, ut nos a
superbia ad humilitatem, ab inobedientia ad obedientiam in-
clinaret, sed potius subleuaret. Ergo ad humilitatem Domini
confundatur elatio serui. Avgustinus. Intueamur, karissimi,
Domini humilitatem. Intueamur, inquam, dulcem natum Dei,   640
toto corpore in crucis patibulo pro nobis extensum. Cernamus
manus innoxias, pio manantes sanguine. Consideremus inerme
latus, crudeli perfossum cuspide. Videamus immaculata uest-
igia, que non steterunt in uia peccatorum, sed semper am-
bulauerunt in lege Domini, diris terebrata clauis rubente   645
f. 16va sanguinis unda. O mirabilis / censure conditio! O inestimabilis
misterii disp[osi]tio! Nos inique agimus et ipse pena mulctatur.
Nos facinus admittimus, et ipse plectitur ultione. Nos crimen
committimus, ipse torture subicitur. Nos superbimus, ipse
humiliatur. Nos tumemus, ipse attenuatur. Nos prelatis nostris   650
inobedientes sumus, ipse patri suo obediens scelus luit
inobedientie nostre. Nos obedientes gule diuersa fercula queri-
mus, et ipse inedia pro nobis afficitur. Nos ad illicitam arborem
rapit concupiscentia, ipsum perfecta caritas pro nobis ducit ad
crucis supplicia. Nos presumimus uetitum, et ipse subit   655
eculeum. Nos iocando delectamur cibo, et ipse condolendo
nobis laborat in patibulo. Nobis [nam] lasciuiens conridet Eua,
ipsi uero plorans compatitur Maria. Dic, age, dic, cenobita, qui
dum corriperis, dum ad emendandum ad ueniam petendam
citaris, recusas, recalcitras, reclamans inflaris, prorumpis in   660
uerba malitie, ad excusandas excusationes in peccatis. Dic,
queso, quid superbis cum sis puluis et cinis? O ceca elatio! O
insens`i´bilis tumor, ad quem compungendum sunt obtunsi
tam acuti aculei. Conpungamur ergo, karissimi, et humiliemur
coram ipso qui pro nobis humilis et obediens factus est, non   665
tantum Deo Patri, sed etiam hominibus. Scriptum quippe est,
'Et erat subditus illis.' Dulce quod mandatum dedit nobis ut
diligamus inuicem. Et nouimus quis ait, 'Increpasti superbos;
maledicti qui declinant a mandatis tuis'. Preceptum quoque
dedit nobis desiderabile dicens, 'Petite et accipietis'. Quid   670

---

645   terebrata] terebratis S,   647   dispositio] R, dispensatio LS.
649   torture] turture S.   654   rapit] rapuit S.
657   nam] RS *om.* L.   660   prorumpis] prorumperis R.
663   insensibilis] a *subpuncted before* b;   tumor] timor S.

precipit ut petamus? Aurum, argentum, pretiosam mundi
substantiam? Absit. Non enim expedit ut ea petamus que se
petentes interimunt. Quid ergo? Veniam. Non igitur erubes-
camus nos ab eo ueniam petere pro propriis delictis, qui pro
ipsis innocens tot et tan/-tis affectus est obprobriis. Quicumque   675
igitur animo ueniam postulauerit, presto est ut tribuat. Et qui
non ex animo petit, [uel omnino non petit], certe non accipit.
Ipse enim nouit abscondita cordis. Ve tumidis in presenti
ueniam petere contempnentibus. De hiis procul dubio scriptum est, 'Peccator cum in profundum uenerit, contempnet.'   680
Hii quoque in laboribus hominum non sunt, et cum hominibus
non flagellabuntur. Sed quia hic eos tenuit superbia, sepel-
ientur in puteo in iniquitate et impietate sua. Attendat caritas
uestra. Dictum quippe est militi. Vniuersi qui pro peccatis
purgandis, extra os putei, in quibuslibet locis cruciantur, hii   685
sunt qui in presenti uita penitentiam egerunt, et nondum
peracta [sibi] iniuncta penitentia ab hac uita discedentes pro
culparum qualitate in tormenti detinentur. Statim ergo post
commissa ducti uera penitentia ueniam postulantes, statim aut
hic aut in futuro liberantur. Qui si corde duro `et´ in-   690
penitenti usque ad extrema uite presentis penitere non uidean-
tur, timendum ualde est ne etiam eorum tormenta usque ad
huius seculi finem perdurent. Hii tamen omnes per beneficia
que pro ipsis in presenti fiunt a predictis suppliciis cotidie
liberantur. Transeamus igitur, karissimi, sepius mente per hec   695
loca tormentorum. Patres nostros et matres, fratres et sorores,
ceterosque cognatos amicosque nobis quondam carissimos qui
forsan ibi torquentur uisitemus, crebris uigillis et orationibus
insistendo, missarum solempnia cum concentu psalmorum
celebrando, elemosinas largiendo, scientes quia quicquid pro   700
ipsis laboris subierimus, nobis ipsis inpendimus. Et si eos in
corpore cruciari cerneremus, et, cum possemus, a tormentis eos
eruere negligeremus, nonne infideles filii, cognati, et amici
iudicaremur? Multo quidem infideliores sunt qui, [d]um possunt, missis, psalmis, precibus, elemosinis de predictis tor-   705
mentis suos quondam karissimos eruere non satagunt. Testatur
enim sanctus Gregorius penas eorum qui saluandi sunt istis

674 nos] uos S.   677 uel ... petit] R, *om*. LS.   679 hiis] *om*. S.
683 iniquitate / impietate] *inverted* S.   687 sibi] R, sub LS.
690 et] *om*. S.   691 non] distulerit ei si uere penitere R.
697 quondam nobis R.   698 forsan] forsitan RS;
uisitemus] *last four letters written over an erasure*, uisitantes RS.
701 laboris] laboribus S.   704 dum] R, cum LS.
705 elemosinis] elemosinis et S.

mitigari et annichilari remediis. Nobis ergo summopere /
f. 17ra cauendum est ne, dum hec in ecclesia pro eorum liberatione
fiunt, rebus ociosis potius quam orationi uacemus. Hec autem   710
ad eorum correptionem dico, qui pro causis minimis inter
missarum sollempnia chorum psallentium sine necessitate sepissime deserunt, quos nullius obedientie sollicitudo, sed sola
mentis extrahit et expellit euagatio. Terreant nos, karissimi,
tormenta supradicta, sed multo magis dies illa omnium ex-   715
trema. Quid torpemus, peccatores? Dies iudicii uenit. Juxta
est dies Domini magnus, iuxta et uelox nimis. Dies ire dies
illa, dies tribulationis et angustie, dies calamitatis et miserie,
dies tenebrarum et caliginis, dies nebule et turbinis, dies tube
et clangoris. O uox diei Domini amara! Quid dormimus,   720
tepidi? Quid dormimus? Qui non expergiscitur, qui non con-
tremit ad tam terrificum tonitruum, non dormit, sed mortuus
est. Ibi, ibi apparebit iudex uiuorum et mortuorum, Ihesus
Christus, nunc patientissimus, tunc districtissimus; clement-
issimus nunc, iustissimus tunc. Ve ibi ueniam petere con-   725
tempnentibus hic. O angustie! Hinc erunt accusantia peccata,
inde terrens iusticia; subtus patens horridum chaos inferni,
desuper iratus iudex; intus urens conscientia, foris ardens
mundus. Si iustus uix saluabitur, peccator sic apprehensus in
quam partem se premet? Constrictus ubi latebit, quomodo   730
parebit? Latere erit inpossibile, apparere intolerabile. Illud
desiderabit, et nusquam erit; istud execrabitur et ubique erit.
Quid? Quid tunc? Quid erit tunc? Quis eruet de manibus Dei?
Vnde consilium? Vnde salus? O! Quis est qui dicitur 'magni
consilii angelus'? Quis est qui dicitur 'saluator', ut ante quam   735
ueniat dies illa nomen eius uociferemur? Iam ipse est, iam ipse
est Ihesus. Ipse idem est iudex, inter cuius manus tremimus.
Respira iam, o peccator; respira ne desperes. Ipse pius Ihesus,
ipse est cuius nominis non inmemor miles noster a tot et tantis
f. 17rb tormentis misericorditer eripitur; cuius audito nomine / for-   740
titudo demonum eneruatur, penarum asperitas hebetatur, ab
ipsius infernalis putei gurgite miles mirabiliter liberatur. Pro-
sequamur ergo, karissimi, militem nostrum, a quo tam neces-
sario tam longe digressi sumus, qui eodem pio Ihesu duce iam
pertransiuit per ignes et aquas, et uideamus si forte eduxerit   745
eum adhuc in refrigerium; ut cuius miseriis et calamitatibus
conpatiebamur, illius etiam solatii participes efficiamur, et

711   correptionem] correctionem W.   714   karissimi nos R.
723–4   Christus Ihesus RS.   729   sic] sic et S (sic *corrected from* hic (?)).
733   eruet de] est qui dicitur saluator S.
743   tam] *om.* RS.   744   iam] *om.* S.

quorum corda ad conpassionem pietatis forte non flexerunt
tristia tormentorum, deuotione saltem et affectu flectant suc-
cedentia gaudiorum.   750

De Purgatorio Patricii

Procedens igitur miles, iam liber ab omni demonum uexatione,
uidit ante se murum quendam magnum et altum in aere a terra
erectum. Erat autem murus ille mirabilis et inconparandi
decoris structure. In quo muro portam unam clausam uidebat,   755
que metallis diuersis lapidibus[que] pretiosis ornata mirabili
fulgore radiabat. Cui cum appropinquasset, sed adhuc quasi
spacio dimidii miliarii abesset, porta illa contra eum aperta est
et tante suauitatis odor ei occurrens per eam exiit ut, sicut
uidebatur, si totus mundus in aromata uerteretur, non uinceret 760
huius magnitudinem suauitatis. Tantasque uires ex ea percepit
suauitate ut existimaret se tormenta, que pertulerat, iam posse
sine molestia sustinere. Respiciensque intra portam patriam
solis splendorem claritate nimia uincente lustratam uidit et
nimirum introire concupiuit. Beatus homo cui talis aperitur   765
ianua! Nec fefellit militem qui illum eo uenire permisit. Cum
enim adhuc aliquantulum longius esset, egressa est in occur-
sum eius cum crucibus et uexillis et cereis et quasi palmarum
aurearum ramis processio talis ac tanta quanta in hoc mundo,
f. 17va prout estimauit, / nunquam uisa est. Ibi uidit homines 770
[unius]cuiusque ordinis ac religionis diuerse etatis et utriusque
sexus. Alios quasi archiepiscopos, alios ut episcopos, alios ut
abbates, canonicos, monachos, presbiteros et singulorum
graduum sancte ecclesie ministros, sacris uestibus ordini suo
congruentibus indutos. Omnes uero, tam clerici quam laici,   775
eadem forma uestium uidebantur induti in qua Deo seruierunt
in seculo. Militem uero cum magna ueneratione et leticia
susceperunt, eumque cum concentu seculo inaudite armonie
secum perducentes, per portam introierunt. Finito uero concentu et soluta processione, secedentes duo seorsum quasi   780
archiepiscopi militem in suo comitatu susceperunt secumque
duxerunt quasi patriam et eius amenitatis gloriam ei ostensuri.
Qui cum eo loquentes primo benedixerunt Deum, qui eius
animum in tormentis tanta corroborauit constantia. Ipsis ergo
illum per amena patrie ducentibus, huc illucque transiens   785

753 a terra] *om.* R.   756 lapidibusque] RS, lapidibus L.
764 splendorem] spendorem R.   765 concupiuit] cupiuit RS;
aperitur talis S.   771 uniuscuiusque] R, cuiusque L, uiuos cuiusque S.
778 seculo] sedulo R ('*Inserted in the margin at the end of the line, by a
different but contemporary hand; a word at the beginning of the next line has been
erased.' Jenkins*).   784 ergo] igitur RS.

multo plura quam ipse uel aliquis hominum peritissimus lingua
uel calamo possit explicare delectabilia iocundaque perspexit.
Tanta uero lucis erat illa patria claritate lustrata ut sicut lumen
lucerne solis obcecatur splendore, ita solis claritas meridiana
posse uideretur obtenebrari lucis illius patrie mirabili fulgore.   790
Finem uero patrie pre nimia ipsius magnitudine scire non
potuit nisi tantum ex ea parte qua per portam intrauit. Erat
autem tota patria quasi prata amena atque uirentia, diuersis
floribus fructibusque herbarum multiformium et arborum de-
corata, quorum, ut ait, odore tantum sine fine uixisset, si   795
ibidem sibi permanere licuisset. Nox illam nunquam obscurat,
quia splendor eam purissimi celi perhenni claritate perlustrat.
f. 17vb Tantamque uidit in ea sexus utriusque mul/-titudinem
hominum, quantam in hac uita neminem estimabat unquam
uidisse mortalium. Quorum alii in hiis, alii in aliis locis, per   800
conuentus distincti, commanebant, et tamen, prout uoluerunt,
alii de istis in illas, alii de illis in istas cateruas cum leticia
transibant. Sicque fiebat ut et alii de aliorum [uisione gauder-
ent et alii de aliorum] uisitacione feliciter exultarent. Chori per
loca choris assistebant dulcisque armonie concentu Deo laudes   805
resonabant. Et sicut stella differt a stella in claritate, ita erat
quedam differentia concors in eorum uestium et uultuum
claritatis uenustate. Alii enim induti uestitu uidebantur aureo,
alii argenteo atque alii uiridi, purpureo, iacinctino, ceruleo,
candido. Forma tamen habitus qua singuli utebantur in seculo.   810
[Forma etenim uestis indicabat militi] cuius[quilibet in seculo]
meriti fuerit uel ordinis. Quorum habitus uarius color uarie
uidebatur claritatis splendor. Alii quasi reges coronati incede-
bant, alii palmas aureas in manibus gestabant. Talium ergo
tantorumque fuit in illa requie iustorum militi delectabilis   815
conspectus nec minor eorundem armonie suauis et ineffabiliter
dulcis auditus. Vndique sanctorum audiuit concentum Deo
laudes perso[na]ntium. Singuli uero de propria felicitate
gaudebant, sed et de singulorum gaudio singuli exultabant.
Tantaque patria illa odoris suauitatis repleta erat fraglantia ut   820

787   perspexit] prospexit RS.   796   sibi] om. S.
801   uoluerunt] uoluerint R.
803–4   uisione ... aliorum] R, om. LS.
811   Forma etenim ... militi and quilibet ... seculo] R, om. LS.
812   *Erasure above* uel ordinis, *which is followed by a caret and* ostendit
interlined above Quorum (*also in bottom margin of f. 17va*); RS *omit* ostendit.
814   ergo] igitur RS   815   tantorumque] et tantorum R.
817   auditus] d *corrected over an erasure.*
818   personantium] R, persolventium L, persoluantium S.
819   et] om. S.   820   fraglantia] fragrantia R (*corrected*), flagrantia S.

inde uiderentur uiuere habitantes in ea. Omnes uero, qui militem intuebantur, Deum benedicentes de eius aduentu quasi de fraterna ereptione a morte gratulabantur. Videbatur ibi quadammodo de ipsius aduentu quasi noua exultatio fieri. Omnes exultabant; undique sanctorum melodia resonabat. Nec 825 estum nec frigus ibi sentiebat, nec quod ullo modo posset offendere uel nocere quicquam uidebat. Omnia ibi placata, omnia placita, omnia grata. Multo plura uidit in illa requie quam aliquis hominum umquam loqui sufficeret aut scribere. Hiis igitur ita completis, dixerunt pontifices ad militem, 'Ecce, 830 frater, auxiliante Deo uidisti que uidere desiderasti. Vidisti

f. 18ra enim / huc ueniendo tormenta peccatorum, hic autem uidisti requiem iustorum. Benedictus sit Creator et Redemptor omnium, qui tibi dedit tale propositum, cuius gratia per tormenta transiens constanter egisti. Nunc autem, karissime, nosse te 835 uolumus que s[i]nt illa que uidisti tormentorum loca, sed et que sit ista tante patria beatitudinis. Patria igitur ista terrestris est paradysus, de qua propter inobedientie culpam eiectus est Adam prothoplastus. Postquam enim inobediens Deo subici contempsit, ultra uidere que uides, immo incomparabiliter 840 maiora gaudia non potuit. Hic enim ipsius Dei uerba sedulo audierat cordis munditia et celsitudine uisionis interne, hic beatorum angelorum uisione perfrui poterat. Cum autem per inobedientiam a tanta beatitudine cecidisset, etiam lumen rationis quo illustrabatur amisit. Et quia, cum in honore esset, 845 non intellexit, comparatus est iumentis insipientibus et similis factus est illis. Huius autem uniuersa posteritas ob ipsius inobedientie culpam, sicut et ipse, mortis suscepit sententiam. O detestabile scelus inobedientie! Motus tandem pietate piissimus Deus noster super humani generis miseria[m] filium 850 suum unigenitum incarnari constituit, Dominum nostrum Ihesum Christum, cuius fidem suscipientes per baptismum tam ab actualibus quam ab originali peccato liberi ad istam patriam redire meruimus. Verum [quod] post fidei susceptionem per fragilitatem creberrime peccauimus, ideo necesse 855 erat ut per penitentiam ueniam actualium impetraremus. Penitentiam etenim, quam ante mortem uel in extremis positi suscepimus nec eam in uita peregimus, post carnis solutionem

821 inde] *om.* RS;   uiuere uiderentur R.
826 estum] estus S (*corrected from* estum);   sentiebat ibi S.
827 placata] pacata W.   831   que] quod RS.   832   hic] hinc S.
834 tale dedit RS.   836   sint] W, sunt LRS.   837   beatitudinis patria RS.
845 illustrabatur] lustrabatur RS.   850   miseriam] RS, miseria L.
854 quod] R, *om.* LS;   post] *om.* R.
855 ideo] *om.* RS.   857   etenim] enim R *with correction erased?*

in locis penalibus que uidisti, alii maiori alii minori temporis
spacio, secundum modum culparum, tormenta luendo persol-   860
uimus. Omnes autem ad hanc requiem per illa loca transiuimus.
O transitus inestimabiliter horribilis! Similiter et omnes quos
f. 18rb in singulis locis penalibus uidisti, preter eos qui infra os / putei
infernalis detinentur, postquam purgati fuerint, tandem ad
istam requiem uenientes saluabuntur. Sed et cotidie quidam   865
purgati ueniunt, quos suscipientes, sicut et te suscepimus, cum
gaudio huc introducimus. Eorum uero qui in penis sunt nullus
nouit quamdiu torquebitur. Per missas autem et psalmos et
orationes et elemosinas, quotiens pro eis fiunt, aut eorum
tormenta mitigantur aut in minora et tolerabiliora transferun- 870
tur, donec omnino per talia beneficia liberentur. Ad hunc
autem locum quietis cum ueneri`n´t, quamdiu hic mansuri
fuerint nesciunt; nullus enim nostrum hoc scire potest de se
quamdiu hic debeat esse. Sicut enim in locis penalibus secundum culparum quantitatem morandi percipiunt spacium, ita et   875
qui hic sumus secundum merita bona plus minusue morabimur
in ista requie. Et licet a penis omnino liberi simus, ad
supernam sanctorum leticiam nondum ascendere digni sumus.
Diem enim et terminum nostre promotionis in melius nemo
nostrum nouit. Ecce hic, ut uides, in magna requie sumus; sed 880
post terminum singulis constitutum in maiorem transibimus.
Cotidie enim societas nostra quodammodo crescit et decrescit,
dum singulis diebus et a penis ad nos et a nobis in celestem
paradysum ascendunt.' Hiis dictis, assumentes militem secum
in montem unum, iusserunt ut sursum aspiciens diceret   885
cuiusmodi coloris ei supra se celum uideretur. Quibus ille
respondit, 'Auro mihi simile uidetur ardenti in fornace.' 'Hec,'
inquiunt, 'est porta celestis paradysi. Hac introeunt qui a nobis
sumuntur in celum. Nec te latere debet quod cotidie pascit nos
Dominus semel cibo celesti. Qualis autem fuerit cibus ille   890
quamque delectabilis, iam Deo donante nobiscum gustando
f. 18va senties.' Vixque sermone finito, / quasi flamma ignis de celo
descendit, que patriam totam cooperuit et, quasi per radios
diuisim super singulorum capita descendens, tandem in eos
tota intrauit. Sed et super militem inter alios descendit et   895
intrauit. Vnde tantam dilect[at]ionis dulcedinem in corde et

859 que uidisti penalibus R;   minori] minoris R.
876 morabimur] *second* m *poorly formed, corrected from* t, morabitur RS.
878 sumus] simus S (*with* u *above first minim of* m).   879   enim] tamen RS.
893 totam patriam RS.
894 diuisim] *with erasure after final letter,* dIuIsum S.
896 dilectationis] S (*with, in* S, ta *added in different ink in the margin, where
the word breaks at the line ending*), dilconis L (*different hand in margin reads*
delectanis), dilectionis R, delectationis W.

corpore sensit ut pene pre nimietate dulcedinis non intellexerit
utrum uiuus an mortuus fuisset. Sed et illa hora cito transiit.
'Hic,' inquiunt, 'est cibus ille unde semel, ut diximus, a Deo
cotidie pascimur. Qui uero in celum a nobis assumuntur, hoc   900
cibo sine fine perfruuntur. Sed quoniam ex parte uidisti que
uidere desiderasti, requiem uidelicet beatorum et tormenta
peccatorum, oportet nunc, frater, ut redeas per eandem uiam
qua uenisti. Et si amodo sobrie ac sancte uixeris, non solum de
ista requie, sed et de celorum mansione securus esse poteris. Si   905
uero, quod absit, iterum illecebris carnis uitam tuam pollueris,
en ipse uidisti quid tibi maneat in penis. Securus ergo redeas;
nam quicquid huc tibi uenienti terroris erat, tibi redeunti etiam
apparere pertimescet.' Ad hec uerba pauescens miles magno
merore pontificibus supplicare cepit ne a tanto leticia ad   910
erumpnas huius seculi redire cogeretur. 'Non,' inquiunt, 'ut
postulas, erit, sed sicut ipse disposuit qui quod omnibus
expediat solus agnouit.' Merens igitur miserabiliter, uolens
nolens egreditur accepta bene[di]ctione, tristis admodum sed
tamen intrepidus, eadem qua uen[er]at uia reuertitur et clausa   915
est ianua.

De Purgatorio Patricii

Eya nunc, dilectissimi, redeunte milite nostro, recordetur
unusquisque qualia et quanta sunt omnia, siue beatorum
gaudia, siue peccatorum tormenta, que adhuc in carne positus,   920
f. 18vb / intuitus et expertus est. Mira certe uidentur immo mira sunt
et inestimabilia. Verum si conparata fuerint ad illa que nec
oculus uidit, nec auris audiuit, nec cor hominis cogitare potuit
que preparauit Deus diligentibus siue contempnentibus se, fere
nulla uel minima parebunt. De tormentis autem inpiorum ad   925
presens sufficiant que superius dicta sunt. Excitemus, igitur, et
erigamus, karissimi, totum intellectum nostrum in quantum
Deus donauerit, [et] cogitemus quale et quantum sit illud
electorum unicum et singulare gaudium. Illud scilicet unum et
summum bonum, omnino sibi sufficiens, nullo indigens, quo   930

897 intellexerit] intellexit S.   903 ut] om. R.
909 apparere] apparare S.
914 accepta] acceptaque RS;   benedictione] RS, benectione L.
915 uenerat] RS, uenit L (with letter erased and ia inserted above); reuertitur
uia R, uertitur uia S.
917 S rubric De beatitudine futuri seculi in Gloria eterna.
918 amor celestium in different hand in the margin (cf. 896).
920 siue] seu S.   925 parebunt] apparebunt S;   impiorum autem S.
926 S rubric in bottom margin with insertion line to Excitemus: De libro sancti
Anselmi qui dicitur Proslogion.
928 et (1)] R, om. L, ei S;   quale] in quale S.   930 omnino] omni S.

omnia indigent ut sint, et ut bene sint. Hoc bonum est Deus
pater; hoc est uerbum, id est filius patris. Hoc ipsum est amor
unus et communis patri et filio, id est spiritus sanctus ab
utroque procedens. Quod autem horum est singulus quisque,
hoc est tota trinitas simul, pater et filius et spiritus sanctus;   935
quoniam singulus quisque non est aliud quam summe simplex
unitas et summe una simplicitas, que nec multiplicari nec aliud
et aliud esse potest. Porro hoc est illud idem unum quod est
necessarium. Porro hoc est illud idem unum necessarium, in
quo est omne et unum et totum et solum bonum. Si enim   940
singula bona delectabilia sunt, cogitate intente quam delecta-
bile sit illud bonum, quod continet iocunditatem omnium
bonorum; et non qualem in rebus creatis sumus experti, sed
tanto differentem quanto differt creator a creatura. Si enim
bona est uita creata: quam bona est uita creatrix? Si iocunda est   945
salus facta: quam iocunda est salus que facit omnem salutem?
Si amabilis est sapientia in cognicione rerum conditarum:
quam amabilis est sapientia que omnia condidit ex nichilo?
Denique si multe et magne delectaciones sunt in rebus delectabilibus: qualis et quanta est delectacio in illo qui fecit illa /   950
f. 19ra   delectabilia? O qui hoc bono fruetur: quid illi erit, et quid illi
non erit! Certe quicquid uolet erit, et quod nolet non erit. Ibi
quippe erunt bona corporis et anime, qualia nec oculus uidit,
nec auris audiuit, nec cor hominis cog`it´auit. Cur ergo per
multa uagamur, querendo bona anime nostre et corporis   955
nostri? Amemus unum bonum, in quo sunt omnia bona, et
sufficit. Desideremus simplex bonum, quod est omne bonum,
et satis, est. Quid enim amas, caro, quid desideras, anima? Ibi
est, ibi est quicquid amatis, quicquid desideratis. Si delectat
pulcritudo: fulgebunt iusti sicut sol. Si uelocitas aut fortitudo,   960
aut libertas corporis cui nichil obsistere possit: erunt similes
angelis Dei, quia seminatur corpus animale, et surget corpus
spirituale, potestate utique non natura. Si longa et salubris
uita: ibi est sana eternitas et eterna sanitas, quia iusti in
perpetuum uiuent et salus iustorum a Domino. Si sacietas: 965
saturabuntur [cum apparuerit gloria Dei. Si ebrietas:
inebriabuntur] ab ubertate domus Dei. Si melodia: ibi chori
angelorum concinunt sine fine Deo. Si quelibet non inmunda

931   et] ut sint et S.   932   hoc ... patris] *repeated* S.
933   communis] communus S.   939   idem] *om.* RS.
943   qualem] quale RS.
944   differentem] differente S (*with* i *inserted above the line after* t (?)).
947   sapientia] scientia S, cognicione] cognitione R *partially over an
erasure.*   949–50   delectabilibus] delectalibilibus S.
966–7   cum ... inebriabuntur] R, *om.* LS.
967   chori] chorus S;   concinunt] *om.* S.

sed munda uoluptas: torrente uoluptatis sue potabit eos Deus. Si sapientia: ipsa Dei sapientia ostendet eis seipsam. Si ami- 970
cicia: diligent Deum plus quam seipsos, et inuicem tamquam seipsos, et Deus illos plus quam illi seipsos; quia illi illum et se et inuicem per illum, et ille [se et] illos per seipsum. Si concordia: omnibus illis erit una uoluntas, quia nulla eis erit nisi Dei sola uoluntas. Si potestas: omnipotentes erunt sue 975
uoluntatis ut Deus sue. Nam sicut poterit quod uolet per seipsum, ita poterunt illi quod uolent per illum; quia sicut illi non aliud uolent quam quod ille, ita et ille uolet quicquid illi uolent; et quod ille uolet non poterit non esse. Si honor et diuitie: Deus suos seruos bonos et fideles supra multa consti- 980
tuet, immo filii Dei et dii uocabuntur et erunt; et ubi erit
f. 19rb unicus eius, ibi erunt et illi he/-redes quidem Dei, coheredes autem Christi. Si uera securitas: certe ita certi erunt nunquam et nullatenus ista uel potius istud bonum sibi defuturum, sicut certi erunt se non sua sponte illud amissuros, nec dilectorem 985
Deum illud dilectoribus suis inuiti`s´ ablaturum, nec aliquid Deo potentius inuitos Deum et illos s[e]paraturum.

Gaudium uero quale et quantum est, ubi tale ac tantum bonum? Cor humanum, cor indigens, cor expertum erumpnas immo obrutum erumpnis: quantum gauderes, si hiis omnibus 990
habundares? Interroga intima tua, si caper`e´ possunt gaudium suum de tanta beatitudine sua. Sed certe si quis alius, quem omnino sicut teipsum diligeres, eandem beatitudinem haberet, dupplicaretur gaudium tuum, quia non minus gauderes pro eo quam pro teipso. Si uero duo uel tres uel multo plures idipsum 995
haberent, tantundem pro singulis quantum pro teipso gauderes, si singulos sicut teipsum amares. Ergo in illa perfecta caritate innumerabilium angelorum et hominum, ubi nullus minus diliget alium quam seipsum, non aliter gaudebit quisque pro singulis aliis quam pro seipso. Si ergo cor hominis de tanto 1000
suo bono uix capiet gaudium suum: quomodo capax erit tot et tantorum gaudiorum? Et utique quoniam quantum quisque diliget aliquem, tantum de bono illius gaudet: sicut in illa perfecta felicitate unusquisque plus amabit sine comparatione Deum plus quam se et omnes alios secum, ita plus gaudebit 1005
absque estimatione de felicitate Dei quam de sua et omnium

972 *Three or four words erased after* illi seipsos S;   quia ... se] *om.* S.
973 se et] R, *om.* L, se S.
975 potestas] potesta + *blotted letter* + *long* s + ur *abbreviation, all following*
omnipotentes S.   985 certi] certe R.
986 inuitis] s *added in different ink.*
987 separaturum] RS, superaturum L.   991 po§sunt capere S.
998 et] *om.* S.   1003 illius] eius RS.   1005 Deum *follows* se S.

aliorum secum. [Sed si Deum sic diligent toto corde, [tota
mente,] tota anima, ut tamen totum cor, tota mens, tota anima
non sufficiat dignitati delectionis: profecto sic gaudebunt toto
corde, tota mente, tota anima, ut totum cor, tota mens, tota   1010
anima non sufficiat plenitudini gaudii. Et hoc fortasse est
gaudium de quo dicit nobis pater per filium suum: 'Petite et
accipietis, ut gaudium uestrum sit plenum.' Ecce, karissimi,
inuenimus gaudium quoddam plenum, et plusquam plenum.
Pleno quippe corde, plena mente, plena anima, pleno toto   1015
homine gaudio illo: adhuc supra modum supererit gaudium. O
si forte hoc gaudium est in quod intrabunt serui boni, qui
intrabunt in gaudium Domini sui. Sed gaudium illud certe
quo gaudebunt electi Dei, nec oculus uidit, nec auris audiuit,
nec in cor hominis ascendit. Nondum ergo dixi aut cogitaui,   1020
quantum gaudebunt illi beati serui Domini. Vtique enim
gaudebunt, quantum amabunt; tantum amabunt, quantum
cognoscent.] Quantum tunc boni agnoscent Deum, et quantum
amabunt eum? Certe neo oculus uidit, nec auris audiuit, nec in
cor hominis ascendit in hac uita, quantum cognoscent eum in   1025
f. 19va   illa uita. Ergo miles noster, licet mira et merito deside/-randa
gaudia uiderit, non dum illud summum bonum et singulare
beatorum gaudium uidit. Orandum ergo nobis est summopere,
karissimi, ut de Deo gaudeamus. Et si non possumus in hac
uita ad plenum, uel proficiamus in dies usque dum ueniat illud   1030
ad plenum. Proficiat hic in nobis noticia Dei, et ibi fi[a]t plena;
crescat hic amor ipsius, et ibi [sit] plenus: ut hic gaudium
nostrum sit in spe magnum, et ibi sit in re plenum. Deus enim
per filium suum iubet immo consulit petere et promittit
accipere, ut gaudium nostrum sit plenum. Petamus, igitur,   1035
quod consulit per admirabilem consiliarium nostrum; ac-
cipiamus quod promittit per ueritatem suam, ut gaudium
nostrum plenum sit. Meditetur interim mens nostra, loquatur
inde lingua nostra. Amet illud cor nostrum, sermocinetur os
nostrum. Esuriat illud anima nostra, desideret tota substantia   1040
nostra, donec intremus in gaudium Domini Dei nostri. Amen.

De Purgatorio Patricii

Occurramus modo, fratres karissimi, militi nostro redeunti et
uideamus si forte sine inpedimento redierit.

Egressus itaque, sicut supradiximus, miles de paradyso,   1045
lugens eo quod a tanta felicitate ad huius uite miseriam redire

ɪɪɪɪ ᴀ1   Sᴇd ɪ ɪ ɪ ᴇᴏᴍɴᴏᴄᴄᴇɴt] ᴅᴇɪ ᴊɪɪɪɪ Lɪ

1007–8   tota mente] *Anselm, and* S *with* mente *subpuncted and followed by*
anima).   1009   gaudebunt sic S.   1012   nobis] uobis R.
1016   illo] illo et S.   1021   gaudebunt] S, gaudium R.
1023   boni] *om.* RS.   1025   eum] illum RS.
1031   fiat] RS, fiet L.   1032   sit] fit RS, fiet L (*with* i *interlined*).
1033   sit (*1*)] fit S.   1034   petere] petente S.
1035   plenum sit RS.   1035–8   Petamus ... sit] *om.* S.

cogeretur, per eandem uiam qua uenerat reuersus est. Quem redeuntem quidem demones undique discurrentes terrere conati sunt, sed ad eius aspectum ut auicule territi per aera diffugerunt. Sed nec eum tormenta quicquam ledere 1050 potuerunt. Cumque uenisset ad predictam aulam, in qua demones eum primitus inuaserunt, ecce uiri illi quindecim qui

f. 19vb ibidem ei primo apparentes eum instruxerant, subito / apparuerunt. Qui Deum laudantes eiusque uictorie congratulantes dixerunt, 'Eya, frater, nunc scimus, quoniam per tor- 1055 menta que sustinens uiriliter uicisti, ab omnibus peccatis tuis purgatus es. Et ecce iam in patria tua lucis aurora clarescit. Ascende ergo quamtocius. Nam si prior ecclesie, post missarum solempnia cum processione sua ueniens ad portam, te redeuntem non inuenerit, statim, de reditu tuo diffidens, 1060 obserata porta redibit.' Accepta itaque ab eis benedictione, protinus ascendit. Eadem uero hora qua prior portam aperuit, miles de intro ueniens apparuit. Quem cum gaudio magno prior suscipiens in ecclesiam introduxit, in qua eum aliis quindecim diebus orationibus insistere constituit. Deinde, 1065 signo dominice crucis in humero suscepto, dominici corporis sepulchrum Ierosolimis uisitare perrexit. Et inde rediens, regem, dominum suum, cui prius familiaris extiterat, utpote uirum industrium et prudentem adiit, quatinus eiusmodi quem sibi consuleret ipse religionis habitum susciperet. Eodem 1070 autem tempore pie memorie Geruasius, abbas cenobii Ludensis, qui a prefato rege locum ad construendum monasterium inpetrauerat, monachum suum nomine Gilebertum de Luda cum quibusdam aliis (qui scilicet Gilebertus fuit postea abbas de Basingewerch) ad eundem regem in Hyberniam misit, ut et 1075 locum susciperet et monasterium fundaret. Qui cum ueniens ad regem susceptus esset, conquestus est quod illius patrie linguam ignoraret. Quod audiens rex ait, 'Optimum interpretem tibi commendabo.' Et accito prefato milite, iussit ut cum monacho maneret. Quam iussionem libentissime miles sus- 1080 cipiens ait ad dominum suum, 'Gratanter ei seruire debeo. Sed et uos cum magna gratiarum actione monachos Cysterni

f. 20ra ordinis in regno uestro susci/-pere debetis, quoniam, ut uerum fatear, in sanctorum requie non uidi homines tanta gloria

1048 demones] *om.* S.   1049 ut] ait S.
1052 primitus eum demones S.   1057 in] *om.* R.
1058 ergo] igitur RS.   1061 redibit] diffidens S.
1063 ueniens] ueniens ad portam S.   1064 ecclesiam] ecclesia S.
1070 consulerit sibi S.   1074 postea fuit RS.
1075 Basingewerch] Basingwerc S; et] *om.* S.   1080 miles] *om.* S.

preditos ut huius religionis uiros.' Mansitque cum eodem   1085
Gileberto miles ille, sed nondum monachus uel conuersus fieri
uoluit. Ceperunt igitur monasterium construere et manserunt
simul ibidem duobus annis et dimidio. Gilebertus uero domus
illius erat celerarius, miles autem forinsecus in omnibus pro-
curator erat et minister deuotus ac interpres fidelissimus,   1090
uixitque sancte ac satis religiose, sicut idem testatur Gilebertus. Et quando soli simul erant familiariter alicubi, ipsius
Gileberti rogatu ob edificationem hec omnia dilegentissime
narrare consueuerat. Postea uero monachi qui cum eo missi
fuerant ad Ludense cenobium in Angliam redierunt militem-   1095
que in Hybernia honeste et religiose uiuentem dimiserunt.

  Hec autem omnia cum sepedictus Gilebertus coram multis,
me quoque audiente, sepius sicut ab ipso milite audierat,
retulisset, affuit inter alios unus qui hec ita contigisse dubitare
se dixit. Cui Gilebertus, 'Sunt quidam', inquit, 'qui dicunt   1100
quod aulam intrantes primo fiunt in extasi et hec omnia in
spiritu uidere. Quod omnino sibi miles ita contigisse con-
tradicit, sed corporeis oculis se uidisse et corporaliter hec
pertulisse constantissime `testatur´. Sed et ego in monasterio
cui prefui aliquid oculis meis huic rei non ualde dissimile   1105
multique mecum conspexere.'

De monacho a demonibus uerberato
'Erat [enim] in eodem monasterio monachus quidam ualde
religiosus. Cuius sanctitati demones inuidentes dormientem
nocte quadam e dormitorio corporaliter tulerunt. Qui tribus   1110
diebus et noctibus ab ipsis detentus est, fratribus nescientibus
quid de eo factum fuisset. Post tercium uero diem in lectulo
suo a fratribus inuentus est, pene ad mortem usque flagellatus
f. 20rb   horribiliterque / a demonibus uulneratus. Michi quoque con-
fessus est se stupenda et horrenda uidisse tormenta. Vixit   1115
autem postea quindecim annos. Sed uulnera ipsius nullo
potuerunt medicamine curari. Semper enim aperta et quasi
recentia uidebantur, quorum quedam ad mensuram longi-
tudinis digiti unius profunda fuerunt. Hic autem, cum uidisset
aliquando iuniorum aliquem immoderatius ridentem uel iocan-   1120
tem uel quolibetmodo inordinate se habentem, aiebat, "O si

1085   preditos] predictos S.   1086   uel] nec S.
1087   monasterium] manesterium S.   1088   et] ac RS.   1091   ac] et W.
1092   quando] R, qm L *with first minim of* m *erased,* quoniam S; simul erant
soli S.   1098   sicut sepius RS.
1100   se] *added in the margin with insertion mark interlined, om.* RS.
1107   S *rubric* De quodam monacho.   1108   enim] RS, *om.* L.
1113   flagellatus] flagellatus est S.   1119   unius] illius S.

scires quanta huic inordinate dissolutioni maneat pena, forsitan
gestus tuos tam incompositos et mores emendares in melius."
Huius monachi uulnera uidi et manibus meis attrectaui ipsum-
que post obitum ego ipse sepeliui. Huius itaque uiri tam sancti,   1125
tam religiosi mihique tam familiaris relatio, si quid superioris
relationis mihi dubietatis inerat, penitus extersit.' Hucusque
Gilebertus.

Item de Purgatorio Patricii
Ego [autem], postquam hec omnia audieram, duos de Hybernia   1130
abbates, ut adhuc certior fierem, super hiis conueni. Quorum
unus, quod numquam in patria sua audier[a]t talia, respondit.
Alius uero, quod multociens hec audierit et quod essent omnia
uera, affirmauit. Sed et hoc testatus est quod idem Purgatorium
raro quis intrantium redit. Nuper etiam affatus sum episcopum   1135
quendam, nepotem sancti Patricii tertii, socii uidelicet sancti
Malachye, Florentianum nomine, in cuius episcopatu, sicut
ipse dixit, est idem Purgatorium. De quo cum curiosius
inquirerem, respondit episcopus, 'Certe, frater, uerum est.
Locus [autem] ille in episcopatu meo est et multi pereunt in   1140
eodem Purgatorio. Sed qui forte redeunt ob immanitatem
tormentorum que passi sunt languore siue pal/-lore diuturno
tabescunt. Sed si postea sobrie et iuste uixerint, certi sunt alias
pro peccatis suis penas se non esse perpessuros. Est et aliud
haut longe ab eodem loco quiddam ualde memorabile, quod   1145
etiam tibi libenter narro.'

. 20va (left margin note)

Rubrica
De uno heremita bono et malo alio cuius mala opera a demonibus audiuit bonus
'Manet [autem] ibi iuxta quidam heremita, uir magne sanctita-   1150
tis, cui uisibiliter unaquaque nocte demonum apparet multitudo. Statim uero post solis occubitum conueniunt in ipsius
cellule curia. Et quasi concilium tota nocte tenentes, singuli
cuidam principi sui quid egerint in die referunt et sic ante solis
ortum recedunt. Ille uero uir uidet eos manifeste et eorum   1155
narrationes intelligit. Ad ostium autem eius ascendunt, sed,

1123 emendares] emandares S.   1130 autem] RS, *om.* L.
1132 audierat] R, audierit LS.   1133 hec multociens S.
1140 autem] RS, *om.* L.   1141 Sed] Et RS.
1142 *In the top margin of f. 20va*: De bono heremita et malo.
1147–9 Rubrica ... bonus] *Inserted in the left-hand margin*; S *rubric* De
quodam heremita.   1150 autem] RS, *om.* L.   1152 uero] enim R.
1154 cuidam ... sui] coram quodam principe suo R, quodam principe suo
S.   1155 Ille] Illic S.   1156 ascendunt] accedunt R.

intrare non presumentes, quasi nudas ei sepissime mulieres
ostendunt. Fit etiam ut eorum relatu multorum uitam actusque
secretissimos in prouintia nouerit.' Hec cum dixisset
episcopus, ait capellanus ei, 'Ego eundem sanctum uirum uidi   1160
et narrabo uobis, si placet, quod ab eo didici.' Iubente uero
episcopo ut narraret, sic intulit, 'Centum miliaribus distat cella
uiri illius a pede montis sancti Brandani. Iuxta quem montem
manet alius quidam heremita, quem, sicut predictus uir dixit,
plus desideraret alloqui quam alium quemquam in hac mortali   1165
uita. Quem cum interrogarem que causa fuerit et cur ipsius
alloquium eatenus optauerit, "quia demonum," inquit, "narratione didici non eum sicut heremitam uiuere. Gaudent enim
in concilio suo et congratulantur ad inuicem quod eum tam
facile seducunt." Sed et hoc quod ab eis nuper audisse contigit   1170
et uidisse narrabo.'

Rubrica
De demonibus rapientibus escam ab illo qui eam negauerat pauperi

f. 20vb | 'Cum quadam nocte congregati fuissent et magistro suo
singuli precedentis opera diei retulissent, affuit inter alios unus,   1175
cui qui princeps eorum uidebatur ait, "Nun quid portas aliquid
ad manducandum?" Et ille, "Porto." "Et quid", inquit, "portas?" "Porto", ait, "panem et caseum, butirum et farinam." Cui
magister, "Vnde hec tibi?" Et ille, "Duo", inquit, "hodie clerici
uenerunt ad domum cuiusdam rustici diuitis et petebant   1180
elemosinam in caritate Christi. Rusticus autem, habens hec
omnia in conclaui, iurauit per sanctam caritatem Christi se
nichil habere quod posset eis largiri, et ob eius periurium
amisit quod habuit. Nam ut ea surriperem, mihi concessum
est." "Mane igitur egressus repperi que audieram a demone   1185
nominari, scilicet panem et caseum, butirum et farinam. Sed
nolens ut inde quisquam gustasset, omnia proieci in foueam."'

Rubrica
De quodam sacerdote quem illudere uolebat demon ut quandam
puellam quam nutrierat corrumperet   1190
'Est et aliud quod tue dilectioni refero. Quod et te mente
retinere cupio illudque referre ceteris ut eorum insidias caueant

---

1160 uirum sanctum R.   1167 optauerit] optauerat S.
1170 me *interlined in different ink after* eis;   nuper] repeated S.
1172–3 Rubrica ... pauperi] *Inserted in lower margin of f. 20va. In the top
margin of f. 20vb in later hand responsible for running-heads;* 1 Demones
rapiunt escam auari 2 Sacerdos et filia eius spiritualis, *and figures* 1 *and* 2 *in
the left-hand margin of col.* 2 *next to paragraphs 1174 and 1191.*
1180 diuitis rustici S.
1188–90 Rubrica ... corrumperet] *In the lower margin of f. 20vb.*

memento. Sacerdos quidam sancte uite et honeste parrochiam
regebat in hac prouincia, cuius erat consuetudo ut cotidie,
summo mane surgens, prius ecclesie cymiterium circuiens, .vij.   1195
psalmos pro fidelibus defunctis decantaret. Castissime uixit et
sollicite doctrine et operibus bonis operam dedit. Demones
uero multociens conquesti sunt quod illum a proposito casti-
monie et sancte conuersacionis nullus eorum flectere ualeret.
Vnde magister eorum grauiter eos increpabat. Accedens autem   1200
unus eorum ait, "Ego eum decipiam. Ego enim ei iam preparaui mulierem, per quam eum a proposito deiciam. Sed non
nisi infra quindecim annos id facere potero." Cui magister eius,
"Si infra .xv. annos illum deiceres, rem grandem faceres." Illis
f. 21ra autem / diebus quibus hec a demonibus tractata sunt, surgens   1205
mane quadam die sacerdos cymiteriumque de more circuiens
repperit iuxta crucem in cymiterio infantulam unam expo-
sitam. Quam accipiens commendauit cuidam nutrici, ut eam
quasi filiam suam propriam nutriret. Ablactatam uero eam
litteras discere fecit, cuius integritatem Christo consecrare   1210
proposuit. Que cum ad pubertatis annos peruenisset et illius
pulcritudini presbiter assuete et nimis familiariter intendisset,
cepit in eius exardescere concupiscentia, quia secundum carnis
pulcritudinem sed potius putredinem nimis erat speciosa. Et
quo secretius et familiarius eam alloquebatur, eo feruentius in   1215
ipsius amorem rapiebatur. Contigit autem nuper ut eius assensum peteret et impetrauit. Et licet acrius ureretur post im-
petratum assensum, pauefactus tamen ad opus tam insolitum,
actum distulit in crastinum. Eadem uero sequenti nocte congregatis demonibus, prosiliens in medium, sacerdotis incentor   1220
ait, "Ante quindecim annos dixi quod per mulierem deicerem
sacerdotem, et ecce iam illum ab ea feci petisse consensum,
quam sibi adoptauerat in filiam. Sed et ipsa me suggerente
concessit, et cras eos in meridie deiciam." Hiis auditis omnes
quasi gaudio magno cachinnantes et constrepentes ei con-   1225
gratulabantur. "Visne", inquit magister eorum, "socios habere
tecum?" "Non est", ait, "necesse. Solus enim hoc opus perficiam." Gratias agens igitur illi magister eius uiriliter eum
egisse dicebat. Die uero crastina predictus presbiter aduocans
puellam in cubiculum suum introduxit eamque super lectum   1230
suum locauit. Stetit igitur ante lectum aliquandiu, quid ageret
hesitans. Tandem uero non illo instigante qui eum ad hoc opus

1195 circuiens] circumiens R.
1198 proposito] *Second* o *blotted and* o *written above.*
1201–2 ei *follows* preparaui S.   1206 circuiens] circumiens R.
1209 eam] *om.* RS. 1214 sed] uel W. 1216 ut nuper S. 1222 ea] illa S.
1224 deiciam] diciam S.   1228 igitur agens R.

f. 21rb perduxerat, sed ipso inspirante qui non permittit hominem
supra modum tempta/-ri, pensans animo presbiter huius
enormitatem sceleris ait puelle, "Exspecta, filia, paululum,   1235
exspecta donec redeam." Procedens itaque presbiter ad ostium
cubiculi cultrum arripuit, uirilia sibimet abscidit forasque
proiecit, dicens, "Quid putastis, demones, quod uersutias
uestras non intellexerim? De perditione mea uel filie mee non
gaudebitis, quia nec me nec illam habebitis." Sequenti uero   1240
nocte, congregatis iterum demonibus, interrogauit magister
discipulum si peregisset quod se facturum spoponderat. Ille
uero ingemiscens incassum se laborasse respondit, et quomodo
presbiter eum preuenerat omnibus enarrauit. Jussu igitur
magistri sui ab aliis grauissime flagellatus est. Et ita cunctis pre   1245
ira turpiter eiulantibus et horribiliter cachinnantibus concilium
eorum dissipatum est. Sacerdos uero uirginem, quam Deo
seruituram nutrierat, in monasterio uirginibus commendauit.'

Hec itaque, pater uenerande, que a predictis uiris ueracibus
et ualde religiosis audiui, sensum uerborum sequens et rel-   1250
ationis eorum seriem, prout intelligere potui, sanctitati uestre
cunctisque in amorem et timorem Dei proficere cupientibus,
sicut iussistis, ecce litteris significo. Si quis igitur quod scribere
talia presumpserim me reprehenderit, iussioni uestre me
obedientiam nouerit exhibuisse. Peccator et ego precor hu-   1255
militer, qui sanctorum patrum exhortationes interserens
opusculum istud per capitula distinxi, caritatem uestram,
uidelicet qui illud legitis uel auditis, Deum exorare, quatinus
me, a peccatis omnibus in presenti purgatum et a supradictis,
f. 21va et si que sunt alie, penis extorrem, una uobiscum / post huius   1260
mortis horrorem transferat in prefatam beatorum requiem
Ihesus Christus, dux et dominus noster, cuius nomen
gloriosum permanet et benedictum in secula [seculorum].
Amen.

1234   huius presbiter S.   1237   cubiculi] cubili R.
1245   Et] ut W.   1246   turpiter] om. S.
1248   seruituram nutrierat] nutrierat Deo seruituram RS.
1253   igitur] autem W.
1255   exhibuisse nouerit RS; Peccator ... precor] Precor et ego peccator RS.
1256   exortationes patrum RS,   1257   capitula] capitulam S
1258   uidelicet ... auditis] illud uidelicet legentium simul et audientium RS;
Deum] om. RS.   1259–60   me follows extorrem RS.
1259   et] om. RS.   1261   mortis] mortens S.   1263   seculorum] RS, om. L.

COMMENTARY

OWAYNE MILES (*OM*1)
AUCHINLECK

1 The opening stanzas of the poem have been lost with the excision of
the folio which originally preceded the present f. 25. Very likely 32 lines
of text are missing: see Introduction, p. xxii. Some indication of what
these lines may have contained may be inferred from the opening of F.
(All quotations from F are taken from Zanden, *Etude*, pp. 90–135, which
I have checked against the manuscript.)

> En honurance Ihesu Crist,
> Ke tut le mund furma e fist,
> Un aventure voil cunter
> Dunt plusurs se porrunt amender
> Ki cest escrist voudrunt oïr
> E en lur quers bien retenir.
> Le oïr ne vaut une chastanie,
> Ki del retenir ne se penie;
> Eynz vaut meuz de tut lesser
> Ke oïr e tost ublïer.   10
> Seignurs, pur ceo le vus ay dist
> Ke vus ky orez cest escrist,
> Si bien i ad, sil retenez
> E, si n'i ad, si l'amendez.
> Ceo voil a tuz iceus requere
> Ki meuz de moy le saverunt faire.
> De ceo ne voil jo plus parler,
> A mun purpos voil repeirer;
> Deu vus doint bon achevement,
> Ore oyez le comencement.   20
>   Si cum jo l'ay escrist truvé,
> Vus voil dire la verité,
> Ne ja de ren n'i mentiray
> Sulunc l'escrist ke truvé ay.
> En Yrlaunde* esteit jadys
> Un hom ky ert de grant pris;
> Sen Patriz esteit sun dreit nun,
> Mult ert de grant religiun;
> En Deu servir s'entente mist,
> Ki pur luy meint miracle fist;   30

> Taunt cum il ert en ceste vie,
> A muz pur luy dunat aÿe.
> En icel tens ceus de la terre
> Vers Damnedeu teneyent guere,
> Kar bien faire ne voleient,
> Si repleni de mal esteint.

*—Zanden reads *Yrlande*.

1:4–5 These lines have no source in *T*, but closely resemble F37–38 *Seyn Patriz en out grant dolur | Kant il les vist en tel errur* . . .

2:1 Cf. F41 *Mult se pena de sermumier* . . .

2:4 Cf. F57 *Mes plein furent de felunnie* . . .

2:5 No doubt influenced by F58 and F61–62 *Sun sen turnerent a folie | . . . Tute sa predicaciun | Ne luy vaut un butun* . . .

2:5–6 'They regarded what he said as only nonsense about nothing' rather than 'There was nothing that he said that they did not regard as nonsense'.

3:1 Cf. F66 *Tuz luy distrent comunement* . . . *T* merely reads *dicebant* (L112). On F67 following a β text of *T*, see Introduction, p. xlviii.

3:4 *sum man*: It looks as if the scribe first wrote *nman* and then squeezed in *o* over the second minim. KA retains MS apparent *roman* and KB says, 'don that roman: das abenteuer ausführen'. E. Willson, *The Middle English Legends of Visits to the Other World and their Relation to the Metrical Romances* (Chicago, 1917), p. 5, translates this note as 'carried out that adventure', and quotes this line as an example to show that 'certain writers of legends were romance readers'. Such a proposition is doubtless true, but this line so translated is doubtful testimony. There is no record of such a usage of *roman* in French or English; it does not occur in F; and the syntactic deficiency which juxtaposes *roman | Into helle* . . . presupposes corruption in the text. Z's emendation *sum man* could have yielded *roman* via *so man* with a missing abbreviation mark; the sense is well supported by *T* and F. In *T* the pagan Irish say that unless one of them (*nisi aliquis eorum* (L114)) may experience the torments and bliss of the other world, then they will not believe Patrick. Cf. F69–70 *S'il ne face akun de lur | Veer d'enfer la grant dolur* . . . The causative *dede* follows F's *face*. Alternatively, an earlier reading may have been *oo man*, for *oo* as a reduced form of *on* 'one' before a consonant frequently appears before *man*: see *OED* O, Oo, *numeral adj.*

4:4–5 For *repenti* in rhyme cf. F73–74 *Ke ne se volent repentir | Ne lur pecché ici joïr* . . ., speaking of the souls in hell.

5:1–3 Not in *T*. Cf. F85–86 *Quant sein Patriz iceo oÿ,* | *Mult en fu dolent e marri* . . .

5:4–5 Cf. F89–90 *E fud mult en aflictiuns,* | *En juines e en oreissuns* . . ., after L117–18.

6:2 *wende*: transitive with object *hem* (6:4) and *folk* (6:6).

7 The stanza expands F95–96 *Si cum il vint pur Deu preer,* | *Il s'endormist devant l'auter* . . . This detail appears neither in *T* nor in any other English or French version. The subsequent references to sleep (10:3, 12:6) are found only in A.

8:1–3 The dream is mentioned in F97 *Si li esteit avis en sunge* . . ., but not in *T*, where Christ *uisibiliter apparuit* (L120).

9:1 *þat nas nouȝt lite*: a novel little physical detail, typical of many that the English poet introduces into this version.

9:2 Cf. F104 *Nus hom ne le vus savereit descrire* . . . Maybe the English poet understood *escrire* for *descrire*, though the latter could also mean 'to write'. This is not in *T*.

9:4–6 Expand F106 *U les evangelies sunt escrist*, which follows *textum ewangeliorum* (L120).

10:2 *a wel feir staf*: cf. F108 . . . *un bel bastun* . . .

10:4–6 Cf. F110–11 *Le bastun Deu le unt apelé;* | *Unkore sunt il en Yrlande* . . . *T* calls the staff *baculus Ihesu* (L124), which more closely resembles the Irish name *Bachal Isa*. See Commentary C64.

11:1–4 Cf. F119–21 *Quant Deu li out cel dun doné,* | *Od sei l'en ad d'iloc mené;* | *En un desert dreit s'en ala* . . ., after L127–8.

12:1–2 Cf. F123–4 *Ke tut esteit obchure e runde;* | *Tel n'i avoit en tut le munde.* L128 has no equivalent for F124.

13:2–4 Cf. F126–7 *Ke cil ke ad fet mortel pecché,* | *S'il seit veray repentaunt* . . ., and *quia quisquis ueraciter penitens* (L129).

14:5 Cf. F136, 138 *De(s) ses pecchez averat relés* | . . . *Trestuz li erent parduné*, and *ab omnibus purgaretur tocius uite sue peccatis* (L131–2).

15:1–2 Cf. F139–40 *E s'il eit ferme creance* | *Bone e pure sanz dutance* . . ., after *si in fide constanter egisset* (L133), which F and A bring forward to precede the sight of the tormented. *MED* creaunce *n*. cites 15:1 under 1.(a) Belief (in sth.), faith, trust, as its first quotation. *OED* gives this line as the first citation s.v. Creance, *sb.* †2. Credit, reputation, *Obs. rare*. *MED*'s reading is clearly the correct interpretation. Neither dictionary takes account of the word's recurrence in lines 32:1 and 47:4.

15:6 Only in A. As Owein discovers, this is not strictly true. In this stanza the substance of lines 3 and 6 is newly introduced to complete the rhyme scheme. The time element in 15:4 is also new in A, developing F141 *Kant il serat iloc dedenz* ...

16:1 Cf. F143 *U les peccheurs serunt jetez* ..., not in L132–3.

16:4–6 Cf. F145–8 *E ensement rever pura | La duce joye ke fait ha | Damnedeu a ses amis, | Ki sunt la sus en paraÿs.* T merely has *gaudia beatorum* (L134).

17:1–2 Cf. F149–50 *Kant li Syres out si parlé | E tut apertement mustré* ... No true equivalent in *T*.

17:3–6 Only in A. Cf. F151–2 *Li Sauvers Ihesu Crist | De cel seint home s'envanist*, and *Domino disparente* (L134).

18 The whole of this stanza follows F153–9 (which have no close equivalent in L134–6):

> E quant sein Patriz s'eveilla,
> Enseignes bones i truva
> Ke i n'out mot de mensunge
> De kanke il out veü en sunge:
> Ceo fut le livre oud le bastun
> Dunt Deu li aveit fait le dun.
> Il en ad mut Deu mercïé ...

19:1 Not in *T* or F.

19:4 *Wharþurth*: *þurth* is spelt thus throughout this poem and always by Auchinleck scribe 1. KA always reads *þurch*. See A.J. Bliss, 'Notes on the Auchinleck Manuscript', *Speculum*, xxvi (1951), 658 n. 5, and O.D. Macrae-Gibson, EETS, 279 (1979), 78 n. to l. 249.

19:5–6 Cf. F164 *Al pople fere amendement* ...

20:1, 3 Cf. F167 *En icel lu, sanz demurance* ..., after *Statimque in eodem loco* (L137–8).

20:5 I have emended according to F170; see Introduction, p. l. *T* gives no indication of the church's dedication (L137–9). It is possible, though unlikely, that the author of AN knew that St Patrick founded St Peter and St Paul's, Armagh, and adapted this knowledge. St Patrick had brought relics of saints Peter and Paul from Rome and laid them in their shrine at Armagh; see *Trip. Life*, II. 474–5. The Lough Derg priory on Saints' Island was a dependency of this foundation at Armagh. More probably, however, *seint Pere* was simply employed to rhyme with *sa mere*, which in A becomes *our leuedy*, not found in *T*.

21:2 Cf. F172 *Ceo sevent bien cels de la tere*. Not in *T*.

21:4 *Regles*: is spelt the same here as in F174, and A follows F in giving the name at this point rather than after telling that the hole is called St Patrick's Purgatory (24:3, F193), as is the order in L150-2. On the name *Regles*, see Commentary Y85.

21:5–6 Not in *T* or F.

22:1 *White chanounes*: are properly the Premonstratensian order of canons regular. F175 reads *Chanoynes riulers* ... The Saints' Island priory, which oversaw St Patrick's Purgatory on Station Island, adopted the Rule of St Augustine (properly Black Canons) *c*.1132. See L138–9 and Commentary.

22:3 This probably owes something to F177–8 *Ke tut dis deivent sanz feintie | Des apostles tenir la vie*. F here follows the β text of *T, uitam apostolicam sectantes* (L139). These words are omitted from α.

22:4–6 Only in A. See Commentary C54ff and C64 on the book and staff.

23:1–2 Cf. F179–80 *Dreit pres de l'est, pres de l'eglise, | Est cele fosse grant assise*, which translates L139–41.

23:3 Only in A.

23:4–5 Cf. F181–4 *Sein Patriz trestut entur | Le fit clore de un bon mur; | Une grant porte fere i fist | E serure bone i mist ...*, which translates *muro circumdedit et ianuas serasque apposuit* (L141–2).

24:2–3 Cf. F192–3 *L'um l'apele la entur | Le purgatorie seint Patriz* ... The 'entrance' is not mentioned in *T*. A ignores the prior to whom St Patrick gives the key (F188, L143–4).

24:4 Cf. F195 *En icel tens ke cest avint ...*, after L145.

24:6 This tag renders F194 *Si cum recuntent les escriz*.

25:1 Cf. F197–8 *Ki pur les pecchez espeinir | La peine volt pur suffrir ...*, where *T* merely reads *penitentia ducti* (L145).

25:2, 6 The repetition here of the visitors' return stems from β *T regredientes* (L146, not found in α), via F196 *Meint i entra ke puys revint ...* (cf. A24:5), and F199 *E quant il furent revenu ...*

25:3–5 Cf. F200–4:

> Si unt bien dist e coneü
> Ki il unt veü apertement
> La grant dolur e le turment,
> U tuz ceus soffrent la penance
> Ki n'unt fet lur penitance ...

Both F and A do not agree exactly with *T* which says that visitors suffered rather than merely saw the torments, and saw the joys (L146–7). Whereas the author of AN is meticulous in explaining that visitors saw the penance of what must be souls in purgatory, the author of *OM1* twice refers simply to hell (24:5, 25:5). Purgatory is specified at 42:6. See below, Commentary A67:6.

26 This stanza expands on F. Cf. ll. 2 and 5 with F205–6 *E la joie reveü unt | De paraÿs, u tuz ceus sunt* ... A ignores St Patrick's instruction to write down the accounts of those who visit the Purgatory (F210–12, L147–8 and cf. L174–5).

26:5 I.e. the Earthly Paradise.

27:1 Cf. F213 *Kant ceus ke el pays esteyent* ...

27:4 Cf. F215 *A seint Patriz dreit en alerunt* ... (In F f. 16r begins with l. 217 not 214 as in Zanden's text.)

27:5 Not in *T* or F. 27:1–28:3 follow F213–24 which greatly expand *Eorum ergo attestacione ceperunt alii beati Patricii predicationem suscipere* (L148–50).

28:1–2 Cf. F220 *Se sunt il trestuz convertuz* ...

28:4–6 This formula for recitation also occurs at this point in F225–34. A follows F in omitting the rest of the preamble concerning the ritual procedure for the entry to the Purgatory (see L176–204). The fact that the details were to follow, concerning Owein's visit in particular, would have made the repetition of this information idle. At this point *T* has the tale of the one-toothed prior (L154–71).

29:1 Cf. F235 *El tens le rey Estevene avint* ...

29:2–3 Not in *T*. Cf. F236 *Ki guardat Engletere e tint* ...

29:4 In *T* Owein was an Irish knight subject to an Irish king; the reference to King Stephen is only to give a date. The idea of linking Owein with Northumberland is entirely our poet's own; see Introduction, p. lv, and see further Easting, 'Owein at St Patrick's Purgatory'. There is no evidence that the poet himself was from the north. Northumbria, of course, had potent links with Ireland, and both were fertile of other-world legend. (On Drihthelm being from Melrose, and Fursey (see *BEH*, III, 19) from Ireland, and the possible transmission of Gregory's *Dialogues* to Northumbria via Ireland, see A.G. Van Hamel's review of Verdeyen and Endepols (1914) in *Neophilologus*, iv (1919), 152–65 (pp. 154–5).) The *OM1* poet may have meant only that Owein fought in Northumberland, and still have regarded the *cuntre þer he born wes* (30:2) as Ireland.

29:5 Cf. F238 *Ke mult ert hardi e fier*. No such description, however brief, is found in *T*, though some effort to rectify this deficiency was made by Roger of Wendover: see my article cited in the previous note.

29:6 *rime*: rather than *storie* (24:6) is more specific and accurate considering the debt to AN.

30 Not in *T*. Cf. F239–43:

> En cele terre u il esteit né
> Par nun esteit Owein apelé.
> Mult ert de grant chivalerie,
> Mes pecché aveit par folie
> Emveer sun creatur mespris . . .

Tnugdal was also *genere nobilis . . . militari arte non mediocriter instructus*, and sinful; see *Visio Tnugdali*, p. 6 ll. 15ff.

31–32 Not in *T*. Cf. F245–52:

> Mes a un jur se purpensa
> K'il la folie guerpira,
> E voudra par confessiun
> De ses pecchez aver pardun.
> Kant il issi purpensé fu,
> Par aveture est avenu
> A cel esvesque ki maneit
> El paÿs u le fosse esteit . . .

32:3–5 In adapting AN the English author has arrived at a false statement. The bishop did not reside at an abbey where the *hole* was, but at the seat of the bishopric in which the Purgatory lay, i.e. Clogher; see Commentary L208–9. The Latin says Owein went *ad episcopum, in cuius episcopatu prefatum est Purgatorium* (L208–9); cf. F251–2, quoted above. In so far as the poet omits the business of the bishop sending a letter to the prior of the Purgatory (L225–32, F297–320) it is, however, more fitting that Owein should be represented as finding the bishop on the site. Note the transition in stanzas 37 and 38 from *bischop* to *priour*.

33:1–3 Cf. F255–7 *E tut li cunut sa folye, | E pur amur Deu merci luy crie, | Ke il luy doint confessiun . . .*

33:5 Cf. F260 *E guerpira tut sun pecché.*

34:1–2 Cf. F261–2 *E le evesque grant joie en a, | Mes del peché mult le blama . . .*, which elaborates *cum pro peccatis increparet episcopus* (L209–10).

35:4 Cf. F273 *Si vus le volez comander . . .* See Introduction, p. xlvii.

36 Neither in *T* nor in *F* is this reply by the bishop in direct speech. One may compare Marie de France's version (ll. 543–6) for the same use of direct speech here, but she has none of the cordiality of A36:1.

36:3 Cf. F280 *E la grant peine luy mustra . . .* A ignores the bishop's suggestion that Owein should adopt the habit of a monk or canon in preference to entering the Purgatory (L222–3, F285ff).

38:1–2 Cf. F324–6 *U quince jurz dust sujurner | Pur fere a Deu ses oreisuns | En juines e en afflictiuns* ..., after L233–4, and A5:4–5 and Commentary.

38:4–5 Cf. A193:1–2.

38:4 Cf. F331 *Le priur a processiun* ...

38:5 Only here in A; cf. the same rhyming phrase in the Auchinleck *Roland and Vernagu*, l. 873, quoted in *MED* s.v. gounfanoun *n.* 1. (c).

39:1–5 Cf. F339–44:

> 'Frere, fait il, vus enterez
> En la fosse ke vus veyez.
> Quant vus serez un poy alé,
> Tut averez perdu la clarté,
> Mes vus truverez la veye grant,
> Si en irez tut dreit avant.'

There is no equivalent in *T* for F341–2, A39:4–5.

39:6 Not in *T*, nor is the north mentioned in F, see F344 quoted above. Although the subterranean geography of the tale is somewhat confused, it is fitting that Owein should be made to go north in order to encounter the demons, the north being traditionally the domain of Lucifer.

40:1 Cf. F345–6 *Et tant siverez le grant chemin | Ki est desuz el suzterin* ..., after β *per concauitatem subterraneam* (L240), where α reads *per concauitatem terre*, though α has *subterraneam* later (W48:13) when Owein reaches the hall.

40:3–4 A has brought the mention of the hall forward. In F the field is at 353 (though mentioned earlier at 347), and the hall at 354; they are preceded by the description of the half-light (F350–2) translated in A41:1–3. The mention of stone (A40:4, 43:6) is only in A.

40:6 Cf. F348 *U poy de clarté truverez* ...

41:1–3 See Introduction, pp. xlvii–xlviii.

42:1–2 No number of *Godes seriaunce* is given by the prior in *T* or F, and A alone specifies thirteen. F386 follows L269–70 (see Commentary) in subsequent narrative (cf. A45:4) giving fifteen. It would seem that *pritten* or *xiii* already existed in the A scribe's exemplar for it is repeated at 45:4 and 190:5. At some stage either *fiften* or *xv* must have been misread. No *T* manuscript known to me gives the number thirteen. There is no evidence for a link with the number thirteen found in two manuscripts of a French prose

version, which seem rather to have added to the figure twelve
usually found in that version; see Owen, *Vision of Hell*, p. 140 n.
146: he suggests that thirteen 'may be due to an analogy with
Christ and the twelve disciples'. The same analogy may justify the
A reading.

A follows F in not mentioning at this point that *temptatores*
(L244) will arrive after the departure of *Godes seriaunce*.

42:6 Not in *T* or F.

43 A follows F in the sequence of events and in omitting the
declining and reviving light found in L258–60. Cf. F365–73:

> Quant alad e enz se mist,
> Sis comandat a Ihesu Crist;
> E cels se sunt tuz returné,
> Si unt la porte refermé.
> Le chivaler de aler se avance,
> En Deu ad mis sa fiance;   370
> Tant ad sun dreit chemin tenu
> Que dequ'al champ en est venu
> E la grant sale i ad truvé ...

F370, which has no equivalent in A, stems from β *confidens in
Domino* (L257), not found in α.

44:2 This line may conceivably show that the A poet knew an α
T text which includes at about this point *Sicut enim estimauit, in
hoc seculo aula talis uisa ab homine uel facta numquam fuit*
(W50:31–34), though the commonplace nature of the line and the
lack of corroborative evidence for the use of an α text, or of any
text of *T*, makes this most unlikely. No such line occurs in F.

44:3 Cf. F378 *Kar sur pilers ert tute asise* ..., which translates
columpnis (L263).

44:6–45:3 Cf. F379–82 *Nule pareys ert fermé, | A merveille l'ad
esgardé. | Quant il out aukes demuré, | Iloc de hors si est entré* ...

45:3 *þare*: for *þere* to rhyme with *bere* < *beren*, with long close ẹ̄.

45:5 Not in *T* or F. F386 calls the messengers *homes de religiun*,
after *quasi religiosi* (L270).

45:6 Cf. F388 *E de blans dras erent vestuz*, after *albis uestibus
amicti* (L270), and see Commentary L270–3.

46:1 Cf. F387 *Tuz furent res e haut tunduz* ..., after *nuper rasi*
(L270).

46:2 *Her most maister*: translates F392 *Le plus haut de eus* ..., cf.
L273.

46:3   Cf. F389 *Il le salurent bonement* ..., after *salutantes illum* (L271). *salud*: A antedates first manuscript reference in *MED* s.v. saluen *v.* (a).

46:6   Cf. F393 *Mult ducement l'aresuna* ...

47   Cf. F399–402:
> Mes de une rien garnir vus voil,
> Si cum les autres faire soil:
> Ke vus ayez ferme creance,
> Estable e bone sanz dutance ...

Cf. also A15:1–2. 47:4–6 translate: 'that thou be of firm belief, (that) thy true allegiance (faith) to God (be) certain and pure, without doubt'. KB interprets *fay* as imperative 'follow' from OE *fegan*, and translates thc line 'füge deine treue zu gott, d.h. vertraue fest auf gott'. This seems unnecessarily tortuous.

48:1–3   Cf. F405–8 *Kar quant nus serum departiz,* | *Verez de mavés esperiz* | *Ceste grant sale tute pleine,* | *Ke vus voudrunt fere grant peine* ...

49:2–3   Not in *T* or F. Reverence for Christ's wounds is shown also at 196:5, again only in A, and cf. 143:4.

49:5   Cf. F425 *E alme e cors perdu serez* ..., after *et corpore et anima pariter* ... *peribis* (L284–5). Only A mentions *helle*.

50:1   Cf. F432–3 *Reclamez Deu omnipotent,* | *De Ihesu numez le nun* ..., after *inuoca Dominum Ihesum Christum* (L291–2). In F this speech by the leader of God's messengers is very long—54 lines; cf. A's 21 lines. A omits the promise that Owein should see paradise if he is constant in purgatory, F444–8, L290.

50:4–51:2   Cf. F449–53:
> Quant il li out tut ceste mustré,
> Il n'i ad pas plus demuré,
> Mes il e tuz si compaingun,
> Li unt duné lur beneiçun,
> Si s'en issi hastivement ...

In *T* the leader of the men in white says that they can stay no longer (L293–4); A follows F in making this notion part of the narrative. F418 also includes the idea in the middle of the speech.

51:3–6   A omits the section on how Owein was armed with the armour of God (F456–64, shortened from L295–305). A makes Owein a much more fearful human figure than the strong knight of Christ (*miles Christi*), awaiting battle with the demons, presented in *T*. See Introduction, p. lvi and Commentary A61:1–2.

52:2   Cf. F466 *Crïer e braire oÿ fortment* ...

52:4–6 Cf. F469–71 *Si tut le mund deust trebucher | E ciel e tere deust asembler, | Greinur noyse pas ne freit ...,* after *si totus commoueretur orbis* (L309). Both F and A omit *T*'s mention of men and beasts, though *ciel e tere* and *firmament to þe mold* may derive from β *omnia animantia terre, maris et aeris* (L310), not found in α.

53 A omits that God's help prevented Owein from going mad with the noise (F473–6, L312–14). F expands on this by having Owein recall the messengers' comforting advice to call on Christ (F477–86). Details in A53:3, 6 are newly introduced.

54:2 Not in *T* or *F*. Grinning backsides presuppose that the poet visualises the demons as wearing a face *Bihinde and eke bifore* (53:6). Representations of demons with faces not only on the backside but on the stomach and limb joints were common in the fourteenth and fifteenth centuries. See e.g. A.N. Didron, *Christian Iconography,* II (London, 1886), figs. 171, 192, and L. Réau, *Iconographie de l'art chrétien,* II (1) (Paris, 1956), p. 61. Cf. also *VWS* SR89–91, SA91–3.

54:3 Cf. F495–6 *Il le vunt tuz mult escarnisant | E par echar li [v]unt disant ...,* after *cachinnando ac deridendo illum salutare et quasi per obprobrium dicere* (L319–20).

54:4 A brings this forward from the fiends' speech in F506 *En char e en os a nus venistes ...*

54:5–55:3 Not in *T* or *F*.

55:1 *most maister-fende*: The compound *maister-fende* (attested in *MED* s.v. maister *n.* 1. (f)) has probably been amalgamated with the expression *most maister* (cf. 46:2 and see *MED* most *adj.* 2. (a)).

55:4–5 Cf. F511–12 *E pur vos pechez espeinir, | Venistes ça peine sufrir.* T does not mention amendment, nor do *T* and F mention Owein's *dedli sinne* (56:3). The English poet throughout lays more stress on Owein's sins and his expiation of them.

56:1–2 Cf. F514 *Dolur e peine od nus averez.*

56:5 Not in *T* or *F*. On the devils' dance, cf. *The Sowdone of Babylone,* ed. E. Hausknecht, EETS, ES 38 (1881), ll. 3188–90: *His soule was fet to helle, | To daunse in þat sory lande | With develes, þat wer ful felle.* Cf. also C282 and Commentary. The dance of the devils introduced by the A poet here contrasts neatly with the carols danced in the Earthly Paradise (141–142), which are also introduced only in A.

57 Cf. F515–20:

> E nepurquant, si vus volez,
> Pur ceo ke servi nus avez,

E ke nus trestuz vus avum,
Hors de la porte vus meterum
Tut sein e sauf, par unt venistes
Quant vus del priur departistes ...

57:4 *wiþ fine amour*: see Introduction, p. liv. Like the references to *þe ioie of helle* (54:5) and *solas* (107:4), the malicious
incongruity of the romantic phrase on the lips of the fiends
parallels the ironic inversion of values practised by the lying
ministers of King Gulinus's court who torture another knight
visitor to St Patrick's Purgatory; see Easting, 'Peter of Cornwall's
Account', pp. 414–15. On demonic irony see also T. McAlindon,
'Comedy and Terror in Middle English Literature: The Diabolic-
al Game', *MLR,* lx (1965), 323–32, and Tom C. Gardner, 'The
Theater of Hell: A Critical Study of some Twelfth Century Latin
Eschatological Visions', unpublished Ph.D. dissertation, University of California, Berkeley, 1976.

58 Not in *T* or F. In 58:3 the poet begins the enumeration of
Owein's sins which are not mentioned in *T* nor in any other
account of Owein's visit. The poet has taken the idea mainly from
the *Vision of St Paul*, and is followed indirectly in this by William
of Stranton; see Introduction, p. li.

58:5 Cf. 119:3.

59:2–3 Only in A does Owein speak at this point, though cf.
*OM*2 C291–2, Y286–7. In *T* it is specifically stated that he
remains silent (L337).

59:5–60:2 Cf. F539–42 *Dunke firent il demeintenant | En la mesun
un fu mult grant; | E piez e poinz dunc luy lïerent, | Einz en le fu
puis le geterent* ..., after L340–2. In *T* the demons then drag
Owein back and forth through the flames with iron hooks (L342
and F543–4); cf. A58:5.

60:5 Cf. F550–2 ... *trestut le fu | Issi esteint demeintenant, | Ne
truvisez petyt ne grant,* after *ut nec scintilla inueniretur* (L350).

61:1–2 Cf. F553–4 *Quant le chivaler out ceo veu, | Assez le plus
hardi en feu* ... A then omits the idea found in L350–3 and
F557–60 that Owein felt *Michel þe balder* because he knew he
could so easily dismiss the fiends and escape torment by virtue of
his prayer. The poem thus preserves greater dramatic tension in
Owein's encounters with the fiends; see also Commentary A51:
3–6. A even has three new lines (61:4–6) emphasising the *fendes
trecherie* and the testing of Owein's heart (faith); 61:4 probably
depends on F555 *En sun quer le purpensa* ... The unusual
expression *þou3t wele in his memorie* may mean simply 'remembered well', for his release from the flames calls to mind the
advice he was given in the hall (47–50:3). It also seems to suggest

that Owein 'committed (this experience) firmly to mind', as a safeguard against future perils.

62:1–2 Cf. F561–2 *Les debles dunc s'en alerent,* | *Le chevaler od eus menerent* ..., after L355–6.

62:3 Cf. F569 *En une estrange regyun* ..., and *per uastam regionem* (L357–8).

62:4–6 Not in *T* or F. The extra physical discomforts are added by the English poet. The fact that there are no trees to be seen again contrasts with the high trees in the Earthly Paradise (145:2).

63:1–3 Cf. F572–6:

> E mult i aveyt grant freydure
> D'un vent ke si petyt esteyt
> K'il a grant peine le oeyt,
> Mes il li sembla nepurquant
> Le cors luy ala perzant.

This follows L360–1. A emphasises the physical pain of the piercing by omitting F *il li sembla* (575, after *T uidebatur perforare*). Cf. the bitter wind in the *Poema Morale* (Lambeth MS), ed. J. Hall, *Selections from Early Middle English 1130–1250*, I (Oxford, 1920), 38 l. 136, and see Owen, *Vision of Hell*, Index s.v. winds, infernal.

63:5 A omits the geographical details of the journey, first travelling NE and then SE (L362–5, F581–90).

63:6 Cf. F588 *Par mi un val ke mut lé fu* ..., after *per uallem latissimam* (L364).

64:1–2 Not in *T* or F. The poet speaks of hell, i.e. Owein thinks he is in hell, but it is really purgatory; see A42:6, 67:6, 72:6, 79:5, 82:2, 160:6, 165:1, 166:2, 179:1, 194:5. In mistaking purgatory for hell, Owein follows a pattern for other-world visitors set by Drihthelm, *BEH*, V, 12 (Plummer, p. 305); see further Easting, 'Purgatory and the Earthly Paradise', pp. 36–37.

64:3–6 Cf. F591–4 *E quant le chivaler aproza* | *A cel liu, dunkes escuta;* | *Pleintes i oÿ e dolurs,* | *Crïer e braire e mult grant plurs* ...

64:6 *schriche and grede*: The syntax here suggests these are nouns, 'shrieking and lamentation', but *grede* exists only as a verb (cited in combination with *schrichen* from Auchinleck *Floris*, l. 449, in *MED* s.v. skriken *v.*), so we have to understand these words as infinitives or supply a subject such as 'folk' after *herd*. The phrase renders F594 *Crïer e braire*, quoted above, but see also the combination with the adjacent nouns *Pleintes* ... *dolurs* ... *plurs*.

65:1–2 Cf. F603–4 *Le champ esteit tut repleni* | *Des homes e de femmes autresi* ..., after L373–4.

65:3 Cf. F610 *A grant dolur, si erent nuz.*

65:4 Cf. F605 *Tuz ventrez turnez ver la terre . . .*, after L374–5.

65:6 A alone has 'iron bands'. L375 and F607 have burning iron nails, but A hereby avoids repetition with the second field of torment; see A70:2.

66:1–3 Cf. F616–17 *Crïerent dolerusement: | 'Merci, merci de nus aiez . . .'.*

66:4 See Introduction, p. xlix.

66:5–6 Not in *T* or F; 66:5 after *fletus et stridor dentium* of Matthew 8:12, 13:42 etc., and Luke 13:28.

67 Not in *T* or F. The first of the stanzas introduced in A detailing the sins for which the various pains were prepared; see Introduction, p. li. This is in place of the fiends' attempts to make Owein turn back (L381–5, F625–30).

67:3 Sloth does not appear in *VSP*, used by the *OM1* poet for the remainder of his list of sins.

67:6 Note the poet specifies purgatory at the beginning of the torments so that we have no doubt ourselves that what is described is not *hell*. See above, Commentary A64:1–2.

68:1–3 Not in *T* or F, where the devils attempt to nail Owein down but are prevented when he calls on Christ. It is not really the first pain because Owein has been thrown on the fire in the cloister-like hall (59–60), but it is the first pain suffered by the other souls and the first pain of purgatory.

68:4 A omits the reiteration of the invocation of Christ after every torment, thereby speeding up the narrative.

68:5 Cf. F643 *Dequ'en un autre venu sunt . . .*

69:1 Cf. F645 *Des homes e femmes plein le virent . . .*, after L391–2.

69:2–3 Not in *T* or F. *OED* s.v. Lore *sb.*[1] 2.†c. cites this instance as 'A form of doctrine, a creed, religion.' *Obs.*

69:4–5 Cf. F649–50 *Les dos de ceus vers tere sunt | E des autres turné amunt*, after L393–5.

70:1–3 A's elaboration.

70:4–5 Cf. F651–2 *Le chivaler sur les uns | Vit sér ardanz dragunts . . .*, after *Dracones igniti* (L395).

70:6 This is a stock line in ME romance, in which *herd* derives from OE *hired* 'household'; hence the sense 'in a household nothing may be hidden' becomes 'there is no secret about it', i.e.

'this is the plain truth'. See *MED* hired n. 3 (c); *OED* Hird, Hired *sb*. 1; Whiting H281.

71:1   Cf. F665–6 *E sur les uns crapouz seeient | Ardanz e neirs …*, and *Buffones … quasi ignei* (L400).

71:2   Newts appear in hell, along with adders, snakes and frogs, in *Poema Morale*, (Trinity MS) l. 277, ed. Hall, *Selections*.

71:3   A's paraphrase of an extended passage, F653–72.

71:4–6   Not in *T* or F. Here the glutton is suitably punished, 'Not where he eats, but where 'a is eaten.'

72–73   The cold wind and the demons with hooks belong to the third field of torment (L422, F724–6 (cf. F683)), though the poet has omitted to move Owein on, and has omitted the repetition of the nail torment (L416–19, F705–12—F elaborates). We can infer that stanzas 72 and 73 do deal with field three for in 73 we are told that these pains are for the sin of lechery, and in 76:5 we have moved on to the fourth field. Altogether there are seven 'fields' of torment: 1. 65–68:4 (sloth), 2. 68:5–71 (gluttony), 3. 72–75 (lechery), 4. 76–82 (backbiting, false witnesses), 5. 83–89 the wheel (covetousness), 6. the mountain and river (90–95), 7. the bath house (96–104). See also, Introduction, pp. li. (On the parallel with the seven seals and the seven-fold furnace of *VSP* and the seven zones of hell in the ON *Solarlioð*, see further D.D.R. Owen, 'The Vision of St. Paul: The French and Provençal Versions and Their Sources', *RP*, xii (1958), 36 n. 10 and ref. to Asin Palacios, Pt. II, ch. III.) There follow the false 'pit of hell' (pride) and the perilous bridge.

72:2   *cold*: cf. *uento frigido et urente* (L422). F724 translates only *urente*: *U vent ki fu bruillant esteit …*

72:3–6   Not in *T* or F.

72:5   *ouerþrewe*: an early use, first citation in *OED* s.v. overthrow *v*. 1. *MED* first cites *Arth. & M.* from the Auchinleck manuscript.

73:2   Cf. F726 *Ke de lur crocs les demaglerent*, after *flagrisque demonum cruciabantur* (L422–3).

73:3–74:3   Not in *T* or F. Lechers appear in *VSP* stanzas 7 and 10.

74:2   *lichoure*: a small hole in the manuscript has recently destroyed the upper part of *l* and the ascender of initial *b* in *bacbiters* (81:4) on the verso (see also the facsimile); photographs supplied to me some years ago show the manuscript undamaged at this point.

74:4–6   No direct speech in F, but cf. L423–4.

75:1–3 Not in *T* or F.

75:4–6 A paraphrases F733–8, after L424–7.

76 A paraphrases and expands on F739–42.

77:1 Cf. *VSP* 3:1 *Some bi þe fiet weren an hongue*, and F753 *Les uns i pendent par le piez* ... The agreement is because *T* itself draws at this point on the *Visio Sancti Pauli*; see Commentary L431–3.

77:2 A substitutes hooks for chains at this point; cf. F754, 759; L431, 434.

77:3 Cf. F756 *Les uns ... par le cous* ...

77:4 A's variation on the tradition, though cf. F767 ... *u par le dos* ...

77:5–6 The poet was truly faced with a plethora of torments catalogued in both *T* and F, the latter (F743–800) even fuller than L430–47. Cf. F779–80 *Il sunt peyné en meinte guise,* | *Ne ne vus say faire devise* ...

78:1–2 Cf. F769–70 *Enz esteit les esquanz* | *En furneyses de suffre ardanz* ..., after *Alii fornacibus sulphureis cremabantur* (L435–6). A's *molten ledde* picks up F775 *E de plum chaud* ...
    quic brunston: *MED* quik *adj.* 5. (b) 'free or native sulfur' (first reference *c.*1330 *SMChron.* 181).

78:3 Not in *T* or F.

78:4 Cf. *VSP* 3:6 *And some bi heore tounges hienge.*

78:5–6 Not in *T* or F. Souls in purgatory cannot pray for themselves; they depend on the prayers of their living friends and relatives to assist them.

79:1 Cf. F771 *Sur gridils sunt les uns rosti* ... Gridirons are not mentioned in *T*, which has frying pans and spits (L436–7).

79:2 A's detail.

79:3–5 Cf. F786–8 *Homes mult k'yl bien cuniseit,* | *Ki furent de sa cunisance* | *E la suffrirent lur penance.* This follows *uidit quosdam de suis quondam sociis et eos bene cognouit* (L441–2).
    queyntaunce: antedates *MED* queintaunce *n.* first reference a.1425 *KAlex.* (LinI) 4897.

79:6 Not in *T* or F.

80:1–2 Cf. F745–6 *Le champ de fu tut pleine esteit,* | *Quanque il ateint tut ebraseit* ...; not in *T*.

80:3–6 Not in *T*, F or *VSP*.

80:4 Refers back to 77:1, 3.

81–82   Not in *T* or F. 81:1–2 refer to 78:4–5.

81:4   Cf. *VSP* 17:4 *þulke weren bacbitares in heore liue.*

83–84:2   Cf. F801–8.

84:3   Cf. F821 *De ambes parz dunc debles curerent …*

84:4–6   A paraphrases F824–30.

85   A omits the fact that the wheel was half submerged in the earth (L452–3, F810). Cf. F811–14 *Neyre flamme de suffre ardant / Hors de la tere vint surdant, / Tute la roe enviruna, / Ceus ke pendirent turmenta.* This follows L453–5. A85:3 and 6 are not in *T* or F, though the sulphur suggests A's 'stink'.

86–87:3   Not in *T* or F. On the wheel as the fitting pain for the sin of covetousness, cf. the Y MS copy of *Adrian and Epotys*, ll. 371–82 (*Common-place Book*, p. 37), attributing the idea to St Paul.

86:3   [covetousness] *regnes now oueral*: *MED* regnen v. 4 (e) of a vice: to be rife, cites nothing before Chaucer except Mannyng (*c.*1303); under 1. (c) of a quality, an element, or activity: to rule, govern, prevail, predominate, the first reference is (1340) *Ayenb.*

86:5   *plouȝ*: the most likely meaning here is plough-land, a unit of land for assessment; see *OED* Plough *sb.* B. †3a, and Plough-land, and *MED* plough *n.* 3. (a). *OED* A.1.a cites *Saxon Leechdoms* *c.*1100 *Ne plot ne ploh*, and then, like *MED*, nothing before *c.*1410 (*c.*(1350) *Gamelyn*, 57,59, which A86:5 clearly antedates. This sense might be reinforced by *OED* B.1.c. †(a) and 2c (a) and *MED* 1b. (c), the means of earning one's living; neither cite anything before *c.*1375. KB noted the sense 'gewinn', gain, profit, after Norse *plógr*, used metaphorically for gain or produce, e.g. *virð lítils veraldar plóg*, cited Cleasby and Vigfusson, *An Icelandic–English Dictionary*.

87:3   *lond and lede*: 'landed property', see *MED* led(e *n.* (2) 3; an alliterative phrase < OE *land and leode*, probably cognate with Old West Norse *land ok lýðr*. See also *OED* Lede *sb.* 1(b), and E.S. Olszewska, 'Illustrations of Norse Formulas in English', *Leeds Studies in English*, ii (1933), 79 and 83.

87:4–6   A's elaboration based on F817–18 '*Ansi cum cels peiné serez / Si vus returner ne volez …*', after L455–6.

88   This expands F835–6 *Sur la roe dunc li geterent / En l'eir turnant sus le leverent …*, after L461–2.

89   The stress on physical pain is not found in *T* or F, and nor is the angel.

90–95 These six stanzas on the mountain, wind and river should follow stanzas 96–104 on the bath-house, if the order is to follow that in *T* and F; see Introduction, pp. l–li.

90:1–2 Cf. F913–15 *Le chevaler od eus menerent; | La dreit veie tant alerent | K'il sunt venu desqu'a un munt* ..., after L489–90.

90:3, 5–6 Not in *T* or F.

90:4 Cf. F918 *Homes e femmes nuz ester* ...

91:1–2 Cf. F928–30 *L'un des debles luy diseyt: | 'Mult vus semble merveile grant | Ke cele gent vunt attendant* ...', after L495–6. The rhyme may be a slip for *þen/men*, as the noun must be plural, but *OED* Man *sb.*[1] records the uninflected form, albeit (*north.*), and see Introduction, p. xxiv. *Þan* is A's usual form for 'then'; there is one instance of *þen* at 128:6.

91:3 *Þat make so dreri mode*: 'That make such doleful lamentation', i.e. lament so sorrowfully. *MED* does not record a collocation *make* ... *mode* (cf. *maken mon*), yet it seems unlikely that one could construe the line with *make* as the v. 'cry out' (or fiendish irony for 'compose a song'?) and *dreri-mode* (recorded only as an adj.) as an adv.

91:3–6 Not in *T* or F. The metaphorical beverage of evil (*MED* beverage *n.* (c) a bitter experience; sorrow, suffering) is related to the drink of pain or death prepared by Satan for the inhabitants of hell; see Carleton Brown, '*Poculum Mortis* in Old English', *Speculum*, xv (1940), 389–99. Cf. such bitter drinks as that in *The Revelations of St. Birgitta*, EETS, 178 (1929), 108 l. 21; *An Alphabet of Tales*, EETS, 127 (1905), 295 ll. 15ff; and *Piers the Plowman*, B.XVIII.361–2. Cf. also *Pricke of Conscience*, l. 6737 *Þe flamme of fire þai sal drynk* ...; Psalm 10:7 (Vulgate) and Deut. 32:33. The introduction of the 'beverage', which comes in the form of a biting wind, contrasts well with the heavenly food, which comes to those on the top of another mountain, in the Earthly Paradise (A182ff).

92:1, 3–5 Cf. F933–5, 937–9, 941 *A peine out finie sa resun | K'il ne veeit un esturbilun | De vent venir* ... *Le chevaler ad sus levé | E les debles ki l'unt mené, | E tut le pople* ... | *Si porta tuz en l'eyr amunt* ..., after L498–500.

92:6–93:1 Cf. F943–4 *Tuz les jeta sanz nule atente | En une ewe ke fu pulente* ..., after L500–2.

93:2 Not in *T* or F. *MED o prep.*(2) 5b. (e) cites this line alone for *o fer* 'to a distance'. Alternatively, the phrase could mean 'of fire' (cf. 70:5, 105:2, 174:1, 183:2, 184:1), applied to the blood-red mountain (90:2–3). With this new detail A emphasises the contrast between the fire and the icy cold river (93:4). For alternation of heat and cold in purgatorial pains, cf. e.g. *VWS* SR366ff, SA368ff and Commentary, and the two baths in Easting, 'Peter of Cornwall's Account', pp. 414–15, ll. 104ff.

93:3 Not in *T* or F; cf. 189:5. A proverbial expression; see Whiting Q7, which cites this alongside other Auchinleck texts.

93:4–6 Cf. F945–8 *E tant ert freide e redde e neire | Ke nuls ne pot dire veire | De la grant ewe la freidur | Ke les turmenta a grant dolur.*

94:1–3 Not in *T* or F. This is the first of four occasions (see Introduction, p. lvii) where *seyn(t)* is applied to Owein, in the sense of 'holy' or 'blessed', scarcely as the title 'saint'. Such an epithet qualifying Owein is found in no other English, French, or Latin account, as far as I know. It is obviously somewhat premature to regard Owein as holy at this stage of his trials (unless retrospectively); it is more fitting at the end of the poem when he is fully purged and his place in heaven is assured. It has been pointed out (E. Dorn, *Der sündige Heilige* (Munich, 1967), p. 25) that Tnugdal is like a saint insofar as he provides a model for imitation; the same can, of course, be said of Owein.

94:2 *mad*: see *OED* Mad *a.* †3, stupefied with astonishment, fear or suffering; dazed; *MED* mad *adj.* 2. (b) stupefied, amazed, bemused, dumbfounded.

94:4–6 A paraphrases F957–64.

95 Not in *T* or F.

95:2 *niþe and ond*: a set phrase for 'envy and spite' as one of the deadly sins; see *MED* nith *n.* 2. (a), and *OED* Nith(e) *sb.*, and following note.

95:4 It is appropriate that the *windes blast* should be retribution for *ond*, as this word (*MED* ond(e *n.*(1)) < OE *anda* is cognate with *MED* onde *n.*(2) < ON *andi* 'breath', and means ill-will, 'animus'; see also *OED* Onde *sb.* 4 and Ande *sb.*

96:1–2, 4 Cf. F843–4, 6 *Le chevaler vunt traïnant | Vers une sale ke esteit mult grant | ... Si en issi mult grant fumé*, after L465–7.

96:5–6 Not in *T* or F.

97:1 Cf. F849 *Mult se duta d'aler avant ...*

97:2–3 Not in *T* or F.

97:4–6 A has concocted this speech from the demons' former taunts. At this point in L470–2 and F852–8 the demons force Owein onward rather than tempt him to turn back.

98:1–3 Cf. F865–8 *Quant en la sale fu entré, | Greinur dolur i ad truvé | E maiure peine, vis li fu, | K'il avant n'aveit vëu ...*

98:4–6   Not in *T* or F.

99:1–2   Cf. F869, 871 *Kar l'eire e tut le pavement,* | . . . *Ert plein de fosses tutes rundes* . . ., after L474–5.

99:3–6   A expands on F880–1 *Kar els erent tutes pleinnes* | *De plusurs metals ke bulirent* . . ., after L477–8.

100:1–2   Cf. F862–3 *En la mesun oÿ criant* | *Homes e femmes ensement* . . .
   schrist: pa. t. pl. of *MED* skriken *v*. Z suggested emendation *schriȝt*, but the spelling *-st* for *-ȝt* (for earlier *-ht*) is found elsewhere in Auchinleck scribe 1's work; compare e.g. the metathetic form *schirsten* (*Of Arthour and of Merlin* l. 4739) and *douster* (4472) and see note, Macrae-Gibson, EETS, 279 (1979), p. 118.

100:3–6   Cf. *VSP* 8:4–5, 9:3, 6, describing the souls immersed in the river beneath the bridge: *Some to heore kneos woden.* | *And some to hore naueles stoden.* | . . . *And some to heore chynne.* | . . . *For heore dedlich sunne.* The closest parallel here from F is 893 *Les uns bullirent par le piz* . . . with A100:5.

101:1–3   Cf. *VSP* 17:1–3 *Sunfole soules for heore gult.* | *Weren in þat put ipult.* | *Heore tongues forto hete*, and F895–6 *Checun home sulunc sa fesance* | *Peine i aveit u aliance* . . . Not in *T*.

101:4–102:1   Not in *T* or F. In medieval art the usurer or miser was usually represented with his neck-pouch in scenes of the Last Judgement or of hell torments from at least the twelfth century on. For English examples, see J. Bilson, 'On a Sculptured Representation of Hell Cauldron, recently found at York', *Yorkshire Archaeological and Topographical Journal*, xix (1907), 435–45, especially p. 439 n. 1, and plate opp. p. 435; E. Trollope, 'The Norman Sculpture of Lincoln Cathedral', *Archaeological Journal*, xxv (1868), fig. 12 opp. p. 14; F. Saxl, *English Sculptures of the Twelfth Century* (London, 1954), pp. 47, 67, 74 n. 29, and plates XLVIII, XCIII, XCV. See also V. Leroquais, *Les Psautiers Manuscrits*, 3 vols. (Macon, 1940–1), plate XLV (Amiens, Bibl. mun. MS 19 f. 12v, hell's mouth with flames and a figure with a neck-pouch standing in a circular pit); and references to tales in Tubach, *Index Exemplorum*, 5044. For feeding on the pence, see the parallel in Dante, *Inferno*, XVII. 55–57, and the figure of Avarice in the wall-painting (*c*.1200) at Chaldon, Surrey: see Torkel Eriksson, 'L'Échelle de la perfection: une nouvelle interprétation de la peinture murale de Chaldon', *Cahiers de civilisation médiévale Xe–XIIe Siècles*, vii (1964), 439–49. There are many tales of usurers being fed on their pence or molten gold: see e.g. Caesarius of Heisterbach, *Dialogus Miraculorum*, XI. xxxix, xlii, and *Hortus Deliciarum*, ed. J. Walter (Strasbourg and Paris, 1952), plates XLIV, XLIII, and for another English example, the *Vision of the Monk of Eynsham*, cap. xxi, ed. H.E. Salter, p. 318 ll. 124–6.

102:2   Cf. 81:5.

102:2–6   Not in *T* or F.

102:4 *ȝede vpriȝtes*: i.e. these souls are floating on their backs on the boiling metal with fiends sitting on them.

102:5 *misours*: 'misers'; the manuscript reading is unambiguous. *OED* dates 'miser' *adj.* and *n.* from the mid-sixteenth century, and its current sense (B.2) 'one who hoards wealth' from *c.*1560. In accordance with this *MED* does not record any such word. The context here suggests an early, previously unrecorded occurrence of the word 'miser': its syntactic relationship to *soules* and *wiȝtes* show that it means a human agent; the punishment of the fiery pence, the *gauelers* (102:1) and *okering* (103:4) all confirm the agent as avaricious.

103 A elaborates in direct speech on F900–2, after L484–5; cf. L468–72 and F852–8. There is no mention of usury in *T* or F.

103:4 See 102:1 and cf. the old man in *VSP* 15:1 *He was an hokerere in is liue*. This man bears not a purse round his neck but fiends: *VSP* 13:4 *Feondes in is necke he bar*; cf. A102:6.

104:1–2 Not in *T* or F, where Christ is invoked.

104:3 Owein includes Mary in his prayers here and at 127:3. Cf. 109:5, 143:6, 197:2 and F492, 736, 1012, 1083. No mention of Mary is made in *T*, nor at this point in F.

104:4–6 Not in *T* or F.

105 Cf. F972–7:
> Le chevaler ad eguardé:
> Une mult grant flamme veit
> Ke mult puante e neire esteit;
> Ansi pueit, ceo li ert vis,
> Cum soffre ardant i fut espris;
> Hors de une fose grant surdeit ...,

after L509–10.

105:1–2 Cf. 183:1–2. *flaumme of fer* (and *flaumbe* (183:2)): these are early uses of 'flame'; *MED* and *OED* earliest reference is Rolle, *Psalter*, 28:7, *a.*1500 (*c.*1340).

106 The seven-coloured flame derives not from *T* or F but is adapted from *VSP* where the pit has seven seals over seven holes and the fire glows through; see Introduction, pp. lii–liii.

106:6 Cf. the fifth in the list of the seven holes of the seals of the pit of hell in *VSP* 24:5 *þat fiȝfte ase naddres on to seone*. A's list is more colourful though only five colours are given and no attempt is made to follow the different forms of snow, hail, fire, etc. of the other seals in *VSP*. The fifth, given here, follows the Latin *quinta serpens*; see *VSP* IV, p. 75 ll. 11–13 and note on p. 98. See also T. Silverstein, *Visio Sancti Pauli*, pp. 72–75, and D.D.R. Owen 'The *Vision of Saint Paul*', p. 34 n. 5.

107 Not in *T* or F, though the parallel address by the devils begins at F991, L515, where they call the pit the entrance to hell.

108:1   Not in *T* or *F*. The image of the soul as a bird in the snare of the
fowler (the Devil) is derived ultimately from Psalms 90:3 and 123:7
(Vulgate), and is a not uncommon iconographical motif. E.g. in the *Hours
of Catherine of Cleves*, f. 107 (facsimile ed. with introduction by John
Plummer, New York, 1971, no. 48), a miniature depicts the release of
the souls from hell-mouth; in the lower border a man snares birds with a
string trap; two decoy birds are below in a cage and an open trap awaits
new victims on the right. See also B. G. Koonce, 'Satan the Fowler',
Medieval Studies, xxi (1959), 176–84, and *MED* fouler(e *n.* and grin(e *n.*
(b).

108:1   *caghe*: on this spelling of 'cage' (unrecorded in *MED*) cf. Bliss,
'The Auchinleck *Life of Adam and Eve*', p. 408 note to ll. 141, 143.

108:2–3   These lines adapt F993 *Ici est nostre mansiun . . .*, after *T Hic est
habitacio nostra* (L515–16). This is the first usage of *courtelage* recorded
in *MED*.
   The Devil had a castle opposite God's, the *castellum diaboli*
constructed from the Seven Deadly Sins; see Owst, *LPME*, p. 93, and
below, Commentary *VWS* SR366ff.

108:4–6   Not in *T* or *F*.

109   A's elaboration. 109:3 has the closest source: F1005 *Ke vus ja mes
ne isterez . . .*

109:5   Devils were, of course, in awe of the Virgin in her capacity as
Empress of Hell. E.g. *alle the dewels ther dredys the name of this glorious
virgyne and ben subdewed to hur power, and she letteth hem to tempte hur
servaundes to the uttrest entente of here malice*; quoted by Owst, *LPME*, p.
19.

110:1   Cf. F1013 *Trestut lur conseil despiseit . . .*, after *illorumque promissa
spernente* (L521).

110:2–6   A elaborates on F1015, 1017 *Dunc unt il pris le chevaler | . . . El
puz ardant le trebucherent . . .*

111:1–3   Cf. F1019–21 *E tant cum il plus avala | De tant le plus chaut tut
truva, | E greniur peine il suffri . . .*, after *quo profundius descendit . . .
grauiorem penam pertulit* (L522–4).
   Þe hatter þe fer on him last: 'the more hotly the fire attacked him'. This
use of *last* (*on*) antedates *MED*'s sole ref. s.v. lasten *v.*(1) 7. (d), *Partonope*
(Add.) 4139, late 15th century.

111:4–6   Cf. F1028–9 *A la parfin numa e dist | De quer veraie le nun Ihesu
. . .*, after L526.

112:2–6   Not in *T* or *F*. KA's emendation is unnecessary: the relative
pronoun *þat* is to be understood at the beginning of line 112:5.

113:1   *Biside þe pit*: cf. F1037 *Delez le puz . . .*

113:2, 3, 6   Not in *T* or *F*. See below, Commentary A128.

113:4–5 Cf. F1041–2 *Qu'il ne sout que part aler,* | *Ne quel chimin, ne quel senter,* after *ignorans quo se uerteret* (L529).

114:1 Not in *T* or F. Cf. 79:6.

114:2 Cf. F1045–6 *... veeit* | *Debles qu'il pas ne cuniseit ...,* after *demones ... ab eo ... ignoti* (L530–1).

114:3–6 Not in *T* or F. This is typical of the greater detail in the visualisation of demons which increases from the twelfth to fifteenth centuries in accounts of St Patrick's Purgatory. Cf. *VWS* p. 103. On sixty as a common number simply meaning 'very many', see S.I. Tucker, 'Sixty as an Indefinite Number in Middle English', *RES*, xxv (1949), 152–3.

115 A adapts F1049–52 *'Tut sul, funt il, ici esteez,* | *Mes pas de nus eschaperez* | *Si cum des autres avét fet* | *Ki ça vus unt mené e tret.'* A omits the rest of the speech in *T* and F where the new devils explain that the pit was not really hell at all: see L531–5 and F1053–68.

116:1 Cf. F1069 *Le chevaler vunt amenant ...,* after L537.

116:2 Cf. F1074, 1076 *Ke dekes a une fluvie sunt venu* | *... Sur tute choses ert puant ...*

116:3–6 Not in *T* or F.

116:4 A proverbial expression: see Whiting H592. Cf. Jesus College, Oxford, MS 29, *XI Pains of Hell,* ed. R. Morris, EETS, 49 (1872), 150 ll. 123–4 for the *deop fen* that *stinkeþ fulre þane þe hund.* | *For Brunston walleþ at þe grund.*

116:6 See Whiting P235. The *OMI* poet has substituted a comparison to stress blackness in place of the burning sulphur of which the river is composed: see L539 and F1079, and cf. F1081 *Mut par esteit bleue e pulente.*

117:1–3 Cf. F1085–8 *Le chevaler revist un punt* | *Utre le fluvie, ke ert parfund.* | *Les debles l'unt fet arester* | *Si diunt dunc al chevaler ...,* after L541–3. The narrow bridge of judgement separating hell/purgatory from heaven/paradise is a well-nigh universal feature in post-mortem mythologies. See P. Dinzelbacher, *Die Jenseitsbrücke im Mittelalter,* Dissertationen der Universität Wien, 104 (1973), pp. 41–46 and *passim,* and my thesis, p. 248.

117:4–5 Not in *T* or F. The bridge is here so called because it leads, for the saved, over the river, beneath which lies hell, into the Earthly Paradise. Cf. F1089–90 *Desuz ceste fluvie ke veeiz,* | *Est enfer ...*

117:6 Cf. F1091–2 *E vus estuvera trespasser* | *Cel punt ...*

118:1 Not in *T* or F. A adapts F1094 *E nus vus muverrum grant turment ...* In *T* the demons throw their hooks, *uncos suos* (L572–3). Cf. *Handlyng Synne,* EETS, 119 (1901), ll. 5271–2.

118:2–3 *þe winde þe schal ouer blowe*: 'the wind will blow (up)on you'; the sense 'the wind will blow you over', i.e. blow you down and/or off the bridge, was not available until *c.*1400, unless this is an early use of the expression: see *OED* Over *adv.* 4 and *MED* over *adv.* 1.(c) (d). Cf. F1095–7 *Nus vus ferum commuvant | Esturbiluns e vent si grant, | Ke vus ne porez sustenir* . . . See Introduction, p. xlviii.

118:4 *midnerd*: KA misreads *miduerd*. Cf. 174:6 and see Commentary.

118:4–6 A verb of motion is omitted after *schalt* (cf. 113:4). Translate: You shall not (pass over) for all this world, unless you fall in the middle (i.e. from the middle of the bridge into the river) to (where are) more of our fellows.

119:1–2 Cf. F1098–1101 *Del punt vus estuvera chaïr | Aval el fluvie k'est desuz, | E quant vus serez la venuz, | Nos compainuns ke la sunt* . . ., after L544–5.

119:3–5 Not in *T* or F.

119:6 Cf. F1102 *Deckes enfer vus plungerunt*, after L545.

120:1 Cf. F1107–8 *Al pié del punt l'unt dreit mené; | Le chevaler ad eguardé* . . .

120:2 Adapts F1114 *Le ewe, desuz, lee e parfund* . . .

120:3–6 Not in *T* or F.

120:4–5 Rhyme *ʒeme/beme* after OE *ʒieme/beam* 'may possibly depend on ME ę̄ in *beam* owing to the influence of *leam* (OE *lēoma*)', Dobson, II. § 120 note.

120:5–6 Cf. Y459 and see Whiting M709. Such a comparison is not uncommonly applied to demon hordes: e.g. devils *flye above in the eyer as thyke as motis in the sonne* in Lincoln Cathedral Library, MS A.6.2, f. 133, quoted by Owst, *LPME*, p. 112.

121:1 Cf. F1113 *De grant haltur esteit le punt* . . .

121:2 Cf. F1116 *K'il fu trenchant cum un rasur* . . ., and see Whiting R53.

121:3 See Introduction, p. xlix.

121:4–123:6 Not in *T* or F.

123:1 MS *dmcl* (possibly *dincal*, the abbreviation mark is over the second and third minims) has been expanded to *dominical*, an adjectival noun which means something like 'Sunday (readings)'. The whole stanza follows *VSP* 20: see Introduction, p. liii. *VSP* 20:1 *dominical* is the sole reference given in *MED* s.v. dominical *adj.* & *n.* (b) 'as noun: ?a book containing the liturgy for Sunday', a meaning also given for Latin *dominicale* in *Lexicon Latinitatis Medii Aevi* (Turnholt, 1975). In the manuscript of *VSP* (Bodleian MS Laud Misc. 108, f. 199vb) the word is

spelt out in full, and is singular, governing *it tellez*, which forms a false
rhyme with *helle*. The copy of *VSP* used by the author of *OM*1 may have
reserved a plural verb in *telle*, this being transmitted to A. The A scribe's
contracted form may indicate uncertainty about the word. An alternative
expansion of the form to a plural *dominicals* could be argued as a
derivation from an expression like *sermones dominicales*. The *Visio Sancti
Pauli* was recounted on Sundays because Paul obtained rest on Sundays
for the souls in hell; in the Lambeth Homilies the tale is headed *In Diebus
Dominicis*: see *Old English Homilies*, ed. R. Morris, EETS, 34 (1868),
41–47. This version omits the bridge; the seven seals of the furnace have
become *þe see of helle*: see *Selections from Early Middle English
1130–1250*, ed. J. Hall, I (Oxford, 1920), 76 l. 24, and II. 417 note, and
on the Sunday Letter II. 415. Whereas in the *Visio Sancti Pauli* hell is in
the pit, in *T*, *F*, *A*, and *OM*2 hell is beneath the river flowing under the
perilous bridge. See T. Silverstein, 'The Passage of Souls to Purgatory in
the *Divina Commedia*', *Harvard Theological Review*, xxxi (1938), 57–58,
and Easting, 'Purgatory and the Earthly Paradise', section II, and esp. p.
37.

123:5 *redempcioun*: this retains the same rhyme sound as *VSP* 20:5
mencion, which follows *VSP* IV, p. 78 ll. 2–4: *Si quis mittatur in hoc
puteo, non fiet commemoracio eius in conspectu domini*. A's use of
redempcioun must be an early occurrence of the word: earliest *MED* and
OED references are Rolle, *Psalter*, 20:1, *a*.1500 (*c*.1340), and, appositely,
Pricke of Conscience, (1340) l. 7251, '*Ffor in hell*,' he says, '*es na
redempcyoune*'.

124 Cf. F1123–8:

> Les debles dunc dist li unt:
> 'Vus estuvera passer cest punt;
> Mes si unkore vus voillez crere
> E lesser ester cest eire,
> Vus poriez bien returner
> E tut cest turment eschaper.'

after L167/18–19.

125:1–3 Cf. F1129–31 *Le chevaler se est purpensé | Cum Deu l'ad suvent
deliveré | De peines e de grant dolurs ...*, after L167/20–21.

125:5 See Introduction, p. xlix.

125:6 Cf. F1141 *Avant ala tut sanz poür ...*

126:1–3 Cf. F1155, 1157, 1160 *Mes quant le debles unt veü ... | Le plus del
punt ert tut passé, | ... Si leverunt un mult grant cri ...*, after L567–8.

126:4–6 This direct speech is not in *T* or *F*, though 126:5 is based on
F1156 *K'il unt le chevaler perdu ...*, which is not in *T*. A has omitted the
widening of the bridge: see Introduction, pp. xlix, under 3:5.

127:1 Cf. F1175–6 *Quant le chevaler passé fu | Trestut le punt ...* and
F1173 *Il ad le punt trestut passé ...*

127:2   Cf. F1170 *A Dampnedeu mult le mercie* ..., and 1174 and 1185 where Owein thanks Christ. In *T* no mention is made of Owein offering thanks for his delivery.

127:3-4   Not in *T* or F.

127:5   Cf. F1184 *K'il fust delivré del turment.*

127:6   Not in *T* or F.

128   Not in *T* or F. See 113. The significance of this robe sent from God is clearly to indicate that Owein is now a new man, cleansed of his sins, *fyned als gold þat shynes clere* (*Pricke of Conscience*, l. 2632). To enter heaven earthly clothing must be divested and heavenly clothing donned: see D.W. Bossuet, 'Die Himmelreise der Seele', *Archiv für Religionswissenschaft*, iv (1901), 139-41. There is a close parallel to the change of clothes and the healing of wounds in the *Visio Alberici*, cap. xx, where, on Alberic's entering paradise, *omnia membra et vestimenta eius que in illius campi asperitate discerpta sibi et scissa videbantur, redintegrata sanantur* (*Miscellanea Cassinese*, xi (1932), 95).

129:1, 4-6   Not in *T* or F, though see below, Commentary A130:5.

129:2-3   Cf. F1190-1 *Il ad devant li esguardé;* | *Un mur de grant beauté veeit* ..., after L753-5.

130:2-3   Cf. F1194, 1196 ... *une porte* ... | *Ke en tut le mund n'aveit pier* ..., not in *T*.

130:4   Not in *T* or F.

130:5   Cf. F1198 *D'or e de peres aürné* ... *T* makes no mention of gold. The gold in F may have suggested A129:6.

130:6   Not in *T* or F.

131-133   A has here greatly expanded F1198 (quoted above) and *T*, which says that the gate *metallis diuersis lapidibusque pretiosis ornata mirabili fulgore radiabat* (L756-7). The whole of the description of the Earthly Paradise is amplified in A: see Introduction, pp. liv-lv.

131   This stanza resembles the catalogue of precious stones on the gate in another Anglo-Norman version of *T*, found in BL MS Harley 273.

> Porte i out molt bien assise,
> Ffeite de merveile guise,
> Tot ert de divers metals,
> Molt i out jaspes e cristals,
> Sardoines et alabandines,
> Topaces e cornelines
> Berils, safirs e charbocles,
> Adamantz, smaraudes, onicles.

See '*Le Purgatoire de Saint Patrice' des manuscrits Harléian 273 et fonds français 2198*, ed. J. Vising (Göteborg, 1916), p. 42 ll. 615-22. The ultimate source for such lists is Apoc. 21:19-20, which includes jasper,

sapphire, chalcedony (*causteloines?*), and topaz, also listed by A, and cf.
Exod. 28:17–20.

131:1 *Jaspers*: first reference in *MED* s.v. jaspre *n.* 'A precious stone,
usually of green color'.

cristal: first reference in *MED* s.v. cristal *n.* 2. (b) 'a small piece of
crystal used as a gem; crystal regarded as a precious stone'. It may have
been prompted here by the biblical crysolite?

131:2 *margarites*: This is an early use, one of only three listed in *MED*
before 1350.

coral: second reference in *MED* s.v. coral *n.*1 (b) 'coral used
ornamentally', after *Cokaygne* 70.

131:3 *safer-stones*: first reference in *MED* s.v. saphir(e *n.* (c) 'a
sapphire'.

131:4 *ribes*: first reference in *MED* s.v. rubi(e *n.* 'The precious gem,
ruby'.

salidoines: first reference in *MED* s.v. celidoine *n.* (2) 'A fabulous
stone, of two kinds, said to be found in the stomach of a swallow.' Cf.
OED †Celidony[2] *Obs.* and see s.v. Chelidonius in Index of Stones in
English Medieval Lapidaries, ed. Joan Evans and Mary S. Serjeantson,
EETS, 190 (1933), 192.

131:5 *causteloines*: sole instance in *MED* s.v. causteloin *n.* [?Vr. of
calcedoine.] 'Some kind of precious stone: ?chalcedony.'

131:6 *diamaunce*: an early usage. *MED* diamaunt *n.* (a) first references
c.1325 *Ichot a burde in a* 6 and (1340) *Ayenb.* This plural form antedates
MED's instance a.1475.

132   Not in *T* or F.

132:1   As the poet is still describing the gate of paradise the sense of
tabernacles seems to be *OED* 4.b, 'A canopied niche or recess in a wall or
pillar, to contain an image', the first reference being Chaucer, *Hous of
Fame*, III. 100 (1190), some fifty years after A.

132:4 *Arches*: This is the second reference in *MED* s.v. arch(e *n.*, the
first being from *pa* (MS Laud Misc. 108, l. 106) describing the
cloister-like hall that Owein first enters, *With pilers and with qvoynte
Arches*; this translates *columpnis et archiolis* (W a 50:19–20, cf. L263–4).

charbukelston: This is the first reference in *MED* s.v. carbuncle *n.* 2.
(b) 'a material made of (or resembling) carbuncles'. On carbuncles'
power of giving off light, see M.A. Owings, *The Arts in the Middle
English Romances* (New York, 1952), pp. 143–4.

132:5 *Knottes*: first reference in *MED* s.v. knotte *n.* 4. (b) 'an embossed
ornament of wood or stone on a wall, pillar, ceiling, etc.'

132:6 *pinacles*: first reference in *OED* s.v. Pinnacle sb.; not cited in, and
hence antedating, *MED* pinacle *n.* (a), first reference Wyclif *Bible*. It

would seem from the high concentration in this one stanza of five words that are all very early usages that the poet was at some pains to make his description as up-to-date and elaborate as possible; see Easting, 'Some Antedatings'.

133   Not in *T* or *F*, though an expansion of the common sentiment in F1199–1200 *Ke nul ne le poreit descrivere, | Ne la beauté cunter ne dire.*

133:1–2   An interesting instance of Christ as *il miglior fabbro*, reflecting the idea of God as architect of the universe. See E.R. Curtius, *European Literature and the Latin Middle Ages*, trans. W.R. Trask (London, 1953), pp. 544–6, 561–2. Cf. the apparition of St Michael to George Grissaphan in St Patrick's Purgatory, where the author's imagination seems similarly to have been stimulated in the first instance by artistic representations: *non est nec esse potest homo depictor nec in arte pingendi doctissimus, qui sufficienter ad depingendam pulchritudinem et formositatem illius esset sufficiens* (*Visiones Georgii*, p. 163).

133:2   On the group *tþ* in *goldsmitþe*, see Bliss, 'Notes on the Auchinleck Manuscript', p. 658 n. 6.

134:1   The detail *bi hemselue* is not in *T* or *F*.

134:2–3   Cf. F1205–7 *Si en issiz une fleirur | Ke tant esteit de grant duchur, | Si tut le mund fust enbaumé . . .*, after β *si totus mundus in aromata uerteretur* (L760); cf. α *si res totius mundi converterentur in aromata* (W108:18–19).

134:4–135:3   Cf. F1211–15:

> E il receust de la duçur
> Si grant force e si grant vigur
> Ke li semble, tut pur veir,
> K'il put suffrir, sanz mal aveir,
> La peine e la dolur grant . . .,

after L761–3.

135:4–6   Not in *T* or *F*.

136   Cf. F1221–7:

> E quant plus pres venu esteit,
> Hors a la porte issir veeit
> Muz genz a processiun,
> Unkes greinur ne vist nuls hom.
> Encuntre luy trestuz veneient,
> Gunfanuns e croyz porteient,
> Chandelabres e paumes de hor . . .,

after L767–70.

136:3   I have added *in*, doubtless omitted accidentally following the minims of *mani*; cf. F1223. *OED* gives 1691 as first date for *procession* as a verb.

136:3, 6   Cf. 38:4–5 and 193:1–2.

136:4 *chaundelers*: an early occurrence of this word antedating *MED* first reference Wyclif's *Bible*; *OED* Chandler first reference is *c*.1325.

136:5 This line appears to be an adaptation of either F1224 (quoted above) or F1229–30 *Il ne quidat ke en tut le mund | Tant fusent gens cum ilokes sunt*. Cf. *talis ac tanta quanta in hoc mundo, prout estimauit, nunquam uisa est* (L769–70).

137 *T* specifies archbishops, bishops, abbots, canons, monks, and presbyters (L772–3); F1233–7 lists bishops, archbishops, priests, canons, abbots, monks, and kings. Kings occur later in L813.

137:5 *frere Prechours*: Friars Preachers or Dominicans appear also as *Frere ... Jacobins* (138:1).

138:1–3 Not in *T* or F. *MED* frer(e *n*. 4. (c) gives the first occurrence of this rhymed list of the four orders of friars from the song *Why werre* in the Auchinleck MS (f. 330r). Cf. *OED* Jacobin *sb*.[1] and *a*.[1] A. *sb*. 1. Friars Minor are Franciscans.

138:4–6 Cf. 1231 *De checun ordre il veeit gent ...*, after L770–1.

139:1 Not in *T* or F. Cf. the separate place of joy in the *Vision of Tundale*, ed. Mearns, ll. 1787–90:

> 'Thys ioye', sayde þe angell bryȝte,
> 'Is ordeyned for wedded men ryȝte
> That lyue in clene maryage
> And kepes her body from owtrage ...'

and cf. *Visio Tnugdali*, 46/3ff.

139:2 Cf. F1232 *Homes e femmes ensement ...*, after *utriusque sexus* L771–2.

139:3–5 Cf. F1257–8, 1260–2, spoken by the two archbishops (though there is no direct speech here in *T*):

> 'Ihesu Christ, funt il, seit loé,
> Ke cele grace vus ad duné ...
> Ke dekes ça estes venu,
> E des turmez vus ad jeté,
> De debles vus ad deliveré.'

139:6 Not in *T* or F.

140 Cf. F1249–53:

> Quant il ourent le chant fini,
> Hors des autres s'en sunt parti
> Deus erce[ves]ques meintenant;
> Al chevaler vindrent alant
> E ovekes eus l'unt dunkes pris ...,

after L779–82.

140:2, 5 *tvay*: for the spelling (also at 158:2) cf. Bliss, 'The Auchinleck *Life of Adam and Eve*', p. 409 note to l. 282.

140:3   Cf. F1227, quoted above, Commentary A136, and L768–9.

141:1–2   Cf. F1263–4 *Amunt aval le vunt menant; | Joie e delit* . . .

141:3 – 152:6   Not in *T* or F, though see Commentary A147:1–2.

141–143   See Commentary A153–154.

142   The dance of the blessed *al bi line* led and accompanied by angels is well illustrated in Fra Angelico's famous painting of the Last Judgement in San Marco, Florence (reproduced e.g. in Colleen McDannell and Bernhard Lang, *Heaven: A History* (New Haven and London, 1988), Plate 21). The sense of *carol* (141:4, 142:1) as a ring-dance accompanied by a choral song sung by the dancers and spectators is first recorded in *MED c.*1325 (*c.*1300). The infinitive form *caroly* (143:1, 5, 144:6) is not recorded in *MED* or *OED*.

142:5   For glosses on the musical instruments, see H.H. Carter, *A Dictionary of Middle English Musical Terms* (Indiana, 1961), who has not, however, cited or consulted *OM*1.

  sautry: *MED* sautri(e *n.* (a) first reference is from Auchinleck *Reinbrun*.

143:4   See Commentary A49:2–3.

145:4   *breke her notes*: Carter s.v. Breken glosses 'to utter the notes of a song; to sing', his first of two quotations being *c.*1410: *But syngars in the fendis chirche breken curiouse nootis* (*Lant. of Liȝt*, 58.15). *MED* breken *v.* 4. (a) reads 'to trill or modulate (a note)' with references from the fifteenth century. These meanings do not seem adequately to cover the case here. The technical terms *Burdoun, mene*, and *hautain* (145:5–6) for the voices in a three-part composition all come from the early fourteenth century. (*mene*: second reference in *MED* s.v. mene *n.*(3) 6., antedates (?) Carter's first reference, Mannyng, 1338.) By *breke her notes* it seems that the poet was referring to the contemporary 'modern' practice of *fractio modi*, breaking the rhythm of the breve into ever smaller units; see e.g. A.T. Davison and W. Apel, *Historical Anthology of Music* (Harvard, 1947), no. 43. That such music should be sung in the Earthly Paradise is interesting in view of the Papal Bull *Docta Sanctorum* (1326) which forbade the use of descant and elaborate 'breaking' of the rhythmic values because of thereby 'intoxicating the ear'.

> The music therefore of the divine offices is now performed with semibreves and minims, and with these notes of small value every composition is pestered.

See H.E. Woolridge, *The Oxford History of Music*, 22nd ed., I (1929), 295. The relevant passage from the Bull (wrongly dated 1322) is there quoted, pp. 294ff. This probably explains why in Carter's quotation *c.*1410 the broken notes are *curiouse* (unduly ornate) and *in the fendis chirche*. It would seem that the musical activity of the birds in paradise, like the architecture of the gate, is both splendid and very up-to-date.

145:6 *wiþ heiȝe steuen*: applied to *hautain* (treble) is not tautological, but more likely means loud in volume, a fairly highly prized musical attribute in the Middle Ages; see Carter, s.v. High, *adj.* II, and *MED* heigh *adj.* 7.(a). (I am indebted to Dr. Patrick Little for advice on medieval musical matters.)

146:4–6 This clearly establishes the setting as the Earthly and not the Celestial Paradise; cf. 170:2.

147:1–2 Cf. F1289–90 *Des roses e des autres flurs | Ki ourent diverse colurs . . .*

147:3 *primrol*: second reference in *MED* s.v. primerol(e *n.* after *Ichot a burde, c.*1325: *þe primerole he passeþ, þe peruenke of pris* (*The Harley Lyrics*, ed. G.L. Brook, (Manchester, 1956), p. 31 l. 13).
   paruink: third reference in *MED*; the form *paruenke*, after the Anglo-Norman, would form a true rhyme with *biþenke* 147:6.

147:4–5 *Mint*: earliest ME usage outside glosses in *MED*.
   feþerfoy: second reference in *MED*.
   eglentere: first usage in verse in *MED*.
   Colombin: second reference in *MED*, misspelt *calombin* following KA. (This note corrects slips in Easting, 'Some Antedatings', p. 168.)

148:6 *licorice*: see Whiting L229 (where A148:6 is misdated *c.*1450, the date he assigns to C and Y).

149:2 See Whiting M431, where again this line is wrongly dated *c.*1450. The date for *OMI* usually given by Whiting, *a.*1325, makes this the earliest of his examples. (On p. xl he dates *OMI c.*1300.)

149:5 See Gen. 2:10ff. Cf. also *VSP* I, p. 69 ll. 24ff, and note, p. 93.

150:1–3 MS *dison* is a misreading for *Pison* (i.e. Ganges), first of the four rivers in Gen. 2:11–12: *ubi nascitur aurum, et aurum terrae illius optimum est.*
   The rhyme *strem/lem* from OE *strēam/lēoma* possibly shows variant *ę̄* for *ē* in *lem*; see B. Mackenzie, 'A Special Dialectal Development of O. E. ēa in Middle English', *EStn*, lxi (1927), 387–8, and Dobson, II. § 120, note.

150:4 MS *fison* for *Gihon* (i.e. Nile), no doubt contaminated by 150:1.

151:1, 4 In Genesis, Tigris is third, Euphrates fourth.

152:1–3 Cf. 144:4–6.

153–154 The mention of *chori* and music, which comes at this point in *T* (L804–6) and is taken up by F1317–20 (where *karolent* occurs, l. 1317), seems to have been transferred by the English poet to 141ff, where it is expanded.

153:1–2   Cf. 162:6. Not in *T*, which has *per conuentus distincti* (L801).
Cf. F1309–12 *Tuz ensemble pas ne seieint,* | *En diversis lius partiz esteint;* |
Par cuvenz furent destraité | *E par treszeins devisé* ...

153:3–5   Cf. F1314–16 *Les uns als autres tost venir,* | *E mult grant joie*
entre eus feseient | *Kant il issi se entreveeint.*

153:6   Not in *T* or F.

154–155   In *T* and F the list of colours and the account of the clothing
follow the analogy with the stars, A156–157.

154:1–3   Cf. F1353–4 *Li un sunt vermail cum sanc,* | *U vert, u neir, u*
purpre, u blanc ..., after L808–10.

154:4–5   Not in *T* or F. *Tonicles*: antedates *OED* Tunicle *sb.* 2. *Eccl.*,
first ref. *c*.1425, and non-ecclesiastical, *Piers the Plowman*, B.XV.163.

154:6   Cf. F1356 *De dras de seye e d'or batuz* ...

155   Cf. F1363–8:

> Par la furme de la vesture,
> U le chevaler mist grant cure,
> Apertement e bien veeit
> De quele vie chescun esteit
> E cum checun out Deu amé,
> Tant cum en secle aveit esté.

After L810–12.

156:1–3   Cf. F1325–7 *Si vus dirai une semblance* | *E assez bone*
concordance | *Des esteiles* ...; not in *T. semblaunce* antedates *MED* only
reference under sense 4., 'Comparison, analogy', from *a*.1550 *Chartier*
Treat. Hope 76/25. *acordaunce* antedates *MED* accordaunce *n.* 2. (b)
(*a*.1449) Lydg. *SSecr.* 1357.

156:4–6   Cf. F1329ff which expands L806–8. The closest parallel is
perhaps F1338 *Kar l'une est plus de autre clere.*

157   Cf. F1339–47:

> Ansi est il, bien le sachez,
> De ceus dunt vus oÿ avez,
> Ky sunt el duz paÿs manant
> Dunt jo vus cunctay avant,
> K'il nen unt pas tuz uelement
> Delyt e joie ensement;
> Mes al meins ad nepurquant,
> Al sen avis, ad autant
> Cumme nus home put de joie aver ...

Not in *T*.

158   This takes up the narrative from 140–141. Cf. F1418–22:

> Dekes al chevaler sunt venu
> Les deus evesques, kil menerent

E ducement l'aresunerent:
'Frere, funt il, la Deu merci
Vostre desir est acompli ...'.
After L830–1. For 158:5 cf. also F1438 *Pur vostre volenté furnir.*

159:1–2   Contraction of F1423–32; cf. F1425, 1429 *Kar vus avez veü la peine ... E la joie ...*, after L831–3.

159:3   Cf. F1433 *Beneit seit Deu e sa pusance ...*, after L833.

159:4–5   Cf. F1439, 1441 *... ore vus dirum, | ... Queus lius ces sunt u vus venistes ...*

159:6   Not in *T* or F.

160   In *T* and F Owein is told first about the Earthly Paradise and Adam: see A171ff.

160:2   Metre and *amorwe* both suggest that the emended reading has been lost by haplography. (Cf. Auchinleck *Life of Adam and Eve*, l. 367, *Boþe an euen & a morwe* (and l. 510), ed. C. Horstmann, *Sammlung Altenglischer Legenden* (Heilbronn, 1878), p. 143 (and 144). MS *auen* does not therefore qualify as sound evidence for a special development of OE *ēa*, as claimed by MacKenzie, 'A Special Development', p. 389, and see also Jordan § 50, Anm. 1.

161   Cf. F1444–8:
Quel liu c'est ke ci veiez,
U nus avum cest grant desport
E ceste joie e ceste confort.
Cest duz païs e cest bel estre
Est numé païs terestre ...
See also A170:1–2.

162:1–3   Cf. F1531–2, 1535–6 *Si ne put nuls ça einz entrer | Ke li n'estot par la passer. | ... U checuns home s'estot purger | Einz k'il puse a nus entrer.* 162:2 *spourged* after *purger* is an early and uncommon usage; see *MED* spurgen *v.* (d).

163:1–3   Cf. F1551–3 *Mes ces ki sunt en cel turment | Ne sevent pas cum lungement | Demurer deivent en la peine ...*, after L867–8.

163:4–6   Cf. F1555, 1557–8 *Kar par messes e par preeres | ... E autres biens ke sunt fesanz | Ceus ke en tere sunt vivanz ...*, after L868ff. *do* (163:5) is causative: friends pay for others (clerics) to sing masses for the souls of their departed fellows.

164   A shortened account based on F1565ff.

165   Cf. F1605–10:
Kar plusurs venent ça dedenz
Hors de dolurs e de turmenz,
E plusurs vunt de ci amunt
En la joie u les seinz sunt

     El paraÿs celestïen,
     U nul entre for cristïen.
After L882–4.

165:4 *celestien*: is the sole occurrence in *OED* and *MED*.

166 Based on F1579ff, but no close parallels. This stanza spells out the idea of the delay in the Earthly Paradise, on which see Easting, 'Purgatory and the Earthly Paradise', pp. 43–46.

167 Not in *T* or F. Cf. *Vision of Tundale*, ed. Mearns, ll. 867–70:
     Not a chylde, þe sothe to say,
     That was borne & dede þys day,
     That he þe paynes shall se ryȝte wele,
     Allþowȝ he hem not fele.
Cf. also the early SEL section on *Alle soulene day*, ed. C. Horstmann, EETS, 87 (1887), 429 ll. 296–8, which speaks of young children:
   For huy ne berez with heom no sunne : þat drawe heom bihinde;
   Also quicliche ase liȝhttingue : þoru purgatorie huy doz gon,
   And heouene-dore findez opene : and wiendez in anon.
and *Pricke of Conscience*, ll. 3312–25.

167:3 *ouerfle*: first citation in *MED* s.v. overflen *v.* (1).

168 Expands F1613–16 *Le chevaler avant menerent; | Dekes a un munt tut dreit alerent | Ke mult esteit haut e grant, | Dequ'al sumet le vunt* [MS *wnt*] *menant* ..., which in turn expand L884–5.

169–170 Not in *T* or F, though see Commentary A170:1–2. These stanzas introduce the account of Adam (171–9), for which the equivalent place to *T* and F would be following A160; see Commentary A171ff. 170:1–2 parallel 161 (and see Commentary A161).

169:5 *croupe*: Welsh *crwth*, a stringed instrument probably at first plucked, later bowed; see Otto Andersson, *The Bowed-Harp: A Study in the History of Early Musical Instruments* (London, 1903), pp. 228, 239, 243, and Mary Remnant, *English Bowed Instruments from Anglo-Saxon to Tudor Times* (Oxford, 1986), 42–55. The name appears to be first used in English in the early fourteenth century, though the instrument was known on the continent before the twelfth century; see *MED* croud *n.* (2) 1; *OED* Crowd, *sb.*[1]; Carter, s.v. Croude, and *The King of Tars*, l. 509 and note.

170:1 *honestly*: this word antedates *MED* references. The adverbial form, demanded by the rhyme with *terestri* can perhaps best be accommodated by throwing the weight on *is* and translating the phrase, 'that exists so beautifully'. The couplet renders F1447–8, quoted above, Commentary A161.

170:6 *aboue þe aire*: Heaven proper, the celestial paradise, as opposed to that *þat is in erþe here* (170:3), lies beyond the regions of air, which mark the outer limit of the world of mutable Nature. See C.S. Lewis, *The*

Discarded Image (Cambridge, 1964), pp. 4 and 108, and below, Commentary C464, Y511. From the mountain summit Owein views only the gate of heaven (181:6, 183:3).

171ff The following discussion of Adam is given here in A by the narrator (171:2), whereas in *T* and *F* it forms part of the opening speech of the two 'archbishops' (L837ff, F1447ff). A's account is largely independent of *F*.

171:3 Cf. F1449 *Dunt Adam fu desherbegé* ...

171:6 Sense unclear, but best read: ... [had Owein done according to God's will]—as (much as) he took against (i.e. opposed) him (i.e. God)—... *MED* nimen *v.* 4. (a) gives *nimen ayen* 'attack (sb.)', and cf. *OED* Take *v.* 20.b. *to take against* 'to oppose'.

172:3 *it*: i.e. God's will, being the prohibition on the Tree of Knowledge.

172:4–174:6 Not in *T* or *F*.

174:6 *midnerd*: from OE *middangeard*, via *middenerd*, q.v. *MED*, which does not record this contracted spelling. KA's reading *miduerd* (also at 118:4) is patently wrong, and was noted by Z. MS clearly gives *n* not *u*. Kölbing's reading would have to be *OED* Midward †B. *sb.* 'The middle, the middle part', which makes only minimal sense. Cf. *The Life of Adam and Eve*, ed. Horstmann (1878), p. 140 ll. 128–30, who makes the same mistake as KA: *He sent to hem an angel bri3t | Wiþ a brenand swerd, | And drof hem in to miduerd* ..., and see Bliss, 'The Auchinleck *Life of Adam and Eve*', p. 408 note to l. 130.

175:1–2 Cf. F1485, 87 *Kar eus tut lur parenté | ... En enfern trestuz alerent* ... The rest of this stanza and F1485ff follow β in speaking of Christ's incarnation and redemption. Note *per fragilitatem* (L855) and F1507 *par frelleté*, not found in α.

176 See Introduction, p. xlviii.

177:3–179:2 The missing lines would very likely have said that all Adam's kin would never have had the chance to return to the Earthly Paradise had it not been for God's mercy in sending Christ to redeem us from original sin, but that he who has sinned since baptism still requires repentance and confession, and a time *In þe paine of purgatori*. See F1479–1522.

179:5 A reference to the weighing of souls at the Day of Judgement which is not found in *T* or *F*.

180 Cf. F1617–22:

> Puis comandé e dist li unt
> K'il esguardast tut dreit amunt
> E ke il lur deit a sun avis
> Lequel le ciel fust blanc u bis,

Vert u bloye, vermail e neir,
A sun avis lur deist le veir.

Cf. *iusserunt ut sursum aspiciens diceret cuiusmodi coloris ei supra se celum uideretur* (L885–6).

180:5–181:3 Owein's direct speech is matched by L887, but not by F1623–4 *Le chevaler lur ad puis dist | K'il fust tut autel cum or quit* …

181:4–6 Cf. F1627–30 '*Veire, funt il, de veire sachez | Ke la clarté ke vus veez, | Est la porte de paraÿs | Celestre* …', after L887–8.

182:1–3 Cf. F1635–8 *Par unt descent chescun jur | A un hure mult grant duçur | Ke jus del ciel descendant vient | E nos vies ci nus sustent* …

182:4–5 Not in *T* or F. The idea of a sweet smell sustaining life is found frequently in medieval visions of paradise; see e.g. *Dialogues*, IV, 37 (and below, Commentary L820–1); the Vision of St Salvius; and *Fís Adamnán*, trans. C.S. Boswell, *An Irish Precursor of Dante* (London, 1908), p. 30 § 5, and p. 34 § 13, and see Patch, *The Other World*, Index s.v. perfume. Cf. A134 and F1292–6:

> … la fleirur ert si grant
> Ke avis esteit al chivaler
> Ke tut sanz beivre e manger
> Il pureit tut diis remaner
> Einz en la duçur sanz mal aver …

182:6 A adapts F1641–2, which follow L891–2.

183:1–2 Cf. 105:1–2.

183:1–5 Cf. F1644–8:

> Le chevaler utre eus veeit
> Cum si se fust flamme de fu;
> Del ciel avalant est venu,
> Par raies ardant se departi
> E tut le paÿs coveri …,

after L892–3.

183:6 *smal*: this spelling is repeated at 182:4 and 134:2; it is recorded in *MED* s.v. smel *n.*, but no instances are cited. Only A refers here to the 'smell' of the flame.

184:1–3 Only A refers to the heavenly flame directly as the Holy Ghost, though the pentecostal origin of the idea is clear in L893–5, and F1650–6 emphasise the rays descending on each of the souls and on Owein. Cf. Acts 2:3–4.

184:4–6 Not in *T* or F.

185–186:3 Cf. F1663–8:

> Dunc li unt les evesques dist:
> 'C'est la joie e le delit
> Dunt Dampnedeu, nostre seignur,

> Nus pest un ure checun jur;
> Mes ceus ke sunt od Deu manant
> Sanz fin sunt cest delit sentant . . .',

after L899–901.

186:1 *Þe soules*: dative construction, 'for the souls . . . that joy shall last . . .'.

186:4 *most*: implies an infinitive, 'go' or 'do'; see *MED* moten *v.*(2) 5b.(c) or (d).

186:5–6 Cf. F1675–7 *Ore vus estuvera repeirer | E par la veie arere aler | Par unt venistes deke ça . . .*, after L903–4.

187:1 Cf. F1682 . . . *ne facét mortel pechez . . .*, not in *T*.

187:2–3, 6 Not in *T* or F.

187:4–5 Cf. F1687–8 *La sus en ciel od Deu serez | E la sanz fin od li meindrez . . .*

188:1–3 Cf. F1704–5 *E si requist en plurant | Ke pur Deu ne l'en jetassent . . .*

188:4–6 Not in *T* or F.

189:4 *last*: This transferred or figurative usage antedates *MED*'s sole reference (s.v. last *n.*(2) (e)), Chaucer, *CT*, B.1628 *a thousand last quade yeer*. *OED* (s.v. Last, *sb.*[2] 2. b.) quotes as its last example an equivalent usage to A's from 1712, Arbuthnot, *John Bull*, III. ix: *Ten thousand last of devils . . .*

189–191 Loose adaptation of F1715–62, though there is no source in *T* or F for A189:4–5 and 190:1–3.

190:1 *No nere þan a quarel miȝt fle*: No fiend might approach him closer than the distance a cross-bow bolt might be shot. This is the sole citation for this comparison in *MED* s.v. quarel *n.*(1) (d); see also A93:3 and Commentary.

190:5 *britten* (see Commentary A42:1–2): F1734 reads *quinze*.

192–194 Not in *T* or F. It is notable that the poet uses the expression *as ich finde in þis stori* (192:1) just at that point where it is not true.

192:2 *Þe priour*: dative construction, 'a sign came to the prior . . .'.

193:6–196:2 Adaptation of F1773–82, though 195:6 only in A.

196–197 Expansion of F1783–4 which merely mention *Le Seint Sepucre*.

197:1 In L1067 and F Owein visits not Bethlehem but Jerusalem, *Þat ich holy stede* (196:1).

197:2 It is not Christ who is the flower and Mary the thorn, but Mary who is as a flower (rose, or lily?) from the thorn, *flos de spina*; see e.g.

Adam of St Victor, 'Sequence for the Nativity of the Virgin Mary', in *Oxford Book of Medieval Latin Verse*, no. 163, l. 8, and also Whiting R206, L280 and R.T. Davies ed., *Medieval English Lyrics* (London, 1963), pp. 375–6.

197:5   Cf. F1786 *Abit de moyne ad receü.*

197:6   Not in *T* or F. Seemingly *seuen* is used for rhyming purposes only.

198:1–3   Cf. F1789–91 *Dekes sa alme del cors departi; | E Dampnedeu l'ad recuilli | La sus en paris celestre . . .*

198:4–6   Cf. the ending of F, 1793–4 *Ore nus doint Deu par sa merci | Ke nus le façum altresi. Amen.*

OWAYNE MILES (*OM2*)
COTTON AND YALE

C1–28, Y1–24 The introductory progression of teachers from God to St Patrick via the prophets, Christ, apostles, and bishops is not in *T*. See Easting, 'Middle English Translations'.

C11, Y7 Based on the Gospels, thirty-three is traditionally the age of Christ at the Crucifixion. For traditions calculating Christ's life at thirty-two years and three months or thirty-three years, see Thomas N. Hall, 'The Ages of Christ and Mary in the Hyde Register and in Old English Literature', *NQ*, NS, xxxv (1988), 4–11.

Y12 *dede hymselfe*: *ded(e* is Y's spelling for 'did' (e.g. 81, 82, 86), here used quasi-causatively, for 'put' himself. The reading is perhaps preferable to the more straightforward C16 *dyed hymself* on idiomatic, and even theological, grounds. Cf. the Y copy of *Adrian and Epotys*, ll. 330–1, *The juvys toke hym at the laste, | And ded hym vp on the rode ...* (*Common-place Book*, p. 35).

C18 Emended according to Y, as *vs* (C17) and *All hem* (MS C18) in apposition are inconsistent. Christ redeemed us from *hym* (i.e. Satan) who was lost through pride.

C19–20, Y15–16 There is little to choose between these two readings, though Y may be preferable. Y15 is more convincing as narrative than C20; Y16 *forth* seems to be weakened to *forsoþe* in C19; C19 and 21 are padded by initial *And*; and the syntax of Y *he sente | To telle* is more straightforward than C's *he sende | That þey shulde ... amende | And to tell* ... Though pa. t. sg. *sende* was replaced by *sente* in ME the overlap in usage does not necessarily justify taking C's rhyme as an earlier, let alone better, reading.

Y19 Emendation takes up C23 *hadde*. MS reading *Ʒet we and* is scarcely defensible as 'And we got ...', both because of the awkward syntax, and because there is no instance of initial *Ʒ* for *g* in 'get' in this scribe's usage in the text. *MED* posits West Saxon, Mercian or Northumbrian influence for forms of 'get' with initial *Ʒ* and this does not normally apply in this East Anglian copy.

Y25 *In þe lond*: is patently wrong; cf. C29 *In Irlonde*.

C33ff, Y29ff In *T* St Patrick preaches of infernal torments and the bliss of paradise, in that order (L81–2).

Y32 *Who*: appears to be neither a representation of C36 *Howe* or *wo* (cf. Y313), but simply the interrogative pronoun 'who'. This reading is supported by the nominative *he* replacing the dative construction *wo þem* *ys*, cf. C36. Y31–32 must be read paratactically: 'and afterwards he spoke of the pain of hell—who (i.e. what kind of person) he is that comes therein'.

C37–38, Y33–34   Not in *T*, despite Y34. That St Patrick ever preached of purgatory is most unlikely, nor is he likely to have read much about it in *hys story*! Y34 is metrically preferable to C38.

C39–44   *þe folke*: are the 'bestial Irish' of the anecdote told by Gilbert in L82–108.

C39   *þys*: *sic* K, but in K4 Kölbing changed his mind and interpreted MS as *þe* while acknowledging 'die züge der schreibung þˢ ähnlich sind'. In fact, the second letter is distinctly different from that in *þe* earlier in the line.

Y37   The figure *1* presumably derives from earlier *one* representing *ony* 'any'; cf. *eny* C42, after *aliquis eorum* (L114). MS repeats *myth*, a scribal error probably caused by the initial *m* of *man*.

C48   Preferable to Y43. Cf. *pro salute populi deuotior* (L117) and *dum talibus pro salute populi intenderet bonis* (L118–19). The line can be restored metrically by omitting the first *þe*.

Y44   *throwr*: Though it is not recorded in *OED* I accept this spelling for 'through'; it is matched in (*c.*1500) *St. Anne(3)*: *Mari … þat was weddyd aftyrward throur goddes grace to joseph …*, quoted in *MED* s.v. gentil-man *n*. 2. *OED* Through *prep*. A a gives *thour* as a variant reading in *The Franklin's Tale*.

Y44–45   *beheue/beleue* (cf. Y240–1 *behaue/beleue*). Luick § 493/A2 and Dobson II. § 115 n. 1 quote Dibelius's use of this rhyme (*Anglia*, xxiii (1901), 188) as evidence of the identification of the earlier sounds ā/ę̄, reading *beheue* as '"behave" sb.'. *MED* gives no example of *behave* as a noun, and *OED*'s first and only reference is 1615 Chapman, meaning 'behaviour'. I am not convinced that we have here far earlier occurrences of this isolated form. Rather I believe *beheue* (Y44) and *behaue* (Y240) represent *biheue* 'behoof', even though *MED* biheve *n*. does not mention this noun following 'through' and a possessive, as in both these instances. Y44 might best be translated: That he (Patrick) might through his (Christ's) benefit/favour. Note that in the equivalent lines C49 and C245 *beheue* does not occur. I take C49 to mean: That he (Patrick) might through his (own) faith. Alternatively, *hys leue* could mean 'Christ's consent/permission'.

C50, Y45   *þe ryȝth beleue*: I take this to be the correct reading. For the phrase *riht bileue* (see *MED* bileve *n*. 2. (a)) following Latin *fides recta*, see H. Käsmann, *Studien zum kirchlichen Wortschatz des Mittelenglischen 1100–1350* (Tübingen, 1961), p. 91. Y's *a beter beleue* is a weakened expression, probably recalling the 'better' from C48.

C52 *bedys*: 'prayers', a reading preferable to Y47 *bed* which has perhaps lost the abbreviation mark for final *ys*. There is no evidence to connect Y's reading with A7:5. Cf. L118–20.

C54, Y49 Books containing the four Gospels were 'often found in the early centuries, when full copies of the New Testament were rare and copies of the Bible almost non-existent' (L.M.J. Delaissé, *Medieval Miniatures* (London, 1965), p. 18). Y49 *gospell* may have lost the plural abbreviation sign.

C54ff St Bernard writes of

> insignia quaedam sedis illius [i.e. Armagh], textum scilicet Evangeliorum, qui fuit beati Patricii, baculumque auro tectum et gemmis pretiosissimis adornatum, quem nominant baculum Iesu, eo quod ipse Dominus, ut fert opinio, eum suis manibus tenuerit atque formaverit. Et haec summae dignitatis et venerationis in gente illa. Nempe notissima sunt celeberrimaque in populis, atque in ea reverentia apud omnes, ut qui illa habere visus fuerit, ipsum habeat episcopum populus stultus et insipiens.

Vita Sancti Malachiae in *Sancti Bernardi Opera*, ed. J. Leclercq and H.M. Rochais, III (Rome, 1963), 334 ll. 7–13. See also H.J. Lawlor, *St. Bernard of Clairvaux's 'Life of St. Malachy of Armagh'* (London and New York, 1920), p. 53 n. 10. The gospels are (falsely) identified with the early ninth-century Book of Armagh in Trinity College, Dublin.

Y50 *yt*: with plural antecedent is well attested in ME; see *MED* hit *pron.* 1. (e).

Y52–55 Badly corrupted. MS *ʒowre* (Y52) is meaningless and is probably a corruption of *þore* (cf. *þere* C57). The rhyme word *ʒere* (C58) has been lost and the verb *bere* been substituted after *bore* (C59). MS *bere* (Y53) is probably a reminiscence of the required rhyme sound for the couplet, but has been emended after *bore* (C59) as a past participle form is required by the sense, and to rhyme with conjectural *þore*. Having thus used the verb 'bear' in Y53, the scribe has inverted the following couplet: Y54 after MS 53 *bere* just as C60 follows C59 *bore*. Because of the need for the verb 'bear' in the same line as 'procession', a new subject has been required and hence *boschoppys* repeated, after Y50. Y55 *baryth* means 'bore it', with enclitic object pronoun. Both here and at Y50, *yt(h)* refers to the plural object book and staff (Y49). I have supplied *yn* from C59 to complete the sense. I have punctuated with a semi-colon after Y53 in order to keep the sense of the following couplet as a unit (cf. C59–60), but it would also be feasible to place a comma after Y53 and colon after Y54. I have retained MS *heyr* (Y53) as the comparative 'higher', i.e. only at the more important feasts were the relics shown, though this spelling is not attested in *OED* and *MED*. *heyr* might otherwise be an anomalous spelling of *hey(e* with the fricative represented by final *-r*; cf. *throwr* (Y44). For the whole passage, cf. L152/8–9.

Y55 *prosessun*: the spelling may indicate the shift from [sj] to [ʃ]. See also Y185 and cf. 528, 653.

C64 *Jhesu staffe*: the correct reading, cf. Y59, the *baculus Ihesu* of L124. See above Commentary C54ff and Lawlor, *op. cit.*, p. 54 n. 1 for references. It was older than the Book of Armagh and its presentation by Christ to St Patrick was recorded by the tenth century. Giraldus Cambrensis says of the staff: *Per quem, vulgari opinione, sanctus Patricius venenosos ab insula vermes ejecit* (*Top. Hib.*, III. xxxiv). In *Trip. Life*, I. 30–31, the *bachall Iosa* or *Isa* is connected with Patrick's stay on Mt. Hermon, where he was told to preach to the Gaedhil, the Gaelic people; see E. O'Curry, *Lectures on the Manuscript Materials of Ancient Irish History* (Dublin, 1861), pp. 600ff. This connection between the gift of the staff and Patrick's preaching to and conversion of the natives is preserved by *TACY*.

In the *Life of Ciaran of Saighir* the *bachall* is said to be given to Patrick by Christ on Mt. Sinai (see C. Plummer ed., *Lives of Irish Saints*, II (Oxford, 1922), 100), and elsewhere, by a married pair on an island in the Tyrrhene sea (see *Lives of Saints from the Book of Lismore*, ed. W. Stokes (Oxford, 1890), p. 155 ll. 219ff). Cf. *Trip. Life*, II. 420–1, and Index Rerum s.v. Bachall Isu, II. 577. *T* was the first to suggest that the gift took place at St Patrick's Purgatory.

On bachalls, pastoral staffs, which were among the chief instruments of the saint's art as a superior medicine man, see C. Plummer ed., *Vitae sanctorum Hiberniae*, I (Oxford, 1910), pp. clxxv–clxxvi. For examples of Irish statues of figures bearing bell and crosier, see John Sharkey, *Celtic Mysteries: The Ancient Religion* (London, 1975), plates 33 and 39. Giraldus tells how bells and crosiers were held in more esteem by the Irish than the Gospels (*Top. Hib.*, III. xxxiii). *Jhesu staffe* was the most venerable of them all.

In 1177 *Jhesu staffe* was seized from the Archbishop of Armagh and kept at Dublin 'as a permanent symbol of the Norman victory' (A. Gwynn, 'Saint Laurence O'Toole as Legate in Ireland (1179–80)', *AB*, lxviii (1950), 234). Laurence Rathold, pilgrim to St Patrick's Purgatory in 1411, visited the relics and saw the *baculus Ihesu* in Trinity College, Dublin (see *AB*, xxvii (1908), 45). It was publicly burned in Dublin in 1538. See also J. Healy, *The Life and Writings of St. Patrick* (Dublin, 1905), pp. 633–6.

In *Legenda Aurea*, cap. 50 (ed. Th. Graesse (Leipzig, 1850), pp. 213–14) and hence in John of Tynmouth, *Nova Legenda Anglie*, ed. C. Horstmann, II (Oxford, 1901), 293 ll. 8–10, and in *pa*, Christ or St Patrick describes the circle of the pit of the Purgatory with the staff:

> In þe eorþe he made mid is staf . a cercle al aboute
> Þer bicom a put swuþe dep . þat men hadde of gret doute

EETS, 235 (1956), p. 87 ll. 45–46. Leslie, *Saint Patrick's Purgatory*, opp. p. xvii reproduces a woodcut from Petrus de Natalibus, *Catalogus Sanctorum* of St Patrick revealing the pit with the Staff of Jesus. Cf. Ariosto, *Orlando Furioso*, X.92.

Y61 MS has lost *wyth hym*, presumably because of the repeated *hym*.

C68, Y63   Y's reading seems preferable, and presupposes the original rhyme form *wes*, probably *ne wes*. Zupitza (Z1) suggested emending C's *reste* to *beste*, but I have retained C's reading as it makes its own adequate sense.

C70–71, Y65–66   See below, Commentary L128.

Y66–67   For the rhyme, cf. Y658–9. The scribe frequently uses *y* for earlier /e/: cf. the rhymes in 146–7, 336–7, 422–3.

Y69   MS *howo*: could be *howe*. Either way the MS reading is nonsensical in context and is either a bad guess on the scribe's part or an inaccurate recall, either in transcription or at some earlier stage of oral transmission, of the emended reading, taken from C74. Cf. *uera fide armatus* and *in fide constanter* (L130, 133).

Y70   MS *he note wyll*: betrays the same kind of error as Y69. C75 seems correct, though the repeat of 'dwell' from C73 is clumsy. The change from *þat he ne dwell* to *he note wyll* seems more likely to have been an aural error than simply a visual confusion resulting in false word division. Intermediate stages, written, spoken, or self-dictated, could have been *he no dwell, he not well*. Y frequently uses *y* for /e/ in 'well', e.g. 64, 86, 144.

C77, Y72   *T* nowhere actually states that St Patrick's Purgatory was a place of pilgrimage, though a claim for its early popularity is made in 1200 (see Easting, 'Peter of Cornwall's Account', p. 416 ll. 160ff) and its European-wide fame was well established by the end of the thirteenth century, probably a good hundred years before the composition of *OM2*.

C77–79, Y72–74   C seems basically a better reading, despite the shift from plural to singular, and the metre of C77 may be improved by the omission of *And. man* (Y72) suits ill with *man, woman* (Y74). The social opposition of *sqwyer or knaue* (C79), implying anyone and everyone of high or low estate, is lost in Y74. *doth* (C77) is perhaps preferable to *goth* (Y72), though for the construction *gon (a) pelrinage* see *MED* gon *v.* 3. (d). For the late southern pr. pl. in -*th* (*doth* C77) cf. *oweth* C232. *ore* (Y74): MS long *r* and flourish; all other occurrences of *or* in Y use 2-shaped *r*.

C80, Y75   This spells out clearly the purpose of a pilgrim's visiting St Patrick's Purgatory. *T* only says as much at this point by implication (L131–2). This opinion incurred the scorn of Trevisa in an addition to his translation of Higden's rehearsal of Giraldus Cambrensis:

> He telleþ [þat] who þat suffreþ þe peynes of þat purgatorie, ȝif it be enioyned hym for penaunce, he schal neuere suffre þe peynes of helle, but he dye fynalliche wiþ oute repentaunce of synne … *Treuisa.* Þei þis sawe myȝt be sooth, it is but a iape. For no man þat dooþ dedely synne schal be i-saued, but he be verrey repentaunt, [what sommeuer penaunce he doo; and euery man that is verray repentaunt] at his lifes ende of al his mysdedes, he schal be sikerliche i-saued and haue þe blisse of heuene, þey he neuere hire speke of Patrik his purgatorie.

Polychronicon, I. xxxv, ed. C. Babington, RS 41.i (London, 1865), 363.

C84   Preferable to Y79 which weakens *stynte* to *stode* and is metrically deficient with loss of *ner*.

Y81   *ded*: is causative rather than periphrastic.

C87–88, Y82–83   See below, Commentary L138–9.

Y85   *Regelys*: (cf. Y412) after *Reglis* (L152). Cf. Commentary A21:4. The Irish word *reiclés* signifies an oratory, small church, or monastic cell. *Thus* (Y84) implies the false derivation of *Reglis* from *regula* (cf. *cunsel* (Y83)), the 'rule' of St Augustine: see Easting, 'Peter of Cornwall's Account', pp. 402-3. This view has been widespread, from e.g. the B MS of *T* (*locus regularis*) to S. Malone in *Journal of the Royal Historical and Archaeological Association of Ireland*, III, 4th series (1874), p. 259 n. The word caused other scribes some difficulty, e.g. *Rigles*, Marie de France (ed. Warnke, l. 377), and *Regulis* H. CCCC MS 462 f. 152v glosses *reglis iuxta linguam patrie memorate*. See further, Pontfarcy, in Haren & Pontfarcy, pp. 13–14.

     hath: 'is called'. This spelling, unrecorded in *MED*, represents either a syncopation of *hateth*, or *hat* with Y's *-th* for *-t*, cf. examples, Introduction, p. xxxi.

Y86–87   *wyll/stell*: on the uncertainty of the rhyming vowel in such instances, see Davis, EETS, ss 1 (1970), lxvi–lxvii, and cf. Y150–1 *wyll/sell* 'seal' < OF *seel* (L *sigillum*).

Y91   *loket*: 'lock it'. See Introduction, p. xxxii.

Y94   *seynt*: For the aphetic form of *assent* see *MED* sent *n.* (1) which cites this instance.

C99   After L177–84. The practice of obtaining episcopal permission for pilgrimages applied not only to St Patrick's Purgatory. See C. Plummer ed., *Vitae sanctorum Hiberniae*, I (Oxford, 1910), pp. cxxii–cxxiii, and also Cross, *Motif-Index*, Q527.

C101–2   After L150–1.

Y98   *rememure*: first of only two references in *MED* s.v. rememori *n.*

C103–10   After L145–8.

Y103   *God wyth þem*: probably an error for *God wote, þey* (cf. C106), but I have retained the MS reading for the possible sense: God (being) with them, (they) told (on their return) of much sorrow …

Y104   See Introduction, p. lxix on the loss of the following line.

Y105–6   The first *þey* refers to the pilgrims; the second two to the canons at the Purgatory. Y is probably closer to the original here than C: cf. L147–8, 174–5. C's *wente yn* (109) could well be a corruption of *witen* or *weten*.

Unfortunately, no trace remains of any books written at Lough Derg, though there is a record of one listing the names of visitors, seen there by Chiericati in 1517: see trans. by J.G. Smyly in J.P. Mahaffy, 'Two Early Tours in Ireland', *Hermathena*, xl (1914), 13. See now also M. Purcell, 'St Patrick's Purgatory: Francesco Chiericati's Letter to Isabella d'Este', *Seanchas Ardmhacha*, xii, 2 (1987), 1–10.

Y106   *hant*: represents *han yt*, 'have it'. For enclitic 'it', see Introduction, p. xxxii. For *han* cf. Y138, 584, 587. Close inspection of the pen strokes reveals that Miss Toulmin Smith's reading *haith* (her l. 110) is erroneous. The final letter is *-t* with a downward flourish (cf. *that* 107). It lacks the top loop which distinguishes *h* in this scribe's hand; cf. *-th* in *whath* (105) and *seynth* (99). The last two letters lack the horizontal normally found through final *-th*. The sweeping tail of *y* in *seyn* (105) may have caused confusion here. What may at first sight appear as *-ith* is in fact the two minims of *n* plus final *-t* with a long cross stroke and long downward tail.

C111, Y107   C is preferable to Y which substituted *bodyn care* for *bolde wore*. C retains the point that despite being bold some visitors still never came back from the Purgatory, an elaboration on the disappearances reported in L174, 203–4. Y's rhyme *care/more* must be on the northern form *mare*.

C113–15, Y109–11   See L206–7 and Commentary.

C114   Correct reading, not Y110 which idly repeats *þer wos a knyth* (cf. C115) before *A knyth þer wos* (Y111). There is no justification in *T* for regarding Owein as an English knight, despite his apparent knowledge of Anglo-Norman or English (or even Latin?), required when acting as interpreter for Gilbert (L1078–80). See also Commentary A29:4, and see further Easting, 'Owein at St Patrick's Purgatory'.

Y111   *klepynd*: *MED* does not record this form. I take it as a metathetic contraction of *klepeden* (the pa. t. pl. form attested in *MED* clepen *v.* 1. (a) and 4. (b)), analogous to *cryend* (Y313, see Commentary).

Owein/Howyn is called *Syr* in his capacity as *miles* (L207 and *passim*), translated in *pa*, *OM1*, and *OM2* as 'knight', its usual medieval sense, not soldier. See *Revised Medieval Latin Word-List*, prepared by R.E. Latham (London, 1965), s.v. Miles.

C118   Here the terminology is general rather than strictly correct: the tale really tells of purgatory, with a glance at hell, and of the Earthly Paradise, with a glance at heaven, the celestial paradise; see Easting, 'Purgatory and the Earthly Paradise' for a discussion of the separation of these categories.

Y122   MS *sete*: for *se* is typical of Y's careless handling of rhymes in many places; see Introduction, p. lxxi.

Y124   *At hys myth*: 'according to his ability'. For the construction, see *MED* might *n*. 3. (e). The awkwardness of the phrase in context and the preservation of *of all* in the second half-line suggest C128 is the more authentic.

C132, Y128   Not in *T*.

Y132   *sowle leche*: for the OE gen. sg. *sawle* retained in this combination, see *MED* soul(e *n.* 1c. (b).

C140   *ʒour*: pl. does not agree with the rest of the speech addressing the bishop as *þou* sg. Y136 is superior as a whole to C140, and Y uses the plural throughout the speech, which seems more suitable. Note that in reply the bishop uses 'thou' in both manuscripts.

C146–8   Cf. L222–3, and see below, Commentary C170–4.

Y143–5   See Introduction, p. lxiv.

C152   MS *of heuen*: is a careless substitution for what must be the correct reading *so hende* (cf. Y147, and for the rhyme C287–8). K retained MS reading and added *aʒen* as a rhyme at the end of C151.

Y148   *thowe*: an anomalous spelling for *tho* 'then' (unrecorded in *OED*), presumably by confusion with 'though'.

Y150   *worthe*: I take this as a metathetic variant of *wrohte*, cf. *made* (C155). On Y's use of *-th(-e)* for earlier *-ht* see Introduction, p. xxxi. Alternatively, though perhaps less likely, the scribe may have meant 'wrote'. *T misit per ipsum epistolam* (L226) does not help significantly.

C156, Y151   Not in *T*. This independent detail is almost paralleled by F311–12 where the prior breaks the wax on receiving the letter, on which Owen (*Vision of Hell*, p. 72) has aptly commented, 'A small touch, but one which enlivens the telling.'

Y151   *selydyth*: 'sealed it'; see Introduction, p. xxxii, and on the rhyme, see above, Commentary Y86–87.

C157–8   I have inverted the MS order of these two lines to comply with Y's better sense.

C162   The emendation *knyʒthes* follows Y157 after *cognita ipsius causa* (L228–9). Cf. C166.

C164ff, Y159ff   No direct speech in *T*. On this whole section, see Introduction, pp. lix–lxii.

Y159   *hethyr*: is a careless alteration for *her*, destroying the full rhyme on the stressed second syllable of *maner*.

C167–8, Y162–3   Y is metrically inferior to C, but *perellys* suggests that Y163 is closer to the original reading: cf. *ei plurimorum perditionem periculumque proposuit . . .* (L229).

C170–4, Y165–7   *. . . per ingressum religionis aliquis consequatur remissionem omnium peccatorum* (Aquinas, *Summa theologiae*, 2a.2ae.189.3. resp.3.). The acceptance of monachism was equivalent to a second baptism. CY here repeat the bishop's advice in C146, Y142. In *T* the prior makes no such suggestion, though cf. L184–6.

Y167   This line is followed by a lacuna both here and at Y144.

Y168–9   Y169 seems a good line apart from the problematical MS *wytte*. If *wytte* means 'wit' it is nonsensical; if it means *wite* 'blame', then it forms an imperfect rhyme with *thyke*, with assonantal *t* and *k*, and long and short /i/ (though *-tt-* might possibly indicate shortening). It would also be possible, though improbable, to read *wytte/thyte*: see *OED* Thight *a*. 'thick-set, dense'. The spelling *thyte* is attested in Norfolk in *EDD*, and this would be suitable here as the fricative appears to have been lost in the Y scribe's speech. See also *Promptorium parvulorum*, s.v. Thight, and n. 2327 on p. 719. But there seems to be no good reason for substituting dialectal *thyte* for the perfectly acceptable *thyke*. I have therefore emended *wytte* to *wykke*, which could easily have been misread. For *wykke* 'evil, wickedness', see *OED* Wick *a*. 3b as *sb*. Sm suggested *me wyke* (in note to her l. 175), but there is no need to alter MS *my* (168) if one takes *wykke* as a noun and not as an adjective.

C175–8, Y168–71   Y seems more authentic. C's rhyme *well/wyll* is inexact; C176 *dyþur y wyll* is a pre-echo of the following half-line; C177 *for my synnus* echoes C176 and displaces *what so befalle* to the second line of the couplet.

These lines nicely reflect the fact that until its temporary closure in 1497 St Patrick's Purgatory was a last resort for desperate sinners from all over Europe, for to enter purgatory in the flesh was clearly to undergo *penitentiam omnibus penitentiis grauiorem* (L215).

C184, Y177   C's *almesse-dedes* are not mentioned here in *T*. Y's *fastyng* is correct: see *quindecim diebus ieiuniis et orationibus uacauit* (L233–4).

Y179   For the rhyme cf. Y66–67 and see Commentary.

C187, Y180   Cf. L189. It may well be that this was Owein's own Requiem mass performed as a rite of severance. This was the case with later pilgrims, e.g. George Grissaphan in 1353 (see *Visiones Georgii*, pp. 94–95) and Antonio Mannini in 1411 (see L. Frati, 'Il Purgatorio di S. Patrizio', *Giornale Storico della Letteratura Italiana*, viii (1886), 159).

Y180–1   *messe/wos*: should perhaps rhyme on /a/, though if Y63 is authentic the archetype may have rhymed on /e/. C uses only *masse*, Y only *messe*; neither uses *wes*. The spelling *wos* suggests the progress of retraction and rounding. Y uses the spelling *was* 45 times (6 in rhyme), *wos* 17 times (only here in rhyme).

C188–9, Y181–2   C is correct in preserving *Wyth*, but *asoyled* is most likely a corruption of Y's *howsyld* which renders *munitur ... sacra communione* (L190). Cf. *Piers the Plowman*, B.XIX.1–3: *I ... dede me to cherche, | To here holy the masse . and to be houseled after*, and see Skeat ed. note.

C190, Y182   No relics are mentioned in *T*. Y's *he* is doubtless an error for *þey*, though as dramatically effective as it is improbable.

C191   MS *man*: emended in accordance with Y to preserve the rhyme.

C193–4   See Introduction, p. lxi.

C200   *OM2* omits the prior's speech (L239–46) telling Owein of the hall he will find, thereby sacrificing expectation to achieve narrative surprise.

C201   *þore*: Zupitza (Z1) suggested *dore*, but was unaware of C's interchangeable use of *þ* and *d*: see Introduction, p. xxviii.

C202, Y195   L254–5 does not help a choice between C *lafte* and Y *preyed*.

C208, Y201   Not in *T*.

C211, Y204   C is correct; Y idly repeats *A lytyll lyght* from Y203.

Y207   *the sunne-reste*: *OED* Sun *sb.* 13 cites this as the second of only two occurrences, the first being from Love's *Bonaventura's Mirrour* (*c*.1400). *MED* sonne *n.* 1b. (d) adds only Chaucer *CT.Mch*.E.2174. Y's noun construction matches *post solis occasum* (L262) more closely than C214.

C217–18, Y210–11   Not in *T*. Cf. A62:6 and Y62–63. C218 substitutes *grasse* for *gresse*.

Y216–17   After L263–4. Y substitutes *bare* for *bere* pa. t. pl., with levelling of the vowel of the singular lengthened in an open syllable.

C223–4, Y218–19   C's line order follows *T* more accurately. *selkowth/sylkeweth* translates *mirabilem* (L265). On Y's odd spelling of this word, cf. the *Paston Letters* use of *ew* for ME *u* noted by Dobson, II. § 160 n. 3.

C225–6, Y220–1   After L269–71. See Introduction, p. lxix on the re-use of this couplet formula at C395–6, Y334–5, 446–7.

C227   Preferable to Y222 which repeats *sey* from Y223 *seyd*. Cf. *qui quasi prior et eorum dux esse uidebatur* (L272–3).

C233–4, Y228–9   C is preferable. Y has inverted the rhymes giving *befall* as an unsatisfactory pa. t.

C235–6, Y230–1   Not in *T*.

C239, Y234   There is a pre-echo of C253, Y248 which renders L293–4.

C240–2, Y235–7   Not in *T*. Y236 MS *Jhu* is difficult to account for. If it is an address to Jesus it is nonsensical; if an exclamation, tortuous, and there is no evidence for *befall* as a transitive verb. It is possibly an absent-minded error, conceivably aural in origin, for *shall* (C241), as emended.

C245–6, Y240–1   Mention of *God* in C suggests that C may be closer to the original: cf. *Si uero firmiter in fide spem totam in Domino posueris*

(L285-6). The spelling of C's rhyme *styffe*/*belefe* seems to suggest that the final consonant is unvoiced, though *OED* Belief *sb.* gives the 16th century for the modern distinction between the voiced verb and unvoiced noun. *MED* bileve *n.*, under 2. (b), gives only one occurrence of *belefe*, from *c.*1450 *Alph.Tales*. The rhyme perhaps demands *stef* or *steve*, see *OED* Steeve *a.* and *adv.*, now Sc. and dialectal, 'firm, unyielding, resolute'.

Y's rhyme requires *beheue* (cf. Y44-45 and Commentary) and suggests *ẹ̄* variant in *beleue* (see Dobson, II. § 120). Translate *throw thy behaue* 'through(out) thy (time of) need'.

C249-50, Y244-5 Not in *T*. Cf. the prayer given to William of Stranton: *Jhesu Christe, fili Dei viui, misereri michi peccatori* (*VWS* SR13).

For the syncopated genitive in *God sun* (Y244) see *MED* s.v. god *n.* 4a. (a). C's *synfull* (250) is clearly preferable to Y's *gentyll* (245 and 293, 331) which is wholly inappropriate in the mouth of a penitent sinner, and smacks of a careless response to 'reading on romance'.

Y246 MS *hath*: a false imp. sg. probably caused by the proximity of *hath* in the next line.

C256, Y251 Here *OM2* omits the passage (L295-304) where Owein, *ad noui generis militiam instructus* (L295-6), is prepared to fight against demons rather than men, and is armed with the armour of God (Eph. 6:13ff).

C257-8 After L307-9. The rhyme requires *helf* (cf. *Sir Firumbras*, EETS, ES 34 (1879), l. 1909, *Beryn*, EETS, ES 105 (1909), l. 2178): see Jordan/Crook § 61.

C259-62, Y252-55 Not in *T*, but cf. L309-12. With C261-2 cf. *Pricke of Conscience*, ll. 4784-5.

C263 *For*: should perhaps read *Þurȝ* to make stronger sense following *ac si totus commoueretur orbis* (L309). Cf. Ld141 *Ase al þe world to borste and to breke*, and A52:4 *Þei alle þe warld falle schold*. The MS reading makes good sense, however, and has been retained. For parallels, see e.g. Chaucer, *Hous of Fame*, l. 1932 and cf. l. 1525.

Y256 *wedyr*: might be a corruption of *worlde* (C262), but it carries the unfavourable connotations of *OED* Weather *sb.* 1.g. Cf. Y476.

C264, Y257 C must be the authentic reading, with *crye* suggested by *tumultuarent* (L311). *faryd* (Y256) evidently put the Y scribe, or an earlier copyist, in mind of Owein being *aferde* (Y257); cf. Y267, C273, 352.

C265-6, Y258-9 Cf. L312-14.

Y259 *rewyd*: i.e. reft, taken away, carried off (from this life) (<OE *reafian*), see *MED* s.v. reven *v.* 2.(d). Cf. *We schall rew the of þi liffe*, in Y MS copy of *St Margaret*, l. 31, *Common-place Book*, p. 111.

C268–9, Y261–2 Y261 is deficient; the C reading must be correct. However, Y262 *owte of* is probably correct and C *I wote, fro* a corruption, for the narratorial interruption is awkward and unnecessary. On the question of demons from hell tormenting souls in purgatory, see Easting, 'Purgatory and the Earthly Paradise', pp. 40–41.

C270, Y263 C is correct, following *innumera multitudo demonum* (L318). Y is corrupt and has merely retained the rhyme word. Beyond the general idea 'There he now needs courage', the sense of Y is uncertain, the *OED* recording no use of *tell* that fits convincingly. The line seems to be either the wish 'May courage there fully tell/count for him/in his favour' or 'May courage there proclaim (or direct) him' or the (under)statement 'There courage may be of great help to him/tell in his favour'. *Tell* 'to count for something' implied in some of these paraphrases is a modern sense, *OED* Tell *v.* 26, and not strictly available, but see also senses 11, 22d, 24.

C271–2, Y264–5 Y is corrupt with MS *Full* for *They fylled* (C271) repeated from Y263; the inappropriate plural *howsys*; and the walls, for the building had no proper walls (see L262–3), cf. Y215–19. The *gostys* should be pictured as filling and overflowing the courtyard. In this respect C's *two rowes* sounds rather too orderly for *so mony* crowding devils, and probably misrepresents Y's better phrase *rowys be rowys*. Y265 is an invention to make up for the loss of a line equivalent to C274. C272 and Y266 follow *cachinnando ac deridendo* (L319).

Y266 *gernyd*: is a well-attested metathetic form of *grenned*: see *MED* s.v. grennen *v.*, and Dobson, II. § 439.

C274 *For*: is metrically superfluous.

Y269–70 *by/hey*: the rhyme is either a half rhyme on *be* and a diphthong, or a full rhyme on [i:]. The latter seems more likely considering Y's rhyme of *cry/hey* (496–7). Y's only spelling of 'high' is *hey(e* (214, 305, 368, 374r, 464).

C277–8, Y270–1 The metre of Y is good and has a good rhyme (cf. Y448–9). The occurrence in Y271 of *betyme*, however, C's rhyme word, may betoken that C is closer to the original, and that Y was making do with a corruption to a simpler concept and rhyme. The metre of C278 is easily restored by omitting *For*. *lyme* I take to mean 'bird-lime, lime(-trap)': see *OED* Lime *sb.* 1, and *MED* lim *n.*(2) 3.(a). *beleue* therefore means 'stay, remain'. Cf. A108:1 (and Commentary) where devils speak of trapping souls like birds in hell: *Þis ben our foules in our caghe*.

C277–90, Y270–85 *OM2* considerably alters the implications of this speech; cf. L320. C283–4 suggest that Owein had done evil and the devils will reward him justly, that is, with pain. This is confirmed in C285–6 (not in *T*). But nevertheless they will let him return to earth and spare him while by his evil living he earns more pain. *OM2* increases the irony,

notably in the second line of each couplet. The explicit statement *habebis
... pressuras ... et dolores* (L328–9) is made implicit in C278, 282, 284–6.
Cf. *VEL* p. 25 where the first devils to see Edmund say: *Behold, ʒondir
commyth on of vs, and he has done vs seruice. Wher for he shall abyd and
dwell with vs* ... On the devils' capacity for irony, see also Commentary
A57:4.

C282, Y275　Not in *T*. Cf. A56:5 and Commentary. Dancing was
frequently castigated as a devilish activity, leading to the deadly sin of
lust, and the dance of devils is found elsewhere, e.g. *Partonope*, EETS,
ES 109 (1911), l. 5087. Cf. the vision seen by a young man in St Patrick's
Purgatory where dancers are tormented, in J. Herolt, *Promptuarium
Exemplorum*, C.ix (not E.ix, as quoted by G.G. Coulton, *Five Centuries of
Religion*, I (Cambridge, 1923), 534). See also J.A. MacCulloch, *Medieval
Faith and Fable* (London, 1932), pp. 24–26.

Y277　*ʒyldyth*: i.e. *ʒyld yt*, 'reward/repay it', after L325–7.

C285–6, Y278–9　The common line C285, Y279 is based on *Recipies ergo
a nobis habundanter que meruisti* (L326–7); see also Whiting H185. Y's
seruyd 'deserved' is the closer equivalent for *meruisti*; see *MED* s.v. serve
v.(2). C286 is not in *T*; Y278 is based on the notions of service recurrent
in this speech in *T*.

Y282–3　*down/sunne*: the spelling of *down* suggests the completion in this
rhyme of the shift from [ō] > [uː].

Y284–5　This couplet seems to be misplaced here (see Introduction, p.
lxviii), for although the irony is appropriate (the devils would prefer
Owein body and soul), when it occurs in C343–4 (see Commentary) the
succeeding couplet provides a fuller context. It is possible that originally
the couplet appeared in both speeches. There is no equivalent for the full
sense in *T*, though cf. L324–5 and 277–8.

C291–2, Y286–7　*T* expressly states that Owein remains silent here,
nichil penitus respondens (L337). Y's reading seems preferable in terms of
the dramatic *Nay*; the *wyll* responding to Y281; the metre and word
order of Y287; and the *bowte* being both appropriate and common in such
a context: Owein's salvation rather than his creation is uppermost in his
mind.

C297–8　*powʒth/mowʒth*: seems to rhyme on [uːχ] with analogical influence of *puhte* (< OE *pyncan* 'to seem') on *pohte* (< OE *pencan* 'to think');
see Dobson, II. § 177. *mowʒth* could be 'was able', from 'may' (*OED* May
v.[1] 3; *MED* mouen *v.*(3)), or 'was permitted', by confusion from *mote*
(*OED* Mote *v.*[1] 1; *MED* moten *v.*(2)).

C301–2, Y294–7　See Introduction, p. lxix. There is no equivalent for
C302, Y294 in *T*.

C304 I.e. as if there were nothing wrong with him. See *MED* eilen *v.* 3. (d). Wu (p. 23 l. 50) is quite wrong and punctuates solely with a comma after *nowʒt*; see also Wu2 note p. 236.

C307 Cf. L351.

C309–10, Y297 Not in *T*, where the same devils drag Owein off.

Y300 *therke*: this word is attested in Norfolk and is therefore unsurprising in the Book of Brome from near the Suffolk/Norfolk border: see *OED* Therk *a.*; *EDD* Thark, and A.J. Bliss, *Sir Orfeo*, 2nd ed. (Oxford, 1966), p. 54 note to l. 370.

C314–16, Y301–3 Not in *T*. Cf. L360–1.

C315–16, Y302–3 Corrupt. Common elements are the conditional construction; 'clothes' in the first line; and C's *wolde be colde* and Y's *xulde be colde* in the second. C's rhyme and metre are awkward, and Y is perhaps to be preferred. Y303 MS *thyrth* is an obvious error, and I have emended to *herte* as nearest in form and required sense. Y frequently uses *y* for /e/ but initial *t* is hard to explain. *throte* I think an unlikely reading because of the vowel change. Miss Toulmin Smith does not emend at all. Y's rhyme *purfuld/colde* is inexact, and *purfuld* takes initial stress. See *OED* Purfle *v.* for the spelling *purfulle* (1502). For the sense of *colde* here, see *MED* colden *v.* 2. (a), and cf. the threat in the note of possession in BL MS Royal 18 A xvii: *He that this booke stelle wolde, Sone be his herte colde* (see T. Wright and J.O. Halliwell, *Reliquiae Antiquae*, II (London, 1843), 163. It is possible that an earlier version read *purfyld/chyld* or *purfeld/cheld* 'chilled', avoiding the same rhyme sound as the previous couplet.

C317–18, Y304–5 C is closer to L360.

C321–2 *knewe/nowe*: depends on rhyme sound [u:], with *knewe* representing variant *knowe* < OE *cneow*. (*MED* knouen *v.* lists (EM) *knuʒ*, *knogh* & (M) *knu* and (late) *knou(e).*) Perhaps this couplet is a rewriting and Y308–9 is to be preferred. *tell* rather than *knewe* may perhaps better render *Finis ... non potuit ... uideri* (L371–2), though there is little to choose between them.

C322, Y309 'go' is to be understood after 'must'. On omission of verbs of motion, see T. Mustanoja, *A Middle English Syntax* (Helsinki, 1960), pp. 543–4.

C324, Y311 Not in *T*.

Y313 *cryend*: I take this as a metathetic form of pa. t. pl. *cry(e)den*; cf. *klepynd* Y111 and Commentary. The whole line is typical of many metrically deficient lines in Y, where the copyist seems to have been content with the barest sense alone.

Y314 *loyn*: (cf. *loyne* Y345) cited *MED* s.v. lien *v.*(1) 3. (a) 'to be down or cast down; lie wounded or unable to move'.

Y315 Here Y loses the rest of the first field of torment, though later lines obviously belonged to it and have been misplaced: cf. C331–4 and Y346–9.

C329 *brasse*: (cf. *clauis ferreis* (L375)) made a useful rhyme with *was*; cf. C387–8, Y436–7.

C330 Cf. *pre dolore uidebantur terram comedere* (L376–7).

C331 Cf. *uentre ad terram uerso* (L374–5).

C332 *Spare þey*: As Wu2 (p. 236 note v. 78) pointed out, this could well have been written for *Spareþ þey*, considering the plural *deueles* in C333, but each soul may be taken as addressing a single devil, so the MS reading has been retained.

C333–4 Cf. *Demones enim inter eos et super eos uidebantur discurrere, qui non cessabant flagris eos dirissimis cedere* (L380–1). As here, *T* frequently has more detailed action than the English versifier was prepared to try and match.

C339–46 This expands *T* (L382–5) by reference to the previous tempting speech of the demons: *quatinus uiuens adhuc in mundo gaudeas, ne totum quod suaue est corpori tuo funditus amittas* (L332–3). Cf. C289. C340's imputation of *gyle* is not found in *T*.

C343–4 Seen here in context (cf. Y284–5), this couplet reminds us that Owein is in purgatory in the body, not rapt in spirit.

C346 *Thus*: For this spelling of 'this' see *OED* This *dem. pron. & adj.* A.5.

C348–50 No direct speech in *T*. The English heightens the dramatic conflict verbally even though it decreases it physically.

C350 Figuratively speaking, i.e. intent on God.

C351–2 *clawe/trowe*: This rhyme is perhaps on a variant plural *clowe*, usually *clowes* (see K3 and *MED* claue *n.* (1)) rather than the northerly *trawe* (*OED* Trow *v. arch.*) and *clawe* pl. < OE *clawa*.

C357–8 Cf. *inuocato Ihesu nomine* (L387).

C361–2 Not in *T*. Cf. Y444–5.

C366 Not in *T*. This neatly reminds us that Owein is a warrior and of his role as a knightly adventurer.

C367–8 Cf. *alium campum, maiori miseria plenum* (L390–1).

C368–9, Y316–420 On the omissions and arrangement see Introduction pp. lxvi–lxviii.

Y320–1 *turne/mone*: this inexact rhyme suggests an earlier *turne/morne*, cf. e.g. Lydgate, *Temple of Glas*, ll. 480–1, 639–40, with *mourne* v. See *MED* morne *n.*

Y328 *streynyd*: there seems to be a deliberate echo of Christ's being stretched for nailing on the cross, suggesting a parallel between Owein's purgation and the suffering of Christ. Cf. C328, 355 and the stress on remembering the Passion both here (C251–2) and in *VWS* SR46, 82, 98–9, 118–19 etc. See *OED* Strain *v.*¹ II.10.†b. For a discussion of the 'straining' of Christ at the Crucifixion, see F.P. Pickering, *Literature and Art in the Middle Ages* (Glasgow, 1970), pp. 238ff.

Y329 The scribe deleted *wos* and substituted the theologically sounder *ys*.

Y336–7 *fylde/behylde*: rhyme (cf. Y356–7) is probably on *ẹ̄*, for the scribe's use of *y* for the reflex of OE *e* is conspicuous throughout this text, and elsewhere in the MS: see N. Davis, EETS, ss 1 (1970), pp. lxvii–lxviii.

Y338 The copyist began another stint here with change of ink and pen.

Y341 *tode*: cf. *todys* (Y352) after *Buffones* (L400). Along with snakes, toads are stock inhabitants of tombs, demonic visions, purgatory, and hell in medieval literature and iconography. See e.g. Guy de Tervarent, *Attributs et symboles dans l'art profane 1450–1600* (Travaux d'Humanisme et Renaissance, XXIX, Geneva, 1958), pp. 135–6.

Y344–5 *lene/kyne*: there is no source for *kyne* in *T*, and this may be a desperate and inexact rhyme. However, it may depend on *ẹ̄* with a close variant in *lene*, and *kyne* with *y* for /e/ in an easterly development of OE *cinu* > *chine* > *chene*. See *OED* Chine *sb.*1. For initial *k* see *MED* chine *n.*(1) and *OED* Kin *sb.*2, given as northern dialect, though there is no record of a form *kene* apart from in MDu.

Lean men and women are tantalized in the Vernon MS version of *þe visions of seynt poul*, ed. C. Horstmann, *The Minor Poems of the Vernon MS.*, EETS 98 (1892), 225, ll. 163ff.

Y350–4 Not in *T*, and corrupt, with the outstandingly hypermetric line 350 probably due to memorial transmission, and the awkward syntactic relationship of the two couplets. This attack on high living is of the same brand as that found in *VWS*. Cf. Bromyard: *In place of a soft couch, they shall have a bed more grievous and hard than all the nails and spikes in the world ... Instead of wives they shall have toads*, quoted by Owst, *LPME*, p. 294, and see pp. 411ff for attacks on 'soft and delycat beddying' and hair combing.

Y353 *vetyn*: = *wetyn* = *wyten*, 'know'. See Introduction, p. xxxii, for the interchange of *v* and *w*, and for the *e* cf. *wete* Y58.

Y360–1 Translate: The knight saw the torment of every man as he went (along).

Y362 *wyll*: in context seems a little odd and perhaps should read *yll*, but there are no firm grounds for emendation.

Y368–9 *lowe/sawe*: This rhyme requires *lawe* < ON *lágr*, which is possible in this scribe's speech along with other northern features. The couplet may be a reworking of a less northerly rhyme in the archetype, e.g. *Summe hynge lowe and summe hynge hye, | Many he knewe that he þer sye.* Cf. Y374–5, C415–16.

Y370 *hokys*: cf. *uncis ferreis* (L434). Y follows the Latin closely here, distinguishing the hooks from the chains, *schenys* (Y364), *cathenis igneis* (L431).

Y372 Cf. *Cumque transissent inde* (L449).

Y375 MS *And nedys*: is an evident error for the emended reading *Vneþe*, cf. C416. As with the bridge, the height is emphasised by Owein's difficulty in seeing the top. There is no compulsion about him seeing the *ourest ȝend*. *ȝend* shows the development of a glide [j] before initial *ĕ* or *ę̄* variant. See Wyld, *History of Modern Colloquial English*, p. 308, and Dobson, II. § 430 n. 5.

Y376 Cf. L451–3.

Y379–80 *bernyth*: may represent earlier *bernyd*, or may indicate the ever present burning of the purgatorial flames, and as such it has not been emended. MS *semyth* probably represents pa. t. *semyd* (see Introduction, p. xxxii), and has been so emended for the reader's convenience.

Y380–1 Not in *T*. The rhyme *ȝarn/qwerne* requires *ȝerne* < OE *ȝeorn*. MS deletion *faste* shows the scribe's mind and pen racing ahead without initial regard for the rhyme.

Y384–5 I have retained the MS reading, though the lines are metrically deficient, and Owein's being well does not match his being fixed on the wheel. The repetition of *Anon* in 385 and 387 suggests confusion; Owein's well-being (384) should (chrono-)logically follow his prayer (386). The rhyme in the archetype may have been *yll/styll*, i.e. Owein suffered while he was stuck on the wheel. The rhyme *wyll/styll* suggests raising: *wyll* is Y's usual spelling of 'well'. I take *stoke styll* to mean 'remained fixed', with *stoke* from *OED* Steek *v.*[2] 6 *intr.* or 7. The strong pa. t. also influenced the weak inflexions of *OED* Stick *v.*[1], see 4. *intr.* Cf. L461–3.

Y389 MS *in wode* makes a false rhyme with *spede*. Emendation with the verb *wede* (*OED* Wede *v.*), supplies the required sense, and it would seem that Y's reading is a corruption derived from an intermediate form with the adj. *wode* 'mad', itself a corruption of the verb *wede*. Devils are not infrequently likened to 'wood' (mad) wolves as it makes a neat alliterative phrase, e.g. *Þai grennede for gladschipe euchan toward oðer as wode wulues þat fainen of hare praie. Þe Wohunge of Ure Lauerd*, ed. R. Morris, *Old English Homilies ... First Series*, EETS 34 (1868), 277 ll. 8–9. Cf. also *Vision of Tundale*, ll. 192–4: *He sawe come an vggly rowte | Of fowle fendes harde grennande, | As wylde wolfes þey come rampande.*

Y392   See Introduction, p. lxx.

Y398   *wythstod*: 'came to a halt'; cf. *substitit, procedere formidans* (L469–70). See *OED* Withstand *v.*4.

Y402   The question is ironic, addressed to the immobile Owein. *And* = if. Sm punctuates with a question mark only after *halte*.

Y403   The emendation is required to make sense, and is based on *Velis nolis illuc usque progredieris* (L471).

Y405   *bate fatys*: 'bath vats' or tubs (*MED* fat *n.*). The spelling *bate* may be simply erroneous, or represent a dialectal shift from [þ] to [t]; cf. Dobson, II. § 374. The idea for the bath vats comes from *balnearium* (L470–1). They are in fact the 'pits' of C370, Y421 (*fosse* L475, 477).

Y406–9   Not in *T*. The idea of the king of the devils being seated in the bathhouse is only found in Y. In the *Legenda Aurea* version of Nicolaus's visit to St Patrick's Purgatory the devils say that in the pit of hell *dominus noster Beelzebub habitat*: see ed. Th. Graesse (Leipzig, 1850), p. 215.

Y407–13   There are signs of corruption in the repeated ideas of 407 and 409; in the contorted sense of 410–11; in the repetition of *ageyn* in 411 and 412; and in the hypermetric line 413. The reference by name to *Regelys*, which floored the scribe (MS *relegys*), is not found at this point in *T*. Cf. Y85 and Commentary.

Y410–13   Not in *T*. The sense is: If you wish to see your home (cf. 408) or if you want to go back again to the gates of Reglis, *then* you may say that you have been chez the Devil (i.e. our master and king, of Y406). An alternative reading, taking *Or* (411) as 'before', could mean: If you will see your home [used ironically of the bathhouse] before you turn back again to the gates of Reglis, *then* you may say that you have been chez the Devil. The devils are tempting Owein to turn back and boast of his adventure, but this would also mean that Owein would fail to complete his purgation, and therefore he rejects the idea and presses on (Y414–17).

Y414–17   Not in *T*.

C372, Y423   Cf. L476. Translate Y 'All without a foot between them'. It seems that at an intermediate stage either in the translation process or the transmission the sense may have been that 'one could not put a foot between (the vats)'.

C373–4, Y424–5   C *metall/wall* suggests the form of the verb 'well' derived from OE *weallan* (*OED* Wall *v.*¹). Y *metell/wyll* uses the form derived from OE *wiellan*, Anglian *wellan* (*OED* Well *v.*¹) with Y's typical *y* for /e/.

C379–80   I have inverted the MS order of the lines in this couplet to accord with the otherwise strict progression from head to foot observed here, following L480–2.

C384, Y433   Cf. C388, Y437. In *T* the devils do not succeed in their attempt to throw Owein into the pits: see L485–7.

C390   *turnemente*: This form was frequently used in the fifteenth century for 'torment' (q.v. *OED*) by confusion with *tournament*. Cf. C574.

Y440   See Introduction, p. lxx.

Y444–5   See C361–2.

C394–5, Y445–6   Between these lines are omitted the mountain, the north wind, the stinking river, and the 'false' pit of hell. See L489–528. K rightly added dots after *faste* to indicate an omission of unspecified length. W2 objected, p. 236 v. 140; K3 replied, p. 500.

C395–6, Y446–7   Cf. C225–6, Y220–1, and see Introduction, p. lxix.

C398   Preferable to Y449; cf. L532–3. C's *false feere* picks up the idea of the lying devils who had told Owein that the pit was hell. See following note.

C399, Y450   This refers to the episode of the 'false' pit of hell omitted by both C and Y, and possibly also by the archetype of *OM2*, though if this was the case it was careless to include this reference without the event to which it refers. See Introduction, pp. lxv–lxvi.

C401   Wu2, pp. 236–7, needlessly posited *sowth* as a spelling for *suthe, sið*, 'while', 'time'. But Y452 plainly shows it simply means 'south'. The geography of the other world is vague and perhaps there is no greater reason for this turn here to the south than that it rhymes with 'mouth'. But see *traxerunt eum contra austrum* (L509), at the beginning of the episode of the 'false' pit, and cf. F970: *Si l'unt tut dreit mené vers le suth.* Cf. also the southward path taken to the river by the Virgin in *The Apocalypse of the Virgin, ANT*, p. 563.

C403–4   *hatere/water*: I take *hatere* (cited *MED* s.v. ha_ter(e n. (1)) to represent a collective singular 'clothing', rather than the plural 'clothes', < OE *hæteru*. On Y's substitution of a formula (454–5), see Introduction, p. lxx. MS *water* looks at first sight as if it has -*tt*-, but the apparent first *t* is in fact the downstroke of the partially obliterated two-compartment *a*.

C408, Y459   C is scarcely apt. Y reiterates a simile not infrequently applied to numerous devils: see Commentary A120:5–6.

C409   Cf. *fetidum* (L538).

C411–12   Not in *T*, but cf. L503–5.

C413–18, Y460–5   C413/Y460 translate L541–2, but the rest of this passage has been moved forward, for in *T* the description of the bridge (L548–54) follows the speech of the devils (C419–24/Y466–71). *OM2* does not translate their second speech (L554–6).

Y461 *glyddyr*: This is the only recorded usage of this word in *MED* s.v. glidder *adj*. 'Slippery'. It represents *lubricus* (L549). See also OE examples in *OED* s.v. Glidder *a*. The Wulfstan instance is a particularly close analogue (quoted by Dinzelbacher and Kleinschmidt, 'Seelen-brücke und Brückenbau im mittelalterlichen England', *Numen*, xxxi (1984), 242). Cf. *sledyr* in *Handlyng Synne*, ll. 5257–60.

Y463 Sharpness is not mentioned in *T*. Cf. A121:2.

C417, Y464 Interesting analogues may be found in 'The Wooing of Emer' (Cross and Slover, *Ancient Irish Tales*, p. 165); *Fís Adamnán*, § 22; *The Adventure of St. Columba's Clerics*, § 35; and the fresco at Loreto Aprutino, Italy (see Peter Dinzelbacher, 'The Way to the Other World in Medieval Literature and Art', *Folklore*, xcvii (1986), 70–87, fig. 4 and p. 76).

C418, Y465 Not in *T*.

C420, Y467 Cf. *Sub isto flammante flumine noueris infernum esse* (L540–1).

Y468 *wynd*: i.e. *wend*, with Y's characteristic *y* for /e/.

C422, Y469 Translation of *nos autem, uentos et turbines commouentes* (L543–4). For Y's alliterative phrase (cf. Y476) see *OED* Wind *sb*. 1. 5. The repetition of 'we shall thee send' and 'wind' preserved in the following line in both MSS may well be authentic and a weak attempt to render the force of *T*.

C427–36, Y474–83 This direct speech by Owein is not in *T*.

C428–30, Y475–7 There is no clear way of determining whether C428 or Y475 is the authentic reading. C follows the pattern found at Y292–3, C357–8, Y330–1; Y (though metrically deficient) more individually fits the sense of the following couplet, which in Y is corrupt. C429–30 seem to have preserved the correct reading. Y476 has lost *rayne* (C429), and substituted *weder* (cf. Y469), which should come in the following line (cf. C430). To pad Y477 the scribe has repeated *For to blow* from its final position in Y478 (cf. C431).

C430 *And all wederes lowd and styll*: In the Glossary I have interpreted *lowd* and *styll* as adjectives, but *lowd and styll* could equally be an adverbial phrase meaning 'at all times', see *MED* loude *adv*. 1. (c).

Y483 *travell*: 'travail', makes an uneasy half rhyme with *fall*. This is a good example of the sense being retained in Y (cf. *labour* C436) but the exact form and rhyme word being lost. For the expression *lese labour/travail* see *MED* lesen *v*.(4) 7a. (a).

Y484 *3ydde*: (cf. *3yd* Y310) shows Y's typical *y* for /e/, though the *-dd-* may suggest raising and shortening.

C438, Y485 Not in *T*.

Y486   For the use of the numeral *1*, cf. Y37.

C443–4, Y490–1   Both texts are metrically corrupt. The original may have read something like: *He calde to hym at euery pas, | Þat euer shall be and euer was.*

Y492–3   *broder/glader*: requires the northerly *brad(d)er*, as in C445.

Y494   MS *myde bryge*: see Introduction, pp. lxx–lxxi.

C449–50, Y496–7   C's order and rhyme are probably authentic. On Y's rhyme see Commentary Y269–70.

C452, Y499   C's *payne* is correct: see L568–70.

Y502   *was*: probably for *wax* (cf. C455) after *creuit* (L562).

C456, Y503   Y preserves the correct reading. See Introduction, p. lxx.

C458   *deuell*: an uninflected genitive plural, a reduction of *deuele* < OE *deofla*. Cf. *liber ab omni demonum uexatione* (L752). For the phrase *develes* (gen. sg.) *power* see *MED* devel *n.* 1b. (c).

Y505   *pray*: cited *MED* s.v. prei(e *n.*(2) 3. (d) 'the act of holding a spiritual captive', which also quotes the phrase *þe develys pray* from *Ludus C.* 300/829.

C459–60, Y506–7   Not in *T*, which at this point contains the first homily (L577–750).

C462, Y509   C is correct; cf. *spacio dimidii miliarii* (L758), being Owein's distance from the wall when the doors open.

Y511   *thow*: I accept this as a pa. t. 3 sg. form (< *þuhte*); it recurs at Y557.

C464, Y511   After *murum ... altum in aere a terra erectum* (L753–4). This seems to mean that the wall reaches into the upper air that *perteyneth to heuenlych kynde* (Trevisa, quoted *MED* s.v. air *n.*(1) 1.) Cf. A170:6 and Commentary.

C465–6, Y512–13   See Introduction, p. lxiv. The details of C465 are not in *T*, but are unexceptional in other-world literature: see Patch, *The Other World*, Index s.v. wall. Note that the wall here is not made of glass, but is 'bright as glass', a common comparison: see Whiting G108 and *MED* glas *n.*1. (a), which quotes *Gawain & CC* 607, *The wallys glemyd as any glasse*, and cf. Y461.

C467–8   This closely follows *Cui cum appropinquasset ... porta illa contra eum aperta est* (L757–8).

C470   Cf. L756.

C473–6, Y516–19   Both MSS are corrupt, and though at first sight C might appear the more plausible reading, Y seems to be a corruption of a text inherently superior. Cf. *tante suauitatis odor ei occurrens per eam* [i.e.

porta] exiit ut, sicut uidebatur, si totus mundus in aromata uerteretur, non uinceret huius magnitudinem suauitatis (L759–61). The archetype of *OM2* may have read something like:

> Þouȝ all þe floures and þe erbery,
> And all þe worldly spycery
> Worþed a smell, by a honderd folde,
> Yt myȝt not to þat sauour be tolde;

and an intermediate stage between that and CY could be envisaged as:

> Þouȝ all wer floures and erbery,
> And all þe world a spycery,
> Such swetnes by a honderd folde
> Myȝt not to þat sauour be tolde.

Apart from the MS reading *flowyr(e*, and the metrically superfluous second *all* in 516, Y516–17 are good lines with a secure rhyme. (*MED* cites this passage s.v. herberi *n.* (a).) The sense of the Latin *totus mundus in aromata uerteretur* has been changed, but *mundus* has passed into *wardly*. MS Y518–19 are corrupt. MS *Yt myth not* from my putative archetypal reading has been moved forward to replace *Worþed a*, which itself at an intermediate stage may have yielded *Wer ther*, as emended. MS Y has lost the concession clause required by *Thow* (516) and this I have supplied with the verb *Wer* (518). MS Y repeats *myth* in 518 and 519.

C has lost the good rhyme *erbery/spycery*, and has picked up Y's *flowyrys* and contrived a new rhyme *flourres/sauourres*. Note the corrupt repetition of *sauour* again in C475 and 476. MS C's *Such was þat* is corrupt as a plural verb is required, and I have used the *Such* in emending Y518, *swech*. C475 *erdely* is a variant of *wardly* (Y517). C476 *Myȝth not* retains the negative in the final line of this passage, as I suppose in the archetype, and forms an emphatic double negative with *Non* in 475. In MS Y 'might not' has been moved forward to 518, and I have restored it to the second line of the couplet.

The texts as printed are emended in the simplest way to yield the sense at which I take the copyists to have been aiming, bearing all these relationships in mind. One might compare the *pa* renderings: Ld468–9 read: ... *þei al þe world : swote spices were, | So muche swotnesse ne miȝte ȝiuen, : ase þat suote smul dude þere.* MS Egerton 1993, ll. 513–14 read: ... *in al þe world. such spices nere | þᵗ suc swetnesse miȝten ȝeue, . as þat breþ þere.* See C. Horstmann, *Altenglische Legenden* (Paderborn, 1875), pp. 200–1. Cf. also the close parallels for a similar idea in Malory, *Works*, ed. E. Vinaver, II (Oxford, 1967), 789, ll. 30–31: *and there was suche a savoure as all the spycery in the worlde had bene there*, and *Vision of Tundale*, ed. Mearns, ll. 1785–6: *The swete sauour, þat þer was, | All þe swetnesse of þys worlde [d]yde passe*. In the *Visiones Georgii*, p. 242, from the souls in paradise—*tanta odoris suauitas emanabat, quod, si minima pars illius in hoc mundo sentiretur, totus mundus sic saciaretur, quod eius sacietas perpetuo famem aufferret et sitim.*

C479–80, Y522–3   There is no way of determining which text preserves the original order. Y *peynys* more accurately follows *tormenta* (L762).

C483–6, Y526–9   Cf. L766–71.

Y528–9   *proseyssun/relygyoun*: I have expanded to *n* the tail on the final two minims in each word.

C487–8, Y530–1   Cf. L774–5.

C490ff, Y533ff   *T* specifies only archbishops, bishops, abbots, canons, monks, and presbyters. *OM2* shows a good deal of amplification. MS Y capitalizes the initial letters of *Mvnkys, Schanonys, Nonnys, Prystys*.

C491   I have glossed this (s.v. oþer *adj.*) as 'each one followed the next in turn', i.e. they went one by one, in single file; see *MED* bi and bi *phrase* (c), which also gives 'in sequence, in orderly fashion'. Alternatively, it could mean they went 'in pairs', 'side by side', see sense (a).

C491–2, Y534–5   Y is closer to *T, et singulorum graduum sancte ecclesie ministros* (L773–4).

C494, Y537   Not found here in *T*. Cf. C231, Y226.

Y539   MS *songys*: another example of Y's careless disregard for the rhyme; cf. Y652.

C499, Y542   For the mention of kings, cf. a later passage in *T, Alii quasi reges coronati* (L813). There is no mention of dukes, earls, and barons in *T*, but *laici* as well as *clerici* are present (L775).

Y543   MS clearly reads *Devkys*, though Miss Toulmin Smith misreads *Devlys*. The distinguishing mark is the ligature between the *k* and *y*; cf. *ly* in *castelys* in the same line and *ky* in *kynggys* in the previous line. The top tail of *k* in *Devkys* is partially obscured by the trailing tail of -*y* in *sey* in 542.

C505, Y544   Not in *T*, though as with the nuns (C496, Y539) *OM2* is given the hint by *utriusque sexus* (L771–2).

C506–8   Cf. *magna ueneratione et leticia* (L777). That Owein 'hears' the *solempnyte* is probably suggested by contrast with *cum concentu seculo inaudite armonie* (L778).

C509ff, Y546ff   C follows more closely the narrative sequence of L779–829. Y545–76 is jumbled. In order to restore the proper order in Y one should read after Y545: Y554–61 (= C509–16: Y has lost C507–8); Y564–5 (= C517–18); Y562–3 (= C519–20); Y566–75 (= C521–30); Y546–53 (= C533–40: Y has lost C531–2); Y576ff (= C545ff: Y has lost C541–4).

Y547, 550   *clothyn*: n. pl. is unrecorded in *OED*, and *MED* cloth *n.* gives only *clathen* as 'early', e.g. 3. (a) Lay. *Brut* 3187. The word is more likely to be a reduction of *clothyng* ger.; see Dobson, II. § 377 iii and n. 2.

C509, Y554 C *wellcomed* is preferable to Y *spokyn*: cf. *susceperunt* (L778).

C512, Y557 In *T* the two men are *quasi archiepiscopi* (L780–1).

C516 *fayrnesse*: is correct, not *forest* (Y561); cf. *patriam et eius amenitatis gloriam* (L782).

C517–30, Y562–75 This expands L792–5, which makes no mention of the Tree of Life or of the 'fruit of wisdom', i.e. of the Tree of the Knowledge of Good and Evil.

C531–2 Cf. L786–7 and 798–800.

C533 *cloded*: i.e. *cloþed*; see Introduction, p. xxviii.

C536, Y549 C's *wonede* is perhaps a corruption of Y's *wonte to were*, which is closer to *Forma tamen habitus qua singuli utebantur in seculo* (L810).

Y552–3 *lesse/wasse*: C67–8, Y62–3 suggest the original rhyme here was on *wes* not *lasse* (as at C539–40).

Y572 The copyist perhaps began another stint here, but certainly changed his pen.

C540, Y553 C is a poor padding line, having lost the correct reading preserved by Y. Cf. *cuiusquilibet in seculo meriti fuerit uel ordinis* (L811–12).

C541–4 Cf. L788–90, 796–7, and 812–13.

C545–6, Y576–7 Cf. L830.

C547–8, Y578–9 Y579 is closer to *qui tibi dedit tale propositum* (L834). CY alter *Benedictus sit Creator et Redemptor omnium* (L833–4).

Y582 Y has lost C551 and adapted C552 to make a triplet.

C554, Y584 C is closer to *Omnes autem ad hanc requiem per illa loca transiuimus* (L861). Y *all tho pas*: I have emended MS *all thow pas* for *pas* is inadequate as a pa. t. 2 sg. The phrase could be an error for *all tho plas* (cf. C's *þat ylke plas*) 'all those places'; *MED* place *n.* records pl. form *plase*. As emended I accept *pas* as an attested pl. of *MED* pas(e *n.*(1) 3. (a) 'a road, path or passageway', combined with (h) 'a dangerous or difficult situation; a predicament, an ordeal, death'. MS *thow* for *tho* (cf. Y427) is an easy error following *thow* 'thou' in the previous line.

C557–64, Y587–90 Loosely based on L854–61. In the first couplet here, where only 'many' and the inverted rhyme words *alyue* and *lyve* are common, Y (though awkward) seems preferable in sense and preparation for the following couplet. Y's *lyve* has to be taken as a distributive singular, with voicing of the final consonant.

C568 *do*: is causative, i.e. unless a friend pays for masses to be sung or read for the deceased. Based on L868–70.

C569   *dyuyne*: I take this to be an absolute use of the adjective, standing for 'divine service', alluded to in the previous line. See *OED* Divine *sb.*[1] †B. *sb.*[1] *Obs.*

C571-2   *alyue/swythe*: assonantal rhyme; cf. C661-2 *blyþe/alyue*.

C574-8, Y591-4   Cf. L835-9. CY have altered the order of elements within this speech, for in *T* the discussion of Adam precedes the account of penance.

C578-9, Y594-5   *T* does not mention Eve or the apple. Y *dede amyse* follows *per inobedientiam* (L843-4).

C581-92, Y597-604   Not in *T*. The length of Adam's sojourn in hell/limbo is variously calculated. The same figure as that given here, 4,604 years, is found also in e.g. the Y MS copy of *Adrian and Epotys*, ll. 316ff, *Commonplace Book*, p. 35; the C MS copy also, ed. Horstmann (1881), p. 519, ll. 320-1 (variants in MSS Arundel 140, Ashmole 61, and Cotton Titus A xxvi are all in error); BL MS Royal 17 A xvi, f. 20v (and copy in MS Harley 2332 f. 20v), above the picture of hell-mouth (not, I believe, 'that of the devil (?)', G.F. Warner and J.P. Gilson, *Catalogue of Western Manuscripts in the Old Royal and King's Collections in the British Museum*, II (London, 1921), 217 item 4); *Ludus Coventriae*, ed. K.S. Block, EETS, es 120 (1917), 97; and *John de Foxton's Liber Cosmographiae* (1408), ed. John B. Friedman (Leiden, 1988), p. 291 l. 8. (I am indebted to Professor Friedman for this reference.) According to Gen. 5:5 Adam died aged 930 years. Given Eusebius's calculation of the Creation in 5198 B.C., then Adam died in 4268 B.C. and spent 4,302 years in Limbo before Christ harrowed Hell in A.D. 34. This figure is given by Dante, *Paradiso*, XXVI.120. The figure 4,604 presupposes the Creation in 5500 B.C. An approximation to this figure, 4,600 years, is given in the York *Harrowing of Hell*, ll. 39-40 and 354: see K. Sisam ed., *Fourteenth Century Verse and Prose*, repr. (Oxford, 1955), pp. 173, 183 and note on p. 259. *Fowre thowsand wynter* was 'a traditional estimate': see the MS Sloane 2593 lyric *Adam lay ibowndyn*, ed. D. Gray, *A Selection of Religious Lyrics* (Oxford, 1975), p. 1 no. 2 l. 2 and note on p. 98. In the A MS copy of *Adam and Eve*, Adam is in hell 5,228 years, a figure calculable from Eusebius's Creation date to Christ's harrowing Hell A.D. 30: see C. Horstmann ed., *Altenglische Legenden* (Heilbronn, 1878), p. 145 ll. 551-2. See also Skeat ed., *Piers the Plowman*, II (Oxford, 1886), 259, note to C.XXI.311 for further examples.

C589   First *hem* = *all hys kynde* (587); second *hem* = Adam and Eve.

C593-4   Cf. L880-1.

Y605-6   605 is a variant of C598, and 606 is made up of the first half of C592, *abyd* from C598, and a new rhyme word. 605 *we dwellyd* pa. t. is acceptable if the bishops are thought to speak on behalf of Adam's *kynne* (603) who have been in the Earthly Paradise since the Harrowing of Hell.

C595-6, Y607-8   Cf. L882-4.

C597–600, Y609–10   Cf. L877–8.

C603–5, Y611–13   Cf. L889–92. For Y612 *bled* against C's *shedde* cf. the Y MS copy of *Adrian and Epotys*, l. 532: *The blood wos bled fore owre mysse be-leve . . ., Commonplace Book*, p. 43. There is no equivalent phrase in *T*.

C605–14, Y614–20   Cf. L892–8. There is no source in *T* for C612, Y618, though Y's jingle of *ded* with *dede* (619) suggests that C612 is the more authentic. Conversely, Y620 seems superior to C614 which pads with *hym þowȝte*. The 'rich bread' is the body of Christ, the food of the blessed: see John 6.

C616   *þowstedest*: for *þo(w)ȝtest*. Z1 suggested *þowȝtedest*, but I have retained the anomalous spelling and form. For *s* representing *ȝ* cf. *schrist* A100:2 and Commentary.

C620, Y626   Cf. L903–4. The rest of this speech in CY differs totally from that in *T*.

C627–30, Y631–4   Cf. L913–14. Y632 is preferable, for C628 *ȝode* sits uncomfortably with the following line. At this point *T* introduces the second homily (L918–1044).

C633, Y637   C's *hole* is incorrect; Y's *halle* is correct, for 'there' (C635, Y639) refers to the hall where Owein meets the fifteen messengers of God before he reaches the hole of the Purgatory entrance.

Y641–4   This is an expansion of C637–8, following L1054–5.

Y645–6   Corrupt. *hom* has been transferred from the beginning of the following line (cf. C641) in an attempt to secure a rhyme.

Y647   The second half of this couplet has been lost and *For now* has been recalled from it (cf. C642) and inserted at the beginning of the following line, Y648. C642 derives from part of the following speech, L1057.

C643, Y648   There seems to be an omission here introducing the direct speech of the (leader(?) of the) fifteen men, though the sudden introduction of direct speech is not uncommon in ME narrative verse.

Y648   *prime bell*: *MED* prim(e *n.* 1b. (b) cites this as the only usage after *a*.1225 *Wint. Ben. Rule*.

C643–50, Y648–55   Cf. L1058–61.

Y648–9   Corrupt. C643–4 preserves the correct rhyme. Y *syngth* = *syng yt*, see Introduction, p. xxxii.

Y652   MS *chanownys* shows a careless disregard for the rhyme; cf. Y539.

Y653   Corrupt (cf. C648), making the sentence anacoluthic.

C651–6, Y656–61   Not in *T*.

C657–8, Y662–3   Cf. L1062–3.

C659–62, Y664–5   Expansion of *cum gaudio magno* (L1063). The phrase 'a weeping tear' (C660) is rare in the singular: see *OED* Weeping *ppl.a.* 3. †a, citing Shakespeare, *Lucrece* 1375. Cf. Malory, *And there was many a wepyng ien, Works*, ed. Vinaver, III. 1196, l. 25.

C663–4, Y666–7   In C the second half of each line has been transposed.

C665–70, Y668–71   Not in *T*.

C671–2, Y672–3   Cf. L1066–7.

C673, Y674   The first half of the line follows *Et inde rediens* (L1067). The rest of the poem is not in *T*.

Y678–9   *held/onwylld*: another instance of Y's use of *y* for /e/. For the rhyme *eelde/unweelde* see e.g. Chaucer, *Canterbury Tales*, I (A) 3885–6, and *Romaunt of the Rose*, ll. 359–60. Noun *held* < OE *eldo*; cf. Y552 for the adj. *held*.

Y681   *leste*: syncopated < *lesteth*.

THE VISION OF
WILLIAM OF STRANTON

SR1–9, SA1–9 On names and dates at the opening of *VWS*, see Introduction, pp. lxxiv–lxxv.

SR2 *Patrik is*: For the use of the poss. pron. see *chanons is* (SR25 and Commentary), and also *man is* (SR526) and *ladi is* (SR564).

SR10 *precession*: cited second under *MED* precessioun *n.*, where quotations suggest a northerly distribution for the form (<ML *precessio*).

devougte: (<OF *devo(u)t* and L *devotus*); the non-etymological -*g*- is by analogy with words from OE -*oht*, and is presumably a back-formation indicating the loss or instability of the fricative in the latter cases, e.g. *thowt* SR571. See also *devowght* SR434, and cf. *moughthes* 'mouths' SR445 and Commentary.

SR11 *toke*: (cf. SA11 *techyd*) 'entrusted', 'gave', see *OED* Take *v.* †60. trans.

SR12 *in forehede*: cf. *Pearl* 871–2 after Apoc. 7:3, 14:1, 22:4 etc. By writing the first word of the prayer, i.e. Jesu, 'in my forehead' is probably meant simply making the sign of the Cross, the sense of 'bless' in the preceding phrase: see *MED* blessen *v.* 5. This is corroborated by the phrase *marked my forehede* (SR27 and see Commentary). *MED* quotes *VWS* for this usage s.v. marken *v.*(1) 7.(a) and (b). Cf. *T propriaque manu fronti sue signum crucis inprimens* (L196–7 and see L252–3).

SR19–22 Cf. the description of the Purgatory given after his visit in 1517 by Chiericati, who says the 'grotto turns aside for two cubits, where, they say, St Patrick used to sleep', translated in J.P. Mahaffy, 'Two Early Tours in Ireland', *Hermathena*, xl (1914), 11.

SR22 William sleeps, so we can take it that, unlike Owein, he only claims to have had a dream-vision, and not to have entered purgatory bodily. See Introduction, p. lxxx.

SR23–24, SA22 Cf. L259–60, and *VEL* p. 24, *hit semyd the dawnyng of a morninge in his springing first.*

SR25 *chanons is*: For this double gen. form see *MED* his *pron.* (1) 6.(b).

SR27, SA26–27 See above Commentary SR12 and Introduction, p. lxxvi. The verb *mark* in this sense of 'make the sign of the Cross' is far less common than the verb *blessen*; SA's evidence is prominent in *MED* s.v. marken *v.*(1) 7. The efficacy of the sign of the cross for dispelling demons is well attested, e.g. *horribilem malignorum spirituum turbam* is so put to flight in Peter the Venerable's *De Miraculis*, II.xx, *PL*, clxxxix, 930–1, and also in the Vision of Bonellus, *PL*, lxxxvii, 435A. See further Ward, *Catalogue of Romances*, III. 370, 396 nos. 421, 479, 485, and *Handlyng Synne*, ll. 8220ff. Cf. Ezek. 9 where the Tau cross is inscribed on the foreheads of the innocent whom God wishes to spare. When George Grissaphan entered the Purgatory he had a cross tied to his left hand: see *Visiones Georgii*, pp. 97–98. Cf. on the power of the name of Jesus, *VEL* p. 26: *if hit myght be possible that a dampnyd saule in hell had power ther of God euer to call this name Jhesus, j wot wil all the deuelis ther shuld neuer have power ouer hym to do hym desese or payn*, and also the *Vision of the Monk of Eynsham*, cap. xxii, ed. Salter, p. 319 ll. 21ff.

SR28, SR27 The saints' laughter here is indicative of the kindly familiarity with which St John and St Hild treat William throughout.

SR33–36, SA32–35 SA has the correct reading. SR has mistakenly changed round the descriptions of the two ways and made them both *faire*. It is the right-hand path which is the straight and narrow and *sumdele fowle in the begynnyng* because it leads through purgatory to paradise. The left-hand, sinister, way is the fair and broad path to hell. Cf. Matt. 7:13–14 and *Aeneid* VI.540–3. On the choice of left and right ways, see further the discussions by Barbara Maurmann, *Die Himmels-richtungen im Weltbild des Mittelalters* (Münstersche Mittelalter-Schriften 33, Munich, 1976), pp. 165ff, and Wolfgang Harms, *Homo Viator in Bivio: Studien zur Bildlichkeit des Weges* (Medium Aevum Philologische Studien 21, Munich, 1970).

SA38 *Sertenly*: SA frequently has a freer and more striking use of direct speech.

SR48–51 *If it myght be plesyng ... be thi will*: This sentence is anacoluthic, though comprehensible. SA49–53 preserves a better reading.

SR52–54, SA54–57 St John of Bridlington was an Augustinian Canon of St Mary's Priory. He was thus especially suitable as a guide in the Purgatory at Lough Derg held by the Augustinian Canons of Saints' Island. On St John, see Introduction, p. lxxix.

SR substitutes St Ive of Quitike for what I take to be the true reading, SA's St Hild of Whitby; see Introduction, p. lxxviii. Quitike is Quethiock in East Cornwall, four miles east of Liskeard. The village is reputedly named after Cadoc, the Welsh abbot of Llancarvon. The name is, and seemingly always has been, pronounced as a disyllable, early occurrences appearing as Quedoc (1201), Queidike (1230), Quedik (1291), Quedic (1317), Quedyk (1381), and Quedek (1399). In 1259 the church was rededicated to SS. Peter and Paul, and after rebuilding dedicated in 1288 to St Hugh of Lincoln (d. 1280). See E. Ekwall, *The Concise Oxford Dictionary of English Place-Names*, 4th ed. (Oxford, 1960), and D.A. Henwood, *St. Hugh's Church, Quethiock* (1970) [church guide].

St Ive (pronounced [i:v]) parish church lies one and a half miles north of Quethiock. The Ive of the dedication is uncertain. Krapp (*The Legend of Saint Patrick's Purgatory*, p. 58) assumes the figure is identical with Ia, better known from St Ives in west Cornwall. Other possibilities are Ivo (*Sancti Ivonis*, 1291), from Welsh Ivon 'John', eldest son of Brechan, king of Wales, and brother of St Keyne, or Ivo, the Persian bishop reputedly honoured at St Ives in Huntingdonshire. (See Ekwall, *Concise Oxford Dictionary of English Place-Names*, and P.M. Wenmouth, *The Parish Church of St. Ive* (1968) [church guide].) From 1259 to 1314 the church was in the patronage of the Grand Master of the Templars, and from 1314 to 1558 of the Prior of the Hospital of St John of Jerusalem in England, under the Augustinian rule. Another nearby Augustinian connection is the priory of St Stephen's, Launceston, where in 1427 the prior John Honyland erected a chantry at the altar of St Margaret and St John of Bridlington; see R. Peter and Otho B. Peter, *The Histories of Launceston and Dunheved* (Plymouth, 1885), p. 16.

SR56   MS cancellation of *to* after *dayneth* suggests the copyist's confusion about the sense of the verb. See *MED* deinen *v.* 2 from *disdeinen*. Instead of the positive 'deign' we have the double negative 'not disdain'.

SR59   *ligh*: -*gh* is here a spelling of -*th*, for *lith* < *liggeth* 'lieth'. For other uses of this spelling in SR see Commentary SR445. MS has a curved flourish above, which Kr expands to *ligheth*.

SA58–60   Whereas in SR55 William invokes St John, in SA he invokes God for having sent St John. Note MS deletion *be god* after *lovyde*. The object of pa. t. sg. *sende*, i.e. St John, is left unexpressed, the verb being used absolutely.

SA59   *sympyll*: may well be the original reading, emphasising St John's condescension, and SR57 *synful* a commoner substitute. Cf. use of 'simple' at SR120, SA122.

SR58–60, SA61–63   It would certainly have *desesyd* William to visit St Ive *often* in Cornwall. It is more likely that William should often have made the pilgrimage from Stranton to Whitby and Bridlington, a round trip of some 125 miles.

SA69   *know*: The present tense (cf. SA658 and knew SA87) is significant. The devils appeared in the form of William's friends who were still living when he wrote his vision. This personal detail is omitted from SR. See SR38–41, SA39–41.

SA69–70   *as by schappe pycturede*: This use of *pycturede*, to mean represented or figured forth, antedates *OED* first reference *c*.1489 in Caxton; *MED* does not record the word at all.

SR67, SA71   SR drops the personal address to *Wyllyam* found in SA. This happens frequently and is perhaps a result of greater rewriting than is found in SA.

SR70, SA75   SA includes *fleschely*, cf. SA81, which is perhaps original and makes a stronger point than SR.

SA71   Emendation matches SA76–77.

SR77–81   A seemingly corrupt and certainly otiose repetition not found in SA. See Introduction, p. xxxvi.

SR84–85   *And þan appered to me evel spirites*: This is a corruption of SA85–86 *in likenes of evyll sprettys*. SR introduces the new devils twice, SR85 and 87–88.

SR89–91, SA91–93   This description of the devils accords with the common manner in which they are depicted in late-fourteenth- and fifteenth-century iconography. The plurality of heads, horns, and faces, especially on the limb joints, is a popular form of demonic deformity. Cf. Commentary A54:2.

SR96, SA97–98   The *noyse and crye* of the devils at this point probably derives from the *tumultus* in L309. Compare this with *VEL* pp. 24–25, *crying, roring, and ȝelling as all the world ther shuld have fallid . . .*

SA102–3   *mark . . . hevene*: This passage has been lost in SA because the copyist's eye must have jumped from *hevyn* in l. 102 to the repeat in l. 103.

SA122   *ouersympul*: sole usage in *MED* s.v. oversimple.

SR123, SA125   I suspect the true reading is *Holy fader*.

SA140   Emended after SR because of scribal error through eye-skip with repeated *kynne*.

SR137ff, SA141ff   On those who hinder matrimony cf. *Jacob's Well*, EETS, 115 (1900), 15 ll. 9ff.

SR141–50, SA144–54   St John's explanation sounds rather confused, especially in SA.
i)   William had neither shrift nor penance for his sin.
ii)   But if he had thought of it, he would have done both.
iii) Therefore, by St Patrick's prayer and the grace of Christ, William is permitted to shrive himself and do penance when he returns to the prior of the Purgatory.
iv)   But if he had had shrift, but not done the penance, then he would have had to pay his penance in purgatory there and then before returning to the world.

SA158   MS reads *fyr*, but this might be an error for *syr*.

SR159–60, SA163–4   For the phrase to 'turn the hand up and down/about', meaning 'a very short time' (cf. 'in the twinkling of an eye'), see *MED* hond(e *n*. 1b. (h). Cf. *al þe lif of man, þouȝ he myȝt lyue a þousand ȝer, nys but a turnyng of a mannes hond as to þat oþer lif, þat euer lasteþ* *wiþ-outen ende* ..., *The Book of Vices and Virtues*, EETS, 217 (1942), 68 ll. 32ff.

SR163–5, SA167–9   As might be expected, it is a commonplace of vision literature that the visionary meets some of his acquaintances in the pains of hell or purgatory: cf. Y369, L441–2 and Commentary, and *Visiones Georgii*, pp. 187–8.

SR166, SA170   *colors/colers*: See *MED* coler *n.* 2, chains worn about the neck as a ornament.

SR166ff, SA170ff   There follows a detailed catalogue of extravagant attire. For the tradition of attacks on such *false plesynge of vayneglory of pride and aray* (SA201), see Owst, *LPME*, pp. 390ff, 409ff. On the *jaggis, daggis* and bells see e.g., Herbert Norris, *Costume and Fashion, Volume Two, Senlac to Bosworth, 1066–1485* (London, 1940), p. 362, fig. 500 and see Index. In the fifteenth-century BL MS Additional 37,049 f. 47v a miniature illustrating pride depicts a youth in a tall hat, blue puffed jacket, red breeches, long *pyked* shoes, with a sword, seized by two devils. Cf. *VEL* pp. 25, 29.

SR168, SA172   *harneist/hernessede hornes*: see *MED* harneisen *v.* (b) 'to adorn'.
   iagges/jaggys: SR here and at 177 and 388 form the second reference in *MED* s.v. jagge *n.* (a), after *Promptorium parvulorum*.

SR169, SA174   *gyngeles/gyngyles*: antedates *OED* Jingle *sb.* 2., first reference 1615. No recorded usage in *MED* as *n.*

SR170   *pokes on hire sleves*: The pouch shape of the full hanging cloth on fashionable sleeves gave the whole sleeve the name *poke*, q.v. *MED n.* (b), which cites SR182.

SA184–5   There is a complex (confused?) image here of the jags first turning into adders and toads etc., which suck, bite, and gnaw the souls' bodies and squeeze and drain more fiends out of the ornamental bells, like a juice and its residue. *streynynge* could be a duplet for *dreynynge*, i.e. *OED* Strain *v.*[1] 14., but I take it as sense 9, 'to extract by pressure', 'to squeeze out' (first reference 1483). Draining, in the sense of straining a liquid is a fairly rare word, and this instance has previously gone unrecorded. *MED* dreinen *v.* (a) offers only one instance apart from Trevisa to modify *OED*'s statement s.v. Drain *v.*: 'It is remarkable that, after the OE period, no example of this word is known to occur for 500 years, till the 16th c.' For the idea of the clothes becoming snakes cf. *Pricke of Conscience*, ll. 6943ff.

SR182, SA187–8   Cf. *Gesta Romanorum*, EETS, ES, 33 (1879), 384: *and my brennynge skynne drawene of, and folowyng me, is for my large trayne of clothe, that I was wonte to drawe aftire me* ...

SR192   *disworship*: An early occurrence of a word not recorded before the fifteenth century: see *MED* disworshipen *v*. first reference Pecock, *c*.1443.

SA205   *redy tyll hus*: The sense is 'immediately available (to help)' *OED* Ready *a*. 9. There is no need to suppose the loss of a verb like 'to help/assist' after *tyll*.

SR202ff, SA216ff   On souls being dismembered and reforged with molten metal, cf. *Vision of Tundale*, ll. 1045ff. On a similar theme see Mircea Eliade, *The Forge and the Crucible*, trans. Stephen Corrin (London, 1962), pp. 84 and 105–7, and refs. on devils as smiths. On attacks on 'dismembering' Christ by swearing, see Owst, *LPME*, pp. 414ff, and see M.D. Anderson, *History and Imagery in British Churches* (Edinburgh, 1971), p. 143 plate 55 for the wall painting at Broughton, Buckinghamshire. The complaint of the arms and other members against the heart and tongue resembles the exemplum of the insurrection of the members against the stomach: see J.B. Pitra, *Analecta Novissima Spicilegii Solesmensis*, II (1888), 448–9.

SA219, 225, 228   *bowlynge*: 'boiling'; this spelling is unrecorded in *MED* and *OED*. It must derive from OF *boulir*.

SR213   *drow*: 'drew' (cf. SA227 *threw*). At SR464 *draw* pp. (<*drawen*) picks up the verb 'throw' from *ythrow* SR446, which suggests possible confusion between these two verbs.

   on þat: 'and those'; I accept *on* as representing 'and' with reduced stress (cf. Commentary SR576); for *þat* + pl. see Commentary SR365.

SA244   *fowynge*: I have found no other use of this form in the sense required here, as glossed: sewage, that which is cleaned out of privies. This noun is an adaptation of the verbal noun, *fowyng*, the act of clearing/cleansing (something of filth). *Promptorium parvulorum*, p. 171, gives *ffowyng*: Mundacio; see *OED* Fow *v*. and Fay, feigh *v*.[2] <ON *fǽgja*, 'to cleanse' and *MED* feien *v*. (2) and feiing(e ger. (2). I take this extension of meaning to be analogous to the formation from 'leave' of 'leaving' (q.v. *OED, vbl. sb.* 2) meaning 'residue', which goes back to the 14th century.

   SR230 reading *fen* is recorded only from the late 14th/15th century: see *MED* fen *n*. (2).

SR235   *wullepak*: *OED* Wool-pack quotes this as the only reference between 1297 and 1600.

SR238ff, SA251ff   On the violation of Holy Days and going to the tavern, see Owst, *LPME*, pp. 435ff and 425ff, and on gluttony in particular, pp. 442ff.

SA254ff   On 'janglers', those who chatter in church and prevent others from praying, see Owst, *PME*, pp. 172–8 and Index s.v. Chattering.

SR250 MS *brondes*: SA260 appears a more likely reading, as it would be difficult to bind anything with fire brands, or bonds of fire, even in purgatory!

SR251 *stowpeng*: this transitive use in the sense of 'lowering' antedates *OED* Stoop *v.*¹ II.

SR251ff, SA261ff Excretory attacks by demons, though absent from the other major medieval visions, are known from at least the 12th century; e.g. the *Vision of Fulbert*, see G.-J. Witkowski, *L'art profane à l'église*, II (Paris, 1908), 35.

SR255–6, SA266–7 SR is probably correct, SA's *God* being perhaps a misreading caused by the following *God* at the end of the sentence.

SR271 *þei*: i.e. the thieves and robbers; *hem*: i.e. the goods.

SA275–84 The text is corrupt in places here. I have supplied passages from SR where SA is clearly deficient. SR seems to distinguish correctly between the robbers, who are taken out of one pain *and cast to other* (SR265, omitted by SA), and the robbed, who are taken out and set by, i.e. put on one side. SA simply has both groups taken out of their pains and set next to each other, thereby losing the contrast found in SR between the continued punishment of the thieves and the relief accorded to their victims. SR's use of *set(t) by* (266, 268) antedates *OED* Set *v.* 142 †a.; *MED* does not record the collocation under setten *v.* 2d.

SR274ff, SA285ff SA preserves a clearer explanation of the evil executors. SR276 *for* means 'before'. SR286 MS marginal note *Quest-mongers* are those who made a profit out of initiating unjust actions or giving false witness; see *MED* quest(e *n.* 1b. (b). Executors, their dilatory dealings and false appropriations are another constant object of criticism in contemporary literature; see Owst, *LPME* references in Index; *PME*, p. 343; *Handlyng Synne*, ll. 6243ff; and SEL, EETS, 87 (1887), 430–1.

SR275 *þe dethis will*: the will (as in will and testament) of the deceased; cf. *þe dedes goodes* in the following line. The scribe's cancellation of *ded* before *dethis* suggests that the form with *-th-* was in his exemplar.

SR283–5 I have emended taking *oþer* as pron. pl., but alternatively the MS reading could be retained with *oþerwhere* meaning 'elsewhere'.

SA299 *landys and feese*: the sense of *feese* here is most likely money taken as bribes, *MED* fe *n.*(1) 3.(a). Under sense 2 no inflected plurals are recorded for this noun (< OE *feoh*) in the phrase *land and fe* 'landed and movable property'. In effect, however, both senses coalesce in this instance. Senses under fe *n.*(2) seem less likely.

SR291 *smolder*: first reference in *MED*.

SA310 *tomangylde*: not recorded in *OED*. *MED* first instance of manglen *v.* is *c.*1450 (?*a.*1400) *Destruction of Troy*, l. 5704.

SR309ff Cf. the souls of the murdered watching the torment of their murderers in the *Apocalypse of Peter*: *And the souls of them that were murdered stood and looked upon the torment of those murderers and said: O God, righteous is thy judgement. ANT*, p. 509 section 25.

SR317, SA320 Sulphur burns with a blue flame.

SR319, SA322 Cf. L431.

SR322ff, SA323ff The threefold division of SR is lost in MS SA, making two groups tormented in the eyes. SA has been restored by reference to SR.

SA329–34 It is impossible to say whether the return here to the subject of *gay* and *stowte aray* is part of the original text lost by SR or an expansion by SA. SR certainly adheres more closely to the immediate subject of lechery.

SR330–45, SA336–48 The basis of this section is the popular didactic literature founded on Prov. 13:24, *Qui parcit virgae odit filium suum; Qui autem diligit illum instanter erudit.* See also *Dialogues*, IV, 19, and e.g. *Fís Adamnán*, p. 42 § 28; *Handlyng Synne*, ll. 4849ff; *Pricke of Conscience*, ll. 5544ff; and Owst, *LPME*, pp. 460ff. Souls are accused by their children in the Vision of Thespesius in Plutarch, *De sera numinis vindicta*, Loeb ed., *Moralia*, VII, 297.

SR350 *noselyng*: first reference in *MED*.

SR352 *backes*, **SA356** *wombys*: SR doubtless preserves the correct reading as it is evidently suitable that backbiters should be bitten on their backs not on their stomachs. This is facilitated by SR's having the souls lying face downward (SR350); SA has them flat on their backs (*wyde oppyn* SA353), hence their stomachs are easy prey.

SR353 *arders*: a spelling not recorded in *MED*; the closest to this form with *r* before *d* is *erdur*, marked as (?error): see naddre *n.*

Cats and beetles are novel additions to the usual hellish menagerie. Cats appear in the Irish *Tidings of Doomsday*, ed. W. Stokes, *RC*, iv (1879–80), 253. This instance of *bitellis* may antedate *MED* first reference s.v. bitil *n.* to *Promptorium parvulorum* (1440). Before this date *OED* records only OE uses up to 1050.

SA357 *dyspetyusly*: this spelling, with /i/ after *t*, is probably antedated only by *Destruction of Troy*, l. 13,173, quoted in *MED* despitousli *adv.* 2.(a). A variant spelling with *u* after *t* occurs in the same poem and the York and Chester plays.

SR356 *stompyng and tredyng on here backis*: cited as third reference in *MED* stampen *v.* after Wyclif Bible and the nicely comparable *Pricke of Conscience*: *Þe devels salle ay opon þam gang, | And ay on þam stamp with þair feth omang (8590–1). OED* Tread *v.*B. 4 *intr.*, records nothing between Chaucer's *Hous of Fame*, 2153 and Caxton *c.*1489. Under sense 5. trans. †a., 'to step on so as to crush, trample', there is nothing from the fifteenth century. Cf. the quotation from Hampole, Psalter 24:1 *Wha sa ligges þare in, þe deuel tredis him.*

SR358–60, SA359–63   On backbiters, see Owst *LPME*, pp. 450ff.

SA361   *speykyne*: On the reduction of final [iŋ] to [in] see Dobson, II. § 377 n. 2.

SA365   *þis*: dem. adj. pl., see *OED* These *dem. pron.* and *adj. (plural).* A.γ.

þat: dem. adj. used with a plural noun, see *OED* That *dem. pron., adj.,* and *adv.* II.1.c. Cf. the instance at SR213, and also A80:5, 81:4.

SR366ff, SA368ff   The towers are related to the idea of the devil's castle: cf. A108:3. See illustrations e.g. in *Scriptorium*, xxiii (1969), plates 104, 105, and Glynne Wickham, *The Medieval Theatre* (London, 1974), plate 25, from the Hours of Catherine of Cleves. See also Owen, *Vision of Hell*, Index s.v. architecture of Hell. For the castle and towers as used in stage settings, see M.D. Anderson, *Drama and Imagery in English Medieval Churches* (Cambridge, 1963), pp. 127–9, and see Index s.v. Hell-Mouth, and also D.C. Stuart, 'The Stage Setting of Hell and the Iconography of the Middle Ages', *RR*, iv (1913), 330–42.

The alternation of fire and ice is one of the most widespread hell/purgatory pains, e.g. Vision of Drihthelm, *Poema Morale* (Trinity MS) ll. 236–8. It derives support from Job 24:19. See also J. Vendryes, 'L'enfer glacé', *RC*, xlvi (1929), 134–42.

SA378   *vemunsume*: MS *vemūsūe*. Of the five minims preceding *s* the first three are clearly *m*; the last two look like *n*, but I have interpreted them as *u* as these are frequently indistinguishable in this hand. *OED* records *venomsome* 1660 and the form *vemon* in dialect. *EDD* records *vemonsome* in north Yorkshire, interestingly from the neighbourhood of Whitby. This localized form may well be from the original text of William of Stranton (who claims to have visited Whitby frequently). The MS abbreviation here may indicate the SA copyist's uncertainty about the word.

SA392   *fyre-brongdys*: Dobson quotes a comparable 15th-century East Midland spelling, *mankyngde*: see II. § 377.

SR388–91, SA394–6   Cf. SR177–80, SA182–4 on this suitable transformation of the jags and dags into snakes etc.

SA400   *tobownede*: not recorded in *OED*. It clearly means the same as SA393 *toswollyn*, and is formed by the addition of the intensive prefix *to-* to a variant of *bolned*, pp. of *bulnen* or *bolnen v.*, q.v. *MED*. See Dobson, II. § 425, for the vocalisation and loss of [l] in the fifteenth century after ME *u* or *ou*. *MED* 1.(b) quotes pa. t. pl. *bownyd* from *Alphabet of Tales, c.*1450.

SR393, SA400–1   SR must be the correct reading, for it is appropriate that those who *shuld haue lyved in continence and abstinded of here bodi*

(SR406–7) and did not, should swell up like a *pipis or tonnes*, both types of large wine cask. SA's *towrys* must be a misreading for *tonnys* by confusion of the four minims of *-nn-*.

SR394, SA401 *toes/tayllys*: SA's *tayllys* is probably the true reading, for the reason given in the previous note, and SR's *toes* an easy error whose only appropriateness is the complement to *fingers*.

SA410 *thyes pepul*: the copyist's superscript addition of *pepul* along with the *-e* of *thyes* shows that *pepul*, though sg. in form, was construed by him as a collective noun, and 'this' therefore changed to 'these', for which *thyes* is SA's usual spelling.

SR407 *abstinded*: *MED* absteinen *v.* does not record this pp. form, though it gives *abstinen* as an alternative form of the infinitive, e.g. Capgrave under 1.(b), and cf. pa. t. 3 sg. *abstined* under 4.(a). The false double weak ending may have been formed by spurious analogy with *blinded* or *blended*.

SA415 *contemplacyon*: is probably the original reading, although there is no way of proving this; cf. SR406–7 *continence*, which loses the inclusiveness of SA's mind/body duality, but also reinforces the notion of abstinence.

SR408 *wormen*: this weak pl. is unrecorded in *OED* except in the gen. *wurmene mete* from *Hali Meidenhad* and the *Aȝenbite*, s.v. Worm *sb.* 6. c. This is the only occurrence in SR which usually uses *wormes*. SR uses the weak pl. *-n* in *sustern* (666) and *shone* (678).

SR416, SA424 SA seems to preserve the correct reading, SR having lost the appropriately punished 'hearts' because of the repeated 'into their'.

SR421, SA429 *xvj/xj*: As with the date of William's visit to St Patrick's Purgatory (SR3–4, SA4, and see Introduction, p. lxxv), there is no way of knowing which, if indeed either, of these figures is correct.

SA441–3 *Goddys/dewlys knyghtys*: See *MED* knight *n.* 2.(c) for the well-established expression *Goddys knyghtys*; the analogous *dewlys knyghtys* is not recorded elsewhere, but conforms to the pattern of *develes child/chapelein* etc., see *MED* devel *n.* 1b.(a) and (b). SA444 further develops the imagery by apparently coining the phrase *Goddys traytores*.

SR435 *behouefull*: *MED* bihoveful *adj.* (a) 'helpful, serviceable', not recorded before 1425.

SR440 *open aboue*: I have emended according to SA for the important point is not that the house is elevated, but that, like the ill-kept churches, the roofs of which have fallen into decay (cf. SR471–6), this house is open to the destructive elements.

SR443, SA455 *pressis/pressys*: SR cited in *MED* s.v. presse *n.* 7. SA *pylyde*: unrecorded in *MED*, which lists SR's *ipiled* as the sole instance s.v. pilen *v.*(3) (b).

SR444, SA457 'Moths' and 'worms' are frequently found in combination: see *MED* mothe *n.* 1.(a) (cites SR460–1) and *OED* Worm *sb.* 5.

SR445 *moughthes*: cited in *MED* s.v. mouth *n.* 1a.(a). -*gh*- here duplicates the -*th*-; cf. *youghe* 'youth' SR360, *ligh* for *lith* 'lieth' SR59, and *strenghe* 'strength' SR486, the equivalent of *strenthe*.

SR460–79 Cf. Jas. 5:1–2. On this whole section on the abuses of the rich clergy at the expense of the poor people cf. Owst, *LPME*, pp. 298ff.

SR483ff, SA472ff In *VWS* the perilous other-world bridge is modified to become the personal purgatory of a vainglorious bishop and his household. For the punishment of a priest on a bridge, cf. Vision of Sunniulf; *Dialogues*, IV, 37, 12, ll. 91–94; *Vision of Tundale*, ll. 473–4.

It is a commonplace of vision literature and accounts of purgatory that objects of good deeds assist the soul in purgatory: cf. William's own cord, SR589–92, SA581–3. The *makynge ... of brigges and causyes and amendement of perilous weyes in savyng of mennes lyves and eke of bestes* (quoted by Owst, *LPME*, p. 556 n. 3) was a recognized form of public charity; cf. *Piers the Plowman*, B.VII.27–28. For the idea that a bridge built in this life for the common good, not for vainglory, assists the soul's passage in the other world, cf. *Wulfstan: Sammlung der ihm zugeschriebenen Homilien*, ed. A. Napier (Berlin, 1883), Homily XLVI, p. 239 ll. 1–15; the stone on which Judas sits: *Petram in qua sedeo, illam misi in fossam in publica uia sub pedes transeuncium ...*, in *Navigatio Sancti Brendani*, ed. Selmer, p. 68 ll. 46–47; *Godeschalcus*, in *Godeschalcus and Visio Godeschalci*, ed. E. Assmann, p. 64 ll. 16–21; and for this whole passage see the discussions by Dinzelbacher, *Die Jenseitsbrücke im Mittelalter*, pp. 68ff, 153ff, 182–3, and 191, and Dinzelbacher and Kleinschmidt, 'Seelenbrücke und Brückenbau', esp. pp. 244–5, 268.

SR487, SA476 *pilers of þe brigge*: *OED* does not record this sense of 'pillar' as the pier of a bridge; *MED* piler(e *n.* 1.(j) records only two instances, *c.*1390 and 1421.

SR489–90, SA478–9 The angel's act betokens the preservation of the sanctity of the office of bishop irrespective of the personal sins of the holder.

SR492 *plunchyng*: cited *OED* Plunge *v.* sense 1. *trans.* β as the first occurrence of the spelling with -*ch*-; *OED* dates SR *c.*1440. *MED* plungen *v.* 1.(a) also gives an instance from Lydgate *c.*1435. For other and earlier instances see senses 2. fig. β and 5. intr. β.

SA486 *gave*: pp., recorded *OED* s.v. Give *v.* A.8.γ. from the 16th century.

SA491–7 A complicated and probably corrupt passage, especially in the starkly paratactic parenthesis (ll. 493–4); something may have gone astray at the column change. The hindering of marriage contracts picks up William's concern on pp. 84–85. *lettyde* (l. 493) I take as a pa. t. sg. following *toke* (l. 489) and *sufferd* (l. 491): translate '[for gold and silver the bishop] suffered men and women to continue in their sin, unpunished in lechery, and (he) hindered other contracts of matrimony—(this was) an evil deed, (which brought) money (i.e. bribes) for them' (i.e. the bishop and his officers). The *partys* (l. 494) are those contracted to marriages which the bishop prevented. These people were therefore obliged to trail about from court to court to seek permission, until they had exhausted their funds and had *to leve þer trew maters*, i.e. abandon their marriage plans.

I have added *chapetor to* (l. 495) and made MS *consistorise* singular as this would seem to be necessary for the balance of the passage. The copyist having written and cancelled *chapyeo* probably felt he had completed the necessary repeat of *chapetor*.

For attacks on the evils of the consistory courts, and on those who paid bishops to maintain themselves in lechery, and on false marriages, divorces, and other injurious arrangements fixed at ecclesiastical courts, see Owst, *LPME*, pp. 222–3, 251–5, 280–2, and on the lechery of the clergy see pp. 267ff.

SR508 *worldly lucor*: cited in *MED* s.v. lucre *n.*(b); an early and infrequent use in the sense 'illicit gain'.

SR513ff, SA506ff At this point in *T* occurs the first homily, and here St John's discussion of purgatory fulfils a similar function. Cf. especially L693ff.

SR521ff, SA516ff *Placebo and Dirige*: *Placebo domino in regione viventium*, Ps. 114:9 (Vulgate), Vespers antiphon in the Office of the Dead. *Dirige, Dominus meus, in conspectu tuo uitam meam*, Ps. 5:8, first nocturn at Matins in the Office of the Dead. Commendations, the recital of psalms with collects and versicles or litany to commend the soul of the deceased (*commendatio animae*) to God, developed from Luke 23:46 (Ps. 30:5). The seven Penitential Psalms are (Vulgate) 6, 31, 37, 50, 101, 129, 142. In *Spiritus Guydonis* the seven psalms with the litany are said against the seven deadly sins, plus the Pater, Ave, and Crede; ed. Horstmann, *Yorkshire Writers*, II. 314–15. The fifteen Psalms are those of the Gradual, (Vulgate) 119–33. See E.T. Donaldson, *Piers Plowman: The C-Text and its Poet* (Yale, 1949), pp. 208–10.

SR526–34, SA520–8 For the image of the water of alms on the fire of sins cf. Ecclus. 3:33 *Ignem ardentem extinguit aqua, et eleemosyna resistit peccatis.*

SR535–6, SA529 The disappearance of the guide leaving the soul to face the assaults of the demons alone is a common feature of many visions; see e.g. Vision of Drihthelm, *Visio Tnugdali*, p. 33 l. 3, and the Vision of the boy William in Vincent of Beauvais, *Speculum Historiale*, Lib. XXVII cap. lxxxiv. Cf. also the Vision of Thespesius, *Moralia*, VII, 293.

SA531–3 William seems here to be referring to the second bridge which features in the *Vision of Tundale*, ed. Mearns, ll. 609–10, *Wyth scharpe* *pyles of iren & stele | Hyt was þykkesette, & greuows to fele*. (This follows, ultimately, *Visio Tnugdali, clavis ferreis acutissimis* (p. 19 l. 20). See the illustration by Simon Marmion in Thomas Kren and Roger S. Wieck, *The Visions of Tondal from the Library of Margaret of York* (Malibu, California, 1990), p. 46.) For *pyles* three MSS read *pykes*, as does Cotton Caligula A ii at l. 627: *The pykes prykkede hys fete full sore*. Cf. the saw-like punishment in the Chaldon wall-painting (see reference in Commentary A101:4–102:1); the punishment of *accidia* (which must be based on *Visio Tnugdali*) in the Todi fresco (see Mac Tréinfhir (1986), p. 152 Fig. 4); and see also the bridge in the *Visio Thvrkilli*, p. 12 ll. 22–25: *deinde restabat pons magnus aculeis et sudibus per totum affixus, quem pertransire quemlibet oportebat, antequam ad montem gaudii perveniret*. Parallels are also to be found in *Visio Godeschalci* and *Draumkvæde*: see Dag Strömbäck, 'Om Draumkvædet och dess källor', *Arv* 2 (1946), 35–70, and Peter Dinzelbacher, 'Zur Entstehung von Draumkvæde', *Skandinavistik*, x (1980), 89–96, and see further, Dinzelbacher, *Die Jenseitsbrücke*, pp. 46–48, and Dinzelbacher and Kleinschmidt, 'Seelenbrücke und Brückenbau', pp. 267–8.

SR555–6, SA548   There is a close coincidental parallel to William's searching for the bridge over the river, in the Visions of Ailsi, ed. Easting and Sharpe, ll. 278–95.

SR565, SA558   The ladder is a variant of the bridge for crossing the river or ascending into heaven. Its use is widespread in vision literature from Jacob's ladder (Gen. 28:12) and the *Vision of St. Perpetua*, ed. J. Armitage Robinson, *Texts and Studies*, I.2. (1891), 66–68. For discussions see H.R. Patch, 'Anglo Saxon Riddle 56', *MLN*, xxv (1920), 181–2; F. Cumont, *After Life in Roman Paganism* (Yale, 1922), p. 154; Arthur Bernard Cook, *Zeus: A Study in Ancient Religion*, 3 vols., II.1 (Cambridge, 1925), 114–40. Cf. *VEL* p. 27, and see also Dinzelbacher, *Die Jenseitsbrücke im Mittelalter*, p. 153 and Index, p. 255 s.v. Leiter.

SR574–9, SA568–71   John Hennig misconstrues the rescue of William here as evidence to parallel the rescue from the pit of the Purgatory of the canon of Eymstadt (1494) and the hero of the 1509 Volksbuch *Fortunatus*: see his 'Fortunatus in Ireland', *Ulster Journal of Archaeology*, 3rd series, xiii (1950), 93–104 (p. 104 n. 36).

SR576   *an*: unstressed form of *and* q.v. Glossary, and cf. *on* SR213 and *and* SR685 where *-d* has been added as a correction.

SR580, SA572   *thowsandfold/thowsande more folde*: I have emended SR by transferring SA's *fold*; cf. SA564. SA's reading, an attempt to exceed the already exaggerated (SA564–5), stands as an adaptation of the use of *folde* as noun, derived from a false analysis of *mani-fold*; see *MED* folde *n.* (2). For this noise, cf. when Owein is on the bridge in L568–70.

SR589–92, SA581–3   There are two questions here: (1) was the merchant robbed by thieves (SA) who were Jews (SR), and (2) who was asking alms, the merchant or William?

(1) I have retained the SR reading: 'robbed with (by) Jews', as this makes its own sense (accepted as such by Kr, p. 38 and hence Félice, p. 67 n. 1). If SR is correct it has the advantage of being the *lectio difficilior*, and it is easy to see that *robbid with iwes* could, via *robbid with thiwes*, become SA's *robbyde of thevys*. A difficulty in SR is MS *wiht*, not because of the form in *-ht*, for *wiht* is a well attested spelling, nor for the construction of the passive and instrumental 'with' (see *OED* With 40), but because this is the only occasion in SR where the word is spelt *wiht*. The usual form (79 instances) is the abbreviation w^t, which I have expanded to *with* on the basis of the 17 instances spelt thus; *wyth* occurs once only at SR443. The odd spelling suggests that *wiht iwes* might result from an inversion of the process just outlined, stemming, that is, from an exemplar reading 'robbid with thiwes', where the palindromic first eight letters of 'with thiwes' could readily cause confusion. In this case, SA's *of thevys* is closer to the original reading.

(2) Was the merchant (a) robbed when he came where William was asking alms, i.e. when the merchant was about to give alms to William (SR, without commas after *iwes* and *were*), or (b) (with comma after *iwes* only), robbed, and then came where William was asking alms, or (c) (with comma after *were* only) robbed when he came to ask alms of William, or (d) (with commas after *iwes* and *were*), robbed, and then came asking alms of William? (a) and (b) seem unlikely because there is nothing else specific to indicate that William was a mendicant or impoverished. (c) also seems unlikely if only because a merchant impecunious enough to be begging alms would be a poor catch for thieves. (d) appears the most sensible reading and best matches SA. I have punctuated accordingly.

SA appears to retain the better readings. *gud* would mean 'money' (*MED* god *n.* 2. 12(c)), but the word can also mean 'alms' (*MED* 10 (c)), and this ambiguity may also have led to the reading in SR.

SA586   This tree is the Tree of Life.

SR597-8, SA587-8   For this comparison, cf. Commentary C473-6, Y516-19. SA 587 *spysse*: MS has a cross through the two final long s's. *MED* spicer *n.* cites this as *spyssers*, following Kr.

SA589-90   *many swete noyse*: see *MED* mani *adj. & n.* 2a.(a) for many preceding a sg. noun without the definite article.

SR604-5, SA595-6   This fair company parallels the procession in L767.

SR611-12   William, or a (Lollardly?) scribal adaptor, is careful to emphasise that reverence is paid not to the image, but to the saint depicted; for the debate on images, see Owst, *LPME*, pp. 136-48, and Anne Hudson ed., *Selections from English Wycliffite Writings* (Cambridge, 1978), pp. 179-81.

SR615   *revershid*: 'wearing ecclesiastical garments', is a composite of *reversed* (*OED* Reverse *v.²*) and *reveshed* (*OED* Revesh, Revess), itself a back-formation from *revest* (q.v. *OED* *v.¹*), the final *-t* having been misunderstood as a participial ending. This instance is the only one with

-sh- cited by *MED* s.v. reversen *v.*(2) (b). The meaning is well illustrated in the *Vision of Tundale*, ed. Mearns, ll. 1679–80: *All reuesched, as þey sholde synge messe, | In ryche cloþes of holynesse.* (For *reuesched* the Royal MS, ed. Wagner, reads *revested*, l. 1649.)

The bishop here in *VWS* serves the same function as the two *quasi archiepiscopi* in L780–1.

SR626–8 The placing of excessive trust in God's mercy deeming 'Howsoever great thy sins be, greater is His mercy', is, according to Bromyard, a 'deception of the devil's' that 'deceives many, nay rather well-nigh the whole world'; translated Owst, *PME*, p. 335 and see n. 3. It is the mistake made by the prioress whose judgement William witnesses, SR686–8, SA658–9.

SR652ff, SA624ff Cf. L903ff.

SR664, SA635 SR's reading is probably correct, as it is in her role of prioress rather than merely as an individual that she is being judged.

SA638 *agayn ... gylte*: 'he had done very little wrong towards her'. This is an awkward construction, presumably intended ironically, as if to say that however strict the examination, the bishop was entirely justified in his accusations against her behaviour. This reading understands *gylte* as pp.; see *MED* gilten *v.*(1) (a).

SR676 *costluer*: unrecorded comparative of *costloue*, see *MED* cost-leue *adj. OED* does not record a comparative of *Costly* before 1577. This passage is quoted in *MED* s.v. overgilden *v.* (c).

SR677 *siluers*: I have retained the MS reading of the inflected adj. even though this is not of French origin.

SR679–80, SA651–2 Cf. *A Revelation of Purgatory*, ll. 289–94 and 308–10.

SA669 *v inwyttys*: will, reason, mind, imagination and thought. See first quotation from Wyclif in *MED* s.v. inwit *n.* 3.(b).

SR701–2 Cf. C621–2 and L147–8. The injunction to the visionary to report what he or she has experienced is, unsurprisingly, a stock element in visions of the other world: see e.g. Gregory, *Dialogues*, IV, 32 and 40; Vision of Drihthelm; Dante, *Purgatorio*, XXXII.104–5; and, in a different mode, Douglas, *The Palice of Honour*, l. 1464. Cf. Bodleian MS Fairfax 17 f. 80r where a peculiarly horrific vision of demonic assault seen by a monk is to be related: *in capitulo coram omnibus recitaretur, ut hoc meo exemplo alii a uiciis terrerentur et ad uirtutes excitarentur. Quod et factum est.* The vision was then written down for future benefit. See Hugh Farmer, 'A Letter of St Waldef of Melrose concerning a recent vision', *Studia Anselmiana*, xliii (1958), 91–101 (p. 100). William's audience, *them þat þis bilongith to*, could be glossed by the Virgin's words to St Birgitta: *thou arte suffred to knowe som paynes in helle and in purgatorie, for warnes and amendement of euel lyuers and to the comforte*

and profyte of thaim that bene good (*Revelations of St. Birgitta*, ed. W.P.
Cumming, EETS, 178 (1929), 117).

TRACTATUS DE PURGATORIO
SANCTI PATRICII

1 The rubric is for the first book of Peter of Cornwall's *Liber Reuelationum*, in which *T* is the first item.

3-4 *.H. abbati de Sartis*: Hugh, abbot of the Cistercian house of Old Warden or Wardon, Bedfordshire, c.1173–81; on Hugh, see *HRHEW*, p. 146; on Warden, see *MRHEW*, p. 127. The rubricator in S correctly glosses with *hugoni* in the margin. This is the only manuscript I know which does so.

   .H., monachorum de Saltereia minimus: H., usually known for convenience as Henry, of Sawtry (Saltrey), Huntingdonshire, a daughter house of Old Warden, near Ermine Street midway between Peterborough and Huntingdon; on Sawtry, see *MRHEW*, p. 125. On Hugh and Henry, see Easting, 'Date and Dedication'. By way of correction to n. 7 there, I am now convinced that Matthew Paris did not refer to the author as 'Henricus', as claimed by, for instance, James F. Kenney, *Sources for the Early History of Ireland* (1966), p. 355; Emile Brouette in *Dictionnaire des auteurs cisterciens*, ed. E. Brouette, A. Dimier, and E. Manning, I (Rochefort, 1975), cols. 356–7; Pontfarcy, 'Le *Tractatus*', p. 460 n. 1, citing Luard's edition of *Chronica Majora*, RS 57.ii, p. 192, and Zaleski, *Otherworld Journeys*, p. 217 n. 22. The marginal annotation in the RS edition, which seems to be the origin of this attribution, is Luard's and has no authority in the MSS (I have checked BL MSS Harley 1620 (f. 156vb) and Cotton Nero D. V (f. 137rb), and am indebted to Professor R. I. Page for checking that Corpus Christi College, Cambridge, MS 26 (f. 117v) also contains no gloss or rubric mentioning Henricus Salteriensis. In fact, Luard follows a tradition of calling the author Henry which goes back to John Bale (1495–1583): see *Scriptorum illustrium maioris Brytannie catalogus* (Basle, 1557), p. 189, and *Index Britanniae scriptorum*, ed. Poole and Bateson, p. 167, though a 15th-century manuscript (The Hague, Royal Library, MS K 33 H) of a Dutch prose translation of *T* had independently made the same expansion: *brueder heynrijc die mynste vanden monnichen van psalterien*: see Verdeyen and Endepols, II (1917), 181 ll. 12–13.

13-14 See *Dialogues*, IV, esp. cap. 37.

18-33 From Hugh of St Victor, *Summa de sacramentis christianae fidei*, Lib. II, pars xvi, cap. ii, *PL*, clxxvi, 582D–583A. On Henry of Sawtry's use of Hugh of St Victor see Easting, 'Purgatory and the Earthly Paradise', pp. 28–34, and Spilling, *Die Visio Tnugdali*, pp. 210–12.

18-21   Cf. *Dialogues*, IV, 37, 12, ll. 97–100 and on the power of *exempla*, see I, Prol., 9, ll. 73–74: *Et sunt nonnulli quos ad amorem patriae caelestis plus exempla quam praedicamenta succendunt* ...

28-29   Cf. e.g. *Dialogues*, IV, 37, 8–9, ll. 60–75.

34-40   Based on Hugh of St Victor, *De sacramentis, PL*, clxxvi, 580D.

39-40   Cf. Augustine, *De Civ. Dei*, I.xi: *Mala mors putanda non est quam bona vita praecesserit.*

41-45   From Hugh of St Victor, *De sacramentis*, Lib. II, pars xvi, cap. iv, *PL*, clxxvi, 586D.

45-47   From Hugh of St Victor, *loc. cit., PL*, clxxvi, 586A.

47-50   From Hugh of St Victor, *loc. cit., PL*, clxxvi, 586B, and see discussion also in *Dialogues*, IV, 44.

51-53   From Hugh of St Victor, *loc. cit., PL*, clxxvi, 586B.

57-60   From Augustine, *Enchiridion*, Lib. I, cap. cix, *PL*, xl, 283, cited by Hugh of St Victor, *loc. cit., PL*, clxxvi, 589B.

60-61   See *Dialogues*, IV, 30, and Augustine, *De Civ. Dei*, XXI.x. Hugh of St Victor (*PL*, clxxvi, 588–9) cites Augustine, *De Civ. Dei* and Gregory, *Moralia*.

64-65   See above, Commentary L57–60.

66-71   From Hugh of St Victor, *De sacramentis*, Lib. II, pars xvi, cap. ii, *PL*, clxxvi, 584AB. Gregory, for example, speaks of corporeal images to assist in understanding the spiritual *per similitudinem* in *Hom. in Ezek.*, I.viii, *PL*, lxxvi, 868B.

78   Henry of Sawtry distinguishes St Patrick as *Magnus* and *secundus*, referring to the early tradition that Palladius, the precursor of the British-born apostle of Ireland, was also called Patrick, hence 'Old Patrick' (Irish Sén-Patric). On the second Patrick, see *AASS*, Mart. II. 588, paragraphs 40–41, and Colgan, *Triadis thaumaturgae ... acta*, II. 280 col. 2. The vexed question of the 'two Patricks' is even yet not finally resolved. For brief recent accounts see L. Bieler, *St. Patrick and the Coming of Christianity* (A History of Irish Catholicism 1, Dublin, 1967), pp. 41ff; R.P.C. Hanson, *St. Patrick His Origins and Career* (Oxford, 1968), ch. VII and 'The Date of Patrick', *Bulletin of the John Rylands University Library of Manchester*, lxi (1978), 60–77; E.A. Thompson, *Who was Saint Patrick?* (Woodbridge, 1985), 162–75; and the references in Picard & Pontfarcy, p. 45 n.

   Some later medieval writers misconstrued this sentence in *T*, as Thomas Wright (*Saint Patrick's Purgatory* (1844), pp. 133–4) pointed out, and ascribed the founding of the Purgatory to a 9th-century abbot Patrick: see Higden in *Polychronicon*, VII.xx, RS, 41.viii, ed. J.R. Lumby (London, 1882), p. 20, and I.xxxv, RS, 41.i, ed. C. Babington (London, 1865), p. 370, and hence John Bromton and Henry de

Knighton, in R. Twysden, *Historiae anglicanae scriptores decem* (London, 1652), cols. 1076 and 2390; for Edmund Campian, *Historie of Ireland*, cap. xiii, who speaks of 'holy Abbot Patricius secundus', see A. Davenport, in *NQ*, clxxxii (1942), 67. The translator of the Middle Dutch version of 1387 seems to have read *primo* as *Paulo* in an effort to make sense of this passage: see G. Waterhouse, 'St. Patrick's Purgatory: A German Account', *Hermathena*, xliv (1926), 38 n. 22 and cf. the same author's 'An Early German Account of St. Patrick's Purgatory', *MLR*, xviii (1923), 321 n. 2.

83   *relator horum*: refers to Gilbert who retold the story to Henry of Sawtry; see L73-75 and 1073-1128. Henry's report of Gilbert's account of the bestial Irishman runs from l. 83 to l. 107. In St Bernard's *Vita Sancti Malachiae* (referred to in a texts of *T*: see below, Commentary L124) we are told of the unbelieving state of the 12th-century Irish:

> Nusquam adhuc tales expertus fuerat in quantacumque barbarie; nusquam repererat sic protervos ad mores, sic ferales ad ritus, sic ad fidem impios, ad leges barbaros, cervicosos ad disciplinam, spurcos ad vitam: christiani nomine, re pagani.

Sancti Bernardi Opera, ed. J. Leclercq and H.M. Rochais, III (Rome, 1963), p. 325 ll. 9–12. Cf. *Top. Hib.*, III.xix. For an account of the backward state of the Irish given by a 15th-century pilgrim to the Purgatory, see J.P. Mahaffy, 'Two Early Tours In Ireland', *Hermathena*, xl (1914), 1–16.

91–92   Presumably the interpreter is Owein: cf. L1077–80.

114–16   Cf. *Dialogues*, IV, 36, 12, ll. 79–82.

120–1   *textum ewangeliorum et baculum unum*: see above, Commentary C54ff and C64.

124   After *est* a includes *De quibus etiam in Uita sancti Malachie scriptum inuenimus* (W22:95–97).

127   *in locum desertum*: It is tempting to see here some trace of the use of *in desertum*, Irish *disert* to mean 'the solitary place where the anchorite took up his abode' (G.T. Stokes, *Ireland and the Celtic Church*, 6th ed. rev. H.J. Lawlor (London, 1907), p. 178). This expression was adopted by the Irish in emulation of Egyptian ascetics, whose influence passed through Copticized France: see A.K. Porter, *The Crosses and Culture of Ireland* (Yale, 1931), pp. 19–20. Note that Henry of Sawtry nowhere mentions a lake or island. See further Easting, 'Peter of Cornwall's Account', p. 402.

128   *fossam rotundam*: Félice, *L'Autre-Monde* (pp. 83–84), notes that the words used in early accounts to describe the Purgatory (e.g. *puteus, antrum, spelunca, fovea,* and *fossa*) suggest a man-made hole (*OM1*) or ditch (*OM2*) rather than a natural cave, a term common in later usage only through poetic license. This is supported by *muro circumdedit et ianuas serasque apposuit* (L141–2) and by 14th- and 15th-century descriptions of an oblong cut-out passage, roofed over, with a door at one end and a pit at the other; for the dimensions see L. Bieler's assemblage of witnesses, in 'St. Patrick's Purgatory: contributions towards an historical topography', *IER*, xciii (1960), 137–44, at pp. 140–2. See also A.T. Lucas, 'Souterrains: the Literary Evidence', *Béaloideas*, 39–41 (1971–73), 165–91, and for possible relationship with the Early Irish *uatha* or 'cave' tales, Christa Maria Löffler, *The Voyage to the Otherworld Island in Early Irish Literature*, 2 vols. (Salzburg, 1983), I. 109, 117.

138–9 *beati patris Avgustini canonicos*: α texts omit the name of Augustine: *canonicos regulares* (BU), *canonicos regularem uitem ducentes* (HAr). Zanden (*Etude*, p. 85) explained the presence of *Augustini* in R by the inscription on the last flyleaf of that MS: *liber Sancti Augustini extra muros cantuar[iae]*, cf. Ward, *Catalogue of Romances*, II. 435. Zanden, however, ignores the other α texts. Moreover, St Augustine of Canterbury is not to be confused with his namesake of Hippo, credited with the formation of the canons' rule which was adopted by the Lough Derg community: see *MRHI*, p. 193, and above, Commentary A22:1. The order of Augustinian canons was established in the mid-eleventh century; the anachronism of attributing their arrival at Lough Derg to St Patrick revealingly indicates their part in propagating the fame of the Purgatory. See further Pontfarcy, in Haren & Pontfarcy, pp. 31–32.

140–1 I take the church to mean the chapel on Station Island and the cemetery to indicate the *lectuli* or 'beds' of the saints found there: see Easting, 'Peter of Cornwall's Account', pp. 401–3.

152 On the name Reglis, see Commentary Y85.

157–8 *Licet ... infirmus*: I have not been able to discover the source for this sentiment. For confirmation that it is not to be found in Gregory, I thank Professor Paul Tombeur, 'Thesaurus Sancti Gregorii', CETEDOC, Université Catholique de Louvain (private communication, 1987).

169–70 This asceticism is entirely characteristic of early Irish monasticism; cf. e.g. Easting, 'Peter of Cornwall's Account', p. 413 ll. 59–64.

177–8 Cf. L208–9 and Commentary.

188 *.xv. diebus ieiuniis uacet*: according to L201–2 a fifteen-day vigil also followed a penitent's sojourn in the Purgatory. On the preparatory fast see also *Visiones Georgii*, p. 94; Thomas Messingham, *Florilegium insulae sanctorum* (Paris, 1624), p. 95 col. 1 and *PL*, clxxx, 983ff. A fifteen-day fast was evidently still the standard practice in 1411: Laurence Rathold had it commuted to five days in honour of the five wounds of Christ *ne forte pre nimia cibi vel potus abstinencia sui vires animi vel sensus verisimiliter vacillarent* (H. Delehaye, 'Le Pèlerinage de Laurent de Pasztho au Purgatoire de S. Patrice', *AB*, xxvii (1908), 48 ll. 8–13). Erasmus speaks of three days' fasting at the Purgatory (*Adagiorum* (Basle, 1526), p. 249), and Pierre le Brun in the eighteenth century speaks of the effects of an eight-day fast: 'on entroit dans la caverne, ou le Purgatoire, l'estomac vuide, le cerveau creux, & fort susceptible de visions' (*Recueil de Pièces pour servir de supplément à l'histoire des pratiques superstitieuses*,

IV (Paris, 1751), 39). Nowadays, following regulations issued by the prior, 17 March 1977, 'The pilgrim observes a complete fast from all food and drink (plain water excepted) from midnight prior to arriving on Lough Derg. The fast continues for three full days during which one Lough Derg meal a day is allowed.'

206–7 *diebus scilicet regis Stephani*: Owein visits the Purgatory during the reign of King Stephen of England (1135–54), *c*.1146/7; see Easting, 'Owein at St Patrick's Purgatory'.

Owein is the first named figure known to visit St Patrick's Purgatory: see the list of named medieval pilgrims in Haren & Pontfarcy, pp. 5–6; they are all men. There is a brief mention (*c*.1323–4) by Philip of Slane, bishop of Cork (1321–7) of an anonymous woman visiting the Purgatory (BL MS Additional 19,513, f. 173r, noted by W.C.M. Wüstefeld, 'Two Versions of the Purgatory of Saint Patrick and their Relation to Avignon', in *Non Nova, Sed Nove: Mélanges de civilisation médiévale dédiés à Willem Noomen*, ed. Martin Gozman and Jaap van Os (Medievalia Groningana, Fasciculus V, Groningen, 1984), pp. 285–98, at pp. 290–1).

208–9 St Patrick's Purgatory lies near the junction of the boundaries of the bishoprics of Raphoe, Derry, and Clogher, and now lies in Clogher (cf. SR7). Henry of Sawtry's circumlocutions here and at L178 may indicate uncertainty or ignorance about which bishopric was concerned. See also Easting, 'Date and Dedication', p. 782; 'Peter of Cornwall's Account', p. 411 ll. 15–16 and n. 2, where Peter specifies the bishopric of Down; and Pontfarcy, in Picard & Pontfarcy, pp. 24–26.

246 *constans esto*: Acts 23:11.

248 After *formidat* a includes: *Uis quippe interni doloris pro peccatis contempnit uniuersa que ei ostenduntur foris. Culpe que ab eo sentiuntur intrinsecus contempnunt tormenta que audit exterius* (W46:107–12).

249–50 Cf. L299–301.

261–2 The dusky half-light of this subterranean world is found also in William of Newburgh's account of the two green children from St Martin's land: *sol, inquiunt, apud nostrates non oritur: cujus radiis terra nostra minime illustratur, illius claritatis modulo contenta, quae apud vos solem vel orientem praecedit vel sequitur occidentem* (*Historia Rerum Anglicanum*, I.xxvii, ed. R. Howlett, RS, 82.i (London, 1884), p. 84). When Ralph of Coggeshall recounts the same tale, the girl says of her land: *quod nullum solem cernebant, sed quadam claritate fruebantur, sicut post solis occasum contingit* (*Chronicon Anglicanum*, ed. J. Stevenson, RS, 66 (London, 1875), p. 119). Cf. Giraldus Cambrensis, *Itin. Kambriae*, I.viii, ed. James F. Dimock, RS, 21.vi (London, 1868), p. 75.

262–4 Cf. *Visio Tnugdali*, p. 42 ll. 19–20 and p. 43 ll. 2–3; the other-world palace of Gulinus in Easting, 'Peter of Cornwall's Account', p. 414 ll. 68–69; and also the *domum sublimem* in E. Craster, 'The

Miracles of St. Cuthbert at Farne', *AB*, lxx (1952), 15. *T* clearly influenced the *Visio Thvrkilli*, p. 10 ll. 9–10: *eratque basilica nimis spatiosa et grandis, sed absque parietibus per girum dependens sicut claustrum monachorum*, probably via the reading in Roger of Wendover's version of *T*: *aula parietes non habebat, sed columnis erat per gyrum subnixa, ut claustrum solet monachorum* (*Flores Historiarum*, ed. H.O. Coxe, II (London, 1841), 259). Schmidt, *Visio Thvrkilli*, adduces other parallels.

269 After *ammirans* α includes: *Sicut enim estimauit, in hoc seculo aula talis uisa ab homine uel facta numquam fuit* (W50:31–34).

269–70 *quindecim uiri*: As W50:36 (apparatus) indicates, α MS U reads *XII uiri* (Zanden, *Etude*, p. 11), and α MS B *uiri duodecim* (Mall, 'Zur Geschichte', p. 157), a reading shared by β MS Vienna, National-bibliothek, Bibl. Pal. Vind. Codex 592. All other *T* MSS known to me give fifteen. Zanden claimed that the U reading, 'twelve', is the original, listing several examples of twelve being a significant number in a gathering: 'Auteur d'un manuscrit latin du *Purgatoire de Saint Patrice* de la Bibliothèque de l'Université d'Utrecht', *Neophilologus*, x (1925), 244 n. 7. His supposed scribal error of XV for XII could, however, work as easily *vice versa*. J. Hennig defends the figure twelve erroneously. He combines the two guides in the Earthly Paradise who are *quasi archiepiscopi* (L780–1) and the twelve messengers in white, whom he, but *not T*, calls bishops, and thereby contrives an invalid interpretation of this group as 'an illustration of the ecclesiastical organisation established at [the Synod of] Rathbrassail': 'Cataldus Rachav. A Study in the Early History of Diocesan Episcopacy in Ireland', *Medieval Studies*, viii (1946), 242–3.

    pa, which is based on an α *T* text, gives twelve as the number of men in white (Ld110, ed. Horstmann, *The Early South-English Legendary*, p. 203).

    W (p. XXXII) argues for fifteen as the earlier reading, and I agree on the basis of the earlier manuscript authority and the almost universal diffusion of this reading. See also above, Commentary A42:1–2.

270–3 It is surely no accident that these messengers *ex parte Dei* (L242) closely resemble Cistercian monks. See below, Commentary L1082–5. Cf. *Vision of Gunthelm*, p. 107, where the Cistercian novice Gunthelm led by St Benedict sees *quaedam capellam in aera dependens ... Erat autem in illa cella chorus quasi uirorum candidatorum in circuitu consedentium*. Both texts doubtless echo Apoc. 4:4.

274–5 *qui ... incepit*: cf. Acts 11:23 and Phil. 1:6.

279 *replebitur inmundorum spirituum domus ista*: cf. *Visio Tnugdali*: *tantam immundorum spirituum multitudinem, ut non solum totam domum et atrium replerent* (p. 9 l. 20–p. 10 l. 1)

279–80 The psychological effects of threats are well deployed by the devils. Cf. *Vision of Gunthelm*, p. 111: *Terribile est ualde quod intueris, sed ecce iam terribiliora uidebis.*

280–2   The demons throughout tempt Owein to give up his adventurous penance. (For an illustration of a devil tempting St Patrick, taken from *Le Purgatoire Sainct Patrice* (Paris, 1530), see Ernst and Johanna Lehner, *Devils, Demons, Death and Damnation* (New York, 1971), illustration no. 33.)

297–302   Cf. Eph. 6:11–17.

309   Cf. *VSP*, IV, p. 78 ll. 28–29: *Et clamor factus est contra animam iustam, quasi celum et terra commoverentur.* The image was a popular one; cf. the devils in *Speculum Laicorum*, cap. IX.59, ed. J. Th. Welter (Paris, 1914), p. 14: *advenit sonus quasi grunitus multorum porcorum adeo horribilis quod videbatur sibi celum et terram concuti sono illo.* This sound, compared with the harmony of heaven, convinces a Cistercian monk that hell *is* more unbearable than *ordinis gravitatem* (cf. L583–6). Cf. also e.g. *Vision of Gunthelm*, p. 111: *factusque est tantus fragor in Tartaris, ac si totus mundus cum suis aedificiis funditus, occumberet, et celum desuper cum firmamento corrueret.*

316–17   The distinction of sound and sight as two aspects of the horror of demons in hell is found in Honorius Augustodunensis, *Elucidarium*, III.xiv–xv, ed. Lefèvre, pp. 447–8. Rubrics in Paris, BN MS f. lat. 3338 alert the reader to this distinction in *T* (ff. 169v–178v): *Prima pena de auditu, Secunda pena de uisu.*

318   *innumera multitudo*: cf. Judg. 6:5.

335   *miles Christi*: cf. 2 Tim. 2:3.

341   *ligatisque ... pedibus*: cf. Matt. 22:13.

347   *Ihesu nomen inuocauit*: according to Roger of Wendover (II. 261) Owein says, *Jesu Christe, miserere mei.* See also above, Introduction, p. lxxv.

358–9   Cf. Vision of Drihthelm, *BEH*, V, 12 (Plummer, p. 305), where it grows so dark *ut nihil praeter ipsas aspicerem, excepta dumtaxat specie et ueste eius, qui me ducebat.*

360   *Ventus quidem urens*: cf. e.g. Exod. 10:13, Ezek. 17:10, Jer. 4:11, 18:17. Owen, *Vision of Hell*, p. 41, renders urens as 'hot', but the association with *rigiditate* (361) suggests that a burning cold is more appropriate. This is how both *OM1* and *OM2* translate it: see A63:1–3 and Commentary, and C316–18, and Paris BN MS f. lat. 5137 reads *frigiditate*. Cf. L422.

362   Cf. Vision of Drihthelm, *BEH*, V, 12 (Plummer, p. 304): *Incedebamus ... contra ortum solis solstitialem.*

364   The *uallem latissimam* is also from Vision of Drihthelm, *BEH*, V, 12 (Plummer, p. 304).

364–5   Cf. Vision of Drihthelm, *BEH*, V, 12 (Plummer, p. 307): *qui mox conuersus ad dextrum iter quasi contra ortum solis brumalem me ducere* *coepit.* See further on the south-easterly direction leading ultimately to heaven, Antonette diPaolo Healy ed., *The Old English Vision of St. Paul* (Speculum Anniversary Monographs 2, Cambridge, Mass., 1978), pp. 55–56.

378–9   Cf. the souls crying for mercy in *VSP,* IV, p. 78 ll. 31–32, and *Visio Esdrae,* 28, ed. Wahl, p. 53: *Et de igne clamabant dicentes: Domine, parce nobis. Et non miserebitur eis.*

381   Cf. *Aeneid,* VI.557.

393–5   Cf. L374–6. With these souls staked out as if crucified, cf. Caiaphas in Dante's *Inferno,* XXIII.111.

416–19   Souls tormented by numerous fiery nails are found in the Irish *Vision of Laisrén,* p. 118; cf. *Fís Adamnán,* § 27; *The Adventure of St. Columba's Clerics,* § 40; and see Pontfarcy, in Picard & Pontfarcy, p. 30, for speculation on such Irish connections. See also Vision of Thespesius, p. 297.

419–21   Cf. *Aeneid,* VI.492–3.

431–3   Cf. *VSP,* IV, p. 75 ll. 8–9 for souls suspended from the fiery trees: *Alii pendebant pedibus, alii manibus, alii capillis, alii auribus, alii linguis, alii brachiis.*

436–7   Cf. II. Macc. 7:5; *Apocalypse of Peter,* trans. James, p. 510, section 34; *Visio Tnugdali,* p. 13 l. 7; the *Vision of the Monk of Eynsham,* cap. xvi, ed. Salter, p. 305; and *Visio Thvrkilli,* p. 21 l. 4.

441–2   Cf. *Visio Tnugdali,* p. 39 ll. 12–14. See above, Commentary SR163–5, SA167–9.

449–55   The *rota ignea* is derived from *VSP,* IV, p. 76 ll. 3–5: ... *rota ignea habens mille orbitas. Mille vicibus uno die ab angelo tartareo volvitur, et in unaquaque vice mille anime cruciantur in ea.* The *Demones* (L457) are replaced in the text of *T* published by Migne by *Ministri* ... *Tartarei* (*PL,* clxxx, 994A) who seem to derive from the *angelo tartareo.* On the relationship of this to the *angelo tartarucho* in the fragmentary Priscillianist apocalypse (printed by De Bruyne, 'Fragments retrouvés d'apocryphes priscillianistes', *Revue bénédictine,* xxiv (1907), 323 ll. 11ff), thought to be of Celtic origin by M.R. James (in *Journal of Theological Studies,* xx (1918), 15ff), see Silverstein (1935), pp. 76–77. See also Seymour in *PRIA,* xxxvii.C.15, pp. 306–7, and Rudolf Willard, 'Two Apocrypha in Old English Homilies', *Beiträge zur englischen Philologie,* xxx (1935), 1–149, pp. 20–22, 24–25. David N. Dumville has more recently doubted that the 'seven heavens apocryphon' was the source for the wheel episode in *VSP* IV: see 'Towards an Interpretation of *Fís Adamnán*', *Studia Celtica,* xii/xiii (1977–78), 62–77, at p. 68.

Compare the wheel as seen in St Patrick's Purgatory in 1358 by Ludovicus de Sur: see Voigt in *Palaestra,* cxlvi (1924), p. 234 ll. 12ff. For this vision see also Frati (1891). The wheel as an infernal torment is widespread: see Owen, *Vision of Hell*, Index s.v. wheels, infernal, and also the *Visio Thvrkilli*, p. 26 ll. 2–6, which repeats *ministris Tartareis*, and *Visiones Georgii*, p. 148.

Compare also the picture of the wheel from the stalls at the Château de Gaillon now in St Denis, showing two wheels, half below rock level, with the mouth of hell breathing flames below, reproduced in G.-J. Witkowski, *L'art profane à l'église*, p. 121 fig. 116h. For other depictions of the pains of hell in the *Visio Sancti Pauli* as incorporated in *T*, see J. Baltrušaitis, *Réveils et prodiges: Le gothique fantastique* (Paris, 1960), fig. 17, p. 129 (Gloucester Psalter, Munich Clm. 835); fig. 12, p. 281 (Cambridge, Trinity College MS B.11.4); fig. 9, pp. 276–7 (Paris, BN MS f. français 9220); p. 275 (Toulouse, MS 815); and cf. also P. Meyer, 'La descente de saint Paul en enfer: poème français composé en Angleterre', *Romania*, xxiv (1895), 357–75, after p. 368.

461 After *esse* α includes: *Planxerunt miserrime et fleuerunt omnes qui rote infixi fuerunt* (W82:30–32).

466ff Compare with this house the *hospitium* of Phristinus in *Visio Tnugdali*, pp. 23ff, on which see Owen, *Vision of Hell*, pp. 34–35; Spilling, *Die Visio Tnugdali* (1975), p. 121; Mearns, *Vision of Tundale*, pp. 24–25; and Picard and Pontfarcy, *The Vision of Tnugdal*, pp. 73–74. It recurs in the Visions of Ailsi, ed. Easting and Sharpe, § 15, and with typical elaboration becomes the subject of the eleventh vision in *Visiones Georgii*, pp. 150ff.

469–70 Owein's stopping here recalls the injunction to St Paul to stop before the seven-sealed pit in *VSP*, IV, pp. 77–78. Cf. also Tundale before the house of Phristinus: *accedere propius nullo modo valebat* (*Visio Tnugdali*, p. 23 ll. 12–13).

470–1 *Balnearium*: cf. Easting, 'Peter of Cornwall's Account', pp. 414–5 ll. 104–20, and see Owen, *Vision of Hell*, Index, s.v. baths, infernal.

479–83 For this motif of graduated immersion, cf. *VSP*, IV, p. 76 ll. 16–27 for souls in the river beneath the bridge; *VSP*, I, p. 65 l. 22–p. 66 l. 9; and cf. Silverstein (1935), p. 153 ll. 20ff, pp. 166–7 ll. 13ff, and see discussion, pp. 12–13. The list in *T* is fuller and ordered to progress from top to toe. As in *T*, there is no designation of sins for this punishment in the Vision of Sunniulf or Vision of the Monk of Wenlock, where immersion in the river beneath the narrow beam is purgatorial in function. See also T. Silverstein, 'Dante and the *Visio Karoli Crassi*', *MLN*, li (1936), 449–52. Dante uses the motif in *Inferno*, XII.

489–90 On the purgatorial mountain (compare the mountain in the Earthly Paradise, L885), see Patch, *The Other World*, pp. 129–30, and for the combination with the wind see the sufferings of the abbot in *Visio Wettini*, cap. X, MGH PLAC, II (1884), p. 270.

498–502   Ezek. 1:4. For the north wind cf. also *The Adventure of St. Columba's Clerics*, § 39, and Ezek. 1:4.

503–5   Cf. Dante's Centaurs, *Inferno*, XII.73–5, and *Inferno*, XXI.55–57.

509–14   On the pit cf. Apoc. 9:1–2; *VSP*, IV, pp. 77–78; Vision of Drihthelm, *BEH*, V, 12 (Plummer, pp. 305–6); *Visio Esdrae*, 35; and *Visio Tnugdali*, p. 33 ll. 18–22. See also Hildegard of Bingen, *Liber vitae meritorum*, II.lxxi, ed. Pitra, p. 96; *Visio Alberici*, VIIII, p. 91 (and see Dinzelbacher, 'Die Vision Alberichs und die Esdras-Apokryphe', p. 439), and the *Vision of the Monk of Eynsham*, ed. Salter, p. 307 ll. 17ff, or in the 15th-century English version, *The Revelation to the Monk of Evesham* [*sic*], p. 40. See also Owen (1970), Index, s.v. pit of Hell.

528–9   Cf. Drihthelm standing by the pit: *cum diutius ibi pauidus consisterem, utpote incertus quid agerem, quo uerterem gressum* (*BEH*, V, 12 (Plummer, p. 306)). As in *T*, devils emerge *de abysso illa flammiuoma*, and surround Drihthelm. See also the Visions of Ailsi, l. 281, and p. 217.

532–4   On the Devil as a liar and the father of lies, see John 8:44. Cf. *Visio Tnugdali*, p. 34 ll. 19–20: *Qui huc te duxit, ipse te decepit . . .*

534–5   Cf. *BEH*, V, 12 (Plummer, p. 305), where the angelic guide informs Drihthelm that the purgatorial valley of fire and ice is not hell: *non enim hic infernus est ille, quem putas*. See further Easting, 'Purgatory and the Earthly Paradise', pp. 36–37, and add Paul Gerhard Schmidt, 'Die Vision von Vaucelles (1195/1196)', *Mittellateinisches Jahrbuch*, xx (1985), 155–63 (p. 160 ll. 32–34).

541–2   See above, Commentary A117:1–3. Souls passing over the perilous bridge to paradise, some of them being hooked by devils into the water beneath which lies hell, can be seen in the Simon Marmion Hours miniature (f. 153r) facing a depiction of the Last Judgement: see John Harthan, *Books of Hours and their Owners* (London, 1977), p. 147. Harthan (p. 148) dates the MS (London, Victoria and Albert Museum, Salting Collection no. 1221) 1475–81.

549–51   Cf. Vision of Sunniulf: *Erat enim et pons super fluuium positus angustus, ut uix unius uestigii latitudinem recipere possit.*

562–3   Cf. *Fís Adamnán*, § 22, see further Dinzelbacher, *Die Jenseitsbrücke im Mittelalter*, pp. 30, 42, and also the 'Bridge of the Eel' in the early Welsh version (*c.*1200) of *Y Seint Greal*, cap. cxxv, ed. and translated by R. Williams (London, 1874–6), p. 594 (Welsh text, p. 242). A bridge broad enough to allow two carts to pass in opposite directions was noteworthy in the early Middle Ages; e.g. note the mention in the Norse *Heimskringla* chapter 12 of such a bridge between London city and Southwark: see M. Ashdown, *English and Norse Documents* (Cambridge, 1930), p. 154.

568–73 Cf. Visions of Ailsi, ll. 390–6, which I suggest is based on this passage in *T*.

577–750 It has not before been properly recognized that the two homilies (L577–750 and 918–1041) are, as the epilogue says, *sanctorum patrum exhortationes* (1256, cf. 620), being largely excerpts from Anselm and John of Fécamp, referred to as Augustine. (Warnke, 'Die Vorlage des Espurgatoire', p. 141, dismissed them as the outpourings ('Expektorationen', 'Ergüsse') of a monk who was inspired to write them by reading *T* shortly after its composition!) These homilies have clearly been added to the story of Owein for the benefit of a monastic audience, probably by Henry of Sawtry for the monks at Old Warden. (Paris, BN, MS f. lat. 11759, from St Germain des Prés, has an interesting rubric to its copy of *T* (ff. 200v–205r), which suggests that the text was read in the refectory on All Souls' Day: *Incipit uisio de narratio de purgatorio sancti Patricii legenda ad mensam in commemoratione fidelium defunctorum.* This manuscript lacks the homilies, however.) The homilies are tied to the main narrative by references to Owein at 684, 739, 743, 918, 1026, and 1043.

579–81 Cf. Job 6:2–3.

601ff There follow extracts from Anselm. References are given to *Opera Omnia*, ed. F.S. Schmitt, 6 vols. (Edinburgh, 1946–61).

601–5 *Vtinam ... paruum?*: adapted from Anselm's first meditation, *Meditatio ad concitandum timorem*, III. 77, ll. 34–37.

605–9 *Quid ... cogitacionem*: adapted from singular to plural, from Anselm, III. 77, ll. 38–42.

611–26 *Ve, quot ... mallei!*: adapted from Anselm, III. 77, ll. 43ff.

618 Cf. Ps. 101:14.

619–20 *Hec ... uerba*: interpolation by ?Henry of Sawtry.

626–31 *Augeamus ... peccauerit*: adapted from Anselm, III. 78, ll. 63–66.

633 Matt. 5:26.

636 Phil. 2:8.

639–45 *Avgustinus. Intueamur ... clauis*: adapted from the sixth chapter of the *Liber Meditationum* attributed to Augustine, *PL*, xl, 905, now understood to be by John of Fécamp: see J. Leclercq and J.-P. Bonnes, *Un maître de la vie spirituelle au XIe siècle: Jean de Fécamp* (Paris, 1946), p. 44 n. 1.

644 Cf. Ps. 1:1.

645–6 *rubente sanguinis unda*: adapted from the famous passage *Candet nudatum pectus* in the same sixth chapter of the *Liber Meditationum* (*PL*, xl, 906): *rubet cruentum latus ... beati sanguinis unda.*

646–7   *O mirabilis . . . dispositio!*: *Liber Meditationum*, cap. vii, *PL*, xl, 906.

647–58   *Nos . . . Maria*: adapted from singular to plural from *Liber Meditationum*, cap. vii, *PL*, xl, 906.

662   Cf. Gen. 18:27.

662–4   *O insensibilis . . . aculei*: adapted from Anselm, III. 78, ll. 53–54.

667   Luke 2:51.

668–9   Ps. 118:21.

670   Matt. 7:7.

678   Ps. 43:22.

680   Prov. 18:3.

681–3   Cf. Ps. 72:5–6.

707–8   E.g. *Dialogues*, IV, 59, 6.

716–23   *Quid . . . est*: adapted from Anselm, III. 77, ll. 23–29.

716–21   Soph. 1:14–16.

723   Acts 10:42.

724–5   See Anselm, III. 78, ll. 67–68.

726–38   *O . . . desperes*: adapted from Anselm, III. 78, l. 72 – 79, l. 81.

729   Cf. I Petr. 4:18.

733   Cf. Deut. 32:39, Job 10:7.

734–5   Cf. Is. 9:6 and Luke 2:11.

740   Cf. 2 Cor. 1:10.

742   The pit, in fact, in Owein's account is *not* the real hell, but part of purgatory: see L534–5, Commentary and my article there cited, n. 60.

745–6   Cf. Ps. 65:12.

748–50   Cf. L16–17.

753–7   Cf. Vision of Drihthelm, *BEH*, V, 12 (Plummer, p. 307); *Visio Tnugdali*, p. 51 ll. 20ff; *Vision of Gunthelm*, p. 108.

761–3   On fortifying and satisfying odours in paradise, cf. L795–6, and see L820–1 and Commentary.

767ff   For the procession which meets Owein, cf. Vision of Boso. Boso *raptus*, lies ill three days as if dead, and visits *horrenda simul et amoena loca*:

> Erant omnes hujus ecclesiae monachi quodam in loco congregati, ante quos multum ex sese splendoris emittens veneranda crux portabatur, quam

omnes vestiti, ordinata sollenniter sicut solent, processione incedentes et
cantes sequebantur.

Symeon of Durham, *Historia Dunelmensis ecclesiae*, IV.ix, ed. T. Arnold,
RS, 75.i (London, 1882), p. 130.

768–9   As the *Visiones Georgii*, p. 225 explain, the *palmas aureas* are
carried *in signum victorie triumphantis*. Cf. Ecclus. 50:14, Apoc. 7:9, and
see L814.

775–7   Cf. also L810–12 and *Visio Tnugdali*, p. 51 ll. 5–6: *et erant vestiti
talibus vestimentis, qualibus ante monachi induti fuerant.*

788–90   Cf. Vision of Drihthelm, *BEH*, V, 12 (Plummer, p. 307): *Tanta
autem lux cuncta ea loca perfuderat, ut omni splendore diei siue solis
meridiani radiis uideretur esse praeclarior.*

791–2   Cf. Visions of Ailsi, ll. 401–2: *campum infinite magnitudinis, cuius
longitudo uel latitudo peruideri non poterat.*

796   Cf. Apoc. 21:25 and *Visio Tnugdali*, p. 41 l. 7: *nox ibi non fuit neque
sol illic occidit.*

798–803   Cf. the blessed in groups in *Dialogues*, IV, 37, 8 l. 65 *albatorum
hominum conuenticula*, and in Vision of Drihthelm, *BEH*, V, 12
(Plummer, p. 307): *Erantque in hoc campo innumera hominum albatorum
conuenticula sedesque plurimae agminum laetantium.*

806–8   See 1 Cor. 15:41. This section on the blessed *per conuentus
distincti* (801) stems from John 14:2 *in domo patris mei mansiones multe
sunt*. This and the Corinthians text are often taken together: see e.g. Peter
Lombard, *Sententiae*, IV.dist.XLIX.i, or Augustine, in *PL*, xl, 410. Cf.
also *Visiones Georgii*, p. 235 ll. 18–19: *Sicut enim stella differt a stella in
claritate, sic eciam sanctus differt a sancto in sanctitate, merito et caritate.*
See also *Dialogues*, IV, 36, 13 on the single bliss but unequal reward
enjoyed by the saved for different degrees of good works.

808–10   The different colours of the clothing of the blessed is not a
common feature of descriptions of paradise. One may compare the
different colours representing different sins in the souls seen in the
Vision of Thespesius: see Plutarch, *De sera numinis vindicta*, 565C. See
Visiones Georgii, pp. 228–9: the angels are in green; apostles, martyrs, and
seraphim in *scarletho rubei*; virgins and widows are *niuei et candidissimi*;
and confessors, patriarchs, and prophets are *crocei*. Cf. also *Navigatio
Sancti Brendani*, cap. 17, p. 50, and Honorius Augustodunensis, *Elucidarium*, III. 81, ed. Lefèvre, p. 464. Silverstein (1935), p. 122 n. 58,
refers also to Gregory, *Moralia*, xxx, 24 on Exod. 35:23.

813   After *splendor* α includes: *hoc enim quod uidebatur esse uestium color
et forma, uidebatur uestis uniuscuiusque potius esse nitentis claritatis gloria*
(W116:137–118:1).

820–1   Cf. e.g. *Dialogues*, IV, 37, 8, ll. 66–68: *Tantusque in loco eodem
odor suauitatis inerat, ut ipsa suauitatis fragrantia illic deambulantes*

habitantesque satiaret; *Vision of Gunthelm*, p. 107: *mirae suauitatis odore fraglantia*; and Gen. 8:21. See also above, Commentary A182:4–5.

821   After *ea* α includes: *Ibi uidebantur mansiones uariorum conuentuum; erant singule magnitudine lucis replete* (W118:161–4). This follows *Dialogues*, IV, 37, 9, ll. 69–70: *Ibi mansiones diuersorum singulae magnitudine lucis plenae.*

825–7   The negative formula is well-nigh universal in descriptions of paradisal bliss: see e.g. Patch, *The Other World*, Index s.v. formula, negative.

829   Cf. Apoc. 7:9.

837–8   On the Earthly Paradise in *T*, see Easting, 'Purgatory and the Earthly Paradise', esp. pp. 42–46.

839ff   The account of Adam is derived from *Dialogues*, IV, 1, 1:

> Postquam de paradisi gaudiis, culpa exigente, pulsus est primus humani generis parens, in huius exilii atque caecitatis quam patimur aerumnam uenit, quia peccando extra semetipsum fusus iam illa caelestis patriae gaudia, quae prius contemplabatur, uidere non potuit. In paradiso quippe homo adsueuerat uerbis Dei perfrui, beatorum angelorum spiritibus cordis munditia et celsitudine uisionis interesse. Sed postquam huc cecidit, ab illo, quo implebatur, mentis lumine recessit.

See also the succeeding passage of Gregory, followed more closely by α *T*, W122:22–124:31.

845–7   Ps. 48:13/21.

863–4   The pit here is clearly still thought of as the entrance to hell, as in the *Visio Sancti Pauli* and Vision of Drihthelm; in fact, in *T* hell lies under the river beneath the bridge. Henry of Sawtry has not been entirely consistent in adapting his sources. See above, Commentary L534–5.

867   After *introducimus* α includes: *De eis uero qui ibi sunt alii aliis maiori uel minori tempore erunt. Qui uero bene purgati de corpore exeunt, statim huc ad nos ueniunt* (W126:66–70).

877–8   Cf. Vision of Drihthelm, *BEH*, V, 12 (Plummer, p. 308): *non tamen sunt tantae perfectionis, ut in regnum caelorum statim mereantur introduci*. The whole of the explanatory speech by the two 'archbishops' is modelled on the speech delivered to Drihthelm by his angelic guide.

885–8   The vision of heaven seen from the summit of a mountain is a commonplace of other-world literature. See Patch, *The Other World*, Index s.v. mountain, on the,.

893–4   Cf. Acts 2:3–4.

899–901   Cf. Lambeth Palace Library, MS 51 f. 126r col. 1, where souls in paradise, not *in superiori paradyso celesti in conspectu Dei*, are fed daily: *Ex odore ... quodam qui hora prima singulis diebus de celo descendit, et pro*

differentia meritorum singulos sui dulcedine ita satiat et reficit ... See C.J.
Holdsworth, 'Eleven Visions connected with the Cistercian Monastery of
Stratford Langthorne', *Cîteaux: Commentarii Cistercienses*, xiii (1962),
200, and cf. *Visio Esdrae*, 59b: *Et cotidie habent manna de coelo.*

901   After *perfruuntur* a includes: *Ibi miles libenter permansisset, si
permanere licuisset. Sed post talia et tam iocunda referuntur ei tristia*
(W132:41–45).

909–11   The desire to remain in paradise is not surprisingly frequently
found in vision literature, e.g. visions of Salvius, Drihthelm, Maximus,
the monk of Wenlock, Adamnán; *Visio Tnugdali*, p. 55 l. 1: *domine,
obsecro, sine me hic esse*; and the Visions of Ailsi, ll. 438–41.

918–1041   The second homily; see above, Commentary, L577–750.

922–3   1 Cor. 2:9.

926–9   *Excitemus ... gaudium*: adapted from singular to plural from
Anselm's *Proslogion*, cap. xxiv, ed. Schmitt, I. 117, ll. 25–26. Most of the
second homily (L926–1041) is essentially the last three chapters (24–26)
of the *Proslogion*.

929–31   *unum ... bene sint*: Anselm, I. 117, ll. 1–2.

931–2   *Hoc ... patris*: Anselm, I. 117, ll. 6–7.

932–4   *Hoc ipsum ... procedens*: Anselm, I. 117, ll. 11–12.

934–40   *Quod ... bonum*: Anselm, I. 117, ll. 16–22.

938–9   Cf. Luke 10:42.

940–51   *Si ... delectabilia?*: Anselm, I. 117, l. 26–118, l. 9.

951–1026   *O ... uita*: Anselm, I. 118, l. 12–121, l. 13.

953–4   I Cor. 2:9.

960   Matt. 13:43

961–2   Matt. 22:30.

962–3   I Cor. 15:44.

964–5   Sap. 5:16.

965   Ps. 36:39.

966   Ps. 16:15.

967, 969   Ps. 35:9.

980–1   Cf. Matt. 25:21, 23, and 5:9.

982–3   Rom. 8:17.

1012–13   John 16:24.

1018   Matt. 25:21.

1019–20 and 1024–5   I Cor. 2:9.

1026–8   *Ergo ... uidit*: Interpolation by ?Henry of Sawtry between the two paragraphs of *Proslogion*, cap. xxvi.

1028–41   *Orandum ... Amen*: adapted from Anselm, I. 121, l. 14–122, l. 2, i.e. to the end of the *Proslogion*.

1035, 1037–8   John 16:24.

1041   Matt. 25:21.

1057   As with later pilgrims, Owein must have stayed twenty-four hours in the Purgatory emerging at dawn; see L130–1. William of Stranton says he entered eight hours before noon, SR7–8.

1066–7   *signo dominice crucis in humero suscepto*: Opinion is divided on whether this means that Owein travelled as crusader or as pilgrim, but perhaps that distinction was less secure than we like to think. See Easting, 'Owein at St Patrick's Purgatory', pp. 166–7, and 'Middle English Translations', and in addition, Dinzelbacher, *Vision und Visionsliteratur*, pp. 201–2 n. 997.

1068   *regem, dominum suum*: most likely Diarmaid Mac Murchadha, King of Leinster.

1069   *uirum industrium*: cf. Gen. 41:33.

1071–2   *pie memorie Geruasius, abbas cenobii Ludensis*: Gervase, first abbot of Louth Park, Lincolnshire from 1139: see *HRHEW*, p. 137 and *MRHEW*, p. 121. The date of his death is unconfirmed: it is reported as 1160–70 in C. de Visch, *Bibliotheca scriptorum sacri ordinis cisterciensis* (Coloniæ Agrippinæ, 1656), p. 124, and as 1150 in Troyes MS 224.

1072–3   *locum ad construendum monasterium inpetrauerat*: most likely Baltinglas, founded 1148.

1074   *cum quibusdam aliis*: Gervase was certainly able to send generous assistance for by 1148 Louth Park was a flourishing community of over one hundred monks: see C.H. Talbot, 'The Testament of Gervase of Louth Park', *Analecta Sacri Ordinis Cisterciensis*, vii (1951), 32–44, p. 37.

1074–5   *Gilebertus fuit postea abbas de Basingewerch*: Gilbert is attested as abbot of Basingwerk, Flintshire in 1155: see *HRHEW*, p. 126 and *MRHEW*, p. 115. For fuller discussion of this whole passage see Easting, 'Owein at St Patrick's Purgatory', esp. pp. 164–6.

1082–5   Henry of Sawtry, Hugh of Sartis, Gervase of Louth Park, and Gilbert of Basingwerk were all Cistercians, so the propaganda here on behalf of their order is not surprising. Cistercians were particularly convinced that they *omnes sine dubio salvabuntur* (*PL*, clxxv, 1323C); indeed, as Henry says here, that they were pre-eminent in glory. Cf. *Inter precipuos autem spiritus beatorum, quantum in se maiori gloria precellit, ordo monachorum cisterciensium*: see Holdsworth (1962), p. 200, and cf. also

pp. 189, 195. In another vision Cistercians have their own special
purgatory and heaven: see Brian Patrick McGuire, 'A Lost Clairvaux
Exemplum Collection Found: The *Liber Visionum et Miraculorum*
Compiled Under Prior John of Clairvaux (1171–79)', *Analecta Cisterci-
ensia*, xxxix (1983), 26–62, pp. 54–55. Cf. Caesarius of Heisterbach,
Dialogus Miraculorum, I.xxxiii; Giles Constable, 'The Vision of a
Cistercian Novice', *Studia Anselmiana*, xl (1956), 95–98; and see
Dünninger (1962), p. 45, and Dinzelbacher, *Vision und Visionsliteratur*,
pp. 218–20. Note also, of course, the similarity to Cistercian monks of the
fifteen men in white who instruct Owein in the underground hall
(L269–70 and Commentary), and see the comments by Zanden, *Etude*,
pp. 71–75.

    Bodleian Library, MS Fairfax 17, from Louth Park, second half of the
twelfth century, contains five visions, including Orm, the Monk of
Wenlock, and Drihthelm (as well as the *Testament of Gervase* (see
Commentary, L1074)), and gives a good sense of the kind of reading that
was available to Gilbert: see Hugh Farmer, 'A Letter of St. Waldef of
Melrose concerning a Recent Vision', *Studia Anselmiana*, xliii (1958),
91–101, and 'A Monk's Vision of Purgatory', *Studia Monastica*, i (1959),
393–7.

1095–6 For suggestions on Owein's choice of life after the return of
Gilbert to England, see Easting, 'Owein at St Patrick's Purgatory', pp.
166–9.

1115–18 This incident in Basingwerk was misunderstood or adapted to
form the exemplum of the monk who entered St Patrick's Purgatory, *and
evur after whils he liffid he had wowndis all ffressh & new, whilk he tuke
þer*, in *Alphabet of Tales*, EETS, 127 (1905), p. 343. See Tubach, *Index
Exemplorum*, no. 3998. *T* was used extensively for exemplum material:
see J.-Th. Welter, *L'Exemplum dans la littérature religieuse et didactique
du moyen âge* (Paris, 1927), pp. 219, 227, 278 n. 135, 280 n. 140, 299 n.
36, 313 n. 64, 438 n. 35.

1127–8 *Hucusque Gilebertus*: indicates the end of the material Henry of
Sawtry heard from Gilbert.

1130 *Ego*: i.e. Henry of Sawtry.

1130–4 Cf. *Visio Thvrkilli* referring to this passage: *super purgatorio hoc
abbates Ybernenses ad capitulum Cisterciense euntes interrogati, nonnulli
eorum respondent omnia vera esse, que de predicto purgatorio narrantur*, p. 3
ll. 7–9.

1136 *sancti Patricii tertii*: bishop Patrick of Dublin. See A. Gwynn, *The
Writings of Bishop Patrick 1074–84* (Dublin, 1955).

1137 Florentianus is usually identified with Fogartach Ua Cerballáin,
bishop of Tír Eoghain 1185–1230; see Pontfarcy, in Picard & Pontfarcy,
pp. 24–26. Henry of Sawtry could have consulted him for a revised
version of *T*. See also Easting, 'Date and Dedication', p. 782. Brian de

Breffny has proposed another candidate, Florence—Flaithbhertach—O'Broclan, abbot and bishop of Derry, d. 1175: *In the Steps of St. Patrick* (London, 1982), p. 111. On the ecclesiastico-political situation and on St Malachy's introduction of the Augustinian Canons into Ireland, see Pontfarcy, 'Le *Tractatus*', pp. 476–9, and in Haren & Pontfarcy, pp. 30–34.

1141–3 Cf. the evidence given in the early 16th century by Chiericati: see J.P. Mahaffy in *Hermathena*, xl (1914), 12–13.

1153 For a later appearance of the devils' *concilium*, cf. EETS, 24 (1867) p. 42, and see R. Woolf, *The English Mystery Plays* (London, 1972), p. 423 n. 11 and references.

1162–1248 These lines are all spoken by bishop Florentianus's chaplain. They are based on what the chaplain was told by the hermit first introduced by the bishop (1150).

1162–3 St Patrick's Purgatory is more like two hundred miles from Mount Brandon, Co. Kerry, which lies on the Dingle peninsula on the southern side of the Mouth of the Shannon. Both places feature prominently on early maps: see e.g. T.J. Westropp, 'Early Italian Maps of Ireland', *PRIA*, xxx.C.16 (1913), especially pp. 415, 426.

Alexander Neckham probably confused the two:

Asserit esse locum solennis fama dicatum
Brandano, quo lux lucida saepe micat.
Purgandas animas dant hic transire per ignem,
Ut dignae facie judicis esse queant.

De laudibus divinae sapientiae, V. 893–6, ed. T. Wright, RS, 34 (London, 1863), p. 461.

Other links have been made, some erroneously, between St Patrick's Purgatory and Brendan. In the *Navigatio Sancti Brendani* the saint meets Paul the hermit, who says: *Fui nutritus in monasterio sancti Patricii per quinquaginta annos et custodiebam cimeterium fratrum* (ed. Selmer, p. 73, cap. 26, ll. 51–52, and see p. xix and n. 14). In SEL *pa* this becomes:

In þe Abbeye of seint paterich : Monek ich was, i-wis
And of is churche a wardein : þare is purgatorie is.

EETS, 87 (1887), 237 ll. 625–6. Ld MS mistakenly says that the twenty-four monks fed with loaves are also 'Fram seint paterikes *Abbeye* : þat in yrlonde is al-so' (EETS, 87 (1887), 228 l. 303), instead of *Fram seint paterikes dai : & seint Ailbi also* after *Navigatio*, p. 32, cap. 12, l. 62 *a tempore sancti Patricii et sancti Ailbei*; cf. EETS, 235 (1956), p. 190 l. 299.

In SEL section *Alle soulene day* St Patrick's Purgatory is said to be next to Mount Brandon:

Seint patrik on vrþe ȝwilene : ane stude þar-of founde,
Ase god wolde, bi-side þe hul : of seint brendan in his londe.

EETS, 87 (1887), 423 ll. 87–88.

1174–87   For analogues to this tale, see Tubach, *Index Exemplorum*, T3643.

1185–7   The chaplain reports the first hermit's own words.

1191–1248   For analogues to this tale, see Tubach, *Index Exemplorum*, T4744.

1195–6   *.vij. psalmos*: see above, Commentary *VWS* SR521ff, SA516ff.

1233–4   Cf. 1 Cor. 10:13.

1249   *pater uenerande*: i.e. Hugh of Sartis (Old Warden). *predictis uiris*: i.e. Gilbert, bishop Florentianus, and his chaplain.

1252   Cf. L12–13.

1253–5   Cf. L7–9.

GLOSSARY

A and C are important manuscripts; Y and SR are of special interest for preserving very localized forms of the language; and SA, though less immediately localizable, has not been read for the *MED*. For these various reasons the Glossary aims to give a complete record of words and forms, and to show the senses and principal uses of each word.

Except for common words usually three occurrences of each word are recorded and subsequent occurrences indicated by 'etc.'. Where possible, senses are placed close to the words they gloss, but where the number of variant spellings and meanings precludes an arrangement on these lines, the senses have been grouped at the beginning and the spelling variants follow, usually in alphabetical order, except for eccentric spellings, which are often relegated to the end of a sequence or entry.

Line references for each spelling are usually given in the order of the printed texts, A, C, Y, SR, SA. To facilitate comparison with KA, references to A are by stanza and line number, without siglum, e.g. 109:6. Line references to the other four manuscripts follow the appropriate siglum, e.g. C125, SA129. Where second and subsequent references to one of these four manuscripts occur in a string, the siglum is omitted, e.g. Y26, 139, SR208, 413, 425.

Where convenient, parentheses have been used to indicate variant spellings and save space, e.g. **aȝeyn(e)** C363, 75. In such cases line references to the full spelling precede references to the spelling(s) which omits the letter(s) in parentheses. Thus, in this example, *aȝeyne* occurs at C363 and *aȝeyn* at C75.

The Glossary deals with five separate manuscripts, and sufficient information is given to indicate which spelling variants are to be found in each; e.g. *about* occurs only in A; *abouten* only in A in rhyme; *abowt* only in SA; and C, Y, and SR use only *abowte*.

Within an entry, different forms of words with the same meaning are separated by a comma; words with the same form but different meaning are separated by a semi-colon; different forms with different meanings are separated by a full point. Headwords are under the form most frequently found in the texts or the form closest to modern English. The swung dash signifies the headword of an entry, or occasionally, as with the different parts of a verb, the headword for the subdivision of an entry. An asterisk indicates an emendation in the text. (sim.) means 'similarly', i.e. in a similar construction to the preceding item, but often with variant spellings. The suffix ^{r} to a line reference indicates an occurrence in rhyme, where the form appears to be distinctively so used; when suffixed to a form it means that at least three-quarters of such forms occur in rhyme in all the texts instanced thereafter; when this proportion applies to only some of the texts, the ^{r} precedes the appropriate line number in the reference(s). The suffix ^{n} refers the reader to a note in the Commentary. Cross references are liberally, though not universally, supplied.

$_3$ has a separate entry after g, and þ and th a separate entry after t. I and y as vowels take the order of i; i representing a consonant, modern j, and j itself are placed together after i/y representing a vowel. Initial y as a consonant follows w. Past participles beginning with y- (representing the reflex of OE ge-) are listed under the initial letter of the stem of the verb, unless only the pp. form is recorded, in which case it is recorded under i. U/v representing a vowel precede u/v representing a consonant.

An Index of Proper Names follows the Glossary.

a *interj.* ah! Y623, SR55.
a *indef. art.* (+ cons.) 9:1, etc.; *an* (+ vowel or aspirate) 11:5, etc., (+ cons.) 11:4, Y219; (+ vowel) **on** Y595, SA12.
a *prep.* see **on**.
a *v.* see **haue(n)**.
abate *v. intr.* reduce SR529, SA523, 524.
abbay *n.* abbey, 20:2, etc., **abbey** C86, etc., Y153, **abey(e)** Y84, 81, 651; *gen.* ~ 21:4.
abbotes *n. pl.* abbots 137:4.
abyde *v. intr.* remain, stay, wait C267, SR17, SA16, etc., **abyd** Y260, 606, **abide** SR653. ~ *subj.* *2 sg.* C345. **abide** *imp. sg.* 182:6. **abydynge** *pr. p.* waiting SA632. **abode** *pa. t. sg.* SR22, 662, SA21. *tr.* ~ endure C566. ~ *pr. pl.* await C598. **abydyng** *pr. p.* enduring C376. **abode** *pa. t. 3 sg.* faced SR20, SA19.
abydynge *vbl. n.* dwelling, abode SA623.

abite *n.* habit, garb, monastic order or profession 45:6, 197:5, SR25, **ab(b)ett** SA24, 25, **abbyt** C88; **take (þe) abyte** enter the monastic life C146, 170, Y165, (sim.) **abyth** Y142.
aboue *adv.* on high 198:5, at the top SR440, **abown** SA452; **abowne** overhead SA576. *prep.* above ~ 78:3, 170:6, SR583, SA349, 352, **above** SR346, 348.
about *adv.* about, around 17:2, etc., **abouten**^{r} 23:4, **abowte** C225, 395, Y220, etc., SR414, 440, SA164; about (of quantity) SR628; (of motion) ~ 83:4, 88:4; around the outside ~ 12:1; **abowt** all around SA421, 633. *prep.* around ~ 53:4, etc., **abouten**^{r} 54:1, **abowt** SA300, etc., **abowte** Y297, 390, SR166, etc., SA170, 172.
abstinded *pp.* abstained SR407^n.
abstynence *n.* abstinence SA415.
abundance *n.* abundance SA640, **habundaunce** SR670.

ac *conj.* but 15:6, etc.
accusid *pa. t. pl.* accused SR668, **accusyde** SA639.
acordaunce *n.* comparison, correspondence 156:2[n].
acordaunt *adj.* = in accordance SR196.
adders *n. pl.* adders SR395, **addres** SR178, **arders** SR353[n], **edder** *sg.* Y341. **edderys** *pl.* Y354, **eddyrs** SA182, etc., **eddyrse** SA394. See also **nadder**.
adoun *adv.* down 46:4, etc., **adon** 92:6, **adown** C197, Y472, 633, SR487, **adowne** C425, 629. See also **doun**.
adrede *v. intr.* to be afraid 31:3. *ppl. adj.* ~ afraid SR541, SA533; ~ (+ of) SA46; **adred** SR536, **adradde** SR45.
afer *adv.* at a distance SR23.
aferd *pp.* (*adj.*) afraid, frightened 52:3, 174:3, Y267, etc., SR41, 94, **aferde** C273, etc.; (+ of) SA16, 117. **afered** SR89, (+ of) SR16. Cf. **fere** *v.*
afyre *adv.* on fire C354.
afliccioun *n.* penitential bodily pain *5:4, 38:1.
afliȝt *pp.* frightened, disturbed 12:5.
afore *adv.* previously SA573.
after *adv.* after, afterwards, subsequently SR22, etc., SA18, etc.; behind one (after motion) SR661, SA584, 633, **aftur** C230, etc. *prep.* in accordance with ~ 2:3, etc., SR664, SA129, etc., **aftur** C169, *wryten* **aftur** *hys mowth* = wrote down what he said C669; after (time) ~ SR2, etc., SA22, **aftyr** Y585, 650, **aftur** C555, etc. See also **þerafter**.
afterward *adv.* subsequently, afterwards SR44, 278, SA609, **afterwarde** SA44, **afturwarde** C188, 644, **aftyrward** Y119, 601, **aftyrwarde** Y11.
agayn(e) *adv.* back (again) C336, 116, etc., SA305, etc., **ageyn** C43, Y38, etc., **aȝeyn(e)** C363, 75, etc., **aȝen** Y102, **oȝain** 25:2, etc.; once more ~ SA112, etc., C625, **ageyn** Y412, etc., **aȝeyn(e)**

C545, 412, **aȝen** SR79, etc., **oȝain** 158:1, 186:6; in reply ~ SA343; = on the contrary ~ SA653. *prep.* against, contrary to, in opposition to ~ SA135, etc., **agane** SA297, **agene** SA127, **aȝen** SR125, 131, **ogain** 135:5, **oȝain** 30:6, 171:6[n]; towards ~ Y527, **oȝain** 144:3; with regard to ~ SA638; facing, in full view of ~ C468, **ageyn** Y663; = to meet ~ C649; in exchange for **aȝen** SR696.
agast *ppl. adj.* frightened, terrified SR114, 541.
age *n.* (mature) age SR361, SA209.
aghte *pa. t. pl.* owned SA288.
ago *pp.* see **go**.
agrise *v.* be(come) afraid, dread (*impers.*) 67:5. **agros** *pa. t. 3 sg.* 105:5.
aȝenst *prep.* against SR137, 697, **oȝaines** 13:3, 179:6; towards ~ SR604, **agaynste** SA607; **oȝaines** facing 190:6; **oȝains** over against, next to 79:2.
ay *adv.* forever 16:5, 112:6, **aye** C680, *euer and* ~ Y681.
ayled *pp. impers.* troubled, *As hym hadde* ~ *nowȝt but gode* = As if nothing was wrong with him C304[n].
aire *n.* air, sky 170:6[n], **ayr** C464, **eyere** Y513, **eyr** SR452, **eyre** Y511.
al *adj. and n.* (1) *adj. sg.* ~ all, every 75:6, 79:6, etc., C198, SR179, 559, etc., SA577, 600, **all** C132, 259, etc., Y26, 124, etc., SR157, 338, etc., SA353, 552, etc., **alle** 12:2, 27:1, etc., Y596; *pl.* all ~ 46:1, 89:5, etc., SR105, 253, etc., SA344, 351, **all** C128, 261, etc., Y254, 516, etc., SR134, 680, etc., SA2, 104, etc., **alle** 72:5, 128:5, etc., C177, 261, Y226; (+ relative that, tho) ~ 175:2, SR617, **all** SR240, **alle** 80:2, 177:1. (2) *n. sg.* ~ all, everything 130:6, **all** C242, 481, etc., Y442, 524, etc.; *pl.* all men (things) ~ 175:6, **all** C77, 231, SA395, **alle** 55:6; **alle** *and some* every one 25:3, 42:2.

al *adv.* all, altogether, completely 14:5, 39:5, etc., SR170, 212, etc., SA225, 270, etc., **all** C22, 305, etc., (vague intensive) Y102, 255, etc., SR186, SA182, 310, etc., **alle** 70:5.

alas *interj.* alas! SR626, etc., SA204, etc., **allas** 65:5, etc., ∼ þat SR694, SA440, 664, **allas** þat 126:4.

alblast *n.* arbalest, cross-bow 93:3ⁿ, 189:5.

aldermest *pron.* most of all 157:5.

aleche *adv.* see **yliche** *adv.*

algate *adv.* at any rate, nevertheless C322, 564, 620, **allgatys** Y626.

aliȝt *v.* spring up, mount 166:6.

alyue *adj./adv.* alive C557, 571, 662.

alle see **al** *adj. and n. and adv.*

allwey *adv.* all the while Y665.

almes *n. pl.* alms SR591; **almes-dede** charity SR523, 524, **almys-dede** SA518, **almos-dede** 164:1, **almus-dede** SA519; **almesse-dedes** *pl.* C184.

almiȝtʳ *adj.* almighty (following God) 60:6, etc., **almiȝten** 13:1, 113:2, **almiȝti** 26:4.

almost(e) *adv.* almost C11, 386, **all-most(e)** Y7, 435, 515, **almest** 92:5.

alone *adj./adv.* alone C257, 305, 360, Y296, **alon** 115:1, Y295, 333.

also *adv.* also, as well 16:4, etc., C23, etc., Y133, SR120, etc., SA185, etc., **allso** Y285, 572, **alsoo** Y19; ∼ *as* in the same manner as SR667; just as 157:6.

am *v. intr. pr. 1 sg.* am C139, SR52, 53, 116, SA54, etc. See also **ar, art, be, is, was.**

ame *v.* estimate Y394.

amen *interj.* amen 198:6, SA5.

amend *v.* amend, correct Y129, **amende** 36:6, 37:3, 55:5, C20, 133; ∼ *pr. t. pl.* SR699; **amendid** *pp.* SR509.

amendement *n.* come to ∼ = convert to Christian living 6:4, 19:6; = make amends (by repentance) SR140, **amendementt** SA143.

amiddes *prep.* in the middle of 194:1.

amidward *adv.* into the middle 60:2, 88:6, 110:6, **amidwerd** 118:5; *prep.* ∼ in the middle of 59:5.

amysse *adv.* astray Y30; (after *ded(e)*) wrongly C528, **amys(e)** Y594, 573.

among *prep.* among 72:2, 141:5, 169:2, C120, SR205, etc., **amonge** Y538, SA219, 425, 454, **amonges** 115:6. *adv.* **amonge** at the same time C660, Y665, together SA263; during this time Y359.

amorow *adv.* next day C187; **an euen and* **amorwe** evenings and mornings, i.e. all the time 160:2.

amour *n. wiþ fine* ∼ = with loving care 57:4ⁿ.

an *indef. art.* see **a.**

an *prep.* see **heiȝe** *adj.*

an *conj.* see **and.**

and *conj.* and 1:5, etc., C2, etc., Y2, etc., SR10, etc., SA2, etc., **ande** SA400, 668, **ant** (before *then*) SA556, (weakened forms) **an** SR576, 622, **on** SR213ⁿ; ∼ *if* 48:5, Y402, SR129, SA49.

angel *n.* angel 89:4, 174:1, **angell** SR489, SA478. angels *pl.* 26:3, 142:4, 187:6, SR674, **angeles** C596, **angellis** SR21, **angellys** Y608, SA20, 645.

ani *adj.* (+ *sg.*) any 20:3, etc., **any** C405, SA14, etc., **eny** C42, **ony** C316, 414, 544, Y461, 463, SR15, etc. (+ *pl.*) SR108. *pron. pl.* ∼ 148:2.

aniþing *n.* anything 48:5, 108:6. Cf. **onything.**

anon *adv.* straightway, at once 43:3, etc., C155, etc., Y123, etc., SR663, **anone** C138, etc., SR571, 706, **anoon** C440; *sone* ∼ 40:2, 64:4; ∼ (+ *right*) 166:3, C83, 637, Y78, 432, **anone** *ryȝte* C383, 629; *euer* ∼ constantly Y379, 487.

anoþer *adj.* another, a second C365, **another** Y356, 489, SR202, etc., SA113, etc., **anothir** SR111, **anothyr** Y336; (as *pron.*) ∼ 68:5, **another** Y337, SR34, **anoþur** C320; something else C169,

another another thing SR290, *mani* ∼ many others 47:2.

anouȝ *adj.* enough, abundant 56:1, (absol.) sufficient 86:4. *adv.* (vaguely intensive) 145:1.

answerd *pa. t. sg.* answered 35:1, **answerde** SA71, 160, **answarde** SA511, **answered** C347, **answeryd** SA118.

ant *conj.* see **and**.

aperceiued *pa. t. pl.* noticed 97:2.

apert *adj.* open 11:5.

apertliche *adv.* clearly 25:5, 26:2.

apliȝt *pp.* (*adv.*) assuredly, truly (a tag × 5 in rhyme) 40:3, 68:1, 74:2, etc.

apon *prep.* see **vpon**.

apostollys *n. pl.* apostles Y16, **apostelus** C19.

appered *pa. t. 3 sg.* appeared SR15, 165, **apperyde** SA15. ∼ *pl.* SR85, 87, **apperyde** SA68, 89, 169. **apperand** *pr. p.* SR65.

appyll *n.* apple Y595, **appull** C579.

aqueld *pp.* destroyed 65:2.

ar *prep., conj.* before, see **er**.

ar *v. intr. pr. pl.* are C398, SA40, etc., **are** C520, SA44, etc., **arn** Y52, 574, **or** SA526, **er** 133:5.

aray *n.* attire, dress SR192, 391, SA201, etc., **araye** SA394, **areye** SA330.

archebysshop *n.* archbishop C61, **hercheboschoppe** Y56. **erchebischopes** *pl.* 140:6.

arches *n. pl.* arches 132:4[n].

arders *n. pl.* see **adders**.

aryȝth *adv.* properly *C74, **arythe** Y69.

arise *v.* get up SR679. **aros** *pa. t. 3 sg.* rose up 105:4.

arliche *adv.* see **erly**.

armes *n. pl.* arms SR211, etc., SA225, 231, **armys** SA227, 239.

arn *v. intr. pr. pl.* see **ar**.

arn *v. pa. t. 3 sg.* see **renneþ**.

arses *n. pl.* arses SR449, SA460, **erses** SR251, 252, SA262, **ersis** SR257, **ersys** SA261, **ercys** SA268.

art *v. intr. pr. 2 sg.* art 55:4, etc., C136, etc., SR31, 119, 623, SA121, 619, **arte** C249, 575, Y409, 591, 658; **harte** Y159, 280.

as *conj.* as, like 93:3, etc., C223, etc., Y389, etc., SR127, etc., SA404, etc.; as, while 8:4, C52, 257, Y212, 296; as if (also with subj.) 83:5, 90:6, etc., C259, 304, etc., Y252, SR23, 234, SA69, 244, 598; as, since C136, 249, Y201; just as, in the same manner 154:4, C285, SR27; such as SR224, 521, 676, SA217, 515; (at the time) when C109, Y372; ∼ ... ∼, **als** ... ∼ as ... as 90:3, C81. **os** SA46, 67. *adv.* ∼ *by/bi* (manner) = judging by, according to SR65, 66; ∼ *now* for the present (time), right now SR653; ∼ *to* as far as ... concerned SR520. See **also**.

ascaped *pp.* escaped SR648

askys *pr. 3 sg.* demands SA642. **aske** ask *pr. 1 pl.* SA316, **axen** SR309. ∼ *pr. 3 pl.* SA417, **axe(n)** SR312, 409. **aske** *pr. subj. sg.* SR654, SA626. **asking** *pr. p.* SR591. **askid** *pa. t. sg.* SR620, 665, **askyd** required SA484, 583. **asked** *pl.* required SR496, **askid** SR618.

asoyled *pp.* absolved from sin C188.

asonder *adv.* apart SR262. Cf. **sundyr**.

assente *n.* assent C97, (aphetic) *at the* **seynt** with the approval Y94[n].

assisis *n. pl.* assizes SR287, (aphetic) **syses** SA297.

asta(t)te *n.* see **estate**.

at *prep.* (mod. uses) e.g. 195:4, C185, Y207, SR375, SA574; in C362, 390, etc., Y485; *chez* Y413; (after *in* and *out*) through 109:2, C471; ∼ *oonus* at one stroke, into a heap C262, **at-***tonys* Y255; ∼ *hys myth* to the utmost of his power Y124; ∼ *hom* = in his own world Y661; (under) C591; ∼ *what tyme* until such time as SR362. **att** SA205. **ate** at the 154:4, 182:1, **atte** SR198. See **assente**, **conseil**.

aubes *n. pl.* albs (eccl. vestments, usually white linen reaching to ankles) 154:5

Aue (Maria) *n.* (Latin prayer) an Ave, Hail Mary SR524, SA519. (five) **Aues** *pl.* SR563, **Ave Maria** SA555.

auncestres *n. pl.* ancestors SR134, **auncetorys** SA138.

Austines *adj.* see **frere**.

auter *n.* altar 7:6. **auters** *pl.* SR473, SA464.

aventur(e) *n.* danger C622, 236; *par* **auenture** maybe, perhaps SA620.

aviis *n.* opinion 180:6.

away *adv.* away C302, SR152, etc., SA85, etc., **awaye** C394, **awey** C359, Y443, **oway** 60:4.

awne *adj.* see **owne**.

awreke *imper. sg.* avenge SR402. Cf. **wreyke**.

axe(n) *pr. t. pl.* see **askys**.

bac *n.* back 71:3. **backes** *pl.* SR259, 352, 354, **backis** SR356.

bacbiters *n. pl.* backbiters 81:4, SR358, *bakbyters SA359.

bad(d)(e) *pa. t. sg. and pl.* see **bid**.

bagges *n. pl.* (money) bags 101:4.

bayli *n.*[1] torment 73:6, **bayly** 98:5.

baylie *n.*[2] power, charge, dominion 126:6, 127:6.

balaunce *n.* scales (of judgement) 179:5.

balder *adj. comp.* see **bold**.

bandys *n. pl.* fetters SA260. Cf. **bendes** and **bond**.

bare *adj.* + *of* devoid of 98:6.

bare(st) *pa. t. sg. and pl.* see **bere**.

barefote *adj.* barefoot SR617.

bargynnes *n. pl.* business transactions SA252.

barones *n. pl.* barons C501.

baryth *pa. t. sg.* (+ it) see **bere**.

batayle *n.* fighting 30:4.

bate *n.* bath Y405[n].

batte *pa. t. pl.* see **bytte**.

baþi *v.* bathe 103:2.

baume *n.* balm 134:3.

bawdrykes *n. pl.* baldrics, girdles (worn crosswise, over one shoulder and under the opposite arm) SA179, **bawderikes** SR175.

be *prep.* see **bi**.

be *v. intr.* be: *inf.* ∼ 9:3, etc., C40, etc., Y36, etc., SR15, etc., SA39, etc., **ben** 31:5, etc., **bene** C371, **byn** Y422. ∼ *pr. pl.* C57, etc., Y132, etc., SR70, etc., SA669,

ben 4:3, etc., C59, SR40, etc., **byn** Y405, 449, 563, **beþ** 81:6, 149:1, 186:1, (*it* beþ *erbes*) 148:1, **beth** SR410. ∼ *subj. sg.* 73:5, etc., C79, etc., Y74, SR30, etc., SA52, etc., **ben** 15:1, 47:4. ∼ *pl.* SA504, **byn** Y578. ∼ *imp. sg.* 95:6, C246, 651, Y656, SR645, 653. ∼ *pl.* 24:1, etc., **ben** 76:4. ∼ *pp.* 167:6, C265, 382, Y258, etc., SR23, etc., **ben** 52:6, etc., C266, etc., Y522, SR231, 466, 539, SA213, 499, **bene** C480, 622, 666, SA146, etc., **byn** Y413, 509, 669, **ybe**[r] 161:4, 166:4. See **am**, **ar**, **art**, **is**, **nas**, **was**.

become, becum see **bicome**.

bed *n.* bed Y47.

bede *pa. t. sg.* see **bid**.

bedys *n. pl.* prayer(s) C52, Y676, **bedes** C675.

befalle *v.* befall, happen C241, be fitting (for) Y227, **befall** Y236, **bifalle** 50:3. ∼ *pr. subj. sg.* C178, Y170. **befall** *pa. t. sg.* Y229, **befell** Y309, **bifel** 32:2, **bifelle** 24:4.

before *adv.* (of time) before, earlier C452, 636, Y339, etc., SR86, 347, SA47, etc., beforehand, first Y258, **befor** SA535, **bifore** 69:6, etc., SR543, **byfore** C265, 368, SR84; **bifore** (of place) in front 53:6, **biforn** ahead 46:2. *prep.* ∼ (of time) before SA9, 429, 655, **bifore** SR8, 684; (of place) ∼ in front of Y204, SA578, **bifore** SR611, **byfore** C593, ∼ in the presence of C600, **befor** Y610, **bifor** 198:6.

befor-sayde *ppl. adj.* aforementioned SA351. Cf. SA507.

begynne *v.* start (up), = appear (*intr.*) C210, Y203, **biginne** begin (to) (play) 56:6. **begynnes** *pr. 3 sg.* begins, starts SA1, **begynneth** SR1. **began** *pa. t. 3 sg.* (+ *inf.*) set about C186, (without *inf.*) commenced Y251, **bygon** C256, **bigan** (+ *inf.*) started to. **begonne** *pl.* C296.

begynnyng *n.* in the ∼ at the start SA34, **bigynneng** SR36.

behaue, beheue *n.* see **biheue**.
behynd(e) *prep.* see **bihind** *adv.*
beholde *v.* look at Y362. **behelde**
pa. t. 3 sg. C219, **biheld** 120:1,
129:4, **behylde** Y212, 337, 357.
behold *pa. t. pl.* SA331, **biholden** SR326.
behouefull *adj.* useful SR435[n].
behovys *pr. 3 sg. impers.* (+ dat.) is
necessary SA346, etc., **behovysse**
SA241.
belef(f)e *n.* see next.
beleue *n.* belief, faith C50, Y45, 241,
belefe C246, **beleffe** SA122, **be-
leve** SR120, **bileue** 15:3, **byleue**
C74.
beleue *v.*[1] believe C44, Y36, **be-
leuyn** Y39. **beleued** *pa. t. pl.*
C40. Cf. **leue** *v.*[2].
beleue *v.*[2] *intr.* remain, stay C278,
bileue 50:5. *tr.* **bileft** *pa. t. 3 sg.*
left behind 17:6. *pp.* abandoned
51:4, **belefte** C305, **bileued** left
behind 60:5.
belyve *adv.* immediately SA547,
566.
belyys *n. pl.* bellies Y316.
bell(e) *n.* bell Y648, C643. **belles** *pl.*
142:6, SR170, SA186, **bellys**
SA174.
ben(e) *v.* see **be**.
bendes *n. pl.* fetters 65:6. Cf.
bandys.
benedicite (L. *imper. pl.*) *interj.*
bless you! Y223, **benedycyte**
C228.
benesoun *n.* blessing (prayer of
benediction) C198, 229, **benesowne** C630, **benysun** Y224,
benycyoun Y191, **benycyun**
Y634.
benethyn *adv.* below Y378.
bent *ppl. adj.* bent C418, Y465,
ybent 132:4.
bere *v.* carry C62, Y57, SR568,
SA561; ~ (witness) 82:5; ~ ...
company keep (someone) company
C514. **berys** *pr. 3 sg.* SA2, **berþ**
123:3. **bereþ** *pr. t. pl.* wear 154:5,
baryth carry it (with suff. obj.
pron.) Y55. **bare** *pa. t. 2 sg.* bore,
gave birth to SA344, **barest**
SR338. **bare** *pa. t. 1, 3 sg.* SR334,

SA341, carried 89:4, C366. **bare**
pl. Y217, (witness) SR286,
SA297; ~ wore 45:6, carried
101:4, etc., **bore** (company) Y559.
bore *pp.* carried C59, **born** born
30:2, etc., SR5, **borne** SA5, **born**
given birth to SA130, **ybore**
carried 94:6, **yborn** 104:4, 112:1,
born 167:1. **born(e)** *ppl. adj.* born
SA598, SR606.
bery *v.* bury Y628.
berne *v.* burn Y290 (MS.). **bernyth**
pr. 3 sg. Y379[n]. **bernyng** *pr. p.*
Y327, 364, **burnynge** SA370. Cf.
brenne.
beschoppys *n. pl.* see **bischop**.
beseche *pr. 1 sg.* request, beg (person for action, etc.) C135, Y131,
SR650, 708, SA622, **beseke**
SA52. **besow3th** *pa. t. 3 sg.* C46,
besowth Y41.
besely *adv.* eagerly, assiduously
SR399.
besy *adj.* meddlesome, officious
SA360.
besyd *adv.* away, to one side Y442,
bisides moreover 156:5. *prep.* **besyde** in *loked hym* ~ looked to his
side C369, (sim.) Y420, **biside**
beside 113:1.
besschopp(e) *n.* see **bischop**.
beste *adv. sup.* see **wel**.
beste *n.* beast Y63. **bestes** *pl.* SR178,
261, SA183, 357, **bestis** SR354,
bestys SA273, 402, 403.
betake *pr. 1 sg. refl.* commend, entrust C292. **betoke** gave to, entrusted to C93. Cf. **byteche**.
bete *v.* beat C247, Y242, SR341,
bette SA338, 347. **betyng** *pr. p.*
SR320, 332, **bettyng** SA324.
betid *pa. t. 2 pl.* SR341, **bett**
SA347. **beten** *3 pl.* SR377, 380,
bett SA382. *pp.* SA385. *gold* ~
ppl. adj. (adorned with) beaten
gold 154:6.
bete *pp.* atoned for C378.
beteche *pr. 1 pl.* see **byteche**.
betyde *v.* happen C32, 346, Y28.
betyme *adv.* in good time C277,
Y271.
betokyns *pr. 3 pl.* signify SA433.
bitokened *pa. t. 3 sg.* represented
SR612.

bethow(3)t(h)e *pa. t. sg.* see **bi-þenche**.

bett(e) *pa. t. pl., pp.* see **bete** *v.*

better *adj. comp.* better 127:6, 179:4, Y273, **beter** Y45, **bettur** C280. **beste** *sup.* C213, Y206. See **gode** *adj.*

better *adv. comp.* (the) ∽ (the) better 14:6, 164:2, C100, Y97, SR603, SA213, 594, **bettur** C48, **bettyr** C343, Y284. See **wel** *adv.*

betwene *prep.* between C372, SA164, **betwyn** Y423, **bitven** 158:2, **bitwene** SR160.

beuereche *n.* drink, bitter draught 91:5ⁿ.

bi *prep.* by (mod. uses) 134:1, etc., SR6, etc., **by** C66, etc., SR9, etc., SA9, etc., **be** C403, 475, Y264, 550, SA214, 442(2); ∽ according to 3:3, 57:2, etc.; ∽ *hem* = according to their will 48:5; (after *com*) through 82:1, 160:3; (with numeral) in groups of 153:2, 162:6; ∽ with 156:3; in company with SR73, **by** C587, Y603; ∽ to the extent of SR175; on account of SR543; (swearing by) SR223, etc.; in (era) 29:1; ∽ *line* in a line 142:1; ∽ *þan* by that (time) 194:3; **by** by means of C165, **be** Y160; **by** next to C230, Y268, SA276, 279, **be** C615, Y621; alongside C513; nearby Y311; past Y638; ∽ (defining a part of the body held, etc.) 77:1, etc., SR318, etc., **be** Y365, etc. See **as** *conj. adv.* **by** to one side SR266, 268. See **fast**, **oþer** *adj.*, **þerbi**.

bicome *pa. t. 2 sg.* (after *way*) went 159:5, (travelled) 186:5. **becum** went to (question where) Y140. **become** *imp. sg.* become C170. **bicom** *pa. t. pl.* became 28:1.

bid *v.* pray SR239. **bad** *pa. t. 3 sg.* 7:4, commanded, entreated Y91, SR346, 575, **badde** C66, etc., **bade** Y61, SA349, 569, **bede** 36:4. **bad** *pl.* 191:4, Y646, **badde** C310, **bade** SA27.

biden, bydden *pp.* see **bodyn**.

bifor(e), -n, byfore *adv., prep.* see **before**.

bigileth *pr. 3 sg.* beguiles SR627.

bigan, -inne, -ynneng, bygon see **begynne, -yng**.

biheue *n.* advantage, *to our* ∽ for our good 182:3; (after through + *poss.*) **beheue** favour Y44ⁿ, **behaue** need Y240ⁿ.

bihinde *adv.* ∽ *and eke bifore* all round 53:6, **byhynde** behind SA176. *prep.* ∽ behind SR171, 546, **bihind** SR542, **byhinde** SR185, **byhynde** SA190.

byinge *pr. p.* buying SA252. **boghte** redeemed *pa. t. 2 sg.* SA104, **bowghtest** SR102. **boght** *pa. t. 3 sg.* SA203, **bou3t** 8:5, 17:4, 196:2, **bow3te** C17, **bowth** Y13. **bowght** *pp.* C252, **bowte** Y287, **bowth** Y247, 323.

biis *adj.* grey 180:3.

biknewe *pa. t. 3 sg.* confessed 33:1.

bileft, -leue(d), byleue see **beleue** *v.*² and *n.*

bilongith *pr. 3 sg.* (+ *to*) concerns SR702.

bynd(e) *v.* bind, fetter (person) Y242, C247. **bounde** *pa. t. pl.* 60:1, 88:3, 110:3. **bonden** *pp.* SA353, **bondon** SA260, **bounden** SR250, ***bownden** fastened (door) C90, **bowndyn** Y87, **ybounde** 65:6, 163:1.

byrdys *n. pl.* birds SA588, **breddes** SR598.

bischop *n.* bishop 32:3 etc., **byschop** C55, **byschoppe** SA634, 660, **bis-schoppe** SA663, **bysschop(e)** SA472, C99, **bysschopp(e)** SA476, 479, 482, **bysschyppe** SA615, **bisship** SR652, **bisshop** SR484, etc., **bysshop** C153, **bys-shoppe** C82, etc., **besschopp(e)** SA631, 480, 624, **bochoppe** Y77, **boyschoppe** Y96, **boschope** Y121, **boschoppe** Y125, 137, 148, **bosschoppe** Y50. **bis-chopes** *pl.* 137:6, 158:1, 180:1, **byschoppus** C27, **bysschoppys** SA388, **bysshopes** C490, 545, **bisshoppes** SR381, **bysshoppus** C23, 512, **beschoppys** SA397, **bochoppys** Y23, **boysschoppys**

Y557, **boschepys** Y19, **bos-choppys** Y55, 533, 576.

bise *imp. sg.* (*refl.*) $\sim$ þe be on your guard 48:4.

biside(s) *prep. and adv.* see **besyd**.

bisshopriche *n.* bishopric SR7, **bis-shopryche** SR5, **bysschoppryke** SA6, **bysshoppryke** SA8.

byteche *pr. t. pl.* commend, entrust (to God) C254, **beteche** Y249. **bitauȝt** *pa. t. pl.* 43:2, 51:2. Cf. **betake**.

bitellis *n. pl.* beetles SR353.

bithink *v. tr.* conceive SR514, **bi-þinke** 122:2, **biþenke** 147:6; *refl.* **biþenche** consider 125:1. **biþouȝt** (+ *of*) *pa. t. 3 sg.* 31:1, **beþowȝth** C45, **bethowt(h)e** Y40, 119.

bitokened see **betokyns**.

***bytte** *v.* bite SA406. **byten** *pr. t. pl.* SR389. **bityng** *pr. p.* SR179, 261, **byttynge** SA184, 273. **batte** *pa. t. pl.* SA403, **bootte** SA386.

bitter *adj.* cutting (wind) 72:4; cruel SR340, **bytter** SA346, **byttyr** SA203.

bytterly *adv.* bitterly SA407.

bitven, bitwene *prep.* see **betwene**.

bitvix *prep.* between 140:5.

biwent *pa. t. 3. sg. refl. him* $\sim$ turned round 83:1.

blac *adj.* black 106:4, 120:2, **blak** 12:1, SR316, 481, 492, SA319, 470, **blake** 71:1, 138:3, Y289, 456, **blakke** C294, 405.

blamed *pa. t. 3 sg.* blamed, re-proached 34:2, **blamede** C129, **blamyd** Y125.

blast *n.* blast 92:3, 95:4.

bled *pa. t. 3 sg.* bled Y612.

bleryng *pr. p.* sticking out the tongue in mockery SA94. $\sim$ *vbl. n.* SR92.

blesse *v.* bless (with the sign of the cross), cross (oneself) SR11, **blysse** SA12. **blyse** *imp. sg.* SA540. **blissede** *pa. t. 1 sg. refl.* SA83, **blyssede** SA107, **blyssyd** SA546, 556, 566, (non *refl.*) SA26. **blissid** *pa. t. 3 sg.* SR60, 621, **blyssyd** SA63, conferred wellbeing on Y620. **blyssyd** *pl.* Y645. **blessed** *pp.* C547, **blessid**

SR116, **blyssed** SA108, **blys-syd(e)** SA118, Y578.

blessyng *n.* (act of) blessing SR619, 620; *in the/þe* **blissyng** with the blessing SR656, 701.

blew(e) *adj.* blue 180:4, SR317. **blew** as *n.* (after *of*) SA320.

blynne *v. tr.* stop, leave off 4:6.

blis *n.* joy 98:6, etc., **blys** SA448, **blisse** 152:2, **blysse** C174, etc., Y591, etc., SA439. Cf. **heuen-blis**.

blisful *adj.* blessed SR97.

blissid *ppl. adj.* blessed SR546, **blys-syd** SA99, 538, 623, **blyssyde** SA505, **yblisced** 152:6, 196:6.

bliþe *adj.* happy, glad 34:1, 182:2, **blyþe** C661.

blo *adj.* blue-black 85:2, 106:4.

blod *n.* blood 90:3, **blode** C604, Y612, SR103, SA105, **blody** *adj.* bloody C17, Y13.

blow *v. intr.* blow Y477, **blowe** C317, 431, Y304, 478. *tr.* 118:2[n]. **blowyng** *pr. p.* SR398, **bloynge** SA405. **blewe** *pa. t. 3 sg.* 63:1, 72:2, 4, Y305.

bodi *n.* body 49:5, 113:6, SR103, etc., **body** C344, 678, Y285, 679, SR59, etc., SA62, etc., **bode** SA200. **bodies** *pl.* SR234, etc., **bodyes** Y355, SA236, etc.

bodyn *pa. t. pl.* endured, suffered Y107, 343, 427. **biden** *pp.* re-mained SR602, **bydden** SA592.

boiland *pr. p., ppl. adj.* boiling 78:3, **bowlynge** SA219[n], 225, 228.

bok *n.* book 9:1, 18:4, **boke** 22:4, etc., Y49, etc., SR664, SA1, 635, **book** C110, 189, **booke** C54, 56. **bokys** *pl.* Y106.

bokeles *n. pl.* buckles SR677, **bokyllys** SA649.

bold *adj.* bold C5, Y115, **bolde** C111, etc., Y196, **boold** Y301. **balder** *comp.* 61:2, **bolder** C307, SA86.

bond *n.* bondage, captivity 6:3; union SR133. **bondes** *pl.* fetters SR250.

bone *adj.* ready, eager Y325.

bone *n.*[1] boon, request Y133.

bonys *n.*[2] *pl.* bones Y628, **bonus** C624.

bootte *pa. t. pl.* see ***bytte**.
bore, born(e) see **bere**.
bot(t) *conj., prep., adv.* see **but**.
both *adj.* both Y558, **boþe** SR24,
bothe SA23. *adv. conj.* ~ ... *and*
both ... and C13, etc., Y143, etc.,
SA491, **boþe** 95:2, etc., C56, etc.,
Y305, SR318, **bothe** C118, etc.,
Y9, etc., SA198, etc., **bowth**
SA293.
bouȝ *n.* bough 145:2.
boght(e), bouȝt, bow(ȝ)(gh)t(h)e(st)
see **byinge**.
bowe *n.* bow C418, Y465.
bowlynge see **boiland**.
brac *pa. t. 3 sg.* failed to observe
(God's will) 172:3. **brake** *pl.* (holy
days) SA251, **broken** SR237,
breke ... *notes* sang with elaborate ornamentation 145:4[n].
brandys see **brond**.
bras *n.* brass 99:5, Y437, SR203,
brasse C329, 388, SA195, 218.
breddes *n. pl.* see **byrdys**.
brede *n.* bread 185:2, food (for the
soul) C614, Y620.
breke *pa. t. pl.* see **brac**.
brenne *v. tr. and intr.* burn C295,
brene Y383, **bren** SR290.
brend(e) *pa. t. 3 sg.* 83:5, 121:5,
193:5, **brent** 80:2. **brening** *pr. p.*
77:2, 85:2, **brennyng** C356,
SR93, etc., **brynneng** SR163,
etc., **brynnyng** SR184, etc.,
SA168, etc., **brynnynge** SA180,
etc. **ybrent** *pp.* SR186. Cf.
berne.
brenstone *n.* sulphur, brimstone
C294, **brynston** Y378, **bronston**
99:6, SA320, **brunston** 78:2,
***brymeston** Y289, **brymston**
SR317.
brerdes *n. pl.* brims 99:4.
brest *n.* breast SA342. **brestes** *pl.*
100:5.
brigge *n.* bridge 117:2, etc., SR483,
etc., **bryg(e)** SA472, etc., Y460,
468, 481, **brygg(e)** C413, etc.,
Y502, SR483, Y484, 492.
briȝt *adj.* bright 150:2, etc., **bright**
SR489, **bryȝth** C465, 607, etc.,
bryth Y615. **briȝter** *comp.* 156:4,
181:2. *adv.* **bryȝth** brightly C543.

bring *v.* bring 3:6, take 38:6, etc.,
bryng Y45, 453, **brynge** C338. ~
pr. 3 sg. subj. 26:6, **brynge** C681,
Y682. **brouȝt** *pa. t. 3 sg.* 175:5,
browght SR315. **browte** *pa. t. pl.*
C195, **browth** Y188, **browȝte**
C319, 353. **broght** *pp.* SA576,
***brought** SR583, **browȝth** C460,
browte Y507, **ybrouȝt** 94:5, etc.
brochis *n. pl.* skewers, spits SR205,
fire ~ SR211, **brochys** SA220.
brocking *n.* complaint 65:5, 78:5.
brod *adj.* broad Y374, etc., **brode**
C319, 455, Y306, etc., SR35, 483,
SA472, **broode** C405. **bradder**
comp. C445, **broder** Y492. **brod-**
est *sup.* Y357.
broder *n.* see **broþer**.
broken *pa. t. pl.* see **brac**.
brond *n.* piece of burning wood,
flaming torch 83:5. **brondes** *pl.*
SR233, etc., **brondis** SR377,
brondys SA381, 382, **brandys**
SA339. See **fire-brondes**.
brose *v.* crush, smash SR291. **brusid**
pp. SR471.
broþer *n.* brother 47:1, etc., **brother**
SR124, etc., (eccl.) Y164, **brodur**
C170; **broder** SA126, 131.
brunston *n.* see **brenstone**.
brusid *pp.* see **brose**.
burdon *n.* burden, fate SR641.
burdoun *n.*[1] low pitched undersong
accompanying melody, bass
145:5[n].
burdoun *n.*[2] pilgrim's staff 195:6.
but *conj.* but C7, etc., Y80, etc.,
SR31, etc., **bot** 50:6, etc., SA37,
etc., **bott** SA30, etc.; unless ~
C567, Y37, SR699, **bot** 49:4, 74:5,
179:4, **bott** SA143, ~ *ȝyf* (with
subj.) C41, 97, ~ *yf* Y94, 320, ~
if SR429, **bot** *ȝif* 3:4, etc., **bot** *þat*
143:2; nevertheless, yet C316; but
if SR142; without Y423. *prep.*
nowȝt ~ nothing but, except
C304, *nothyng* ~ only SR557, *no*
... *thyng, nothynge* ... **bott**
SA549, 651, *nis* **bot** is only 181:6;
bot only 2:5, 165:5. *adv.* **bott** only
SA638.

caghe *n.* cage 108:1[n].

calle *v.* summon C601. **call** *pr. t. pl.* name SA55, $\sim$ C64. **calde** *pa. t. 3 sg.* called Y440, **called** C298, etc. *pl.* C115, 596. *pp.* C101, **callyd(e)** SA442, 669, 441.

cam(me) *pa. t. sg.* see **com.**

can *pr. 1, 3 sg.* am/is able to 9:2, 44:2, 77:5, Y569, SR93, 514, SA95, 450, 507. **kanste** *pr. 2 sg.* C431. **couþe** *pa. t. 3 sg.* knew 30:4, was able to 37:1, (with *v.* of motion understood) 113:4, **cowþe** C466, **kowþe** C534, **cowd** Y308, etc. **kowþe** *pp.* known C670.

candell *n.* candle SR610.

card *pa. t. 3 sg.* sorrowed 5:2.

cardinals *n. pl.* cardinals 137:2.

care *n.* misery 98:3, Y107, SA341, etc., **kare** C180.

Carmes *adj.* see **frere** *n.*

carol *n.* round dance accompanied by singing 142:1. **carols** *pl.* 141:4.

caroly *v.* dance and sing in a carol 143:1, 5, 144:6.

cartys *n. pl.* carts, wagons Y503.

caste *v.* throw, fling C424, Y471. **castyng** *pr. p.* SR371, 418. **cast** *pa. t. 3 sg.* 92:6, 95:5. *pl.* 88:6, etc., SR376, SA248, **cast** *vp* vomited SR245, $\sim$ C295, etc., **casten** 60:2, **kest** SA262, etc., **keste** Y433, SA426, **kestyn** Y383, **kyste** Y290. **cast** *pp.* raised Y316, SR230, etc., SA243, poured, SA293, $\sim$ C393, Y442.

casteles *n. pl.* castles C500, **castelys** Y543.

castel-tour *n.* castle tower 108:3.

cattes *n. pl.* cats SR353.

cause *n.* cause, reason SR130, 310, SA133, 317, 487.

causteloines *n. pl.* chalcedony stones? 131:5[n].

celestien *adj.* celestial 165:4.

certeyn *adj.* steadfast 47:5. *adv.* $\sim$ assuredly SR72, 157, **certayn** SR77, 667, **seyrteyn** Y137. *yn* **certayn** quasi-*sb.* truly SR681.

certenly *adv.* certainly SA206, **sertenly** SA38, 638.

cese *v.* cease SR18, **sece** *of* SR359.

chanon *n.* canon SA24, 29, **chanoun** C647, **chanown Y652, **schanown** Y184. **chanons** *gen.* SR25[n]. **channons** *pl.* SR604, **chanones** C493, **chanons** SR406, SA414, **chanonus** C87, etc., **chanouns** 137:5, SA596, **chanownys** Y667, **schanonys** Y82, 536, **schanownys** Y664, *white* **chanounes** Augustinian canons 22:1.

chansell *n.* chancel SA463. **chauncelles** *pl.* SR473.

chapel *n.* chapel 8:1.

chapeletes *n. pl.* wreaths for the head **SR172, 188, **chappelettys** SA177, 194.

chapetor *n.* ecclesiastical court SA495.

chapman *n.* trader, merchant SR590, SA582.

charbukelston *n.* material made of carbuncles 132:4[n].

charge *n.* duty, responsibility SR475, SA439.

charite *n.* Christian love 144:2.

chastement *n.* chastisement SR340.

chasten *pr. pl.* amend by discipline SR343. **chastyd** *pa. t. pl.* SA345, **chastynde** SR339.

chaunce *n.* (person's) fate 179:4, *a* $\sim$ by chance 32:2.

chaundelers *n pl.* candlesticks 136:4[n].

chaunged *pa. t. 3 sg.* changed (hue) 79:6, 114:1.

cheynes *n. pl.* chains SR319, **chenys** SA322, **schenys** Y364.

chele *n.* cold 62:5.

chere *n.* manner, demeanour 17:3, etc., C55, **chyre** Y50.

chewyd *pa. t. 3 sg.* see **shew(e)** *v.*

chide *v.* find fault 81:6. *to other* **chyd** *pa. t. 3 sg.* railed against the others Y495, *wyth oþur* **chydde** C448.

child *n.* child 167:1, SR334, **chyld** SA340, 341. **children** *pl.* SR158, etc., **chyldren SR332, **chylder** SA162, etc.

chin *n.* chin 100:6, **chyn** Y428, **chynne** C377, Y370. **chynnys** *pl.* Y366.

chirch *n.* church SR611, **chirche** 7:1, etc., SR238. *holy* ~ Holy Church SR125, etc., *holy* **chirche** SR137. Cf. **kyrke**.

cladde *pp.* (*adj.*) see **clothed**.

clawe *n. pl.* claws C351[n].

clene *adj.* free (of sin) 143:2, 162:3; free of filth SR36, SA35; complete SA612. *adv.* completely SR634, SA604.

clenesse *n.* chastity, purity 152:1.

clepeing *vbl. n.* crying out 109:5.

clepi *v.* call out 51:5. **clepeþ** *pr. 3 pl.* name 10:5, etc., **clepete** (with suffixed obj. *pron.*) name it Y59. **cleped** *pa. t. 3 sg.* called out 60:3, etc., **clepyd** Y329, **klepyd** Y386, 487, 490. **clepyd** *pl.* named Y84, **klepynd** Y111[n]. **cleped** *pp.* 161:6, SR52, **klepyd** Y99, **ycleped** 24:2, 170:2.

clere *adj.* clear, bright 156:3, SR595, SA585. *adv.* clearly C543.

clerk *n.* learned man 9:2, 122:1. **clerkes** *pl.* clerics SR484, **clarkys** SA473, 517.

clevid *pa. t. pl.* cut, split SR220, **clevyd** SA235.

clingeþ *pr. 3 sg.* shrivels up, withers 148:5.

cloyster *n.* cloister C223, Y219.

close *v.* close C95. **closid** *pa. t. pl.* enclosed SR477(2), **closyd** SA466. **closid** *pp.* enclosed SR349, etc., **closyd(e)** SA421, 352, 465.

cloþ *n.* garment 128:1, 4, 173:2, fabric C534, **cloth** SR169, **clothe** SR443. **cloþes** *pl.* clothes 113:3, **clothes** SR461, SA455, 456, **clothis** SR169, etc., **clothys** Y302, SA173, 175, **cloþus** C315, 537. See **gold**.

clothed *ppl. adj.* clothed, dressed SR177, **clothid** SR605, **clothyd** Y546, **cloded** C533, **ycloþed** 155:5; **cladde** SR24, **clede** SA23, 173, etc.

cloþeing *n.* clothing 155:2, **clothynge** SA200, **clothyn** Y547, 550[n].

cold *adj.* cold 63:1, etc., SR442, etc., SA523, **colde** C313, 316, Y300, 303, SA522, **cowlde** SA369,

kowld SA374. *adv.* ~ coldly 72:4.

cold *n.* cold SR380, 385, 459, **colde** SA391, 454.

cole *n.* live coal 60:5, 105:6. **coles** *pl.* SA248

colers *n. pl.* collars SR174, SA170[n], **colors** SR166.

colombin *n.* columbine 147:5[n].

colour *n.* colour SR40, 66, **colowre** SA40, 70. **colorys** *pl.* Y565, **colours** 106:1, 147:2, **colowres** C518, SA589.

com *v.* come 6:4, etc., **come** 42:1, C43, etc., SR56, etc., **cum** Y38, etc., SA565, etc., **cume** Y415, **comen** 162:1, **commyn** Y70. **cum** *pr. 1 sg.* Y135. **comest** *pr. 2 sg.* SR145, **comeste** C281, **comys** Y582, **comyst** Y274, **cummyste** SA149. **comeþ** *pr. 3 sg.* C603, *ous* **comeþ** (there) comes to us 182:2, **comyth** Y32, 589, ***cumyth** Y611. ~ *pr. 1 pl.* 166:2, **come** C593, **comen** 166:1. ~ *pr. 3 pl.* 41:5, 165:5, **come** C279, **comeþ** 162:4, 165:1, C36, **comyn** SR461, **cum** Y272, 653. ~ *pr. 2 sg. subj.* 187:2. **come** *pr. 3. sg. subj.* SR139, **cum** SA143. **come** *imp. sg.* C401, **cume** Y452. **comyng** *pr. p.* C6, SR235, etc., **cummyng(e)** SA376, 568, 22. ~ *pa. t. 1, 3 sg.* 8:6, etc., Y6, etc., SR581, SA114, 320, **come** 197:4, C10, etc., Y112, SR63, etc., **comme** Y395, 494, **cam** 175:2, Y154, 209, 514, etc., SR19, etc., SA18, etc., **camme** Y447. ~ *pa. t. 2 sg.* 57:5, **cum** Y270. ~ *pa. t. pl.* 25:2, etc., Y221, 261, SA248, **come** 45:4, 158:1, C105, etc., SR394, etc., **comme** Y335, **comyn** Y108, **cum** Y102, SA401, **cam** SR594, SA456, 634. **cum** *pp.* Y591, SA61, **cumme** Y409, **comen** 54:4, C139, 575, SR58, etc., **comyn** SR134, 135, 142, SA119, **commen** SA138, **commyn** SA139, **cummyn** SA146, 629, **ycome**●[r] 25:6, etc., **ycomen** 55:4. Cf. **comyng** *vbl. n.*, **welcome**.

comandy *v.* command 35:4.

comen *adj.* common (people) SA433, 457, 499, **comyn** SR383, 468, **commyn** SA458, 486; **comoun** shared by all 186:4, **comun** 159:4.

comyng *vbl. n.* coming SR60, **cumynge** SA63; $\sim$ arrival Y407, **comynge** C650.

commendacyon *n.* one of the Offices of the Dead in which souls of the dead are commended to the mercy of God or the Virgin SA517. **commendacions** *pl.* SR522.

commounliche *adv.* unanimously 3:1.

company *n.* company, band SR604, etc., **compeny** SR621, **compeynie** 58:6, 140:2, **cumpany** SA595, etc.; *bere hym* $\sim$ keep him company C514, *bore ... cumpany* Y559

complaint *n.* complaint SR124, **complentt** SA126.

conseil *n.* advice 110:1, **conseyl(e)** 59:2, 88:1, **counseill** SR198, **consell(e)** SA208, 214, M*zat swiche a* $\sim$ *to be* to follow such a course of action 173:6; **cunsel** rule Y83, **cunsell** plan Y320.

conseily *v.* advise 42:4, **conseyl** 47:1. **counsaill** *pr. 1 sg.* SR654. **conseyld** *pp.* 50:4.

consistor(i)e *n.* bishop's court SA495.

conteyni *v. refl.* restrain oneself (from yielding) 42:5.

contemplacyon *n.* contemplation SA415.

continence *n.* continence, chastity SR406.

continually *adv.* continually SA312, **contynually** SA230, 405, **continu(e)lich** SR306, 216, **continulych** SR398.

continue *v.* continue SR638, **contenue** SA492, **contenew** SA609.

contractys *n. pl.* $\sim$ *of matrimonie* solemn agreements to enter into matrimony SA493.

contre(e), -ye *n.* see **cuntre**.

cop *n.* summit 168:5.

coper *n.* copper 99:5, SA218.

corage *n.* courage Y263.

coral *n.* coral (as ornament) 131:2[n].

cord *n.* rope SR589, **corde** SR574, etc., SA568, etc.

correcte *v.* correct SR390, SA502.

costluer *adj.* *comp.* (after *more*) more lavish, extravagant SR676[n].

councelyng *vbl. n.* giving of counsel SR361.

countre *n.* see **cuntre**.

cours *n.* turn, time 103:6.

courtelage *n.* courtyard 108:2[n].

couent *n.* convent 43:1, Y95, **couente** C98, SA11, **covent** SR11, **coventt** SA637.

coueytous *adj.* covetous 86:4, **couaitise** 87:2.

couþe *pa. t. sg.* see **can**.

covete *v.* covet SR655, **covytt** SA627. *pr. t. pl.* SA332.

covetise *n.* covetousness SR508, **couaitise** 86:2, **covytys** SA334.

cowd *pa. t. sg.* see **can**.

cowlde *adj.* see **cold**.

cowntre *n.* see **cuntre**.

craftyly *adv.* ingeniously C469.

creatour *n.* creator 30:6, 176:5.

creaunce *n.* belief, faith 15:1[n], 32:1, 47:4.

Crede *n.* the Creed SR524, SA519.

cri *n.* cry 52:2, 53:1, **crie** crying out 109:4, SR479, **cry** C450, Y310, etc., SA314, **crye** C264, etc., SR308, SA98. **creyes** *pl.* SR92.

crie *v.* cry (out) 73:3, etc., SR217, **crye** C193, SA468. **crid** *pa. t. pl.* 66:2, 100:2, etc., **cride** 90:6, **cryde** C332, SA231, **cryed** C326, **cryend** Y313[n]. **cryeng** *pr. p.* SR400, **cryenge** SA408.

cryinge *vbl. n.* shouting SA94.

cristal *n.* (rock) crystal (as precious stone) 131:1[n], 132:6, **cristall** SA585; (as *adj.*) **cristal** *ston* SR595.

cristen *adj.* Christian 28:2, 165:5, SR238, 707, SA602. Cf. **evyn-cristen**.

cristendome *n.* state of being a Christian SR138.

ycristned *pp.* christened 27:5.

croice(s) *n.* see **cros**.

crokes *n. pl.* hooks, grappling irons SR300, **crokys** SA307, 372.

cros *n.* Cross SR490, 615, **crosse** C671, Y672, SR3, SA478, **croice** 38:5, 193:2. **croices** *pl.* 136:6, 137:6.

crouþe *n.* fiddle 169:5[n].

crownes *n. pl.* crowns (top of the head) C231, 494, **crownys** Y226, 537, **crounes** 46:1.

cummandement(t)ys *n. pl.* (ten) commandments SA202, 668.

cunsel(l) *n.* see **conseil** *n.*

cuntre *n.* country, land 30:2, Y121, 647, SA617, 645, **cuntray** 21:2, **contre** C39, Y35, SA40, 55, **contree** SR40, **contreye** C641; ~ region Y298, 561, SA585, 592, 593, **cuntray** 113:5, **cuntere** Y209, **contre** SR601, SA623, **contree** SR594, etc., **contreye** C311, **countre** C125, 216, **cowntre** C516.

curates *n. pl.* curates SR467, **curetys** SA388.

cursyde *ppl. adj.* cursed SA142.

cut *pa. t. pl.* cut SR183. **cuttyng(e)** *pr. p.* SA190, SR437, **kittyng** SR183. ~ *pp.* SR185.

cuttyng *n.* that which has been cut off SR186. **cuttyngys** *pl.* ornamental slashes in the cloth of garments SA173.

daggis *n. pl.* ornamental divisions made by slashing the lower edge of a garment SR389. Cf. **iagges**.

day *n.* day 14:4, etc., C73, etc., Y276, etc., SR23, etc., SA434, etc., **daye** Y299, **dai** SR200; ~ = reign 29:1; lifetime C555, Y585; in (vp)on a ~ 31:1, C51, Y46 one day; (after neg.) in ner ~ ne nyght = (not) at any time C84, in ~ nor nygth Y79; in boþe ny3th and ~ = all the time C171, Y143, (ditto) **daye** Y166; in to þis ich ~ = until today 10:6. **days** *pl.* 38:1, **dayes** C183, 663, Y176, 666. *gen.* C185, Y178. See **dome, ending-day, Ester, fest, Holyrode**.

dayneth *pr. 2 sg.* disdains SR56[n].

daynyng *pr. p.* condescending SR679.

dayng *n.* dawning, daybreak SR23.

daunce *n.* dance 56:5, C282, **dawns** Y275.

de *pron.* see **þou**.

ded *adj.* dead 187:4, Y658, **dede** C279, etc., Y272, 619, SR110, 421, SA113, 429. **dede** as *n. pl. gen.* dead people's SA287, **dedis** SR276. See **deþ**.

dede *n.* deed 13:2, SR272, etc., SA142, etc. **dedes** *pl.* 155:4, SR531, SA345, 635, **dedis** SR519, etc., **dedys** SA514, etc. See **almes, indede, misdede**.

dedli *adj.* deadly, mortal (sin) 56:3, 187:1, **dedeli** 1:3, 100:3, **dedely** SA668. *adv.* **dedly** (after v. sin) mortally SA141.

defaute *n. in* ~ *of* through the lack of SR340; *for* ~ for lack, need SR404, **defawte** SA412.

defens *n.* defence, excuse SR668.

defowled *pa. t. pl.* polluted, made dirty SR472.

degre *n.* rank, grade in Church hierarchy C492, Y535, 553, SR496, SA483; social rank SR635.

dey(e)d, deyen *pa. t. sg., v.* see **dye**.

dekys *n. gen. sg.* ditch's Y66. Cf. **diche**.

del *n. a þousand* ~ a thousand times 135:2. Cf. **haluendel, sumdel(e)**.

delay(e) *n.* delay C645, Y650.

delayn *pr. pl.* delay SR275. **delayde** *pa. t. pl.* SA286.

delycate *adj.* dainty, luxurious SA652, **dilicate** SR680.

delys *n. pl.* see **deuell**.

deliuerd *pp.* ~ *fro(m)* saved from 127:5, 139:5, **delyuerid** *owt of* SR534, **delyueryd** *owt(e) of(f)* SA289, 527.

ydelt *pp.* divided 157:1.

delue *v.* dig 172:4.

depe *adj.* deep C71, Y66, SR538, **deppe** SA530. **deppest** *sup.* 64:2.

dere *adj.* dear 57:3. *adv.* dearly 8:5, etc., C252.

derk(e) *adj.* dark C313, 110:5. Cf. **therke**.

desert *n.* wilderness 11:4, Y598.

deserued *pa. t. pl.* deserved 91:4. ~ *pp.* 16:2, **deservyde** SA232. Cf. **servid**.

desesyd *pa. t. sg.* see **disese**.

desire *n.* desire, lust SR324, **desyre** SA327.

desyre *pr. 1 sg.* desire SA51. **dessyrynge** *pr. p.* SA650.

desmay *v. intr.* become discouraged 5:3.

deþ *n.* death 86:6, **ded** 196:4. **dethis** as *gen. pron.* dead person's SR275.

dette *n.* debt SA334.

devkys *n. pl.* see **dukes**.

deueling *ppl. adj.* grovelling 65:4.

deuell *n.* devil C419, 448, **dewyll** Y495. **deuelus** *gen.* (the) Devil's C402, **dewlys** SA443; *at þe* **develys** at the home of the Devil Y413. **deueles** *pl.* C268, etc., **delys** Y335, **deuelus** C412, **deuelys** Y297, **devellis** SR355. ~ *gen. pl.* C458[n], **develys** Y505.

dever *n.* duty SR509.

deuine *adj.* see **diuine**.

deuine *v.* conjecture, guess 122:3, 142:2.

deuise *v.* conceive, imagine 93:5. **deuised** *pp.* looked attentively 45:2.

deuocion *n.* devotion, reverence, devoutness SR425, etc., **deuocioun** C60, **deuocyon** SA434, 554, **deuocyoun** C145, 676, **devociun** Y141, **devocyon** SA435, 641, **devocyun** Y54. **deuocions** *pl.* acts of worship SR431.

deuote *adj.* devout SA10, **devougte** SR10[n], **devowght** SR434.

dewrynge *prep.* see **duryng**.

diamaunce *n. pl.* diamonds 131:6[n].

diche *n.* ditch 172:4. **dyches** *gen.* C71.

dye *v.* die 97:5, C623, **deyen** Y627. **dyed** *pa. t. 3 sg.* 175:1, C16, 237, **dyede** C679, **deyd** 198:1, **deyed** Y232, 680.

dignite *n.* dignity, worthiness, rank in order of esteem 137:1, 176:6, **dygnyte** C490, 599, Y533, 609.

diȝte *v.* make 23:6. **diȝt** *pa. t. sg.* = ordered, controlled 29:2. *pp.* made 44:1; put, cast 74:4, 87:4, **dyth** treated Y319, **ydiȝt** furnished 83:6; transported 167:2.

dilectable *adj.* delightful, pleasant SR599, **dilectabyll** SA590.

dyn *n.* loud noise C258.

Dirige *n.* Matins in the Office for the Dead SR522, SA516.

dirt *n.* ordure SR231, 450, 469, **dyrtt(e)** SA263, 244.

disese *v.* molest SR705. **disesyng** *pr. p.* causing hardship, discomfort SR59. **desesyd** *pa. t. 3 sg.* SA62.

disgisyng *n.* newfangled or elaborate fashion SR387. **dysgysyngys** *pl.* SA393.

dishonour *n.* dishonour SR257.

dishonour *pr. pl.* dishonour SR255. **dyshonord** *pa. t. pl.* SA267.

dismembrid *pa. t. pl. tr.* divided limb from limb SR225, **dysmembyrde** SA238.

dyspende *v.* waste, squander SA496. **dyspendyd** *pa. t. pl.* SA419, **dispendid** spent, occupied (time) SR242.

dyspetyusly *adv.* mercilessly SA357[n].

dysplesse *v.* displease SA627. **displesyng** *ppl. adj.* SR655. **displesyde** *pa. t. pl.* SA198.

dyssese *n.* discomfort SA304.

distroyed *pa. t. pl.* destroyed SR310, **dystrevd** SA316, **distroied** SR312.

disworship *pr. pl.* dishonour SR192[n].

dyþur *adv.* see **þider**.

diuers *adj.* different, various 77:6, etc., SR65, etc., **diuerse** SR163, **dyueres** SA217, 455, 456, **dyuers** C518, Y565, SA68, **dyuerse** SA167, etc., **dyvers** SR443.

diuerslich *adv.* in various ways SR458.

diuine *adj.* divine (with *service*) SR474, **deuine** SA433, 464; as *n.* **dyuyne** divine service C569[n].

do *v.* do, act, perform 2:3, etc., C124, etc., Y165, etc., SR32, etc., SA545, 613, **doo** Y162, SA31, etc., **don** 35:2, Y590, **done** 172:6; ∼ work (shame etc.) on 50:2, 89:6, C244, *334, Y329, SR47, **don** Y325, 349; ∼ (+ *inf.*) cause (person) to ... 6:4, **doo** SA48. **doose** *pr. 3 sg.* SA63, **doþ** 153:6, **doth** C544, **dothe** SR60. ∼ *pr. pl.* 163:4, SR697, (+ *inf.*) cause to be performed 163:5, **doth** C77. ∼ *pr. subj. sg.* 48:5, 49:4, C167; (auxil. forming periphrastic *pr.*) C551, Y657; (+ *inf.*) cause (person) to ... 86:6; (+ *inf.*) cause to be performed C568. ∼ *imp. sg.* C169. **doyng** *pride pr. p.* committing the sin of pride SR697. **diddest** *pa. t. 2 sg.* SR131, 141, **dyde** SA134, 145. **ded** *pa. t. 1, 3 sg.* Y573, 618, **dede** C504, Y594, **did** SR500, **dyde** SA349, etc., **dud** SR693; **dede** worked (woe) on C410; placed C87, Y82; (*refl.*) put Y12; **dede** *on* put on 128:4; **ded** (+ *inf.*) caused to be performed Y81, 86; **dyde** *worschyppe* paid homage SA114. **dede** *pa. t. pl.* 76:2, C528, **deden** SR196, **did** SR241, etc., **dide** SR215, **dyd** SA390, **dyde** SA132, etc., **didden** SR129; **dede** worked (pain) on 68:2, **dyde** (offence) SA234. **dede** *pa. t. subj. sg.* (+ *þat*) brought it about that = caused (person) to ... 3:4. ∼ *pp.* 188:5, SR531, 630, **don** 13:2, 177:2, C277, etc., Y391, etc., SR509, **done** (*adj.* ended) C458, Y130, etc., SR147, etc., SA147, etc., **down** Y282, **ydo** 155:4, put 16:1, **ydon** 78:1. Cf. **penaunce-doyng**.

doctrine *n.* instruction, learning SR456.

doleful *adj.* sorrowful SA314, **dulful** SA307.

dome *n.* judgement, opinion 45:5, 159:4, 186:4; (day of) ∼ Day of Judgement, Doomsday SR201, etc., SA213, etc.

domesday *n.* Day of Judgement 179:5.

domyd *pa. t. 3 sg.* condemned SA660.

dominical *n.* Sunday reading 123:1[n].

domysman *n.* supreme judge, i.e. Christ on the Day of Judgement SA410, **doumsman** SR401.

donge *n.* dung SA263.

donward *adv.* face downward 69:5.

dore *n.* door 98:1, C90, etc., Y87, etc., SR706, **þore** C201[n].

dotaunce[r] *n.* doubt 15:2, 47:5.

douhti *adj.* doughty 29:5, **dowȝty** C119, **dowty** Y115.

doun *adv.* down 86:6, **down** C230, Y225, *515, SR182, etc., SA247, etc., **downe** C472, Y324, SR234, **downg** Y190; *al* ∼ from head to foot 154:6; *vp and* ∼ to and fro 141:1, 158:3, *turne ... honde vp and* **downe** = turn (one's) hand over SR160.

dowb(e)lettes *n. pl.* man's tight-fitting garment, covering body from neck to hips or thigh SR447, 446, 464, 465.

dowte *n.* fear C348.

dowte *pr. 1 sg.* fear C291.

dragons *n. pl.* dragons SR178, 353, **dragonse** SA183, **dragouns** 70:5, *dragownes** SA356.

dravyng *pr. p.* see next.

draw *v.* pull SR504, 498. **drawyng** *pr. p.* SR182, 183, tearing to pieces SR492, **dravyng** pulling SA187, **drayng** SR209, forcing SR175, **drawynge** SA180. **drow** *pa. t. 1 sg.* withdrew SR571. **drewe** *pa. t. pl.* dragged C403, forced C412, pulled SA223, **drow** SR213[n]. **draw** *pp.* ∼ *on* put on (clothes) SR464.

drede *n.* fear, terror 51:4, 53:1, C559, Y589, SR584, SA563, 577.

drede *v.* (*refl.*) dread, fear, be afraid 120:3. ∼ *imp. sg.* SR703. **dredyng** SR27. ∼ *pa. t. 1 sg.* SA90. **drad** *pa. t. 3 sg.* 104:1, 125:6. **dred** *pp.* SR89, **dredde** SA26.

dreynynge *pr. p.* draining, squeezing SA185[n].

dreynt *pp.* submerged, drenched 94:1.

dreri *adj.* doleful 91:3.
driȝt *n.* Lord 60:3.
drinkes *n.* *pl.* drinks SR680, **drynkys** SA652.
drof *pa. t. 3 sg.* drove 174:6. ⁓ *pa. t. pl.* 54:3. **dryuen** *pp.* C355.
dronknesse *n.* drunkenness SR242.
dueling *vbl. n.* delay 20:3.
duelle *v.* wait, remain, delay 41:5, 188:3, **dwell** Y164, etc., **dwelle** C73, etc., **dwellyn** Y68. **dwelle** *pr. 3 sg. subj.* C75. **dwellyng(e)** *pr. p.* SA645, SR674. **dwelled** *pa. t. 3 sg.* C183, 663, lived C12, **dwellid** SR675, **dwellyd** Y8, 594, 605, remained Y176, 667.
dukes *n. pl.* dukes C500, **devkys** Y543.
dulful *adj.* see **doleful** *adj.*
duryng *prep.* in ⁓ the will(-ing) of God = for as long as God wills SR227, etc., **during** SR247, **durynge** SA460, **dewrynge** SA268.
dwell(e), -ed, -id, -yd, -yn, -yng(e) see **duelle** *v.*
dyþur *adv.* see **þider** *adv.*

eche *adj.* every, each Y424, etc., SA308; *on* ⁓ *half* all around C258; *on* ⁓ *a syde* on every side C407. ⁓ *pron.* each one Y551. Cf. **ich** *adj.*[1].
edder(ys), eddyrs(e) *n.* see **adder**.
eder *adj.* (*pron.*) see **ether**.
eene *n. pl.* see **eiȝen**.
eese *n.* see **ese** *n.*
eft(e) *adv.* again 33:6, C552, SA620.
eftesone *adv.* repeatedly SR397; **eftsunne** afterwards Y283, **efteson** C290.
egge *n.* edge 125:5.
eglentere *n.* briar rose 147:4.
eiȝen *n. pl.* eyes 114:4, 159:1, **eene** SA323, 329, **eyne** SA222, etc., **yen** SR206, etc,, **yne** SA221.
ey(e)r(e) *n.* see **aire**.
eke *adv.* also 21:6, 53:6.
elbowe *n.* elbow SR91, SA93. **elbowis** *pl.* SR585.
eldes(t) *adj. sup.* see **old(e)**.
elles *adv.* otherwise 4:4, etc., C100, **ellys** Y97, SA512, **els** SR517.

elleswhere *adv.* elsewhere C350, 562.
eme *n.* uncle SR420, SA428.
emperour(e)s *n. pl.* emperors C499, SR135, **emperowres** SA139, **emprorys** Y542.
emperyce *n.* empress SA650, **emprise** SR678.
encrese *v.* see **increyse**.
ende *n.* end 23:1, etc., C71, etc., Y66, etc., **end** Y504, **ȝend** Y375. **endys** *pl.* Y464.
ending *n.* end 54:6.
ending-day *n.* day of death 112:3.
endure *v.* endure, last SR159, 363, **indewre** SA163. **endurys** *pr. 3 sg.* SA241. **enduryng** *pr. p.* SR689.
engendred *pa. t. pl.* bred SR461.
eny *adj.* see **ani**.
enioyned *pa. t. 3 sg.* condemned SR689.
enmy *n.* enemy SA205.
enquestes *n. pl.* inquests SR287, **enquestys** SA298.
ensample *n.* see **exemple**.
entente *n.* heart, mind C454, **yntente** Y501; **entent** faith C573; *wyth good* ⁓ faithfully C389, (sim.) **yntent** Y438.
entre *n.* entrance 24:2, etc., C70, etc., Y65, etc., **hentre** Y92.
entred *pa. t. 1 sg.* entered SR6, **enterde** SA7.
entring *n.* entrance 12:3.
er *adv.* before 96:3, etc., **ere** 115:4. *prep.* ⁓ *þen* 128:6, **ar** *þan* 103:3. *conj.* ⁓ 159:6, 167:2, C656, SR150, 657, **ar** 109:2, 166:2, Y661. See also **her(e)**.
er *pr. pl.* see **ar**.
erbery *n.* garden plants (herbs collectively) Y516.
erbers *n. pl.* arbours 147:1.
erbes *n. pl.* plants 148:1.
erchebischopes *n. pl.* see **archebysshop**.
ercys *n. pl.* see **arses**.
erdely *adj.* see **erþely**.
ere see **her(e** *adv.*
eres *n. pl.* ears SR188, **erys** SA193.
erles *n. pl.* earls C501.

erly *adv.* ᵔ *or late* sooner or later C563; **arliche** *and late* at all times 22:2.

ermytes *n. pl.* hermits C495, **ermytys** Y538.

erþe *n.* earth (mod. uses) 9:5, etc., C70, etc., **erth** Y317, 628, **erthe** Y65, 376, SR56, etc., SA59, etc.

erþely *adj.* earthly 144:4, **erþly** C577, **erþelich(e)** 44:2, 184:5, **erdely** C475, **ertely** Y593.

ese *n.* idleness, sloth SR670, **eese** SA651, **esee** SA641.

ese *v.* (*refl.*) rest, refresh oneself C411.

esement *n.* the advantage, convenience SR499, SA486.

esy *adj.* slothful SR678.

est *adj.* east 23:1.

estate *n.* rank SA484, **astate** SR496; **astatte** means SA333.

Ester day *n.* Easter Day SA8.

ete *v.* eat SA467. **etynge** *pr. p.* SA357. ᵔ *pa. t. 3 sg.* Y573, 595. ᵔ *pa. t. pl.* 101:6, C330, 579.

ether *adj.* (*pron.*) each (of two persons) SR126, **eder** SA129; ᵔ *odere* each other SA141, **other** *otheir* SR137.

euen *adv.* straight, directly 39:3, 39:6, **evyn** SR593. See **hold**.

*euen *n.* see **amorow**.

euer *adv.* (1) always Y445, SA257, **euur** C95, **ever** SR291, **evir** SR697; ᵔ constantly, all the time 78:5, 81:2, SA531; ᵔ perpetually, for ever 164:5, Y247, 491, 683, **euur** C312, etc.; ᵔ *anon* continually Y379, 487; ᵔ *þe ... þe* (with comparatives) in proportion as ... so 111:1. (2) ᵔ at any time, ever 175:2, 181:2, Y357, SA535, etc., **euur** C260, **ever** SR441, etc.; ᵔ at all times SA205. See **ay** *adv.*, **pasce** *n.*, **what** *adj.*, **who** *pron.*

euerych *adj.* every SR194, 301, (as *pron.*) in **euerich** *com til oþer* = (they all) came towards each other 153:3; **euery** every C58, etc., Y215, etc., SR91, etc., SA434, etc., **euury** C191, etc., **every** SR91, **heuery** Y53.

euerychon *pron.* (*quasi-adj.*) every one (of them) C359, Y578, 645, **euerichon** 27:4, **eueryschon** Y294, **euurychone** C302.

everlestyng *adj.* everlasting SR703.

euermo *adv.* for ever, always 4:2, 174:5.

euermore *adv.* for ever, always 49:6, etc., Y243, etc., SR200, **euurmore** C251, etc., **evermore** SR363, 690.

euetes *n. pl.* newts 71:2.

evil *adj.* evil, bad SR17, 704, **evyl** SA108, **evyll** SA15, etc., **evylle** SA41, **euyll** SA45, **evel** SR14, etc., **evell** SR109, poor, unsatisfactory SR118; **evel** as *n.* evil (things) SR359, **evyl** SA361, **euyll** = punishment C346. *adv.* **evel** miserably SR41(2), 114.

evyn-cristen *n. pl.* fellow Christians SA297, **evyn-crysten** SA361, 366.

Exaltacion *n.* ᵔ *of þe Crosse* Church Feast (of the Exaltation of the Holy Cross) observed on 14 September SR3.

examinacion *n.* examination, interrogation SR657, **examynacion** SA629, 637.

examynde *pp.* examined, questioned SA636.

executo(u)res *n. pl.* (legal) executors SA287, 286, **exccutores** SA285, **executours** SR274, 276, SA290.

exemple *n.* example SR456, **ensample** SR432, 467, **ensampell** SR383, **insampyll** SA390.

ey(e)r(e) *n.* see **aire**.

eyne *n. pl.* see **eiȝen**.

face *n.* face 166:5, etc., (with plural possessive) C331, SA427. **faces** *pl.* SR418, **facys** Y346.

fader *n.* father SR255, etc., SA340, 598; = God the Father Y685; = priest SR55, 362, 649, SA125, 508, 621. **faders** *pl.* SA338, 339, 343, = priests SA215.

fay *n.* faith 47:6ⁿ.

faile *v.* (+ *of*) lose SR705. **faylyd** *pa. t. 3 sg.* lacked Y198. **failed** *pa. t. pl.* slackened SR253; **failidden**

failed (to support) SR543, **faylyde** SA536.

fayn *adj.* pleased Y526, **fayne** C483; ~ (+ *of*) pleased, delighted with Y555, etc., **fayne** C510, etc. *adv.* ~ gladly, willingly C44, 140, Y39, etc., SR601, **fayne** C382, SA592, **feyn** 35:2.

fair *adj.* splendid 20:2, **fayr** C86, etc., **fayer** Y530, **fayur** Y213; ~ beautiful 147:1, **faire** SR326, etc., **fayre** SR560, etc., **fayer(e)** Y510, 564; ~ good 156:1; **faire** fine SR34, 604, **fayr(e)** SA595, C485, **fayer** Y528, **feir** 10:2, **ffayre** SA34; **fayr** courteous C163, **fayer** Y158; **faire** (as term of address) SR333, 334, **fayre** SA340, 341. **fairer** *comp.* 130:2, 136:5. **fairest** *sup.* SR596, **fayryst** SA586.

fair *adv.* gently, courteously 124:6, **fayr(e)** C195, 509, 546, **fayer(e)** Y577, 554, 634.

fayrnesse *n.* beauty C516.

fall *v.* fall Y497, SA295, **falle** 55:2, 86:6, collapse 52:4, befall C233, **falle** *by* fall off C449. **falleþ** *pr. 3 sg.* 123:4. **fallys** *pr. pl.* SA299. **fall(e)** *pr. 1 sg. subj.* C435, Y482. **falle** *pr. 2 sg. subj.* 118:5. **fallyng** *pr. p.* SR284, etc. **fel** *pa. t. 1, 3 sg.* SR585, 7:5, 183:3, **fell** SA578, C121, etc., Y117, 515, **felle** SA264. ~ *pa. t. pl.* SA463, **fel(l)** SA477, 334, **fellen** SR618, **fillyn** SR327. **yfalle** *pp.* 119:1.

fallyng(e) *vbl. n.* falling, *in the/þat* ~ as he fell SA477, SR489.

fals *adj.* false, deceitful 82:5, 102:5, SA297, **false** C398, SR286, SA201, etc., pretended SA434.

falslich *adv.* improperly SR501, **falssely** SA489.

fande *pa. t. 1 sg.* see **finde** *v.*

fardyr *adv.* see **forþer**.

fare *adv.* see **fer** *adv.*

fare *v.* fare (well) SR32, SA31. **fore** *pa. t. 3 sg.* behaved (fig., burned) 105:6. Cf. **ferde**.

faryd *pa. t. 3 sg.* see **ferde**.

farthermore *adv.* (+ comp.) ~ ... *þe better* the farther ... the better

SA593, *þe* **ferthermore** SA594.

fast *adv.* swiftly 84:6, Y392, SR572, 602, SA593, **faste** C215, 394, Y402, 443; ~ firmly, securely 110:3, Y315, 317, SA353, **faste** C328; hard (freezing) C318; earnestly C46, 639; ~ *by* close by SR33, SA31; *as* ~ *as* as soon as, immediately SA566.

faste *v.* fast C132, Y128.

fasting *vbl. n.* fasting 5:5, 38:2, **fast-yng** Y177, SR525, SA519.

fatys *n. pl.* vats, (bath-)tubs Y405[n].

fawe *adj.* (+ *of*) pleased (with) 97:3.

fawte *n.* lack, want SR270, *in* **faute** *of* for lack of SA497.

febyll *adj.* feeble Y344.

fechen *v.* fetch 54:5, **fecche** C586. **fyttyn** *pr. t. pl.* Y608. **fettyn** *pa. t. pl.* Y326. **fechyde** *pp.* SA279.

fed(d)(e) *pp.* see **fet** *pr. t. 3 sg.*

feere *n.* see **fere** *n.*[1].

feese *n. pl.* fees SA299[n].

feght(t)ys *pr. t. pl.* see **fiȝt** *v.*

feyle *n.* failure, *wiþouten* ~ certainly 59:1.

feyn *adv.* see **fayn**.

feynt *adj.* faint 94:2.

feir *adj.* see **fair**.

fel *n.* see **flesche**.

felawes *n. pl.* companions, comrades 57:6, etc., **felowys** Y449.

feld *n.* field 40:3, etc., **felde** C319, etc., **fylde** Y336, etc., **fyuld** Y306.

fele *adj.* many 8:2, C13, etc., **felle** Y9, 574.

fele *v.* feel C605. **felle** *pr. 1 sg.* Y168. **felyng** *pr. p.* SR293. **feld** *pa. t. 1, 3 sg.* SR441, 577, 125:5, **felde** SA453, C611, **felyde** SA571, **felte** C388, 441, Y304, 437, **felth** Y488. **felde** *pa. t. pl.* SA162, **felden** SR158.

fellawered *n.* body of companions 51:1. Cf. **ferrede**.

felonie *n.* wickedness 2:4.

feloschyppe *n. in* ~ in company (together) SA474.

felowde *pa. t. 1 sg.* see **folowyng** *pr. p.*

felowys *n. pl.* see **felawes**.

felthe *n.* see **filthe**.

fen *n.* dung SR230[n], 252.

fende *n.* fiend, devil 55:1, etc., SA185, the Devil SA205; **fynd** Y466. **fendes** *gen.* 6:3. **fendes** *pl.* 48:2, etc., C293, etc., SR175, etc., SA633, **fendis** SR232, etc., **fendys** SR542, SA180, etc., **fyndys** Y266, etc.. **fendes** *gen. pl.* 61:5, 125:2, 139:5, SR257, **fendys** SA267, 460, **fyndys** Y643.

fer *adv.* far 110:5, SR154, **ferre** C365; *so* **fare** = to so great a degree 133:4; ∼ *and neiȝe* = widely 129:4, 183:4.

fer *n.* see **fire**.

ferde *pa. t. 3 sg.* happened C263, **faryd** Y256, (indef.) = stretched across (of a bridge) Y465, ∼ C418, *wyth hem* ∼ = surrounded, accompanied them C507.

ferder *adv.* see **forþer**.

ferdfull *adj.* see **fer(e)ful**.

fere *n.*[1] companion Y271. ∼ *pl.* 80:5, 155:6, **feere** C398.

fere *n.*[2] company, *yn* ∼ together Y449.

fere *v. tr.* frighten C349. **ferde** *pp. intr. (adj.)* afraid SA96. Cf. **aferd**.

fer(e)ful *adj.* fearsome, terrifying SR88, 18, **ferdfull** SA2.

ferrede *n.* company, crowd 53:2. Cf. **fellawered**.

ferþ *num. adj. ord.* fourth 76:5, 151:4, **fort** SA259.

ferther *adj.* far, more distant SR558. See **forþer** *adv.*

ferthermore *adv.* see **farthermore**.

fest *n.* feast 186:1, Church Feast(-day) SR2, **feste-day** C58, *heuery heyr* **feste** at every major feast-day Y53.

fet *pr. 3 sg.* feeds 185:2. **fed** *pp.* SR463, **fed(d)e** SR680, SA652.

feþerfoy *n.* feverfew 147:4[n].

fier(e), fyer(e) *n.* see **fire**.

fiften *num. adj.* fifteen 38:1, **fyftene** C183, etc., Y176, 639; as *n.* C226.

fiften *num. adj. card.* used as *ord.* fifteenth 195:4.

fifti *num. adj.* fifty 53:3.

fiȝt *v.* fight 135:5. **feght(t)ys** SA667, 441.

fillyng *pr. p.* filling SR206, etc. **fylled** *pa. t. pl.* C271, **fyllyd(e)** SA226, 235, 222, **filt** SR221. **yfilt** ... *of pp.* filled with 99:3.

fillyng *vbl. n.* being filled SR246.

filthe *n.* filth SR233, 247, **fylthe** SR231, SA246, **felthe** SR234. **fylthys** *pl.* SA245, **filthes** obscenities, ill behaviour SR245.

finde *v.* find 40:2, **fynd** Y569, SR38, **fynde** C524, SR33, SA32. ∼ *pr. 1 sg.* 192:1. **fande** *pa. t. 1 sg.* SA67, **fond** SR64. **fond** *pa. t. 3 sg.* 18:2, etc., Y122, etc., **fonde** C38, etc. **yfounde** *pp.* 41:1, etc.

fine *adj.* see **amour** *n.*

fynger *n.* finger SR569, SA562. **fingers** *pl.* SR209, etc., **fyngers** SA223, 401, **fyngyrs** SA649.

fyngermele *adv. bi .ij.* ∼ (to the depth of) two fingers' width SR176.

fire *adj.* fiery SR211, **fyre** SA186.

fire *n.* fire SR155, etc., **fyr** C392, SA158, **fyre** C293, 301, SA156, etc., **fier(e)** SR304, etc., SR154, etc., **fyer(e)** Y288, 364, 378, **fer(e)** 193:5, 59:6, 93:2[n], etc. **fires** *pl.* SR347, 351, **fyres** SA351, 354. See **afyre** *adv.*

fire-brondes *n. pl.* fire-brands SR342, 386, **fire-brondys** SR372, **fyre-brondys** SA247, 376, **fyre-brandes** SA348, **fyre-brongdys** SA392. Cf. **brond**.

firmament *n.* heavens, sphere of the fixed stars 52:5, 92:5.

first *adj.* first 68:1, SR12, 568, **fyrst** SA12, 562.

first *adv.* first, in the first place SR26, etc., **fyrst** C187, Y223, SA25, 179, **fyrste** C5, etc., Y29, etc., **furste** C228.

fyttyn *pr. t. pl.* see **fecchen**.

fiþel *n.* a bowed stringed instrument (fiddle, violin) 142:5, 169:5.

fyuld *n.* see **feld**.

fiue *num. adj.* five 196:5.

flame *n.* flame Y395, **flaumbe** 183:2, **flaumme** 105:2[n].

fle *v.*[1] flee C267, **flyen** Y260. ∼ *imp. sg.* 124:4. **fled(d)yn** *pa. t. pl.* Y443, 294, 332.

fle *v.*[2] fly 190:1. **fleiȝe** *pa. t. 3 sg.*
183:5. **flewe** *pa. t. pl.* SA85,
flowe 189:5, **flowen** C302, etc.
flowe *pp.* C274.
flesh *n.* (man's dead) flesh C624,
flessh (living) flesh SR176, etc.,
fleche SA181, **flesche** SA187;
flesche *and fel* flesh and skin, i.e.
the whole body 54:4.
flesshly *adj.* carnal, sensual SR426;
fleschely mortal SA75, 81.
flood(e) *n.* river C424, Y471.
flour *n.* flower 197:2. **flour(r)es** *n.*
pl. C473, 147:1, **flowres** C408,
517, **flowerys** Y564, *****flowyrys**
Y516.
fode *n.* food C603, Y611. See **soule**
n.
folde *suff.* used absolutely in *a thows-*
ande more ⁓ a thousand more
times SA572[n]. Cf. **hundre-fold,**
þousandfold.
fole *n.* fool C142. **foles** *pl.* 141:5,
*****follys** Y138.
folk *n.* people 6:6, 19:5, **folke** Y45;
(construed as pl.) ⁓ 27:1, SR84,
241, **folke** C7, etc., Y35, etc.
folly *n.* folly, foolishness Y117, **foly**
143:3, SA398, 670. **folies** *pl.* 4:6,
foliis 13:6.
folowyng *pr. p.* following SR62. **fol-**
owde *pa. t. 1 sg.* SA64, 584,
folowid SR593, 661, **felowde**
SA633.
fond(e) *v.* test 61:6, C308.
fonston *n.* font 27:5.
for *conj.* because 24:4, 91:4, etc.,
C206, 267, etc., Y106, 138, etc.,
SR383, 425, etc., SA131, 238,
etc., **ffor** SR129, 194, etc., SA16,
87, etc.
for *prep.* for (mod. uses) 7:4, etc.,
C15, etc., Y186, etc., SR50, etc.,
SA107, etc., **fore** Y259, 313; ⁓ *no*
by (means of) any 109:4, 5, 6; ⁓
in order that C449; on account of
Y14, 399; *þe* **fore** on your account
49:3; *adv.* ⁓ before (time) SR276;
⁓ *as moch(e) as* seeing that SR477,
500, ⁓ *as myche as* SA466. See **no**
and cf. **forsoþe, þerfor, wher-**
fore.

forbede *pr. 3 sg. subj.* in *God* ⁓ *it*
God forbid it SR517; (used *absol.*
as exclamation) *God* ⁓ SA511.
forbrent *pa. t. 3 sg.* burned up 85:5,
106:2. ⁓ *pp.* 113:6, 128:6.
forde *adv.* see **forþ.**
fore *pa. t. 3 sg.* see **fare** *v.*
forest *n.* forest Y561.
foreto *inf. particle* see **forto.**
forgat *pa. t. 1, 3 sg.* forget SA536,
forȝate C386, **forȝete** lost, forsook Y596. **forȝete(n)** *pp.* forgotten C481, Y524, **forȝette** Y435,
forȝete neglected SR148, **for-**
getyn SA152.
forgyff, forȝiue see **foryeven.**
forȝeuenes(se) *n.* forgiveness C104,
178, 550, Y101, 171.
forhede *n.* forehead SR27, 83, SA13,
27, 84, **forehede** SR12.
forlast *pr. 2 sg.* (fut. sense) lose 39:5.
forlore *pp.* 49:6, 94:3, **forlorn**
112:2, 126:5, 175:6.
forlete *pa. t. pl.* abandoned, forsook
C580.
forneise *n.* furnace 78:1.
forsayde *ppl. adj.* aforesaid SA354.
forsake *v.* give up, refrain from 34:5,
SR690, SA661. ⁓ *pr. 1 sg.* refuse,
reject 59:2; shun SR687, SA659.
forsoke *pa. t. 3 sg.* refused
110:1; abandoned SR691, SA662.
forsakyn *pa. t. pl.* gave up
SR641. **forsaken** *pp.* refused 88:1.
forsoþe *adv.* in truth 8:4, 66:4, C19,
etc., **forsothe** SA118, **forsowthe**
SA135, 560; ⁓ *ywis* truly indeed
(tag) 5:2, 122:4, etc., ⁓ *to say* to
tell the truth (and sim., tags) 23:2,
32:5, etc., 151:2.
fort *num. adj. ord.* see **ferþ.**
forto *conj.* until SR198, 362, 691, ⁓
þat SR397, 661.
forto *inf. particle* 20:6, etc., C232,
etc., Y149, etc., SR325, etc.,
SA50; in order to 7:2, etc., C133,
514, Y129, 497, SR356, 398, etc.,
SA200, 640.
forþ *adv.* out, on, forward, away 39:3,
etc., C364, **forþe** SR107, **forth**
C186, etc., Y16, etc., SR202, etc.,
forthe Y326, SR87, etc., SA89,
etc., **forde** C353; **forth** hence-

forth C651; ∼ ... *wiþalle* straightaway 96:1.

forþer *adv.* farther 64:5, 76:1, etc., **furþur** C209, **fardyr** SA368, **ferder** Y202, 372, etc.; *þe* **ferther** ... *the* (+ comp.) the farther ... the SR603.

forþermore *adv.* moreover 130:1, *forþermar* still farther 75:2.

forþeward *adv.* presently 134:6.

foryeven *v.* forgive SR240. **forgyff** *imp. sg.* SA544. **forȝiue** *pp.* 14:5, **foryeve** SR241.

fot *n.* foot 125:4, **fote** C328, Y486, 489, SR526, **foote** C439, 441, 442, **fute** Y315; **fote** foot-measure C372, Y423; foot (of a ladder) SR575, SA568. **fet** *n. pl.* 60:1, 70:1, etc., **fete** C355, Y328.

foule *adj.* foul, evil, dirty 54:2, 67:2, etc., **fowle** C311, Y298, SR36, 354, 481, SA34, 185, etc., **fowlle** Y602.

foule *adv.* foully 85:3, **fowle** C409, SR450. **fouler** *comp.* 116:4.

foules *n. gen.* bird's 169:4. ∼ *pl.* 108:1, 145:3. ∼ *gen.* 146:1, **foulen** 169:1.

foure *num. adj.* four 149:5, **fowr** C583.

fourme *n.* form 184:1.

fowynge *n.* sewage SA244[n].

fowndyng *vbl. n.* (trial by) temptation C241. Cf. **fond(e)** *v.*

fram *prep.* from 17:5, 52:5, etc., **from** 139:5, *Y497, SR269, 379, SA308.

frende *n.* friend 36:1, C567, SA206. **frendes** *pl.* 163:4, SR70, etc., SA81, **frendys** SA75, 514.

freres *n. pl.* friars C494, SA414, **fryerys** Y537; **frere** *Prechours* Friars Preachers, Dominicans 137:5; **frere** *Menours* Friars Minor, Franciscans 138:1; **frere** ... *Jacobins* Dominican friars 138:1; **frere** *Carmes* Carmelite friars 138:2; **frere** *Austines* Augustinian friars 138:2.

frese *pa. t. 3 sg.* froze C318.

frete *pa. t. pl.* ate 71:3.

Friday *n.* Friday SR2, 8.

fryuth *n.* see **frut(e)**.

fro *prep.* from 127:5, C180, etc., Y14, etc., SR84, etc., SA17, etc., **froo** SA57; ∼ (postponed) 74:6, etc., C82, etc., Y238, 250, SR184, 581, **froo** C596, Y77, 608.

from *prep.* see **fram**.

frut(e) *n.* fruit (lit. and fig.) Y567, 568, SR466, **fruyte** C522, **frwyte** C523, 527, **fryuth** Y572. **frutys** *pl.* Y574, **frwytes** C529.

ful *adj.* full (with *of*), 76:6, 98:4, etc., SR169, 221, etc., SA369, 370, etc., **full** C1, 299, etc., Y244, 564, etc., SR367, SA174, 246, etc.; ∼ complete SR683, 684, SA656, **full** SA502, 654; ∼ *a feld* a field full 65:1.

ful *adv.* (intensive modifying *adj.* or *adv.*) completely, very 11:3, 44:1, etc., SR651, 694, 698, SA90, 589, etc., **full** C10, 31, etc., Y54, 86, etc., SR372, SA448.

fulfil *v.* perform SR637, **fulfyll** Y136, SA608. **fulfillyn** *pr. t. pl.* SR275. **fulfylle** *pr. subj. sg.* C238, **fullfyll** Y233. **fulfild** *pp.* 158:5, (+ *of*) filled up with 2:4.

gaffe *pa. t. sg.* and *pl.* see **gefeth**.

gay *adj.* gay, bright SR167, 172, 174, 188, SA194, 330, **gaye** SA171, 177.

gain *adj.* straight, direct (way) 39:2.

gain *n.* see **gette** *v.*

game *n.* amusement, delight 21:5, Y358, **gamen** 168:3, C340.

gan *pa. t. 3 sg.* began (with *to* and *inf.*) 51:5, 52:2. etc.; (with plain *inf.*) 5:3, 27:2, etc., **gane** Y679; (*refl.*) *him* ∼ 31:3, 125:1, (+ *to*) 120:3; (with *forto* and *inf.*) Y222; (with plain *inf.* forming *pa. t.*) 38:6, 129:2, etc., C210, Y556; (+ *to*) 55:2; (*refl.*) 8:2, **gon** C127.

gan *pl.* began (with *to* and *inf.*) 88:5, Y186, **gun** 66:1, 73:3, etc.; (with plain *inf.*) Y291, 297, 390, **gun** 59:6, 84:6, 146:6. Cf. **begynne**.

gare *v.* make, cause (with *inf.*) SA406. **gartt** *pa. t. 3 sg.* SA485.

gate *n.*[1] gate 23:5, 43:3, etc., Y514, 527, 662. **gates** *pl.* 133:4, 134:1,

gatys Y402, 412. See **helle-**$\sim$, **heuen-**$\sim$, and cf. **3ate**.
gate *n.*[2] way, path 39:2.
gauelers *n. pl.* usurers 102:1.
gefeth *pr. 3 sg.* gives SR147. ***gyf** *pr. subj. sg.* SA602. **gyfe** *imp. sg.* SA544, **gyff** SA106. **gaffe** *pa. t. 2, 3 sg.* SA582, 152, **geffe** Y148. **gaffe** *pa. t. pl.* SA317. **gave** *pp.* SA486^n, **geve** SR383, **gevyn** SA305, **gyffyn** SA389. Cf. **3eue**.
gent *adj.* elegant, beautiful 132:3.
gentyll *adj.* noble Y245, 293, 331.
gentylly *adv.* courteously SA598.
gernyd *pa. t. pl.* see **grenne**.
gette *v.* get, obtain Y101, 171, **gete** C148, **gett** SA671. **gett** *pr. 3 sg.* in *alle gett þe no gain* (it) all profits you nothing 55:6. **gat(t)** *pa. t. 1 sg.* begot SA340, SR333. **gast** *pa. t. 2 sg.* begot SR337, **gatt** SA343. **get** *pa. t. 3 sg.* got Y80, **gatte** C85, **gat** ... *no gain* profited nothing 189:1. **geten** *pp.* begotten SR127, **geton** SA130, obtained SA491, **getton** SA280, **goten** SR501, 505, SA489, **gotyn** SA499.
geve, -yn *pp.* see **gefeth**.
gy *v.* guide, lead 142:4.
gyf(e), gyff, -yn *pr. subj. sg., imp. sg., pp.* see **gefeth**.
gyle *n.* guile, treachery C340.
gilt *n.* guilt SR297, **gylte** SA658.
gilt *pp.* wronged, sinned against SR241, **gylte** committed offence SA638^n.
gilti *adj.* guilty SR686.
gyltyde *ppl. adj.* overlaid with gold SA170.
giltles *adj.* innocent SR313.
***gyngel** *n.* ornament that jingles SR180, **gyngyll** SA185. **gyngeles** *pl.* SR169^n, **gyngyles** SA174, **gyngyllys** SA187.
ginne *n.* trick, stratagem 109:6.
girdels *n. pl.* belts, girdles SR167, 175, **girdelles** SR676, **gyrdyls** SA171, **gyrdyllys** SA174, 179, 648.
gyse *n.* manner, fashion Y218.
glad *adj.* cheerful, happy C55, 212, Y205, 407, 409, SR107, **gladde**

C661, SR561, **glade** SA110, 553.
gladder *comp.* C446, SA595, (þe) **glader** Y493.
gladly *adv.* gladly SR52, SA54.
gladnes(se) *n.* gladness SR567, SA559.
glasse *n.* glass C414, 465, Y461.
gle *n.* pleasure, mirth, in $\sim$ *and game* 21:5, *gamen and* $\sim$ 168:3; (skill in) music making, minstrelsy 145:4.
gleme *n.* ray of (spiritual) light C607, Y615.
glyddyr *adj.* slippery Y461^n.
glyde *v.* glide, pass C611.
glori(e) *n.* glory 20:4, 152:5, 179:6, 165:2.
glori(o)us *adj.* glorious SR547, SA539.
glotoni *n.* gluttony 71:4, **gloteny** SR242.
glotoun *n.* glutton 74:3.
glowand *pr. p.* glowing 79:2, **gloweand** 70:2, 101:5, **glowyng** C329, 354, **gloynge** SA260.
gnawyng(e) *pr. p.* gnawing SA357, SR354, **nowynge** SA184.
go *v.* go, walk 39:2, 41:4, etc., C42, 66, etc., Y134, 646, SR67, 238, etc., SA78, 360, etc., **goo** C548, Y61, 93, etc., SA71, 72, 75, **gan** 75:2, **gon** 40:1, 64:5, etc., C639, Y37, 145, etc., **gone** C137, Y282, 297. **gos** *pr. 2. sg.* 49:5, **goste** Y402. **goþ** *pr. 3 sg.* 41:2, **goth** C214, goes on Y72^n. $\sim$ *pr. subj. sg.* 103:3, C605, Y30, **goo** Y613, SR657. $\sim$ *pl.* C34. **go(o)** *imp. pl.* SA164, SR160. **goyng(e)** *pr. p.* SA251, SR484. $\sim$ *pp.* 172:2, SR485, **goo** C456, **gon** C572, Y238, SA253, 474, **gone** C553, SR537, **ago** 48:1, **ygo** 126:2, **ygon** 39:4.
God *n.* God 2:2, etc., C1, etc., Y22, etc., SR29, etc., SA30, etc., **Gode** SA5, 28, etc. **God** *gen.* in $\sim$ *service* SA651, in $\sim$ *sun* Christ Y244, **Goddes** C28, etc., SR6, etc., SA444, **Goddis** SR101, etc., SA232, **Goddys** Y27, etc., SA6, etc., **Goddus** C200, 387, **Godes** 7:2, etc., **Godys** Y24. **God** *dat.* in

bitau3t him $\sim$ 43:2, 51:2, (sim.) C254.

gode *adj.* good 15:2, etc., C23, etc., **good** C389, etc., Y54, etc., SR14, etc., **goode** C676, SR108, **gud** SA14, etc., **gude** SA514; $\sim$ = firm (faith) 15:1, etc.; = strong (wall) 23:4, **goode** (wind) C423; **good** long (while and sim.) C339, Y675, SR485, 644; *wyth* **good** *chyre* cheerfully Y50. See **better** *adj. comp.*

gode *n.* good (deed(s)) 76:2, good (things) 182:4; *yn all* $\sim$ = for your benefit C238, (sim.) **goode** Y233; *it was for non* $\sim$ it was not for any good purpose 90:5; **good(e)** welfare, benefit C15, Y11; **gud** money SA583. **godes** *pl.* (worldly) goods SR264, 505, **goodes** SR259, etc., **gowdys** SA270, **guddys** SA280, etc., **gudys** SA287, etc., **gude** SA412. See **ayled**.

godenisse *n. do* = live righteously 163:4, **goodnesse** goodness SR532, 630.

godspelle *n.* (the) Gospel(s) 9:4, **gospell** Y49. **gospellus** *pl.* C54.

goinfainoun *n.* see **gonfanoun**.

gold *n.* gold 136:4, etc., SR166, etc., **golde** SA171, 177, *red(e)* $\sim$ gold alloyed with copper 129:6, 130:5, 132:5; $\sim$ *and siluer* SR282, (sim.) 86:5, SR167, 287, 502, SA293, 298, 491; *a clop of* $\sim$ a garment of cloth of gold 128:1. See **bete** *v.*

golde *adj.* $\sim$ *rynges* gold rings SA648.

goldsmiþe *n.* goldsmith 133:2ⁿ.

gonfanoun *n.* banner 38:5, **goinfainoun** 136:6, 193:2.

gonges *n. pl.* privies SR231.

goodnesse *n.* see **godenisse**.

gospell(us) *n. (pl.)* see **godspelle**.

gost(e) *n. holy* $\sim$ Holy Ghost Y685, 184:1. **gostes** *pl.* spirits C269, **gostys** Y262.

gostely *adj.* spiritual (father) SA215, **goostly** SR362, (devotions) SR431.

gouerna(u)nce *n.* behaviour, mode of living SR686, 691, SA443.

gouernyde *pp.* governed SA636, **gouerend** SR667.

gownes *n. pl.* gowns, dresses SR171, **gownys** SA176.

grace *n.* grace (of God) 6:1, 31:4, etc., C152, 306, etc., Y237, 436, etc., SR104, 552, SA7, 78, etc., **gras** 25:2.

gracious *adj.* merciful SR587.

gras *n.*[1] see **grace**.

gras(se) *n.*[2] grass C218, SR595, **gres(se)** SA586, Y211.

graunt *v.* grant C78, **grante** Y73. **graunte** *pr. subj. sg.* C242. **grante** *pl.* Y133. **graunt(e)** *imp. sg.* C137, SR103, 143:5, 198:5. **graunted** *pp.* SR144, **grantyd** SA148.

grede *v.* cry out, shout 51:5, 64:6ⁿ.

grediris *n. pl.* gridirons 79:1.

greis(e)ly(ch) *adj.* see **griselich(e)**.

grene *adj.* green 106:3, etc., C517, etc., Y562, 566.

grenne *v.* grin, grimace C296, Y291. **grenned** *pa. t. pl.* 54:2, C272, **grenyd** Y389, **gernyd** Y266ⁿ.

gresely *adv.* in a frightful manner Y401.

gret *adj.* great, large, big 11:4, etc., C60, etc., Y231, SR393, etc., **grete** 53:2, etc., C130, etc., Y126, etc., SR31, etc., **grett** SR365, SA30, etc., **grette** Y163, SR505, **greytte** SA334; $\sim$ *and smal* = every one 99:4. ***gretter** *comp.* SA551. **greettys** *sup.* SA439, **gretyste** SA534. See **periil**.

gretelich *adv.* very much, greatly SR140, **gretely** SR448, **grett(e)ly** SA51, 116, 144, SA127.

greue *v.* harm, injure 15:6, **greve** SR530, SA524. **greveth** *pr. 3 sg.* offends SR140, **grevose** SA144. **greuede** *pa. t. 3 sg.* caused pain C451, **grevyd** Y525, SA383. **greued** *pa. t. pl.* 68:3.

grinding *n.* grinding (of teeth) 66:5.

grypyng *vbl. n.* holding on SR579.

griselich(e) *adj.* horrible, ghastly (causing fear) 11:6, etc., 12:3, **grislich** SR542, **greislych** SR538, **griseli** 66:6, **grisly** SR44, **gryesely** SA357, **gryselly** SA565,

grys(s)ely SA337, 530, SA90, etc., greis(e)ly SA45, SR538, gres(e)ly SA600, SR308, etc.
groped pa. t. 3 sg. groped C208, gropyd Y201.
grounde n. = floor 99:1; (river) bottom 116:5, 150:6, grownde C412; grownd(e) ground, earth C331, SA558, Y346, SR350, 566; goþ to ∿ sets (sun) 41:2. See helle-∿.
groueling ppl. adj. grovelling, prone SR350.
groweþ pr. 3 pl. grow 148:2. growyng(e) pr. p. SA586, C521, SR595. grewe pa. t. 3 sg. C218, growyde SA587. growid pa. t. pl. SR596.
gudly adv. courteously SA597.

3a interj. yes 181:4, 3e SA158. Cf. 3ys.
3af(fe) pa. t. sg., pl. see 3eue.
3alu adj. yellow 106:3, 180:4.
3are adj. ready, prepared Y349.
3arn adv. quickly Y380[n].
3ate n. gate C468, 471, 3atte SA379, yate SR375. Cf. gate n.[1].
3e pron. 2 pl. you C349, SA53, 72, ye SR67, 339, etc.; ∿ (men in general) 24:1, 28:6, etc., ye SR708. 3ou acc., dat. 28:5, 156:1, C117, 3ow SA50, you C291, yow Y113, SR117, 342, 708, SA50, 52, etc. 3our poss. adj. 59:2, C348, yowre SR340, 708. Used as polite form to one person: 3e Y132, 133, SA125, ye SR123; 3ow Y131, yow SR124, 586, 587, 650, SA126, 579, 622; 3our C140, 3owre Y136, yor SA54, 580, yowr(e) SR587, 588.
3ede pa. t. (serving as past of go) 1, 3 sg. went 46:2, 173:4, C437, SR537, 602, 603, yede SR576, 3yd(de) Y484, 310, 3ode 136:1, C628, yode C320. 3ede pa. t. pl. 51:2, 102:4, etc., 3eden 54:1, 142:4, 3ode 100:5, C513.
3efe imp. pl. see 3eue.
3ellyng pr. p. yelling SA470, yellyng SR482.
3eme n. heed (after 'take') 120:4.
3end n. see ende.

3eon adj. that ... over there, yon SA156, 3yn yonder, those Y404.
3eondyr adv. see 3ondyr.
3ere n. year C58, SA4, yere SR3. 3er pl. 58:2, C11, 81, 3ere C583, Y7, 597, 599, SA429, 3eres (adj. follows) 197:6.
3ete adv. still, to this or that time, yet 10:6, 22:6, 3et C39, 57, etc., Y491, 3ett SA40, 69, 628, 3ette C64, 314, 3yt Y52, 98, 3yte Y609; ∿ moreover, besides 72:1, 3et Y19, 3yt Y33, 305; 3et at some future time C336, 3yt Y417; ∿ forþermar still farther 75:2. 3et conj. (after and or but) nevertheless, but C378, Y174, 3ett SA210, 644, 3yt Y96, yet SR448, 657.
3eue pr. 2 sg. subj. give C150. 3eyffe pr. 3 sg. subj. Y237. 3if pr. subj. pl. 163:5. if imp. sg. SR552. 3efe imp. pl. Y145. yavest pa. t. 2 sg. SR590. 3af pa. t. 3 sg. 9:1, 10:1, etc., C53, 153, 3affe Y48, yaf SR619. 3af pa. t. pl. C229, yoven SR432. 3if pp. 11:1, yeve SR149, yevyn 456. Cf. foryeven, gefeth.
3if conj. if 15:1, 28:6, etc., 3yf C147, 179, etc., (+ þat) C308, 345; if C561, SR16, etc., yf C247, Y242, 277, etc., SR527, SA15, etc., yff SA132; all 3yf although C597. See but.
3yldyth v. (with suff. obj. pron.) repay it, requite it Y277.
3yn adj. see 3eon.
3ynge adj. see 3ong(e).
3ys interj. yes SA511. Cf. 3a.
3yt(e) adv. see 3ete.
3ondyr adv. yonder SA156, 3eondyr SA158, yender SR153, 156, etc., yendur SR322, yonder SR263, yondyr SA160. Cf. yender adj.
3ong(e) adj. young, ∿ and olde = all of them C539, Y18, C22, (and sim.) 3ownge Y552, 3ynge Y363.

habundaunce n. see abundance.
haill n. hail SR472, hayl SA463.
hailstonis n. pl. hailstones SR471, haulstones SR452, holestones SA462.

hakyng *n.* see hawkynge.

half *adv.* half(-way) 126:2.

halfe *adj. the* ~ *wylle* half of the wheel Y376; as *n.* half C462.

halfe *n.* see eche.

hali-day *n.* Church festival day SR238, haly-dai SR242. haly-daies *pl.* SR238, haly-des SA251, holi-dais SR246.

halidom *n.* holy relic 82:4.

halle *n.* hall 40:4, etc., C220, Y213, 637.

halte *pr. 2 sg. subj.* hesitate Y402.

haluendel *n.* half (the amount of) 98:3, 122:6.

ham *pron., acc.* see hye.

hamers *n. pl.* hammers SR190, hamerys SA324, hamours SR321.

hand(e), -ys *n., -pl.* see hond.

hand-brede *n.* hand's breadth SA180.

hangyng *pr. p.* hanging SA350, 377, hyngyng SA322, honging 77:1, 84:2, hongyng SR318. hange *pa. t. pl.* SA384, henge 80:4, 81:1, hing 78:4, hynge Y365, 368, 370, hyngyn Y377. hanged *pp.* SR324, hangid SR323, hangyd(e) SA328, 326.

hant *pr. pl.* (+ suff. obj. *pron.*) see haue.

har *poss. adj.* see hye.

hard *adj.* harsh, severe 34:6, 56:2, herde SA104.

hard *adv.* tightly, fast (bound) 60:1, 88:3, 163:1.

harm(e) *n.* harm, injury SA48, 362, SR47, herme pain, suffering Y387.

harmelese *adj.* without injury C460.

harneist *ppl. adj.* furnished with silver or other metal adornments SR168[n], hernessede SA172.

harp(e) *n.* harp 142:5, 169:5.

harte *pr. 2 sg.* see art.

harte *n.* see hert.

harvest *n.* autumn SR9.

hast *n.* haste, *in* ~ quickly 93:6.

hastily *adv.* hastily 13:5.

hatere *n.* clothing C403[n].

hatte *pr. 3 sg.* is called/named C63, hath Y85[n]. hi3t *pa. t. 3 sg.* 30:1, hyte Y58. hete *pa. t. pl.* commanded 180:1.

hatter *adj. comp.* see hote *adv.*

haue *v.* have (mod. uses) 56:1, 5, etc., C80, 99, etc., Y279, 604, etc., SR344, 698, etc., SA39, 630, etc., have SR539, SA418, etc., hauen 115:2, hauyn Y227, a (*auxil.*) Y391, 397, 431, 497, 509; ~ *ioye of* enjoy SR129, (sim.) SA132; ~ *knowlage of* know SR49, (sim.) SA50; ~ *thonke of* be thanked by SR640, (sim.) SA487. haue *pr. 1 sg.* C166, 348, Y161; (with prefixed *pron.*) ichaue 47:2. has *pr. 2 sg.* 58:2, hase SA29, 610, hast 39:4, etc., C285, Y278, 279, SR31, etc., SA61, haste C277, etc., Y270, etc., hate Y580, ~ SR49. haþ *pr. 3 sg.* 43:4, 68:4, etc., hath C142, 252, 558, Y130, 287, etc., SR57, 124, 143, etc., hathe SA148, hatht C292, hase SA127, 498, 666. hathe *pr. 2 pl.* SA51. haue *pr. 1, 3 pl.* 16:2, 58:4, etc., C525, 553, etc., Y571, 609, SR218, 241, etc., SA232, 304, 606, have SR636, SA257, 391, etc., han 47:3, 63:4, etc., Y138, 584, (have as a duty, *refl.* with *inf.*) Y587, hant (with suff. obj. *pron.*) have it Y106[n], hase SA605, hath Y253. haue *pr. subj. sg.* 179:4, C248, Y284, SA46. haue *pr. subj. pl.* SA449. haue *imp. sg.* 49:1; ~ *mercy* C250, 358, 428, Y245, 293, 331, SR103, 551, SA105, 543; ~ *mynde* (*of*) remember SR547, SA539, SR98; ~ *yn mynd* Y243, (sim.) SR42, 46, SA42; ~ *yn þy þowght* C251, (sim.) Y246, SA47, 101. hauyng *pr. p.* SR373, havynge SA361. haddest *pa. t. 2 sg.* SR118, 148, 150, haddeste C548, hade SA120, 151, 154, (with suff. *pron.*) haddestow 56:4. had *pa. t. 1, 3 sg.* 17:1, 113:2, Y76, 197, etc., SR23, 82, etc., SA305, 499, etc., hadde 1:4, 11:1, etc., C23, 81, etc., SR94, 239, SA666, hade

SA96, 124, etc. **had** *pa. t. pl.*
138:6, Y255, 548, SR89, 90, etc.,
SA301, 366, 438, **hadde** 25:4,
50:4, etc., C231, 378, etc., **hade**
SA91, 92, etc., **hadden** SR402,
haddyn Y372, 454, 530, **hadyn**
Y371, 392, 418. **hade** *pa. t. subj.*
sg. would have SA146, **haddest**
SR142. **had** *pp.* SR126, 149,
hadde SA129, **hade** SA153, 440,
hadden SR194.

hautain *n.* treble (voice in music)
145:6[n].

hawkynge *n.* hawking SA435, **hakyng** SR430.

he *pron.* he 2:1, etc., C3, etc., Y10,
etc., SR60, etc., SA3, etc., **hee**
C207. **him** *acc., dat., refl.* 6:1,
etc., SR126, etc., **hym** C30, etc.,
Y14, etc., SA128, etc., (intensifier)
Y212. **his** *poss. adj.* 2:3, etc.,
SR21, etc., **hys** C5, etc., Y13,
etc., SA21, etc., **hyys** Y610; **is**
SR509, = its 151:5; **his** (as absol.
pron.) his saints 26:4; (following *n.*
(with *gen.* inflexion)) *Patrik* **is**
SR2, *chanons* **is** SR25[n], *man* **is**
SR526, *ladi* **is** SR564. Cf. **him-
self.**

hede *n.*[1] head SR26, 346, SA349,
heued 70:1. **hedes** *pl.* SR172,
183, etc., **hedeys** SA189, **hedys**
Y350, **heddys** SA91, etc.

hede *n.*[2] heed (after **take**) SR193,
630, 695, SA665.

hede *v.* take care of, guard 119:3.

heder, -yr *adv.* see **hider.**

hey *adv.* high up Y368; *boþe* ~ *and
lowe* (implying totality) = very
strongly (of wind blowing) Y305,
(sim. with) **hye** = completely,
everywhere C318. See next.

hei3e *adj.* high, tall 121:1, 145:2, etc.,
hey(e) Y374, 214, 464, **high**
SR477, 558, etc., **hye** SA466,
562, **hyghe** SA551, 632, **hy3e**
C415, 417; ~ exalted 50:1, 165:3,
198:2; ~ noble 176:6, **high**
SR136, **hyghe** SA139; **hyee**
splendid SA466; ~ loud 145:6[n];
from **hey** from (a place) high up
Y497; **hyee** *auters* High Altars
SA464. **heyr** *comp.* in *heuery*

heyr *feste* (at) every major/very
solemn Feast-day Y53[n]. **hei3e** (as
n.) *an* ~ in heaven 152:5, *on* ~
185:6; *on* **hy3e** loudly C276, *on*
hey Y269, *wiþ* **heye** 26:1.

hei3e *v.* hasten 191:4.

heyll *adj.* healthy Y397, ~ *and sound*
Y674.

heyll *interj.* hail! SA125.

held *n.* old age, in *full wyll of* ~ far
advanced in age Y678[n]. See
3ong(e).

hele *v.* save, purify C14.

hell *n.* hell Y450, 467, SR675, **helle**
3:5, etc., C118, etc., Y114, 262,
SA646, 672.

helle-gate *n.* the gate of hell 109:2.

helle-grounde *n.* the abyss of hell
64:2.

helle-peyn *n.* the pain of hell Y31.

helle-pyne *n.* the torment of hell
C35.

hell-mowth *n.* the mouth of hell
Y453.

help *n.* help 198:3, C85, SR68, etc.,
SA38, etc., **helpe** Y80, SA289,
580, **helppe** SA72.

help *v.* help 111:5, 172:5, SR95,
helpe C443, **helppe** SA97. **helpest** *pr. 2 sg.* C362, **helppyst**
Y445. **help** *imp. sg.* C300, 435,
438, **helpe** C390, Y439, 482, 485.
helpyd *pa. t. 3 sg.* SA290. **holpe**
pp. Y416, **holpen** SR462, 518,
SA458, **holpyn** SA513.

hem *pron. obj.* see **hye.**

hemselue *pron.* themselves 134:1,
hemself C143, SR243, 260, 297,
478, **hemselfe** Y139.

hende *adj.* gracious C287, **hynd(e)**
Y147, obedient Y280.

henge *pa. t. pl.* see **hangyng.**

hennes *adv.* hence (motion) 103:3,
159:6, **hens(e)** SA154, SR150.

hentyd *pa. t. pl.* seized Y432. **hent**
pp. 75:4.

her(e) *adv.* here 58:1, 39:2, etc.,
C164, 25, etc., Y234, 164, etc.,
SR123, etc., SA1, etc., **hyre**
Y321, **ere** Y624; ~ = in this
world 148:2, 169:5, etc., C12, 536,
544, Y8, 549; = in my story

171:2. ⌣ *ouer* over here, over this (bridge) 117:6.
her(e) *poss. adj.* see **hye, she.**
hercheboschoppe *n.* see **archebysshop.**
herd *n.* household, in *in* ⌣ *is nouȝt to hide* it is very true (it cannot be kept secret) 70:6[n].
herd *pp.* praised, honoured 158:4, **heried** SR622, **yherd** 159:3.
herde *adj.* see **hard** *adj.*
here *v.* hear 52:2, 134:6, 190:2, SR44, 658, **yhere** 28:6, 30:3, 63:2; ⌣ listen to SR479, SA467. **heryn** *pr. t. pl.* SR707. **herd** *pa. t. 1, 3 sg.* 5:1, 64:6, etc., SR15, 217, etc., SA339, **herde** C187 (*masse*), 258, etc., SA3, 15, etc., **hard** Y180, 310, SA531, **harde** SA535, etc. **herd** *pp.* SR609, 701, **herde** C260, **harde** SA532, **yherd** 59:4.
hereyn *adv.* into this place Y67, **herin** 108:4, **heryn** C72; in this place Y594, **herinne** 14:4, 103:5, **hyryn** Y68.
hereof *adv.* about/of this 176:1.
heried *pp.* see **herd** *pp.*
herken *imp. sg.* listen to 158:6. **herknes** *imp. pl.* 28:4, **herkneþ** 76:4.
herme *n.* see **harm(e).**
hernessede *ppl. adj.* see **harneist.**
herre *n.* hair Y352.
hert *n.* heart SR220, 320, etc., **hertt** SA235, 425; ⌣ (as seat of emotions, etc.) 49:1, 61:6, etc., SR98, 192, etc., *****herte** Y303[n], **hertt** SA200, 600, etc., **harte** Y506. **hertes** *pl.* SR417, 435, etc., **herttys** SA233, 332, etc.
hert(e)ly *adv.* sincerely, earnestly SR239, 607.
hete *n.*[1] heat 96:4, 101:3, 163:3, SR230, 370, etc., SA371, **hette** SA522, 524.
hete *n.*[2] vehement rebuke C129, Y125.
hete *pa. t. pl.* see **hatte** *pr. 3 sg.*
heþeing *n.* scorn, mockery, in *drof him to* ⌣ ridiculed him 54:3.
hether, -yr *adv.* see **hider.**
heued *n.* see **hede** *n.*[1].

heuen *n.* heaven 9:5, etc., C148, etc., SR642, 682, SA59, **heuene** C118, SR99, 550, **heuyn** Y15, 114, **heven(e)** SR101, 56, etc., **hevyn** SA102; ⌣ *vndur* = on earth C260.
heuen-blis *n.* the joy of heaven 8:3, 198:5, ⌣-**blysse** C4, 33, **heuyn-blysche** Y4, **heuyn-blysse** Y29.
heuen-gate *n.* the gate of heaven 183:3.
Heuen-king *n.* the King of heaven 18:6.
heuen-ryche *n.* the kingdom of heaven C21, **heuyn-reche** Y17.
heuery *adj.* see **euerych.**
heui *adj.* grievous, hard to endure 167:4.
hewe *n.* colour, complexion 79:6, 114:1.
hewyng *pr. p.* hewing, cutting SR303.
hide *v.* hide 70:6. See **herd** *n.*
hider *adv.* hither 162:4, 167:2, **hydur** C281, 625, **heder** SR71, 76, etc., **hedyr** SA81, **hether** SR658, SA76, 626, 630, **hethyr** Y159, 235, etc.
hidowus *adj.* frightful, terrifying SR580, **hudious** SR92, 280, 438.
hye *pron.* they 4:4, etc., **hy** 43:2. **hem** *acc., dat.* 3:2, etc., C8, etc., Y5, etc., SR26, etc., **ham** SR222. **hem** *refl.* C411, Y587, SR633. **her** *poss. adj.* 4:5, etc., C14, etc., SR270, etc., **here** SR39, etc., **hir** 1:5, SR172, etc., **hire** SR159, etc., **hyr(e)** Y346, 355, 533, **har** C229. Cf. **hemselue, þai.**
high, hyghe, hyȝe, hyee *adj.* see **heiȝe.**
hiȝt *pa. t. 3 sg.* see **hatte.**
hill *n.* hill SR661, **hyll** SA632. **hilles** *pl.* SR284, **hyllys** SA294.
himself *pron.* himself SR665, **hymcelfe** Y6, **hymself** C10, etc., (*refl.*) C45, **hymself(f)e** SA490, Y37, (*refl.*) Y12, **himselue** 172:5.
hing, hynge, hyngyn(g) see **hangyng.**
hir(e), hyr(e) *pron. acc., dat., poss. adj.* see **hye, she.**

hirself *pron.* herself SR667, 668, **hyrselfe** SA636.

hit *pron.* it SR130, 254, 567, **hyt** C40, etc., SA49, 52, *133, 246, **hytt** SA51, etc., **it** 2:5, etc., Y210, etc., SR142, etc., **yt** Y34, etc.; (with *pl.* complement) **hyt** C512, **it** 140:6, 148:1, **yt** Y50, 327.

hyte *pa. t. 3 sg.* see **hatte**.

hoghe *adj.* see **howge**.

hokes *n. pl.* hooks, awls 58:5, 73:2, etc., (meat-)hooks 77:2, **hokys** Y370.

hold *v.* keep SR325, ∽ ... *vnder* = smother SR291; **holde** maintain, adhere to (belief) C74. **holt** *pr. 3 sg.* + *him* considers himself 157:6. **hold** *imp. sg.* in **hold** þe euen norþ keep (going) due north 39:6. **hild** *pa. t. 1 sg.* in **hild** forþe my way continued on my way SR107. **held** *pa. t. 3 sg.* held 19:1. **held** *pa. t. pl.* considered 2:5; held 191:1. **yhold** *pp.* in **yhold** him stille = held his peace, abstained from action 171:4.

hole *adj.* healed 128:5; ∽ and sownde uninjured C338, 673; complete, uncut SR169.

hole *n.* pit, entrance 11:5, 14:1, etc. **holes** *pl.* eye sockets SR206, **holles** SA222.

holestones *n. pl.* see **hailstonis**.

holy *adj.* holy 7:1, 22:3, etc., C27, 184, etc., Y20, 182, etc., SR123, 431, etc., SA508, 621, **holi** 195:1. See **chirch**, **gost(e)**, **kyrke**.

holi-dais *n. pl.* see **hali-day**.

Holyrode day *n.* Feast of (the Exaltation of) the Holy Cross, 14 September SR8.

hollely *adv.* completely SA657, **holy** SR687.

hom(e) *adv.* (to) home C641, 656, SR700, Y636, 646.

hom(e) *n.* home Y410, at ∽ Y408, 661.

homewarde *adv.* towards home SR704.

hond(e) *n.* hand C62, etc., SR160, 10:2, etc., Y315, SR61, etc., **hand(e)** SA64, etc., Y57, 160, SA520, 571. *lefte* ∽ left side

SR34, (sim.) SR35, 37, SA32, 34, *right* ∽ right side SR556, (sim.) C219, Y212, SR33, 34, 37, etc., SA32, 33, 36, etc. *take on* ∽ undertake(n) SR121, (sim.) SR31, SA122, *an* ∽ 32:6. **hondes** *pl.* SR373, **hond** 60:1, 70:1, 114:6, 191:1, **handys** Y382, SA377.

hondred(de) *n.* see **hundred**.

honestly *adv.* fairly, beautifully 170:1[n].

honour *n.* honour 176:4.

honoureþ *pr. t. pl.* honour 176:5.

honowred *pa. t. 1 sg.* greeted respectfully SR113.

hope *n.* hope Y323.

hope *pr. t. 1 sg.* hope C151, Y146, 417.

hornes *n. pl.* (animal) horns SR90, SA92; (hunting?) horns SR168, SA172.

horrible *adj.* horrible, frightful SR88, 226, **horrabyll** SA233, 363, etc., **horrabyl** SA506, **horribull** SA460, **horrybyl** SA262, **orible** SR639, **orrabyll** SA183, 384, 547, **orrible** SR178, 374, 379.

horses *n. pl.* horses SR261, SA272.

hote *adj.* hot C388, 609, SR221, 316, etc., **hott** SA521, **hoote** Y437, **howt** SA319.

hote *adv.* hotly SR415, **hott** SA225, **hoth** SA260. **hatter** *comp.* 111:2.

hotte *n.* heat SA391, **hoytte** SA243.

hou *adv.* how 42:5, 108:5, etc., **how** C616, Y319, 622, SR634, 665, 695, SA339, etc., **howe** C36; ∽ by means of which 6:2.

hounde *n.* dog 116:4.

hous *n.* house SR439, 440, 441, 451, **hows(e)** SA360, 361, etc., C271, **howsse** Y393. **houses** *pl.* SR478, **howses** SA467, **howsys** Y264, 355.

hovyng *ppl. adj.* hovering, suspended in the air SR347.

howge *adj.* great SA447, **hoghe** SA550. **howgyste** *sup.* SA534.

howyn *adj.* see **owne**.

howsyld *pp.* given sacrament of Holy Communion Y181.

howso *pron. indef.* see **whoso**.

hudious *adj.* see **hidowus**.

hundred *num. adj.* hundred 84:1, Y599, **hondred(de)** C581, 583, **hundyrd** Y597.

hundre-fold *n. be a* ∼ by a hundred times Y518.

hunger *n.* hunger 62:5.

huntyng *n.* hunting SR430, **hunt-tynge** SA435.

hus(e), hvs see **we**.

husbondys *n. pl.* husbands SA333.

I *pron.* I C78, etc., Y73, etc., SR9, etc., SA5, etc., **y** 40:5, etc., C113, etc., SR5, etc., **ich** 10:4, etc., and (fused forms) see **haue, wyll. me** *acc., dat., refl.* 35:3, 4, 181:1, C137, etc., Y245, etc., SR11, etc., SA11, etc., **my** SR489. **mi** *poss. adj.* 28:4, 59:3, **my** C136, etc., Y145, etc., SR27, etc., SA13, etc., **min** 180:6, **myn** C165, **myne** Y323, SR578, 597, SA113; as *n.* SR110, 656, 701, 709. See **to-ward**.[1]

ich *adj.*[1] each, every 44:6, 95:6, 101:1, etc., **iche** Y184, 360, 585, **yche** C555. Cf. **eche**.

ich *adj.*[2] (after *þis* or *þat*) same, very 7:4, 10:6, 14:1, etc.

ichil *pr. 1 sg. see* **wyll**.

ydyll *adj.* idle, foolish, vain SA436, 446.

yen *n. pl.* see **ei3en**.

if, yf *conj.* see **3if**.

if *imp. sg.* see **3eue**.

yfere *adv.* together 57:6.

yhere *v.* see **here**.

yknewe *pa. t. 3 sg.* recognized, was familiar with 79:3. **yknawe** *pp.* 58:4.

yliche *adj.* like 21:3, 165:6.

yliche *adv.* alike, equally 157:3, **ylyche** C22, **aleche** Y18.

yliche *n.* equal 170:5.

ylke *adj.*[1] each, every SA93, 185.

ylke *adj.*[2] (after *þat*) same, very C554, SA481.

ilkone *pron.* each one C491.

yll *adj.* evil SA111, bad (repute) SA363, **ylle** severe (penance) C597.

ymage *n.* picture (of a saint) SR612; carving (crucifix) SR615.

in *adv.* in (of motion) 24:5, 45:3, etc., SR9, 62, SA9, 248, 380, **inne**[r] Y372, 418, **yn** C109, 111, etc., Y193, 261, SR375, **ynne** Y202, SR707.

in *prep.* in, into 1:3, etc., C29, etc., Y9, etc., SR2, etc., SA4, etc., **inne**[r] 1:6, 143:1, C236, 549, Y580, **yn** C7, etc., Y45, etc., SR265, etc., **ynne** Y231, SR57, 177, 675; ∼ on 44:6, SR35; ∼ *þat* in as much as SR138.

inclyned *pa. t. 1 sg.* bowed SA578.

increyse *v.* increase SA358, **en-crese** SR356.

indede *adv.* assuredly SR138.

indewre *v.* see **endure**.

injones *pr. 3 sg.* imposes, prescribes (penance) SA150.

ynke *n.* ink 122:1.

inoght *adj.* enough SA257.

insampyll *n.* see **exemple**.

yntent(e) *n.* see **entente**.

intil *prep.* into 62:3, 87:6, 127:6.

into *prep.* to, into 3:5, 11:4, etc., C70, 311, etc., SR6, 142, etc., SA187, 195, etc., **ynto** C50, 67, etc., Y298, 494, etc.; ∼ until SR364.

inwarde *adj.* inward, earnest SA603, **ynward** SR633.

inwyttys *n. pl.* inner faculties SA669[n].

ypilt *pp.* thrust 101:2.

iren *adj.* (made of) iron 65:6, 70:2, 77:2.

iren *n.* iron C90, **yren(e)** SA260, 421, 423, SR189, 210, etc., SA308, **yryn(e)** SA322, Y87.

is *poss. adj.* see **he** *pron.*

is *v. intr. pr. 3 sg.* is 16:6, etc., SR12, etc., SA33, etc., **ys** C1, etc., Y22, etc., SA158, 503, 581; with *pl. subj.* ∼ 156:5, SR432.

ise *n.* ice 93:4, **yse** SR367, 370, 371, SA370, 374.

yse *v.* see 129:2, 130:1, 166:5. **yseye** *pa. t. 3 sg.* 12:4, **ysei3e** 61:1, 152:4. **ysei3e** *pl.* 126:1. ∼ *pp.* 159:1, 161:5.

it, yt see **hit**.

ywerd *pp.* protected 113:2.

ywis[r] *adv.* (rhyming tag) certainly 5:2, 8:6, 16:3, etc., **ywysse** C589.

Jacobins *adj.* see **frere.**

jaggys *n. pl.* ornamental points on edges of garments, produced by cutting wedge-shaped incisions SA172, 182, 395, **iagges** SR168[n], 177, **iaggis** SR388.

jangyllynge *pr. p.* chattering SA254.

jaspers *n. pl.* jaspers (precious stones) 131:1[n].

ioie *n.* joy, pleasure 16:5, 26:5, 54:5, etc., **ioy(e)** SR129, 703, **yoy** Y515, **joy** Y532, 575, etc., **joye** C108, 472, etc., SA132. **ioies** *pl.* 26:2, 27:2, etc., **joyes** C668; five joys of the Virgin SA556, **ioyes** SR564.

ioifull *adj.* joyful SR642.

jugement *n.* (particular) judgement SA630, 659, **iugement** SR659, 687.

iugge *n.* judge SR218, 309. **juges** *pl.* SA2.

jvrours *n. pl.* those sworn to give evidence SA303.

iwes *n. pl.* Jews SR591[n].

kanste *pr. 2 sg.* see **can.**

kare *n.* see **care.**

key(e) *n.* key 23:5, Y88, C91, 93, Y90.

kempte *pp.* combed Y350.

kende *pa. t. sg.* taught 37:6.

kene *adj.* sharp SA309. **kener** *comp.* C414.

kepe *v.* obey (commandment) SA202; *to* ⁓ *with þat charge* with which to perform that duty SR475. ⁓ *pr. subj. sg.* protect C180. ⁓ *imp. sg.* (*refl.*) guard 187:1. **kepyd** *pa. t. pl.* kept SA329.

keper *n.* keeper SA10.

kest(e), kestyn *pa. t. pl.* see **caste.**

kyll *v.* kill SA79. **killyn** *pr. t. pl.* SR313. **kylden** *pa. t. pl.* SR310. **kilde** *pp.* SR312.

kynde *n.* species C523; race, stock C587. **kynd** *pl.* Y568.

kindenesse *n.* (act of) kindness SR49, 631, 655, 696, **kynd(e)nes**

SA665, 50. **kyndnesse** *pl.* acts of kindness SR335.

kyne *n.* crack, fissure (in earth) Y345[n].

king *n.* king 29:1, **kyng** C114, Y406; = God Y22, **kynge** C26, 682. **kinges** *pl.* 137:3, **kingis** SR135, **kynges** C499, **kyng(g)ys** Y542, SA138. See **Heuen-king.**

kinne *n.* race 177:1, **kynne** Y603; parentage, stock SR136, SA140; relatives C286.

kyrke *n.* church SA253. *holy* ⁓ Holy Church SA130, 388, 411.

kyste *pa. t. pl.* see **caste.**

kittyng *pr. p.* see **cut.**

klepy(n)d *pp.* see **clepi.**

knaue *n.* boy Y74; (low) servant C79, **knawe** Y278.

knaw *v.* see **know.**

kne *n.* knee C381, Y430, SR91, **knee** SA93. **knes** *pl.* 55:2, **knesse** SA554, 578, **kneis** SR561, 585, 618, 620.

knel(e)d *pa. t. sg.* kneeled C197, 425, 19:1, **knelid** SR561, 566, **knelyd(e)** SA559, Y190, 472, 633.

kniȝt *n.* knight 29:4, 35:1, etc., **knyȝt** C115, 119, **knyȝte** C121, 160, etc., **knyȝth** C186, 197, etc., **knyȝthe** C384, **knyth** Y110, 111, etc. **knyȝtes** *gen.* C256, **kny3thes* C162, **knythtys** Y157, 251. **kniȝtes** *pl.* 137:4, **knyghtys** SA441, 443.

knitte *v.* tie SR575, **knytt** SA569.

knyves *n. pl.* knives SR205, 260, 302, **knyvys** SA220, 271.

knokkyd *pa. t. pl.* knocked SA379. **knockyng** *pr. p.* SR375.

knolege *n.* see **knowlage.**

knottes *n. pl.* embossed ornaments 132:5[n].

know(e) *v.* know, recognize 84:5, C48, 537, Y550, SR162, **knaw** SA166. **know** *pr. 1 sg.* SA69, 658; (*refl.*) acknowledge SR686. **knowes** *pr. 2 sg.* SA75, 80, **knowest** SR75, 80. **know** *pr. 1 pl.* SR338, SA344. **knowe** *imp. sg.* SR69. **knowyng** *pr. p.* SA490. **knew** *pa. t. 1 sg.* SR164, SA87,

168, **knewe** SR111, SA113.
knewe *pa. t. 3 sg.* 114:2, 155:2, Y157, 369; perceived C321ⁿ.
knoue *pp.* SA653, **knowe** Y43, SR43, **knowen** SR673, 682, SA44, **knowne** SA644. Cf. **yknewe**.
knowlage *n. forto haue* ~ *of* to know, be informed about SR49, (sim.) **knolege** SA50.
kowld *adj.* see **cold** *adj.*

labour *n.* effort, pains C436.
ladder *n.* ladder SR565, 567, 569, 574, etc., **ledder** SA558, 569, **leddyr** SA560, 567, 570.
ladi *n. owre* ~ Our Lady SR116, (sim.) **lade** SA119, **leuedy** 20:5. **lade** *gen.* SA556, ~ *is* SR564.
lafte *pa. t. 3 sg.* see **leue** *v.*[1].
lay(e), layne, layen *pa. t. sg. and pl.* see **lye** *v.*
layte *n.* lightning C259.
lak *n. in* ~ *of* for lack of SR270.
lakkyde *pa. t. 3 sg.* (*impers.*) *theme* ~ they lacked SA212.
lande, landys see **lond(e)**.
last *n. pl.* cartloads (fig. as intensifier of number) *ten þousand* ~ = an immense number 189:4ⁿ.
lasse *adj. comp.* see **litel**.
last *adj. sup.* (as *n.*) *atte* ~ in the end, finally SR198, *at þe* **laste** C15, 123, 131, etc., Y127, (sim.) Y589.
lasten *v.* continue, last 112:6, **lest** 186:2. **lasteþ** *pr. 3 sg.* 16:5, **lastes** C680, **lastys** SA258, **leste** Y681ⁿ. **laste** *pa. t. 3 sg.* (+ ind. obj.) SR362; *on him* **last** attacked him 111:2ⁿ; **lasted** extended C464.
lat *pr. 3 sg.* see **lete** *v.*[1].
late *adv.* see **erly** and **or** *conj.*[2].
latyne *n.* see **letaney**.
laughed *pa. t. pl.* laughed SR28, **loghe** SA27.
law *n.* law, rule followed in a nunnery SR664; *þe riȝt* **lawe** the true faith 37:6; *Godes* **lawe** 13:3; *þe* **law** *of* God the Scriptures SA389; *in þe* **law** *of* God according to God's law SR127, SA137, (sim.) with *after* SA129, 483. **lawes** *pl.* 115:3.

lawnes *n.* see **lownesse**.
lece *pr. 1 sg. subj.* see **lese**.
leche *n. sowles* ~ confessor C136. See **soule** *n.*
lecherie *n.* lechery 58:3, SR503, **lechery(e)** SR323, SA326, 459, 492.
led *pa. t. sg.* see **lede** *v.*
ledde *n.* lead 78:2, **lede** 103:2, SR203, **leyde** SA217.
ledder, leddyr *n.* see **ladder**.
lede *n.* landed property, *lond and* ~ 87:3ⁿ. See also **ledde** *n.*
lede *v.* lead, convey 119:6, 124:6, 162:5, 187:6, C207, 402, Y200, (dance) C282, Y275. **lad** *pa. t. 3 sg.* SR281, 299, 348, 365, **ladde** 11:2, 37:4, C67, **led** Y62, SR249, 258, 330, 480, **lede** SA216, 242, etc., **ledde** C589, SR202, 229. **ladde** *pa. t. pl.* 62:2, 76:1, 90:1, etc., C311, 364, **lede** SA325, **led(d)yn** Y356, 298, 306, 336.
lef *adj.* pleasing, *þat* ~ *beþ* who like 81:6; *whoso is* ~ whosoever likes 82:4; **leue** dear 47:1, **leue** *and dere* 57:3.
lef *n.* leaf 173:3. **leuys** *pl.* Y566.
lefe see **leue** *n.* and *v.*[1].
left *adj.* left SR37, SA32, **lefte** SR34, SA34, **lifte** SR35. See **hond(e)** *n.*
lege *adj.* ~ *lorde* superior lord to whom service is due SA442.
legge *n.* leg SA520.
legge *v.* ~ *on* impose (penance) 33:4. **leydyn** *pa. t. pl.* laid Y324. **leyd** *pp.* (told) 92:2. See **lye**.
leyde *n.* see **ledde**.
leyen *pa. t. pl.* see **lye**.
lem *n.* brightness 150:2; gleam, ray 193:6; **leme** lightning *Y252; flame SR235, 347. **lemes** *pl.* SR316.
lene *adj.* skinny Y344.
lenge(r) *adj., adv. comp.* see **long(e)** *adj., adv.*
lenghte *n.* length C321, **lenkyt(h)** Y308, 394.
lengur *adj., adv. comp.* see **long** *adj. adv.*
lepe *pa. t. pl.* leapt SA385, **lopen** 73:1, SR379.

lernyd *ppl. adj.* learned (men) SR521. **ylernd** *pp.* 115;4.

les *n.* untruth, *wiþouten* ~ truly (tag) 30:1, 151:2.

lese *v.* lose, ~ ... *labour* waste ... effort C436. **lece** ... *travell pr. 1 sg. subj.* Y483ⁿ. **les** *pa. t. sg.* 171:3, 184:5. **lorn** *pa. t. pl.* 75:6. **lorn** *pp.* C18, Y14. See **lost**.

lesing *n.* untruth, *wiþouten* ~ truly (tag) 38:3.

lesse *adj. comp.* see **litel**.

lest *adj. sup.* see **litel**.

lest(e) *v., pr. 3 sg.* see **lasten**.

letaney *n.* litany Y187, **letanye** C194, **letenye** SR523, **latyne** SA518.

lete *v.*¹ ~ *be* give up, avoid 36:4; **leten** leave off, eschew 31:6, abandon 37:2, C147. **lat** *pr. 3. sg.* (+ *be*) 144:4. **lete** *pr. 2 pl. subj.* 102:3. **let** *imp. sg.* let, allow C618; **let** *be* leave off, speak no more of that SR652. **lete** *impl. pl.* allow Y624. **lete** *pa. t. 3 sg.* (+ *inf.*) caused to be performed 20:2, 23:6, SR498, **lette** C89; ~ allowed (person) to ... Y193. **let** ... *alon pa. t. pl.* left (someone) by himself Y333, **lettyn** Y295; **leten** gave up, ceased 27:6. **lete** *pa. t. 3. sg. subj.* (+ neg.) should not fail/forbear 180:2. **let(t)yn** *pp.* (+ *in*) admitted SA380, SR375; **ylete** left behind 163:6. **leten** *ppl. adj.* 143:3.

lete *v.*² (+ *inf.*) prevent (somebody) from (doing something) SR38, **lett** SA37, hinder SA39. **letteth** *pr. 3 sg.* SR132, 138, **lettys** SA136, 141. **lettid** *pa. t. 3 sg.* SR128, **lettyde** SA493, **lett** SA131; **letyd** (*refl.*) delayed Y118. **lettyd** *pa. t. pl.* SA255.

lett *n. wiþouten* ~ without delay 20:1.

letter *n.* missive C155, Y96, 150, etc., **lettur** C99, 160, 165. **letters** *pl.* alphabetic characters SR414, 424, SA422, 431.

leue *adj.* see **lef**.

leue *n.*¹ faith C49.

leue *n.*² permission C150, 153, Y148, **lefe** Y145; ~ leave (see **nam** and **take**) 189:2, C157, **leve** SR706.

leue *v.*¹ leave (in place) C624; **lefe** leave off, abandon SR632, **leve** SR197, 684, 690, SA207, 210, 364, etc. **leve** *pr. 3 sg. subj.* SA603. **lefe** *pr. pl. subj.* SR633. **leve** *imp. sg.* SR37, SA35. **levyng** *pr. p.* SR360, 430. **left** *pa. t. 3 sg.* 173:2, **lafte** C202. **lefte** *pa. t. pl.* C360, SR130, SA133. **levyde** *pp.* SA214.

leue *v.*² believe 6:5, 182:6. Cf. **beleue** *v.*¹.

leuedy *n.* see **ladi**.

leuyd, -yn(g), leved(en), -id, -yd(e), -yng(e) see **liue** *v.,* **lyffyng(e)** *vbl. n.*

lewid *adj.* wicked, unchaste SR433; unlearned, secular SR523, **lewde** SA518; **levde** secular, foolish SA435.

libbe *v.* see **liue**.

lic(c)houre *n.* lecher 73:4, 74:2.

lich *adj.* see **lyke**.

licorice *n.* liquorice 148:6.

lye *v.* remain C432, ~ *in syne* SA502; *lyen lie Y321, **ligge** 65:1, 117:1, **legge** 67:6. **lyes** *pr. 3 sg.* SA62, **ligh** SR59ⁿ. **lay** *pa. t. 3 sg.* 10:3, C52, Y47, *600, resided 32:4; (in sin) C122; lead (way) C633, **laye** Y637. **lay** *pa. t. pl.* 65:4, 69:1, 4, 72:6, SR350, *SA353, **layen** 79:1, **layne** Y351, **leyen** C327, **loyn(e)** Y345, 314ⁿ. **ly** *pp.* 69:5.

lieng *vbl. n.* lying (abed) SR678, **lyggynge** SA649.

lif *n.* life SR322, **lyf** C132, **liif** 73:4, 95:3, 102:1, **lyffe** SA114, 199, **liue** 33:6, 81:4, 196:4, **lyue** C128, 651, Y656, **lyve** Y128, 588, **lywe** Y124; *with þe* **lyfe** alive SA163; *lede þer* **lyfe** spent their life SA325; *on* **lyve** alive SR499; *tre of* **liif** Tree of Life 146:4, (sim.) **lyf(f)e** Y570, C525. *with hire* **lifes** *pl.* alive SR159.

lyffers *n. pl. oder gud* ~ others who live righteously SA215.

lyffyng(e) *vbl. n.* conduct, way of living, *synfull* ~ SA459, *gud* ~ SA390; **leuyng** SR646; *good (ensampell of)* **levyng** SR383, 638;

lewid/vnklene **levyng** SR433, 468; (*gud*) **levynge** SA609, 617.
lifte *adj.* see **left.**
lyggynge *vbl. n.* see **lieng.**
light *n.* light SR23, 559, **lyght(e)** SA22, Y204, 206, SA551, **liȝt** 40:6, 184:4, 194:1; **liȝt** *of day* 39:5; *lem of* **liȝt** ray of light 193:6; **lyȝth** C204, 205, 210, 213, **lyte** Y198, **lyth(e)** Y208, 197, 203. **lyghttys** *pl.* SA320.
liȝt *pa. t. 3 sg.* (+ upon) descended on 184:2.
lyȝte *adj.* (+ *of*) delighted (with) C477; (sim.) **lyt** Y520.
liȝting *vbl. n.* bright light 85:1; lightning 121:5.
liȝtnesse *n.* light, brightness 41:1.
like *adj.* like, ~ *to* SR182, **lyke** C30, Y26, 219, SA39, (*vnto*) SA320, 650, **lich** SR39. Cf. **yliche** *adj.*
like *adv.* likely SR155, **lyke** SA158. Cf. **yliche** *adv.*
likeing *n.* enjoyment 185:4.
likid *pa. t. 3 sg. impers. me* ~ I was pleased SR603.
liknes *n. in* ~ *of* like, in the form of SA85.
lili *n.* lily 147:2.
lym(m)e *n.* limb SR301, SA308. **lymmes** *pl.* SR226, 254, 355, **lymmys** SA310.
lyme *n.* (bird-)lime (trap) C278[n].
line *n. bi* ~ in a line 142:1.
lyst *pr. 2 sg.* wish, choose C432. **lyste** *pa. t. 3 sg.* desired, wanted Y660. **lyst** *pa. t 3 sg. impers. hym* ~ he wished C655.
lyt *adj.* see **lyȝte.**
lite *adj.* small 9:1.
lyte, lyth(e) *n.* see **light.**
litel *adj.* small, little, short SR23, **litil(l)** SR535, 667, **lytull** C204, 337, 461, etc., **lytyll** C181, 332, Y197, 508, etc., SA120, 522; **litill** slender, fragile SR567. **lesse** *comp.* less C342; (after neg.) *more ne* ~ = none at all C68, (sim.) 123:6. (As *n.*) *more and* ~ the higher and lower in rank, i.e. everyone Y552, (sim.) **lasse** C539, **lasse** *and more* 28:1.

lytyll *adv.* (and *n.* in *adv.* phrases) *a* ~ *sowth* a little way towards the south C401; *a* ~ *froo the* a little distance from thee SA157; *bott* ~ *gylte* = had done very little wrong SA638[n]; *a* ~ *bradder* a little broader C445, (sim.) Y492; *a* **lytull** *more* C211.
liue, lyue, lyve, lywe *n.* see **lif.**
liue *v.* live 146:2, 152:1, SR507, **lyue** C289, **lyve** SA398, **lyfe** C339, **libbe** 164:6, **leuyn** Y282. **lyve** *imp. sg.* SR702. **lyffynge** *pr. p.* SA393, 515, **lyveng** SR387, **levyng(e)** SA69, SR40, 520, SA41. **liued** *pa. t. 3 sg.* 197:6, **lyued(e)** C674, 582, **lyffyd** SA483, **leuyd** Y675, **leved** SR495, **levyd** Y598, SA486. **liued** *pa. t. pl.* 1:3, 174:5, **lyffyde** SA416, **leved** SR112, 322, **leveden** SR65, 478, **levid** SR164, **levyde** SA168. **lyved** *pp.* SR406, **levid** SR665, **levyde** SA415. Cf. **lyffyng(e).**
lo *interj.* see **lo(o).**
locke *n.* lock 23:5, **lok** Y88, **lokke** C91.
loghe *pa. t. pl.* see **laughed.**
loyn(e) *pa. t. pl.* see **lye.**
loke *n.* appearance 174:2. See also **locke.**
loke *v.* look SA346, SA349. **loke** *imp. sg.* Y467; consider 48:4, 173:5, SR147, 161, SA165; make sure C245, 248, etc., Y240, 657, SA46, 617, etc., **lowke** SA151. **lokynge** *pr. p.* + *to* looking towards SA553. **loked** *pa. t. 1, 3 sg.* looked 64:4, 129:2, C225, 395, SR173; **lokid** *to* looked toward/at SR560, 565, etc., (sim.) **lokyd(e)** SA178, 567, 557, 663; **lokyd** Y220, 334, etc.; = looked to find out Y311; + *after* looked for (sb.) SR161, (sim.) SA154, looked out for (sth.) SA531. **lokyd** *pa. t. pl.* + *on* looked at SA330. See **besyd.**
lokke *n.* see **locke.**
lokke *v.* lock C94, **louken** 23:5, (with suff. obj. *pron.*) **loket** lock it Y91. **loked** *pa. t. 3 sg.* Y92, **lokked** C201, ***lokkyd** Y194.

lond(e) *n.* (the) land, country C7, 30, etc., 44:5, 62:3, etc., C61, 608, Y25, 26, etc., SR581; (opposed to water) 94:6, 169:6, **lande** SA573; *on euury* ~ (vaguely) all about, everywhere C327, (sim.) Y314. **londes** *pl.* = fields, landed property SR284, 289, **londys** SA303, **landys** SA295, 299. See **lede** *n.*

long(e) *adj.* long (of dimension) C221, SA175, 190, C353, Y214, 327, SR170; (of duration) 163:2, C122, SR274, 297. **lenger** *comp.* Y338, **lengur** C367.

long(e) *adv.* (for) a long time SA163, 285, 550, 15:4, 45:1, etc., Y118, 661, SR110, 159, 557. **lenge** *comp.* (after *no*) 50:5, **lenger** C253, Y234, 248, **lengur** C239.

longyng *ppl. adj.* ~ *to* befitting, appropriate to SR432.

lo(o) *interj.* see, look SA237, 278, etc., 117:4, SA250, **lowe** SA266.

lopen *pa. t. pl.* see **lepe**.

lord(e) *n.* Lord C361, etc., SA58, Y439, etc., SR55; ~ *God* C427; *our* ~ C51, SR624, SA4, etc., SR42, etc.; ~ *and kynge* C682. **lordes** *gen.* Lord's SR46, SA47, **lordis** SR563, **lorde** SA556. See **lege**.

lore[r] *n.* teaching, belief 69:3[n]; (God's) ~ 28:2, C28, Y24; *holy* ~ C184, Y177.

lorn *pa. t. pl., pp.* see **lese**.

lost *pa. t. pl.* were dispossessed of (lands) SA303. **loste** *pp. ben* ~ perished C266. Cf. **lese**.

loþly *adj.* horrible, ugly 53:5, **loþli** 70:5, **loþeliche** 114:5.

loþly *adv.* fiercely 88:5.

loude *adv.* loudly 73:3, 81:3, etc., **lowd(e)** C193, 326, Y313.

louken *v.* see **lokke** *v.*

loue *n.* love 144:2, 4, SR508; *for his* ~ for love of him SR640, (sim.) **love** SR631, *for þe* **luffe** *of Gode* SA210; (in entreaty) *for his* ~ SR650, *for Godes* ~ for the love of God 71:5, (sim.) 198:4; *for the* ~ *of God* SR708, (sim.) **love** SR50, **luffe** SA52, 583.

loue *v.* see **luffe**.

lovyde *pa. t. 1 sg.* praised SA110. ~ *pa. t. pl.* SA599. ~ *pp.* SA58, **loved** *an heried be God* God be praised and honoured SR622.

low *n.* flames SA351.

lowde *adj.* loud C264; stormy (weather) C430[n]. See **loude** *adv.*

lowe *adj.* low C417, Y464; not loud (wind) Y479; low in social status SR136.

lowe *adv.* quietly (wind) C432; low down Y368. See **hey** *adv.*

lowe *interj.* see **lo(o)**.

lowke *imp. sg.* see **loke** *v.*

lownesse *n.* humility, lowliness SR671, **lawnes** SA642.

lowtid *pa. t. pl.* knelt down SR607.

lucor *worldly* ~ filthy lucre SR508[n].

luffe *v.* love SA204. **loueþ** *pr. t. 3 sg.* 144:5, 152:1. **loue(n)** *pr. t. pl.* SR81, 75, 136, ~ SA140. **loued** *pa. t. 1, 3 sg.* SR126, **loved** SR112, 126, **luffyde** SA114, 128.

lust *n.* delight SR426, SR435. **lustes** *pl.* pleasures SR426.

mad *adj.* dazed 94:2[n]; **made** (+ *man*) foolish SA100.

madman *n.* madman SR98, 547.

mageste *n.* (after 'his') majesty, = glory of God C600, **magyste** Y610.

may *pr. 1, 3 sg.* am/is able to, can, may 16:4, etc., C76, 434, etc., Y263, 481, etc., SA626, **mai** 147:6, 162:1; (in question) SR514, SA508; *y can or* **may** I know how to or am able to (do sth.) SR514. **may** *pr. 2 sg.* C148, 171, 339, etc., Y413, 466, SA624, **mayis** Y625, **maist** SR652, **miʒt** 107:4, 124:2, **myth** Y143, 166. **may** *pr. pl.* 30:3, etc., C34, etc., Y234, SR518, 530, 531, SA512, etc. *pr. subj. pl.* C284, Y277. **might** *pa. t. 1, 3 sg.* SR569, **miʒt** 6:2, etc., **myght** C8, SR48, 162, etc., SA562, etc., **myghtt** SA523, **myʒte** C267, 270, 392, **myʒth** C40, 48, etc., **myte** Y36, **myth** C42, Y37, 43, etc., **mowʒth** C298[n]. **might** *pa. t. pl.* SR462, **miʒt** 89:6, **myght** SR429, 460,

533, SA255, 418, etc., **my3th(e)**
C537, 193, 371, 456, **myth** Y353,
388, etc. *3yf he hadde* **my3th** *pp.* if
he had been able (to) C274.
mayne *n.* see **meyne.**
maynteneng *pr. p.* supporting,
abetting SR502.
maister *n.* scholar, learned man
122:3; **maystyr** master, leader
Y406; *most* ⌁ chief personage
46:2; *most* ⌁*-fende* most important leading devil 55:1ⁿ. **maysterys** *pl.* learned ecclesiastics
Y534.
make *n.* equal (thing) 151:5, **mack**
12:2.
make *v.* (mod. uses) 59:6, 182:2,
etc., C89, 667, Y86, 670; build
44:2, Y81, SR498, SA485; *sarmoun to* ⌁ to speak, ?deliver sermon 2:1; ⌁ ... *mone* lament, weep
Y321ⁿ; *solas* ⌁ rejoice 107:4; (+
to and *inf.*) cause (sb. or sth. to do
sth.) C431, SR399; recite
(prayers) 195:3. **make** *pr. 1 sg.* ⌁
... *complaint* complain SR123,
(sim.) SA126. **makyst** *pr. 2 sg.*
Y478. **makyth** *pr. 3 sg.* Y2. **make**
pr. pl. ⌁ ... *dreri mode* = lament
sorrowfully 91:3. **makyng(e)** *pr.
p.* SA471, SR207, 482, 600,
SA253. **made** *pa. t. 3 sg.* 172:6,
174:3, C86, 91, Y88, 257, SA209;
created Y475, SA203; ⌁ *his praier*
said his devotions 7:3; ⌁ *of nou3t*
created out of nothing 130:6; ⌁
ryght put (things) right C2; wrote
(letter) C155; ⌁ *his orysowne*
prayed C426, (sim.) Y473;
maked 21:1, 51:6, **mad** Y498.
made *pa. t. pl.* C293, SA93, etc.,
⌁ ... *blis* rejoiced 153:5; ⌁ *mowes*
made faces C272, ⌁ *a mowe* Y266;
⌁ ... *melodyes* sang ... songs,
played melodiously C498, (sim.)
madyn Y541; ⌁ ... *satesfaction*
= performed penance SR271,
(sim.)SA282; **mad** Y579, **maden**
SR91, **madyn** Y288, *merthys*
madyn sang songs Y545. **made**
pp. C224, Y218, 397, SR368, 500,
etc., SA488, 499, *þis melody* thus

rejoiced 140:1; **ymade** 162:3, in-
flicted (torment) 122:4.
makyng *vbl. n.* building SA487.
maleyce *n.* hatred SA475.
man *n.* (a) man 29:5, etc., Y8, etc.,
SR24, etc., SA23, etc., **mon** C12,
etc.; ⌁ person 3:4, etc., C314,
etc., **mon** C72, 557, 676; (generic,
without art.) ⌁ 80:6, Y63; (voc.)
173:5, SA539. **manys** *gen.* Y11,
mannes 155:6, **mannys** SA520,
man *is* SR526, **monnus** C15,
610. **men** *pl.* 22:3, etc., C3, etc.,
Y221, etc., SR38, etc., SA39, etc.;
(people in general) 10:5, etc., C14,
etc., Y59, etc., SR674, etc.,
SA104, etc., **man** 91:2ⁿ. **menis**
gen. SR264.
man *pron. indef.* (not always distin-
guishable from **man** *n.*) one, a
man, a person 22:6, C569, SR159,
etc., SA521, etc.; *no* ⌁ no one,
nobody 93:5, etc., C96, Y89, etc.,
SR132, SA136, *no* **mon** C92, etc.;
ani ⌁ anyone, anybody 63:2,
147:6, (sim.) C42, SA208.
mane *adj.* see **many.**
maner *n.* way 128:2, 157:1, SR313;
yn fayr **maner(e)** in a courteous
manner C163, (sim.) Y158; *yn all*
⌁ in every way C535, (sim.)
Y548; ⌁ species 148:1; kinds of
106:1, C529, 563, ⌁ *of* Y424,
SR162, 231, SA166; *no* ⌁ no kind
of (sth.) whatever 62:4, 109:6; *al*
⌁ *every* kind of, all kinds of 9:4,
138:4, 169:1, (sim.) C486,
manere C530, *all(e)* ⌁ *of* C373,
473, Y575, SR259, 584, SA70,
270. **maners** *pl.* ways SR290,
409, **manere** 77:6.
mani *adj.* (+ *sg.* or *pl.*) many 47:2,
102:4, etc., **many** Y21, 126, etc.,
SR88, 475, etc., SA68, 456, etc.,
mane SA89, **mony** C130, 315,
etc., SR400, etc.; ⌁ *a(n)* 24:5,
etc., **many** *a(n)* Y341, 276, etc.,
mony *a* C76, 142, etc.; (as
pron.) ⌁ 136:3, **many** Y39, etc.,
SR627.
manifold *adj.* great, intense (of penance) 34:6.
mankinne *n.* mankind 144:3.

margarites *n. pl.* pearls 131:2[n].

mark *imp. sg. (refl.)* mark (oneself with the sign of the Cross) SR99, 549. **marked** *pa. t. 1 sg.* SR83, **markid** SR105, 554, 564, 572; (non *refl.*) made the sign of the Cross (on forehead) **marked** SR27.

masse(s) *n. (pl.)* see **messe**.

maters *n. pl.* affairs, business SA497.

matrimonie *n.* see **contractys**.

mede *n.*[1] mead 149:2.

mede *n.*[2] *for* ～ by bribery, for a fee SA502; profit, gain SA493[n].

medys *n.* (with *pl. v.*) middle part(s) Y464.

medowys *n. pl.* meadows Y563, **medewus** C520.

meyne *n.* household servants, retinue SR390, 488, **meny** SA476, **mayne** SR485.

mekely *adv.* humbly SR147, 637, SA608.

mekenes(se) *n.* meekness, humility SR195, 671, SA641.

mekill, mekyl(l) *adj., adv.* see **mykel(l)**.

mele *n.* meal 182:2.

melodye *n.* music(-making) 141:3. **meladys** *pl.* Y541. See **make** *v.*

meltte *v. intr.* melt SA371, **mylt** SR369. **meltyng** (metals) *pr. p.* (*tr.*) SR282. **molten** *pp.* mixed, fused SR203, **molton** SA217, 293. **molten** *ppl. adj.* melted (metal) 78:2, SR210, 212, 288, **molton** SR214, **ymelt** 99:6.

membris *n. pl.* limbs, parts of the body SR213, 225, 227, **membyrs** SA227, 240, **menbres** SR224; **membrys** genitals Y367, **menbris** SR323, **membyrse** SA327, *prevy* ～ SR319, *prevey* **membyrs** SA322.

memorie *n.* (faculty of) memory 61:4[n]; *yn* **memorye** in commemoration (of sb.) C101.

mendede *pa. t. 3 sg.* put right, atoned for (wrong) C2.

mene *n.* middle voice in a three-part harmonized composition 145:5[n].

Menours see **frere**.

menstracie *n.* musical merriment 141:6.

mercy *n.* mercy C250, etc., Y293, etc., SR32, etc., SA213, etc., **merci** 66:4, SR121, 582, **mersy** SA366; (as *interj.*) ～ have mercy! Y623, **merci** 66:2, 3.

merely *adv.* joyfully SA589. Cf. **miri**.

mery *adj.* joyful, cheerful C496, 498, 659, Y520, 539, 664, SA594, blissful SR651, SA593, full of perfect joy SA623, **meri** SR601, **miri(e)** 141:4, 145:4.

merthys *n. pl.* see **myrthe**.

meruayle *n.* marvel C76.

meruellys *adj.* astonishing Y71.

meschaunce *n.* see **mischaunce**.

messe *n.* Mass 163:5, Y180, 649, 650, **masse** 154:4, C187, 644, 645. **masses** *pl.* SR521, SA516.

mesure *n. owt(e) of* ～ excessively SR244, extremely SR316, (sim.) **mesore** SA319.

metal(l) *n.* metal C373, 470, SR207, etc., 99:5, **met(t)ell** SA223, Y424, 441, SA218, etc. **metals** *pl.* SR203, **metellys** SA217.

mete *n.* food 101:6, 163:5, SR463. **metes** *pl.* SR680, **mettys** SA652.

mete *v. impers. him gan* ～ he dreamt about 8:2.

metely *adv.* fittingly, handsomely Y217.

metyn *v.* meet Y556, **mette** SA36. **mett** *pa. t. 1 sg.* SA111, 112, **mette with** SR109.

me-warde see **toward(e)**.

michel *adj.* big, large 83:4, 161:2, **mych(e)** Y373, 393, 455; ～ much, great 121:6, 169:2, **miche** 141:3, 153:5, **mych(e)** C489, 506, 508, Y253, 632, 396, 427, 532, **mychell** SR699, **moch(e)** SR49, 270, etc., SR139, 695; **moche** many C531, SR503; ～ (as *n.*) much 30:4, **miche** 172:6; (in phrases) *yn so* **moche** *þat* to the extent that SR610, *bi as* **miche** *as* 133:1; *for as* **moch(e)** *as* since, because SR500, 477, (sim.) **myche** SA466. Cf. **mykell** and see **space**.

michel *adv.* greatly, much (modifying *v.*) 5:2, **mochel** SR536, **moch(e)** C143, SR88; ~ (modifying compar.) 61:2, **miche** 150:5, **mych** Y338, 493; ~ very 11:5. Cf. **mykyll.**

myd(d)e *n.* middle C447, Y494.

myddyll *n.* middle C417; waist SA569, **myddell** SR576.

midnerd *n.* (our) world 118:4, 174:6[n].

miȝt *n.* power, strength 75:6, etc., (appeal) 141:2, **myght(e)** SA184, SR180, SA665, **myth** Y643, *full of* **myght** C1, (sim.) **myȝte** C357, etc., **myȝth** C249, **myth** Y244, etc.; *at hys* **myth** with (all) his might, as best he could Y124[n]. **mythtys** *pl. lord of* ~ *moste* Lord of greatest power Y684. See **more** *adj. comp.*

miȝt, myght(e), -(t), myȝte, myȝth(e), myth *pa. t. 1, 3 sg.* etc. see **may.**

mykell *adj.* great C106, SR57, **mykyll(e)** SA448, C108, 410, Y103, 371, 419, **mekyl(l)** SA87, etc., SA449; much SA50, 665, etc.; **mekill** many SR626. Cf. **michel** *adj.*

mykyll *adv.* greatly, much (modifying *v.*) C120, Y139, **mykel** SR244, **mekyll** Y116, SA46, 90; ~ (modifying compar.) C594. Cf. **michel** *adv.*

mild(e) *adj.* gracious, kindly 17:3, 5, 136:2, 51:3.

myle *n.* mile C462, SR109, SA111, **myll** Y509. **mile** *pl.* 116:5.

mylt *v.* see **meltte.**

mynd(e) *n.* mind SR142, SA146; (in phrases) have *in* ~ = remember C248, SR42, SA42, Y243, SR46, have ~ *on* = (also) think of, reflect upon SR82, have ~ *of* SR98, 547, SA539; have *no* ~ *on* = fail to remember, have no thought of SR94, 544, have *lytyll* ~ *of* give little thought to SA120, have *evell* ~ *on* = badly fail to remember SR118.

myne *v.* undermine (foundations) SA475.

mint *n.* mint (plant) 147:4[n].

miri *adv.* joyfully 142:6. Cf. **merely.**

miri(e) *adj.* see **meri.**

myrthe *n.* eternal bliss, happiness C526. **myrthes** *pl.* delights, joys SR427, **myrthys** SA436, **merthys** *madyn* made merry, were joyful Y545.

misbileue *n.* heathen religion 1:5.

mischaunce *n.* adversity 36:4, (have) **meschaunce** (suffer) evil fortune 56:4.

misdede *n.* (number uncertain) wrong-doing(s), sin(s) 4:5, 14:3, etc., **mysdede** C133, 567, **myssedede** Y129. **misdedis** *pl.* SR683, **mysdedes** SR341, **mysdedys** SA655.

mysdoers *n. pl.* malefactors, offenders SR313.

mysdone *pp.* done wrong C134.

myself *pron.* myself SR620.

misgilt *n.* sin, wrong-doing 101:1.

mysgouernance *n.* misconduct SA647, 658.

myskepeng *vbl. n.* inadequate care SR473.

misours *n. pl.* misers 102:5[n].

missays *n.* pain, suffering 164:3.

mysse *v.* lack, fail to find C34.

myter *n.* mitre SR490, SA479.

myth(tys) *n.* (*pl.*) see **miȝt**; *pa. t. 3 sg.* etc. see **may.**

mytigacion *n.* alleviation of punishment SR515, **mittigacyon** SA509.

mo *adj. comp.* greater in amount SR93, 559, more 139:2, 160:5, C24, 309, SR168, 514, **moo** Y20, SA507, ~ other 118:6; as *n.* more (people) 41:5, etc.

moch(e), mochel see **michel.**

mode *n.* sorrow 91:3[n].

moder *n.* mother 104:3, etc., SR256, 332, etc., SA341, etc. **moders** *pl.* SA338, 339.

moghtys *n. pl.* see **mothis.**

mold *n.* earth, world 52:5[n]; *on* ~ (tag) in the world 136:5.

molten, -on *pp.* see **meltte.**

mon *n. to* ~ as companion 115:2. See **man.**

mone *n.*[1] moon C206, Y199.

mone *n.*[2] *make þi* ∼ = lament Y321.

monkes *n. gen. sg.* monk's 197:5. ∼ *pl.* 137:5, C493, **monkis** SR604, 663, **monkys** SA414, 596, 634, **monkous** SR406, **mvnkys** Y536.

monnus *n. gen. sg.* see **man**.

mony *adj.* see **mani**.

moo *adv.* to a greater number C595, Y607. See **euermo**.

more *adj. comp.* more 56:4, etc., C594, Y387, SR44, etc., SA22, etc.; greater 52:6; larger C367; = wider SR35. As *n.* more 152:4; *no* ∼ nothing more C124, Y120, SA496. **most(e)** *sup.* greatest Y1, 684, SR441, SA453, *for þe* ∼ *parte* in most instances SA489. See **maister** and **namore**.

more *adv. comp.* more 135:2, C9, 308, etc., Y5, SR59, etc., SA62, etc.; moreover 10:1; (modifying compar.) SR85, 675, SA86; *no* ∼ never again 33:5, C551; *ferder* ∼ = to a more distant point Y392, *forth* ∼ Y454. **most** *sup.* most SR104, 553; (modifying sup.) SA534. Cf. **almost(e)**, **euermore**, **farthermore**, **moreouer**.

moreouer *adv.* moreover SA614.

morwe *n. on þe* ∼ in the morning 192:5, (sim.) **morow** C105, Y102, *on* **mowrow** Y180. Cf. **amorow**.

most(e) *adj./adv. sup.* see **more**.

mot *n.* speck of dust 120:5. **motys** *pl.* Y459.

mote *pr. 1 sg.* may (equiv. subj. after request) C137. **mote** *pr. 2 sg.* (expressing wish) SR55; **most** must 103:2, etc., (elliptical for) must do 186:4, C623, **moste** C181, 421, 620, **muste** Y468, 626. **mot** *pr. 3 sg.* (in blessing) 196:6, SR586. **mote** *pr. pl.* must C565, must go (*inf.* understood) C564, (+ *nede*) must necessarily C560. **most(e)** *pa. t. 3 sg.* C99, 132, had to C267, etc., = must go C322, 34:4, 188:3, **muste** Y96, etc., = must go Y309; **moste** *nede* = was obliged to C208. **muste** *pa. t. pl.* (with *pr.* sense) SR340, **muste** *nede* Y590.

mothis *n. pl.* moths SR444, 461, **moghtys** SA457.

moughthes *n. pl.* see **mouþe**.

mounteyn *n.* mountain 90:2, 93:2, 168:2.

mouþe *n.* mouth (bird's) 169:4, **mowth** (devil's) C402, *aftur hys* **mowth** according to his words/ report C669, **mowþe** C610. **mouthes** *pl.* SR352, **mowtes** SA245, **mowthes** SA193, 355, **mowþis** SR187, **moughthes** SR445[n]. Cf. **hell-mowth**.

mowe *n. made a* ∼ made a face, grimace Y266. *made* **mowes** *pl.* C272.

mowntenance *n.* (time taken to walk a certain) distance C462.

murderars *n. pl.* murderers SA313, **murdres** SR307.

na *interj.* no SA624.

nadder *n.* an adder, a serpent 106:6. **neddren** *pl.* 71:2. See also **adders**.

nay *interj.* no 36:1, 75:1, C619, Y286, etc.

nailes *n. pl.* (metal) nails 70:2, SR189, 428, **nayles** C329, 353, 356, SR181, 415, **naylles** SA186, **nayl(l)ys** SA195, Y326, **nalys** SA423; **nayles** fingernails SR209, 225, **naylles** SA240, **nalys** SA223.

nayled *pp.* nailed C328, 331, **naylyd** Y315, 317, **ynayled** 70:3.

naked *adj.* naked 65:3, 173:4, **nakid** SR442, 459, **nakyd** SA454.

nam *pa. t. 3 sg.* took Y155, **nome** C160; ∼ *his leue* took his leave 189:2; *oȝain him* ∼ opposed him 171:6[n]; ∼ went 175:1. **nom** *pa. t. pl.* seized 110:2, **nome** took, lead 158:2. **nome** *pp.* taken 140:5, **ynome** (way) 43:4, 168:4, taken, lead 63:4, 107:1, 116:1.

name *n.* name 20:4, 21:4, 50:1, C391, SA5, 606; *by* ∼ (specifically) C66, (sim.) Y61; *on Goddes* ∼ in God's name C154, (sim.) Y149; reputation SR360, SA363.

namore *adj.* no more 41:1.

narrow *adj.* narrow SA33, **narowe**
C415, **naru** 117:2, 121:3.
nas *pa. t. 3 sg.* see **nis.**
nat(t) *adv.* see **nouȝt** *adv.*
nauel *n.* navel 100:4. **novelys** *pl.*
Y367.
nawȝte *adv.* see **nouȝt** *adv.*
ne *adv.* not (before *v.*) 15:5, C8, 84,
etc.
ne *conj.* nor C613, SR94, 141, etc.,
SA208. See **litel.**
neckes *n. pl.* necks SR168, **neckis**
SR166, **nekkys** SA170, 172, 270.
neddren *n. pl.* see **nadder.**
nede *n.* necessity 124:3, 187:3; need,
want SR57 (also) peril, distress,
SA60; *had* ∿ was obliged Y201;
hadde ∿ needed to SR239; *had* ∿
of needed to SR194; *had(e)* ∿
were poor or needy SA291,
SR279; *at* ∿ in time of trouble or
peril C362, 438, Y445, 485,
SA206.
nede(s) *adv.* of necessity SA460,
C208, 560, Y590, **nedys** Y631,
SA497, 628.
nedid *pa. t. 3 sg. impers. (t)hem* ∿
was necessary for them, they
needed SR244, 403. **nedyde** *pa.
t. pl.* needed SA411.
nedy *adj.* poor SR462, 479.
nedys *adv.* see **nede(s).**
negh *adv.* see **neiȝe.**
neghebor *n. gen.* neighbour, fellow
Christian SA362. **neghbours** *pl.*
SR359, **neghburse** SA255.
neiȝe *adv.* nearly, almost 94:3, **negh**
SR96. **neigh** nearby, close
SR618, **nygh** SR162. (quasi-
prep.) ∿ close to, near 64:3, as
prep. **nyȝ(e)** C275, 467. See **fer,
noure, well** and cf. **ner(e)** *adv.
comp.*
neyses *n. pl.* noses SA355. Cf. **nose.**
neyther *conj.* ∿ ... *nor* neither ...
nor Y63, 199, etc., **neyþur** ... *ner*
C206. Cf. **nother.**
nekkys *n. pl.* see **neckes.**
nel *pr. 3 sg.* will not SR629. ***nyll** *pr.
2 sg. subj.* in *wyll þou* **nyll** *þou*
willy nilly, whether you wish to or
not Y403. **nold** *pa. t. 3 sg.* would

not 37:2, 59:1. **nold** *pa. t. pl.*
SR197, **nolden** 4:4.
nempne *imp. sg.* call 50:1.
ner *adv.* ∿ ... *ne* neither ... nor C84.
ner(e) see **nis; neyther; neuer;
noþur.**
ner(e) *adv. comp.* nearer 190:1,
136:1. As *pos.* near, close SA166;
almost, nearly Y399.
neþer *adv.* lower, deeper 111:1.
neuer *adv.* never 9:3, etc., C488,
542, Y299, etc., SA144, etc., **neuur**
C312, etc., **never** SR141, etc.,
ner(e) Y618, 588. (emphatic neg.)
∿ *so* no matter how SR136,
SA139.
neuermo *adv.* never again 172:1.
neuermore *adv.* never again 188:4,
Y108, 582, **neuurmore** C112.
neuertheles(se) *adv.* nevertheless,
however Y500, SA145, **neuerþelesse** Y280, SA41, **neuurþelesse**
C287.
neuurþelatter *adv.* nevertheless
C453.
new *adv.* see **newe** *adv.*
newe *adj.* new 115:3, 119:4, C231.
newe *adv.* (modifying *pp.*) newly
46:1, C494, **new** Y226.
next *adv.* ∿ *after* immediately following SR2, 8.
nice *adj.* foolish SR685; **nyse** extravagant, self-indulgent SR193,
197, 390, 465, SA207.
nygh *adv.* see **neiȝe.**
nyght, -es, -tys, -gth *n.* see **niȝt.**
nyȝ(e) *adv.* see **neiȝe.**
niȝt *n.* night 14:4, **nyght** C84, **nygth**
Y79, **nyȝth** C73, etc., **nyte** Y166,
nyth(e) Y68, 299, 475, and see
day. (adverbial) *þat* ∿ 192:3.
nyghtes *pl.* (adverbial) *in* ∿ at
night SR678, *on* **nyghttys** SA650,
651.
nyll *pr. 2 sg. subj.* see **nel.**
nyne *adj.* nine C581.
nis *pr. 3 sg.* is not 9:2, 41:1, etc., **nys**
SR132. **nas** *pa. t. 3 sg.* 9:1, 60:5,
etc. **ner(e)** *pa. t. pl.* 141:5, 173:5.
nyse *adj.* see **nice.**
nist *pa. t. 3 sg.* see **nite.**
nite *pr. pl.* do not know 163:2. **nist**
pa. t. 3 sg. 128:2.
nyte, nyth(e) *n.* see **niȝt.**

niþe *n.* malice, envy, in $\sim$ *and ond* 95:2[n].

no *adj.* no, (with neg.) any ($+$ cons.) 9:2, etc., C68, etc., Y89, etc., SR94, etc., SA39, etc., ($+$ vowel or aspirate) 44:2, SA48, 75. **non** (postposited) 66:4, 130:4, ($+$ vowel or *h*) 129:5, 187:5, C321, 475, Y659, **none** SR47, etc., (separated from *n.*) C317; **non** (as *pron. sg.* or *pl.*) none (of persons) 3:2, 114:2, etc., C30, Y26, (of things) 15:6, 130:2, C80, 488, Y531, SA533, **none** SR541. See **thing**.

no *adv.* (before *v.*) not 2:5, etc., (following aux.) SR74; (modifying comp.) 50:5, etc., C239, etc., Y234, 248. $\sim$ *for þan* nevertheless 57:1. See **more, nother**.

no *conj.* nor 130:4, 148:5, etc., (after neg.) 4:6, 9:3, etc. See **nother** *conj.*

noder *pron.* see **nothir** *pron.*

noght, no3t *adv.* see **nou3t** *adv.*

noise *n.* noise, sound 109:4; unpleasant din SR539, 554, **noyse** SR15, etc, SA94, etc. **noyses** *pl.* SR93, 400, SA95, **noyse** (construed as *pl.* after *many*) melodious sounds (bird-song) SA590.

noiþer *conj.* see **nother** *conj.*

nold(en) *pa. t. sg./pl.* see **nel**.

nom(e) *pa. t. sg./pl.* see **nam**.

non(e) *adj.* (and as *pron.*) see **no**.

none *n.* noon SA9, *þe* $\sim$ SR8.

nones[r] *n. for þe* $\sim$ (practically meaningless tag) indeed 131:6, C469.

non(e)skines *adj.* (in adv. phrases following neg.) *for* $\sim$ *nede* not for any (kind of) necessity/reason at all 124:3, 187;3.

nonne *n.* nun SR26, 681, SA25; **nonnes** *gen.* SR664. **nonnes** *pl.* 138:3, C496, **nonnys** Y539.

nor *conj.* (after neg.) nor Y79, 619, SA96, etc. See **neyther, nother**.

noreschyde *pa. t. 1 sg.* suckled SA342, **norshid** SR334.

norþ *adv.* (to the) north 39:6.

northcontree *n.* the north of England SR53.

nose *n.* (with *pl. poss.*) nose SA193. **noses** *pl.* SR187, 352. Cf. **neyses**.

noselyng *adv.* face downward SR350[n].

not(e), nott(e), noth *adv.* see **nou3t**.

notes *n. pl.* musical notes 145:4, bird song SR600.

nother *adj.* (after *no*) no other 78:6; as *pron.* Y165.

nother *conj.* $\sim$ ... *nor* neither ... nor SA256, **noþur** ... *ner* C168, 218, **noiþer** ... *no* 123:6; **nothir** (after neg.) nor SR272. Cf. **neyther**.

nothyng(e) *adv.* not at all SA524.

nothing *pron.* nothing SR654, **noting** 2:6, 125:6, **nothyng(e)** SA561, 626, 650, Y200, SR557, SA97.

nothir *pron.* $\sim$ ... *other* neither (of two persons) ... (the) other SR129, **noder** ... *oder* SA132.

nou3t *adv.* not at all, not 4:5, etc., **nowght** SR343, **now3t** C34, **now3th** C141, etc., **nowt** Y260, **nowte** Y137, etc., **nowth** Y258, etc., **naw3te** C267, **noght** SR457, 703, **no3t** C378, **nat(t)** SA74, etc., SR638, SA79, etc., **not** C8, etc., Y79, etc., **SR56**, etc., SA651, **note** Y388, 394, **nott** SA77, etc., **notte** Y625, **noth** Y512, etc.

nou3t *pron.* nothing 37:1; *of* $\sim$ out of nothing 130:6; *ayled* **now3t** *but gode* = there was nothing wrong with C304[n]; *sette ry3th* **now3th** = thought nothing of it C482.

noure *adv.* $\sim$ *nei3e* nowhere near, not nearly 185:3.

novelys *n. pl.* see **nauel**.

now *adv.* now 86:3, etc., C670, Y404, 648, SR288, etc., SA60, etc., **nowe** C322, SR437; just now, recently 161:4; *ry3th* $\sim$ at that time C642; (emphatic in exhortation) 28:4, etc., C651.

nowynge *pr. p.* see **gnawyng(e)**.

nunnery *n.* nunnery SR658.

o see **of** *prep.*, **oon** *adj.*

occupacyonys *n. pl.* activities, pastimes SA436.

occupied *pp.* ~ *in* engaged in, kept busy with SR429, 434, 436, (sim.) **occupyde** SA446.

oder(e), odyr(e) *adj.* see **oþer** *adj.*

of *adv.* off SR183, 185, 209(1), 211, SA191, 223(1), etc.; of, about (after speak) SA532, **off** SA67.

of *prep.* from C99, 160, 604, Y155, SR640, (after *ask*) SA626; off, from 123:4, 127:1, out of, from 93:3, SR231(1), 466, SA244, **o** 18:1; ~ *wronge makyth ryth* = creates good out of evil Y2; (made) of SR231, SA195, **off** Y289, **o** 93:2ⁿ, 129:6; ~ *him cam* descended from him 175:2, (sim.) SR135, **off** SA139; *abstinded* ~ (body) abstained from (bodily pleasures) SR407; *sece* ~ cease from, leave off SR359; of (mod. uses) 3:2, 6:3, 40:4, etc., C1, 61, 329, 523, etc., Y101, 244, 434, etc., SR3, 110, etc., SA1, 92, etc., **off** SA8, 148, **o** 70:5, etc.; ~ (because) of, on account of 67:5, C478, SA142, 362, 647(1), **off** C478, Y521; ~ by (means of), from 134:4; ~ ... *get* ... *no gain* profited ... nothing by 189:1; of, about, concerning 2:6, 8:2, 30:4, 84:4, 176:2, 3, C28, 33, 528, Y120, SR419, 665, 666, 703, SA2, 126, **off** C6, 348, Y236; ~ in SR5(2), (rejoicing) SA362, (pride) SA214*, *haue ioye* ~ enjoy, have pleasure in SR130, ~ *dome* in judgement 45:5, *made* ~ *sylkeweth gyse* made in a strange manner Y218; *haue mercy* ~ have compassion on (sb.) Y245; *haue in mynd* ... ~ remember SR46 (see also **mynd(e)**); *in trust* ~ trusting in SR627; *space* ~ space of time for SR199, 362, SA662; *correct* ... ~ = punish ... for, reprove SR390; *power* ~ authority over (soul) SR240; on (pity) 1:5, (vengeance) SA316; *amende* ... ~ atone for C134; (adjectival) SR577, 676(1); some of (in partitive phrase after *toke*) SR186; by (instrument) SR289, SA267, *swerynge* ~ SA239, (agent) SR447, SA397, 504, 582,

foryeve ~ forgiven by SR241; ~ *vertu* powerful SR86, SA87; ~ *grete stenche* = very evil smelling SR230; ~ *myche wondre* with great astonishment Y253; *full wyll* ~ *held* = very aged Y678. See also **bare, faile, fayn** *adj.*, **fulfil, knowlage, nede, point, priis, rede, schriue, sette, si3t, speyke, telle, thanke, ware.** Cf. **hereof, þerof.**

office *n.* *bi his* ~ on account of his position of responsibility (as bishop) SR502.

officers *n. pl.* ecclesiastical officials SR485, 510, **offecers(c)** SA504, 473, 490, 497.

ofspring *n.* (Adam's) descendants, i.e. the human race 172:1.

oft(e) *adv.* often C652, 667, Y350, SR529, 607, 635, SA523, 2:1, 5:4, SA599.

often *adv.* often SA61, 605, **oftyn** Y657, 670.

often-tymes *adv.* many times, frequently SR58.

oftok *pa. t. 3 sg.* caught up with, overtook 80:2.

ogain, o3ain *adv.* see **agayn(e).**

o3ain(e)s *prep.* see **a3enst.**

okering *n.* usury 103:4.

old(e) *adj.* old C677, 167:5. **eldest** *sup.* C233, **eldes** Y222, 228, (as *pron.*) **eldest** C227. See **3ong(e)** and cf. **held.**

omnipotentʳ *adj.* *God* ~ Almighty God 6:5, 75:5, 104:2, etc.

on *adj.* see **oon** and **a** *indef. art.*

on *adv.* on SR210, etc., SA224, etc., (of clothes) C315, 487; ~ *to sene* to look at 106:6, 156:4, (sim.) SA530; ~ *tweyne* in two SR220.

on *conj.* see **and.**

on *prep.* on (mod. uses) 70:4, etc., C222, etc., Y212, etc., SR8, etc., SA83, etc., ~ *fire* on fire SR212, etc., SA192; on, onto Y383; in SR598, (after 'believe') 6:5, (sim. with 'thought') C245, (after 'remain') C278, ~ *carol* in a dance 142:1, ~ *Goddys name* in God's name C154, **a** *Goddys name* Y149, ~ *a row* in a row Y551, (sim.

'rout', 'belief') Y221, 335, SR120, (with 'manner', 'wise') Y548, 219, (sim.) SA37, 314, etc.; at (after 'grin') 54:2, C272, 296, Y291, 389, (sim. 'look') SR173, SA330, ('laugh') SA27, ∼ *nyghttys* at night SA649(2), 651; on, by (with 'swear') 82:4; of, about (with 'think') 89:3, SA83, (sim.) SA96; about, concerning (after 'make complaint') SR124; ∼ *a day* one day 31:1; ∼ *slepeing* a-sleeping 7:5. See do, eche, hei3e *adj.*, hond(e), lasten, legge, lif, myd(e), morwe, sonder *adv.* and cf. afyre *adv.*

on *pron.* one (person) Y332, SR419, 663, SA425, 634, (thing) 149:3, SA32(1,3), (opposed to 'the other') SR366, SA369, one SR33, 290, oon *and* ∼ one by one C601; *such* ∼ such a one C366, (sim.) Y307.

ond *n.* hatred, malice 95:4[n], and see niþe.

onded, ondoo *v.* see vndo.

one *adj.* see owne.

one *pron.* see on *pron.*

oneþe, onnethe *adv.* see vn(n)eþe.

ony *adj.* see ani.

onicles *n. pl.* onyxes 131:5.

onys *adv.* at some (future) time or other Y627, onus C623. See at.

onything *n.* anything SR568. Cf. aniþing.

onkindenesse *n.* see vnkyndeness.

only *adv.* only SR95, etc., SA97, solely SR685.

onlokked *pa. t. 3 sg.* unlocked C199.

onto *prep.* see vnto.

onus *adv.* see onys.

onwylld *adj.* feeble, weak Y679.

onwyn *n.* sorrow, distress Y419.

oo *interj.* o! C617.

oon *adj.* one SR606, 607, o 120:4, o *sithe* = once 182:1; = first 150:1; (as opposed to 'two') 103:6; on (as opposed to 'other') C439.

oonus *adv.* see at.

oore *n.* see ore.

open *adj.* open 44:6, C222, *SR440, SA452, opyn Y215, unconcealed

SA243; *wyde* oppyn stretched out flat on the back SA353.

openede *pa. t. 3 sg. intr.* opened (of a gate) C468; opend *tr.* SR664, opynde SA635.

opon *prep.* see vpon.

or *pr. pl.* see ar.

or *conj.*[1] or 82:5, etc., C79, etc., Y242, etc., SR14, etc., SA111(2), etc., ore Y74.

or *adv., conj.*[2] before C605, SR564, SA111(1), 154, 557, 603; ∼ *than* Y15; ∼ *that* Y613; ∼ *to late* before it is too late 109:1.

ordende *pa. t. 3 sg.* created SA670.

order *n. þat* ∼ *had ytake* that had received ordination 138:6; *þe* ∼ *of wedlake* = (those in) the wedded state 139:1; ordyr religious rule or order SA416, 647.

ordynaunce *n. at hys* ∼ at his command C591.

ore *conj.* see or *conj.*[1].

ore *n.* mercy 188:2; *þyn* oore! have mercy! C617.

orible *adj.* see horrible.

orisoun *n.* (act of) prayer 5:5, 38:2, SA12, orison SR11, oryson Y676, SA14, orysowne C426, 675, orysun Y473.

orrabyll, orrible *adj.* see horrible.

os *conj.* see as.

oþer *adj.* other, another, other kinds of 28:5, 36:5, etc., Y75, 297, SR231, etc., other Y534, 574, SR93, etc., SA178, etc., othyr Y335, 354, 447, SA276, oþur C24, etc., (postposited) C309; second C80, 442; previous C634; owþer Y320, oder SA215, 331, odyr(e) SA183, 194, 244, 272; ∼ *þre* = three others 156:5; other *his membris* = other parts of his body SR225; (as or approaching *pron.*) other (the) other SR126, 130, etc., SA129, 369; ∼ second, other (one) 150:4, 170:4; *other* otheir each other, one another SR137; *eche lyme from* ∼ = limb from limb SA308; *ilkone wente* oþur *be and be* = each one followed the next in turn C491[n]. ∼ *pl.* others, other (things) 69:5,

Y272, SR283, 379, **other** Y239,
SR172, 233, 625, etc., SA177,
240, 297, (or adverbial = otherwise), **oþur** C244, 279, **odyr**
SA256. See **chide, ether** *adj.*,
euerych *adj.*, **nothir** *pron.*, and
cf. **tother.**
oþer *conj.* or 73:5, 133:2, 164:1(1),
169:6; **oþur** ... *or* either ... or
C568.
oþerwise *adv.* in different ways 77:5;
oþurwyse differently C400,
owtherweyes Y451.
ouer *adv.* over, across Y507, **ouur**
C460, (up)on 118:2^n. See **her(e)**
adv.
ouer *prep.* over, across 124:2, 183:5,
C320, Y460, etc., SA188, etc.,
over SR347, etc., **ouyr** Y307,
ouur C413, etc.
oueral *adv.* everywhere 86:3.
ouercum *v.* overcome Y643, **ouurcome** C242. **ouercomen** *pp.*
192:4.
ouerest *adj. sup.* highest, uppermost
Y375.
ouerfle *v.* escape, flee 167:3^n.
overgilt *pp. adj.* covered with gold,
gilded SR676, 677.
ouermoche *adv.* immoderately
SA393.
ouerschaken *pp.* shaken off (pain)
68:4.
ouersett *pp. adj. with* ... ∿ covered,
decorated ... with (ornaments)
SA175, **oversette** SR170.
ouersympul *adj.* too weak or witless
SA122.
ouerþrewe *pa. t. 3 sg.* knocked down
(sb.), overwhelmed 72:5^n.
ouȝt *adv.* at all 94:4; by any chance
108:5.
our, ous *poss. adj., pron. acc.* see **we.**
ourn *pa. t. pl.* ran 84:3.
out *adv.* out 25:6, 105:2, 106:1, etc.,
C112, 382, 393, **owt** SR92, 206,
etc., SA94, 311, etc., **owte** Y431,
496, SA372, 385; ∿ *at* out via, out
of C471; ∿ + 'say' to the end,
completely 17:1. See **þurthout.**
out *prep.* out of 105:4.
out of *prep.* out of, from 6:3, etc.,
C570, etc., from out of 126:6, **owt**

of SR152, 252, etc., SA109, etc.,
owte of Y262, etc., SR244,
SA185, 276, **owte off** SA527,
owth of Y527. See **mesure.**
oway *adv.* see **away.**
owene *adj.* see **owne.**
owere *poss. adj.* see **we.**
oweth *pr. t. pl.* (+ *inf.*) ought C232.
owght *pa. t. 3 sg.* (present sense)
SR195. **owght** *pa. t. pl.* SR672.
owne *adj.* own C156, 641, SR40,
etc., SA279, 338, 638, **owene**
C540, 590, 632, **owhen** 87:6,
owyn Y636, **howyn** Y151, 647,
one SA21, 287, 617, **awne**
SA135; *quasi-sb.* in *of myne* ∿ of
my own SA113.
owners *n. pl.* owners SR277.
owre *poss. adj.* see **we.**
owre *n. þe .viij.* ∿ the eighth hour
SR7, *the viijte* ∿ SA9.
owt(e) (of), owth of *prep.* see **out
(of).**
owther *adj.* see **oþer** *adj.*
owtherweyes *adv.* see **oþerwise.**
owyr *poss. adj.* see **we.**
oxen *n. pl.* oxen SR261, **oxon**
SA272.

pace *v.* see **passe.**
pay *n.* satisfaction, in *serue God ... to*
∿ serve God well C172, Y144,
(sim.) **paye** Y167.
pain(e) *n.* pain, torment, punishment
179:3, SR616, 4:1, etc., **payn(e)**
C297, etc., SR219, etc., SA198,
etc., SR139, etc., SA282, etc.,
pein 25:1, 101:2, **peyne** C334,
Y325. **paines** *pl.* 15:5, etc.,
paynes SR163, etc., SA179, etc.,
paynys SA276, 279, **payns**
SR347, SA513, **payens** SA438,
peynes 82:6, **peynys** Y104, etc.,
peynus C107.
paynes *pr. t. pl.* torments SR289,
payneth SR290, 386, 437. **payn-
eng(e)** *pr. p.* SR506, 409. **payned**
pa. t. 3 sg. SR372. **payned** *pa. t.
pl.* SR377. **payned** *pp.* SR328,
etc., **paynyd** SA285, **ypayned**
SR282, etc.
pays *n.* see **pes.**
paintour *n.* painter 133:2.

palmes *n. pl.* palm leaves 140:3.
pappis *n. pl.* (woman's) breasts SR335, **pappys** (non-specific) breast Y429, **pappus** C379.
par *prep.* see **aventur(e)**.
paradis *n.* paradise 16:6, etc., **paradys** 26:5, **paradyse** C668, **paradysse** Y671; ∼ *celestien* Celestial Paradise 165:4; ∼ *terestri* Earthly Paradise 170:2, *Erþly* **Paradyse** C577, (sim.) Y593.
parcels *n. pl.* parts, pieces SA192.
parte *n.* see **more** *adj. comp.*
parti *n.* (in phrases) *a* ∼ partly, somewhat 103:5, *a* ∼ *of* some 14:2. **parties** *pl.* parts (of the body) SR303; **partys** = persons contracted to a marriage SA494.
paruink *n.* periwinkle 147:3ⁿ.
paryche *v.* see **peressh**.
pas *n. pl.* dangerous paths Y584ⁿ.
pasce *n. euer a* ∼ at every step Y490.
passe *v.* (*tr.*) cross (bridge) C434, **pace** Y481; ∼ traverse, go along (this/that way) SR73, SA20, 38, 79, **passen** SR79; (*intr.*) advance, go, get by SR39, SA37, 38. **pas** *pr. 2 sg.* go 159:6, **passist** SR704. ∼ *pr. t. pl.* 165:2. ∼ *imp. sg.* go SR645, 700. **passynge** *pr. p.* exceeding, going beyond the bounds of SA332, surpassing SA590.
passid *pa. t. 1 sg.* SR108. **passed** *pa. t. 3 sg.* SR21, **passyd** exceeded SA375. **passed** *pa. t. pl.* SR62, **passyde** SA65. **passed** *pp.* (*tr.*) C554, 574, **passyd** Y584, **passid** SR623, (*intr.*) (motion) **passed** SR150, **passid** SR277, **passyde** SA154, (*adj.*) **passed** over, past 53:1, **passid** SR584, 608, **passyde** SA600, past SA577.
passyng(e) *ppl. adj.* extreme SA371, 454, SR370, 442, 451, 459, = very large SR451; (*adv.*) marvelously SA593.
passion *n.* suffering, Passion (of Christ) SR42, etc., SA83, etc., **passyon** SA42, etc., **passioun** 175:4, **possion** SR46.
Pater noster *n.* Lord's Prayer SR524, SA519. ∼ *pl.* SA555, **Pater** SR562.

pein, peyn(e)(s), peynys, peynus *n.* see **pain(e)**.
pelleure *n.* fur SA648, **puler** SR676.
penance *n.* penalty enjoined as a penance SA150, 152, etc., **penaunce** 13:5, 33:4, etc., SR143, 637; ∼ *with do* = carry out one's penance SA147, 613, **penans** Y581, 588, **penaunce** C281, SR141, 148, **penawns** Y274, **pennanse** SA145; *space of* ∼ time in which to carry out one's penance SA662, SR363, (sim.) SR199; ∼ punishment C597, SA153, 233, 391, **penanse** SA354, **penaunce** 14:2, C560.
penance-doynge *vbl. n.* performance of penance SA211, **penaunce-doyng** SR692.
pens *n.* coins, pennies 101:5.
people *n.* mankind generally SR157, **pepyll** SA161, ∼ people SR402, etc., **pepul** SA410, **pepull** C48, SA389, 488, 515, **pepyl** SA468, (the common) ∼ SR383, 457, 468, 499, (sim.) **pepull** SA486, **pepyll** SA458.
perced *pa. t. 3 sg.* pierced 63:3.
peressh *v.* perish SR423, **paryche** SA412. **perisshid** *pp.* killed, destroyed SR72, **peryshyd** SA77, **pershid** SR77. Cf. **perishyng**.
peryd *pa. t. 3 sg.* appeared Y46.
periil *n.* peril 124:4, **peryll** SA600.
perelles *pl.* C182, **perellys** Y175, 231, 236, **peroles** SR608, *grette* **perellys** *it is* it is very dangerous (to do sth.) Y163.
perilous *adj.* dangerous SR623.
perishyng *vbl. n. in point of* ∼ on the verge of dying SR96.
perle *n.* pearl SA194, **perlle** SA177.
perles *pl.* SR173, **perlous** SR188.
person *n.*[1] person SR635, SA606; *agayn hyr owne* ∼ = with regard to her personally SA638.
person *n.*[2] parson SR420, SA428.
persons *pl.* SA431, 462, **persones** C497, SR423, 455, 472, **personys** Y540.

pes *n. ben in* $\sim$*!* be silent! 76:4; *in* pays in peace 164:6.

pestilence tyme *n.* time of plague SR111.

piche *n.* pitch, wood tar 105:6, pych(e) C294, SR316, pyke Y289; (in comp.) *as swart as* $\sim$ as black as pitch 116:6, (sim. with 'black') pyke C405, Y456, SA319, 470.

pycturede *pp.* represented, figured forth SA70[n].

pike *n.*[1] pick-axe 172:4. pykys *pl.* spikes SA533.

pyke *n.*[2] see piche.

pilers *n. pl.* pillars 44:3, 132:3, pyllerys Y216; $\sim$ piers (of a bridge) SR487[n], pyllers SA476.

pilgrimage *n.* pilgrimage SR523, 525, pylgramage SA518, pylgrymage C77, pylgrymmage Y72.

pylyde *pp.* piled up, filled SA455[n], ipiled SR443.

pyllowys *n. pl.* pillows Y351.

pinacles *n. pl.* pinnacles, small ornamental turrets 132:6[n].

pine *n.* punishment, torment 36:3, 48:3, etc., pyne C570. See hellepine.

pyned(e) *pp.* tortured, punished SA437, 335, 337, pynyde SA207, 444, (+ of) by SA397.

pipis *n. pl.* large wine casks SR393.

pit *n.* pit 64:2, 107:2, etc., pytte C384. pittes *pl.* 99:2, pyttys Y421, 425, 427, 433, pyttus C370, 374, 376.

pyte *n.* pity C299.

place *n.* place 184:3, C305, 443, 586, Y602, SR421, etc., plas 139:6, C554. places *pl.* SR212, 215, 243, SA229. See also restyng(e)place.

Placebo *n.* $\sim$ *and Dirige* = vespers and matins of the Office of the Dead SR521, SA516.

play *n.* game 119:4. playes *pl.* (theatrical) plays SA251, amusements, pastimes SA436.

play *v.* (or *n.*?) play (a game) 56:6. plas *n.* see place.

plates *n. pl.* (iron) plates SR413, SA421, 422, platis SR414, platees SA432.

pleyng *vbl. n.* merrymaking, dalliance SR426.

plente *n. gret* $\sim$ a great many 137:2, 145:5.

plesaunt *adj.* pleasing SR553.

plese *v.* please (God) SR195, SA202; pleyse satisfy, delight SA200. plesyng(e) *pr. p.* acceptable SA621, SR48, 104, SA49, etc., plesing SR649.

plesyng(e) *vbl. n.* gratification SA201, satisfaction SR496.

plou3 *n.* plough-land 86:5[n].

plukkyng *pr. p.* pulling at SA481.

plunchyng *pr. p.* plunging, thrusting SR492[n].

point *n. in* $\sim$ *of* on the verge of SR96; *in* poynte *forto* to the point of, ready to SR368; poynt item SR665.

pokes *n. pl.* full, elongated sleeves SR170[n], 182, pokys SA175, powkys SA188.

pomp(p)e *n.* $\sim$ *and pride* ostentation and display SA640, SR669.

ponesches *pr. t. 3 sg.* punishes, torments SA298. poneschys *pr. t. pl.* SA500. poneschyde *pp.* SA304, etc., ponyschyd(e) SA620, 504, punysshid SR274, 279, etc.

popes *n. pl.* popes 137:1.

porcatory *n.* see purgatori.

pore *adj.* poor C22, SR459, 479, SA467, powre SA418; as *n. pl.* in inclusive phrase $\sim$ *and ryche* everybody C556, (sim.) Y586; *wiþ* pouer *and eke wiþ riche* = for everybody 21:6.

possible *adj.* possible SR157.

possion *n.* see passion.

pottes *n. pl.* pots SR235, pottys SA248.

poudre *n.* powder, ash 85:6.

pouer *adj.* as *n.* see pore.

pouerte *n.* poverty SA209.

poure *adj.* pure 15:2, 47:5.

pourper *n.* cloth of purple 154:2.

power *n.* strength, power C458, pouwere 156:6; $\sim$ authority

SR634, **powre** SA502, 605; *hath* ⌣ *of* has authority over SR240; *hath no* ⌣ *to* = is not able to C558, (sim.) SA39; *by here* ⌣ = with all their might SR39.

powkys *n. pl.* see **pokes**.

powre *adj.* see **pore**.

pray *n.* depredation Y505[n].

pray(e) *v.* pray (to) (God, Christ) SA256, 5:6, **prey** Y186. **pray** *pr. 1 sg.* request C149. **prayd** *pa. t. 3 sg.* entreated 33:2, 188:2. **prayde** *pa. t. pl.* C639, SA254, **preyed** Y195.

prayer *n.* prayer SR12, 14, 27, 545, SA43, 84, etc., **praier** SR43, 86, etc., **preiere** 78:6; *haue me in yowre* **praier** = pray for me SR709; ⌣ intercession SA148, **praier** SR144, **preier** 28:3; entreaty 189:1; *maked his* **preier** said his prayer 51:6. **prayers** *pl.* SR10, 431, etc., SA11, 254, 525, **praiers** SR434, (+ *gan make*) = said (his) prayers 195:3. See also **make**.

praysyng *vbl. n.* the approbation SA488.

precession *n. with* ⌣ accompanied by a procession SR10[n]. Cf. **processioun**.

preche *v.* exhort C253, talk Y248. **preched(e)** *pa. t. 3 sg.* preached C31, 29, 33, etc., **prechyd** Y25, 27. **prechid** *pp.* SR382, **prechyde** SA389.

precherys *n. pl.* preachers Y20, **prechorus** C24.

prechyng(e) *vbl. n.* admonition, persuasion SA364, SR197, 361, SA208.

Prechours *n. pl.* see **freres**.

precious *adj.* precious (blood) SR103, **preciose** SA105, ⌣ **ston(es)** precious stones 130:5, SR173, 189, (sim.) **preciuus** SA194, **precyvse** SA178, **presyous** C470.

prede *n.* see **pride**.

preier(e) *n.* see **prayer**.

prelates *n. pl.* ecclesiastics of high rank SR382, 390, SA388, 397.

presse *n.* chest for clothes SA455. **pressis** *pl.* SR443[n], **pressys** *off*

clothes SA455.

prest(e) *n.* priest C647, 154:4, C191, SR149, **pryst(e)** Y184, SA152. **prestes** *pl.* C232, 497, SR455, 465, **prestis** SR424, **prestys** SA431, 440, 515, 596, **pristes** SR432, 467, 605, **prystys** Y540, 652, (*dat.*) Y227.

presyous *adj.* see **precious**.

prevays *n. pl.* privies SA244.

prev(e)y, preuy, preuely *adj./adv.* see **membris, pryue, pryuely**.

prey(ed) *v., pa. t. pl.* see **pray(e)**.

preyor(e) *n.* see **priour**.

pride *n.* (sin of) pride 58:3, SR197, SA657, **pryde** C18, Y14, **prede** 112:5, ⌣ *of hert* SR192; ⌣ opulence SR387, 685, **pryde** SA393; ⌣ ostentation SA199, 201; ⌣ *of* pride in SA214; *in* **pryde** proudly SA395, 398. See **do, pomp(p)e**.

priis *n. of* ⌣ splendid 149:3; *of much more* ⌣ *of* much more precious/ renowned on account of 150:5; *lest of* ⌣ the least excellent 148:3.

pryme *n.* the canonical hour of prime, *to* ⌣ for the Office of prime C643. **prime** *bell* bell rung for prime Y648[n].

primrol *n.* ?primrose, cowslip 147:3[n].

principally *adv.* principally SR500, SA661, **princypally** SA513, **principallich** SR519.

prioresse *n.* prioress SR657, SA629.

priour *n.* prior 38:4, 192:2, etc., SR11, 146, etc., **pryour** C93, 646, etc., **pryowr(e)** Y154, 172, etc., Y651, 663, **prior** SR9, SA9, 11, 14, 18, 150, **preyor(e)** Y153, 90, 95. **pryowrys** *gen.* Y191. **priours** *pl.* 137:4.

prisoun *n.* prison 110:4, 175:5.

pryst(e), -ys *n.* see **prest(e)**.

pryue *adj.* hidden C70, **preuy** Y65.

pryuely *adv.* mysteriously C10, **preuely** Y6.

priuete *n. Godes* ⌣ divine secrets 9:6.

processioun *n.* (a) procession 136:3, 138:5, C59; *wiþ* ⌣ in a procession 38:4, 193:1; **procession** SA10, **processyoun** C192, 485, 648,

prosessyoun Y653, proseyssyun Y528, prose(y)ssun Y185,
55^n. Cf. precession.

prophetys *n. pl.* prophets C5.

proued *pa. t. 3 sg.* endeavoured, tried
2:1.

psalmes *n. pl.* Psalms SR522^n,
SA517, salmes SR522.

psauters *n. pl.* ~ *sayd* (a selection of)
the Psalms recited SA516. Cf.
sauter.

puler *n.* see pelleure.

pulle *v.* pull SA475. pullyng *pr. p.*
SR486.

punysshid *pa. t. pl.* see ponesches.

purches *v.* (*refl.*) obtain through
merit SA447. purches *them pr. t.
pl.* earn for themselves SA671.

purchese *n.* = something earned or
deserved SA449.

pure *adj.* true, real 123:2.

purfuld *pp.* trimmed with fur Y302^n.

purgatori *n.* (i) purgatory 42:6, 67:6,
194:5, etc., purgatorie SR277,
532, purgatory(e) C80, 549, 564,
37, SA289, purcatory Y580, 582,
porcatory Y33, 75. (ii) Purgatory = St Patrick's Purgatory, a
cave on Station Island, Lough
Derg, County Donegal, Ireland
SA10, 150, Purgatori(e) SR10,
146, 192:2, *Patrikes* Purgatori
35:5, *Patrikes* Purgatorie 24:3,
Patrik is Purgatorie SR2, Purgatorie *of Seint Patrik* SR6, *Patrike* ~ SA3, ~ *of Saynt Patrike*
SA7, *Seynt Patrykus* Purgatorye
C102, (sim.) C138, *Seynth Partrykys* Purcatore Y99.

purpos *n. in ful* ~ *was* fully intended
SR684, (sim.) purpasse SA656.

put *v.* add SR529, SA523. puttyste
pr. t. 2 sg. (*refl.*) put (oneself in
danger) Y231. put *pr. t. 3 sg. subj.*
SR527, SA521. put *pr. t. pl.* put,
thrust 109:2. puttyng *pr. p.*
SR211, 445; puttyng (sb.) *owt of*
(their) *good name* = destroying
their reputation SR359, (sim.)
SA362. put *pa. t. 1 sg.* SA570. put
pl. SR221, SA261, putt SA236.
put *pp.* SR9, 526, putt SA9, 521.

quantite *n.* quantity, amount SR528.

quarel *n.* bolt (shot from a crossbow)
93:3, 189:5, 190:1.

queyntaunce *n.* acquaintance 79:4^n.

queinter *adj. comp.* more skilful
133:2.

quene *n.* queen SA650. quenes *pl.*
137:3.

quic *adj.* alive 139:6, qwykke C613,
qwekke Y619; ~ *brunston* burning or native sulphur 78:2^n, 99:6.

quite *v.* reward SR586, qwytte
SA579; qwyte requite C284.

qweynte *pp.* extinguished C301.

qwerne *n.* a hand mill Y381.

qwhan *adv.* see when.

rayn(e) *n.* rain C422, 429, SA463,
SR472.

ran(ne) *pa. t. 3 sg.* see renneþ.

raso(u)r *n.* razor 121:2, SR570, rasowre SA563.

raþe *adv.* quickly, without delay
C341. raþer *comp. no* ~ no sooner
92:1. raþest *sup.* soonest 6:2.

rebell *adj.* rebellious SR697.

reche *adj.* see riche *adj.*

reche *v.* reach SR570, SA562. reching *pr. p.* extending (from ... to)
SR566, rechyng SA558. reght
pa. t. 1 sg. stretched out (one's
hand) SR577.

red(e) *adj.* red 90:3, 154:1, 180:4,
red-hot SA186, 70:2. See gold *n.*

rede *n. after his* ~ according to his
counsel/advice 2:3, (sim.) C169, *bi*
... ~ 57:2; course of action C280;
plan Y273.

red(e) *v.* discern, make out C534,
Y547; ~ *and sing* read and chant
(church service) (tag) 20:6, (sim.)
C568. *of* ~ *pr. 1 sg.* read about
112:4; advise C145, 167, Y141,
162, 164. redest *pr. 2 sg.* advise
C175. redyn *pr. 3 pl.* read SR707.
rede *pa. t. 3 sg.* read Y156, redde
C161.

redely *adv.* clearly Y5, redylye C9.

redempcioun *n.* redemption, liber-
ation from hell 123:5.

redy *adj.* direct, unimpeded (way)
C631; prepared Y663; ~ (+ *tyll*)
= willing to give help to SA205^n.

refresshid *pp.* provided shelter and refreshment SR460, **refresshyde** comforted SA513.

reght *pa. t. 1 sg.* see **reche** *v.*

regnes *pr. 3 sg.* reigns 86:3[n].

rehersid *pa. t. 3 sg.* recounted SR335; repeated SR628.

reioysed *pp.* gladdened, made more joyful SR29, **reioysyd** SA28, reiosyde SA614.

reiosynge *vbl. n. havynge* ∿ *of* exulting in SA361.

reyth *adv.* see **ri3t** *adv.*

reles *n.* abatement of distress SR278.

relevid *pp.* given relief (from pain) SR410, **relevyde** SA419.

religion *n.* the religious life SR669, *þe* **religeon** SA640, **relygion** SA642; **relygiun** a religious order Y142, **relygyoun** C146, 486, Y529, **relegyon** SA414; *al maner* **religioun** = members of all kinds of religious orders 138:4; **relygyon** devotion, piety Y677.

religious *adj.* belonging to a religious rule or order SR405, 671.

relykes *n. pl.* relics C190, **relykys** Y183, **relekys** Y52, **relyquus** C57.

remedi *n.* relief (from pain) SR515, **remedy** SA508.

rememure *n.* commemoration, (retention in) memory Y98[n].

renneþ *pr. 3 sg.* spins (of a wheel) 86:1; **rinneþ** is current, spreads 71:6; flows (of a river) 151:3. **ran** *pa. t. 3 sg.* flowed 93:2, 121:4; rose (of a wall) Y511; spun (of a wheel) Y380, **ranne** Y376, **arn** 88:4. **vrn** *pa. t. 3 pl.* flowed 149:5.

repentance *n.* repentance SA211, 612, 655, **repentaunce** SR683.

repenti *v.* repent 4:5, *(refl.)* 13:4. **rependede** *pa. t. 3 sg. (refl.)* C123.

*reprevyd *pa. t. 3 pl.* censured, rebuked SA399.

require *pr. 1 sg.* ask, request SR50.

resayuynge *pr. p.* receiving SA350.

resoun *n.* talk, speech 158:6; *told him* ∿ *ri3t* = gave him good advice 46:6; *by* **reson** *of* on account of SA439.

rest *v. (refl.)* remain SR650. **restyde** *pa. t. 3 sg.* was left SA354.

reste *n.* rest, peace C68, SA651; *sonne goth to* ∿ = sun sets C214.

restyng(e)-place *n.* place where one rests SA19, SR19.

reuelacion *n.* revelation SR1, 20, **reuelacyon** SA20.

revershid *pp. adj.* attired in ecclesiastical garments SR615[n].

reuþe *n.* pitiful sight 67:1; **rewthe** pity SA582, **ruthe** SA230, *hadde* **rewþe** *of* had pity on 1:4.

reweful *adj.* see **ruful**.

rewyd *pp.* taken away Y259[n].

ribaudie *n.* idle nonsense 2:5[n].

ribes *n. pl.* rubies 131:4[n].

riche *adj.* costly, precious, splendid 131:3, **ryche** C53, 56, etc., Y183, **reche** Y48, 546; ∿ *well off* 157:6; **ryche** superior, choice C614, **reche** Y620; fine, excellent Y81, 84. **richer** *comp.* more splendid 132:2. See **pore** *adj.*

riche *n.* kingdom 165:3, 170:4. See **heuen-ryche**.

richer *adv. comp.* more elaborately 133:5.

riches *n. pl.* wealth SR670, SA641.

ryffe *v.* tear apart SA307. **ryvynge** *pr. p.* SA273, 481.

rigge *n.* back 77:4.

right, ryght *adj., adv.* see **ri3t**.

ryght *n.* justice, that which is right C2, 34, **ry3th** C541, **ryth** Y2; *be* ∿ *of* on account of SA443.

rightful(l) *adj.* just SR401, 309, 687.

rightfully *adv.* properly SR702.

ryghtwasness *n.* righteousness SA315.

ryghtwys *adj.* righteous SA659, **rightwous** SR218, ***ryghtewose** SA409.

ri3t *adj.* true, proper 24:2, 37:6, 46:6, **right** SR71, 76, **ryght** C4, Y467, SA77, **ry3te** C420, 679, **ry3th** C50, **ryth** Y4, 680; ∿ *just* 29:1, **ryth** Y644. See **hond(e)** *n.*

ri3t *adv.* straight, directly 11:3, 39:3, 74:5, 151:3, etc., **ry3th** C590, 632; **ry3th** at once C608, **ryth** Y616; **rythe** correctly Y59; ∿ *as* just as if 83:5, (sim.) **right** SR526, **ryght**

Y381, **ryth** Y465; **ryght** just, exactly SA524, **ry3th** (now) C642; **right** very SR107, 561, **ryght** C89, SA560, **ryghtt** SA110; (intensive with *adv., adv. phr.*) ∿ 194:1, **ryght** SA593, **ry3th** C262, 440, **ryth** Y146, 362, **rythe** Y161, **reyth** Y327, (with negative) ∿ at all, whatever 89:6, **ry3th** C482; *anon* **ryght** straightaway Y78. See **anon, ary3th**.
rime *n.* poem 29:6.
rynge *v.* ring (*tr.*) C643. **ryngyth** *pr. 3 sg.* (*intr.*) Y648. **rong** *pa. t. pl.* (*tr.*) 142:6.
ringes *n. pl.* rings SR677, **rynges** SA648.
rinneþ *pr. 3 sg.* see **renneþ**.
rysyng *pr. p.* rising SR351, SA651.
rose *pa. t. 1 sg.* SR565, 567, SA557, **rosse** SA64, 559, **roos** *me* (*refl.*) SR61. **ros** *pa. t. 3 sg.* 196:4.
riuer *n.* river 93:1.
ryvynge *pr. p.* see **ryffe**.
robbers *n. pl.* robbers SR264, **robbars** SA274.
robbyd *pa. t. 3 pl.* robbed SA280, **robbeden** SR269. **robbid** *pp.* SR590, **robbyde** SA582.
roch(e) *n.* rock, rocky height SR348, 557, SA350, 352, 550, SR347. **roches** *pl.* SA295, **rochis** SR284.
rode *n.[1]* þe ∿ the Cross C16, 237, Y12, 232, SR616.
rode *n.[2]* complexion, facial colour 114:1.
rode-tre *n.* þe ∿ the Cross 196:3.
rode *pa. t. 3 sg.* rode Y307.
rong *n.* rung (of a ladder) SR569, 570, 577.
roppe *n.* rope SA569.
rose *n.* rose 147:2.
rounde *adj.* round, circular 12:1, 99:2.
rout *v.* roar 88:5.
row(e) *n.* (*vp*)*on a* ∿ in order C538, Y551. **rowes** *pl.* rows C271, **rowys** *be* **rowys** row upon row Y264.
row *pp.* rolled Y255.
rowte *n.* troop, band C347, 396, Y447, (*vp*)*on a* ∿ in a troop C226, Y221, 335.

ruful *adj.* doleful, rueful SR628, **reweful** 52:2.
rule *n.* rule (of a religious order) SR664.
rulid *pp.* (*refl.*) ∿ *her* conducted herself SR666.
ruthe *n.* see **reuþe**.

sacred *pp.* consecrated SR474.
safer-stones *n. pl.* sapphire stones 131:3[n].
say *v.* say 37:1, SR14, SA14, 37, **sai** SR217, **scyn** Y413, **sigge** 77:5; **sey** speak Y222; ∿ tell 180:6; *that is to* ∿ SA127, 532; *herd* ∿ heard men relate SR540. ∿ *pr. 1 sg.* SR655. **seyste** *pr. 2 sg.* Y622. **seyt** *pr. 3 sg.* 24:6, 46:4, 84:4, etc., **seiþ** 110:2. ∿ *imp. sg.* SR701, SA43, **sai** SR43. **saing** *pr. p.* SR334, 359, **sayng** SR308, 333, 336, 400. **said** *pa. t. 1, 3 sg.* SR27, 30, etc., **saide** SR52, 118, 547, **sayd** SA78, etc., **sayde** C72, 131, etc., SR307, SA29, etc., **sede[r]** 2:6, 27:3, etc., **seyd** 13:1, 33:5, etc., Y67, 131, etc. **said** *pa. t. pl.* SR28, 66, etc., **sayd** SA254, 339, etc., **sayde** C397, SA70, 74, etc., **sede[r]** 57:1, 103:1, **seyd** 3:1, 4:4, etc., Y187, 448, **seyde** C41, **saiden** SR78, 694, **sayden** C276, 547, **seydyn** Y269, 347, 450. **said** *pp.* SR64, 122, etc., **sayd** SA253, 433, 516, **sayde** C81, 134, SA124, 465, etc., **seyd** Y76, 130, **yseyd** 17:1, 92:1.
saing *vbl. n.* saying, recitation (of the Psalter) SR521.
Saynt *adj.* see **Seint**.
salidoines *n. pl.* celidonies 131:4[n].
salmes *n. pl.* see **psalmes**.
saluacion *n.* salvation SR553, **saluacyon** SA545, **saluasyon** SA107, **sauacion** SR104.
salud *pa. t. 3 sg.* greeted 46:3[n].
same *adj.* same SR9, 10, etc., SA25, 65, etc. (as *pron.*) Y85, SA267.
Sant(e), Santt *adj.* see **Seint**.
sarmoun *n.* ∿ *to make* to preach a sermon 2:1.

satesfaction *n.* satisfaction (payment of temporal punishment due to sin) SR272, **satisfaccyon** SA283.
save *prep.* except (by) SA122.
saue *v.* save C286, SA81. **saue** *pr. subj. sg.* Y173. **saued** *pp.* 125:3, C662.
saueour *n.* Saviour 133:1.
savyng *prep.* ⁓ *only* except (by) SR121.
saunfayle *adv.* certainly (tag) 30:5.
sauour *n.* perfume C475, 476, 478, SR597, **savor** Y521, **sauere** SA587. **sauourres** *pl.* C474.
sauter *n.* psalter 176:1. *saing of* **sawters** *pl.* recitation of (a selection of) the Psalms SR521. Cf. **psauters**.
sautry *n.* psaltery (plucked stringed instrument) $142:5^n$.
scaldyng(e) *ppl. adj.* and *vbl. n.* see **skalde** *v.*
scarlet *n.* rich cloth of bright red colour 154:1.
schake *v.* go (descend) 107:5.
schal *pr. 1, 3 sg.* shall, will (*auxil.* forming fut.) 9:3, 15:5, 6, etc., SA78, **shal** SR68, 291, **shall** C78, 80, etc., SR139, 290, **xall** Y73, 75, etc.; must, have to **schall** Y57, SA72, 142, **shall** C62. **schal** *pr. 2 sg.* 56:5, SA46, 512, **schall** SA31, etc., = must SA37, **shall** C282, SA31, 36, **xall** Y321, 613, 658, **schalt** 40:1, 2, etc., (*inf.* 'go' understood) 118:4, **schallte** Y279, **shalt** C342, 552, 653, SR32, etc., (*inf.* 'go' understood) C141, = must SR69, 73, etc., **shalte** C278, 285, 605, **xalte** Y174, 275, (*inf.* 'go' understood) Y403; (with suffixed *pron.*) **schaltow** 36:2, 109:3. **schal** *pr. t. pl.* 119:2, SA39, 43, etc., **schall** SA48, 212, etc., **shal** SR47, etc., SA609, **shall** C182, etc., SA36(2), 39, **xall** Y277, 283, etc., **schul** 41:6, 42:1, etc., **shul** SR38, 43, etc., **shull** C349, 400, etc., **shullen** SR39, 200, etc., **shullyn** SR272, 328, etc. **schulde** *pa. t. 1, 3 sg.* SA15, 97, 164, **schuld** 6:1, 14:5, etc., Y89, SA500, = ought

to SA464, **schold(e)** SA130, 132, 52:4, **sholde** C449, (forming equivalent of subjunct.) C639, **shuld** SR15, 127, etc., = ought to SR474, 665, 667, **shul(l)de** C32, 92, **schude** Y28, **xulde** Y303. **schulde** *pa. t. 2 sg.* SA153, **shuldest** SR149. **schuld** *pa. t. pl.* 2:2, SA288, 371, etc., **schulde** SA16, etc., = ought to SA253, 389, etc., **shuld** SR17, 129, etc., = ought to SR382, 406, etc., **shulde** C20, 262.
schalde *v.* see **skalde**.
schame *n. do* (sb.) ⁓ inflict injury (on sb.) 50:2, 76:3.
schano(w)n(ys) *n.* (*pl.*) see **chanon** *n.*
schap(pe) *n.* see **shap**.
schape *v.* escape Y237.
schare *pa. t. pl.* cut SA225. **schorne** *pp.* SA426, (*adj.*) **schorn** (of hair) 46:1.
scharppenes *n.* see **sharpnesse**.
schauyn *pp.* see **shauen**.
schenys *n. pl.* see **cheynes**.
schepparde *n.* see **sheperd**.
schet *pa. t. pl.* shut 43:3.
schewed(e), **-yd(e)** *pa. t.*, *pp.* see **shew(e)** *v.*
schyn *n.* shin Y429.
scholdyrs *n. pl.* see **shulders**.
schon *pa. t. 3 sg.* shone 129:6, Y199, **shone** C206. **shone** *pa. t. pl.* C543.
schone *n. pl.* see **shone**.
schoppys *n. pl.* see **shoppes**.
schorn(e) *pp.* (*adj.*) see **schare** *pa. t. pl.*
schowe, **-yd** *v.*, *pa. t.* see **shew(e)** *v.*
schowffyllys *n. pl.* see **shovelis**.
sc(h)riche *v.* shriek, screech $64:6^n$, 66:1. **schrist** *pa. t. pl.* $100:2^n$.
schryfte *n.* confession SA612, 654, **scrift** SR683, **shrift(e)** SR361, 198, imposition of a penance SR199.
schriue *v.* (*tr.*) ⁓ (him) hear (his) confession 33:3. **schryve** (*refl.*) make confession Y587, SA604, **schrywe** Y123, 657, **shryue** C127, 558, 652, **shryve** SR239.
shryueth *pr. 3 sg.* (*refl.*) C559.

shryve *imp. sg.* SR145, **schryfe** SA149. **shryveng** *pr. p.* SR633. **schrevyn** *pp.* (*pass.*) (been) confessed, received absolution and penance SA146, 151, 211, **schryvyn** SA145, **shreven** SR141, 142, **shryve** SR148, **yschriue** 31:5.

schrode *adj.* malicious SA360.

score *n.* score (numeral) 53:3.

scrift *n.* see **shryfte**.

scrippe *n.* (pilgrim's) bag 195:6.

se *n.*[1] sea 169:6.

se *n.*[2] (bishop's) see C126, Y122.

se *v.* see, look at (and extended senses) 15:5, etc., C43, etc., Y64, 560, SR296, 657, SA230, **see** Y466, 532, SR44, 704, SA45, etc., **sen(e)** 106:6, 16:4, **syn** Y38, 613. **se(e)** *pr. 1 sg.* SA158, SR155. **seeys** *pr. 2 sg.* SA156, 198, **seys** SA165, 299, **seist** SR153, 161, etc., **syst(e)** Y319, 410, 404; (with suffixed *pron.*) **sestow** 117:4. **sees** *pr. t. pl.* SA304. *see* imp. sg. = make sure SR147. **saw** *pa. t. 1, 3 sg.* Y203, 499, SR1, 26, etc., SA3, 99, etc., **sawe** C463, 495, Y113, 213, etc., SR24, 232, 283, SA169, etc., **saghe** SA457, **saue** SA179, 194, **save** SA306, 336, **say** Y455, **sey** Y421, 425, etc., **seye** Y375, **sei3e** 62:6, etc., **sey3e** 153:1, **sye** C227, 627, **sy3** C117, 325, etc., **sy3e** C220, 396, 416. **sawest** *pa. t. 2 sg.* SR639. **seyn** *pa. t. pl.* Y104, 105, 388, **sen** C109, **sei3e** 26:2, 168:1, 193:6, **sy3** C107. **sei3e** *subj. sg.* 188:4. **seen** *pp.* SR348, 702, **sen** 25:4, 98:2, **sene** C479, 621, 665, SA601, 610, **sein** SR609, **seyn** Y253, **syn** Y523, 668.

sece *v.* see **cese**.

secular *adj.* secular SR466.

Seint *adj.* (prefixed to names) Saint SR6, 9, etc., **Seynt** C29, 88, etc., Y60, 78, etc., **Seynth** Y40, 99, 134, **Sein** 5:1, 123:3, **Seyn** 1:4, 18:1, etc., **Saynt** C65, 138, SA7, **Sant** SA56, 66, etc., **Sante** SA19, **Santt** SA100, 115, 359, **Sent** SA156, 216, etc.; **seynt** holy (applied to Owain) 149:4, 188:1, 198:4, **seyn** 94:1[n].

seint *n.*[1] saint SR612. **seintes** *pl.* SR642, **santtys** SA614.

seynt *n.*[2] see **assente**.

seke *adj.* sick Y397.

sekenes *n.* sickness SA209.

sekerer, -ly, sekyr(ly) *adj./adv.* see **siker, sikerliche**.

seyrteyn *adv.* see **certeyn**.

sele *n.* seal C156, **sell** Y151.

seled *pa. t. 3 sg.* sealed C156, (with suffixed obj. *pron.*) **selydyth** sealed it Y151.

selkowth *adj.* marvellous C224, **sylkeweth** Y218[n].

sell *n.* see **sele**.

selly *adv.* marvelously 44:1.

sellyng *pr. p.* selling SA252.

selue *adj.* (emphasising a n.) *bi* ⏜ by themselves 153:1. See also **hem-selue** *pron.*

semblaunce *n.* resemblance (comparison) 156:1[n].

semed *pa. t. 3 sg.* seemed C217, **semyd(e)** SA478, Y210, *380, SA371. *impers. me* ⏜ it seemed to me SR483.

semly *adj.* pleasant 152:3.

send(e) *v.* send 6:1, 35:3, C422, 423, Y469, 470. **sendyth** *pr. 3 sg.* Y3. **send(e)** *imp. sg.* C433, Y480. **sende** *pa. t. 3 sg.* C19, SA59[n], **sent(e)** C3, Y16, 642, SR475. **send(e)** *pp.* SA76, SR81, **sent(e)** C240, SR71, 76, **sentt** SA81, *seynth Y235, **ysent** 19:3, 127:4, etc.

sengyll *adj.* single Y216.

seriaunce *n. pl.* servants 42:2.

serpentes *n. pl.* serpents SR374, 378, 388, 399, **serpenttys** SA394.

serteyn, sertenly *adv.* see **certeyn, certenly**.

seruauntes *n. pl.* servants SR387, **seruandys** SA392, 397.

serue *v.* serve 22:2, C172, Y144, 167. **seruyst** *pr. 2 sg.* Y408. **seruyd** *pa. t. 2 sg.* Y276. **serued** *pp.* 58:2, 119:5, C283, **seruyd(e)** SA312, Y279, **servyd** SA438.

seruice *n.* church-service SR427, *Goddes* ⏜ SR425, (sim.) SR434,

service SR431, **servis** SR679, *God* ∿ SA651, *diuine* ∿ SR474, (sim.) **seruece** SA465, **serues** SA433; *Goddis* ∿ = serving God SR686, (sim.) SA658, **seruise** 67:4, *þe* **seruece** *of Gode* SA437.
servid *pp.* deserved SR219. Cf. **deserued.**
sett *v.* found, build 20:2. **settyng** *pr. p.* placing SR210, 305. **set** *pa. t. 1 sg.* placed SR611; **sett** *me down* = knelt SA554. **sett** *pa. t. 3 sg.* placed, put 125:4; installed 22:1; **sette** placed, put C439, 442, Y486, 489; *of hyt he* **sette** *ry3th now3th* he took no notice of it C482. **set** *pa. t. pl.* put SR215, **sett** SA224, 229, 311; **setyn** *owte* let forth Y496. **set** *pp.* ∿ *on my kneis* = kneeling SR620; ∿ *by* placed to one side SR268ⁿ, (sim.) **sett** SR266, placed SA276, 279, **ysett** decked, clothed 154:2. See **ouersett.**
sethen, seþþen *adv.* see **sythyn.**
seuen *num. adj.* seven 106:1, 197:6.
sexti *num. adj.* sixty 114:4, 6ⁿ.
shap *n.* fashion of dress SR39, **schap** Y548, **schappe** SA40, 69; *as by* ∿ = judging by their garments SR66.
shappus *n. pl.* genitals C380.
shapte *pp.* fashioned, cut (of clothing) C535.
sharp(e) *adj.* sharp 121:2, 125:5, Y463. **s(c)harper** *comp.* SA563, SR570.
sharpnesse *n.* sharpness SR578, **scharppenes** SA571.
shauen *ppl. adj.* shaven C494, **schauyn** Y226, **shafe** C231.
she *pron.* she SR151, 665, 666, etc., SA100, **sche** SA155, 639, 646, etc., **sho** SR691. **hir** *acc., refl.* SR151, 666, 668, etc., **hyr** SA639, 660, 662. **hir(e)** *poss. adj.* SR666, 670, 26, 658, etc., **hyr** SA114, 629, etc.
shedde *pa. t. 3 sg.* shed (blood) C604.
shelde *n.* shield C366.
sheperd *n.* shepherd SR134, **schepparde** SA137.

shew(e) *v.* reveal C47, SR634, **schowe** Y42. **sheweth** *pr. 3 sg.* shows (mercy) SR696. **shewed** *pa. t. 3 sg.* C69, SR366, **shewid** SR412, 439, **schewed** 13:1, **schewyd(e)** SA420, 451, **schowyd** Y64, **chewyd** SA368. **shewed** *pa. t. pl.* C25, **schewed(e)** C515, 141:2, **schewyd** Y21, **schowyd** Y560. **shewid** *pp.* SR50, 513, 632, **schewyd(e)** SA51, 506, **yschewed** 17:2.
shityng *pr. p.* shitting SR252, **shytyng** SR450.
shone *pa. t.* see **schon** *pa. t. 3 sg.*
shone *n. pl.* shoes SR678, **schone** SA649.
shoppes *n. pl.* shops SR598. See **spysse schoppys.**
shovelis *n. pl.* shovels SR371, **schowffyllys** SA373.
shovyng *pr. p.* shoving SR234.
shredyng *pr. p.* shredding SR417, 437.
shrift(e) *n.* see **schryfte.**
shryve, shryue(th), -eng, shreven *v.* see **schriue** *v.*
shulders *n. pl.* shoulders SR182, **scholdyrs** SA188.
side *adj.* spacious 161:2; long SR185.
side *n.* in *ich* ∿ on each side 44:6; side (of body) 63:3, **syde** C17, Y13; *bac and* ∿ = (on the) back and sides 71:3; *bi the water* ∿ = along the bank of the water SR537, 555, 558, (sim.) **syde** SA548–51; *in a* ∿ to one side SR619; *on euery* **syd(e)** C222, 268, etc., Y458, 544, etc., 562, 617, (sim.) **syyd** Y261. **sydes** *pl.* sides (of body) SA239. See **eche** *adj.*
sigge *v.* see **say.**
sight *n.* sight, view SR106, 152, etc., **syght(e)** SA109, 44, 169, **si3t** = thing seen 12:4, 66:6, 152:3, **syght** SA307, **sy3te** C478, **syth** Y521; *bi* ∿ as it appears to the eye SR65, (sim.) SA68; *bi* **si3t** *opon to se* = to look at 181:3; *bi hire* ∿ = by looking at them SR327; *in* **syght** to look at SA35, (sim.) *of* **si3t** 11:6,

23:3, 83:3, *to* ∼ SR36, 481; **siȝt**
opon view of 185:5; *without* ∼ *of*
without seeing SR108. **sightes** *pl.*
SR45, 608, **syghtys** SA45, 600.
sikelatoun *n.* precious cloth (of
gold?) 154:3.
siker *adj.* ∼ *ȝe be* you may be certain
24:1; (or *adv.*) secure, safe 135:4;
sekyr confident SA86. **sekerer**
comp. SR85
sikerliche *adv.* certainly 3:2, 25:4,
sikerly 41:3, 52:1, **sekerly** SA78,
sekyrly SA161.
sylkeweth *adj.* see **selkowth**.
siluer *n.* silver 86:5, SR166, 170,
etc., **syluer** SA174, etc.; *adj.* **sylluer** SA649. **siluers** (with *n. pl.*)
SR677. See **gold**.
simpell *adj.* weak, feeble SR120,
sympyll poor (in modest use)
SA59. See also **ouersympul**.
syn *conj.* seeing that Y172.
sinful *adj.* sinful 13:2, 30:5, SR103,
552, **synful(l)** C250, 358, 428,
SA104, 459, 544, SR57, SA105.
sinfull as *n. pl.* sinful men
SR102, **synful(l)** SA543, SR551.
sing *v.* sing (divine office) 20:6,
(mass) 163:5, **synge** C568, 644,
(with suffixed obj. *pron.*) **syngth**
sing it Y649. **singing** *pr. p.* 26:3,
singyng SR600, **syngynge**
SA589, **singeng** SR599. **song(e)**
pa. t. pl. C194, 81:2, 142:3.
singyng *vbl. n.* singing SR599, *masses* ∼ singing masses SR521,
(sim.) **syngyng** SA516.
sinne *n.* sin 1:3, etc., **synne** C104,
etc., Y117, etc., SR140, etc.,
SA334, 618, 661, **syn(e)** Y581,
SA144, etc., Y101, SA603. **sinnes**
pl. 36:6, 55:5, **synnes** SR245,
etc., **synnys** Y126, 169, SA304,
etc., **synnus** C128, etc.
sinne *v.* sin 33:5. **synneth** *pr. 3 sg.*
SR137, **synnys** SA141. **synneth**
pr. t. pl. SR627, **synnys** SA668.
synned *pa. t. pl.* SR323, 324,
synnyd SA326, 327. **synned** *pp.*
SR125, 636, **synnyde** SA127,
606.
sir *n.* (as polite form of address) sir
108:5, 117:4, **syr** C135, 149, 164,

Y159, **syre** C175, Y131, 168;
(placed before name Owayne) **Syr**
C196, etc., Y111, etc., **Syre** Y189,
etc.
syster *n.* sister SA112, etc., **soster**
153:6, **suster** SR110, etc.; spiritual sister SR54, 59, ∼ SA62,
sister SA56. **sustern** *pl.* SR666.
syses *n. pl.* see **assisis**.
syth *conj.* since, because C287.
sitt *v.* sit 70:4. **syth** *pr. 3 sg.* Y406.
sat *pa. t. 3 sg.* 46:4, C257. **sat** *pa.
t. pl.* 145:3, **sete** 71:1, 102:6,
setyn Y225, (*refl.*) **sette** C230,
sotyn Y352.
siþe *n. o* ∼ one time, i.e. once 182:1.
sythyn *adv.* then, afterwards Y31,
127, etc., **sethen** C35, 131, **seþþen** 92:6, 197:4.
skalde *v.* (*tr.*) burn C392; **schalde**
scald Y441. **scaldyng(e)** *ppl. adj.*
SA521, SR527, 528; as *vbl. n.*
SA522.
skaþe *n.* harm C342.
sky *n.* sky 72:3.
skyn(n)e *n.* skin SR182, SA188.
sleyers *n. pl.* slayers SA313, **sleers**
SR307.
slene *pa. t. pl.* slew SA316.
slepe *n.* sleep 10:3, 18:1.
slepeing *vbl. n.* sleep 12:6; *fel on* ∼
fell asleep 7:5.
slepyde *pa. t. 1 sg.* slept SA22,
slepte SR22. **slepe** *pa. t. 3 sg.*
8:1, 4.
sleves *n. pl.* sleeves SR171, **slevys**
SA175, 188.
slewþe *n.* sloth 67:2.
slowe *adj.* slow, slack 67:4.
slumbered *pa. t. 1 sg.* slumbered
SR22, **slomered** SA21.
small(e) *adj.* small SR396, SA319,
403, **smale** SR316; **smal** fine
(powder) 85:6; slender 132:3. See
gret.
small(e) *adv.* into small pieces
SR418, SA426.
smal *n.* see **smell**.
smeke *n.* reeking smoke Y396.
smell *n.* smell, fragrance C471,
Y514, 518, **smal** 134:2, 182:4,
183:6.

smert *adj.* painful, severe 49:2; sharp 120:1.

smert *v.* (*intr.*) feel pain, suffer 111:3.

smiche *n.* smoke 96:6, **smych** SR158, 351.

smyte *v.* strike, hit SR180; clash C262. **smytyng** *pr. p.* SR190, etc., **smyttynge** SA186, 196, **smyteng** SR206. **smote** *pa. t. 3 sg.* darted C610. **smote** *pa. t. pl.* SR253, **smotte** SA221, 264, 309. **smeten** *pp.* SR416, **smeton** SA228, 432, **smyt(t)en** SA461, SR471, **smyttyn** SA423.

smoke *n.* (a cloud of) smoke SR155, SA158, 350, 354.

smolder *v.* smother, suffocate SR291ⁿ.

snake *n.* snake 71:2. **snakes** *pl.* SR353, 374, etc., **snakys** SA394, 401, etc.

snow(e) *n.* snow SR367, 370, 371, 472, **snaw** SA374, 463.

so *adv.* so (mod. uses) 12:3, 123:1, 155:5, etc., C167, 171, 640, etc., Y256, etc., SR53, 96, 576, etc., SA118, 592, **soo** Y76, etc., SA96, etc.; ∿ thus, in this way 48:4, SR419, SA424; in such a way C95, SR552, SA106; to such a degree Y620; likewise SR289, 617; *what* ∿ whatsoever C178. See **neuer**.

so *conj.* **sone** ∿ as soon as 94:4; ∿ so that C48.

sodenly *adv.* suddenly SR84, 369, SA85, 476, **sodaynly** SR385, 488.

sofferande *ppl. adj.* see **suffre** *v.*

softe *adv.* luxuriously (or *adj.* soft) Y351.

solaci *v.* comfort 41:6.

solas *n.* delight; ∿ *make* = amuse yourself 107:4.

solempnyte *n.* ceremony, celebration C508, 592.

som(e), **somdele** *adj., adv.* see **sum, sumdel(e)**.

somer *n.* (adverbial) in summer 148:5; ∿-*tyde* summertime Y459, **summer**-*tyd* Y563. **someres** *gen.* C408, 520.

somewhat *adv.* see **sumwhat**.

somtyme *adv.* see **sumtyme**.

son *n.* son SA102, etc., **sone** 175:3, SR99, etc.; *þe* **sonne** the Son Y685; ∿ son (as term of address) Y625, **sone** C619. See **God**.

sond *n.* *þonked Ihesu Cristes* ∿ thanked Christ's ordering of events 19:2, 191:2.

sonder *adv.* see **sundyr**.

sone *adv.* soon, straightaway 7:5, 43:4, etc., C81, 162, etc., Y238, etc., SR63, etc., SA89, 404, etc., **sowne** SA380; *conj. phr.* ∿ *so* as soon as 94:4. *comp.* the soner the more quickly C570. See **anon** and cf. **eftesone**.

song(e) *n.* song, singing C496, 659, Y358, 539, 664, 146:1, 169:1. **songys** *pl.* SA590, **songus** SR599.

sonne *n.* sun 41:2, C206, 214, 544, **son** Y199. Cf. **sunne-reste**.

sonne-beam *n.* sunbeam 120:5.

sore *adj.* severe, harsh 33:4, C297.

sore *adv.* bitterly, greatly, severely 5:3, 111:3, etc., C385, *Y119, 257, etc., SR45, 372, etc., SA285, 620, etc., **soore** C123.

sorynes *n.* sorrow SA362.

sorow(e) *n.* sorrow, distress SA257, 342, C106, 479, 582, Y103, 173, 523, SR633, SA450, 604, **sowrow** Y371, 598, **sorwe** 66:5, 67:1, etc.; *turnyd them to* ∿ turned into a cause of sorrow for them SA396.

sowroys *pl.* afflictions SA358.

*****sorowful** *adj.* distressing SA379.

soster *n.* see **syster**.

sothefast(e) *adj.* true C12, 26.

sothefastenes *n.* truth(fulness) SA2.

sothely *adv.* truly, certainly SA77, 318, etc.

sotyn *pa. t. pl.* see **sitt**.

sou3t *pa. t. 3 sg.* see **sowght**.

soule *n.* soul 37:3, etc., **sowle** C173, etc., Y284, 285, SR105, etc., SA135, 240, **sowll** Y629, **saule** SA107, etc., **savle** SA632. *gen.* ∿ *fode* food for the soul 182:5; **sowle** *leche* confessor Y132ⁿ; see **leche**. **soule** *pl.* ? 153:1, **soules** 16:1, etc., **sowles** C14, 406,

SR128, etc., SA221, **sowlys**
SA302, 425, **soulen** 4:2, **soles**
C410, **saules** SA321, etc., **saulys**
SA264, etc., **saullys** SA300,
savles SA261, etc., **sawles**
SA131, etc., **sawlys** SA260, etc.
See **sowll-helle**.
sour *adj. þat hem is aniþing* ⌣ that
anything is unpleasant for them
108:6.
sowght *pa. t. 1 sg.* sought SR603.
souȝt *pa. t. 3 sg.* 196:1. **sow3th** *pp.*
C142, **sowte** Y138.
sowkyng(e) *pr. p.* sucking SA183,
SR179, 396, 408.
sowll-helle *n.* salvation Y10.
sownd(e) *adj.* see **heyll, hole** *adj.*
sowne *adv.* see **sone**.
sowrow, sowroys *n.* (*pl.*) see **sor-
ow(e)**.
sowth *adv.* southwards C401ⁿ.
sowth *n. þe* ⌣ the south Y452.
space *n.* distance SR109, etc.,
SA111, 176; ⌣ *of* time/opportun-
ity for (penance) SR199, 362, 692,
SA211, 662.
spade *n.* spade 172:4.
spak(k)(e), spac *pa. t.* see **speyke**.
spare *v.* spare pains C290, 333,
*Y283, 348. **spare** *imp. sg.* or *pl.*
show mercy C332ⁿ, Y347.
spark *n.* spark 60:5. **sparkys** *pl.*
SA263.
sparkelyng *ppl. adj.* emitting sparks
SA320.
speche *n.* talk SA446.
spede *n.* aid, help (of God) SR29,
SA28.
spede *v. intr.* prosper 14:6; succeed
Y388; *impers.* fare 164:2. *tr. pr. 3
sg. subj. God* ⌣ may God assist
you (as greeting) SR28, SA27.
speyke *v.* speak, tell SA532. **spekeþ**
pr. 3 sg. 9:4, 176:1. **speykyne** *pr.
p.* SA361. **spac** *pa. t. 1 sg.* 171:2.
spak *pa. t. 3 sg.* SR63, **spake**
C234, Y29, etc., SR122, SA125,
spakke C65. **spake** *pa. t. pl.*
Y401, 577, **speke** 142:3, C335,
546, **spokyn** Y318, 554. **spake**
pp. Y640, **speken** C636.
spelle *n.* speech 107:3.

spende *v.* spend SA494. **spendyng**
pr. p. SR474. **spendid** *pa. t. pl.*
squandered SR411.
speris *n. pl.* spears SR302.
spycery *n.* spices Y517.
spicers *n. pl. gen.* ⌣ *shoppes* shops of
dealers in spices, apothecaries'
shops SR597.
spil(lyn) *v.* kill, destroy SR79, 74.
spyll *pr. 2 sg. subj.* SA82.
spirites *n. pl.* spirits SR41, etc.,
spiretes SR108. Cf. **sprit(e)**.
spysse schoppys *n.* apothecaries'
shops SA587ⁿ. Cf. **spicers**.
spourged *pp.* purged 162:2.
spradde *pa. t. 3 sg.* (*intr.*) spread out
C608, **spredde** Y616.
springeth *pr. t. pl.* grow 148:4.
sprang *pa. t. 3 sg.* sprang 105:2,
sprong 183:2; **spronge** dawned
C642.
sprit(e) *n.* spirit SR543, 14, **spret(t)e**
SA14, 536, **sprett** SA111. **sprites**
pl. SR16, 704, **spritis** SR17,
spretys SA45, **sprettys** SA16,
etc. Cf. **spirites**.
sqwyer *n.*¹ squire C79.
sqwyer *n.*² see **swere** *n.*
stable *adj.* constant, stedfast SR326.
stabled *pa. t. 3 sg.* made stable/sec-
ure 29:2.
staf *n.* staff, crosier, baculum 10:2,
18:4, 22:4, etc., C54, 671, **staffe**
C56, 62, 64, Y49, etc., **stafte** Y59,
672.
stalen *pa. t. pl.* stole SR269.
stange *v.* pierce, sting SA406.
stangyd *pa. t. pl.* SA386, 403.
stark *adj.* fierce 105:3.
state *n.* estate, rank 155:3.
stede *n.* place 20:1, 24:1, etc., C101,
Y98; *in Goddis* ⌣ as God's representative SR123, (sim.) **steyde**
SA125. **stedes** *pl.* 82:1. See
stond(e) *v.*
stedfast *adj.* firm, unshaken (belief,
heart) 15:3, C246, Y241, **stedefast** 111:6, SR120, **stedfaste** Y8,
SA121; ⌣ unchanging (of God)
Y22.
stedfastly *adv.* firmly C441, Y488.
steied *pa. t. 1 sg.* climbed SR579.
stiȝe *pa. t. 3 sg.* ascended 197:3.

steyle *n.* see **style.**
stel(e) *n.* steel C90, 130:4, **stell** Y87.
stench(e) *n.* stench SR230, 247, 350, etc.
ster *n.* star 156:4. **sterres** *pl.* 156:3.
stern *adj.* stern 174:2.
steuen *n.* voice 17:5, 145:6.
styffe *adj.* firm C245^n.
sti3e *pa. t. 3 sg.* see **steied.**
stikeng *pr. p.* piercing SR260.
stykkynge *ppl. adj.* $\sim$ on sticking into, piercing SA271.
style *n.* rung (of a ladder) SA562, **steyle** SA571.
styll *adj.* calm (weather) C430^n, Y477; **styll(e)** *adj.* or *adv.* unmoved C161, Y156, 385; still (abide, dwell) C565, Y606, **stil** SR17. See **hold** *v.*
styng *v.* sting SR399. **styngen** *pr. t. pl.* SR389. **styngyng** *pr. p.* SR179, 397. **stongyn** *pa. t. pl.* SR380.
stynk(e) *n.* stink *Y396, 399, SA162, etc., 453.
stinking *ppl. adj.* stinking 95:5, **stin(c)kand** 110:5, 93:1, 116:2, **styngkyng** SR156, **stynkyng(e)** SA160, 354; vague sense indicating disgust (of sin) SR468, SA458. **stank** *pa. t. 3 sg.* 85:3, 116:4, **stonk(e)** C409, SR450.
stint *pa. t. 3 sg.* stopped 97:1, **stynte** C84, **styntyd** Y398.
stoke *pa. t. 3 sg.* remained fixed Y385^n.
stompyng *pr. p.* stamping (with the feet) SR356^n.
stond *n.* see **stounde.**
stond(e) *v.* stand C220, 441, 62:6, Y213, **stand(e)** SA300, Y488; $\sim$ remain stedfast C307. **standes** *pr. 2 sg.* C397, *standyst Y448. **stondeth** *pr. 3 sg.* SR124, 125, **standys** SA127, 128. **stonde** *pr. t. pl.* SR67, **stande** SA72, 74. **stondyng** *pr. p.* SR251, 292, 560, **standyng** SA553. **stod(e)** *pa. t. sg.* 173:4, C161, 303, etc., Y614, SR614, Y156, etc., **stoode** C225; **stode** = delayed Y79. **stod(e)** *pa. t. pl.* 44:3, 90:4, 100:1, C275, 538, Y268, SA226, 261, Y428, 430,

551, stodyn Y265, 458. **stond** *pp.* 45:1, **stande** *in grett stede* been of great help SA500, (sim.) **ystondyn** SR505.
ston(e) *n.* stone C316, SR349, SA353, 40:4, 43:6, attributive $\sim$ (made of) stone 23:4, 129:3, = millstone Y381; (precious) 130:5. **stones** *pl.* 118:1, C261, **stonys** Y254; $\sim$ gems 150:6, 151:6; (precious) $\sim$ C470, SR173, 189, SA178, 194. See **cristal** and cf. **safer-stones.**
stoppe *v.* stuff SR234. **stoppeng** *pr. p.* SR232, 233, 445. **stopped** *pa. t. pl.* stuffed, stopped up SR187, **stoppyd** SA193, 245.
stoppyng *vbl. n.* being stuffed, cramming SR247.
store *adj.* fierce 105:3.
story *n.* story, book C38, Y43, **stori(e)** 24:6, 42:3, etc.
stounde *n.* (a) time, while 163:2, C332, **stownd(e)** C337, 411, 674, Y675; *summe* **stond** for a little while Y347.
stowpeng *pr. p.* lowering SR251^n.
stowte *adj.* splendid SA331.
straytt *adj.* rigorous SA637.
streynynge *pr. p.* squeezing (out) SA184^n. **streynyd** *pa. t. pl.* stretched Y328^n.
strem *n.* stream 150:1, 151:1, 4. **stremes** *pl.* 149:5.
streng𝖇e *n.* strength 134:5, **strenghe** SR486.
stryf(f)e *n.* strife Y571, C526.
strong *adj.* severe, intense 15:5, 56:2, etc.; strong 117:2, Y326; gross, flagrant 74:2, 3; difficult 64:5, 167:4.
strong *adv.* intensely, fiercely C354; **strongely** securely SA451, **stronglich** SR439.
such(e) *adj.* see **swiche.**
suete *adj.* see **swete.**
suffre *v.* endure, suffer, bear C560, SR200, 256, etc., **suffer** SR246, SA241, 346, 365, **suffri** 55:4, etc., **suffyr(e)** SA417, 267, 460; $\sim$ permit, let SR74, 80, **suffer** SA80, 398. **suffren** *pr. t. pl.* suffer SR458, **suffri** 4:2, **suffyr** SA233,

447, **suffers** SA238. **sofferande**
ppl. adj. SA206, **suffreng** SR641.
suffredes *pa. t. 2 sg.* 160:4, **suffredist** SR551, **suffyrde** SA543.
suffred *pa. t. 3 sg.* 25:1, 49:3,
175:4, SR493, 616; allowed
SR507, **sufferd** SA491, **suffyrde**
SA494. **suffred** *pa. t. pl.* suffered
79:5, **suffreden** SR270, 460, **suf-
fyrd(e)** SA416; allowed SA411,
399, 501, **suffred** SR403, 510.
suffred *pp.* suffered SR295, **sufferd** SR297; **suffred** allowed
SR503, **suffyrde** SA498.
sufferyng *vbl. n. penaunce* ∼ enduring penance SR199.
sum *adj.* some, a certain 36:5, 156:4,
summe Y347, **som** C47,
somme C560, 567; with *pl. n.* ∼
Y42, **summe** Y266, 268, SR167,
172, etc., **some** C275; (as *pron.*)
∼ some (part) 106:3, 4, SA583; ∼
pl. some 71:1, 77:1, etc., Y100,
107, SR166, 169, etc., SA90, 91,
etc., **summe** Y266, 366, etc.,
SR90, 164, etc., **some** C103, 111,
etc., **somme** SR417. See **al** *adj.*
and *n.*
sumdel(e) *adv.* somewhat SA33,
SR35, **somdele** C664. ∼ *pron.*
small amount 40:6.
summer-tyd *n.* see **somer**.
sumtyme *adv.* once, formerly Y23,
SR611, SA57, 387, 392, 395,
som(e)tyme C502, 27, 536.
sumwhat *adv.* somewhat SR27, 29,
528, SA21, etc., **somewhat**
SR22, **summewat** Y666.
sumwhile *adv.* sometimes 162:6.
sundyr *adv. in* ∼ apart SA273, *on
sonder* SR304. Cf. **asonder**.
sunne *n.* see **son** *n.*
sunne-reste *n.* sunset Y207[n]. Cf.
sonne *n.*
suster(n) *n.* see **syster**.
swart *adj.* black 116:6, **swert** 120:2.
swech(e) *adj.* see **swiche**.
swerd *n.* sword 174:1, *Y463 (MS
sward). **swerdes** *pl.* SR205, 207,
260, **swerdis** SR302, **swerdys**
SA220, etc.
swere *n.* neck 77:3, 80:4, 101:4,
sqwyer Y365.

swere *v.* swear (an oath) 82:4.
sweren *pr. t. pl.* SR223.
swerynge *vbl. n.* using profane language SR226, SA238.
swert *adj.* see **swart**.
swete *adj.* fragrant 182:4, 183:6,
C474; sweet C609; delightful
SA590, **suete** SR600; ∼ dear,
beloved 198:6, C433, Y329. **swetter** *comp.* sweeter 148:6, 149:2;
more fragrant SR597, *SA587.
swete *adv.* pleasantly 8:1.
swete *v.* sweat 96:5.
swetenisse *n.* fragrance 134:4, **swetnes** Y519.
swcucning *n.* dreaming 18:3.
swiche *adj.* such 44:5, etc., **such(e)**
C320, SR420, SA122, C474, 614,
SR43, 120, **such** *on* such a one
C366, **swech(e)** Y337, *518,
syche SA428, 440, **sweche** *on*
such a one Y307.
swiche *pron.* the like 9:2; the one
171:3, **suche** C524, **swech(e)**
Y206, 531, **syche** SA444.
swiþe *adv.* very 12:5, etc., **swyde**
C220, 485; ∼ greatly 34:2; quickly
96:1, 191:6, **swythe** C572, 655;
þei him were ∼ *wo* though he was
greatly distressed 189:3.
swollen *pp.* swollen SR397.

ta unemphatic form of *inf. particle* to
Y670.
tabernacles *n. pl.* ornate canopied
niches 132:1[n].
tayllys *n. pl.* backsides SA401.
take *v.* take (mod. uses) 195:6,
SA478; *to God* ∼ commit, devote
(themselves) to God 2:2; ∼ *penaunce* accept the penance assigned
by a confessor 13:5, (sim.) 34:4,
etc., SR637, SA608; ∼ *owt* re-
move SR416. **take** *pr. 1 sg. I* ∼
me to I commit myself to Y287,
(sim.) SR687, SA659. **take** *pr. 2
sg. subj.* 74:5, 87:5; ∼ assume
(canon's or monk's habit) C146,
Y142. *imp. sg.* C170, Y165, SR37,
SA35. **takyng(e)** *pr. p.* SA480,
SR233, 304, etc., = eating
SR243. **toke** *pa. t. 1, 3 sg.* C55,
671, Y50, 90, etc., SA564;

received SA489, **tok** 134:5; ⁓ accepted (benediction) *C198, 630, Y224, etc.; (leave) C157, SR706; gave SR11ⁿ; *up* ... **tok(e)** picked ... up 18:2, 5; *to him he* ⁓ = bade him sit next to him 46:5. **toke** *pa. t. pl.* C190, SR444, SA192, etc., **toke** *of* took part of SR186; **toke** *vp* began to utter C450; **token** *owt* removed SR220; **tokyn** Y382, SR276. **take** *pp.* ⁓ *on hond* undertaken SR31; taken SR264, 265, 267; ⁓ *me* committed myself SR685; **taken** 68:5, 88:2, SR501, **takyn** SA30, 275, 657, etc., **ytake** 138:6, SR143. See **ʒeme, hede** *n.*², **hond(e), order.**

talkyng *pr. p.* talking SR614. **talkid** *pp.* SR644, **talkyd** SA615.

talking *vbl. n.* recitation 28:4.

talys *n. pl.* tales Y71, SA360.

tanges *n. pl.* see **tong(e).**

tapers *n. pl.* wax candles 136:4.

taverns *n. pl.* taverns SR243, **tauernys** SA251.

teche *v.* teach 58:1, 115:3, 119:4, C9, Y5, SR71, 76, 459, SA76. **teches** *pr. 3 sg.* SA130, **techeth** SR127. **taw(ʒ)te** *pa. t. 3 sg.* C14, Y10, **taught(e)** *SA14, SR14, 28. **tawʒte** *pa. t. pl.* C28, **tawte** Y24, **techyd** SA11. **tawght** *pp.* SR83, 456, **taghtt** SA84, **tawte** Y258, **ytawʒte** C265.

tech(e)ing *n.* teaching, instruction 3:3, SR467, **techyng(e)** SA18, 208, 364, SR19, 198.

tell(e) *v.* tell 151:2, C117, 182, etc., Y17, 113, C21, Y71, etc., SA95, etc., **tel** 28:5, 156:1, 159:4, **tellen** 180:2; ⁓ describe, count C270, 532, SR93, 514, SA450; reckon Y308; be of advantage to Y263ⁿ; *of* ⁓ tell about C76. **tell(e)** *pr. 1 sg.* 49:4, SA135, **tel** SR132. **telle** *pr. 3 sg.* 123:1ⁿ. **tell** *pr. 2 pl. subj.* SA53. **told(e)** *pa. t. 1, 3 sg.* C32, 665, 667, Y28, 670, SA66, 36:3, Y668, ⁓ *of* 69:6. **told(e)** *pa. t. pl.* C106, 399, 6, **toldyn** Y103. **tolde** *pp.* Y519, = compared C476, **ytold** 34:3; *mykyll of* **told(e)**

greatly esteemed C120, (sim.) Y116. See **resoun.**

temptacion *n.* temptation SA613.

temptacions *pl.* SR642.

ten *num. adj.* ten 80:3, 189:4; *bi* ⁓ in groups of ten 153:2, *be* ... **tene** 162:6.

tenderly *adv.* with tender emotion SR694; **tenderlich** lovingly, with affection SR605.

tendernesse *n.* tenderness SR338.

tendyr *adj.* tender, loving SA344.

tene *n.* suffering C582, Y598.

tere *n.* tear C660. See **wepynge.**

terestri *adj. paradis* ⁓ Earthly Paradise 170:2.

teryng *pr. p.* tearing SR261, 300, 487, 492.

testament *n.* will SA288.

tide *n.* time, *þat* ⁓ then 70:3, (sim.) **tyde** C505, 612, Y545, **tydde** Y618; *someres* **tyde** summertime C408, 520. See **somer.**

tiding *n.* ⁓ *of* information about 3:6.

til *prep.* until 146:3, SR200, 690, **tyll** C290, 559. See **euerych, redy.**

til *conj.* until 86:6, etc., **tille** 41:5, **tyll** C216, etc., Y117, etc.; (so) that (at length) Y435; ⁓ *þat* 162:2, **tyll** *þat* C585. Cf. **intil, þertil, vntil.**

time *n.* time (when something happens) SR422, **tyme** SR111, 396, etc., SA429, etc.; *in þat* ⁓ at that time 24:4; = reign 29:3, **tyme** C113, Y109; life-time C103, Y100, SR21, SA21; while C122; *as long* **tyme** for as long a while SR274, 297. **times** *pl.* occasions (following numeral) 191:3, SR629. Cf. **often-tymes.**

tyne *n.* tin SA218

tine *poss. adj.* see **þou.**

tine *v.* lose 48:6.

to *num. adj.* see **two.**

to *adv.* too 71:6, 109:1, C143, SR120.

to *conj.* until SA209, 216(1), 288, 496(1), 554, 661.

to *prep.* to (mod. uses) 26:4, etc., C4, etc., Y15, etc., SR19, etc., SA15, etc.; at (of throwing) 58:5, SR376, (of making noise) SR92, SA93; for (in various senses) 182:3, C643,

SR128(1), 276, 515, SA131, 509, 627(1); into Y433; ∼ *mon* as a companion 115:2; ∼ *sight* to look at SR36, 481; ∼ ... *warde* see **toward.** Cf. **into, þerto, vnto.**

to *inf. particle* 2:1, etc., C3, etc., Y5, etc., SR11, etc., SA12, etc. Cf. **forto.**

tobownede *ppl. adj.* swollen up SA400[n].

tobrent *pa. t. 3 sg.* consumed (by fire) 89:2.

tobrosid *pa. t. pl.* severely bruised SR453, **tobryssed** *pp.* SA462.

***today** *adv.* nowadays Y85.

tode *n.* toad Y341. **todes** *pl.* 71:1, SR178, 353, 374, etc., **todys** Y352, 354, **toodes** SA394, **toodys** SA356, **towdys** SA183, 377, 402.

toes *n. pl.* toes SR394, **towse** SA224.

tofore *adv.* before SR110.

tofore *prep.* before SR421, in front of SR585.

toforesaid *adj.* previously mentioned SR351.

toforn *prep.* in front of 7:6.

togeder *adv.* together SR129, 133, **togedre** SR203, **togedyr** SA131, 137, into collision Y255, against each other *C262.

togiders *adv.* = into contact 153:4.

tokyne *n.* token, sign C47. **token** *pl.* 18:2, **tokenes** C13, **tokenys** Y9, 42.

tokening *n.* (a) portent, sign 192:3, **tokenyng** C25, Y21.

tomangylde *pa. t. pl.* hacked to pieces SA310[n].

tong(e) *n.* tongue C270, 532, SR219, SA450, 78:4, 81:1, SA425. **tongys** *pl.* Y366, SA94, 234, 235, 445, **tongis** SR433, **tonnges** SR417, **tounges** SR220, **tunges** SR438, **tungis** SR435, **tanges** SR93.

tonges *n. pl.* tongs SR209, **tongys** SA224.

tonicles *n. pl.* tunicles, vestments resembling dalmatics 154:5[n].

toni3t *adv.* last night 167:1.

tonnes *n. pl.* tuns, barrels SR393.

too *num. adj.* see **two.**

top *n.* top SR560, 565, etc., **toppe** SA568, 577, etc.

topes *n.* topaz 131:1.

torent *pa. t. pl.* lacerated 89:1. **torent** *pp.* torn 113:3.

tormentys *n. pl.* see **turment.**

toswollyn *ppl. adj.* swollen up SR393.

totere *pa. t. pl.* tore at 73:2.

toþe *n.* tooth 66:5.

tother *adj.* (in *adv.* phrase) *þe* ∼ *day* the preceding day Y638. As *pron.* *þe* ∼ the other (one) Y339. *all þe* ∼ *pl.* all the other things Y499. Cf. **oþer.**

toucheþ *pr. 3 sg.* is pertinent 176:2.

tou3 *adj.* painful, severe 56:2.

tounges *n. pl.* see **tong(e).**

tourn *v.* see **turn(e).**

tour(res) *n.* (*pl.*) see **towre.**

touten *n. pl.* backsides 54:2.

toward(e) *prep.* towards SA469, Y467, SR251, 449, etc., ∼ *þe erþe* = face downward 65:4; **to me-warde** towards me SA565.

towne *n.* town SA428.

towre *n.* tower SR375, etc., SA370, etc., **towour** SR558, etc., **tower** SR370, **tour** 121:1. **towres** *pl.* SA369, **tow(e)rys** Y543, SA401, **towers** SR366, **tourres** C500. Cf. **castel-tour.**

towse *n. pl.* see **toes.**

trayles *n. pl.* trains (of robes) SR185, **traylys** SA192.

traylyng *pr. p.* trailing SA176, **trayleng** SR171.

traynes *n. pl.* trains (of robes) SA190, 191.

traytores *n. pl. Goddes* ∼ betrayers of God SA444.

trecherie *n.* deceitfulness 61:5.

travell *n.* effort, trouble Y483.

travell *v.* travel SA494.

tre(e) *n.* tree C525, SA586, 589, 62:6, 146:4, 173:3, C218, Y211, 570; wood 130:4. **tre(e)s** *pl.* C261, 521, 145:2, **treis** SR596, 599, **tryn** Y254, 566. Cf. **rode-tre** and see **lif.**

trecherie *n.* deceitfulness 61:5.

tredyng *pr. p.* trampling SR356[n].

trendyll *n.* (mill-)wheel Y380.

trent *pa. t. 3 sg.* (*intr.*) rotated 83:2.

treso(u)r *n.* treasure C94, Y91.

trespas *n.* offence, sin 25:1, SR131, **trispas** 31:5, **tryspasse** SA135, 234, 347.

trew *adv.* ∼ *getton* honestly acquired SA280.

trew(e) *adj.* honest, good SR264, SA497, 314, 497, **true** SR270, 308; ∼ true 47:6.

trewly *adv.* (emphatic) indeed, truly SA231, etc., **trevly** SA185, etc.; **treuly** *gotyn* honestly acquired SA499, (sim.) **trulych** SR505.

trewthe *n.* truth SA305.

tribulacion *n.* misery SR139, 699, SA143.

tryn *n. pl.* see **tre(e)**.

Trinite *n. God in* ∼ = God in three persons 129:1, 144:5, 176:3.

trispas, tryspasse *n.* see **trespas**.

tryste *pr. t. pl.* rely C143.

troste *pr. t. pl.* rely Y139.

trowe *pr. 1 sg.* (in assertions) expect C273, 352, Y267. **trowestow** *pr. 2 sg.* (with suff. *pron.*) do you think 180:5.

trust *n. in* ∼ *of* trusting upon SR627.

turment *n.* torment, torture 104:1, 111:5, etc., Y360, 439, **turnement(e)** C390ⁿ, 574. **turmentes** *pl.* SR366, 493, **tormentys** SA485, 510. See **turmentid**.

turmentid *ppl. adj.* tormented SR227, 296, **turment** SR314. ∼ as *pron.* (*pl.*) tormented ones SR295.

turmentri(e) *n.* infliction/suffering of torture 76:6, 98:4.

turn(e) *v.* (*tr.*) convert C50, 19:5, twist (hand) SR160, SA164; **tourn** rotate (wheel) 84:6. ∼ (*intr.*) change Y320; ∼ ... *to* change into SR177; ∼ *agayne* = go back C336, (sim.) SA616, 135:4. **turnest** *pr. 2 sg.* revert (to sin) SR647. **turnys** *pr. t. pl.* direct SA670. **turn** *imp. sg.* ∼ *o3ain* go back 97:4, 109:1. **turnyng** *pr. p.* ∼ *a3en* going back SR395; turning (*tr.*) SR449. **turned** *pa. t. 3 sg.* ∼ *agayn* returned C201, (sim.) **turnyd** Y194; ∼ changed SR278, (sim.) **turnyde** SA291; directed

SA332. **turned(e)** *pa. t. pl.* ∼ *a3eyne* returned C545, 363; **turnyd** *ageyn* turned round Y400, 576; **turnyde** ... *to* (or *pp.*) turned ... into SA182. **turnyd** *pp.* changed SA195, **yturned** SR189; turned *Y346; ∼ *them to* turned into ... for them SA396.

turnement(e) *n.* see **turment**.

turnyng *vbl. n.* ∼ *a3en* reverting (to sin) SR636.

tvelue *num. adj. bi* ∼ in groups of twelve 153:2, (sim.) 162:6.

twey *num. adj.* two SR366, **tvay** 140:5ⁿ, 158:2. As *pron. pl.* **tvay** two people 140:2.

tweyn *num. adj.* two Y48, 503, 557, 576; *on* **tweyne** in two (pieces) SR221.

two *num. adj.* two C53, 271, 512, 545, SA32, **to** 103:6, **too** SA368, *in* **too** in two (pieces) SA235.

þai *pron.* they 1:6, etc., SR46, etc., SA65, 74, 404, **þay** 189:5, **thay** SA16, etc., **þei** SR16, etc., SA79, **thei** SR28, etc., **þey** C6, etc., Y104, etc., SR197, 198, **they** C59, etc., Y139, etc., SA27, etc., **þi(e)** Y353, 325. **þem** *acc., dat., refl.* C36, 667, Y103, SR73, 184, 619, SA299, **them** Y228, etc., SR66, etc., SA25, etc., **theme** SA212, **thame** SA265. **þer** *poss. adj.* C630, SA91, etc., **ther** Y10, etc., SA94, etc., **þere** SR269, **there** SR428, SA225, **þur** C198. Cf. **hye**.

þan *adv.* then 3:5, etc., Y658, SR28, etc., SA457, **than** Y39, etc., SR58, etc., SA29, 197, 242, **thanne** SR48, etc., **þen** C37, etc., SR397, SA58, etc., **then** C44, etc., *Y382, SR97, etc., SA27, etc., **thenne** C655, 669, SR342, 412. ∼ *when* 41:2

þan *conj.* than 56:5, etc., SR60, etc., **than** Y285, 339, 499, **þen** C414, SA87, 411, **then** C344, etc., SA63, etc. See **er, or** *adv., conj.²*.

þan *demons. pron.* see **þat**.

thank(e) *n.* thanks, gratitude SA611, 487, **thonke** SR640.

thanke *pr. 1 sg.* thank Y444, *I* ∼ *hyt*
þe I thank you for that C361.
thongkid *pa. t. 1 sg.* SR107.
thankyd *pa. t. 3 sg.* Y506,
þonked 18:6, etc., gave thanks for
184:6, 191:2, **þonked** ... *of*
thanked ... for C306. **thankyd**
pa. t. pl. Y641, SA599, **þonked**
139:3, C638, **thonkid** SR607,
610. **thonkid** *pp.* SR613.
þare *adv.* see **þer.**
þat *demons. adj.* that 7:4, etc., C30,
etc., Y45, etc., SR21, etc., SA35,
etc., **that** C451, 505, 556, Y89(2),
etc., SR348, 615, 674, 681,
SA379, 452, 531, ∼ (*pl.*) 80:5, 81:4,
etc., SR213, 365, **that** SA360. (As
def. art.) ∼ *o* 150:1, ∼ *oþer*
150:4. See also **þo** *demons. adj.*
and **þos(e).**
þat *pron.* 21:2, 171:1(1), etc., C43,
Y38, SR19, 367, SA348, **that** C385,
Y414, 613, 617, SA51, 62, etc.;
∼ that which C6, 134, SR104,
SA545; *bi* **þan** by that (time)
194:3, *no for* **þan** nevertheless
57:1, *with* ∼ thereupon SR60, (sim.)
SA63, 384, etc., **that** SR706
∼ (emphatic vicarious usage)
SA456. See **in** and **þo** *demons.*
pron. and **þos(e).**
þat *rel. indecl.* 1:6, etc., C1, etc., Y14,
etc., SR15, etc., SA50, etc., **that**
C2, etc., Y8, etc., SR465, 705,
SA56, 634; ellipsis before **is**
112:5; ∼ ... + *poss.* = whose
SR472.
þat *conj.* that 3:2, etc., C40, etc.,
Y110, etc., SR52, etc., SA23, etc.,
that C42, etc., Y128, etc., SA644;
∼ so that 2:2, etc., C69, etc.,
Y482, SA77, 81, 95, **that** C20,
etc., Y44, SA255; ∼ such that
92:4, 96:5; until 15:5; (introducing
exclamatory clause) SR694,
SA440, 664; (as conjunctive\ particle) see **but, forto** *conj.*, **ʒif, in**
prep., **til, while.**
þe *adv.* the (with compar.) 14:6, 61:2,
111:1, 2, etc., C48, 100, Y493,
SR603, SA534, 594, **the** C570,
SR541, 603.

þe *def. art.* the 4:1, etc., C7, etc.,
Y12, etc., SR3, etc., SA9, etc.,
the Y65, etc., SR2, etc., SA1,
etc.; *dat.* 192:2, (*pl.*) 186:1. Cf.
at(t)e *s.v.* **at.**
þede *n.* country 87:6.
theder, -yr *adv.* see **þider.**
thefes *n. pl.* see **þeues.**
þei *conj.* although 35:4, 52:4, 189:3.
theis *demons. pron.* see **þis** *demons.*
pron.
themselfe *pron. pl.* themselves
SA256.
þen, then see **þan.**
þenche *v.[1]* seem to (with dat. pron.)
91:6. **þenkeþ** *pr. 3. sg. impers. me*
∼ it seems to me 181:1, *me* **thin-**
kith SR651, (sim.) *him* ∼ 157:5.
þouʒt *pa. t. 3 sg. impers. him* ∼
8:4, etc., (sim.) **þowʒt(e)** C464,
etc., 451, **þowʒth** C484, **thowʒte**
C477, **thowght** SR217, 429, *my*
∼ SR489, etc., **thought** SR24,
thoght(e) SA23, 262, etc., **thowt**
SR571, **thowth** Y525, **thow**
Y511[n], 557, ∼ *him* 121:6.
þenchen *v.[2] on* ... ∼ think about
94:4, **thynke** SA507. **þenk** *imp.*
sg. ∼ *opon* consider 49:2. **þows-**
tedest *pa. t. 2 sg.* C616[n]. **þouʒt**
pa. t. 1, 3 sg. 31:4, 61:4, etc.,
þowʒte C124, **þowʒth** C297,
thowt(e) Y120, 362, 509, ∼ (+
on) 89:3, **thoght** SA83. **thowʒte**
pa. t. pl. C334.
þennes *adv.* from there 11:3, **þens**
C255.
þer *adv.* there 41:5, etc., C86, etc.,
Y113, etc., SA21, etc., **þere** 17:6[r],
etc., C57, SR155, etc., **ther** C197,
etc., Y104, etc., SA112, etc.,
there Y190, 623, etc., SR165,
etc., SA586, **þare[r]** 45:3[n], 73:1,
89:5, **þore[r]** C183, 511, 552, etc.,
*Y52. (Unemphatic, preceding *v.*)
∼ 53:2, etc., C210, etc., Y110,
etc., SR132, 466, SA508, **þere**
SR539, 603, **ther** SR87, 515, 614,
SA132.
þer *conj.* where 10:3, 32:4, etc.; **ther**
as C196.
þer *rel. adv.* where, in which 30:2,
32:5, etc., C553, SA464(2),

559, **ther** Y63, *299, **ther** *þat* Y189, **there** SR258.

þerafter *adv.* after that, afterwards 52:1, **þeraftur** C211.

þeramong(e) *adv.* among them C495, 146:2.

þerat(e) *adv.* in that place 22:2; *ny3* ~ near to it C467.

þerbi *adv.* *be war* ~ beware of that 71:5, 81:5, 95:6, 102:2; **þerby** next to it C442, Y489.

þerfor(e) *adv.* for that, for it C212, Y205, SR141, 143, 149, etc., SA153(2), 145, etc., **therfor** SR280, SA152; ~ for this reason, cause, etc. SR41, etc., SR199, SA240, 365, etc., **therfor(e)** SR81, 143, etc., SA391, etc., SA153(1), etc., **therefore** SR256, 427.

therfro *adv.* away from it SR571.

þerin *adv.* in it, in there, therein, there 15:4, etc., SA57, etc., **þerinne** 4:3^r, etc., C122, 377, Y373, **þeryn** C73, etc., Y112, 430, SR161, etc., **þerynne** SR194, etc., **theryn** C526, Y100, 428, SR299, 392, **therynne** Y118; ~ into it C435, **þerinne** 187;2, **þeryn** C96, 295, Y93, 290, **theryn** SR230.

therke *adj.* dark Y300^n. Cf. **derk(e)**.

þerof *adv.* of it 13:4, Y308, 394, SR143, 317, SA147, etc., **therof** Y462, etc., SR141; ~ from it SA301; with that 34:1, 97:3.

þeron *adv.* thereon, on it 90:4, 145:3, C439, 456, Y503, **theron** Y377; ~ of it, to it 129:5; in them 100:1, in it 130:4, **theron** Y216.

þeropon *adv.* on them 132:5; **thervpon** on it Y486.

þerouer *adv.* across it 117:1, **therouer** C322, Y309.

þerout *adv.* outside (it) 45:1.

þertil *adv.* to it 84:3.

þerto *adv.* to it SR527, 529, SA522, 523, 563, **therto** SR570; ~ to them 16:2; for it C91, **þertoo** Y88; ~ in addition C264, 409.

þervnder *adv.* under it 120:2.

þerwhile *adv.* while 174:5.

þerwith *adv.* with it SR187, 196, **þerwyth** SA193, *458.

þeues *n. pl.* thieves 80:5(1), **thefes** SR263, 269, **thevys** SA274, 279, 583. ~ *gen.* 80:5(2).

þider *adv.* to that place 26:6, 35:6, **þydur** C34, 142, **dyþur** C141, 176, **theder** Y30, 163, **thedyr(e)** Y170, 138, **thyþur** C177.

þykke *adj.* dense, numerous C408, **thyk(k)e** C371, 406, Y169, 457. **thykker** *comp.* Y422.

þykke *adv.* densely, thick (on the ground) C327, **thyke** Y314, 345, 459. **þicker** *comp.* 120:6.

þilk(e) *adj.* that (same) 170:5, SR163, etc., **thilk** SR331, etc., **þilche** 186:2. ~ *pl.* those SR84, 274, etc., **thilk** SR196, etc., **þyulk** SR349, **thik** SR472, **þilche** 69:4, 91:2.

þilk *pron.* that one SR420. ~ *pl.* those SR307, **thilk** SR295, 343.

þing *n.* thing(s) 7:4, 28:5, etc., **thinge** SR95, **thyng** SA549, **þyng** = enterprise SR31, **thyng** SA30; *in alle* ~ in all respects 155:1. **þinges** *pl.* 8:2, 53:5, **thyngys** Y48, **þynkes** C53.

thinkith *pr. 3 sg.* see **þenche** *v.*[1].

thyrde *num. adj. ord.* see **þridde**.

þis *demons. adj.* this 10:6, etc., SR53, etc., SA38, etc., **this** SR14, etc., **þys** C39, etc., **thys** C119, Y98, etc., SA55, etc., **thus** C346^n, SA50. **þis** *pl.* SA365, **this** SR497, **þise** SR408, **thyes** Y250, SA237, etc., **þes** SA313, **thes** Y52, SA250, etc., **þese** SR200, etc., **these** C255, SR340, etc., **theys** Y319.

þis *demons. pron.* this 5:1, etc., **this** SR12, 495, 707, **þys** C399, 616, **thys** C577, Y593, 622, SA241, 427. **þis** *pl.* 108:1, **thes** SA296, **þese** SR223, etc., **these** SR381, 405, **theis** SA197, **thyes** SA206, etc.

þiself *pron.* yourself SR80, **þiselffe** SA80, **thiself** SR24, **thyselffe** SA82.

þo *adv.* then 13:1, 64:1, etc., C65, 153, etc., SR86, etc., **tho** Y60^r,

etc., SR85, etc., **þoo** C107ʳ, etc., **thoo** SR346, **thowe** Y148ⁿ.
þo *conj.*[1] when 89:1, 104:6.
þo *conj.*[2] though 128:3, **þow** SR133, **thow** Y516, *as* **þowgh** SR606, **thowffe** SA137.
þo *demons. adj. pl.* those C57, 376, Y425, SR89, 185, etc., **tho** C356, Y427, SR191, 311, 378, **þoo** SR267, 444, etc., **thoo** SR312, **thow** Y175, 576. Cf. **þos(e)**.
þo *demons. pron.* that one 148:3, SR156. ~ *pl.* those 80:4, 108:4, etc., C77, SR237, 279, etc., **tho** SR237, 240, 617, **þoo** SR255, 263, etc., **thoo** SR286, 507, **thowe** Y471. Cf. **þos(e)**.
thoght *n.* see **þowght**.
þole *v.* suffer, endure (*tr.*) 14:2.
þonder *n.* thunder 121:5, **þondur** C259, **thundyre** Y252.
þore *adv.* see **þer**.
þore *n.* see **dore**.
thorht *prep.* see **þorow** *prep.*
þorn *n.* thorn 197:2ⁿ.
þorow *adv.* through C572.
þorow *prep.* through C355, SR415, **thorow(e)** SR253(1), (2), SA186, **þurth** 42:6, 63:3, etc., ~ because of C18, **thorowe** SA199, **throw** Y117; ~ by (means of), with C569, **thorow** C152, 573, SA18, 30, etc., **thowroo** SA148, **thorht** SA6, **throgh** SA38, **throw** Y147, ***throwe** Y601, **throwr** Y44ⁿ, **þurth** 25:2, 28:3, etc.; **throw** throughout Y240; ~ with (permission, consent) C49, 97.
thorowout *prep.* right through SR180, **þurthout** 80:1.
þos(e) *demons. adj. pl.* those SA70, 378, 39, **thos(e)** SR363, SA108, 462, **thows** SA392, **thowys** SA290, 610, **thoys** SA191.
thowes *pron.* SA417. Cf. **þo** *demons. adj. pl. and pron.*
þou *pron.* you (*sg.*) 35:4, etc., C136, etc., Y159, etc., SR44, etc., SA37, etc., **þow** SR31, etc., SA29, etc., **thow** C150, etc., Y142, etc., SR31, etc., SA61, 624, etc. **þe** *acc., dat.* 41:6, 49:4, etc., C135, 182, etc., Y175, 237, etc., SR38,

49, etc., SA62, 136, etc., **the** C244, 649, Y141, 469, etc., SR43, 74, etc., SA43, 616, **de** C167. **þe** *refl.* 36:6, etc., Y231, 657, SR99, etc., SA149, 540, **the** SR549, **de** C652. **þi** *poss. adj.* 39:2, etc., Y161, etc., SR34, etc., SA42, etc., **thi** SR33, etc., **þy** C145, etc., SR645, **thy** Y233, etc., SA40, etc., **they** Y141, **þin(e)** 36:6, etc., 87:6, **þyn** C617, **thyn(e)** SA135, 617, **tine** 55:5.
þousand *num. adj.* thousand 84:1, 135:2, 191:3, **þousend** 48:2, 80:3, **þowsande** C583, **thowsond** Y599. See **last** *n.*
þousandfold *adv.* a thousand times 181:1, ***thowsandfold** SR580, **thowsandefolde** SA564. As *n. be a* **þowsandfolde** C475. See **folde**.
thowe *adv.* see **þo** *adv.*
thowes *pron.* see **þos(e)**.
thowffe, þowgh *conj.* see **þo** *conj.*[2].
þowght *n.* haue yn þy ~ = keep in mind C251, (sim.) **thoght** SA47, 101, **thowth** Y246; **þow3th** mind, thought C245, 459, 481, **thowte** Y415, **thowth** Y506, 524, **thoght** SA96, thinking SA446. **thowghtis** *pl.* SR436.
thowroo *prep.* see **þorow** *prep.*
tho(w)(y)s *demons. adj. pl.* see **þos(e)**.
þowstedest *pa. t. 2 sg.* see **þenchen** *v.*[2].
þrawe *v.* see **þrowe**.
þre *num. adj.* three 156:5, C11, **thre** SA131.
thret *n.* threat, ? torment C348.
þridde *num. adj. ord.* third 151:1, **thyrde** SA242.
thryst *pa. t. pl.* thrust SA246.
þritten *num. adj.* thirteen 42:1, 45:4, 190:5.
þrytty *num. adj.* thirty C11.
throgh *prep.* see **þorow**.
throtes *n. pl.* throats SR446, **throttys** SA247.
þrowe *v.* knock down, cause to fall 118:1; **þrawe** hurl, fling 58:5. **threw** *pa. t. pl.* SA189, 227.

ythrow *pp.* ∼ *of* thrown by SR446.

throw(e), throwr *prep.* see **þorow**.

þrust *n.* thirst 62:5.

þur *poss. adj.* see **þai**.

þurth(out) *prep.* see **þorow, thorowout**.

thus *demons. adj.* see **þis**.

þus *adv.* thus, in this way 28:1, etc., C569, SR122, etc., SA229, etc., **thus** C349, Y271, therefore Y84.

vg(g)ely *adj.* ugly SA261, 45.

vnboolde *adj.* frail C678.

vncouþe *adj.* strange, unknown 62:3.

vnder *prep.* under 40:1, 122:5, SR581, **vndyr** SA573; ∼ at the foot of ? 93:2; in accordance with Y83; **vnþur** = wearing (the habit) C88; ∼ *Godes glorie an hei3e* = on earth 152:5 (see also **heuen**).

vnder *adv.* underneath 121:4, SR292.

vndernome *pa. t. 3 sg.* donned (habit) 197:5.

vnderstond[r] *v.* know how, learn, understand 19:4, 27:2, 61:3, 133:6, SR518, **vndyrstande** SA512, **vnþurstonde** C8. *ich* ∼ *pr. 1 sg.* I know on good authority (tag) 10:4, 95:1, **vndyrstond** Y109, **vnþurstonde** C113. **vnderstode** *pa. t. 1 sg.* SR539. ∼ *pp.* Y161, **vnþurstonde** C166.

vndo *v.* undo, open (*tr.*) C92, **ondoo** Y89. **onded** *pa. t. 3 sg.* unlocked Y192. **vndede** *pa. t. pl.* (*intr.*) opened 134:1. **vndo** *pp.* uncompleted (penance) SR148, **vndone** SA153.

vnkynde *adj.* ungrateful SA667, 669.

***vnkyndenesse** *n.* ingratitude, unnatural conduct SA607, **onkindenesse** SR636.

vnklene *adj.* impure SR468.

vnluste *n.* disinclination SA209.

vn(n)eþe *adv.* scarcely, hardly 63:2, C416, *Y375, **vnnethe** SA211, 562, **oneþe** C372, **onnethe** SR568, 569.

vnponyschyde *ppl. adj.* unpunished SA492.

vntil *prep.* to (with *v.* of motion) 68:5. Cf. **til**.

vnto *prep.* to SR15, 30, etc., SA51, 632, etc., **onto** Y386, ∼ until SR396, SA365, for SA287. See **like** *adj.*

***vntrewþe** *n.* lack of true faith 1:5.

vnwytty *adj.* foolish, unwise SA670.

vp *adv.* up (mod. uses) 19:1, 64:4, etc., C303, 338, 411, etc., Y428, 430, 511, SR61, 348, etc., SA557, 559. See **caste, doun, take**.

vpon *prep.* (up)on C16, Y12, 232, SA385, **vppon** SR284, 320, 579, etc., **apon** SA261, 295, etc., **opon** 84:2, 125:4; concerning 176:4; ∼ in (+ trust) C143. See also **day, row(e), rowte, sight, take**.

vpon *adv.* on one's person (of apparel) Y530.

vpri3tes *adv.* on their back, face up 102:4.

vpward *adv.* face upwards 69:4, upwards Y316.

vrn *pa. t. pl.* see **renneþ**.

vsage *n.* behaviour SR194.

vse *n.* use SR276, SA288.

vsid *pa. t. pl.* used SR465, practised SR245, **vsyde** SA199, **vsidden** SR389, **wsyd** SA395. **vsyde** *pp.* SA202.

vayle *n.* veil SR26, **velle** SA25.

vaynglorie *n.* vainglory, inordinate pride SR500, **vayneglory** SA201, **vaneglory** SA487.

valay *n.* valley 63:6.

vaneshid *pa. t. 3 sg.* vanished SR490, 555, **uaneschyde** SA567, **vanyschyd** SA479, **vanys(s)hid** SR536, 573. **vaneshid** *pa. t. pl.* SR84, 106, **vanyschyde** SA109. **vaneshid** *pp.* removed from sight SR152, **vanyschyde** SA155.

vanite *n.* vanity, idle foolishness SR193, **vanyte** SA332. **vanites** *pl.* worthless things SA329, **vanytes** idle activities SA252, 330, 657, **vaniteis** SR430, 436, 685.

varey *adj.* true SA612.

vax *v.* see **wax(e)**.

velle *n.* see **vayle**.

vemunsume *adj.* venomous SA378[n].
vengance *n.* ~ *of* vengeance on SA316, ~ *on* SA418, **veniaunce** SR309, 312, 410.
verely *adv.* truly, really SR217.
uergyn *n.* see **virgen**.
vertu *n.* power 184:4, 196:5, SA88, *of* ~ powerful SR86.
vessell *n.* vessel SR527, SA521.
vestymentes *n. pl.* vestments C487, **vestemens** Y530.
vetyn *v.* see **wyte**.
viage *n.* journey SR120, **vyage** SA122.
vicars *n. pl.* vicars SA430, 463, **vicaries** SR424, 455, 472, **vycaryes** C497, **vekerys** Y540.
vilanie *n.* infamous deeds 76:3.
virgen *n.* virgin SR546, **virgyn** SR97, **uergyn** SA99, 538.
visage *n.* face SR91, SA92, **vysage** SA262. **visages** *pl.* SR89, SA91.
voces *n. pl.* voices SA408.
voide *v.* depart SR43, **voyde** SR18, SA17, **vode** SA43.
volente *n.* will 158:5.

wage *n.* reward C78, Y73.
way *n.* way (= route one follows) 11:3, 36:2, etc., C4, 150, etc., SR21, 34, etc., SA64, 552, etc., **waye** SA78, **wai** SR37, **wey(e)** Y4, 134, etc., **wye** Y201; ~ distance SA474; *þe* ~ on the way 42:6. **wai(e)s** *pl.* paths SR33, 63, SA32, **wayes** SA66.
wayke *adj.* weak SA560.
waileway *interj.* exclamation of sorrow 69:2.
wayly *v.* wail 66:1.
waynes *n. pl.* wagons C456.
wald *pa. t. pl.* see **wyll**.
walkyd *pa. t. pl.* walked SA597.
wall *n.* wall C463, *C510, SA353, **wal** 23:4, 129:3, SR349. **walles** *pl.* SR477, **wallys** SA466, **walys** Y217, **wowys** Y265.
wall *v.* boil C374[n], **wyll** Y425[n].
wallyd *ppl. adj.* surrounded by a wall SA451, **ywallid** SR440.
wan *conj.* see **when**.
wanted *pa. t. 3 sg.* lacked C205.

war(e) *adj.* aware SR23, SA22, 105:1, 183:1. See **þerbi**.
ward, ward(e)ly, warld(e) *n./adj.* see **world(e), worldly**.
warse *adv. comp.* worse SA383.
was *pa. t. 1, 3 sg.* was 5:4, etc., C6, etc., Y14, etc., SR9, 86, etc., SA3, 22, etc., **wase** SA429, **wes**[r] 30:2, 76:5, **wos** Y26, 110, etc., **were** 85:3, (after *it* with *pl.* antecedent) 140:6. **was** *pa. t. 2 sg.* C553, Y583, SR141, SA116, 144, **were** 115:5, SR114, 591. **wer** *pl.* 46:1, etc., C5, etc., Y226, etc., SA392, **were** 2:4, etc., C371, etc., Y23, etc., SR152, etc., SA86, etc., **weren** 1:6, 53:5, 107:2, 168:5, SR214, 414, 465, 501, **wern** 65:2, 78:1, Y346, 457, (after *yt* with *pl.* antecedent) Y327, **war** 45:5, **ware** SA173, 404, **wore**[r] *C27, 111, (after *hyt* with *pl.* antecedent) C512, **was** 128:6, SA470, **wasse** Y553. **wer** *pa. t. subj. sg.* 191:5, Y94, 97, SA520, **were** 83:5, 129:3, etc., C41, 97, 100, SR157, 393(2), etc., SA209. **wer** *pa. t. subj. pl.* 100:2, *Y518, **were** 90:6, 175:6, SR16, 17, SA16, 17, **weyre** SA333.
wasche *pp.* washed 103:5.
wast *n.* waste, (spent) *in* ~ = squandering SR411, SA419.
wat *adj./pron.* see **what**.
water *n.* water 94:1, 5, etc., C189, 404, Y460, SR481, 527, etc., SA471, 549, etc., **watur** C409, 413, **watyr** Y182, *a* ~ an expanse of water SR480, SA469, (sim.) C404, Y455.
wax *pr. pl.* grow, increase (in numbers) Y607, **wexen** C595. **vax** *inf.* Y679. **wax(e)** *pa. t. 3 sg.* C446, 445, 455, **waxyd** Y492, **wex** 94:2, C678, **wexede** C677. **waxide** *pa. t. pl.* became SA402, **waxyde** SA404.
we *pron.* we 48:1, etc., C182, etc., Y19, etc., SR70, etc., SA74, etc., **wee** SA347. **ous** *acc., dat.* 8:5, 57:3, etc., **vs** C3, 17, Y21, 174, etc., SR60, 646, etc., **hus(e)** SA63, 345, 347, 129, etc., **hvs**

SA317. **our** *poss. adj.* 20:5, etc.,
C51, 170, 594, 603, **owre** C278,
Y164, etc., SR3, etc., SA42, etc.,
owyr Y405, **owere** SA101.
weche *pron./adj.* see **which**.
wed(e) *n. pl.* garments C533, Y546.
*****wede** *v.* rage, go mad Y389[n].
weder *n.* (rough) weather Y476,
wedyr Y256[n], **wether** Y469.
wederes *pl.* C430.
wedlake *n.* wedlock 139:1. See
order.
weght *n.* weight SA561.
wey(e)(s) *n.* see **way**.
weyre *pa. t. subj. pl.* see **was**.
weyryde *pr. 3 sg.* see **were**.
wel *adv.* well (mod. uses) SR32, 75,
etc., SA31, **wele** 21:2, 48:4, etc.,
C155, 277, SA422, **well** C89,
172, etc., SR70, 111, etc., **welle**
SA428, **woll** Y105, **wyll** Y64, 86,
144, etc.; ∼ (intensive, modifying
v.) very much SR112, (modifying
adj. or *adv.*) very 8:1, 29:3, etc.,
SR605, **well** C354, **woll** Y6, 213,
etc., **wolle** Y632, (sim. with
comp.) **well** C217, much C280,
367, **woll** Y273; ∼ much 80:6;
many 48:2; easily 135:1; *as* ∼ also
SR666; *as* **well** *as* in addition to
SA480; **well** *ny3* very nearly
C472.
welcome *adj.* welcome SR30, 31,
623, **wellcome** C164, **welcum**
SA29, **wolcum** Y159.
welcome *interj.* welcome! 55:3.
wele *n.* happiness 62:4, C530, **wylle**
Y575; ∼ riches, wealth C502;
noþur for ∼ *ner for wo* = not on
any account C168.
welfare *n.* prosperity, happiness
SA362.
well *adv.* see **wel**.
wel(l)comed *pa. t. sg.* welcomed
C163, SR605. **wellcomed(e)** *pa.
t. pl.* C637, 509, **welcomede**
C513, **welcumyd** SA597.
welles *n. pl.* wells, springs 149:1.
wende *v.* (1) *tr.* turn, convert 6:2. (2)
intr. go 35:6, 36:2, etc., C72, 173,
etc., *****Y67, 658, **wend** SR656,
wynd(e) Y146, 179, etc., 281,
468, ∼ turn C288, return C151,

653. **wende** *imp. sg.* 39:3. **wende**
pa. t. sg. 193:4, **went** 3:5, 17:5,
etc., Y77, 122, etc., SR62, 87,
etc., SA166, 529, etc., **wente**
C82, 203, etc., Y15, 196, etc.,
wenth Y673, **wentt(e)** SA64,
110, 547. **went(e)** *hys way* took
his way C157, (sim.) SR61, Y152.
went *pa. t. pl.* 43:2, 62:1, etc.,
Y558, SR660, **wente** C109, 111,
etc., Y185, 250, **wentt** SA631,
wenten C255, **wentyn** Y107.
wente *pp.* C243, **ywente** 47:3,
127:1.
wene *adv.* see **when**.
wene *n.* supposition, *wiþouten* ∼
certainly (tag) 180:5.
wene *pr. 1 sg.* think C522, Y567.
wende *pa. t. 3 sg.* 64:1.
wentyr *n.* see **winter**.
wepyng(e) *pr. p.* weeping C628,
SR694, **wepynd** Y665. *ppl. adj.
mony a* ∼ *tere* abundant weeping
C660[n].
wepyng(e) *vbl. n.* weeping SA664,
Y632, SR681.
were *v.* wear (clothes) Y549. **wereþ**
pr. 3 sg. 154:4, **weyryde** SA188.
weryng(e) *vbl. n.* wearing SA647,
SR676.
wereof *adv.* (made) of what Y512.
werkes *n. pl.* doings 82:3, *Godes* ∼
devotions 7:2, 37:5, 195:2.
wesdam *n.* see **wysdom**.
wete *v.* see **wyte**.
wether *n.* see **weder**.
weued *pp.* removed 60:4.
wex, -ede, -en *v.* see **wax**.
whan *adv./conj.* see **when**.
whare *rel./conj.* see **where**.
wharþurth *adv.* by which means
19:4[n], ∼ *þat* whereby 146:5.
what *adj.* what (mod. uses) 128:2,
155:3, etc., C324, Y547, SR162,
SA166, 605, **wat** Y553, 669; ∼
whatever C72, Y67, 72, SR146,
SA150, *at* ∼ *time* till such time as
SR362.
what *pron.* what 35:3, C32, 63, etc.,
Y113, 311, etc., SR161, 459,
SA44, 165, **wat** Y28, 58, etc.,
whath Y105, ∼ *so* whatever

C178, Y170, **whatsoeuer** whoever SA142.
wheche *pron.* see **which.**
wheder *adv.* see **whyþur.**
whele *n.* wheel 83:2, 86:1, 89:4, etc., **wylle** Y373, 376, 383.
when *adv., conj.* when 5:1, 32:1, etc., C139, 159, etc., SR14, 26, etc., SA124, 253, etc., **whenne** C341, 388, 391, **whan** C213, Y208, 678, etc., SR122, 618, 644, **wan** Y436, **wene** SA168, **qwhan** Y135, ~ *þat* 190:4.
wher(e) *adv.* where SA605, C398.
wher(e) *rel., conj.* where 83:2, Y583, SR212, etc., SA646, C68, etc., Y140, SA61, 222, 632, **whare** 105:2, 183:2, SR58.
whereuer *adv.* wherever SA264, **whereever** SR254.
wherfore *adv.* and therefore SR707.
wherynne *adv.* in which SR204.
wheþer *conj.* whether 180:3, **wheþur** C79, (+ *þat*) C613, **wyther** Y619.
whether *adv.* see **whyþur.**
why *adv.* why C324, 397, Y402, SA134, 204, **whi** SR131, 629, **wy** Y448.
which *pron.* (*rel.*) which SR41, 75, etc., **wiche** 16:1, **weche** SA13, 40, etc., *the/þe* ~ SR1, 20, etc., *the/þe* **weche** SA1, 221, who SA36, 69, *the/þe* ~ SR65, 70; (sim.) **wheche** SA11, **whyche** C528, **wyche** Y357. **weche** *adj.* SA669, *þe* ~ SR12, 447, etc.
while *n.* space of time (adverbial) *a* ~ 39:4, SR650, (sim.) **whyle** C204, **wyll** Y174; (+ *adj.* as good, little = a long, short time) ~ SR486, 644, (sim.) C181, 339, 461, Y508, *a grett* **whylle** SA616.
while(s) *adv., conj.* while SR112, 478, 499, *155:6, **whyle** C298, SA485, **whylys** SA445, **whyll** Y328, SA257, 396, 505, **wyll** for a while Y197, as long as Y280.
whilom *adv.* formerly 79:4.
white *adj.* white 45:6, 138:3, 180:3, **whyte** C465, **whytt** SA585, 596. See **chanoun.**

white *n.* (in phr.) *in* ~ in white apparel SR24, 605, (sim.) **whytte** SA24.
whyþur *adv.* whither C144, **wheder** SR67, **whether** SA71.
who *n.* see **wo.**
who *pron.* who Y32, whoever 152:1, ~ *þat* 13:2, 67:4, 73:4, 144:4. **whom** *obj.* whom SR183, SA286.
whoever *pron.* whoever SR138, **whoeuur** C34.
whoso *pron.* whoever 82:4, 123:4, C63, **howso** Y30.
wy *adv.* see **why.**
wick *adj.* wicked 95:3, **wicke** horrible 110:4.
wicked *adj.* wicked 69:3, **wykked** C269, **wykyd** Y262.
wide *adj.* wide 63:6, **wyde** C221, 370, Y214, 421, ~ extensive 161:1.
wide *adv.* wide apart 44:3; far and wide 71:6, **wyde** C31, Y27. See **open.**
wye *n.* see **way.**
wiȝt *adj.* brave 29:5.
wiȝt *n.* being 44:2. **wiȝtes** *pl.* men 102:5.
wiif *n.* woman 73:5, 102:2, **wiue** 81:5, ~ wife 146:5, 172:5.
*****wykke** *n.* wickedness Y168[n].
wykked, wykyd *adj.* see **wicked.**
wikkidnesse *n.* wickedness SR632, **wykkydnes** SA655.
wild(e) *adj.* fierce 80:1, 89:2.
wyldernesse *n.* wilderness C67, 217, **wyldyrnes(se)** Y62, 210.
wilfulli *adj.* willingly SR637.
will *n.* will, purpose, wish, inclination SR272, 273, **wille** 111:6, 171:5, **wyll(e)** C162, 566, 598, Y161, SA503, C140, 238, etc., Y157, 233, SA348, 445, etc., **wil** SR51, 257, etc., ~ testament SR275, **wyll** SA286; *at thy* **wyll** at thy command C429, Y476; *wiþ gode* **wille** eagerly SR619, (sim.) **wyll** SA608, **wyl** SA613; *was in* **wil** intended SR325. See **duryng.**
wyll *pr. 1 sg.* (auxil. of volition or intention) wish, will, intend C117, 140, SA38, **woll** Y113, **ichil** 28:5, 35:2, etc.; ~ am willing SA54, **wil**

SR52; ∼ (of futurity) Y286, 322,
etc., **woll** C151; ∼ (*inf.* of 'motion' understood) C177, Y170.
wyll *pr. 2 sg.* Y403 (and see **nel**),
Y410ⁿ, **wilt** 57:2, SR67, 74, 79,
wylt(e) Y172, 411, etc., C147,
179, 336, **wyllte** SA71, **wolte**
C288. **wyll** *pr. 3 sg.* C63, 72,
SA396, **woll** Y58, SR241; (of futurity) ∼ C601, Y417, **wil** 35:3;
(impersonal) *as prystys befalle* ∼
= as (it) is fitting for priests
Y227. **wyll** *pr. pl.* Y242, SA612,
wil 28:6, **wyl** SA665; (of futurity)
∼ C337, 626, etc., **wil** 159:4,
SR74, 80, **will** SR694, **woll**
C247, 561, Y105, 592. **wold** *pa. t.
1, 3 sg.* 3:2, 13:4, 31:4, 33:5, Y67,
SR72, 78, 126, etc., SA305, 524,
etc., **wolde** C47, 124, 196, etc.,
Y42, 120, etc., SA20, 523, 661,
wol SR690. **wolde** *pa. t. 2 sg.*
SA79. **wold** *pa. t. pl.* Y431,
SR17, 234, etc., SA364, 398, 467,
wolde C44, 308, 333, etc., Y39,
391, SA80, 204, 207, etc.,
wolden SR359, **woldyn** Y348,
wald 75:4. **wost** *pa. t. 2 sg. subj.*
35:4. **wald** *pa. t. 3 sg. subj.* 34:5.
See also **nel**.
wyll(e) *adv.* and *n.* see **whele, wall**
v., **wel, wele, while, while(s)**.
wyllyng *n.* intention SA327; *duryng
the willyng of God* = for as long
as God wills SR227.
win *v.* gain 87:3.
winde *n.* wind 63:1, 72:2, 118:2,
wynd(e) C317, 422, 431, etc.,
SR161, SA165, Y304, 469, 476.
windes *gen.* 92:3, 95:4. **wyndys**
pl. Y470.
winne *n. for Goddes* ∼ by God's bliss
33:2.
winne *v.* go, *out ... ∼ get out* 109:3;
for al þis warld to ∼ = for the
whole wide world (tag) 190:3.
winter *n.* winter 41:3, **wynter** C214,
wentyr Y207, ∼ (adverbial) in
winter 148:5. **wynter** *pl.* after
num. = years SR421.
wirche *v. Godes werkes forto* ∼ to
perform his devotions 7:2, 37:5,

195:2; ∼ (sb.) *wo* do (sb.) harm
118:3. **worthe** *pa. t. 3 sg.* made
(= wrote) Y150ⁿ. **wrouȝt** *pa. t. pl.*
80:6. **wroght** *pp.* made C292,
wrouȝt (pain) done (to sb.) 93:6;
acted 171:5; **ywrouȝt** committed
(sin) 31:2; made 130:3, 132:1,
133:5.
wysche *v.* see **wysse**.
wysdom *n.* knowledge (of good and
evil) C527, **wesdam** Y572.
wyse *adj.* wise C578, 667, **wysse**
Y670.
wise *n.* manner, way 86:1, SR530,
wyse C148, 224; *yn all wyse* in
every way C223, (sim.) with *on*
Y219; *on thys* **wyse** in this manner, thus SA37, (sim.) SA315,
409; *on þe same* **wyse** in the same
way SA525. See also **oþerwise**.
wiselich *adv.* wisely 29:3.
wisemen *n. pl.* wise men 45:5,
wyssemen Y3.
wysse *v.* show, point out (the way)
C3, **wysche** Y3.
wyte *v.* know C63, **wete** Y58, vetyn
Y353ⁿ, ∼ discover C466, Y512.
wot(e) *pr. 1 sg.* C106, 269, 40:5.
wete *pr. 2 sg. subj.* SR52, **wytt**
SA54. **wete** *pr. pl.* Y105, **wite**
21:2, **wote** Y583. **wist** *pa. t. 1 sg.*
SR86, 421, **wyst** SA428. **wyste**
pa. t. 3 sg. C162, 612, 656, Y387,
661, **woste** Y140, 618. **wist** *pa. t.
pl.* 194:3. Cf. **nite**.
witnes(se) *n.* evidence, testimony
123:3, SR287, 82:5, **wyttenes**
SA2, 297.
wittes *n. pl.* senses, wits SR543,
wyttys SA536, 670.
wiþ *prep.* with (mod. uses) 17:3, 57:4,
122:1, etc., **with** SR10, 11, etc.,
etc., **wyth** C17, 55, 66, etc., Y87,
151, 174, etc., SR443, SA64, 92,
94, etc., **wythe** SA12; ∼ among
21:6; **with** by SR349, *590; **with**
her lifes = alive SR159; *God* **wyth**
þem = God being with them
Y103ⁿ. See also **chide, heiȝe, þat**
pron.
wiþalle *adv.* moreover 85:3. See
forþ.

wiþdrawe v. cease, refrain from 13:6. ∿ *pr. 2 sg. subj.* (*refl.*) depart 97:6.

wyther *conj.* see **wheþer**.

withilden *pa. t. pl.* withheld SR279.

wythin *prep.* in, inside SA181, 352, 465, 466, **withynne** SR176.

wythinne *adv.* inside C209.

without *prep.* without SR108, 200, 364, **wythoute** C645, **wythowte** Y650, SA213, 366, outside Y265; **wiþouten** 15:2, 20:1, **wythouten** C654, **wythowten** C174, **wythowtyn** Y571. See also **les, wene.**

wythstand v. withstand SA613. **wythstod** *pa. t. 3 sg.* came to a halt Y398ⁿ. **withstoden** *pa. t. pl.* withstood SR641.

wiue *n.* see **wiif.**

wo *adv. hem was* ... ∿ they were distressed, wretched 106:5, (sim.) 189:3, C36, 330, **woo** C326.

wo *n.* (cause of) harm, pain, distress 4:1, 121:6, 160:4, etc., C180, 376, etc., Y239, 251, 427, 632, SR438, **woo** C343, 410, Y173, 343, 391, SR494, 699. See **wele, wirche.**

wode *adj.* mad 90:6, 100:2, 173:5, SA204, **wod** Y399, **wood** fierce, raging (winds) Y470.

wode *pa. t. pl.* waded 100:4.

wodes *n. pl.* woods SR283, 289, **woddys** SA295.

wofull *adj.* grievous SA417.

woke *pa. t. 3 sg.* (*intr.*) woke 18:1.

wol(l) *adv./v.* see **wel, wyll.**

wolcum *adj.* see **welcome** *adj.*

woluys *n. pl.* wolves Y389.

woman *n.* woman Y74, SR24, 133, etc., SA553, etc. **women** *pl.* Y312, 342, etc., SR158, 672, etc., **wemen** SA167, 176, etc., **wimen** 65:2, 90:4, etc., **wymmen** C325, 375, 505.

wombe *n.* belly 77:4. **wombys** *pl.* SA356.

wond *pa. t. 3 sg.* (*intr.*) turned, spun 83:4.

wond *pr. 3 sg. subj.* hesitate 191:4.

wonder *adv.* exceedingly SR601, 602, 662, **wondyr** C463, SA357, **wonþur** C313, 356.

wonder *n.* have ∿ *of* to marvel at 91:2; *of myche* **wondre** with great astonishment Y253.

wonderd *pa. t. 3 sg.* marvelled 44:4; **wondered** wondered C324.

wonderful(l) *adj.* excellent SR598, amazing SA162.

wonderly *adv.* exceedingly SR378, 380, **wondyrly** Y510, 615.

wondys *n. pl.* see **wounde.**

woni v. dwell, live 153:1. **woneþ** *pr. 3 sg.* 133:3. **woned** *pa. t. 3 sg.* SR54, **wonnyde** SA56, 646. **wonede** *pa. t. pl.* C536.

wont(e) *ppl. adj.* accustomed Y549, 350.

wonþur *adv.* see **wonder** *adv.*

woo *adv./n.* see **wo.**

wood *adj.* see **wode** *adj.*

word(e) *n.* word (various senses) SR12, SA12, 283, 92:1, Y9, = prayer C248, Y243; command Y136, *Goddes* ∿ C31. **wordes** *pl.* C13, SR414, 436, 625, 628, **wordys** SA422, 423, *Goddys* ∿ Y27.

wordy *adj.* worthy C588, Y604.

wore *pa. t. pl.* see **was.**

world *n.* world 16:3, 40:5, 130:3, 151:5, SR66, 112, etc., **worlde** C623, SR145, SA169, 252, **warld** 12:2, 52:4, 190:3, **warlde** SA149, 161, etc., **ward** Y569, 627; *for all þe* **worlde** = (in) exactly (the same way) C263. **worldes** *gen.* 146:3, worldly C502, SR670.

worldly *adj.* worldly SR426, 508, 694, **wardely** SA270, 436, 641, etc., **wardly** of the world Y517.

wormes *n. pl.* serpents, reptiles SR374, 388, 394, etc., SA384, *wormis SR379, **wormys** Y354, SA378, 457, etc., **wormen** SR408ⁿ.

worship *n. in* (*þe*) ∿ *of* in honour of SR563, 612, (sim.) **worschypp** SA555; *dyde* **worschyppe** paid homage SA115.

worship v. honour SR587, 643. **worship** *pp*(*l. adj.*) SR55, 624, **worschyped** worshipped SA464.

worshipful *adj.* in address ∿ *lord*

honourable lord SR55, (sim.)
worschypfull SA58.
worthe *pa. t. 3 sg.* see **wirche**.
wos *pa. t. 1, 3 sg.* see **was**.
wost *pa. t. 2 sg. subj.* see **wyll**.
woste, wote *v.* see **wyte**.
wounde *n.* wound 65:3. **woundes**
pl. 128:5, 143:4, SR207, 208, 224,
wondys SA239, **woundes** *fiue*
(Christ's) Five Wounds 196:5,
(sim.) *.v.* **woundes** SR563,
wondys SA556.
wowys *n. pl.* see **wall** *n.*
wreche *n.*[1] wretch SA59, 105, 344,
544, **wrecche** SR337, 338,
wryche SA343. **wrechys** *pl.*
SA667, **wraches** SA250,
wrachys SA237.
wreche *n.*[2] vengeance 91:4.
wrechyd *adj.* wretched SA264.
wrecchidnesse *n.* base behaviour
SR476.
wreyke *imper. sg.* avenge SA410.
wrenche *n. pl.* tricks 125:2.
write *v.* write 9:2, 122:1, SR12,
wrytte SA12. **wryten** *pa. t. pl.*
C669. **wryte** *pp.* Y106, **wryten**
C110, **wrytton** SA422, **wryttyn**
SA432, **wreten** SR415, **wretyn**
Y34.

wroght *pp.* see **wirche**.
wrong *adj.* (morally) wrong 82:3.
wrong(e) *n.* wrong C2, 541, Y2,
SR295, *wyth* ∼ wrongly, falsely
SA490.
wroþ *adj.* angry 173:1.
wrouȝt *pa. t. pl., pp.* see **wirche**.
wsyd *pa. t. pl.* see **vsid**.
wullepak *n.* wool-pack SR235[n].

xall, xalte, xulde *v.* see **schal**.

yare *adv.* quickly C334.
yate *n.* see **gate** *n.*[1].
ye *pron. 2 pl.* see **ȝe**.
yellyng *pr. p.* see **ȝellyng**.
yender *adj.* that ... over there
SR153, 158, 191, etc., **yonder**
SR246, 268, 313, 344.
yender *n. pl.* þe ∼ = the people over
there SR358. Cf. **ȝondyr** *adv.*
yerlych *adv.* annually SR502.
yet *conj.* see **ȝete**.
yetyng *pr. p.* pouring SR236. **yet** *pa.
t. pl.* SR283.
yevyng *vbl. n.* giving SR467.
yonder, yondyr *adj./adv.* see **yender** *adj.* and **ȝondyr** *adv.*
youghe *n.* youth (period of) SR360.
yow(r) *pron. 2 pl. acc./dat.* or *poss.
adj.* see **ȝe**.

INDEX OF PROPER NAMES

SELECT BIBLIOGRAPHY

I list here only works which I have cited more than once, or in summary form, or which have contributed significantly to this edition, whether cited or not. Other works which I have used less extensively are given a full reference at the point of citation. See also Abbreviations and Short Titles.

The Adventure of St. Columba's Clerics, ed. W. Stokes, *RC*, xxvi (1905), 130–70.
An Alphabet of Tales, ed. M.M. Banks, EETS, 127 (1905).
Annals of the Kingdom of Ireland by the Four Masters, ed. John O'Donovan, 2nd ed., 7 vols. (Dublin, 1856).
Annals of Ulster, ed. William M. Hennessy, 4 vols. (Dublin, 1887–1901).
Anselm, *Opera Omnia*, ed. F.S. Schmitt, 6 vols. (Edinburgh, 1946–61).
Apocalypse of Paul. See *ANT*, pp. 525–55, and E. Hennecke, *New Testament Apocrypha*, ed. W. Schneemelcher, English trans. ed. R.McL. Wilson, II (London, 1965), 755–98.
Apocalypse of Peter. See *ANT*, pp. 505–24, and E. Hennecke, *New Testament Apocrypha*, ed. W. Schneemelcher, English trans. ed. R.McL. Wilson, II (London, 1965), 663–83.
The Apocryphal Old Testament, ed. H.F.D. Sparks (Oxford, 1984).

Bale, John, *Index Britanniae scriptorum*, ed. R.L. Poole and Mary Bateson (Anecdota Oxoniensia: Texts, Documents and Extracts chiefly from Manuscripts in the Bodleian and other Oxford Libraries, Medieval and Modern Series, Part IX, Oxford, 1902).
Bar, F., *Les Routes de l'autre monde: Descentes aux enfers et voyages dans l'au-delà* (Paris, 1946).
Becker, E.J., *A Contribution to the Comparative Study of Medieval Visions of Heaven and Hell, with Special Reference to the Middle English Versions* (Baltimore, 1899).
Benz, Ernst, *Die Vision: Erfahrungsformen und Bilderwelt* (Stuttgart, 1969).
Bernard, St, *Vita Sancti Malachiae* in *Sancti Bernardi Opera*, ed. J. Leclercq and H.M. Rochais, III (Rome, 1963). [See also Lawlor.]
Bieler, L., 'St. Patrick's Purgatory: Contributions towards an Historical Topography', *IER*, xciii (1960), 137–44.
—— *Four Latin Lives of St. Patrick* (Scriptores Latini Hiberniae, VIII, Dublin, 1971).
Bliss, A.J., 'Notes on the Auchinleck Manuscript', *Speculum*, xxvi (1951), 652–8.
—— 'The Auchinleck *Life of Adam and Eve*', *RES*, NS, vii (1956), 406–9.
—— 'The Spelling of *Sir Launfal*', *Anglia*, lxxv (1957), 281–4.
Boswell, C.S., *An Irish Precursor of Dante: A Study on the Vision of Heaven and Hell ascribed to the Eighth-century Irish Saint Adamnan, with Translation of the Irish Text* (London, 1908).
Bousset, D.W., 'Die Himmelreise der Seele', *Archiv für Religionswissenschaft*, iii–iv (1900–1901), 136–69, 229–73.

Brandes, H., 'Ueber die Quellen der mittelenglischen Versionen der Paulus-Vision', *EStn*, vii (1884), 34–65.

Caesarius of Heisterbach, *Dialogus Miraculorum*, ed. J. Strange, 2 vols. (Cologne, Bonn and Brussels, 1851, repr. 1967).

Carozzi, Claude, 'La Géographie de l'au-delà et sa signification pendant le haut moyen âge', *Settimane di Studio del Centro Italiano di Studi sull'Alto Medioevo*, xxix (1983), 423–81.

Carter, H.H., *A Dictionary of Middle English Musical Terms* (Bloomington, 1961).

Caerwyn Williams, J.E., 'Welsh Versions of *Purgatorium S. Patricii*', *Studia Celtica*, viii–ix (1973–74), 121–94.

Ciccarese, Maria Pia, 'Alle origini della letteratura delle visioni: il contributo di Gregorio di Tours', *Studi Storico Religiosi*, v (1981), 251–66.

—— 'La *Visio Baronti* nella tradizione letteraria delle *Visiones* dell'aldilà', *Romanobarbarica*, vi (1981–1982), 25–52.

—— 'Le più antiche rappresentazioni del purgatorio, dalla *Passio Perpetuae* alla fine del IX sec.', *Romanobarbarica*, vii (1982–1983), 33–76.

—— 'Le visioni di S. Fursa', *Romanobarbarica*, viii (1984–1985), 231–303.

—— ed., *Visioni dell'aldilà in occidente: Fonti, modelli, testi*, Bibliotheca Patristica (Florence, 1987).

Colgan, John, *Triadis thaumaturgae seu diuorum Patricii Columbae et Brigidae, trium veteris et maioris Scotiae, seu Hiberniae sanctorum insulae ... acta ...*, II (Louvain, 1647).

Concordantiarum Universae Scripturae Sacrae Thesaurus Auctoribus PP. Peultier, Etienne, Gantois (Cursus Sacrae Scripturae, V, Paris, 1939).

Coulton, G.G., *Five Centuries of Religion*, 4 vols. (Cambridge, 1923–1950).

Cross, T.P., *Motif-Index of Early Irish literature* (Bloomington, 1952).

—— and Slover, C.H., *Ancient Irish Tales* (London, 1936).

Curtayne, A., *Lough Derg: St. Patrick's Purgatory* (London, 1944).

Delehaye, H., 'Le Pèlerinage de Laurent de Pasztho au Purgatoire de S. Patrice', *AB*, xxvii (1908), 35–60.

Dinzelbacher, Peter, *Die Jenseitsbrücke im Mittelalter*, Dissertationen der Universität Wien, 104 (1973).

—— 'Die Vision Alberichs und die Esdras-Apokryphe', *Studien und Mitteilungen zur Geschichte des Benediktiner-Ordens und seine Zweige*, lxxxvii (1976), 435–42.

—— 'Klassen und Hierarchien im Jenseits', *Miscellanea Mediaevalia*, xii (1979), 20–40.

—— 'Reflexionen irdischer Sozialstrukturen in mittelalterlichen Jenseitsschilderungen', *Archiv für Kulturgeschichte*, lxi (1979), 16–34.

—— *Vision und Visionsliteratur im Mittelalter* (Monographien zur Geschichte des Mittelalters 23, Stuttgart, 1981).

—— 'The Way to the Other World in Medieval Literature and Art', *Folklore*, xcvii (1986), 70–87.

—— ed., *Mittelalterliche Visionsliteratur: Eine Anthologie* (Darmstadt, 1989).

—— and Kleinschmidt, Harald, 'Seelenbrücke und Brückenbau im mittelalterlichen England', *Numen*, xxxi (1984), 242–87.

Dods, M., *Forerunners of Dante: An Account of Some of the More Important Visions of the Unseen World, from the Earliest Times* (Edinburgh, 1903).

Dumville, David N., 'Towards an Interpretation of *Fís Adamnán*', *Studia Celtica*, xii–xiii (1977/1978), 62–77.

Dunning, P.J., 'The Arroasian Order in Medieval Ireland', *Irish Historical Studies*, iv (1945), 297–315.

SELECT BIBLIOGRAPHY 331

Dünninger, E., *Politische und geschichtliche Elemente in mittelalterlichen Jenseits-visionen bis zum Ende des 13. Jahrhunderts*, Diss. phil. (Würzburg, 1962).

The Early South-English Legendary, ed. Carl Horstmann, EETS, 87 (1887).
Easting, Robert, 'An Edition of *Owayne Miles* and other Middle English Texts concerning St. Patrick's Purgatory' (unpublished D.Phil. thesis, University of Oxford, 1976).
—— 'The Date and Dedication of the *Tractatus de Purgatorio Sancti Patricii*', *Speculum*, liii (1978), 778–83.
—— 'Peter of Cornwall's Account of St. Patrick's Purgatory', *AB*, xcvii (1979), 397–416.
—— 'Purgatory and the Earthly Paradise in the *Tractatus de Purgatorio Sancti Patricii*', *Cîteaux: Commentarii Cistercienses*, xxxvii (1986), 23–48.
—— 'Owein at St Patrick's Purgatory', *MA*, lv (1986), 159–75.
—— 'Some Antedatings and Early Usages from the Auchinleck *Owayne Miles*', in *Sentences for Alan Ward*, ed. D.M. Reeks (Southampton, 1988), pp. 167–74.
—— 'The Middle English "Hearne fragment" of St Patrick's Purgatory', *NQ*, NS, xxxv (1988), 436–7.
—— 'The English Tradition', in Haren & Pontfarcy (1988), pp. 58–82.
—— 'The South English Legendary "St Patrick" as Translation', *Leeds Studies in English*, xxi (1990), 119–40.
—— 'Middle English Translations of the *Tractatus de Purgatorio Sancti Patricii*', in *The Medieval Translator, Volume II: Papers read at a conference on The Theory and Practice of Translation in the Middle Ages, held at Gregynog Hall, August 1987*, Westfield Publications in Medieval English, ed. Roger Ellis, forthcoming.
—— and Sharpe, Richard, 'Peter of Cornwall: The Visions of Ailsi and his Sons', *Mediaevistik*, i (1988), 207–62.
Eckleben, S., *Die älteste Schilderung vom Fegefeuer des heil. Patricius* (Halle/Saale, 1885).
Endepols, H.J.E., *Die Hijstorie van Sunte Patricius Vegevuer* (The Hague, 1919).
Esposito, M., 'Notes on Latin Learning and Literature in Medieval Ireland—V', *Hermathena*, l (1937), 139–83.
Etienne De Bourbon, *De septem donis*, ed. A. Lecoy de la Marche, *Anecdotes historiques, legendes et apologues* ... (Paris, 1877). [See also Frati (1886).]

Farmer, Hugh, 'A Letter of St. Waldef of Melrose concerning a Recent Vision', *Studia Anselmiana*, xliii (1958), 91–101.
—— 'A Monk's Vision of Purgatory', *Studia Monastica*, i (1959), 393–7.
Félice, P. de, *L'Autre Monde: mythes et legendes. Le Purgatoire de saint Patrice* (Paris, 1906).
Fís Adamnán. See Boswell (translated text), Seymour (1927), and Dumville.
Foster, F.A., 'Legends of the After Life', in *Manual*, 2 (1970), 452–7, 645–9.
Frati, L., 'Il Purgatorio di S. Patrizio secondo Stefano di Bourbon e Uberto da Romans', *Giornale Storico della Letteratura Italiana*, viii (1886), 140–79.
—— 'Tradizioni Storiche del Purgatorio di San Patrizio', *Giornale Storico della Letteratura Italiana*, xvii (1891), 46–79.

Gardiner, E., 'The "Vision of Tundale": A Critical Edition of the Middle English Text' (unpublished Ph.D. thesis, Fordham University, New York, 1979).
—— 'The Translation into Middle English of the *Vision of Tundale*', *Manuscripta*, xxiv (1980), 14–19.

Gardner, Tom C., 'The Theater of Hell: A Critical Study of some Twelfth Century Latin Eschatological Visions' (unpublished Ph.D. thesis, University of California, Berkeley, 1976).

Godeschalcus. See Visio Godeschalci.

Görlach, M., The Textual Tradition of the South English Legendary (Leeds Texts and Monographs, NS, 6, Leeds, 1974).

Gregory of Tours, Historia Francorum. See B. Krusch and W. Levison eds., Gregorii Episcopi Tvronensis Libri Historiarum X, MGH, SRM, I.1 (1951).

Grosjean, P., 'De S. Iohanne Bridlingtoniensi collectanea', AB, liii (1935), 101–29.

Guddat-Figge, G., Catalogue of Manuscripts containing Middle English Romances (Texte und Untersuchungen zur englischen Philologie 4, Munich, 1976).

Gurevich, Aron, 'Au Moyen Age: Conscience individuelle et image de l'au-delà', Annales E. S. C., xxxvii (1982), 255–75.

—— 'Popular and Scholarly Medieval Cultural Traditions: Notes in the Margin of Jacques Le Goff's Book', Journal of Medieval History, ix (1983), 71–90.

—— 'Oral and Written Culture of the Middle Ages: Two 'Peasant Visions' of the Late Twelfth–Early Thirteenth Centuries', New Literary History, xvi (1984), 51–66.

—— Medieval Popular Culture: Problems of Belief and Perception, translated by János M. Bak and Paula A. Hollingsworth (Cambridge Studies in Oral and Literate Culture 14, Cambridge, 1988).

Handlyng Synne, ed. F.J. Furnivall, EETS, 109 (1901) and 123 (1903).

Himmelfarb, Martha, Tours of Hell: An Apocalyptic Form in Jewish and Christian Literature (Philadelphia, 1985).

Holdsworth, C.J., 'Eleven Visions connected with the Cistercian Monastery of Stratford Langthorne', Cîteaux: Commentarii Cistercienses, xiii (1962), 185–204.

—— 'Visions and Visionaries in the Middle Ages', History, xlviii (1963), 141–53.

Honorius Augustodunensis, Elucidarium, ed. Yves Lefèvre, L'Elucidarium et les Lucidaires (Bibliothèque des écoles françaises d'Athènes et de Rome 180, Paris, 1954).

Horn Childe and Maiden Rimnild, ed. Maldwyn Mills (Middle English Texts 20, Heidelberg, 1988).

Horstmann, C. ed., Altenglische Legenden (Paderborn, 1875).

—— ed., Altenglische Legenden: Neue Folge (Heilbronn, 1881).

—— See also The Early South-English Legendary, The Life of Adam and Eve, Spiritus Guydonis, and VSP.

Hugh of St. Victor, Summa de sacramentis christianae fidei, PL, clxxvi, 183–618.

Hughes, Jonathan, Pastors and Visionaries: Religion and Secular Life in Late Medieval Yorkshire (Woodbridge, 1988).

Jacobus de Voragine (Varaigne), Legenda Aurea, ed. Th. Graesse, 2nd ed. (Leipzig, 1850).

James, M.R. and C. Jenkins, A Descriptive Catalogue of the Manuscripts in the Library of Lambeth Palace (Cambridge, 1930).

Jenkins, T.A., 'The Espurgatoire Saint Patriz of Marie de France, with a Text of the Latin Original', The Decennial Publications of the University of Chicago, 1st series, vii (1903), 235–327.

John of Fécamp, Liber Meditationum, PL, xl, 901–42.

Jordan, R., Handbook of Middle English Grammar: Phonology, trans. E.J. Crook (Janua Linguarum, Series Practica 218, The Hague and Paris, 1974).

Kahrl, Stanley J., 'The Brome Hall Commonplace Book', *Theater Notebook*, xxii (1968), 157–61.

Kenney, James F., *The Sources for the Early History of Ireland: Ecclesiastical. An Introduction and Guide* with addenda by L. Bieler (New York, 1966).

The King of Tars, ed. Judith Perryman (Middle English Texts 12, Heidelberg, 1980).

Kölbing, E., 'Zwei mittelenglische Bearbeitungen der Sage von St. Patrik's Purgatorium', *EStn*, i (1877), 57–121.

—— 'Vier romanzen-Handschriften', *EStn*, vii (1884), 177–201. [See also K1, K2, K3, K4.]

Krapp, G.P., *The Legend of Saint Patrick's Purgatory: Its Later Literary History* (Baltimore, 1900). [See also Kr.]

Kren, Thomas and Wieck, Roger S., *The Visions of Tondal from the Library of Margaret of York*, The J. Paul Getty Museum (Malibu, California, 1990).

Laing, D. See *Owain Miles*.

Lapidge, Michael and Sharpe, Richard, *A Bibliography of Celtic-Latin Literature 400–1200* (Dublin, 1985).

Lawlor, H.J., *St. Bernard of Clairvaux's 'Life of St. Malachy of Armagh'* (London and New York, 1920).

Le Goff, Jacques, *La Naissance du purgatoire* (Paris, 1981).

—— *L'Imaginaire médiéval* (Paris, 1985).

'*Le Purgatoire de Saint Patrice' des manuscrits Harléian 273 et fonds français 2198*, ed. J. Vising (Göteborg, 1916).

Le Purgatoire de Saint Patrice du manuscrit de la Bibliothèque Nationale fonds français 25545, ed. M. Mörner (Lund, 1920).

Le Purgatoire de Saint Patrice par Berol, ed. M. Mörner (Lund, 1917).

Leslie, Shane, *Saint Patrick's Purgatory: A Record from History and Literature* (London, 1932).

—— *Saint Patrick's Purgatory* (Dublin, 1961).

The Life of Adam and Eve [Auchinleck], ed. C. Horstmann, 'Canticum de Creatione b)', in *Sammlung Altenglischer Legenden* (Heilbronn, 1878), pp. 139–47. [See also Bliss (1956).]

Loomis, L.H., 'Chaucer and the Auchinleck MS: "Thopas" and "Guy of Warwick"', in *Essays and Studies in Honor of Carleton Brown* (New York, 1940), pp. 111–28.

—— 'The Auchinleck Manuscript and a Possible London Bookshop of 1330–1340', *PMLA*, lvii (1942), 595–627.

Lybeaus Desconus, ed. M. Mills, EETS, 261 (1969).

Lyle, E.B., 'The *Visions of St. Patrick's Purgatory, Thomas of Erceldoune, Thomas the Rhymer* and *The Daemon Lover*', *NM*, lxxii (1972), 716–22.

MacCulloch, J.A., *Early Christian Visions of the Other-World* (Edinburgh, 1912).

—— *The Harrowing of Hell: A Comparative Study of an Early Christian Doctrine* (Edinburgh, 1930).

—— *Medieval Faith and Fable* (London, 1932).

Mackenzie, B.A., 'A Special Dialectal Development of O.E. ēa in Middle English', *EStn*, lxi (1927), 386–92.

Macrae-Gibson, O.D., 'The Auchinleck MS.: Participles in -*and(e)*', *ES*, lii (1971), 13–20. [See also *Of Arthour and of Merlin*.]

Mac Tréinfhir, Noel, 'The Todi Fresco and St Patrick's Purgatory, Lough Derg', *Clogher Record*, xii (1986), 141–58.

Mahaffy, J.P., 'Two Early Tours in Ireland', *Hermathena*, xl (1914), 1–16.

Mall, E., 'Zur Geschichte der Legende vom Purgatorium des heil. Patricius', *RF*, vi (1889), 139–97.
Manuscript Sources for the History of Irish Civilization, ed. R.J. Hayes, 11 vols. (Boston, Mass., 1965), and *First Supplement 1965–1975*, 3 vols. (Boston, Mass., 1979).
Marshall, J.C. Douglas, 'Three Problems in the Vision of Tundal', *MA*, xliv (1975), 14–22.
Marston, T.E., 'The Book of Brome', *Yale University Library Gazette*, xli (1967), 141–5.
Matthaei Parisiensis, monachi Sancti Albani, Chronica majora, ed. H.R. Luard, 7 vols., RS, 57 (London, 1872–1883).
McAlindon, T.E., 'The Treatment of the Supernatural in Middle English Legend and Romance, 1200–1400' (unpublished Ph.D. thesis, University of Cambridge, 1960).
Mearns. See *The Vision of Tundale*.
Messingham, Thomas, *Florilegium insulae sanctorum seu vitae et actae sanctorum Hiberniae* (Paris, 1624).

Navigatio Sancti Brendani Abbatis: From Early Latin MSS., ed. Carl Selmer (University of Notre Dame Publications in Medieval Studies, XVI, 1959).
Non-Cycle Plays and Fragments, ed. Norman Davis, EETS, SS 1 (1970).
Non-Cycle Plays and The Winchester Dialogues: Facsimiles of Plays and Fragments in Various Manuscripts and the Dialogues in Winchester College MS 33, with introductions and a transcript of the Dialogues by Norman Davis (Leeds Texts and Monographs, Medieval Drama Facsimiles, V, The University of Leeds School of English, Leeds, 1979).

Octovian Imperator, ed. Frances McSparran (Middle English Texts 11, Heidelberg, 1979).
Of Arthour and of Merlin, ed. O.D. Macrae-Gibson, 2 vols. EETS, 268 (1973) and 279 (1979).
Os, A.B. van, *Religious Visions: The Development of the Eschatological Elements in Medieval English Religious Literature* (Amsterdam, 1932).
Owain Miles and Other Inedited Fragments of Ancient English Poetry [ed. David Laing and W.B.D.D. Turnbull and others] (Edinburgh, 1837).
Owen, D.D.R., 'The *Vision of St. Paul*. The French and Provençal Versions and Their Sources', *RP*, xii (1958), 33–51.
—— *The Vision of Hell: Infernal Journeys in Medieval French Literature* (Edinburgh and London, 1970).

Palmer, Nigel F., '*Visio Tnugdali': The German and Dutch Translations and their Circulation in the Later Middle Ages* (Münchener Texte und Untersuchungen zur deutschen Literatur des Mittelalters 76, Munich, 1982).
Patch, H.R., *The Other World according to Descriptions in Medieval Literature* (Cambridge, Mass., 1950, repr. New York, 1970).
Peters, E., 'Zur Geschichte der lateinischen Visionslegenden', *RF*, viii (1894), 361–4.
Picard, Jean-Michel. See *The Vision of Tnugdal*, and Picard & Pontfarcy.
Piers the Plowman. See *Vision of William concerning Piers the Plowman*.
Plummer, C., *Venerabilis Baedae Opera historica*, 2 vols. (Oxford, 1896). [See also *BEH*.]
—— *Vitae sanctorum Hiberniae*, 2 vols. (Oxford, 1910).

—— *Lives of Irish Saints*, 2 vols. (Oxford, 1922).

Poema Morale, ed. J. Hall, *Selections from Early Middle English 1130–1250*, I (Oxford, 1920), 30–53.

Polychronicon Ranulphi Higden Monachi Cestrensis, 9 vols., RS, 41 (London, 1865–1886).

Pontfarcy, Yolande de, 'Le *Tractatus de Purgatorio Sancti Patricii* de H. de Saltrey: sa date et ses sources', *Peritia*, iii (1984), 460–80. [See also Haren & Pontfarcy; Picard & Pontfarcy; and *The Vision of Tnugdal*.]

The Pricke of Conscience, ed. R. Morris (Berlin, 1863).

Promptorium parvulorum, ed. A.L. Mayhew, EETS, ES 102 (1908).

Purvis, J.S., *St. John of Bridlington* (The Journal of the Bridlington Augustinian Society, No. 2, August, 1924).

A Revelation of Purgatory by an Unknown, Fifteenth-Century Woman Visionary: Introduction, Critical Text, and Translation, ed. Marta Powell Harley (Studies in Women and Religion 18, Lewiston and Queenston, 1985).

The Revelation to the Monk of Evesham, ed. E. Arber, English Reprints (Westminster, 1901). [See also *Vision of the Monk of Eynsham*.]

The Revelations of Saint Birgitta, ed. W.P. Cumming, EETS, 178 (1928).

Revised Medieval Latin Word-List, prepared by R.E. Latham (London, 1965).

Robinson, P.R., 'A Study of Some Aspects of the Transmission of English Verse Texts in Late Medieval Manuscripts' (unpublished B.Litt. thesis, University of Oxford, 1972).

—— 'The "Booklet": A Self-contained Unit in Composite Manuscripts', *Codicologica*, iii (1980), 46–69.

Röckelein, Hedwig, *Otloh, Gottschalk, Tnugdal: Individuelle und kollektive Visionsmuster des Hochmittelalters* (Europäische Hochschulschriften, III.319, Frankfurt, Berne, New York, 1987).

Rogeri de Wendover Chronica; sive Flores historiarum, ed. H.O. Coxe, 5 vols., English Historical Society Publications (London, 1841–2).

Rüegg, A., *Die Jenseitsvorstellungen vor Dante und die übrigen literarischen Voraussetzungen der 'Divina Commedia'*, 2 vols. (Einsiedeln, Cologne, 1945).

Ryan, J., 'St. Patrick's Purgatory', *Studies*, xxi (1932), 443–60.

—— 'Saint Patrick's Purgatory, Lough Derg', *Clogher Record Album*, ed. Joseph A. Duffy (Monaghan, 1975), pp. 13–26.

Samuels, M.L., 'Some Applications of Middle English Dialectology', *ES*, xliv (1963), 81–94.

—— 'Kent and the Low Countries: Some Linguistic Evidence', in *Edinburgh Studies in English and Scots*, ed. A.J. Aitken, Angus McIntosh and Hermann Pálsson (London, 1971), pp. 3–19.

—— *Linguistic Evolution* (Cambridge, 1972).

Schmidt, P.G., 'The Vision of Thurkill', *Journal of the Warburg and Courtauld Institutes*, xli (1978), 50–64. [See also *Visio Thvrkilli*.]

—— 'Die Vision von Vaucelles (1195/1196)', *Mittellateinisches Jahrbuch*, xx (1985), 155–63.

Selections from Early Middle English 1130–1250, ed. J. Hall, 2 vols. (Oxford, 1920).

Seymour, M.C., 'The English Manuscripts of *Mandeville's Travels*', *Edinburgh Bibliographical Society Transactions*, iv (1966), 185–6.

Seymour, St. John D., *St. Patrick's Purgatory: A Mediæval Pilgrimage in Ireland* (Dundalk, 1918).

—— 'The Seven Heavens in Irish Literature', *ZfcP*, xiv (1923), 18–30.

—— 'The Eschatology of the Early Irish Church', *ZfcP*, xiv (1923), 179–211.
—— 'Studies in the Vision of Tundal', *PRIA*, xxxvii.C.4 (1926), 87–106.
—— 'The Vision of Adamnan', *PRIA*, xxxvii.C.15 (1927), 304–12.
—— *Irish Visions of the Other World: A Contribution to the Study of Mediaeval Visions* (London, 1930).
Shields, H.E., 'An Old French Book of Legends and its Apocalyptic Background' (unpublished Ph.D. thesis, Trinity College, Dublin, 1966).
Silverstein, T., *Visio Sancti Pauli: The History of the Apocalypse in Latin, together with nine texts* (Studies and Documents, IV, London, 1935).
—— 'Dante and the *Visio Karoli Crassi*', *MLN*, li (1936), 449–52.
—— 'Dante and the Legend of the *Mi'rāj*: The Problem of Islamic Influence on the Christian Literature of the Otherworld', *Journal of Near Eastern Studies*, xi (1952), 89–110, 187–97.
—— 'The Vision of St Paul: New Links and Patterns in the Western Tradition', *Archives d'histoire doctrinale et littéraire du Moyen Age*, xxxiv (1959), 199–248.
Sir Eglamour of Artois, cd. F.E. Richardson, EETS, 256 (1965).
Smith, Lucy Toulmin, 'St. Patrick's Purgatory, and the Knight Sir Owen', *EStn*, ix (1886), 1–12. [See also *Common-place Book*.]
Spilling, H., *Die Visio Tnugdali: Eigenart und Stellung in der mittelalterlichen Visionsliteratur bis zum Ende des 12. Jahrhunderts* (Münchener Beiträge zur Mediävistik und Renaissance-Forschung 21, Munich, 1975).
Spiritus Guydonis, ed. C. Horstmann, *Yorkshire Writers: Richard Rolle of Hampole and his followers*, II (Leipzig, 1896), 292–333.
Stanford, M.A., 'The Sumner's Tale and St. Patrick's Purgatory', *JEGP*, xix (1920), 377–81.
Stuart, D.C., 'The Stage Setting of Hell and the Iconography of the Middle Ages', *RR*, iv (1913), 330–42.

Tidings of Doomsday, ed. W. Stokes, *RC*, iv (1879–80), 245–57.
Traill, D.A., *Walahfrid Strabo's 'Visio Wettini': text, translation and commentary* (Lateinische Sprache und Literatur des Mittelalters 2, Berne, Frankfurt, 1974).
Tubach, F.C., *Index Exemplorum: A Handbook of Medieval Religious Tales* (FF Communications 204, Helsinki, 1969).
Tundale: Das mittelenglische Gedicht über die Vision des Tundalus, ed. A. Wagner (Halle, 1893).
Turner, Victor and Turner, Edith, *Image and Pilgrimage in Christian Culture: Anthropological Perspectives* (New York, 1978).

Verdeyen, R. and Endepols, J., *Tondalus' Visioen en St. Patricius' Vagevuur*, 2 vols. (Ghent and The Hague, 1914, Ghent and 's Gravenhage, 1917).
Visio Alberici. Ed. Mauro Inguanez, 'La Visione di Alberico', with introduction by Antonio Mirra, *Miscellanea Cassinese*, xi (1932), 33–103 [text pp. 83–103].
Visio Baronti Monachi Longoretensis, ed. W. Levison, MGH, SRM, V (1910), 368–94.
Visio Esdrae. Ed. O. Wahl, *Apocalypsis Esdrae. Apocalypsis Sedrach. Visio Beati Esdrae* (Leiden, 1977), pp. 49–61. [Trans. R.J.H. Shutt in *The Apocryphal Old Testament*, ed. Sparks, pp. 947–51.]
Visio Godeschalci. Ed. E. Assmann, *Godeschalcus und Visio Godeschalci* (Quellen und Forschungen zur Geschichte Schleswig-Holsteins 74, Neumünster, 1979).
Visio Sancti Pauli. See *VSP* I/IV; Silverstein (1935); and for translation see *Apocalypse of Paul*.

Visio Thvrkilli relatore, vt videtur, Radvlpho de Coggeshall, ed. Paul Gerhard Schmidt (Leipzig, 1978).

Visio Tnugdali, Lateinisch und Altdeutsch, ed. A. Wagner (Erlangen, 1882). [See also *Vision of Tnugdal*.]

Visio Wettini [Heito], ed. E. Dümmler, MGH, PLAC, II (1884), 267–75. [For *Walahfrid Strabo*, see Traill.]

Vision of Adamnán. See *Fís Adamnán*.

Vision of Antonio Mannini. See Frati (1886).

Vision of Drihthelm. Bede, *Historia Ecclesiastica*, V, 12. See *BEH*.

The Vision of Edmund Leversedge: A 15th-century account of a visit to the Otherworld edited from BL MS Additional 34,193 with an Introduction, Commentary and Glossary, ed. Wiesje Fimke Nijenhuis (Capelle aan der IJssel, 1990). [See also *VEL*.]

Vision of Fursey. Bede, *Historia Ecclesiastica*, III, 19. See *BEH*. [See also Ciccarese (1984–1985).]

Vision of Gunthelm. Ed. G. Constable, 'The Vision of Gunthelm and other *Visiones* attributed to Peter the Venerable', *Revue bénédictine*, lxvi (1956), 92–114, text pp. 105–14. [Reprinted with addenda in Giles Constable, *Cluniac Studies* (London, 1980).]

Vision of Laisrén, ed. K. Meyer, *Otia Merseiana*, i (1899), 113–19.

Vision of Laurence Rathold de Pászthó. See Delehaye (1908).

Vision of Maximus. See Valerius of Bierzo, *Opuscula, PL*, lxxxvii, 431–3.

Vision of Orm, ed. H. Farmer, *AB*, lxxv (1957), 72–82.

Vision of Ramon de Perellós. See A. Jeanroy and A. Vignaux, *Voyage au Purgatoire de St Patrice: Visions de Tindal et de St Paul* (Bibliothèque méridionale, 1st series, vol. 8, Toulouse, 1903).

Vision of Salvius. See Gregory of Tours, *Historia Francorum*, VII.i.

Vision of Sunniulf. See Gregory of Tours, *Historia Francorum*, IV.xxxiii.

Vision of the boy William. See Vincent of Beauvais, *Speculum Historiale*, XXVII.lxxxiv, lxxxv.

Vision of the Monk of Eynsham, ed. H.E. Salter, in *Cartulary of the Abbey of Eynsham*, II (Oxford Historical Society, 51, 1908), 257–371. [See also *Revelation to the Monk of Evesham* [sic].]

Vision of the Monk of Wenlock. See Boniface, *Ep.* 10, in *Die Briefe des heiligen Bonifatius und Lullus*, ed. M. Tangl, MGH, ES, I (1916), 7–15.

Vision of Thespesius. See Plutarch, *De sera numinis vindicta*, 563B–568, in *Moralia*, VII, ed. and trans. Phillip H. De Lacy and Benedict Einarson, The Loeb Classical Library (London, 1959), 268–99.

The Vision of Tnugdal, translated from Latin by Jean-Michel Picard with an introduction by Yolande de Pontfarcy (Dublin, 1989). [See also *Visio Tnugdali*.]

The Vision of Tundale, ed. R. Mearns (Middle English Texts 18, Heidelberg, 1985). [See also *Tundale*.]

The Vision of William concerning Piers the Plowman, ed. W.W. Skeat, 2 vols. (Oxford, 1886, repr. 1969).

Visiones Georgii: Visiones quas in Purgatorio Sancti Patricii vidit Georgius miles de Ungaria A. D. MCCCLIII, ed. L.L. Hammerich (Det. Kgl. Danske Videnskabernes Selskab. historisk-filologiske Meddelelser, XVIII.2, Copenhagen, 1930).

Visions of Ailsi. See Easting and Sharpe.

Voigt, M., *Beiträge zur Geschichte der Visionenliteratur im Mittelalter, I.II.*, in *Palaestra*, cxlvi (Leipzig, 1924, repr. New York and London, 1967).

Walsh, Katherine, *A Fourteenth-Century Scholar and Primate: Richard FitzRalph in Oxford, Avignon and Armagh* (Oxford, 1981).
Ward, H.L.D., *Catalogue of Romances in the Department of Manuscripts in the British Museum*, II (London, 1893).
Warnke, K., 'Die Vorlage des Espurgatoire St. Patriz der Marie de France', *Philologische Studien Karl Voretzsch zum 60. Geburtstage* (Halle/Saale, 1927), 135–54.
—— *Das Buch vom Espurgatoire S. Patrice der Marie de France und seine Quelle* (Bibliotheca Normannica 9, Halle/Saale, 1938).
Waterhouse, G., 'An early German Account of St. Patrick's Purgatory', *MLR*, xviii (1923), 317–22.
—— 'St. Patrick's Purgatory: A German Account', *Hermathena*, xliv (1926), 30–51.
Willson, E., *The Middle English Legends of Visits to the Other World and their Relation to the Metrical Romances* (Chicago, 1917).
Witkowski, G.-J., *L'art profane à l'église, ses licences symboliques, satiriques et fantaisistes: France* (Paris, 1908).
Wright, T., *St. Patrick's Purgatory: An Essay on the Legends of Purgatory, Hell and Paradise, current during the Middle Ages* (London, 1844).
Wyld, H.C., *A History of Modern Colloquial English*, 3rd ed. (Oxford, 1936).

Zaleski, Carol, 'St. Patrick's Purgatory: Pilgrimage Motifs in a Medieval Otherworld Vision', *Journal of the History of Ideas*, xlvi (1985), 467–85.
—— *Otherworld Journeys: Accounts of Near-Death Experience in Medieval and Modern Times* (New York and Oxford, 1987).
Zanden, C.M., van der, 'Auteur d'un manuscrit latin du *Purgatoire de Saint Patrice* de la Bibliothèque de l'Université d'Utrecht', *Neophilologus*, x (1925), 243–9.
—— 'Un chapitre intéressant de la "Topographia Hibernica" et le "Tractatus De Purgatorio Sancti Patricii"', *Neophilologus*, xii (1927), 132–7.
—— *Etude sur le Purgatoire de Saint Patrice, accompagnée du texte latin d'Utrecht et du texte anglo-normand de Cambridge* (Amsterdam, 1927).

The following book was published too late for me to be able to make use of it:
Morgan, Alison. *Dante and the Medieval Other World* (Cambridge Studies in Medieval Literture 8, Cambridge, 1990).